Art of the Bedchamber

Art of the Bedchamber

The Chinese Sexual Yoga Classics
Including
Women's Solo Meditation Texts

Douglas Wile

State University of New York Press

Published by
State University of New York Press, Albany

© 1992 State University of New York

All rights reserved

Printed in the United States of America

For information, address State University of New York
Press, State University Plaza, Albany, N.Y., 12246

Production by Dana Foote
Marketing by Theresa A. Swierzowski

Library of Congress Cataloging in Publication Data

Wile, Douglas.
    Art of the Bedchamber : The Chinese Sexual Yoga Classics Including
  Women's Solo Meditation Texts / Douglas Wile.
       p.   cm.
    Includes bibliographical references and index.
    ISBN 0–7914–0885–X (alk. paper).—ISBN 0–7914–0886–8 (pbk. :
  alk. paper)
    1. Sex customs—China—History—Sources.   I. Title.
  HQ18.C6W56 1992
306.7'09—dc20   90-28707
                                                        CIP

10 9 8 7 6 5 4 3 2

Contents

PART TWO
THE CHINESE SEXUAL YOGA CLASSICS

PART ONE
INTRODUCTION

I. MOTIVE AND FOCUS

Sex, like music, is considered something of a universal language, but anyone who has listened to Chinese music will tell you how different *la diférence* can be. To Chinese sexual sensibilities, the Western sexual ideal—two souls striving to be one, who tune their instruments to the same pitch, make beautiful music together for a short duet, share the glory of a crashing crescendo, and console each other through a languorous denouement—is so much adolescent thrashing. How different the Chinese ideal, for here the male conductor rehearses each member of his female orchestra through the entire score, only to rest his baton as she reaches crescendo, absorbing the exhilarating waves of sound, before he retires to his dressing room to count the evening's receipts. As Western culture begins to ask itself, "Now that we can do anything we want, what do we want to do?" Chinese sexual yoga arrives with a fresh perspective that will stimulate even the most seasoned sinologists and jaded satyrs.

This source book in Chinese sexual yoga seeks to make a number of contributions. It is the first comprehensive collection of all published primary material to appear in any language, including Chinese. The translation itself aspires to a new standard of accuracy and felicity,

and the annotations attempt both to elucidate unfamiliar terminology in the text and be fully accountable for differences between the present translation and all previous efforts. Emendations to the original texts are undertaken with full disclosure of the background to the reader. By presenting the broadest possible spectrum of primary sources, the reader is able to witness the evolution of sexual practices in China, the key issues that divide its several schools, and the relationship of the "paired practices" (*shuang-hsiu* 雙修) camp to its detractors. Additionally, this broad base of primary materials will give humanists, scientists, and the general reader a more complete picture of Chinese sexual practices and a more complex matrix of data for comparative studies. The section devoted to women's practices, though of the "solo" rather than "paired" persuasion, marks the debut of these texts in translation and highlights the importance of sexual energy and the reproductive function in Chinese meditation. Finally, this retrospective of traditional teachings attempts to provide a baseline for assessing contemporary publications on Chinese sex techniques and to offer new paradigmatic and practical possibilities at a turning point in Western sexuality.

Methodologically, this work is pri- 3

marily philological and historical rather than anthropological or literary and, accordingly, is not concerned with erotic literature or art, sexual mores or deviance, prostitution, concubinage, gay quarters or harem life, venereal disease, homosexuality, eunuchs, fetishism, or paraphenalia. Neither is it a systematic comparative study of Western and Chinese sexuality or of the esoteric practices of China and other non-Western traditions such as India, Tibet or Japan. The focus of this work, then, is chiefly the written record of Chinese sexual yoga, which may be defined for the present as the practice of sexual intercourse for the purpose of intergender harmony, physical and psychological health, and ascended states or immortality. The introductory chapters attempt to place these sexual techniques in the larger context of medicine and esoteric macrobiotics and provide the reader with the conceptual tools necessary to crack the terminological code.

Judging from the bibliographic catalogues of the dynastic histories and references to sexual titles in secondary sources, the extant corpus is far outnumbered by the missing in action. The various works in this anthology survived through different stratagies. The "Uniting Yin and Yang" and "Highest Tao" are time capsules recently recovered from a Han tomb after more than two millennia. The *Ishimpō* fragments, from which four of the classics in the second section of this collection were reconstructed, survived in the Imperial Library of Japan and returned to China at the beginning of the twentieth century after more than a thousand years in exile. Another group of texts, *The Prescriptions of Su Nü*, "Health Benefits of the Bedchamber," and "The Dangers and Benefits of Intercourse with Women," were granted asylum in the Chinese medical sanctuary, but the *True Classic of Perfect Union*, *Exposition of Cultivating the True Essence*, and *Wondrous Discourse of Su Nü* again were lost in the land of their nativity, surviving only under Japanese patronage. The sexual alchemy texts of Sun Ju-chung, Chang San-feng and Lu Hsi-hsing, all of them Ming, needed to survive only four centuries of secret circulation to be preserved for the present. The sixteen "paired practices" documents in this translation, spanning almost 2,000 years, allow us to approach with some confidence the task of understanding Chinese sexual self-cultivation from very nearly its inception to the present.

These works, essentially instructional manuals, may be analyzed from a number of different perspectives, but to judge them on their own terms would be simply to test them in the bedroom and evaluate their contribution to health, happiness, and enlightenment. To see these texts "through Chinese eyes," of course, is not the same as objectivity; and as the texts themselves reveal, there was more than one pair of "Chinese eyes." The Ma Wang tui manuscripts, dating from the early Han, show no hint of defensiveness, though later authors sometimes were openly apologistic. Chinese detractors—Confucian, Buddhist, and Taoist "pure practitioners"—condemned both the ethics and efficacy of sexual practices, and some Western critics undoubtedly will take exception to them on physiological, psychological, or moral grounds. Some will feel that Chinese sexual yoga elevates sex to the level of spirituality, and others that it degrades meditation to the level of masturbation.

Open-minded Western scholars such as Robert van Gulik have been sufficiently impressed with the basic rationality of Chinese sexual practices to pronounce them "normal and healthy." The empirical observation and analysis of human sexual response found in these documents sound positively "modern," and paradoxically, the earliest texts are among the most strictly "scientific" in their outlook. However, to express our admiration for Chinese sexual practices by appealing to Western scientific categories, as if these represented an absolute and objective standard of authority, is like praising Confucius or Lao tzu on the basis of their approximating Jesus. Issues of methodology and scholarly stance will be discussed at length in Chapter VI of this introduction, but suffice it to say here that the Chinese have done for sex what they have done for the soybean. Taking the raw material of biology beyond the realm of simple stew, they have completely transformed it into a wide variety of nourishing new forms. Confucius said, "Eating and sex illustrate our intrinsic natures"; and it is clear that from the point of view of East-West cultural diffusion, food was first but sex may well be next.

II. THE ETHOS OF CHINESE SEXUAL PRACTICE

The sexual beliefs and practices outlined in the texts in this collection express an ethos shaped by other elements in the culture—medicine, metaphysics, and meditation—but they have also contributed to these elements; as Kristofer Schipper states in his "Science, Magic, and Mystique of the Body": "Sexuality, far from being relegated to a clandestine and apocryphal sphere, is found to be the pivot of ideas and activities." These texts reflect an elite, even esoteric, tradition—based on *coitus reservatus* and multiple partners—but belief in the dangers of sexual excess and the benefits of what Charlotte Furth calls "mild continence" were the common property of all classes. To duplicate the Chinese recipe for sophisticated sex, however, we cannot simply subtract the ingredient of ejaculation from the mix, for this ignores the many cultural values that shaped the Chinese taste. With no attempt to ascribe direct causality, this section explores themes in the texts and clues in the wider culture that help explain the emergence in China of a unique and highly developed set of sexual practices.

Kristofer Schipper has identified three modes of conceptualization in Taoist literature: "the empirical, symbolic and theological." Corresponding to the first two of these, the "Empirical" and "Metaphysical" sections of this chapter look within the sexual literature for the inductive and deductive ideas that informed its development, whereas the remaining five sections examine some of the social factors and values that had an impact on the sexual sphere and gave these texts their language and form.

The Empirical Ground

The empirical or inductive mode of conceptualization is very prominent in the sexual literature. Scientific observation in China, as elsewhere of course, takes place through a cultural filter, and then data are organized into a theoretical framework that reinforces more fundamental values in the culture. This section attempts to analyze the experiential foundations of sexual practices in China and the unique interpretation that the Chinese gave to them. Experience and interpretation are difficult to separate, but insofar as possible, our purpose here is to identify the Chinese response to the most objectifiable aspects of sexual experience.

The first formative datum of experience encountered in these classics is that energy is lost through ejaculation. Postcoital enervation impressed the ancient Chinese more than any heights achieved through orgasm. As the legendary P'eng Tsu states in the *Classic of Su Nü*, "When *ching* is emitted the whole body feels weary." Ejaculation brings enervation not relaxation, homeostatic holocaust not emotional catharsis. Detumescence of the penis is consistently analogized in these texts with death. In precisely parallel passages, the "Shih wen" and *Prescriptions of Su Nü* ask, "Why is it that the penis, which is born together with the

5

body, dies before it?" For the Chinese sexual ideologues there is no glory in fallen heroes. A paradigm of tension-release thus was rejected in favor of one of sufficiency-deficiency (*hsü shih* 虛實). The Yellow Emperor, summarizing the lessons of his sexual initiation in the *Classic of Su Nü*, concludes, "The essential teaching is to refrain from losing *ching* and treasure one's fluids." Because loss of semen depresses the body's entire energy economy, semen is seen as possessing a material (*ching-ye* 精液) and energetic (*ching-ch'i* 精氣) aspect. To use the oil-lamp metaphor of the "Health Benefits of the Bedchamber," "If the fuel is exhausted the flame expires"; however, if the semen is retained, the sexual energy will support superior health. Loss of any of the body's substance, in fact, including breath, saliva, sweat, flatulence, and menstrual blood is regarded as depleting, and even the religious saving and composting of fecal waste may be seen as part of the same conservative mentality. The soporific state following emission also may have inspired the conceptual link in medical theory of *ching* and will (*chih* 志), both associated with the urogenital system (*shen* 腎) and of the urogenital system and the brain.

Second, it was observed that the activation of sexual energy (*ching*) floods the entire system with positive vital energy (*ch'i*). The Ma Wang tui text, "Shih wen," calls this energy "divine wind" (*shen-feng* 神風), and the sexual liturgy of the *Shang-ch'ing huang-shu kuo-tu i* (Yellow book salvation ritual, a Shang-ch'ing scripture) often repeats the formula, "*Yin* and *yang* unite harmoniously and living *ch'i* flows throughout." The release of *ching-ch'i* into the system has a general tonic effect and the power, as the "Uniting *Yin* and *Yang*" states, "to open closures and unblock obstructions." Because *ch'i* is fundamental to the Chinese understanding of the nature of homeostatic health, it was natural that sex be given high points for its ability to promote *ch'i* circulation. These positive effects are immediately negated, however, if the energy elevated through sexual play is lost through ejaculation. It therefore was

necessary to make a yoga of sex, a system of techniques for simultaneously stimulating and conserving sexual energy. Therefore, *The Classic of Su Nü* and *Wondrous Discourse*, in discussing the benefits of sexual practice, both employ the compound *tao-yin* 導引, the traditional term for yoga.

Third is the experience that sexual potency declines with age. As the "Highest Tao" states, "By forty our sexual energy (*yin-ch'i* 陰氣) is halved." What ejaculation is to our short-term experience of *ching* loss, age is to our long-term experience, and both demonstrate the dependent relationship between that which has the power to create new life and our own moment-to-moment state of vitality. This observation led the physicians to conclude that sexual energy is a finite quantum in any organism, hence, as the "Shih wen" states, "What is lost must be supplemented." Taking this reasoning one step further, the inner alchemists believed that it is not age that causes sexual decline, but rather sexual mismanagement that causes aging. In the final stage of thinking, it was concluded that by suppressing the onset of puberty, the aging process itself could be defeated. Describing this state of suspended animation, the notes to the *True Transmission* say, "At this moment [fifteen years], the *ching-ch'i* is replete and the state of pure *Ch'ien* is realized. . . . If he receives enlightening instruction from an adept, then his foundation may be secured by itself."

Fourth, it was observed that ejaculation, although depleting physical reserves, has the opposite effect on sexual desire. After an immediate postcoital letdown, there is a rapid psychological rebound and an intensification of erotic interest. This sexual law of inertia, the tendency of a body in motion to remain in motion, or sexual addiction, is best expressed in the traditional medical metaphor of fire unchecked by water (*yin hsü huo wang* 陰虛火旺) and the Taoist aphorism, "when the *ching* is full one is free of lustful thoughts." It was noted that premature ejaculation (*tsao-hsieh* 早瀉), spermatorrhea (*hua-ching* 滑精), and nocturnal emissions (*meng-i* 夢遺)

were associated not with a high level of sexual energy but with deficiency, often resulting from what the *Classic of Su Nü* calls, "expenditure without restraint." Thus sexual prowess came to be defined not as the ability to expend semen but to save it. Certain herbs, yogic practices, and *coitus reservatus* itself can all contribute to "strengthening and stabilizing the *ching*" (*ku ching* 固精).

Fifth is the belief that sexual energy is capable of transfer from one organism to another, an opportunity to go beyond conservation to acquisition, as the *Summary of the Golden Elixir* states, "saving *ching* means saving one's own *ching*; accumulating *ch'i* means accumulating your partner's *ch'i*." When practicing *coitus reservatus*, as the "Health Benefits" points out, "Constant intercourse with the same women results in a weakening of her *yin-ch'i*." It thus was assumed that the sexual energy released during the fission reaction of female orgasm could be "drunk" (*he* 喝), "consumed" (*shih* 食), or "inhaled" (*hsi* 吸) through the penis of the passive male partner who had learned the proper techniques of absorption. The logic of traditional energetics seemed to suggest, at least to the sexual school, that energy lost through sexual activity could be replaced most efficiently only by sexual energy itself: as the commentary to the *True Transmission* states, "If bamboo breaks, bamboo is used to repair it; if a human being suffers injury, another human being may be used to repair the damage." Lesser potencies of assimilable supplementation also may be absorbed from the woman's breath, saliva, or breasts. Sexual energy is considered a natural resource, to which, like other resources in traditional Chinese society, the elites enjoyed privileged access. Partners are chosen then on the criteria of looks, feel, freshness, and taste—like fruit in the marketplace. However, unlike the energy derived from food, the only limit placed on the amount of *ching-ch'i* that may be absorbed in a single fueling session is the availability of sources. For this reason, the *Secrets of the Jade Chamber* advises, "Even greater benefits are reaped by

frequently changing partners." ... are depleted significantly by or... menses, but intolerably by chil... the *Essentials of the Jade Chamber* states, "Choose women who have not yet given birth."

Sixth is the observation that the period from infancy to puberty is characterized by abundant *yang* energy (*ching-ch'i*) and an absence of seminal (or menstrual) leakage and sexual desire. This is the time of wholeness, of physiological integrity. If we would turn back the clock on aging (*fan-lao huan-t'ung* 返老還童), we must take youth as our model. This is expressed, perhaps, earliest in the *Lao tzu*, which states, "The infant knows nothing of male and female, but its penis erects. This is the height of *ching*." Here then is the innocent hardness (*yang*) that springs to life in the midst of supreme softness (*yin*). The alchemists, inner alchemists, and sexual alchemists all pursued strategies of supplementation to regain sexual essence lost through puberty and subsequent sexual activity; and the most radical "pure practitioners" (*ch'ing-hsiu* 清修) sought to head off puberty itself. Ming sexual alchemists became increasingly focused on capturing the partner's sexual essence just before the "flowers fall," and female solo practitioners declare in the words of the *Correct Methods of Women's Practice*, "Within the human body, pubescent essence is the source for cultivating life."

Seventh, abstinence from intercourse, whether voluntary or enforced, was observed to produce both psychological and physiological aberrations. Exceptions were very advanced age or a high level of yogic attainment. *The Classic of Su Nü* explains, "By abstaining from intercourse the spirit has no opportunity for expansiveness, and *yin* and *yang* are blocked and cut off from one another." Physiologically, abstainers were likely to find their sexual energy "die in its lair," as the *Secrets of the Jade Chamber* puts it, resulting in a general decline in vitality and longevity. Psychologically, frustrated sexual desire could lead to what the "Dangers and Benefits" calls "mental instability" (*i tung* 意動) or even seduction

7

by incubi (*kuei-chiao* 鬼交) and ultimately death. Abstinence, then, is as dangerous as indulgence. It should be noted, however, that the harmful effects of abstinence are attributed to deprivation of sexual contact and not of orgasm, although the early texts concede that repression in the face of repletion may be harmful as well.

Eighth, man's arousal time is faster than woman's, but his own passion is even faster than his physiology. Being *yang*, man is "easily moved and easily stilled," as the *Exposition* says; thus slow and complete arousal is as important when practicing *coitus reservatus* as on the rare occasions when one ejaculates. If it is normally harmful to emit semen, it is even more harmful before the whole system has warmed up. The "Highest Tao's" "three levels" and *Classic of Su Nü*'s "four levels" correlate the size, hardness, and temperature of the penis during foreplay with the sequential arousal of such systems as skin, muscle, and bone. The disastrous consequences of incomplete arousal are among the sex related disorders detailed in such standard symptomology patterns as the "ten exhaustions" and "seven injuries." *Reservatus*, then, cannot be practiced in a passive state, for only with full arousal is the semen secure; as the *Classic of Su Nü* states, "When the four *ch'i* [of arousal] have arrived, and they are regulated by means of the *tao*, then one will not foolishly release the mechanism nor shed the *ching*."

Ninth, the mingling of sexual essences has the power to create new life; as the commentary to the *True Transmission* says, "A human being is endowed with father's *ching* and mother's blood, and from this his body is formed." Conception proves the existence of prenatal essence within the postnatal physical body. The importance of *ching* is experienced in a negative way in the aftermath of its loss and in a positive way through the pleasure of its stimulation and the strength of its preservation. Its power is preeminently manifest, however, in its role in procreation. The link between procreative potential and longevity is expressed

as early as the "Shih wen," which states, "If the penile *ch'i* fails to develop, there can be no reproduction. Therefore, long life depends completely on the penis." Restating this theme in the context of male-female relations, the *Exposition* declares, "When man and woman have intercourse, by practicing absorption long life is gained, and by ejaculating the womb is calmed and conception takes place." Through an inwardization of the concept of male fertility, there is a progression from the *Ishimpō*'s, "obtaining offspring" to the "Dangers and Benefit's," "If the *ching* goes forth, it creates new life, but if it is retained, it gives life to one's own body," until finally reaching in the sexual alchemists the spiritual parthenogenesis of what the *True Transmission* calls "forming the holy fetus."

Tenth, not surprisingly it was observed that sexual compatibility is the foundation of conjugal harmony. The *Exposition of Cultivating the True Essence* says, "Without sexual intercourse there would be no way for man and woman to harmonize their feelings." Harmony requires a detailed understanding of the partner's emotional state and arousal rate; therefore, couples must monitor each other's responses, pace their own level of excitement, and actively promote their partner's pleasure. At very least, the man must delay his climax to adjust for the differential in arousal time between "fire and water" and to ensure the woman's full satisfaction. For the purpose of preserving his own health on most occasions the man should refrain from emission, but the *Classic of Su Nü* notes that avoidance of satiety also contributes to preserving long-term interest in a partner, "Although exercising self-control and calming the passion, love actually increases, and one remains unsatiated." Sexual felicity is a precondition not only for personal pleasure and mutual satisfaction, but for the family fortunes and progeny as well. The "Benefits of the Bedchamber" says, "If couples have intercourse in the proper way, they will be blessed with children who are fortunate, virtuous, wise and good. . . . The way of the family will be daily more prosperous."

To these primarily andocentric experiences of sexual energetics, Chinese sexologists added a series of observations based on female response. As early as the Ma Wang tui era, and continuing through the Ming, the woman was said to love "slowness" (*hsü* 徐) and "duration" (*chiu* 久), and abhor "haste" (*chi* 急) and "violence" (*pao* 暴); all of which, for better or worse, have far-reaching physiological consequences. The woman expresses her desires through "sounds" (*yin* 音), "movements" (*tung* 動) and "signs" (*cheng* 徵 or *tao* 到). In her sexual responses she is compared to the element water, "slow to heat and slow to cool," and in her fertility to the moon, which gave its name, *yüeh* 月, to the menses (*yüeh-ching* 月經, *yüeh-shih* 月事, or *yüeh-hsin* 月信). Her sexual satisfaction was considered an objective condition for timely conception and healthy offspring. Prolonged foreplay always is presented as the necessary precondition for orgasm, whereas orgasm itself always is accomplished through penile penetration. At the same time, she was subjected to rigorous scrutiny for the proper physical characteristics (*ju hsiang* 入相) and disqualified as a sexual partner, in some cases after puberty, after childbirth in others, but certainly no later than menopause.

The language of the sexual literature does not distinguish between "facts" based on the direct experience of the author, the collective experience of generations, or deductive extrapolations from theoretical models of traditional science or cosmology. That enervation follows ejaculation or that virility declines with age may seem nearly universal experiences of sexuality, but knowledge of the more rapid recovery time associated with frequent *reservatus* and occasional emission or the necessity of full arousal for seminal security may be accessible only to those, borrowing Sivin's phrase, "in a heightened state of awareness." Determination of the optimal days of female fertility as the first five after the last day of menstruation would seem to be the product of collective observation and cor-

respond quite closely with curre͟ ern thinking. Other beliefs, such consequences of conception at time͟ traindicated by astrology, geomancy meteorology (lightning produces insa͟ ity, thunder deafness, and so on) may be less a case of empiricism than biological "pathetic fallacy."

The experiential crucible of Chinese sexual practices is best summarized by the legendary P'eng Tsu when he says in the *Classic of Su Nü*:

> When *ching* is emitted the whole body feels weary. One suffers buzzing in the ears and drowsiness in the eyes; the throat is parched and the joints heavy. Although there is brief pleasure, in the end there is discomfort. If, however, one engages in sex without emission, then the strength of our *ch'i* will be more than sufficient and our bodies at ease. One's hearing will be acute and vision clear. Although exercising self-control and calming the passion, love actually increases, and one remains unsatiated. How can this be considered unpleasurable?

The early sexual theorists concluded that orgasms past (and all orgasms are past in seconds) are not so sweet as sweet *ch'i* present. The whole of Chinese sexology may be seen in some sense as a response to the trauma of postejaculatory betrayal. The alternative esthetic of anticlimax they propose offers a solution to the dilemma so vividly portrayed in these texts as going to woman with a hunger and coming away with a hemorrhage, seeking to be full of her but becoming empty of oneself. In a passage in the "Shih wen" one might style, "the education of the penis," the Emperor Shun declares: "Oné must love it and please it; educate it and reason with it, and give it food and drink. Cause its peak to be strong and employ it with slowness. It must be fed but not spent; it must be given pleasure but not ejaculate. In this way resources accumulate and *ch'i* is garnered." Out of this developed a peculiarly Chinese brand of sexual epicureanism, requiring that one "know the white but maintain the black"—in sexual terms, an attitude of black *yin* coolness during the white heat of *yang* sexual combustion.

The drive to "plant one's seed" (*chung*   9

tzu 種子), as important as that was in traditional Chinese society, became for some, less compelling than the desire to live forever. Learning from nature came to mean not repeating nature's mistakes, for if the exoteric process of nature is to bear fruit and die, then the esoteric reversal must be to withhold one's seed and thus preserve one's own life. Procreation may be nature's necessity, but immortality would be mankind's masterpiece. In some texts, the archetype of immortality is taken from the perpetual motion of the celestial spheres and in others from the biological processes of conception, gestation, and birth. In theory, the breach created by puberty could be repaired by limiting future leakage and by supplementation through absorption of female essence. The decision, then was made to shift investment from orgasm to the more profitable and sustainable feeling of strength and health associated with nonejaculation. Orgasm should not be compared with our normal state but rather with our postcoital condition, not the baseline of the curve with the peak but the baseline with the low point. *Coitus reservatus* is then experienced not as an unbearable itch or pressure, but fullness and vigor. Beyond this, the waters of *ching*, an unfailing source of primal sanguinity, could be used to irrigate the spirit.

Consistent with Taoist yoga or the internal martial arts, the emphasis in sexual practices is on arousing and circulating internal energy without engaging in kinetic overkill or allowing the energy to escape. There is an attempt to maximize the anabolic advantages of relaxation, oxygenation and circulation as against the catabolic disadvantages of oxygen debt, lactic acid build-up, and sweat. The concept of climax, so much a part of the Western artistic, athletic, and even religious esthetic, is replaced by a system of positive abstinence in which potential energy is valued over kinetic. An internal esthetic of sustainable whole-body positive *ch'i* replaces the localized and transient pleasure of erogenous titilation and muscular spasm.

Is the practice of *coitus reservatus* merely the logical solution, as many have

speculated, to the burdens of polygamy? If this were the case, we should expect to encounter countless cross-cultural parallels, particularly in view of the prevalence of polygamy throughout history and in widely scattered societies around the world. Although the practice of *reservatus* may be found in other cultures, nowhere else is there comparable evidence for its independent origination or is its theory so elaborated. In her counsel to the Yellow Emperor, the goddess Su Nü teaches that the two-edged sword of polygamous sex can cut either in the direction of burden or opportunity. As a practical matter, the techniques of *reservatus* may be applied to satisfying the sexual needs of many wives, but the motivation can hardly have been altruism or even expedience. After all, why acquire more wives if there is not something to be gained for oneself? Chinese landlords did not acquire more land simply to increase their responsibilities, and certainly the anticipated rewards of polygamy tended to evaporate if it merely increased the opportunities for loss. Somehow, theoretical dissonance resulting from the dilemma that greater consumption leads to greater loss had to be resolved. Whether the origins of polygamy can be explained by the theory of "absorbing sexual energy" (*ts'ai-pu* 採補), or whether the theory represents a resolution of contradictions inherent in the institution itself is a question best left for future studies.

The Metaphysical Ground

Were the sexual practitioners scientists in search of a theory or metaphysicians in search of a practice? In terms of their intellectual orientation, the Ma Wang tui, *Ishimpō*, medical and householder manuals leaned toward the former, whereas the sexual alchemists leaned toward the latter. Both were interested in changing the material conditions of life, and both continually generated theory to account for their experience and project new possibilities. The general theory of *yin* and *yang* was congenial to all sexual practitioners and left plenty of room to maneuver as they struggled to square their theory with the facts of life and changing intellectual trends. Later, the Five Phases, trigrams and hexagrams, Stems and Branches, and so on, provided additional intellectual leverage for the sexual alchemists in constructing their theory. Sexual practice as an evolving system of thought will be analyzed in later sections of this Introduction, but here let us explore some of the fundamental intellectual issues confronting those who sought to make sex the solution to the problems of health and salvation. How many were won over to the sexual school by the force of its theory and how many by personal proclivity is a question that may be asked of any doctrine.

In the beginning was not the "Word," but cosmic sex, the mating of *Ch'ien* (The Creative) and *K'un* (The Receptive), heaven and earth. "One *yin* and one *yang* is called the *tao*," declares the *I ching*, "male and female mingle their *ching* and all creatures are born." It is no wonder, then, that echoing these words, the *Wondrous Discourse* reminds us, "The sexual union of man and woman is the *tao* of *yin* and *yang*." Sex is *yin* and *yang* in action; *yin* and *yang* are sex writ large. The sexual adept could no more enter the bedchamber free of centuries of cosmological baggage than could the connoisseur of art behold a painting in a vacuum. The followers of the sexual school of Taoism encouraged the development of a sexual sensibility that invested every act of coition, indeed, every organ, posture, and sensation with an indelible metaphysical significance. Man and woman are heaven and earth; heart and genitals are fire and water; sexual arousal is the rising sun. Cosmic configurations and celestial movements are reflected in the sex act. As a preparation for their mating, "the man sits on the woman's left and she on his right," for as the *Tung Hsüan tzu* continues, "heaven revolves to the left and earth spins to the right . . . , therefore, the man should revolve to the left and the woman to the right. . . . What is above acts, and what is below follows; this is the way of all things." The individual's role is not larger than life, but one could not

forget (even beneath the quilt) that it was certainly part of the larger life of the universe. As Kristofer Schipper observes in *Le Corps Taoïste*, "Its centrality in the cosmological concepts of *yin* and *yang* indicate, as Marcel Granet was fond of saying, that it was 'more sacred than we regard it!' Each union was taken as sanctified by heaven, and without the intervention of religion or political authority." Chinese sexual theoreticians had the audacity to believe that any metaphysics worth its salt should be valid in the bedroom, and one senses that much of Chinese metaphysics itself was actually inspired by the mundane physics of sex.

It was all well and good to define man and woman as the microcosmic embodiment of heaven and earth, and especially thereby to place man in the superior position, but the *Classic of Su Nü* could not avoid confronting two disquieting dissonances: female sexual superiority and human mortality. The *Classic* says, "Woman is superior to man in the same way that water is superior to fire," and "Because heaven and earth have attained the *tao* of union, they are eternal; because man and women have lost the *tao* of intercourse, they suffer the onset of early death." *Coitus reservatus* addressed the first crisis on a practical level by extending male stamina and, later, by substituting the trigram *Li* for fire, gave additional theoretical clarity to male "weakness in the middle," offering a logical source of supplementation in *K'an*, his mate.

Evening the odds in the "battle of the sexes" was one thing; matching the cosmic standard of longevity of heaven and earth was quite another. Chuang tzu's gentle, "merging with the processes of transformation of heaven, earth and all creation" might satisfy the mystics, and the "Dangers and Benefits" homely, "The *tao* of heaven and earth is to store its *ching* in the winter; if man can emulate this he can live a long time," might satisfy the physicians. However, some like P'eng Tsu, in the "Shih wen," envisioned an immortality both literal and personal, "*Yin* and *yang* do not die . . . thus are men of the *tao*." In the same work, fellow Immortal, Jung Ch'eng, further elaborates this theory of cosmic mimesis:

> The gentleman who desires long life must follow and observe the *tao* of heaven and earth. The *ch'i* of heaven waxes and wanes with the phases of the moon, and therefore it lives forever. The *ch'i* of earth alternates cold and hot with the seasons of the year; the difficult and the easy supplement each other. In this way, the earth endures without corruption. The gentleman must study the nature of heaven and earth and put this into practice with his own body.

No one could dispute that nature was the proper model for humanity, but deciphering her secrets proved to be a bit like interpreting "God's will."

Somehow heaven and earth conduct their relations so as to demonstrate a perfect conservation of matter and energy, or should we say *ch'i*, and thus achieve eternity. Human beings should expect no less of themselves. The spontaneity of sexual response, its independence from conscious will, which so disturbed St. Augustine, was taken by the Chinese as a sign of its naturalness, as the *Tung Hsüan tzu* says, "It is a natural response without the need for human effort." However, emulation of nature could not mean simply "doing what comes naturally." The urge to interact was natural; the urge to ejaculate was like overeating—too much of a good thing. The fact that heaven and earth "mated" without apparent loss to either side implied a kind of cosmic *coitus reservatus*. Human beings rarely arrive at this realization until well past puberty, when sexually speaking, they have already crossed into the postnatal (*hou-t'ien* 後天) realm; and it is for this reason that sexual disciplines are necessary.

The beginning of the *Wondrous Discourse*, echoing the *Su wen*, "Shang-ku t'ien-chen p'ien," speaks of a prehistoric period when every sage was a Methuselah, but even in the present age, immorality still is assumed to be a universal birthright. The universe as a whole possesses these pre- and postnatal aspects—one pure and permanent and the other impure and impermanent—and so does every human being. The emphasis on pre- and postnatal dualism, which does not become prominent in the extant sexual literature until the Ming, helps finally to give theoretical justification for seeming to "go against" nature. By making use of the age-old Taoist concept of "reversal" (*fan* 返), it becomes possible to pull oneself upstream (*ni* 逆) against the current of postnatal nature and to soar with the power of pure *yang* into the prenatal paradise of infinity (*wu-chi* 無極). The inner alchemist's theory of the etheric fetus (*sheng-t'ai* 聖胎), of course, was tailor-made for the sexual practitioners, who could now explain male absorption of female *yang* essence as resulting in a form of spiritual pregnancy.

For the Taoist practitioner, the body is truly the laboratory of the spirit. While the Confucianists honored the body as an inheritance from the ancestors, the Taoists saw the body as a miniature heaven and earth. In matters of sex, both Confucianists and Taoists were more rational than romantic, however, although applying a strict cost-benefit analysis, they came to different conclusions. The Confucianists felt that marriage was too important a social institution to confuse with love, and the Taoists felt that sex was too powerful a spiritual crucible to corrupt with romance. The Confucian sexual mystery is immortality in one's progeny; to the Taoist it is the transformation of one's own body chemistry. The Confucianists take the family as the microcosm; the Taoists take the body. For the later Taoists, by a painstaking technical process of self-transformation, one could become a god, whereas for the Confucianists, a reasonably righteous life and filial descendants was sufficient to secure one's comfort in the other world. Both aspired to another world, but the Taoists did not want to die to get there. For the "paired practices" school of Taoism, it seemed logical to seek the source of life eternal in the "gate of birth" (*sheng-men* 生門), the female vagina.

Although there is a strong metaphysical resonance to Chinese esoteric sex, this should not be confused with sexual mysticism. It may be possible to argue that the conscious enactment of the union of *yin* and *yang*, like, for example, self-identification with Shiva and Shakti, is mystical, but mysticism in the sense of experiencing the dissolution of self in other and bursting through to oneness with the divine does not describe the Chinese sexual ethos. In fact, only one expression of classical mystical experience is found in these texts, and it appears in the women's section. Ts'ui O Hsien tzu is quoted in a note to the *Queen Mother of the West's Ten Precepts on Women's Practice* as saying, "I forgot my own identity. . . . Suddenly I had another revelation and said, 'Heaven and earth are as one body with me.'" In "paired practice" sexual cultivation, however, over and over the man is warned to keep emotional distance from the woman, for what he is really seeking is fuel for his own journey. As for orgasm, it is not a flash of ecstasy that reveals our divine nature or potential for bliss, but a stupefying crash that leaves one dull and depleted.

The closest approximation of mystical longing in the sexual literature is a kind of metaphysical memory of the prenatal state of *wu-chi* (infinity), which preceded the division and interaction of *yin* and *yang*, a noumenal state above forms that one approaches by "transmuting the *ching* into *ch'i* and the *ch'i* into spirit, reverting to the void and becoming one with the *tao*." The goal of sexual cultivation is to isolate the prenatal aspect of each of the "Three Treasures"—the internal *ch'i*, the unexcited *ching*, and the desireless spirit. As the adage has it, "Speaking little preserves the *ch'i*; ejaculating little preserves the *ching*; worrying little preserves the spirit." The early Taoists were content with spiritual liberation in the midst of materiality, but the sexual yogi's ambition, if you will, was to develop sufficient escape velocity to leave the material plane. This was to be accomplished in a succession of booster phases by burning ever more refined physiological fuels.

The Individual and the Imperial Ideals

The private Taoist citizen at times was tolerated and at other times persecuted for engaging in sexual practices; his writings were sometimes more or less freely circulated and sometimes very effectively censored. As late as the early Republican period, Yeh Te-hui, in van Gulik's words, was "branded with the *hic niger est*," for publishing the *Ishimpō* sexology classics, and the Ming *Tao tsang* barred any works on sexual yoga. Mass religious movements, featuring sexual rites as a means to health and salvation, flourished during periods of popular unrest, but were generally stamped out with the reestablishment of strong central authority. However, whereas sex as a spiritual or religious practice always was on the defensive and often driven underground, the public ideal of the Emperor, the embodiment of *Ch'ien* on earth, nourishing his *yang* energy through contact with countless ranks of wives and consorts, was a permanent institutionalized model of the efficacy of *coitus reservatus* and multiple partners.

Based on Marcel Granet's seminal study, *Le Polygynie Sororale et le Sororat dans la Chine Féodale* (1920), van Gulik summarizes the sexual ideology of imperial rule in these words:

> In the human sphere the union of king and queen, the man and woman *par excellence*, epitomizes the balance of the positive and negative elements in the realm and the world. . . . Since the king has a maximum of *te*, he needs a large number of female partners to nourish and perpetuate it through sexual intercourse.

The orthodox ideology reinforced and even prescribed a regimen of self-strengthening sessions with wives of lower rank, culminating with full climax once a month with the Empress. The goal was both a heightening of imperial charisma and a eugenic pursuit of fit male heirs. The Emperor, ever jealous of his prerogatives, combed the countryside for the *13* most beautiful women. As the Emperor and his household were a kind of living museum of the most cherished values of the race, there was a constant tendency for the other members of the aristocracy to arrogate these privileges to themselves. Wang Mou, a twelfth century Confucian conservative, wrote in his *Yeh-k'o ts'ung-shu*, "Nowadays, the princes and nobility keep large numbers of consorts and concubines which they use as a kind of medicine in order to obtain the 'true essence' and thus to strengthen their vitality." Statuary in the form of Tantric "double deities," set up by the Mongol rulers in their Peking palaces during the thirteenth century, was still in evidence well into the Ming, when Shen Te-fu (1578–1642) says of these images in his *Pi-chou-chai yü-t'an*, "They represent pairs of Buddhas, richly adorned, embracing with their genitals touching." Shen tells us that their purpose was to instruct princes in the various methods of sexual congress, and thus answer on a grand scale to the sex manuals of private households. Hence, although the medieval court had no interest in popularizing sexual practices, as the absence of sexual titles from the official histories of the Yüan, Ming, and Ch'ing attests, they also could not help but preserve them in their very way of life.

Judging from the extant corpus and titles cited in secondary sources, the majority of works written during more tolerant periods and addressed primarily to the householder were written in the emperor-counselor dialogue form, whereas those written in a less liberal environment, or for restricted private readerships of connoisseurs (e.g., *Tung Hsuan tzu*), religious devotees (e.g., *Shang-ch'ing huang-shu kuo-tu i*), or serious adepts (e.g., *True Transmission*) adopt an alternative literary form or straightforward expository style. The mytho-imperial convention, then, seems to coincide with the more mainstream transmissions of sexual practices, whereas all other styles represent less sanctioned private practices. The reclusive Taoist was always regarded by the court as one who, so to speak, "sought salvation outside of the Church" and, if he gained a reputation for perfecting any of the arts of longevity, was likely to receive an imperial summons. The biographies of adepts and immortals recount the various ruses employed to avoid the audience hall and the kiss of death of imperial favor. Perhaps the emperor-tutor dialogue form flattered the monarch's sense of self-importance and illustrated a willingness on the part of accomplished adepts to share the secrets of the sex arcana with him.

The Battle of the Sexes

Against a background of economic scarcity and the perception of sexual energy as a natural resource, the "battle of the sexes" in China took on a more than metaphoric significance. In Taoist circles, the sex act was called "the battle of stealing and strengthening" (*ts'ai-pu chih chan* 採補之戰), indicating in somewhat ominous terms the potential for increasing one's own treasury at the enemy's expense. Of course, the methods of engagement follow classical Taoist military strategy, which forbids storming the gates, but employs instead a series of feints and maneuvers designed to sap the enemy's resistance.

On the mythological plane, the initiated hero and his sex quest remained a literary convention from the Han to the Ming. In the "Uniting Yin and Yang," "The Highest Tao," and especially the "Shih wen," the cast of heroes and initiators, including mortals and immortals, is large but exclusively male. By the time of the *Ishimpō* texts, perhaps five centuries later, the Yellow Emperor and his trio of initiatresses have become the central story, and the Queen Mother of the West emerges as the patroness of would-be women adepts. The Yellow Emperor and Queen Mother never meet in the mythology, but the dramatic possibilities of such an encounter are intriguing to contemplate. The rise of Su Nü, Ts'ai Nü and Hsüan Nü does not necessarily signal an advance in gender equality during this period, for the earlier Ma Wang tui texts are almost entirely free of theories prejudicial to women, although beauty contests, multiple female partners, and essence theft already have begun to creep into the *Ishimpō* material.

Metaphysically wedded to the paradigm of *yin* and *yang*, the Taoists were obliged to concede, in the words of the *Ch'ien-chin fang*, that "man cannot be without woman nor woman without man," for as the *Classic of Su Nü* says, "*yin* and *yang* require each other to function; thus when a man is excited he becomes hard and when a woman is moved she opens up." However, even the idea that health is impossible without sexual contact is never as lofty an ideal as "sprouting wings and ascending to heaven." Obviously such tensions could never be fully resolved in practice. *The History of the Former Han* calls sex, "The highest expression of natural feelings, the realm of the highest *tao*," but the *Secrets of the Jade Chamber* warns that, "Those who would cultivate their *yang* must not allow women to steal glimpses of this art." Even though the earlier texts do not turn away from the sensuous joys of sex, they also prefigure the planned obsolescence of the need for physical union between man and woman. In the oft-repeated legend, "The Yellow Emperor had relations with 1,200 women and ascended into heaven," the accent falls upon the ascension rather than the 1,200. The worldly obligation to produce progeny is dealt with somewhat grudgingly, and usually in the back pages, until it disappears altogether in the sexual alchemy texts. The "pure practices" school totally rejected carnal techniques in favor of the mystical marriage of male and female principles within the body of the meditator, and even the later "paired practices" adepts regarded relations with the opposite sex as an expedient to entering a paradise free of sexual desire.

The techniques described in these texts make it possible for the male to surmount his inherent handicap in the bedroom, to triumph over woman, who not only holds the power to bring forth life, but walks away so little diminished (or worse, unsatisfied) from the sex act. They give him courage in the presence of his "enemy," who is "superior to man in the same way that water is superior to fire," and allow him to emerge strengthened from his bouts in the bedroom. For the patriarch of the polygamous household, outnumbered by the adult females, the one chink in his amour is closed, and he is able to uphold his *yang* dominance over the *yin* majority. Each act of coition with emission exposes his "Achilles heel" and saps his will to rule, but multiple contacts without ejaculation reinforce his right to dominance. Perhaps this is compensation or face saving, or perhaps a subconscious primitive fear of the death of *yang* observed in night, in winter and in solar eclipse? In China, male mastery of feminine libido was accomplished not by clitorectomy as in some cultures, but by tapping female energy through *coitus reservatus*.

Once Taoist practices became focused on the pursuit of pure *yang*, then Taoism comes full circle and man once again is enjoined to "play the role of woman," to "play the guest" in sex. Outer *yang* is cultivated through activity, but inner *yang* prospers through passive inaction. Here, however, *yang* is not identified with the hard and aggressive as in the *Lao tzu* and *I ching*, but the light, the spiritual and the heavenly. The mutual longing of *yin* and *yang* for each other that marks the early sexual texts disappears in the writings of the sexual alchemists, who are concerned to steal a bit of masculine *yang* essence from the heart of *yin*, to repair the broken link, and return to the adamantine state of pure *yang*. Woman now is defined as the most convenient source of prenatal *yang* energy. Theft of the feminine principle is philosophical Taoism's subtlest victory for the patriarchy; theft of masculine essence from the female body is the contribution of sexual alchemy.

The Cult of Youth

We are accustomed to thinking of China as a culture that respects age above all else, where status soars as the years accumulate, somewhat softening the sting of old age. The Taoist ideal, however, has nothing to do with status and everything to do with youth. In fact, we might say that the Taoist ideal of eternal youth seeks the best of both worlds: a youthful glow on an old man. This is a common theme in popular iconography and a motif met with more than once in the sexual literature and art. We see, too, the glorification of the infant, the innocent adolescent, the virgin, and finally the fetus itself. The baby boy's spontaneous erections represent the innocent exuberance of the *ching*, the sweet sunrise of the *yang* force. For both sexes, prepubescence is a time not just of innocence but of sexual capital formation. The adept who guards his *ching* can hope to recapture both the function and appearance of adolescence. The higher adept retraces the fetal state by gestating a perfect etheric replica of himself. Nothing seemed more logical to the Taoists than the pursuit of immortality by the attainment of higher and higher states of health, "reversing the aging process and reverting to youth."

Finally, more than sympathetic magic favors partners of peak freshness, for the process of what the *Exposition of Cultivating the True Essence* calls "rejuvenation through grafting" is technique not merely metaphor. Modern man goes to bed with fears of contracting sexually transmitted diseases; the Taoists worried about losing their seminal assets, but also cherished the hope of capturing their partner's youthful essence. Something of the blush of youth rubs off through sexual transmission; as the *True Classic of Perfect Union* says of the Immortal Lü Tung-pin, "the more intimate he was with women, the higher his spirits." Even in solo practice, the adept is advised to gather the inner elixir while it is "fresh" and not yet "old." Youth indeed is the holy grail of Taoist science. If nature bestows it once, the means to reclaiming it a second time must be "available in every home." In sexual practices, the source of "eternal spring" (*yung-ch'un* 永春) is sought in the "springlike youth" (*ch'ing-ch'un* 青春) of young women.

Sexual Practices and Ethics

Confucius expressed his attitude toward sexuality with characteristic irony: "I have never seen a man who loved righteousness as much as sex," and Han Confucianists were already of two minds on the subject of sexual cultivation. The *History of the Former Han* editors were apparently sympathetic, for in commenting on the sexual titles in the "Bedroom Arts" bibliography, they note, "Those who abandon themselves [to sexual pleasure] pay no heed [to the precepts in the sex manuals], thus falling ill and harming their very lives." The *Po-hu t'ung* (Comprehensive discussions in the White Tiger Hall), a record of discussions on the Confucian classics held in 79 A.D., shows a similar atunement to the principles of sexual practices, reminding gentlemen of a concubine's right to regular sexual satisfaction "up to the age of fifty," and the necessity for men over seventy to resume sexual relations, "lest in sleeping alone they not be warm."

There were some skeptical voices in the Confucian camp, however, as rationalist, Wang Ch'ung (27–97 A.D.) protests in his *Lun heng*, "Ming-i," "Su Nü explained the method of the five females to the Yellow Emperor. This art not only brings physical harm to father and mother, but threatens the nature of sons and daughters." A thousand years later, Wang Mou in his *Yeh-k'o ts'ung-shu*, Chapter 29, again warned against the health hazards of sexual practices. However, when Wang laments that even the great Confucian champion, Han Yü, succumbed to sexual teachings, we cannot help but conclude that, in the main, sexual techniques were not seen as incompatible with Confucian values. *Coitus reservatus* could be reconciled with the Doctrine of the Mean, and the *History of the Former Han*'s "pleasure with restraint" perfectly summarizes the Confucian position that moderation, rather than indulgence or repression of natural urges, was conducive to mental balance. Deprived of any sense that sex itself was sinful, and hardly defenders of equality for women, the majority of Confucianists were not about to set themselves four-square against the sexual arts, particularly when these corresponded in principle with medical opinion and just might lead to immortality. Not until the Ming do the handbooks of sex disappear altogether from the official bibliographic catalogues, and the survival of sexual texts seems to have been most precarious during the Mongol and Manchu dynasties.

More serious objections than the Confucianists could muster came from the Buddhist quarter. Apart from the Tantrists, the Buddhists in general were less impressed that sexual practices might lead to the accumulation of *ch'i* than they were certain it would lead to the accumulation of *karma*. However, because of their own celibate stand, the Buddhists could no more attack these Taoist practices as a threat to the family than could polygamous Confucianists, who may have used these techniques to keep the peace at home. Again, given the low status of women in both Confucianism and Buddhism, neither could claim to be defenders of women against the biological raiding practiced by some Taoists. Ironically, rather than the Chinese Buddhists being influenced by native sexual disciplines, a segment of the Taoists from the fifth century on actually embraced celibacy to prevent the Buddhists from capturing the moral high ground in their rivalry. Though the terms "false teachings" (*wei-chiao* 偽教) and "heterodox teachings" (*hsieh-chiao* 邪教) are used in relation to the sexual arts, neither Confucian nor Buddhist arguments have the ring of profound moral outrage. The Buddhist notion that sex was sinful or attachment forming was no more acceptable to the majority of Confucianists than it was to any but the most quiescent Taoists.

The central problems for the sexual theoreticians themselves were practical not ethical: the depletion of female partners and the need for self-control. However, issues that assume the character of ethical dilemmas within the sexual school include the necessity of householders to maintain decorum (*li* 禮) in their sexual relations and the ability of adepts to remain detached and avoid using *reservatus* to merely prolong earthly pleasures. The "Highest Tao" speaks of "excessive roughness and lack of decorum," which all the texts thereafter decry as harmful to the health of both partners and to their emotional bond. The *Wondrous Discourse* warns against the abuse of technical skill: "If this is taken as the secret of relations with creatures of red rough within the bedcurtains, then one will surely suffer the disaster of fanning the flame while reducing the oil." Nevertheless, whatever tension existed between the claims of technique and ethics was generally resolved in favor of technique, especially when immortality was the end that justified the means. Ethical prerequisites are conspicuously absent from the sexual literature, and even in women's solo cultivation, which consistently emphasizes the need for moral development in tandem with practice, we find as in the *Ten Precepts*, "It is not sufficient to be merely good; to attain immortality one must know the art." Because ethics were so closely associated in the minds of the Taoists with the conventional morality of the Confucianists, it is not surprising that they refused to let this stand in the way of their pursuit of the natural, or even as here, supernatural salvation through the techniques of physiological manipulation.

In the Author's Preface to the *True Transmission of the Golden Elixir*, Sun Ju-chung discusses an ethical dilemma that disturbed him prior to putting his father's teachings into writing. Although he hoped that publication of this esoteric lore would save it from extinction, he also agonized over its falling into the "wrong hands." In the early sexual literature, the wrong hands meant committing gender treason by sharing secrets with the "enemy," but for Sun the wrong hands meant, "those who were only interested in using this art to achieve physical health" and did not proceed to the great work of preparing the elixir. It is clear from the sincerity and urgency of Sun's tone that the pursuit of immortality carried the force of ethical imperative.

17

The Sexology Classics as Literature

Taken together, the sexology classics are decidedly didactic, but hardly tedious technical manuals or dry scientific treatises. The original audience for these works, the literati, expected all information to arrive in a pleasing literary package. Dramatic dialogue, verse, and aphorism, as well as the balanced alternation of empirical and theoretical passages all are blended with special delicacy in the sexual literature. As long as the *Kama Sutra* and *Ars Amatoria* are revered as landmarks of world literature, it would be difficult to deny that status to the *Tung Hsüan tzu*, *True Classic of Perfect Union*, or "The Rootless Tree," where literary values have created lively works of lasting beauty. Some day the physiological poetry of Chinese self-cultivation may be recognized as a literary genre in its own right.

The Ma Wang tui and *Ishimpō* texts, representing the early phase of sexual practice, have the clean-edge carved-in-stone quality of classics that were made to last. The dialogue style of these works, reminiscent of the earliest medical classics, contributes to the aura of authority and antiquity. The texts of the third group, being derivative, are more pallid stylistically, and though the *Wondrous Discourse* of the middle Ming returns again to the Yellow Emperor–Su Nü dialogue form, it now merely is a format, giving structure but not life to the work. The texts of the sexual alchemists show a new burst of technical and theoretical innovation, and the pages fairly crawl with bizarre linguistic creatures. How much of the technical jargon of the later texts was a convenient scientific shorthand, how much was intended to put outsiders off the scent, and how much was read as a kind of premodern fantasy or science fiction are questions begging further study. Certainly not all readers of the *True Transmission* and Chang San-feng texts were prepared to follow the instructions to the letter, but many were undoubtedly entertained and perhaps inspired in the bedroom by the compelling language of the writing.

Donald Harper is perhaps the first scholar to look at the sexual texts within the context of literary tradition. I agree from a literary standpoint that the use of verse in the texts is intended to "enchant" the reader and facilitate recitation and memorization, having its origins in rhetoric and magico-religious incantation. At the same time I also concur with Isabelle Robinet's observation in her *Méditation Taoïste*, which although not specifically addressed to the sexual literature, applies equally well: "It appears that in their present form, the great classics are the product of the transcription and codification of a certain number of incantations, formulae, methods or techniques—called *chüeh, fa,* or *tao.*" The sexual aphorisms (*chüeh* 訣), such as "nine shallow, one deep" (*chiu-ch'ien i-shen* 九淺一深), "arousal without emission" (*tung erh pu hsieh* 動而不瀉), or "enter dead, withdraw live" (*ssu ju sheng ch'u* 死入生出) are examples of language in its most distilled and potentized form. Intended to facilitate replication of experience, the *chüeh* are both mnemonic and mantra, altering the subjectivity of the practitioner to catalyze physiological transformation.

Harper, like many other scholars, frustrated by philological headaches in the sexual literature, insists that, "The 'Ho Yin Yang' verse represents the earliest example of cryptic poetry composed in order to conceal a technique in a secret code." Ascribing motives to ancient and anonymous Chinese authors is risky business. We have little enough evidence of reader response to the content of the texts, much less the language. Medical works of the same period are no less difficult for the uninitiated, nor are the sexual texts more difficult than the medical after their terminology has been mastered. Harper himself says of the Ma Wang tui sexual texts, "they do not constitute an isolated set of esoteric teachings." Is the language of physicists or lawyers deliberately hermetical, or rather an attempt to communicate with precision and economy to an initiated readership? I believe what we see in the sexual literature is simply the language of specialists.

III. SEXUAL PRACTICES AND MEDICINE

The medical corpus provides our first glimpse into the principles of Chinese sexual practice. The *Huang-ti nei-ching su-wen* and *Ling shu*, of perhaps the seventh to third centuries B.C., established conservation as the cornerstone of medical advice on sex. The *Su wen*, "Shang-ku t'ien-chen p'ien" decries, "entering the bedchamber in a drunken state and exhausting the *ching* through desire," and the *Ling shu* "Hsieh-ch'i tsang-fu ping-hsing p'ien" warns, "excessive sexual exhaustion injures the kidneys (*shen*, urogenital system)." An interesting case history of "sexual exhaustion" from this period is preserved in the historical annals of the *Tso chuan*:

> The Ruler of Chin requested medical advice from the state of Ch'in. Duke Ching of Ch'in sent Physician Ho to see him. Physician Ho declared: "The illness is incurable for the cause may be found in your entering the women's quarters. . . ." The Duke asked, "Should women be avoided?" Physician Ho responded, "Simply be moderate."

Another pre-Ch'in historical and philosophical work, the *Lü-shih ch'un-ch'iu*, "Ch'ing-yü p'ien," expresses the concept of moderation in the form of a parable, "If one understands how to be sparing in one's early years, the *ching* will not be exhausted. If cold comes early in the autumn the winter will surely be warm. Much rain in the spring means summer drought." The principle of the conservation of sexual energy thus was firmly established during the period of the great philosophers and physicians several centuries before the Common Era. Echoes of this medical advice can be heard in the philosopher Chuang tzu's, "Do not agitate your *ching*" and the *Lieh tzu*'s, "Sickness arises from starvation, satiety and sexual desire."

Although sexual continence as a tenet of medicine appears as early as our earliest medical text, the *Su wen*, sexual practice as a special branch of learning cannot be documented until the Ma Wang tui "Uniting Yin and Yang" and "Highest Tao" and the *Han shu*'s "Art of the Bedchamber" bibliography. The existence of separate sexual texts in the Ma Wang tui corpus and the level of codification and terminological sophistication they reveal suggests a period of development reaching back at least to the late Chou. Though we can say with certainty that by the second century B.C., the "art of the bedchamber" had established itself as an independent state sharing borders with medical science and the yogic practices of self-cultivation, the regulation of sex life remained an important aspect of medical theory and practice. From the pre-Ch'in *Su wen* and *Ling shu* to the late Han *Chin kuei* of Chang Chi (Chung-ching) and Sun Ssu-miao's *Ch'ien-chin i-fang* of the T'ang, we see a consistent emphasis on the role of *ching* conservation in promoting general health. Specialized works such as Chu Tan-hsi's *Se-yü p'ien* (On sexual desire) and Chao Hsien's *Kua yü* (On reducing desire) counsel not only moderation in conjugal relations but late marriage and extreme caution in one's declining years. Although mainstream medicine and esoteric sexual practice share a common emphasis on conservation, where the two part ways is that the former stresses minimizing contact and reducing desires, whereas the latter seeks to maximize contact to stimulate the *yang* principle and absorb sexual essence from female partners. A figure like the great T'ang physician Sun Ssu-miao was able to maintain one foot in each camp. In his *Ch'ien-chin i-fang* he put the conventional medical wisdom on continence in the mouth of the legendary Immortal, P'eng Tsu: "The superior man sleeps in a separate bed and the average under separate quilt. A hundred doses of medicine are not as good as sleeping by oneself. Satiety at night costs one day of life, intoxication one month, but sex a year." However, in his earlier *Ch'ien-chin yao-fang*, "Fang-chung pu-i"

(Benefits of the bedchamber) he described nearly every technique of the sexual alchemists, including the path of "returning the *ching*" and meditative visualizations for use during intercourse.

The most important concept shared by the medical and sexual traditions is *ching*. Western medicine regards sexuality largely in relation to the function of reproduction, but for the Chinese it is not only "what life comes from," as the *Ling shu* says, but in the words of the "Shih wen," "Nothing is more important for the *ch'i* of man than the *ching* of the penis." The theoretical primacy of the *ching* in medicine and sexual practices is illustrated in two Ming texts: Kung Yen-hsien's medical classic, the *Shou-shih pao-yüan* and the anonymous *Wondrous Discourse of Su Nü*. Kung states, "We must not let the desires run wild or the *ching* will be exhausted. The *ching* must not become exhausted or primal purity dissipates. Therefore, *ching* generates *ch'i* and *ch'i* generates spirit." In parallel fashion the *Discourse* asserts, "The *tao* of cultivating life takes *ch'i* as its root. The *ch'i* can mobilize the blood and the blood can be transformed into *ching*. The *ching* can nourish the spirit." There also is agreement between these two works on the special importance of abstinence in adolescence and early manhood, the period when the *ching* is still fragile. As if with one voice, the *Shou-shih pao-yüan* warns, "If a man experiences his first emission too early this harms his *ching-ch'i*", and the *Discourse* cautions, "When a man is young his blood *ch'i* is not yet full and he must abstain from sex." Both medical and sexual practice serve the *ching*, but each in its own way.

If *ching* is the basic unit of sexual substance and energy, *shen* is the locus of its function. The term *shen*, often misleadingly translated "kidneys" or "renal system," is simultaneously a collective designation for the urogenital organs (kidneys and testes designated as "internal *shen*" and "external *shen*," respectively) and a network of interconnected systems of influence extending to include the brain, bones, and marrow, and at its outermost limit, the teeth and hair. Its external orifices are the ears above and penis (or vagina) and anus below . Commenting on the significance of the *shen*'s anatomical location, the *Su wen*, "Chin-kuei chen-yen lun," says, "The abdomen is *yin*, and the organ representing *yin* within *yin* is the *shen*." Another chapter, the "Liu-chieh tsang-hsiang lun" describes its special function, "The *shen* rules the root of hibernation and storage. It is the locus of the *ching*." The *Su wen*, "Hsüan-ming wu-ch'i p'ien," outlines the principal correspondences between the Five Viscera (heart, lungs, liver, spleen, and kidneys) and various external influences and internal interactions. The text explains that when the heart's fire is added to a deficiency in the *shen*, one experiences a feeling of "fearfulness" (*k'ung* 恐). This precisely describes the Yellow Emperor's condition in the opening paragraph of the *Classic of Su Nü* when he confesses his "fear of danger." The external secretion associated with the *shen* is saliva, and thus the *Exposition of Cultivating the True Essence*, Chapter 13, says, "The woman's 'upper peak' is called Red Lotus Peak. Its medicine is called 'jade spring.' . . . The man should lap it up with his tongue. . . . It nourishes the 'mysterious gate' (sexual organ) and fortifies the *tan-t'ien*." The *Su wen*, "Hsüan-ming wu-ch'i p'ien's" statement that, "afflictions of the *yang* principle manifest during the winter," explains the sexual aphorism's advice on coital frequency: "Thrice [a month] in spring, twice in summer, once in autumn, and none in winter." According to the *Su wen*, the aspect of human consciousness centered in the *shen* is "will" (*chih* 志), which explains postcoital enervation and lack of ambition in chronic *shen* deficiency. The relationship among the *shen*, brain, and ears helps to understand the emphasis in the sexual literature on "returning the *ching* to nourish the brain" and the "buzzing in the ears" associated with *ching* deficiency following emission.

The genital function of the *shen* has its *yin* and *yang* aspects. The *yin* aspect, considered postnatal and symbolized by the element water, is associated with semen; the *yang* aspect, considered prenatal and symbolized by fire is associated with sexual energy. The theory of the pre- and postnatal aspects of the *shen* accounts for why the union of *yin* and *yang ching* (male and female) is necessary for conception, and yet the reproductive potential is not immediately operative in the offspring. The prenatal aspect of the *ching* passed on by the parents continues to guide the maturation of the offspring and is sustained by the "*ching* of water and grain" until the postnatal aspect reaches repletion at puberty. Because of the postnatal *ching*'s susceptibility to leakage, it poses a threat to the integrity of the prenatal *ching*, which now depends upon it, and indeed to the well-being of all the organs that look to the *shen* as a kind of reservoir of energy for the whole body. Of course, the heart, or "ruler" (*chün* 君) of the body is the supreme manifestation of the fire principle, but the "ministerial fire" (*hsiang-huo* 相火) of the *shen*, or "true fire within water," earned for the *shen* the title of "lesser heart" (*hsiao-hsin* 小心). The seat of the sexual fire, or "true *yang*" (*chen-yang* 真陽), in the *shen* is called the "gate of life" (*ming-men* 命門), variously assigned in the classical literature to the right kidney or a point between the kidneys. The physiological alchemists, solo and sexual alike, referred to the "true *yang*" as "gold within water" and considered it the raw material of the elixir. For medicine, however, it is sufficient simply to preserve the balance of pre- and postnatal aspects of the *ching*, which may be accomplished by sexual continence and a tranquil mind.

Most of the primary classical definitions of *ching*, *shen*, and *ming-men* are more or less male biased, and it is necessary to cull fragmentary references to female sexuality in the general medical literature and specialized works on traditional gynecology. The *Su wen*, "Shang-ku t'ien-chen lun" explains:

At seven a woman's *shen-ch'i* is replete, her teeth change and hair grows. At twice seven she has reached maturity, her *Jen* meridian is open, her *Ch'ung* meridian full, and her menses flows at regular intervals. Now she is able to bear children. . . . At eight a man's *shen-ch'i* is full, his hair

grows and teeth change. At twice eight the *shen-ch'i* is replete, he reaches sexual maturity, and the *ching-ch'i* overflows. If *yin* and *yang* unite harmoniously, he is able to sire offspring.

This physiological account may be supplemented by an attempt at comparative anatomy from a treatise entitled *T'ai-hsi ken-chih yao-chüeh* found in the *Yün-chi ch'i-ch'ien*, Chapter 58:

The root and origin of the [primal *ch'i*] is opposite the navel, at the level of the nineteenth vertebra, in the space in front of the spine where it approaches the bladder from below. It is called the "stalk of life" (*ming-ti* 命蒂) "gate of life" (*ming-men* 命門), "root of life" (*ming-ken* 命根), or "abode of the *ching*" (*ching-shih* 精室). It is here that men store their semen and women their menstrual blood. This then is the source of the *ch'i* of long life and immortality.

It is axiomatic in Chinese medical parlance that "man is ruled by *ch'i* and woman by blood," thus it is clear from the foregoing that the functional equivalent of the male *ching* for the female is blood. A woman's maturation and fertility are calculated in terms of blood, yet her transferable sexual energy in most of the sexual literature is referred to as *ching*. For the male, *ching*, orgasm, and conception coincide in one spasmodic event; for the female, blood, orgasm, and conception are not so neatly aligned. The *I ching* says, "Male and female mingle their *ching*." But most medical texts describe conception as the meeting of *ching* and blood. The ovaries are not defined as such in Chinese medicine, much less the ovum, but both are subsumed under the categories of "womb' (*pao* 胞) and "blood." For medical practitioners, the concept of the role of blood in female health and fertility was sufficient for most theoretical and practical purposes. However, for sexual practitioners, the object being absorption of sexual energy, the concept of blood must have proven exceedingly inconvenient.

In the early sexual literature and throughout the householder tradition, the focus was on female *ching* released *21* during orgasm without prescribing any schedule linked to her menstrual cycle; however, in the later sexual alchemy texts the menstrual cycle came to be used to calculate a woman's peak ripeness as an object of "medicine" gathering. Accompanying this shift in focus from orgasm to menses is a search for the *yang-ch'i* locked within the female body and an attempt to capture it before overripening into *yin* blood. Women's solo practices, too, seek to refine the "starlike heavenly treasure" before it degenerates into "red pearls" or the "red dragon." The literature of traditional Chinese gynecology is dominated by problems of menstruation, fertility, and childbearing, but two exceptions are the Ming *Wan-mi-chai fu-k'o* of Wan Ch'üan and the Ch'ing *Fu-k'o yü-ch'ih* of Shen Chin-ao, both of which provide detailed analysis of the stages of arousal, the signs of sexual satisfaction, and the symptoms of inappropriate sexual activity, which parallel the sexology classics in this collection.

The medical literature of *shen* dysfunction offers additional insights into the unique therapies recommended in the sexology classics. Medical theory generally attributes sexual dysfunction to deficiency syndrome in the *shen* sphere and, specifically, "deficiency of *yang*." The homeostasis of the *shen* is dependent on the complementary balance of water and fire, the "true *yin*" and "original *yang*." *Yang* deficiency of the *shen* allows the water to operate unchecked, resulting in the following symptoms: premature ejaculation, bloating, incontinence, and spontaneous sweating; *yin* deficiency allows the fire to operate unchecked and produces nocturnal emission, irritability, parched mouth, insomnia, and dizziness. To cure *yang* deficiency, traditional Chinese medicine addresses the *ch'i*; to cure *yin* deficiency it tonifies the blood. The medical syndrome known as "empty fire" (hsü-huo 虛火) explains the anomalous relationship between fire and water principles in the etiology of *shen* dysfunction: a deficiency of water brought about by excessive ejaculation actually allows the fire of sexual desire to rage unchecked

and results in a downward spiral of exhaustion. Thus in the medical literature, sexual excess (*fang-lao* 房勞) is seen as the chief threat to *shen* health and *ching* sufficiency. The Ma Wang tui and *Ishimpō* sexology texts share with the medical literature (e.g., *Chu-ping yüan-hou lun*, "Hsü-lao hou") the use of ejaculation analysis as a diagnostic indicator, usually referred to as the "seven injuries" (*ch'i-shang* 七傷). However, the sexual literature goes beyond the medical in tracing a host of illnesses to improper intercourse and in prescribing sexual yoga as a therapeutic modality. The sexual practitioners reject the conservative strategy of the physicians in treating *shen* deficiency, arguing that restriction may succeed in stemming *ching* loss, but the stagnant *ching* then will become moribund and unable to generate *ch'i* for the body. The "Dangers and Benefits" states the sexual school's position very succinctly: "By seeking to prevent the *ch'i* from becoming excited, they weaken their *yang* principle." This debate is reminiscent of the legend of Bodhidharma who is said to have introduced *kung-fu* exercises into the monastic routine of Shao-lin monks to offset the debilitating effects of sedentary meditation.

An interesting case study in the medical significance of sex-related conditions is revealed in the diaries of the late nineteenth century Manchu Emperor Kuang-hsü, who like many emperors experienced precocious sexual contact and hundred of wives and concubines vying for his favor. He recorded: "I have suffered from nocturnal emissions for twenty years. Ten years ago it would occur as many as ten times a month, but during the past ten years only two or three. Instances of emission without dreams or erection were especially serious during the winter." Here, then, is a perfect example of how, according to Chinese medical theory, spermatorrhea and nocturnal emissions are the result of deficiency and not repletion of *ching*, an instability resulting from the imbalance of fire and water. A similar confession appears in Chiang Wei-ch'iao's *Yin Shih tzu ching-*

tso fa (Master Yin Shih's meditation method), a widely circulated and influential work published in 1914. Correlating his poor health and sex-life, he says, "At twelve I began to masturbate and after habitual practice began to suffer nocturnal emissions, dizziness, waist pain, blurred vision, buzzing in the ears, and night sweats. . . . At twenty-two I was married . . . and was unable to control my sexual desire."

Because the practice of medicine is such a public affair, and because the corpus of received medical literature is so voluminous, it would be tempting to ask the question, What is the influence of medicine on sexual practices? However, the theoretical consonance of the Ma Wang tui medical and sexual texts, their equal level of development, the mixing of sexual and nonsexual modalities in some of the texts, and even their physical proximity on discovery point to a common lineage. That there already were specialized works on sexual practices by the early Han perhaps is natural, given the emphasis on sex life in health, and may be similar to the case of acupuncture and herbology, which existed as somewhat autonomous regions under a common constitution within the borders of medical science. Similarly, the juxtaposition of normal and paranormal health aspirations in the sexual literature parallels the situation of herbology, which at its outer fringe gave rise to the search for the external elixir of immortality, and acupuncture, which at its outer fringe inspired the belief that internal energy could be channeled and transformed to form the inner elixir.

Whether sexual practices should be traced as an independent movement; or whether it should be seen as a branch of medicine, yoga, or meditation or as part of a larger *yang-sheng* enterprise is open to question. What sexual practices share with medicine, for example, is not necessarily borrowed, but often seems to spring from a common matrix. Herbology attempts to influence our physiological state through the digestive and circulatory systems; acupuncture and moxibustion through the meridians; yoga and meditation through the mind, musculature, and respiratory system; and sexual practices through the sex organs.

Though we have seen many examples of medicine and sexual practices sharing a common theoretical platform, it is rare to find a direct medical attack on the foundations of sexual practice. However, in this startlingly clinical analysis, the Ch'ing gynecologist, Shen Chin-ao says.

> The *tao* of concentrating the *ching* consists of (1) reducing desires, (2) moderating intercourse, (3) stilling anger, (4) abstaining from alcohol, and (5) avoiding stimulating foods. Today, those who discuss health often mention gathering *yin* to supplement *yang* and prolonged sex without ejaculation. This is great nonsense! The *shen* is the center of the *ching*. Whenever man and woman have intercourse the *shen* is disturbed. As the *shen* is agitated the *ching* and blood will certainly be set in motion. Even if there is no external emission, the *ching* has already left its center. Even if one succeeds in restraining oneself, there are always a few drops of "true *ching*" which escape as the penis becomes limp. This is based on common experience. Just as fire produces smoke and flame, how could these return again to the log from which they spring?

The normally peaceful relations between medicine and sexual practice, based on a common concern for *ching* conservation, are shattered here by Shen Chin-ao, who denies any advantage to the *ching* resulting from sexual arousal and insists that stimulation, even without ejaculation, causes a tangible loss to the *ching*. Although Shen's argument is unusual in its thrust, it ultimately reinforces the very traditional medical and Taoist quietist positions that continence is the best medicine in sexual matters. This against the sexual school's conviction that an attenuated or homeopathic dose of sexual contact alone was capable of conferring immunity to leakage.

IV. Sexual Practices and Taoism

The Position of Sexual Practices in Taoism

From the point of view of the official dynastic bibliographers, the association of sexual techniques and Taoism was not decisively accomplished until the Sung. After occupying a rubric of its own during the Han and sharing a section with "Medical Works" in the Sui and T'ang, sexual practices finally came to rest under "Taoist Works" in the *History of the Sung*. In fact, the Sung Taoist, Tseng Tsao, writing in his *Tao shu*, "Jung Ch'eng p'ien," associates the propagation of sexual teachings with "Taoist priests" (*fang-shih* 方士), who confuse the scholar class with teachings on the "battle of stealing sexual essences." Looking back to our earliest sexual texts, however, the "Uniting Yin and Yang" and "Highest Tao," apart from such expressions as "immortal" (*hsien* 仙) and "spiritual illumination" (*shen-ming* 神明), which strike us as distinctively Taoist, there is little else to indicate special philosophical affiliation. Even two hundred years later, in the first century of the Common Era, Wang Ch'ung tells us in his *Lun heng*, "Ming-i," that Su Nü transmitted the "method of the Five Females" without associating these practices with any philosophical school, despite ample opportunity to do so in the "Tao hsü" chapter devoted entirely to condemning Taoist macrobiotic techniques.

For Taoist alchemist, Ko Hung (283–363 A.D.), writing another two hundred years after Wang Ch'ung in his *Pao P'u tzu*, Chapter 8, sexual cultivation was enshrined as a desideratum in a trinity of fundamental techniques: "Those seeking immortality must perfect the absolute essentials. These consist of treasuring the *ching*, circulating the *ch'i*, and consuming the great medicine." For Ko, what it meant to be a Taoist in the fourth century

24 was to be deadly serious about the business of immortality, and he had very definite opinions about the role of sexual disciplines:

> There are more than ten masters of the sexual arts. Some use them to cure injury, some to attack illness, some to strengthen the *yang* by absorbing *yin*, and some to achieve longevity. The essential teaching is to "return the *ching* to nourish the brain." This art has been orally transmitted from immortal to immortal without being recorded. Those who consume the most precious medicines, but fail to grasp the essentials of this art, cannot achieve long life. It is also the case that man cannot abstain from intercourse, for if *yin* and *yang* do not interact, this leads to diseases of obstruction. One becomes withdrawn and resentful, and thus sickly and short lived. Giving free rein to one's passions also shortens life, and thus only by restrained balance can one avoid harm. Without receiving the secret oral transmissions of the art, not one man in ten thousand can escape practicing this without injuring himself. The works of Hsüan [Nü], Su [Nü], Jung Ch'eng Kung, and P'eng Tsu record only the rough outline without committing the real secrets to writing. Those who desire immortality must conscientiously seek to discover it. My discussion here is based on the words of master Cheng Chun. They are for the benefit of future followers of the *tao* and are not merely personal conjecture. I have not myself exhausted the secrets of this art. One branch of Taoists seek solely by means of the art of intercourse to achieve immortality without preparing the medicine of the golden elixir. This is sheer folly!

From Ko's discussion, the only one of its kind from the pre-T'ang period, it is apparent that he accepted the general macrobiotic benefits of sex craft as set forth in the Ma Wang tui and *Ishimpō* literature. A confirmed alchemist, however, he saw the chief function of sexual techniques and yoga as extending life to "300 years," the range necessary for completing the true "golden elixir." For Ko, then, without sexual practice the best medicine is useless, but without the elixir, immortality is unattainable. For the purposes of our study, Ko has succeeded in defining the position of the "external elixir" (*wai-tan* 外丹) alchemists and at the same time has given sexual cultivation an ancillary but assured role in the Taoist curriculum. Finally, it is equally clear from Ko's discussion that there existed by the fourth century, if not earlier, a school of immortality seekers based exclusively on the sexual elixir. This development well may have been due to the increasing tendency to pursue technical approaches to immortality, along with the promise of life extension already present in the earliest sexual literature. The sexual elixir school would continue to flourish through the Ming, in parallel with the medical and householder traditions of sexual practices.

While Ko Hung was developing his theories, and apparently experimenting in the laboratory, another movement, also marching under the banner of the *tao*, had arisen among the masses of the common people. Beginning a century before Ko's birth during the late Han, a millenarian religious and political movement led by the Masters Chang and promising to usher in the Great Peace incorporated ceremonial "sexual union" (*ho-ch'i* 合氣, *hun-ch'i* 混氣, or *ho-ho* 和合) as a means of obtaining "absolution of sins" (*shih-tsui* 釋罪). Unfortunately, most of what we know about this extraordinary movement is filtered through the lens of its enemies. The *San-kuo chih* (Annals of the Three Kingdoms), representing the establishment response to these radical teachings, condemned them as "demonic doctrines" (*kuei tao* 鬼道). Its sexual rituals in particular proved to be the exposed soft flank that allowed Buddhist polemicists such as Tao An in his *Erh chiao lun* (Discourse on the two teachings) and Hsüan Kuang in his *Pien huo lun* (Discourse refuting delusions) to attack them as "demonic methods" (*kuei-fa* 鬼法) and "false doctrines" (*wei-tao* 僞道). Perhaps the most complete contemporary account is that of Chen Luan, who in his *Hsiao tao lun* (Ridiculing the

Taoists) describes his personal experiences in a Taoist congregation prior to being converted to Buddhism. Writing in 570 A.D. he says, "We were first instructed in the practice of 'uniting *ch'i*' (*ho-ch'i* 合氣) after the teachings of the *Yellow Book* (*Huang shu* 黃書), and the three-five-seven-nine method of sexual intercourse. In pairs of 'four eyes and two tongues' we practiced the *tao* in the *tan-t'ien*."

Knowledge of the existence of sexual rituals in ancient China has inspired the imaginations of Western scholars such as Granet, Maspero, and Needham, who could not help but be impressed with the sharp contrast between the stereotype of Confucian society and the Dionysian images these practices evoke. However, precisely what Maspero assumed to have been "eliminated from the *Tao tsang*," Kristofer Schipper discovered there under the title *Shang-ch'ing huang-shu kuo-tu i*, simply an elaborated version of the same title mentioned by Tao An and Chen Luan. The text agrees in many details and general tone with eyewitness Buddhist accounts, although I would concur with Schipper's dating as "late medieval." The text, a complete liturgy for sexual ceremonies in the Taoist religion, is a remarkable document for social history, the history of religions, and sexology. For our purposes, it is most interesting as a synthesis of religious ritual and sexual yoga. Let us briefly summarize the ceremony as it is described in the text.

The celebrants, not to exceed twenty in number, first bathe, burn incense, and offer salutations to the officiating priest (*shih* 師) and invocations to the gods. The participants now begin meditative visualizations based on colored *ch'i* (white, yellow, red, green, and black) corresponding to the five directions and five organs. The couples kneel facing each other and carry out more *tan-t'ien* visualizations and petitions to the deities for health and salvation. Following this, the priest helps the supplicants remove their garments and loosen their hair. Now the couples interlace their hands in various ritual patterns and recite formulas,   25 followed by a series of gestures with hands and feet relating to the eight trigrams, twelve Earthly Branches, and organs. After another long sequence of dance, massage, prayers and meditation, there is a passage that translates:

> With his right hand he massages her "lower *tan-t'ien*" three times. Approaching the "gate of birth" (*sheng-men* 生門), he opens the "golden gate" (*chin-men* 金門) with his right hand while lifting the "jade key" (*yü-yao* 玉鑰) with his left and casting it upon the "gate of birth" Now supporting her head with his left hand, he massages the "gate of life" (*ming-men* 命門) up and down and from side to side, while reciting the following three times: "Water flows to the east and clouds drift to the west. *Yin* nourishes *yang* with a *ch'i* so subtle. The mysterious *ching* and nourishing liquid rise to the 'tutorial gate' (*shih-men* 師門)." The first partner now recites: "The 'divine gentleman' (*shen-nan* 神男) holds the gate and the 'jade lady' (*yü-nü* 玉女) opens the door. As our *ch'i* is united, may *yin* bestow her *ch'i* upon me." The second partner now recites: "*Yin* and *yang* bestow and transform, and the ten thousand creatures are nourished and born. Heaven covers and earth supports. May *ch'i* be bestowed upon the bodies of these humble supplicants."

After a complex series of prayers and invocations, the text continues:

> Raising his head and inhaling living *ch'i* through his nose, he swallows *yang* according to the numbers 3, 5, 7, and 9, and recites: "May the *tao* of heaven be set in motion." The second partner now recites: "May the *tao* of earth be set in motion." Following this he enters the "gate of birth" to a depth of half the head, while reciting: "Oh, celestial deities and immortals, I would shake heaven and move earth that the 'five lords' (*wu-chün* 五君) might hear my plea." Now the second partner recites: "Oh, celestial deities and '*tan-t'ien* palace' (*tan-t'ien-fu* 丹田府), I would move earth and shake heaven that the five deities of the body might each be strong." He then penetrates to the greatest depth, closes his mouth and inhales living *ch'i* through his nose and exhales through the mouth three times. Gnashing his teeth, he recites: "May nine and one be born in the midst." Now he withdraws and then returns to a depth of half a head.

After another series of invocations and choreographed postures, gestures, massage, and coition, the ceremony ends. Sexual intercourse is integrated into Taoist shamanism here in the same way that it is grafted onto inner alchemy. It provides powerful symbolic and actual stimulation on both psychic and physiological levels. That part of the ceremony involving intromission is not given undue prominence and does not overshadow the other yogic, liturgical, and ritual elements. There is no specific language suggesting sexual arousal, and neither orgasm nor *coitus reservatus* enter the discussion, though I would feel confident in saying that nonejaculation could be assumed. The survival of the *Shang-ch'ing huang-shu kuo-tu i* in the *Tao tsang*, despite the very thorough suppression or censorship of works on sexual yoga, is a mystery I will not attempt to solve. The living rather than archaic language of the text, together with its late date, is proof that such practices persisted in codified form, and undoubtedly in fact, long after the Han. Circulation of the *ch'i* is not expressed in terms of "microcosmic orbit," but the *tan-t'ien* and *ni-wan* (nadir and apogee of the ellipse) frequently are mentioned.

We have seen that as sexual practices became entrenched in the increasingly variegated landscape of "the *tao* of immortality" (*hsien-tao* 仙道) and religious Taoism, attacks were mounted by alchemists and Buddhists alike. A third antisexual front was opened up by the quietest branch of Taoists themselves, who traced their roots directly to Lao tzu and Chuang tzu and adhered to the doctrine of "purity, stillness, and nonaction" (*ch'ing-ching wu-wei* 清靜無爲). Among these was the Sung Taoist, Tseng Tsao, (twelfth century), who devoted a chapter to sexual practices, "Jung Ch'eng p'ien" (On the art of Master Jung Ch'eng) in his *Tao shu* (Axial principles of the *tao*). Unlike Ko Hung, who granted sexual practices a minor role in preparing oneself for the elixir, Tseng rejected them altogether in both yogic and religious Taoism. The chapter is valuable because it helps, albeit from a negative perspective, to define the position of sexual cultivation within the *tao*, and because it fills a gap in the received literature, extending from the Sung to the Yüan. In particular, it summarizes the teachings of the *Ju yao ching* (Mirror of absorbing the medicine), an early work on sexual alchemy, which survives only in thoroughly emasculated form in the *Tao tsang*. The first section of Tseng's "On the Art of Master Jung Ch'eng" paraphrases the essential principles of the *Ju yao ching* as a preliminary to refuting them, but in the process effectively preserves a glimpse of this early phase of sexual alchemy. I translate the relevant passage:

> I once obtained Master Ts'ui's book, the *Ju yao ching*, which discusses the "battle of mounting women." If "guest" and "host" remain in a state of abstraction, then there is shared awareness and not shared intention, shared perversion but not shared benefit, shared intercourse but not shared bodies, shared bodies but not shared intercourse. All of this refers to facing the sexual partner without becoming excited. Intercourse of the spirit internally and externally without physical excitement is the *tao* of attaining intrinsic nature. If one becomes excited, the spirit departs and the intrinsic nature declines. By remaining unstained and unattached, our primal substance will remain, the *ch'i* will be stable and the spirit fixed, and combining together as form in the "central palace," the *yin* is refined away and the *yang* preserved. The "red snow" is the true substance of the "sea of blood" and is that which becomes a fetus. Within the "palace of children" it is *yang-ch'i*, and when it emerges it is blood. When the "tortoise" enters, it must wait for the moment when this is mobilized and she is emotionally excited. Then the "tortoise" turns its neck, holds its breath, and swallows it, making an effort to draw it in. If the *ch'i* is steady and the spirit concentrated, the *ch'i* will enter the "gate" where the "windlass" and "water wheel" may be used to raise it to the "*K'un*-lun peak," after which it convenes in the "golden gate towers," and enters the *tan-t'ien*, where it then becomes the elixir.

Tseng's refutation of the teachings just translated opens by denying any association between the art of the bedchamber and the ancient immortals and by claim-ing that even religious Taoism abandoned sexual rituals by the time of Chang Taoling. He next quotes from a series of famous Taoists who dismiss sexual practices using empirical, psychological and philosophical arguments. Sexual practices are compared to "clutching a piece of jade and hurling oneself into a fire, or burying a dog in a golden coffin." The great Taoist synthesizer, Wei Po-yang, is quoted as saying, "If one cuts off a piece of flesh and inserts it into the belly, it will not become a fetus. Thus foreign substances cannot become elixir." Putting what must have been a standard argument of the sexual school into the mouth of an imaginary interlocutor he writes, "The lotus does not grow in high places or flat planes, but in river mud." Tseng counters with an analogy of his own, "The lotus in the mud easily decays, unlike the pine that grows in mountain crags and does not wither. In fact, I even have a lotus that flourishes in the midst of fiercest fire." All metaphors aside, in the end, Tseng favors the quietest approach to mediation and regards sexual disciplines as producing only mental perturbation and constituting a dangerous distraction from the *tao*. Although conceding its long history and association with the sage kings of antiquity, he nevertheless denies its efficacy in the pursuit of immortality, which for Tseng no less than Ko Hung was the goal of Taoism.

Theoretical objections from within the Taoist ranks to the position of the "paired practices" school came, then, from a number of different directions. The argument based on "nonaction" holds that any deliberate technique encourages the grasping ego and can only obstruct the flow of the *tao*. The argument of the "pure practices" inner elixir school holds that the gross postnatal secretions exchanged during male-female intercourse are inferior to the prenatal *yin-yang* essences harmonized in the body of the solo practitioner. With all parties agreeing on the fundamental importance of *ching*, the debate centers not so much on the role of the reagents, but under what laboratory conditions they may best be transmuted. The "nonac- 27 tion" camp believed the body fares best when undisturbed, even with the best intentions, by the mind; the "pure practices" people cannot deny the role of sexual energy, but want to separate it from the act of sex and carefully contain the reaction; the sexual school itself held that the interaction of *yin* and *yang* incarnate was necessary to heat the *ching* to the vaporization point and enable it to rise. All parties describe worst case scenarios of the other side, and it is not difficult to imagine actual examples of "pure" practitioners becoming "dry" and stagnant, and "paired" adepts degenerating into licentiousness and exploitation. Wary of dogmatic extremes, however, the majority of Taoists instinctively appreciate that sexuality is not "outside the *tao*," but are bothered by exaggerated claims of efficacy and the potential for abuse. This ambivalence is expressed by contemporary Taoist apologist, Hsiao T'ien-shih, who in his *Tao-chia yang-sheng hsüeh kai-yao* (Outline of Taoist health practices) relegates sexual cultivation to the "side door, left path" (*p'ang-men tso-tao* 旁門左道), but nevertheless concedes that "a side door is also a door, and a left path also a path." Hsiao says revealingly, "When a good man practices a heterodox method, the method becomes good, and when a evil man practices a good method the good method becomes heterodox."

Even among the staunchest "pure practices" opponents of "paired practices," however, we find techniques that strike the Westerner as surprisingly sexual. Theoretically, because of the interrelatedness of the "three primary vitalities"— *ching*, *ch'i*, and spirit—the sexual energy (*ching*) may be strengthened and stabilized by meditation based solely on cultivation of imperturbability of the spirit or by yogic techniques that seek to activate the "*ch'i* function" (*ch'i-chi* 氣機). The most direct nonsexual approach to strengthening the *ching* works with the genitals themselves, as in "iron crotch training" (*t'ieh-tang kung* 鐵襠功) or marital arts methods aimed at developing the ability to resist blows and retract the testicles. However, even the most abstract and detached forms of Taoist meditation anticipate equally tangible physiological effects in the genital domain, as in the phenomenon known as "horse hides its testicles" (*ma ts'ang shen* 馬藏腎), where penis and scrotum shrink to prepubescent proportions and *ching* leakage is banished forever. In women's cultivation, too, the goal is to regain the state of girlhood, so that the breasts of the practitioner shrink and the menses ceases. Thus it can be seen that the debate in Taoism over the role of sexuality finds those who reject sexual intercourse, but none who cast out sexual energy, and even "pure" practitioners engage in genital massage and eagerly await the awakening of the "original *yang*," manifesting in erection during meditation, to set the *ch'i* in microcosmic motion.

The Vocabulary of Sexual Yoga

The previous section examined the uneasy induction of sexual practices into the Taoist fraternity. This section attempts to analyze the adoption by sexual practitioners of later Taoist technical vocabulary and its integration into sexual theory. Approaching the primary texts of later Chinese sexology without an introduction to its vocabulary is like plunging into physics without a background in mathematics. Sexual practice in its early phases shared a common theoretical foundation with medicine, while developing the special terminology necessary to describe the mutual physiological responses of both sexes during intercourse. In the later phases of its development, extensive borrowing from cosmology, alchemy and the *I ching* gave rise to a more complex, and perhaps hermetic, system, but one that allowed adepts to communicate the profound physiological and psychological changes observed to be associated with the simultaneous practice of meditation and sexual activity. What follows, then, is a primer in the vocabulary of sexual yoga.

Yin and Yang

The overarching theme of Chinese sexology, of course, is the union of *yin* and *yang*. Resonating on many levels, it is physically man and woman and metaphysically masculine and feminine. As technical terms in sexology, *yang* may refer to the male gender, the male member, or sexual essence; whereas *yin* may refer to the female gender, the private parts of both sexes, or sexual secretions. Leaner and more abstract than such mythical personifications as Venus and Apollo or Shiva and Shakti, the *yin-yang* paradigm nevertheless gives ample scope for man and woman to play the roles of heaven and earth and adds a metaphysical dimension to the commerce of the bedroom. The early texts are marked by the existential loneliness of *yin* and *yang* for each other, and their union consummates a cosmic synergy; whereas in the later sexual alchemy tradition, *yang* is concerned only to steal a bit of like essence from the heart of *yin* to mend its own missing link.

The glorification of *yin* in early Taoist philosophy, and the emphasis on the balance of *yin* and *yang* in traditional Chinese medicine, gives way to the search for pure *yang* in alchemy, meditation, and sexual yoga. In early Taoism, *yang* in its aspect of hardness was to be avoided and *yin* softness to be cultivated; in later Taoism, *yang* in its aspect of spirit was to be cultivated and *yin* materiality to be avoided. With the development of sexual alchemy, there is a distinct shift from identification of male sexual essence with *yang* to *yin*, and *yin* to *yang* in the female. What appears to be ambivalence or imprecision here, however, actually may illustrate the subtlety of the *yin-yang* paradigm. Thus male sexuality, considered in its *yang* aspect, shows the vital strength-giving qualities of male virility, whereas in its *yin* aspect, it expresses weakness through its instability and susceptibility to leakage.

Trigrams and Hexagrams

Yin and *yang* and the eight trigrams and sixty-four hexagrams of the *I ching* are both the myth and mathematics of Chinese thought. These stacks of straight and broken lines, less colorful than the pantheon of gods of other peoples, or Chinese folk religion itself, nevertheless acquire a metaphysical life of their own and even can be used in very affecting mythopoetic narratives. *Yin* and *yang* expressed as a priori categories in the system of trigrams are *Ch'ien* (The Creative) and *K'un* (The Receptive). In this form they represent the noumenal, precreation realm. According to "Wen Wang's Sequence of Trigrams," the mating of *yin* and *yang* gives birth first to *Chen* (The Arousing) and *Hsün* (The Gentle), and then to *K'an* (The Abyssmal) and *Li* (The Clinging), the second son and daughter. For inner alchemy and sexology, however, the sexual associations with *K'an* and *Li* are reversed, so that *K'an* now represents the watery female aspect and *Li* the fiery male. Only in the texts on women's practice do we find a reversion to the "Wen Wang Sequence" and the use of *Li* for female.

With the mating of *Ch'ien* and *K'un*, pure *yin* and *yang*, the phenomenal world of mixed *yin* and *yang* is set in motion as symbolized by the six offspring of the parent trigrams. The two trigrams, *K'an*, with its strong middle line and weak exterior, and *Li*, weak in the middle but strong outside, now become the focus of inner and sexual alchemy. In this postcreation world, the two trigrams also represent the two "Falls," of humankind. During the fetal stage of human development *Li*, the heart, spirit or fire, is in perfect harmony with *K'an*, the kidneys, *ching* and *ch'i*, or water. Birth signals the first "Fall," as water sinks and fire rises, and body and mind become alienated. The second "Fall" takes place at puberty as the *Ch'ien* or pure *yang* body is decisively "broken" (*p'o* 破) with the onset of menses or the first loss of semen.

Solo meditation seeks to mend the vertical rift through the inversion of *K'an* and *Li*, aided by *Hsün*, the breath. This is the journey from the hexagram *Wei-chi* (Before Completion) to *Chi-chi* (After Completion), where fire is checked by water and water converted to steam (*ch'i*), and finally to total transcendence with the restoration of *Ch'ien*. In sexual cultivation, the search for *yang* is horizontal, as man, *Li* broken in the middle at puberty, attempts to borrow energy from woman symbolized by *K'an*. The 29 harmonious mating of *K'an* and *Li* once again is symbolized by the hexagram *Chi-chi*, and in later texts even comes to be interpreted literally as the female superior position in intercourse. More rarely, the hexagram *T'ai* (Peace), with trigram *K'un* ascendant over *Ch'ien*, is used to indicate this relationship. A final pair of hexagrams encountered occasionally in the later literature is *Chun* (Difficulty at the Beginning) and *Meng* (Youthful Folly). In the *Secret Principles of Gathering the True Essence*, "*Chun* and *Meng*" are used to represent the diversity of pre-pubescent partners, while elsewhere in the sexual alchemy texts, *Chun* and *Meng* stand for morning and evening, or the *yin* and *yang* phases of alchemical firing time.

Use of the trigrams in mythopoesis is best illustrated by the wonderful commentary to the *True Transmission of the Golden Elixir*. Here the "*yang* gold" elixir, symbolized by the middle line in *Ch'ien*, flees its original abode during the mystical mating of *Ch'ien* and *K'un* and lodges in the "palace of *K'un*." *Ch'ien's* conversion to *Li*, whether interpreted as resulting from loss or exchange, is considered a devolutionary state, which can be repaired only by reclaiming the "*yang* gold" from female partners. However, according to the *True Transmission*, it is vain to seek for *yang* in *Ch'ien*, in *K'un*, or even in *K'an*, for only *Tui* (The Joyful), the youngest daughter of *K'un*, is "of one species with *Ch'ien*."

One of the most important functions of the trigrams and hexagrams is as phase markers for the macro- and microcosmic circuits of energy. This makes it possible to synchronize lunar and solar phases with natural biological cycles and meditational and sexual practices. The *Wondrous Discourse of Su Nü* correlates the system of the *I ching* with the Stems and Branches to maximize the advantage of the macrocosmic *yang-ch'i* for eugenic and macrobiotic ends.

The Five Phases

The systems of trigrams and hexagrams interlock with the Five Phases, Branches and Stems, and lunar phases. As in

Chinese medicine, the Five Phases (metal, wood, water, fire, and earth) appear rather late in the history of sexology and then play a relatively minor role. Only when the highly technical language of inner alchemy merges with that of sexual yoga do we encounter it at all. The Five Phases sometimes are used to express correspondences with the hours, seasons, and azimuthal directions, though the Terrestrial Branches, trigrams, and hexagrams also are available for this purpose, and they may be said to reinforce each other. For example, Fu Chin-ch'üan's commentary to the *Ju yao ching* explains that Celestial Stems, *wu* and *chi*, representing the emotions (*ch'ing*) and intrinsic nature (*hsing*, reason), both belong to the earth Phase and need to be brought into harmonious conjunction. Stem, *keng*, belonging to metal, is said to be the "white tiger," and Stem *chia*, belonging to wood, the "green dragon." These must travel from their respective poles in the west and east to mate. According to the "production sequence" of the Five Phases, metal, the mother, produces water, the child, but sexual alchemy, which typically reverses nature in search of the supernatural, seeks the metal born in water, or the *yang* essence in woman. Wood and metal also may be correlated with the trigrams *Chen*, the oldest son and the east, and *Tui*, the youngest daughter and the west.

Sun Ju-chung's long description of the elixir process employs nearly every paradigm in the Chinese metaphysician's repertoire, resulting in a dense multi-dimensional text, which expresses quality and quantity, microcosm and macrocosm simultaneously. For example,

> The first lunar month belongs to the hexagram *T'ai* (Peace), which is three *yang* lines below and three *yin* lines above. This represents *yin* and *yang* poised at the balance point, like the half image of the first quarter of the moon, which is metal within water. Metal flourishes during *yu*. *Yu* begins with the first "climatic period" of the eighth lunar month. After reaching the period of "flourishing metal," the fire is sufficient. "Withdrawing the *yin* tally" should rest during the eighth month.

This passage from Sun's *True Transmission of the Golden Elixir* illustrates how the Five Phases function in relation to *yin* and *yang*, the lunar cycle, hexagrams, Twenty-Four Climatic Periods, and Terrestrial Branches. The sexual elixir is expressed in the Five Phases system as "gold [metal] within water," or *yang* in the midst of woman, who is characterized like the trigram *K'an* as soft on the outside but hard on the inside.

Chang San-feng is especially partial to the Five Phases, using the elements to express everything from the stages of arousal to menstrual cycle and "crucible" quality. The *Summary of the Golden Elixir* correlates water and metal with the lunar phases to determine the precise moment during the woman's menstrual cycle when intercourse is most profitable to the male adept. The Phases fire and water are used by Chang to represent the hot and cold stages of arousal for gathering and processing the woman's elixir. The woman's arousal level may be gauged by the "wateriness" of her tongue and the "fieriness" of her "dates." Water also symbolizes the woman's sexual secretions, and the two Stems, *jen* and *kuei*, belonging to that element, are used to distinguish the precise time and kind to gather. In traditional medicine the Five Phases are correlated with the Five Viscera so that the heart is represented by fire, and the tongue is one of the remote organs within the heart's sphere of influence. Thus, during sexual activity, tongue-to-tongue stimulation causes the fire of the heart to burn strong and also tonifies the other organs within the heart's sphere, such as the small intestine. As the fire of the tongue reaches its peak, it is overtaken by waves of watery secretions, signaling the arrival of the *yang* essence and the opportunity for gathering and absorption. On a somewhat simpler level, Chang San-feng uses the elements gold (metal), fire, and water to distinguish the three grades of "crucible" quality based on the woman's age.

The Five Phases crop up again in the very different environment of women's practice. In the solo context of the *Precious Raft*, woman, considered here *K'un* and not *K'an*, is said to conceal the "true fire," which when activated ignites the "common fire" of sexual longing. The "common fire" threatens to "melt" the "metal" and gives rise to the impulse to quench the fire by releasing the watery secretions of sexual climax. The element fire here is seen as having a lower and higher octave, "common" and "true," which vibrate sympathetically during practice, but must be clearly distinguished to hold the attention unwaveringly on the higher note.

Celestial Stems and Terrestrial Branches

The ten Stems (*t'ien-kan* 天干) and twelve Branches (*ti-chih* 地支) have been used from very ancient times to generate a series of sixty pairs that mark the progression of diurnal and annual cycles. The Terrestrial Branches have strong associations with the points of the compass and can be used geomantically, as in the *Summary of the Golden Elixir*, to indicate the most advantageous alignment of the adept's retreat. Thus if front and back are oriented properly according to the first and seventh Branches, *tzu* 子 (north) and *wu* 午 (south), the "green dragon's" (male) chamber may be situated appropriately on the east wing and the "white tiger's" (female) on the west. In inner and sexual alchemy, the Stems and Branches are used microcosmically to designate spatial and temporal points of interest on the map of meditation. The polar points in this scheme, *tzu* and *wu*, mark in anatomical terms the North Pole (perineum) and South Pole (crown of the head), but in the Chinese conception of phase energetics, *tzu* also connotes the zenith of the *yin* phase and the nadir of *yang*. Having reached its nadir in the north, this also is the direction from which to anticipate the rebirth of *yang*. By evoking *tzu* and *wu*, then, it is possible for inner alchemists to indicate both the poles of microcosmic orbit circulation and the "advancing" and "retreating" (*yang* and *yin*) phases of the cycle. In this conception, Branches *mao* 卯 and *yu* 酉, representing due east and west, symbolize the mid-points in each half of the elixir cycle designated for "rest." The twelve Terrestrial Branches as a paradigm of the phase energetics of meditation may refer to units as small as the inhalation (*yang*) and exhalation (*yin*) of one complete breath cycle, or the longer course of elixir production over hours, days, and months.

Unique to the meditation tradition, and especially dear to sexual adepts, is the concept of the "hour of the living *tzu*" (*huo tzu shih* 活子時). Macrocosmically *tzu* represents the North, midnight, and the winter solstice, the turning point from which *yang* stages its triumphant return. In the microcosm of human physiology, it speaks to the awakening of the *yang* force asleep within the *yin* region of the *shen* (urogenital system), which manifests in spontaneous erection of the penis from midnight to early morning. During sleep it is the unconscious response of microcosmic energies to the rising *yang* power of the sun, but during meditation it signals the awakening of the "primal *ching*" (*yüan-ching* 元精), which is free of conscious sexual desire and may be channeled into the circuit of orbiting energy. Some of the texts and commentaries in this collection insist on the literal synchronization of sexual practice with the midnight-to-dawn macrophase of rising *yang*, but others consider it a matter of individual biology, emphasizing that the "hour of the living *tzu*" is whenever we feel the impulse to practice.

Another critical matter of individual biology for inner alchemy is expressed with the Celestial Stems *jen* 壬 and *kuei* 癸. *Kuei*, the tenth and last Stem, traditionally has been used to represent puberty, as it and *jen*, the ninth, are both assigned to the house of water in relation to the Five Phases. Some of the later texts in this collection contain formulas for calculating the accumulation of blood and *ching* during female maturation. This allows one to predict the onset of puberty and the peak of fertility in postpubescent women, times when the maximum *yang* energy is available to the sexual adept. It usually is stressed that the *jen* stage immediately preceding the menses (*kuei*) should be addressed, and in some pas-

sages we glimpse something like the concept of ovulation, or even a suggestion that the very first menstrual period is perhaps the most potent source. *Kuei* is defined here as "*yin* within *yin*," whereas *jen* is "*yang* within *yin*," or the gold within water, which is the adept's prize. *Jen* also is associated with conception and pregnancy and, hence, perhaps the notion of fertility. Chang San-feng, offering a variation on this theme, tells us that during sexual arousal the woman will first produce a quantity of *kuei* secretion, and that following this the pure *jen* emerges, which alone is suitable for absorption by the male adept.

As *jen* and *kuei* belong to the element water, *wu* 戊 and *chi* 己, the fifth and sixth Stems, are both assigned to earth, or the central region between the four cardinal points. The corresponding organ of the Five Viscera is the spleen, and according to medical theory, the seat of that aspect of consciousness approximating our notion of volition (*i* 意). The "*wu* earth" thus is the center of *K'an* and the "*chi* earth" the center of *Li*. The will (*i*) within each of these, body and mind, seeks to unite with the other. Consistent with the sexual school's assignment of *K'an* and *Li* to female and male sexual energy rather than to *ch'i* and spirit, Chang San-feng in his *True Transmission of the Golden Elixir* uses the term "*chi* earth" for the adept's sexual essence (that is, the middle of *Li*), and "*wu* earth" for that of the female partner.

The auspicious "monarchial and ministerial days," recommended for eugenic purposes in the *Ishimpō* and later householder texts, also are based on the Celestial Stems and their associations. *Chia* 甲 and *i* 乙 are the auspicious days of spring because of their association with spring's phase, wood. Summer is assigned to *ping* and *ting*, or fire; autumn is *keng* and *hsin*, or metal; and winter is *jen* and *kuei*, or water.

Lunar Phases

The concept of lunar phases appears both literally and metaphorically, macrocosmically and microcosmically in these texts.

Most of the early texts in this collection include among the taboo days for intercourse the first and last days of the moon, the two quarters, and full moon. These prohibitions are exclusively eugenic and have little bearing on the participants themselves. The "Health Benefits of the Bedchamber" lists the ten days of every month known as "lunar mansion days" (*yüeh-hsiu jih* 月宿日), which are most favorable for intercourse. These are not strictly speaking a matter of lunar phases, but rather an indication of the moon's position in relation to the twenty-eight constellations. According to the "Health Benefits" table, several months include the first of the month, or new moon, among the auspicious "lunar mansion days," which is forbidden in the earlier texts. This apparent contradiction arises from conceptual dissonance between the one system, which is based on the lunar phases, and the other, which is based on the moon's position. A similar lack of congruence may be found in Sun Ju-chung's *True Transmission of the Golden Elixir*, where the most favorable day for intercourse is considered "the evening of the full moon of the eighth lunar month when *yang* first stirs." This is forbidden in the early system of phase taboos, but again this may be traced to Sun's purposes, which are exclusively alchemical and not eugenic. From this point of view, the full moon is considered "pure *yang*," and the eighth month, associated with the trigram *Tui*, represents the youngest daughter of *K'un*. This then is the perfect macrocosmic match of *yin* and *yang* for sexual practice. Here we are beginning to cross the border from astronomy to physiology.

Chang San-feng completes the shift to microcosmic physiology, using the lunar phases metaphorically as a timetable for computing the woman's highest *yang*-yielding potential. In the early texts, the juncture of the last and first days of the month are ruled out, for it is precisely at this time that the balance of *yin* and *yang* is unresolved, but for Chang San-feng's biological symbolism, this is when the "*ching* of the sun and moon shoot their *ch'i* at each other." At this passage the

woman's *yang* energy is purest and freshest. The commentary to *The Secret Principles of Gathering the True Essence* describing this moment says, "Wait for the right time! The moon will come out and the 'golden flower' appear." The compound *shuo-shih* 朔事 (literally, "new moon affair") is an obscure but not unknown expression for the menses in Chinese. The women's cultivation texts operate in the same metaphorical territory, but here the full moon symbolizes the young woman's state just prior to puberty when the "primal *ch'i*" or "lead *ch'i*," and the accumulation of blood reach their peak. This is "*yang* within *yin*," just as the light of the moon represents the *yang* energy of the sun reflected in the embodiment and emblem of *yin*.

Alchemy

The Taoists, who were deeply impressed with nature's powers of transformation, came to believe during the early Han that humankind could steal this secret from heaven and carry out in the laboratory a process of refining potable gold, "golden elixir," from cinnabar, lead, sulphur, and other reagents. Apparently daunted more by its toxicity than its inefficacy, alchemy eventually gave way after the T'ang to inner alchemy, but not without bequeathing a rich legacy of theory and terminology. Much of the technical vocabulary borrowed from alchemy by the internal alchemists also turns up in the writings of the sexual school, often resulting in three different definitions of the same term. The most important ingredients borrowed from alchemy are lead and mercury. In solo practice, mercury and lead refer to the vertical *yin-yang* dichotomy between heart and kidneys, or spirit and *ch'i*. In sexual texts, mercury becomes the male *ching* and lead the woman's *yang* energy locked within her watery essence. As the *True Transmission of the Golden Elixir* proclaims, "Absorb the partner's lead to supplement your mercury."

Defining the inverted process of conception pursued by the adept, the *True Transmission* explains that normally mer-

33

cury goes forth to impregnate lead, but in the esoteric method lead is induced to visit mercury. In sexual practices, the female partner's "true lead" is then considered the "medicine" that may be absorbed into the adept's system for macrobiotic transformation. During the transition from solo to paired practices, the term "mercury" has changed from spirit to semen. As Chang San-feng describes the process, when mercury reacts with lead, it causes the volatile mercury to solidify, revert to cinnabar, and never again escape the body.

Binary Terms

Some of the binary terms already discussed, *K'an/Li* and *tzu/wu*, for example, emerge from larger cyclical constructs such as the eight trigrams and twelve Terrestrial Branches. Another group of pairs comes out of a more mythological mode of conceptualization, but these are subject to similar shifts as one moves from the solo to sexual school. For example, "tiger" and "dragon," representing *ch'i* and spirit in the solo school, come to mean female and male in the sexual. Prepubescent males and females whose sexual essences are fully intact come to be known as "green dragon" and "white tiger," mythical creatures who in the popular imagination are associated with east and west. In fact, the two cardinal points—east and west—routinely are used as covers for male and female, or their respective sexual essences. Occasionally, too, in the later texts, "dragon" will refer to just the penis, as when it "sports in the water" or "drinks from the tiny spoon." When it comes to women's solo practices, the "white tiger" of *ch'i* must be subdued and the "red dragon" of the menses must be "slain" as a prelude to refining the elixir within the body of the female adept. Another mythical pair, the "scarlet bird" and "mysterious warrior," representing the ruling constellations of the southern and northern skies, are borrowed by inner alchemy from astrology, but retain in the sexual literature the meanings of heart and kidneys without acquiring separate sexual meanings.

Another pair, "eight *liang* and half a *chin*" draw upon the traditional Chinese system of weights and measures to indicate the two halves that make up the whole elixir. Thus "eight *liang* of lead and half a *chin* of mercury combine to form one lump of purple gold elixir." Another set of numerical pairs, "two sevens" and "two eights," represent the numbers fourteen and sixteen, the ages of female and male puberty. By extension, they represent the height of sexual energy, and by further extension the energy itself.

One of the most versatile binary terms in Chinese esoteric studies is the "crucible and stove." Its alchemical origins are obvious, but its metaphoric applications for the inner elixir school may include heaven and earth, mind and body, head and abdomen, spirit and *ch'i*, and *ni-wan* and *tan-t'ien*. In meditation practice, the crucible often is pictured between the kidneys, and the spirit provides the fire of the stove, which is fanned by the breath to heat the *ching* so that it may rise up the spine. With the shift to sexual practices, the term "crucible" generally is used to designate the female partner, but the *Summary of the Golden Elixir* uses it for the male as well. The *Exposition of Cultivating the True Essence* uses "stove" for the female partner and Chang San-feng, too, calls woman the "stove" and man the "sword" that enters it for tempering.

A critical dichotomy for understanding the nature of the sexual elixir is expressed in the terms "prenatal" and "postnatal." In metaphysics, the distinction applies to the pre- and postcreation states of the universe—unity and duality. In medicine, the terms refer to what is congenital or inherited versus what is acquired by effort or influence. Here in the context of elixir production, the "prenatal" is the etheric essence or pure energy residing in the midst of "postnatal" materiality. It is the energetic aspect of the reproductive potential that must be isolated, refined, and transmuted into spirit.

The final pair that appears with great frequency in these texts is based on two philosophical terms: intrinsic nature and life. Intrinsic nature (*hsing* 性) refers to our spiritual nature, sometimes correlated with the superior soul (*hun* 魂), or spirit; life (*ming* 命) refers to our corporeal nature, health, or *ch'i* and is associated with the "inferior soul" (*p'o* 魄). The various schools of self-cultivation in China often are classed according to their emphasis on physical or spiritual development and their respective order. The school of "dual cultivation" advocates simultaneous and balanced cultivation of both natures, and interestingly shares its name—*shuang-hsiu*—with the sexual school, which to avoid confusion, I have translated "paired practices" throughout.

Minor Systems in Phase Energetics

A number of systems appear with less frequency than the ubiquitous Stems and Branches, lunar cycle, and Five Phases, but play a supporting role in explaining various processes in inner alchemy. The *True Transmission of the Golden Elixir* uses the Twenty-Four Climatic Periods (*chieh-ch'i* 節氣), or fortnightly nodes of the solar year, in conjunction with the Phases, Branches, and hexagrams to explain the inner seasons of the elixir "firing time." Another relatively rare system borrowed from inner alchemy, the "Six Stages" (*liu hou* 六候), is based on the ancient Chinese unit of five days and surfaces as another measure of "firing time" in the later sexual alchemy texts. The *True Transmission* defines its function most clearly by explaining that the first "two stages" are devoted to gathering the "external elixir" from the partner and the "last four" to producing the "inner elixir" by uniting the "medicine" with one's own *ching*.

A final concept, "with or against the normal course," (*shun ni* 順逆) does not mark points on a cyclical progression, but the forward or backward flow of movement itself. The "normal course" leads from the prenatal to the postnatal, from perfection to corruption, while the "reverse" leads from the postnatal to the prenatal and the possibility of gestating the mystical fetus in the body of the male adept. Over and over it is announced that if the going out of the male *ching* to meet the female *ching* (or blood in some texts)

is the normal course, then logically if this is reversed, and woman plays the host, it is man who rebirths himself as an immortal. The concrete process of absorbing the "external medicine" and raising one's own *ching* to feed the higher centers in the brain is often analogized as "reversing the flow of the Yellow River" by means of a "water wheel," which pulls it up against the direction of the breath and the normal flow of *ch'i* in the meridians.

Minor Disciplines

Medicine and meditation, of course, are the two disciplines that contributed most to the theoretical and practical foundations of sexual yoga; several others also are called upon in these texts for their special expertise. Physiognomy is used to determine temperament and sexual characteristics in a partner. Astrology and the almanac help calculate auspicious or inauspicious days for eugenic or elixir purposes. Geomancy counsels us on the negative influences of taboo places and helps orient the layout of the elixir retreat. Military strategy, long associated with Taoism, lends a number of concepts to sexual practices. The *True Classic of Perfect Union*, an extended metaphor on the "battle of the sexes," teaches a strategy of feint and parry, whereby the male is able to colonize the "enemy" and exploit her territory for raw materials.

Numerology also comes into play in several ways in these texts. On the simplest level, nine, the highest single-digit odd or heavenly number, symbolizing *yang*, and its multiples of thirty-six and eighty-one are often used for sets of repetitions in sexual regimens. Drawing on the *I ching* tradition, the numbers also correlate with the Five Phases, especially in the later texts, where the association of seven with fire and nine with metal is emphasized. Multiples of seven rule the woman's life: menses at fourteen, menopause at forty-nine, and forty-nine days following parturition to be rid of impurities. The *Exposition of Cultivating the True Essence* applies the "seven" formula to estimating the value of various "crucibles." Those of fourteen, "minor *yin*," are said to "nourish the body," whereas those of twenty-one, "abundant *yin*," merely "increase the lifespan." The ages twenty-eight, thirty-five, forty-two, and forty-nine are designated as "strong," "declining," "major," and "exhausted," and contribute nothing to the "great work." In the *Essentials of the Golden Elixir Method for Women a* complicated set of calculations are used to compute the increments of maturation by *chu* and *liang* that add up at precisely fourteen years to one *chin* of blood. Similarly, counting backwards, the loss through menses is calculated so that at forty-nine the entire *chin* is exhausted and menopause sets in. A man's life proceeds by multiples of eight, the most important passages of which are puberty at sixteen and the "locking of the *ching*" at sixty-four. The ten months of mystical pregnancy required for the birth of the "holy infant" corresponds to the ten months of natural gestation and qualifies one as "earthly immortal." The degree of "heavenly immortal" is reserved for those who have consumed the "mysterious pearl" and nurture it for 5,048 days, precisely the number ordained for one complete reading of the *Buddhist Tripitika*.

Sexual Practice and Meditation

This section will attempt to summarize certain aspects of general meditation theory that merge with sexual practices in the late householder tradition of the Ming and particularly with sexual alchemy and women's cultivation. Again, whether meditation adopted sexual technique in furtherance of its goals or sexual practices adopted meditation for its purposes misstates the case, which appears to be a parallel development of "paired" and "pure" practices. Just as the early sexual literature assumes a knowledge of medical theory, the later sexual alchemy texts assume a background in Taoist cosmology and practical experience in meditation. We will not attempt an exhaustive review of the historical evolution of meditation theory and techniques, but simply describe the main features of the

tradition as it stood during the period represented by the received literature of sexual alchemy, namely the Ming. Beginning with a sketch of the map of the body's inner landscape, we will proceed to a description of the varieties and levels of energy in the body, together with their interactions and conversions. We will then trace the development of the technical processes for refining the inner elixir, culminating in "orbital meditation," and the fusion of this technique with sexual yoga. Finally, we will consider the larger cycle, or "firing time," for refining the elixir over months and years and completing the work of immortality.

The Anatomy of Inner Alchemy

The model of the human body proposed by Chinese meditation theory agrees in many ways with that of medicine, but it is not simply a copy. The goals of medicine are normal health and lifespan, whereas the goals of meditation, especially in the period of inner alchemy, are supernormal health, embodied immortality, or ascension to etheric paradises. Likewise, if the chief modalities of medicine are herbs and acupuncture, those of meditation are breath and mind control. Having said this, it should be noted that medicine attaches great importance to the role of mental factors in health, whereas immortality seekers for their part often are interested in the macrobiotic properties of exotic herbs. Exponents of sexual yoga sometimes presented their art as if sufficient in itself to realize immortality, but most practitioners approved of ancillary exercises and macrobiogens.

Comparing the medical and meditational models of the human body, one finds that meditation adopts all of the points and meridians of acupuncture theory, though only a small number are relevant in practice, and adds to these a host of others that exist only as psychic centers, somewhat analogous to the Indian concept of *chakra*. The acupuncture points can be directly accessed for specific effects by needles, moxabustion, and palpation, whereas the meditation points, both those shared with medicine and those belonging exclusively to meditation, are accessed through mental focus, a process of "turning the vision and hearing inward" (*shou-shih fan-t'ing* 收視返聽) and "focusing the mind in the points" (*shou ch'iao* 守竅) . The circuitry of *ch'i* flow in meditation follows familiar medical meridians, but attempts to direct the energy for macrobiotic ends. Again it should be emphasized that the goals of Chinese meditation are physiological transformation and not simply mental abstraction or the contemplation of such ideals as love, peace, or compassion. Among the most important centers and circuits for mental focus and *ch'i* circulation developed in the meditation tradition are the "elixir fields" (*tan-t'ien*), "yellow courts" (*huang-t'ing*), "three passes" (*san-kuan*), "nine palaces" (*chiu-kung*) and "nine orifices" (*chiu-ch'iao*).

Beginning students of Chinese yoga, if they know nothing else, will be familiar with the *tan-t'ien* ("elixir field") and able to locate it externally by measuring an inch or so below the navel, or internally by fixing the mind, breath, and *ch'i* in the lower abdomen. When the mind is directed to the *tan-t'ien* and the diaphragm relaxed, there is a sensation of centering and fullness of *ch'i* in the lower abdomen. This is the most fundamental technique in Chinese meditation and is described as placing "fire" (spirit) under "water" (kidneys). The term *tan-t'ien* first appears in the *Huang-t'ing wai-ching yü-ching* (Jade classic of the external radiance of the yellow courts) at the beginning of the Chin (third century). A medical work of the same period, Huang Fu-mi's *Chen-chiu chia-i ching* (The elements of acupuncture), locates it two inches below the navel and defines it as a synonym for the *ming-men*. By the end of the Chin (fourth century), Ko Hung outlined a theory of "three *tan-t'ien*" in his *Pao P'u tzu*: "Two- and four-tenths inches below the navel is the lower *tan-t'ien*; below the heart in the region of the 'crimson palace' and 'golden gate towers' is the middle *tan-t'ien*; between the eyebrows at a depth of one inch is the *ming-t'ang*, at two inches the *tung-fang*, and at three inches the upper *tan-t'ien*." The

Huang t'ing nei-ching yü-ching (Jade classic of the inner radiance of the yellow courts) of approximately Ko's time or somewhat later also refers to "three fields" (*san-t'ien* 三田).

It would be lovely at this point to provide one simple diagram of the "three *tan-t'ien*" and leave it at that, but over the centuries various authorities have provided very different definitions. There are those who identify the "upper *tan-t'ien*" 上丹田 as the *yin-t'ang* 印堂 or *hsüan-kuan* 玄關 (between the eyebrows), the *tsu-ch'iao* 祖竅 (between the eyes), the *ni-wan* 泥丸 (center of the brain) or even the *shan-chung* (between the breasts). Of the more than fifty alternate names for the "middle *tan-t'ien*" perhaps the most famous is the "yellow court" (*huang-t'ing* 黃庭), located just below the spleen in the very center of the abdominal organs, which in inner alchemy is considered the womb of the "holy fetus." The "lower *tan-t'ien*" generally is located in the abdomen, but a minority opinion identifies it with the *hui-yin* 會陰 at the perineum, or even the *yung-ch'üan* 湧泉 at the ball of the foot. Among those holding the majority view, estimates of its latitude range from the epicenter of the navel to one to three inches below it, and its depth is variously defined as nearer the navel, the spine, or somewhere in between. This even has led some to a theory of "three lower *tan-t'ien*": one anterior (in line with the *Jen* meridian), one posterior (in line with the *Tu* meridian), and one median (where the *Ch'ung* meridian cuts the plane of the *Tai* meridian). We may conclude then that a *tan-t'ien* is a functional locus whose effects are catalyzed by mental focus. Experience in meditation will confirm the observation of the Ch'ing physician Chou Hsüeh-t'ing, who states in his *San chih ch'an*. "The *tan-t'ien* is below the navel. It can be felt but it cannot be calculated in inches." Taken together as a system, the "three *tan-t'ien*" are seen, according to one scheme, as the seat of the "three treasures"—*ching*, *ch'i*, and spirit, respectively—and by another as the three ventral passes traversed by the *ch'i* during its downward progress, corresponding to the three dorsal passes of its upward ascent. The harmonization and interconnection of the three *tan-t'ien* during meditation then is the perfect fusion of the three energies.

It is clear from various citations in the sexology texts that the authors consider the "lower *tan-t'ien*" to be the primary center and that its locus is the abdomen. The *Essentials of the Jade Chamber* says, "Fondle her *tan-t'ien*," and the *Wondrous Discourse*, "Swallow her saliva to nourish your *tan-t'ien*." The *True Transmission* commentary very specifically defines it as the "sea of *ch'i*" (*ch'i-hai* 氣海), "two fingers above and two fingers below [the navel] and one and two-tenths inches in the middle. . . . It is the place to which water reverts and *ch'i* converges." The *Exposition of Cultivating the True Essence* defines the *tan-t'ien* as the destination of the saliva swallowed during meditation and the *ming-men* as the seat of the *ching-ch'i*, clearly distinguishing a ventral/dorsal dichotomy. Obviously subscribing to the "three *tan-t'ien*" theory, the *Exposition* says, "Inhale a breath and raise it to the upper *tan-t'ien*." The *Summary of the Golden Elixir* and *Secret Principles of Gathering the True Essence* use the terms *tan-fu* ("palace of the elixir") and *tan-t'ien* interchangeably, giving the anterior location.

Though the three *tan-t'ien* are defined primarily by their role in meditation practice and the energies they represent, they are not completely independent of anatomical referents. This is apparent in the *Correct Methods for Women's Practice*, which introduces a different diagram of the "fields" based on the unique features of female anatomy. Here, the "upper *tan-t'ien*" is located in the breasts, the "middle" in the navel, and the "lower" in the uterus.

The theory of the "three passes" (*san-kuan*) is much less controversial than that of the "three *tan-t'ien*." If the *tan-t'ien* are centers of discrete energies and the foci of concentration during meditation, the "three passes" are gates, often thought of as bottlenecks, through which the *ch'i* must penetrate on its upward journey via the *Tu* meridian in the back. The lowest pass is the *wei-lü* 尾閭 located

at the coccyx; the middle is the *chia-chi* 夾脊, located in the middle of the thoracic vertebrae; and the highest, at the occiput of the skull, is called the *yü-chen* 玉枕. It should be noted that whereas the *wei-lü* is defined structurally in Taoist yoga and martial arts as the coccyx, and in meditation as a *ch'i* "pass" on the "microcosmic orbit," in sexual yoga, as in the *Secret Principles of Gathering the True Essence*, it may refer to the pubococcygeal muscle. The literature of inner alchemy is replete with special techniques —posture, breath, visualization, and sphincter contraction—for enabling the *ch'i* to rise against the current through these successively narrower "three passes."

The term "nine orifices" (*chiu-ch'iao* 九竅) used in these texts, as distinct from the more familiar eyes, ears, nostrils, mouth, anus, and genitals, refers to the main points along the complete circuit traveled by the *ch'i* during microcosmic orbit meditation—the three *tan-t'ien* and "three passes," plus three additional points. These last three are the *pai-hui* 百會 at the fontanel, the *hui-yin* 會陰 at the perineum, and the *ni-wan* 泥丸, generally understood to be the center of the brain, but sometimes described or pictured as the crown of the head. Before considering the functional significance of the circuit formed by the "nine orifices," it remains to define a number of points of critical importance in the "inner landscape." The first is a pair of "magpie bridges" (*ch'üeh-ch'iao* 鵲橋), deriving their name from astronomy and mythology and serving as vital links between the *Jen* and *Tu* meridians, which are severed at birth as we enter the "postnatal" world and begin to breathe and defecate. The "bridges" may be repaired by pressing the tongue against the hard palate to seal the nasal duct, or *yin-t'ang* area, and prevent leakage of the "twin columns of jade" (nasal mucus) and by constricting the anal sphincter in the *wei-lü* area to prevent the loss of *ch'i* through flatulence. Two other scenic spots in this "inner landscape" are the "flowery pool" (*hua-ch'ih* 華池), or mouth, which produces the "jade liquid returning elixir," and the "twelve story pavilion" (*shih-er ch'ung-lou* 十二重樓), or throat, which conducts the "elixir" to the chest, stomach, and "lower *tan-t'ien.*"

The Three Treasures

Medicine, meditation, and sexual alchemy all take the body's energies as the fundamental raw materials of health or transformation. By far the most important model of these energies is enshrined in the theory of the "three treasures" (*san-pao* 三寶)—*ching, ch'i,* and spirit— also referred to in some of our texts as the "three primary vitalities" (*san-yüan* 三元). Medicine works with the postnatal "treasures" to maintain health, while inner alchemy meditation takes the prenatal aspect of the "treasures" as the precursors of the elixir.

The importance of *ching* conservation in Chinese medicine already has been discussed, but it is worthwhile to remind ourselves here that the early sexual adepts developed their practices against a theoretical background that assumed that new life begins with the intermingling of male and female *ching.* (Alternate formulations speak of male *ching* and female blood, and also refer to the sexual secretions and energy released during a woman's orgasm as *ching.*) This prenatal *ching* continues to grow from the moment of conception and is sustained after birth by the postnatal *ching* derived from "water and grain" in the stomach and spleen. Prenatal *ching* is stored in all the organs, but chiefly in the "kidneys," or urogenital system. The concept of *ching* also embraces the Western notion of endocrine function and thus is seen as the basis for maturation and development of the organism. When the *ching* is full to repletion at puberty, sexual desires arise and the threat of *ching* loss becomes inevitable. *Ching* is a highly concentrated form of *yang* energy, but highly unstable and easily fissions with passion as a catalyst. There is some ambivalence in the literature as to whether it is *ching* repletion that brings about sexual desire or sexual desire that causes *ching* leakage. With early intervention, however, and proper training, the "pure *yang*" body may be preserved in its prime without resort to supplementation—a kind of short-cut to immortality. Failing this, the amount of supplementation required is proportional to the history of expenditure. The first step is to minimize *ching* loss through limiting of intentional or spontaneous semen emission. The repression of sexual desire by will power is unacceptable as it distorts the spirit and may cause the *ching* energy to atrophy. What is required, then, is simultaneous stimulation and limitation: stimulation of the *ching* to maintain its vitality, and *coitus reservatus* to limit its loss to the system. The *ching* energy may be strengthened by herbs, exercise, and even meditation directed specifically at the genital organs, but for the sexual school, it is the sex act itself that is most efficacious.

Primary definitions of *ching* and *ch'i* often make it difficult to distinguish these two terms at the prenatal level. For example, the *Su wen* says, "*Ching* is the root of the body," and the *Nan ching* declares, "The *ch'i* is man's root." At the secondary or postnatal level, the empirical perspective of sexual practices, "semen and sexual energy" proves to be an adequate working definition of *ching.* *Ch'i,* then, is a less concentrated form of energy, which circulates in the meridians and is related to the front line functions of respiration, absorption, and defense. The state of one's health generally is defined by the sufficiency or exhaustion of *ch'i,* its openness, obstruction, or direction of flow. *Ch'i* is the most generalized term for the highly volatile state of the body's energy directly experienced as a totality and that responds immediately to environmental or emotional influences. As the *Su wen* says: "When one is angry the *ch'i* rises; when happy it relaxes; when sad it diminishes; when fearful it sinks; when cold it contracts; when animated it disperses; when alarmed it is chaotic; when weary its wastes; and when thoughtful it concentrates." Medicine deals only abstractly with the prenatal "treasures" as a theoretical construct, addressing itself in practice to the care and feeding of the postnatal *ching, ch'i,* and spirit. Inner alchemy meditation, for its part, addresses the postnatal only as a preliminary to combining the prenatal elements that form the elixir of immortality.

Among the four primary aspects of *ch'i*—primal (*yüan* 元), thoracic (*tsung* 宗), nutritive (*ying* 營), and defensive (*wei* 衛)—the last two have special practical significance in determining suitable times for sexual relations. The theory of "nutritive *ch'i*," for example, explains the inappropriateness of sex after eating, and the theory of "defensive *ch'i*" forbids sex after bathing. Similarly, *ch'i* connects the organs of the body's interior with their respective "orifices" (*ch'iao*) and explains the sympathetic resonance of heart and tongue during the act of kissing. The kidneys are naturally linked to the salivary orifices, so the *ch'i* of the kidneys stimulated during sex or meditation rises up the *Tu* meridian in the spine, flows into the mouth, and is transformed into sweet salivary elixir.

The third of the "treasures," spirit, refers in functional terms to the mind and nervous system and in traditional medicine is associated with the heart. Although spirit depends for its existence on the material support of *ching* and *ch'i*, it also acts as their "ruler." Spirit rules from its seat in the heart, but each of the other four Viscera are regarded as manifesting an aspect of spirit . As the *Su wen* says: "The heart harbors the spirit, the lungs the superior soul, the liver the inferior soul, the spleen intentions, and the kidneys ambition." Classical medical theory is wholly rational and offers no support for a belief in the survival of the spirit after death. Therefore, the *Su wen* says: "To possess spirit is to live; to lose it is to die." In the popular imagination, the same term, "spirit," is used to refer to the gods, immortals, and ancestors; in esoteric Taoism the "pure *yang* spirit" emerges as the end product of inner alchemical transformation to dwell in distant paradises, or "return to the void and revert to the *tao*."

Traditional medicine stresses the mutual dependence and convertibility of *ching*, *ch'i*, and spirit. Meditation seeks to get behind the postnatal semen, breath and mundane mind to the prenatal sexual energy, internal *ch'i*, and cosmic consciousness, and to mount rung by rung to the realm of pure immortal spirit. As a matter of simple observation, loss of semen was found to result in physical and mental lassitude, therefore *ch'i* and spirit were seen as dependent upon sufficiency of *ching*. Exhaustion of the *ch'i* through overexertion of the physical body, for example, likewise will depress the *ching* and spirit. Emotional perturbation influences the spirit, causing hyper- or hypoactivity of the *ching* and *ch'i*. Medicine is concerned primarily with the interdependence of the "three treasures" and seeks to maintain their collective strength by balancing their mutual interaction. Meditation seeks to exploit the mutual convertibility of the three energies by promoting a deliberate tilt in the direction of spirit through a process of "refining the *ching* into *ch'i* and the *ch'i* into spirit." The *Wondrous Discourse* states: "Blood can be transformed into *ching*, and *ching* can nourish the spirit." "Pure practices" theory holds that conversion takes place naturally when the mind is emptied of desires. "Paired practice" theory holds that repletion of the *ching* excites sexual desire in the mind, which then cannot be emptied without distorting the spirit or devitalizing the *ching*. Desire itself must be harnessed for the upward journey; the beast cannot simply be tethered at the foot of the mountain. The gradual transmutation and drawing up of energy usually is referred to in sexual yoga as "returning the *ching* to nourish the brain." Before the *ching* can be mobilized, the *ching-ch'i* (prenatal sexual energy) must be extracted from the *ching-ye* (postnatal semen) in a kind of steaming process, where the spirit plays the role of fire and the breath, wind. Belief in the separability of the energetic and material aspects of the *ching* is demonstrated in the universal theory of "returning the *ching*" and the relatively rarer teaching on the expendability of semen after it has undergone the energy extraction process. For the sexual school, there is the additional problem of defining whether the *ching* involved is exclusively one's own, the partner's, or a fusion of the two. Most of the early texts in this collection leave this point ill-defined, but some of the later explicitly state that the male *ching* must be actively mobilized to meet the partner's incoming *ching* and convey it upward.

Orbital Meditation

Having discussed the alchemical apparatus (stove and crucible) and "medicine" (*ching*, *ch'i*, and spirit) in the previous section, it remains only to describe the path and timing of the firing process. Though the concept of absorbing *ching* and raising energy up the body appears as early as the Ma Wang tui texts, the model of a complete circuit formed by moving *ch'i* up the *Tu* and down the *Jen* meridians is not described in the literature until the Sung and Yüan. This practice is now generally called "microcosmic orbit" (*hsiao chou-t'ien* 小周天) meditation, but in early inner and sexual elixir texts it more commonly is referred to as "Terrestrial Branches *tzu* and *wu*," "the ecliptic of the sun," "the zodiac," "water wheel," "Big Dipper," "*Jen* and *Tu* meridians," "the movement of water and fire," "advancing the fire and withdrawing the tally," "the ascent and descent of *yin* and *yang*," and "the hexagram *Chun* in the morning and *Meng* in the evening."

The first two groups of texts in this collection represent the state of sexual practices from roughly the Han to the T'ang. The emphasis here is very much on the art of intercourse itself and its role in health. The themes of immortality and "returning the *ching*" are sounded but are by no means dominant. Once inner alchemy advances from a few simple steps to a full-blown choreography, then microcosmic orbit meditation seizes center stage and the sex act itself exists merely to catalyze the elements in the firing process. Microcosmic orbit meditation marks the culmination of a thrust that begins in pre-Ch'in times with the concept of *ching*, *ch'i*, and spirit and the pathways of *ch'i* circulation. By the time of the *Ishimpō* texts, the concept of "returning

the *ching* to nourish the brain," the role of breath in controlling and circulating the *ch'i*, and the value of salivary secretions all are very much in evidence and destined to be equally important in solo meditation. In the third group of texts, roughly from the T'ang to the Ming, we see the addition of specific points—the *tan-t'ien*, *ni-wan*, and *p'ing-i* (*hui-yin*)— and the movement of *ch'i* from the *tan-t'ien* up to the *ni-wan* with the aid of *ch'i* visualization. By the time of the last group of texts, a model of the complete microcosmic orbit is in place, with a clear circuit including the *wei-lü*, *chia-chi*, *ni-wan*, "flowery pool," "storied pavilion," and "lower *tan-t'ien*." *Tan-t'ien* massage, genital gymnastics, and anal constriction also are introduced at this point.

By the time we arrive at the last group of texts in this collection, exclusively Ming, all of the elements of medicine, the *I ching*, alchemy, and inner alchemy have come together with orbital meditation and a comprehensive program of stages, or "firing time," for completion of the elixir through sexual practice. The clearest expositions of the microcosmic method may be found in the following passages in this collection: *Summary of the Golden Elixir* (Chapter 1), *Secret Principles of Gathering the True Essence* (no. 12), *Queen Mother of the West's Ten Precepts* (Precept 4), *Master Li Ni-wan's Precious Raft* (Chapter 2), and *Correct Methods for Women's Practice* (Chapter 3). Constructing a composite of these passages give us the following general picture of microcosmic orbit meditation. After assuming an appropriate meditation posture, relaxing the body, emptying the mind, closing the mouth, and pressing the tongue against the hard palate to form the "upper magpie bridge," one begins to focus the mind in the "lower *tan-t'ien*" (abdomen) while practicing deep diaphragmatic breathing. The descent of the atmospheric *ch'i* (air) during inhalation causes the internal *ch'i* to pass from the "lower *tan-t'ien*" to the *hui-yin* (perineum) where constricting the anus seals the "lower magpie bridge" and encourages the *ch'i* in its upward progress to the *wei-lü* (coccyx), *chia-chi* (thoracic vertebrae), and *yü-chen* (occiput), where it enters the brain and floods the *ni-wan* (midbrain). This completes that half of the orbit known as "advancing the *yang* fire," and one now begins "withdrawing the *yin* tally" by exhaling and allowing the *ch'i* to descend to the *yin-t'ang* between the brows and enter the "flowery pool" (mouth), where a portion of the *ch'i* is translated into "jade liquid" (saliva), which along with the *ch'i*, flows down the "storied pavilion" (throat) past the "crimson palace" (heart) and stomach back to the *tan-t'ien*. In the solo meditation school, the advancing "*yang* fire" manifests naturally at the "hour of the living *tzu*" when the mind reaches perfect stillness. It is the prenatal *yang-ching* dwelling in the region of the lower body that microcosmic orbit practice is designed to unite with the spirit of the heart and circulate throughout the body. The "paired" inner alchemists differ from their "pure" colleagues only in their belief that the most powerful awakening of the prenatal *ching* (sexual energy) takes place concurrent with the stimulation of the postnatal *ching* (semen) during intercourse. The marriage of microcosmic orbit meditation with sexual yoga marks the crowning achievement of Chinese sexology.

Firing Time

Microcosmic orbit meditation is the smallest unit of meditational practice, but there are greater cycles and higher stages of attainment over the course of hours, days, months, and years. If the goal of microcosmic orbit meditation is the conversion of *ching* to *ch'i*, then in the next phase, *ch'i* is transmuted to spirit. This sometimes is called "macrocosmic orbit." The term "macrocosmic orbit" also is applied in some texts to the projection of *ch'i* into the meridians of the four limbs, shifting one's concentration from the "lower" to the "middle *tan-t'ien*," or the mystical mergence of one's own *ch'i* with the *ch'i* of the cosmos. An example of extending the circulation beyond the *Jen* and *Tu* meridians to include the extremities may be seen in the reference to "heel

breathing" (*chung-hsi* 踵息) in the *Essentials of the Golden Elixir*. The mystical mergence of microcosmic and macrocosmic *ch'i* may be seen most clearly in the *Queen Mother of the West's Ten Precepts*.

The deeper stages of absorption leading to the transmutation of *ch'i* into spirit are described in great detail in all of the texts in the fourth group of this collection. As a result of the awakening of the prenatal *ching* and the mergence of the mind with the breath, the "lesser medicine" (*ching* transmuted to *ch'i*) begins to circulate, the mind then detaches from all phenomena and one experiences the "fetal breath," or seeming cessation of breathing and pulse. At this stage, having reached the height of stillness, from within stillness movement once again is born, heralding the emergence of the "greater medicine." Often this manifests in the form of involuntary visual and aural hallucinations, such as flashes of light and peals of thunder. It is considered particularly important at this point to prevent leakage of the "six roots" (*liu ken* 六根) by sealing the nose, eyes, ears, and mind, and particularly by maintaining tension of the tongue and anus to prevent the escape of *ch'i* through nasal mucus and flatulence. The "greater medicine of the golden elixir" also is called the "golden liquid returning elixir" because it is a manifestation of the metal *ch'i* of the kidneys, or "metal in the midst of water," rising up the *yang* arc of the *Tu* meridian and becoming liquid elixir in the mouth as it descends the *yin* slope of the *Jen* meridian. The well-known Sung philosopher, Chou Tun-i (Lien-hsi), summarized this process of spiritualization very succinctly:

> Refine the *ching* so that it is transformed into *ch'i*, and refine the *ch'i* so that it is transformed into spirit. That is, refine the physical *ching* into a subtle form of *ch'i*, and refine the subtle *ch'i* of the breath so that it is transformed into a mysterious spirit, which permeates the Five Viscera and Six Bowels.

The texts in this collection contain a number of other formulations borrowed from the elixir literature for expressing the larger parameters of practice. Prominent among these is the "*chiu-chuan ch'i-fan* 九轉七返" cycle, which depending upon one's interpretation might be translated as "nine revolutions and seven reversions" or "revolution of the nine and reversion of the seven." The first interpretation is based on the methods of external alchemy and calculates a prescribed number of completed cycles of orbital circulations for the perfection of the elixir. In keeping with this interpretation, the *Secret of Gathering the True* takes the "nine revolutions" as nine times nine ascents of the *ch'i*. The second interpretation is based on the numerological association of the number seven with fire and nine with metal, so that the descent during meditation of the spirit's fire and the ascent of the *ch'i*'s metal represents the orbiting of the elements that combine to form the elixir.

During a single meditation session, or over the course of the diurnal or seasonal cycle, the intensity of effort is determined by the theory of "civil and martial fires" (*wen-huo wu-huo* 文火武火). The "martial fire" is employed during the phase of "advancing the *yang* fire" and the "civil fire" for "withdrawing the *yin* tally." At the midpoint in each phase is a period of rest, *mu-yü* 沐浴, literally to bathe, during which the intensity of the fire is not increased. Some authorities in these texts interpret the notion of microcosmic and macrocosmic synchronization literally and advocate the commencement of practice at midnight, or even the winter solstice, when the *yang* force begins its ascent. Others hold that the "hour of the living *tzu*," the individual biological awakening of sexual energy, is independent of cosmic cycles.

Stages of attainment also sometimes are expressed in these texts as levels of immortality. The *True Transmission of the Golden Elixir*, for example, posits three levels—human, earthly, and heavenly—corresponding to three stages each of a ninefold process. There are minor variations in the curriculum of self-cultivation itself among the various texts in this collection, but those elements generally shared by all of them include: "refining the self," "establishing the foundation," "gathering the medicine," and "returning the medicine." The practitioner's task during the first two involves stilling the mind and strengthening the *ching* and *ch'i*, stages shared by the solo and paired practice schools. However, the sexual adept also must be prepared to synchronize his own state with the level of arousal and arrival of the partner's "medicine," the prenatal *ching-ch'i* released along with the postnatal secretions during orgasm. The ecstatic experience of "obtaining the medicine" is captured in a verse by the great Sung philosopher Chu Hsi. Although he is writing of "pure practices" experience, it parallels many descriptions in our own collection:

> Suddenly at midnight a peal of thunder;
> Ten thousand gates and a thousand doors
>   open in succession.
> As if from nothing an apparition appears;
> Behold with your own eyes Fu Hsi comes.

Echoing the words of the *Mirror of Absorbing the Medicine*, a description of the arrival of the "greater medicine" by the famous Ming physician, Li Shih-chen, declares: "Those who receive it feel light and healthy in body, and even the weak appear strong. In a state of complete abstraction, one is as if drunk or fatuous. This is proof."

Having summarized the absorption of meditation theory and techniques into sexual practice, it is interesting to note that "pure" practitioners were not above borrowing a few metaphors from their "paired practices" counterparts. Phrases such as "*ching* and spirit unite like the joyful intercourse of husband and wife" routinely appear in the meditation literature. Taken together, the points, energies, circuits, and stages are the elements of an inner art form—silent music, motionless dance, invisible painting. Artist, medium, and audience are one, and though the goals are most often expressed in terms of health or spirituality, the experience itself may perhaps best be understood as esthetic.

V. THEMATIC PROGRESSIONS

We now have examined most of the key conceptual tools employed in formulating the theory of sexual practice. The works in this collection follow a rough chronological progression, and by isolating certain thematic elements as tracers, we may discern some subtler patterns of development beneath the terminology and between the lines of text. These thematic tracers also will help illuminate opposing doctrines within the sexual school as they developed and shifted over time. Finally, although the number of tracers could be multiplied indefinitely, these four have been chosen because they highlight both the evolution of sexual practices as a discipline and some of the social attitudes that helped shape them.

The Pleasure Principle

The Ma Wang tui and *Ishimpō* texts, representing the Han to T'ang periods, strongly emphasize prolonged foreplay, female orgasm, and male *reservatus* as promoting not only superior health but also greater pleasure than ejaculatory sex. Pleasure is presented in these texts as a basic necessity of life, like food and air. The *Tung Hsüan tzu* attempts to raise sex as a primal pleasure to the level of art, but clearly an art that serves to enhance pleasure as the core of esthetic experience. By the third group of texts, the pleasure principle, as well as the poetic style used to express it, have begun to fade, though not disappear, and the threat of ruin from sexual excess has become the dominant note. At the same time, the prospect of gaining immortality through sexuality is beginning to replace the poetry of the act itself as the most forceful inspiration. Technical interest shifts from postural possibilities and the intricacies of arousal to negative prohibitions and production of the elixir.

In the sexual alchemy texts, the pleasure principle has all but disappeared, and the focus has shifted entirely to technical instructions for a procedure in which joy and love are irrelevant. The sensual pleasure of sex has been completely sublimated and replaced with a transcendental pleasure, which is a function of the meditational process and not the sex act itself. The focus of attention has shifted from foreplay and sexual response to the preliminary phases of entering one's own meditative state. Here pleasure has become just another symptom of readiness in regulating the alchemical "firing time." How far we have come from the "exemption clause" in the reconstructed *Classic of Su Nü*: "With such a woman, even if one does not practice the correct methods of intercourse, there will be no harm!" In this unique passage, a woman who combines both physical beauty and intense passion is able to share a pleasure so perfect that it cancels the effects of seminal loss.

The Position of Women

In the first two groups of texts, although men are unmistakably both authors and audience, women nevertheless play a highly visible if not equal supporting role. A woman's pleasure is a precondition for releasing her *ching*, but recognition of her rights in the bedroom goes beyond simply milking her for sexual secretions. The detailed analysis of women's sexual response bespeaks at least a partial accounting of women's sensibilities and health requirements. Notwithstanding the emphasis on emotional harmonization between partners, it would be rash to equate this with current Western notions of romantic love. The word "love" (*ai* 愛) appears only four times in all of these texts. "The Highest Tao Under Heaven" says, "If one is slow and prolonged, the woman will experience great pleasure. She will feel as intimate as with a brother and love you like a father and mother." *The Classic of Su Nü* tells us that by practicing *coitus reservatus*, "a man's love for the woman will actually increase"; and the *Exposition of Cultivating the True Es-*

sence says that, "engaging in the 'battle of essences' in the proper way, not only strengthens the body, but increases a woman's love for the man." *The Wondrous Discourse* speaks of "respect and love" (*ching ai* 敬愛) and "kindness and love" (*en ai* 恩愛) as the basis for conjugal harmony. Emotional considerations largely disappear in the sexual alchemy texts, but here in the householder manuals, sexual compatibility is emphasized as crucial for marital success and in turn the stability and prosperity of the family and health of the offspring.

Reading the sexology classics as dramatic scripts, the first three groups in this collection show well-rounded female characters, whereas the literature of sexual alchemy portrays women as flat metaphysical props. The earlier texts portray dialogue, postures, and vignettes in which we can imagine human characters, unlike the alchemical agenda of the elixir school, which obscures the possibility of sexuality as human communion. In the early texts, the female partner is called "woman" or "enemy," but by the last she has become "other," "crucible," or "stove." Calculations once employed to determine eugenic possibilities and fertility are now turned to predicting the precise moment of the appearance of the "medicine," an event that may occur only once in a woman's lifetime. There is a concomitant shift in focus from the energy released on orgasm to the rarer "medicine" of puberty or ovulation. In the full-blown sexual alchemy literature, foreplay and female orgasm have all but disappeared, corresponding to a shift in language from regarding the woman's essence as "*yin-ching*" to seeing her as harboring the "true *yang*." In the early texts, one still feels that women hold up half the *tao*, but by the end of the sexual alchemy tradition, she has become a kind of sexual wet nurse.

Kristofer Schipper has identified an interesting psychological ambivalence in the Chinese male response to female sexuality. In *Le corps taoïste* he says:

Making love is good for the health, but in reading these manuals it becomes apparent that the attitude is not fundamentally so positive. Love is also fearful: woman is a vampire who steals man's essence. One shutters to think that it was in this very manner that the Queen Mother of the West, that great goddess, gained immortality.

Around this central ambivalence swirl a host of related contradictions. The faculty of sex tutors in the Ma Wang tui texts is exclusively male, whereas in the *Ishimpō* they are chiefly female. The *Ishimpō* contains both the goddess initiatresses, Su Nü, Ts'ai Nü, and Hsüan Nü, and the Queen Mother: collaborators and separatist. With the emergence of Su Nü as the chief guardian of the sex arcana, there is the implication that the sexual secrets are with woman because they are within woman, but ironically at the same time the *Secrets of the Jade Chamber* warns the man to "conceal his art from his partner." The same work gives the female followers of the Queen Mother, "who understand the art of nourishing *yin* with *yang*," two choices: she may use her power to produce male offspring or enjoy eternal youth herself. These essentially are the same options offered to the male practitioner, though the possibility of immortality for women remains an undeveloped subplot in a story whose real hero is the Yellow Emperor. A second minor theme is what the "Dangers and Benefits" calls "the *tao* of man and woman achieving immortality together." The theme of immortality for women disappears from the sexual literature after the *Ishimpō* and only reemerges in the context of women's solo meditation, where women are instructed to exploit their own internal *yang* essence to revert to girlhood or transform themselves into a man. The theme of shared immortality becomes even less a possibility in "paired practices" with the development of sexual alchemy, and reappears again only in our own time with the synthesis of Chinese sexual techniques and modern Western values.

The importance of physical beauty and feminine temperament remained constant throughout the whole history of classical sexology, but there was a steady   45 downward revision of the requirement for youth until finally in the end we reach the moment of puberty itself. The escape clause in the reconstructed *Classic of Su Nü*, granting exemption from harm when ejaculating with women of exceptional beauty, in later texts becomes advice to train with "ugly stoves" to develop self-control. Contrariwise, as early as the *Classic of Su Nü* we are taught to repress the esthetic aspect of sexual arousal by imagining the "enemy" as "tiles and stone"; while as late as Chang San-feng, "fine women" are specified for the practice of "blowing the flute." The contradiction between beautiful women providing the highest "medicine" and the necessity to repress the esthetic response for ejaculation control was difficult to resolve. Nevertheless, the emphasis on, and at times the ambivalence surrounding, female physiognomy and feminine attributes reveals more than a skindeep esthetic judgment, but indicates the Chinese faith in the goodness of that which nature makes beautiful.

Ejaculation Frequency and Control

Judging from the limited sample of published documents, there is an unmistakable cooling trend in ejaculation frequency as we move from the Han to the Ming. The Ma Wang tui texts allow that "when the *ching* is replete one must ejaculate," but provide no specific numerical guidelines. A significant downward revision accompanies the transition from the *Ishimpō* material to the medical and householder manuals, and most striking, the disappearance of numbers altogether in the sexual alchemists with the tacit assumption of unconditional nonejaculation.

The reconstructed *Classic of Su Nü* contains two prescriptive passages, which are widely divergent in their allowances. If we consider only the first passage, which forms part of the continuous dialogue, and ignore the second, which appears to be interpolated and is identical with the "Health Benefits of the Bedcham-

ber," then comparing the *Classic of Su Nü* and *Secrets of the Jade Chamber* we see only modest belt tightening. The *Essentials* considers limiting ejaculation to twice a month sufficient to attain 200 years of perfect health. The *Classic* allows two ejaculations per day for a "strong lad" of fifteen, while the *Secrets* has no figure whatever for this age . The *Classic* allows two per day at twenty, but the *Secrets* only once in two days. At thirty years of age the Classic permits one per day, while the *Secrets* one in three days. At forty years, the *Classic* and *Secrets* draw close with one in three days and one in four days, and by fifty years converge at one in five days. The *Secrets* pursues a mnemonic progression of one ejaculation in two, three, four, and five days for ages twenty, thirty, forty, and fifty, and closes the curve with zero at age sixty. The *Classic* continues after fifty, allowing one in ten days at age sixty, and one in thirty at seventy. Remembering that these prescriptions apply only to ejaculation and that sexual contact sans ejaculation is strongly encouraged, the *Classic* and *Secrets* tables are liberal indeed. In very rough terms, by the time of the "Health Benefits of the Bedchamber," the intervals between ejaculations have widened by a factor of approximately four. The "Dangers and Benefits of Intercourse with Women" pegs the frequency to season rather than age, but making the necessary adjustments, the factor also is roughly four or five.

The latest work chronologically, *The Wondrous Discourse of Su Nü*, provides not only a schedule of the upper limits of ejaculation frequency, but an important theoretical innovation. All previous texts, though they may differ in numerical detail, are consistent in presenting the optimum interval as widening in a linear progression from youth to old age. *The Wondrous Discourse* harkens to Confucius' admonition, "In youth the blood *ch'i* is not yet full and therefore one must abstain from sex." At twenty, it allows only once in thirty days, the same as the *Classic* allows at seventy, and by contrast with the *Classic*'s twice per day at the same age. At thirty and forty, which the

Wondrous Discourse considers the height of a man's sexual power, it allows fewer than the *Classic* and *Secrets*, but more than the "Health Benefits." Granting the first escape-valve provision since the "Highest Tao," the *Wondrous Discourse* stresses that in midlife the *ching* is full to "overflowing," and repression may lead to illness. The last group of texts, representing radical sexual alchemy, makes no concessions to the householder, and even the word "ejaculation" (*hsieh* 寫) is entirely absent.

To sum up then, the early texts regard the immediate postpuberty years as the peak of sexual vitality and hence allow as many as two ejaculations per day. The "Health Benefits" is far less generous in intervals, but reveals the same incremental tendency. The *Wondrous Discourse*, initiating another school of thought, takes youth as the most vulnerable age and forms an interesting bridge to the last group of texts wherein, by preserving one's seminal integrity, puberty offers the quickest access to immortality.

The Ma Wang tui texts contain no discernable ejaculation control techniques, other than stopping short of inevitability, but by the time of the *Ishimpō* classics the full spectrum of methods already was in place. These methods include mental imaging, breath control, perineal compression, pubococcygeal contraction, teeth gnashing, as well as eye, tongue, nostril, spinal, and abdominal techniques, and such practices as "entering dead, withdrawing live," and changing partners on arousal. This panoply of self-defense methods takes full advantage of emotional, esthetic, and physiological response factors. The third group of texts adds nothing of a practical nature to this list, but the *Exposition of Cultivating the True Essence* makes two important theoretical contributions. The first consists of a condemnation of retrograde ejaculation; and the second, the necessity of simultaneous absorption through the nostrils and penis. As explained in the text, if the "gate of heaven" (nostrils) is left unsealed, then leakage will occur from the "gate of life" (penis) below, but if inhalation and retention are practiced in concert, a kind of pneumatic draw is created that causes the *ching* to rise. Among the last group of texts, the *True Transmission* contains no reference to ejaculation control, but the Chang San-feng texts detail most of the techniques listed earlier, though they are very much overshadowed by the alchemical instructions. The *Summary of the Golden Elixir*, however, does introduce the subtle new retention technique of synchronizing exhalation with penetration and inhalation with withdrawal. In the "art of the bedchamber" texts—Ma Wang tui, *Ishimpō*, and to some extent the medical and householder manuals—the purpose of ejaculation control techniques is twofold: first, to prevent premature ejaculation and guarantee female satisfaction; and second, to conserve semen through *coitus reservatus*. The chaste sexual alchemy texts of Lu and Sun make no explicit reference to ejaculation control, but the *Exposition* and Chang San-feng texts' innovations in this area show that interest continued all the way through the classical tradition.

Sexual Energy

The concept of "returning the *ching* to nourish the brain" long has been considered the centerpiece of Chinese sexual practice. Over the nearly 2,000 years that these texts represent, we can discern a number of developments in the interpretation of female sexual energy and the techniques for effecting the "gathering," (*ts'ai* 採) "refining," (*lien* 練), and "circulating" (*hsing* 行, *huan* 還) of her essence by the male adept. Although the classic formulation does not appear until the *Ishimpō* texts, the concept of absorption of female essence already is in evidence in the Ma Wang tui material. The "Uniting Yin and Yang" says, "Suck the '*ching*-spirit' upward," and the "Shih wen" says, "absorb her *ching*," "draw in *ch'i* to fill the brain," and "all the *ching* rise upward." The various references to energy absorption and circulation in the Ma Wang tui texts leave room for ambiguity as to whether the essences involved are internal, external, or an amalgam of the two. The *Classic of Su Nü* fails to resolve this ambiguity, giving us both, "To be aroused but not ejaculate is what is called 'returning the *ching*,'" and "Gather her overflowing *ching* and take the liquid from her mouth. The *ching-ch'i* will be returned and transformed in your own body, filling the brain." The reconstructed *Essentials* contains one passage describing a procedure for effecting retrograde ejaculation where the diverted "*ching*" apparently is semen and not "*ching-ch'i*" (sexual energy). In the very next fragment of this text we find a wide variety of techniques for "stilling" (*chih* 止) the *ching*, without mention of "returning" or absorbing *ching* from the partner. The *Secrets* makes no reference to "returning the *ching* to nourish the brain," but rather of distributing the *ching* to the "hundred vessels" (*pai-mai* 百脉) for curing specific illnesses. What is absorbed from the woman, as described in the *Secrets*, is called "*ching* secretions" and "*ch'i*," and both male and female sexual essences are called "*yin-ching*." "*Ching*" and "*ch'i*" are used more or less interchangeably here, the woman's sexual energy in one instance being called "*yin-ching*" and in another similar context "*yin-ch'i*." The "nine shallow, one deep" rhythm is specifically prescribed for facilitating absorption, as is shallow penetration. Again no clear linkage is made between absorption of feminine energy and raising or circulating one's own, and again the path and process are vague. The *Tung Hsüan tzu*, the most romantic and least esoteric of the early texts, in only one passage lists a number of standard techniques of ejaculation control, concluding, "the *ching* will rise of itself." Ignoring the unique passage on retrograde ejaculation in the *Essentials* for the moment, to generalize about the early phase of sexual yoga that these texts represent, we may say that the "return," "circulation," or "rising" of the *ching* takes place naturally as a result of simultaneous stimulation and *reservatus*; and that male and female sexual energy usually are treated in separate passages in the texts and never explicitly linked.

The "Health Benefits of the Bedchamber" includes all of the techniques of ejaculation control found in the early texts, but also adds several new elements. First, it introduces the dramatic new discovery that frequent sex with occasional ejaculation is less depleting than occasional sex with habitual ejaculation. This provides additional empirical support for the theory that frequent *coitus reservatus* heightens sexual power. Second, it introduces meditative visualizations and yogic postures for precoital preparation and postcoital absorption. A third element is the emphasis on the importance of absorption from "above"; that is the woman's breath. The "Dangers and Benefits" includes everything in the "Health Benefits," together with some new themes. It is the only text to address the question of postejaculatory remediation, advising that when emission does take place, one should supplement the loss by engaging in exercise to "circulate energy internally." The *Classic of Su Nü* introduced the possibility of immortality for women by reversing the direction of sexual osmosis. The "Dangers and Benefits," however, is the first text to describe a path of mutual immortality for men and women through a combination of deep penetration, low arousal, and *tan-t'ien* visualizations. This is a radical departure from the usual one-sided concept of release and absorption, but unfortunately the text does not explain if there is an exchange of energy or how energy would be released without orgasm. On the issue of abstinence, however, the "Dangers and Benefits" does give theoretical clarification to the earlier teachings, warning that abstinence not only gives rise to "ghost sex" (intercourse with incubi) and nocturnal emissions, but "weakens the *yang* principle."

The *Wondrous Discourse* articulates the full range of topics in sexology, but adds only one significant new theory to our understanding of the nature of sexual energy. By giving us a parabolic curve of sexual vitality, peaking at middle age, it separates the concept of sexual energy from simple ejaculatory potency. This shift in the locus of sexual energy away from the gonads culminates in the theory that the *ching* is concentrated at twenty in the intestines, at thirty in the thighs, at forty in the lower back, and at fifty in the spine. As in the Ma Wang tui and *Ishimpō* texts, the quantity and flow of ejaculate also is seen as a barometer of sexual fitness, specific symptoms indicating injury to specific systems. Similarly, later in the same text we find the novel idea that at midnight the *yang-ch'i* is just beginning to return and thus is too weak to be shed. The analysis of sexual arousal, correlating stages with organ systems, hearkens back to the *Classic of Su Nü*, further reinforcing the conception of the *ching* as diffused throughout the body and aligning it more closely with classical medical theory.

The concept of absorbing a partner's energy is left for the very end of the *Wondrous Discourse* and then simply described as "absorb her *yin-ching* to fortify your *yang-ch'i*." Absorbing the woman's breath is said specifically to benefit one's "spine marrow" and her saliva to nourish the *tan-t'ien*. These are new elements to date, and the former, in fact, unique in all the literature. Explicit reference to mutual absorption is missing, but it does provide a theoretical basis for the possibility of two-way exchange, stating that man by nature is sufficient in *yang-ch'i* but deficient in blood, whereas woman is sufficient in blood but deficient in *yang-ch'i*, concluding suggestively that, "Those who are able to comprehend this subtle mystery use repletion to supplement deficiency." The *Wondrous Discourse* and *Exposition of Cultivating the True Essence* are roughly contemporaneous and, although they reveal some significant differences, share the notion of the importance of simultaneous absorption from above and below. The *Exposition*, however, goes a bit further, propounding a theory of "Three Peaks" in which the breast essence appears as a new element in an expanded three-stage sequence of absorption. This theory of absorbing mouth, breast, and vaginal essences during sex may perhaps be seen as parallel-ing on an etheric level the traditional pharmacological use of menstrual blood, placenta, and human milk as tonic supplements.

The *Exposition*'s radically novel theory of "corrupt *ching*" not only explicitly refutes the retrograde ejaculation method, but holds that, when the sexual energy (*yüan-yang*) has been extracted and circulated through protracted practice, the deenergized semen (*pai-ching* 敗精) may be expelled without loss. The *Exposition* is the first text to clearly state that what is circulated by the adept consists of one's own *ching* and the "medicine" of the partner's "Three Peaks." This applies both to the phase of intromission and to the postcoital exercises prescribed for decompression and distribution.

The *True Classic of Perfect Union* is cast as a strategy for victory in the "battle of absorption," and the commentary interprets the extended military metaphor in a fairly predictable way. Because the emphasis is on capturing the spoils of war, referred to variously as "true fluid," "true *ching*," and "true *yang*," less attention is paid to the role of the male *ching* itself, except to stress the techniques of *reservatus*. The original text is vague concerning the path of "returning the *ching*," but the commentary supplies a complete description of the microcosmic orbit. Though common in the late sexual alchemy literature, this is the first instance in the householder tradition of a reference to the female essence as "true *yang*." This closes an important gap in the early texts by using the theory of similars to explain how female essence can strengthen male virility. This text more than any other clearly expostulates the principles of sexual energetics based on the transferability of sexual essence and the techniques for sealing one's own borders while raiding the "enemy's" territory.

In the fourth group of texts, the *True Transmission of the Golden Elixir* builds on many concepts in the *Exposition*, presenting the most detailed analysis of the source, nature, and manner of refining 49 the sexual elixir of any text to date or of any text in this collection. By the time of the Ming, it had become common to characterize the woman's sexual essence as "true *yang*," but the *True Transmission* borrowing from alchemy and medicine refers to it also as "lead" and "*ch'i* and blood." According to the *True Transmission*, the women's sexual essence is released in two stages: the first, designated by the ninth Celestial Stem *jen*, is described as "*yang* within *yin*;" the second, designated by the tenth, *kuei*, is "*yin* within *yin*." Only the *jen* qualifies as "the prenatal external medicine produced in the postnatal crucible."

Both the *Exposition* and the *True Transmission* throw new light on how male and female—internal and external—energy combine in the body of the adept to form the elixir and eventually the "holy fetus." The *Exposition* asserts: "The *yin-ching* is difficult to make secure and strong, and so requires the lead to control it." Combining the woman's "lead" with the adept's own "mercury" allows him to transmute "quicksilver" into "cinnabar" or "jade paste." Comparing the interaction of the two elements to "the attraction of loadstone for iron," it exhorts the adept to "mobilize a bit of one's own mercury to welcome" the incoming female energy. The implication here is that male sexual energy alone is unstable, and that, only when aroused without bursting out and fused with female essence, does it achieve a stable state, enabling it to serve as the raw material for inner alchemy. The *True Transmission* addresses this very directly, referring to the respective contributions of male and female as "internal" and "external medicine" and even "internal" and "external elixir." The term "external elixir" (*wai-tan* 外丹), of course, is more commonly associated with the classical school of alchemy, but here is used to designate the "external" energy derived from female partners during sexual practice. The male model of spiritual pregnancy also gives theoretical clarity to the process of combining the two energies and the necessity of female *ching*. The

three Chang San-feng texts share much in common with the *True Transmission* in terms of theory and vocabulary, but add two new minor dimensions to the theory of sexual energy. The first is the use of "blowing the flute" (fellatio) to "open the passes" as a prelude to intercourse, and the second is the necessity for "obtaining the medicine" by enacting "earth over heaven" (female superior) postures.

The last question we need to consider in this section is the contribution of women's practices to the overall theory of sexual energy in health and immortality studies. As examples of solo or "pure practices," of course, they deny the efficacy of borrowed *ching*, but fully endorse the notion of self-transformation through the mastery of sexual energy. Because all of the women's texts in their present form cluster chronologically in the Ch'ing, it is difficult to discern much in the way of development, and the minor differences in emphasis do not prevent us from discussing them collectively. There is universal agreement that menstruation is the feminine analogue of ejaculation, and that the blood should be conserved by suspending menses, "slaying the red dragon." However, the focus of one's training is sometimes referred to as blood, sometimes *ching*, and sometimes *ch'i*; the material aspect of female sexual energy is called *yin* and the energetic aspect *yang*. The fundamental difference between man and woman as described in the *Essentials of the Women's Golden Elixir Method* and the *Precious Raft* is that men must control both their passions and naturally active *ch'i*, whereas women also must still their desires, but simultaneously stimulate their *ch'i* to overcome the natural stasis of *yin* and release the *yang* principle. The "red dragon" of menstruation is the product of postnatal *yin-ch'i*, which appears under the influence of mental excitement. By eliminating the excitement and employing practices to stimulate the *ch'i* function, the "red" is said to be transformed into "white phoenix marrow" and sets the stage for the appearance of the "greater medicine," "holy fetus," "pearl," or "*yang spirit.*" Showing their shared theoretical foundations, it is clear that the raw material of training in the women's solo school is precisely the same energetic essence pursued by men in their female partners.

VI. THE DEVELOPMENT OF CHINESE SEXOLOGY

Chinese Studies

Evidence of a renaissance of interest in sexology as a branch of science, together with its broader social dimensions and role in culture, began to emerge in the late nineteenth century in China. Under Western stimulus, late Ch'ing reformers such as K'ang Yu-wei in his *Ta-t'ung shu* (Book of the great unity) and T'an Ssu-t'ung in his *Jen hsüeh* (The learning of love) catalogued the crimes of misogyny and made empassioned pleas for women's equality. Writing in 1896, T'an cites the theory that "men have three stages of arousal and women five" to prove the antiquity of scientific sexology in China prior to contact with the West. Interestingly, T'an's numbers, three and five, correspond only with the Ch'ing gynecological work, *Fu-k'o yü-ch'ih*, of Shen Chin-ao and the recently discovered Han "Highest Tao under Heaven." T'an was martyred before Yeh Te-hui's resurrection of the *Ishimpō* classics, and therefore the source of his information is difficult to establish. Both K'ang and T'an believed that removing all social prohibitions would allow sex to revert to its natural role, obsessions would disappear, and a higher spiritual partnership of the sexes would be possible. They were impressed with Western sexual mores, especially greater gender equality, the right of divorce, and public mixing of the sexes. Yeh Te-hui in the Preface to his reconstruction of the *Ishimpō* fragments tells us that his motivation in seeing these works published was not to incite sexual license, but to demonstrate that at an earlier time in China's history sex was accorded its rightful place in the scheme of human life. He condemned the Sung Confucian "School of Reason" (*li-hsüeh* 理學) for fostering a climate of sexual repression and expressed the hope that publication of the Sui-T'ang handbooks of sex would bring the teachings of the sages back to the land of their origin. A patriot, but archconservative, Yeh did not share K'ang and T'an's vision of lowering social barriers between the sexes, believing it reduced humanity to "bestiality"; he restricted his liberalism to relations within the bedchamber alone. What we see then in the late nineteenth and early twentieth centuries is the beginnings of an attempt to respond to the challenge of Western sexual culture by seeking out Chinese sources of scientific sexology and recognizing the need to curb sexual superstition, footbinding, concubinage, and slavery.

The influence of Western-style scholarship became pronounced during the early Republican era, but I can find no titles on sexual practices from this period. It is not until the late 1960s that popular works begin to appear, which combine the outlook and reasearch methods of modern Western sexologists with some traditional elements. This genre continued in the 1970s and 1980s, when I began to collect this material in Taiwan, Hong Kong, and overseas Chinese bookstores. Because of library acquisition policies, none of these valuable works is available in public library collections, but

51

turn up randomly either over or under the counter in Chinese bookstores. Four of them in my possession contain colloquial Chinese paraphrase translations of some of the texts in the present anthology and have been valuable for insights and comparative readings of difficult passages. Of the four, three are unsigned, all are undated, and the titles bear little relation to the contents. The basic texts appear in multiple editions, each time under a different title, making bibliographic citation highly problematic. Despite their anonymity and grossly commercial format, they nevertheless obviously are the work of knowledgeable sexologists, who are well-acquainted with Western sexology, some of the extant Chinese classics, and bits of the oral tradition. All four works are based on the *Ishimpō* fragments or Yeh's reconstructions, but cut up and reorganized, with colloquial renderings and rambling commentaries. Observations based on Western perspectives often are supported by citing studies and statistics, but textual exegesis of the classics relies solely on native cultural intuition, uninformed by lexical consulation or other hermeneutic techniques. The lack of scholarly care in the handling of the texts themselves results in numerous errors, but also rare flashes of insight. I have taken the contribution of these works seriously enough to include their interpretations of critical issues in my own footnotes.

Another class of recent publications in Chinese are those of contemporary meditation masters teaching traditional techniques of sexual yoga for modern readers. Unlike the authors in the previous group, who seek to introduce and interpret traditional teachings, these adopt the stance of teachers or inheritors of that tradition. Of the three in my posession, one is anonymous, one pseudononymous, and the last, a translation into Chinese of a Japanese work based on the Chinese tradition. All combine sexual techniques with medical information and a wealth of yogic practices. They include concepts and techniques not found in the classics, illustrating not only the great diversity of the unpublished tradition, but in some cases, perhaps, innovations in an ongoing evolution of the art. For students of Chinese sexology, these works, rich in terminology, lore, and general ethos are extremely useful in the initiation and immersion process. Though not written to satisfy scholarly criteria, when it comes to the classic texts themselves, they are no less accurate than some Western scholarly translations and often more accurate than Western popular works. Some buttress their faith in the ability of sexual practices to confer immortality with elements from Western science or parallel practices from Indian yoga and Tantrism.

Among the novel teachings that appear in these works is the theory set forth in Akagi Koichi's *Hsien-jen hui-ch'un ch'iang-ching shu* (Methods of the immortals for rejuvenation and sexual strengthening) that the *ch'i* released during female orgasm and that locked within the male semen must first be extracted and combined within the body of the male adept, after which the semen, now a spent residue, should be ejaculated. Following the woman's orgasm, the adept should bring himself to the brink, thus refining out the *ch'i* from the semen and preventing the woman from simply reabsorbing her own *ching-ch'i*. Simultaneous orgasm, he says, is beneficial only to the woman. Unlike traditional texts, which incidentally are rarely mentioned in his presentation, he does not connect the process of absorption with microcosmic orbit circulation or with the idea of "returning the *ching* to fortify the brain." He recommends a period of sleep immediately following coitus and specifically forbids postcoital love play as a waste of energy. Acknowledging that this method benefits only the male, and in view of the difficulty of obtaining an adequate supply of young girls in the present age, he introduces a modified method for married couples. Following the woman's first orgasm, which is absorbed by the man, she should bring herself to orgasm again to give him a second opportunity to absorb her *ch'i*. Finally, they both reach climax together during which time she uses vaginal contractions to absorb his *ching*.

A second original method is found in Kung Chien Lao Jen's *Chung-kuo yang-sheng ts'ai-pu shu* (Chinese sexual yoga). He contradicts the traditional view that the woman's exhaled breath is a valuable source of sexual revenue, arguing that it is foul and should be strictly avoided. During the woman's climax, the man should use visualization and sphincter contractions to absorb her *yang-ch'i*. This, however, according to Kung Chien Lao Jen, is only the first stage— acquisition—and not yet assimilation. Assimilation takes place following the woman's orgasm as the man continues to move in and out, stopping each time just before the point of ejaculatory inevitability. To climax at this point is to bring harm to both partners, he says, without benefit to oneself. Although it is important to stop short of ejaculation, it is equally important for excitation to reach the point of internal penile contractions. After as many rounds of this procedure as possible (five guarantees immortality) and when climax becomes inevitable, one simply surrenders and, in the author's idiom, "lays down one's armor."

The anonymous author of the *T'e-hsiao mi-fang* (Marvelous prescriptions) touches on nearly every aspect of sexuality within the context of monogamous maritial relations and displays considerable clinical experience in treating sexual dysfunction using both traditional Chinese and modern Western modalities. Among the concepts not found in other sources is the idea that breast milk is chemically altered by sexual excitation, and thus infants should never be nursed during intercourse. He prescribes the traditional compression of the perineum and tongue to palate contact as therapies for premature ejaculation, citing the *Secrets of the Jade Chamber* as *locus classicus*. Describing an acute condition known as *wang-yang* ("loss of *yang*"), resulting from one night's excess after long abstinence, he offers an interesting first aid procedure. When a male partner who has

spent himself to death's doorstep experiences spermatorrhea, cold sweat, and near unconsciousness, the woman should continue to maintain genital contact while pricking the *wei-lü* point at the base of the spine with a needle or sharp object. Failing this, she should bite the *jen-chung* point in the center of the upper lip. He even introduces some basic solo meditation techniques, including microcosmic orbit meditation, genital massage, saliva swallowing, and "locking the gate of *yang*" by gaining voluntary control of prostate and seminal vesicles. He attributes these techniques to P'eng Tsu, Chang San-feng, and Wu Hsien, but barely hints at the possibility of paired sexual practices in the single crytic phrase, "If one can also obtain the nourishment of *K'an-ching*. . . ." One can only wonder how many of his readers are aware that the trigram *K'an* stands for female sexual energy or will catch the import of this lone phrase in a very long work. In all of the books in this genre we see a natural and unself-conscious mixing of Western and Chinese scientific paradigms. "*Yang-ch'i*" and "sex hormones" rub shoulders in the same sentence as if they are simply two different names for the same phenomenon.

Contemporary Chinese monographs on traditional sexology, if they exist, have so far eluded my bibliographic net, and I therefore have to content myself with scraps of scholarship in other works. Hsiao T'ien-shih's *Tao-chia yang-sheng-hsüeh kai-yao* (An outline of Taoist health practices) devotes considerable space to the issue of sexual practices in Taoism. Both a scholar and exponent of Taoism, Hsiao is responsible for seeing countless rare works published, including several included in this anthology, which otherwise would be closed to the public. The attitude that emerges from his discussion of sexual yoga in the *Tao-chia yang-sheng hsüeh kai-yao* and his introductions to the Chang San-feng and Lu Hsi-hsing texts in the monumental *Tao-tsang ching-hua* (Essence of the Taoist canon) is a study in ambivalence. On the one hand, he deprecates sexual techniques as inferior to the more rarified systems of meditation, but at the same time cannot help but respect them for establishing a secure and enduring foothold in the Taoist landscape. In this sense, his attitude is remarkably like Tseng Tsao's a thousand years before him. Hsiao also lists numerous sexual titles in his personal collection that have not yet been published and others that he says he has no intention of seeing published. From scattered references in his book, however, it is possible to catch glimpses of gems not present in the already published material. At times, too, he lets down his guard and presents some passages from unpublished works without prefatory disclaimer and with something like sympathy for the concept of "astral intercourse" involving a kind of spiritual exchange of essences.

Turning to Mainland scholarship, I have seen only one undated, unpublished article on sexology by a physician, Ch'en Hua, entitled "Chung-i yü hsing" (Chinese medicine and sex), which is well researched but confines itself exclusively to the benefits of moderation, the role of *shen* in traditional Chinese medicine, and standard sexual dysfunction. Its sources are mainstream medical classics; and no mention whatsoever is made of sexual *ch'i-kung* therapy, much less the sexual school of immortality. He quotes from the writings of Sun Ssu-miao, represented in this anthology, on the dangers of sexual excess, but omits Sun's prescription of sexual yoga with multiple partners as a good general tonic.

More recently, a collectively authored work entitled *Chung-kuo ku-tai yang-sheng ch'ang-shou mi-fa* (Ancient Chinese secrets of health and longevity) has been published by the Chekiang Science and Technology Press, which devotes an entire chapter to traditional sexual hygiene. Here as with Ch'en's article, the authors prefer to cite sources in the medical literature rather than introducing the reader to the sexual classics. When describing the stages of arousal and the benefits and ills of sexual intercourse, for example, they ignore the *Ishimpō* material, relying instead on obsure gynecological works and the Ma Wang tui texts.

Even Sun Ssu-miao usually is quoted here without crediting the source. As for methods of "cultivating the *ching*," the chapter describes only dietary supplements and herbs, omitting practices outlined in the sexual literature. However, one revealing sentence suggests that the *Chung-kuo ku-tai yang-sheng ch'ang-shou mi-fa* authors were not unaware of the broader spectrum of traditional teachings and practices in this area:

> Our ancestors who examined sexuality from a medical standpoint believed that the appropriate techniques not only provided mutual sexual satisfaction, but even more important, contributed to health and longevity. This is what is meant by, "Among the more than ten schools of sexual disciplines, some use it to relieve injuries and ills and others to cure diseases, some use it to gather *yin* for the benefit of *yang* and others to promote longevity."

It surpasses the Ch'en article, probably written ten years earlier, in its frank discussion of the romantic aspects of sex and the need for an artful and loving approach to intimate relations.

Whatever reticence remains among contemporary Chinese scholars to treat traditional sexual practices as a worthy research topic arises, I believe, from a concern for their own reputations and a fear of rekindling feudal abuses. Are they afraid, perhaps, that just below the surface of the male psyche lurks the attitude described by T'an Ssu-t'ung a century ago:

> It is the brutish custom of men to drool over young girls. Is this not deriving pleasure from their pain, even from their bleeding and screaming? Looking at the period following the Sung dynasty, the races of Mongols and Manchus have alternated as masters of the Chinese people. That these foreigners refrained from footbinding is in itself sufficient to make them worthy of heaven's aid; it is not that heaven is guilty of misplaced partiality.

Internal criticism could be silenced at the executioner's block, but similar statements by foreign observers, such as the following by a nineteenth century missionary, remain a potent source of embarassment to the present: "Girls scarcely twelve years old were given up to the beastly passions of men. Parents prostitute their daughters, husbands their wives, brothers their sisters—and this they do with a diabolical joy." Altogether, there seems to be a lack of confidence in the public's ability to separate the rice from the chaff when it comes to traditional sexual hygiene, and particularly in the area of male prerogatives.

An interesting case of protecting the public from the facts can be found in the editor's introduction to the *Ma Wang tui Han-mu po-shu* (Silk manuscripts from the Han tomb of King Ma), vol. 4. Mysteriously, the editors discuss every text in this *yang-sheng* volume with the exception of the two on sexual cultivation, the "Ho yin-yang" and "T'ien-hsia chih-tao t'an," while listing the "Yang-sheng fang," "Tsa liao fang," and "Shih-wen" as examples of "what the *Han shu* bibliography calls 'art of the bedchamber.'" They then quote the *Han shu* editor's comment on sexual disciplines and conclude in their own words, "Thus it can be seen that the ancients already were aware of the harmfulness of this art, and it was therefore proscribed by later generations." This interpretation is accomplished by taking the phrase 迷者弗顧以生疾而隕性命 as referring to those who become overzealous practitioners of these arts rather than those who ignore them.

Among recent Mainland publications on *ch'i-kung* are several that touch on aspects of traditional women's sexual problems. *Ch'i-kung ching-hsüan* (Selected articles on *ch'i-kung*), edited by Yen Hai, has an article by Hu Yao-chen outlining some techniques and concepts not found in the texts in the present collection. Describing deliberate suspension of menses, "slaying the red dragon," as a technique developed for Buddhist nuns, he mentions various combinations of points used during meditation, including the *ch'i-hai, kuan-yüan, hui-yin,* cervix, *yung-ch'üan, tsu-ch'iao,* and *shan-chung.* Gradually the menstrual period will arrive later and later each month until it disappears altogether. The four women's texts in our anthology present breast mas-

sage as an integral phase of practice, but it is conspicuously absent from Hu's discussion. Massage figures in his technique only as an antidote to feelings of sexual arousal resulting from concentration on the *shan-chung* point between the breasts, and then the point of application is the navel.

Ma Chi-jen's *Chung-kuo ch'i-kung hsüeh* (Chinese yoga), one of the most comprehensive scholarly treatments of the history, theory, and practice of *ch'i-kung* ignores paired sexual practices, but devotes one paragraph to women's solo cultivation. Without citing any of the specialized titles in the present collection, it describes the "slaying of the red dragon" by quoting from the Yüan work of Ch'en Chih-hsü, *Wu-chen p'ien chu* (The *Wu-chen p'ien* with annotations):

> When it comes to women cultivating immortality, the breasts are the site of *ch'i* generation, and the technique is quite simple. The cultivation of immortality for women is called "refining the physical form." Women's practice involves first accumulating *ch'i* in the breasts, then setting up the "stove" and establishing the "crucible" to carry out the method of "*yin* major refining the form."

The *Chung-kuo ku-tai yang-sheng ch'ang-shou mi-fa* takes a very different tack in describing the special problems of women's sexuality, focusing on sex during the woman's "three periods" (*san-ch'i* 三期); viz., menses, pregnancy, and postpartum. General medical theory forbids intercourse during these three periods because of deficiency and cold in the *Ch'ung* and *Jen* meridians and insufficiency of blood. Basing his summary of the tradition on Sun Ssu-miao, he warns that intercourse during the menstrual period can lead to menorrhagia, vaginal discharge, painful periods, as well as diseases of the cervix and uterus. Intercourse also should be avoided during the first and third trimesters of pregnancy. Indiscretions may lead to miscarriage, resulting from the simultaneous fueling of the fire principle and depletion of water. During the postpartum period of recovery and lactation, one should abstain for at least a hundred days before resuming sexual relations.

Western Studies

Students of Chinese sexology will doubtless be familiar with the works of such pioneering scholars as Henri Maspero, Robert van Gulik, and Joseph Needham. Because their studies have become standard sources in the field, I will not attempt to review their positive contributions, but at the risk of seeming unbalanced in my presentation, will confine my survey of these scholars to what appear to be weaknesses, errors, or biases in their analyses. Any review of Western studies of Chinese sexual practices must begin with Henri Maspero's landmark work on Taoist macrobiotics, "Les procédés de 'nourir le principe vital' dans la réligion taoïste ancienne" (1937), and in particular, the section entitled "Pratique sexuelle." Maspero was operating with several fundamental handicaps. First, with the exception of the "Dangers and Benefits," his argument is based solely on the *Ishimpō* fragments, Yeh Te-hui's reconstructions, and scattered references to sexual practices in ancient secondary works. Second, he does not exploit the rich resources on sexual hygiene, sexual dysfunction, and female sexuality in the general medical and gynecological literature. Third, certain limitations in his analysis of Taoist meditation, based exclusively on *Tao tsang* texts, cannot but adversely influence his understanding of sexual practices. Fourth, in discussing the role of sexual rituals in the Taoist religious movement at the end of the Han, he overlooked the very detailed description in the *Shang-ch'ing huang-shu kuo-tu i* preserved in the *Tao tsang*. Fifth, he apparently was unaware of the special branch of women's meditation and its contribution to our understanding of traditional conceptions of female sexual energy.

The first handicap is the most serious. By contrast with the painstaking detail of

his analysis of the evolution of breath techniques, his discussion of sexual practices is ahistorical and monolithic. The lack of Han and Ming texts prevented him from developing a more complete picture of the periods, genres, and debates within the sexual literature. Another side effect of this restricted base of primary sources is a fundamental misinterpretation of the key theoretical aphorism, "return the *ching* to nourish the brain." His error here is compound. First, in taking the *Essentials of the Jade Chamber* passage describing deliberate retrograde ejaculation as *locus classicus* for "returning the *ching*," he has misrepresented the exception for the rule. It is amply clear even from the limited sources available to him, that the orthodox method, in the words of the *Classic of Su Nü*, was "To be aroused but not ejaculate is called 'returning the *ching*,'" or the *Tung Hsüan tzu*, "The *ching* will rise of itself." The orthodox understanding of the "*ching*" that "returns" or "rises" is *ching-ch'i* (sexual energy), and not literally semen, as a minority believed was possible through injaculation. Moreover, Maspero mistranslates the phrase 抑陰囊後大孔前 in the critical *Essentials* passage as, "seize (the penis) behind the scrotum and in front of the anus," failing to recognize this instruction, with countless parallels in both the solo and sexual literature, as indicating manual compression of the perineum. There is no justification for interpolating "the penis" in this context, and the penis certainly is not located between the scrotum and the anus.

Because of Maspero's failure in analyzing solo *yang-sheng* practices to develop a clear conception of "microcosmic orbit meditation" and the process of "transmuting *ching* into *ch'i* and *ch'i* into spirit," he is unable to recognize the same theoretical principles at the core of "paired" practices. His discussion of solo meditation lacks a thorough grasp of the role of *ching* as fuel source, and his description of sexual practice lacks an understanding of the role of *ch'i* energy released from the excited *ching* and circulated throughout the body and upward to

56

the brain. Only this can explain his inability to discriminate between mainstream and minority opinion, and seizing upon the latter, allowing it to define the "art of the bedchamber" for his Western readers.

Maspero's purpose in writing his celebrated "Les Procédés" appears to have been to delineate the boundaries of Taoism as a religious movement, a perspective that may account for his neglect of the more empirical elements in the sexual texts. Unfortunately, the result is that everything in the literature that strikes the modern reader as rational and enlightened is barely hinted at, whereas everything that is exotic and quaint, or fits the stereotype of superstition or religion, is described in great detail. The many pages of translation and commentary devoted to calendrical taboos and highly dubious allusions to sexual practice in the *Huang-t'ing ching* (Yellow court classic) might have been more profitably spent introducing the startlingly scientific analysis of the stages of sexual arousal, harmonization of emotions, sexually induced illness, and sexual yoga therapy.

Following Maspero, the next major contribution is Robert van Gulik's *Erotic Colour Prints of the Ming Period* (1951) and *Sexual Life in Ancient China* (1961), which stand to this day as the only booklength scholarly monographs on sexual customs, erotic art and literature, and esoteric sexual practices in China. They have the further distinction of being virtually the sole source for secondhand studies and translations, such as the works of Etiemble, Won-chan Cheng, Jolan Chang, and Nik Douglas, all of whom trust van Gulik rather than returning to primary sources. The *Erotic Colour Prints* contains many fine reproductions of Chinese erotic art and copies of original texts of several rare sexology classics; the later work consists of the historical survey of the first with an appended essay on the relationship between Taoist and Indian Tantric sexual practices. Van Gulik's thesis in the appendix that China is the original birthplace of sexual yoga, rather than India as commonly assumed,

can be said only to be strengthened by the discovery of the Ma Wang tui texts of the second century B.C. Many readers will be frustrated, however, by the limited circulation (fifty copies) of the *Erotic Colour Prints* and the latinization of all passages describing genital contact in *Sexual Life*, a delicacy that does not wear well with time.

Van Gulik uncovered many texts unknown to Maspero, the most important of which are the "Health Benefits" of the T'ang and the *Wondrous Discourse*, *True Classic*, and *Exposition* of the Ming. Missing from his study are the Ma Wang tui texts (not yet discovered) and the works of Sun Ju-chung, Chang San-feng, and Lu Hsi-hsing, plus the *Shang-ch'ing huang-shu kuo-tu i*, and all works on women's cultivation. His sources, however, were sufficiently diverse and cover a long enough period to begin to analyze the evolution of the sexual school. He introduces the Confucian, Buddhist, and Taoist "pure practices" attacks on the sexual practitioners, although he ignores the theoretical debates within the "paired" school itself. Absent, too, from his discussion is the role of sexual energy in medical and meditation theory, and how the two streams converge in sexual yoga.

Though van Gulik covered a very broad range of topics and materials, his standard of translation accuracy was consistently high, and later translators of sexual literature, such as Ishihara and Levy and Hsia, Veith, and Geertsma, even with the benefit of his models, fell far short of him. Nevertheless, allow me to point out just two errors whose ripples extend beyond local context to create minor theoretical turbulence. First, by misinterpreting the *p'ing-i* 屏翳 acu-point (actually an alternate name for the *hui-yin* 會陰 at the perineum) as "one inch above the right nipple," he was mistakenly lead to claim discovery of a new ejaculation control technique. Second, in the same *Essentials* passage mentioned earlier under Maspero, van Gulik mistranslates *shih* 施 as "activated," when here and in countless parallel passages it means "ejaculate." By committing this

57

small translation error, van Gulik has preserved his innocence of injaculation and avoided promoting it as *the* definition of "returning the *ching*"; Maspero and Needham translate the letter correctly, but seriously misinterpret the spirit. Perhaps van Gulik, having thoroughly grounded his thinking in the essential principle of "stimulation without ejaculation" (*tung erh pu hsieh* 動而不瀉), could not entertain the possibility of a second theory in the classics themselves, whereas Maspero and Needham, with a weaker grasp of fundamentals, could be persuaded that the exception was the rule. It is a pity, however, that van Gulik was not able to bring his difference here with Maspero into sharp focus and to distinguish *coitus reservatus* from retrograde ejaculation, the orthodox from the heterodox.

Van Gulik makes three uncharacteristically simplistic assertions in this otherwise very objective study: the perverseness of sexual practices, the openness of ancient sexual mores, and the inefficacy of sexual yoga. As to the first, in a footnote to his "Sexual Techniques," Joseph Needham mentions disabusing van Gulik "in personal communication" of his view of Taoist sexual practices as "sexual black magic" and "sexual vampirism." Van Gulik evidently took this to heart as his second book, *Sexual Life in Ancient China*, is free of such aspersions. Kristofer Schipper in his *Le Corps Taoïste* seeks to refute the second simplification in van Gulik's outlook; namely, that prior to the Manchu conquest, China was sexually "liberated." Schipper points out that "open love and sexual expression were not favored" in the feudal family, and that the Manchus can hardly bear the full responsibility for centuries of Confucian repression. I would like to challenge the third assertion, which van Gulik sums up in the statement: "The therapeutic properties of sexual congress are, of course, largely fictitious." Such a categorical conclusion is rash and unsupported by any scientific study or even anecdotal evidence based on a fair sample of actual practitioners. Seen in the context of traditional medical theory and as a form of

what the *Classic of Su Nü* calls "*tao-yin*," the ancient term for *ch'i-kung*, one has the basis for beginning to appreciate the preventative and therapeutic potential of Chinese sexual practices.

If Maspero looks at sexual practices from the point of view of their role in Taoism and van Gulik at the wider context of their role in Chinese sexual life, Joseph Needham focuses on sexual practices in the development of scientific theories and social philosophy. Needham's discussion is divided between two volumes of his *Science and Civilization in China*: Volume 2, "Sexual Techniques" and Volume 5, "Sexuality and the Role of Theories of Generation."

The earlier "Sexual Techniques" reviews the primary and secondary sources, outlines the general principles of sexual yoga and the sexual rituals of the Taoist church, and advances the view that sexual practices confirm the profeminine ideology of Taoism. Although he does not follow in Maspero's footsteps by mistranslating the *Essentials* passage cited earlier as "seize the penis," nor repeat van Gulik's error in missing the reference to retrograde ejaculation altogether, he does commit the fatal error of accepting this single passage as *locus classicus* for "returning the *ching*." In doing this he turns away from the mainstream teaching expressed as early as Ma Wang tui, "Shih wen," as "stimulate the penis . . . contract the anus . . . absorb the *ch'i* to fill the brain . . . all the *ching* will rise upward," or as late as Chang San-feng, whose *Secret Principles of Gathering the True Essence* states, "with repeated contractions of the *wei-lü*, the 'sea of *ching*' is aroused and the '*yin* waters' stirred. A pleasurable sensation begins to rise up. . . . Quickly withdraw the 'sword' . . . and the 'medicine' traverses the *wei-lü* . . . , penetrates the 'three passes' . . . , crosses the 'jade pillow' . . . , and arrives at the *ni-wan*." Here in the final phase of full-blown sexual alchemy, microcosmic orbit meditation merges with *coitus reservatus* to assist one's own excited *ching* energy and the "medicine" captured from the woman in rising and circulating.

Needham's much longer treatment of sexual practices in Volume 5, though it offers the widest range of sources and most comprehensive discussion of sexual practices published to date, fails to correct some of the erroneous assumptions of the earlier volume and, in fact, he digs himself even deeper into a theoretical hole. Early in his analysis here, Needham makes two useful distinctions: first, between "semen" and "seminal essence"; and second, between *"coitus reservatus"* and *"coitus thesauratus"* (Needham's neologism for retrograde ejaculation). However, he then proceeds indiscriminently to interpret virtually every appearance of *"ching"* as semen and every *"huan-ching pu-nao"* as *"coitus thesauratus,"* against overwhelming explicit and contextual evidence that what rises is *ching-ch'i* (not *ching-ye*), usually aided by pubococcygeal contractions (not manual compression). Needham, like Maspero, completely overlooks the essential technique of anal constriction, so common in *yang-sheng* training and referred to in the sexual literature as *hsi chou* 翕州 ("Highest Tao"), *suo hsia-pu* 縮下部 (*Secrets of the Bedchamber*), and *ju jen-pien* 如忍便 or *chia wei-lü* 夾尾閭 (*Secrets of Gathering the True Essence*). Furthermore, to say that the passing of the semen into the bladder with retrograde ejaculation, "always escaped the notice of the Taoists" is simply untrue. What escaped Professor Needham's notice is the passage in the *Exposition* that clearly states, "If one attempts to forcibly lock it, then the corrupt *ching* will ooze into the urinary bladder and scrotum."

Once Needham has mistakenly installed injaculation at the center of his thesis, he is now predisposed to go beyond misinterpretation to mistranslation, beyond *"coitus thesauratus"* to "masturbation." Needham's rendering of *tao-yin* 導引 in the *Classic of Su Nü* as "masturbation" is one of those small translation errors with large theoretical consequences. Though it is clear from sources such as Yün Fang Chen Jen, quoted in Hsiao T'ien-shih's *Tao-chia yang-sheng hsüeh kai-yao*, and contemporary informants such as Dr. Stephen

Chang and Mantak Chia that masturbatory injaculation exists as a training technique preliminary to advanced coital practices, there is not a single bona fide reference in the classical literature. Van Gulik, Levy, Schipper, Hsia/Veith/Geertsma, and numerous Chinese colloquial translations all avoid the error of interpreting *tao-yin* (which Needham himself correctly translates no fewer than ten times elsewhere as "gymnastic techniques" and "massage") as "masturbation" in this context. Unfortunately, now with masturbation on the mind, he finds it in an even more unlikely place—women's cultivation. Commenting on the *Queen Mother of the West's Ten Precepts*, he says, "In all matters concerning sex the text is ambiguously worded, so that masturbation (as among the male Taoists) is not positively excluded." There is nothing "ambiguous" in this text (which features an excellent commentary by Min I-te), and it is perfectly consistent with other texts on women's cultivation, which prescribe breast massage but strict repression of sexual arousal. Far from being "not positively excluded," the text of the *Ten Precepts* flatly states, "If there is a feeling of pleasure, one must strictly avoid sexual thoughts," and the commentary adds, "otherwise the labia will open wide and the sexual secretions will flow." Allowing the imposters—injaculation and masturbation—to usurp the rightful rulers of sexual practice—*coitus reservatus* and *tao-yin*—results in the serious skewing of a major study.

Kristofer Schipper is perhaps the first student of Taoism since Maspero to write at length on sexual practices. His most comprehensive treatment appears in an essay entitled "Science, Magic and Mystique of the Body," which was published in Michel Beurdeley's *Les Nuages et la Pluie* (English editions, *The Clouds and the Rain, Chinese Erotic Art*, 1969). In keeping with the title, Schipper divides sexual practices into "science" (art of the bedchamber), "magic" (sexual alchemy and orgiastic ritual), and "mystique" (spiritualized sexual fantasy and mystical marmarriage meditation). Although this classification scheme is the essay's chief scholarly contribution, it is never developed as such, and there is considerable confusion as to whether these categories describe serial or parallel phenomena, stages, or tendencies. Though the scheme embraces the entire scope of sexuality in self-cultivation, translations and citations are exclusively from the *Ishimpō*, leaving out a thousand years of received literature.

Still seeking to distinguish and define the first two categories in his article "The Taoist Body" (1978) Schipper says: "So as I have tried to show elsewhere, there is a difference between the sexual hygiene of say, the *Yü-fang pi-chüeh*, and Taoist practice. The most important difference is that the former looks at sex essentially from the male perspective, while Taoism, at least ideally, identified with the female body." The obvious counterpoint here is Needham's, "No sharp line of distinction can be drawn between arts specific to the Taoists and the general techniques of the lay bedchamber." Although Needham's denial of our ability to make any useful distinctions in this regard may be unnecessarily pessimistic, Schipper's attempts are ambivalent and overly vague. All of the texts from Ma Wang tui through the Ming share at least three elements—male *reservatus*, absorption of female essence, and the achievement of transcendent states through sexual cultivation. However, without taxing our powers of discrimination too much, we can also say that the householder tradition of the "art of the bedchamber" gives equal emphasis to the emotional, medical, eugenic, and macrobiotic aspects of sex, whereas the sexual alchemists focus almost exlusively on sexual practice as a means to immortality. Schipper's distinction based on the practitioner's self-identification as male or female may be supplemented by noting the more fundamental conceptual shift from identification of the male *ching* from *yang* to *yin* and of the female from *yin* to *yang*, along with the increasing prominence of female superior postures, and the model of male pregnancy.

Finally in his *Le Corps Taoïste* (1982)

Schipper attempts to resolve this perceived contradiction between the "art of the bedchamber" and "sexual alchemy" by defining both right out of Taoism. Now he refers to the "art of the bedchamber" as "mistakenly considered Taoist"; and of what he formerly called "Taoist practices," he now says, "It is a mistake to see the idea of nourishing *yang* at the expense of *yin* as Taoist." Is it not unseemly for a Western scholar to take sides in an ancient Chinese debate between "pure" and "paired" practices? This thinly disguised agenda, and the prejudice underlying it, severely compromises the objectivity and balance of his presentation. He is tolerant of the art of the bedchamber, and actually embraces spiritualized sexual fantasies, sexual ceremonies, and mystical marriage meditation, but is thoroughly hostile to sexual alchemy. Although he correctly identifies elements of "selfishness," "impersonality," "exploitation," and "vampirism" in some of the sexual alchemists, he fails to cite a single title or quote a single passage from their literature, or to set them off against the distinctively chaste sexual alchemy of the *True Transmission* and *Seeking Instruction*. Relying exclusively on worst-case scenarios, his efforts to separate the baby from the bathwater yield for the reader far more bathwater than baby. Instead of building on the work of Maspero and van Gulik and going beyond them, he actually exposes far less useful data and exceeds them only in venting personal antipathies. Van Gulik and Needham fundamentally were neutral in their attitude to sexual practices and somewhat disposed to accept their wholesome influence on Chinese society. For this reason, they were in a better position to survey their subject objectively than Schipper, who was so revolted by some of what he saw that it became more important to share and support his personal reaction than to give a complete, much less fair, account of what is there.

Schipper devotes considerable space in *Le Corps Taoïste* to criticizing van Gulik for promoting the view that prior to the Manchu conquest and Western influence, China was "sexually liberated" and free of sexual perversion. Though his description of the Chinese family as characterized by "furtive sex" is based on sound anthropological intuition, it is curious that he singles out van Gulik for "simplistic" thinking on this score rather than Needham, whose views on the humanizing influence of Taoist sexual practices on Chinese society were far more sanguine and sweeping. Just as Schipper realized that the Manchus could not bear sole responsibility for centuries of sexual repression in China, he should have equally acknowledged that the exploitative tendencies in sexual practices were the product of patriarchal society and not the cause.

Donald Harper's "The Sexual Arts of Ancient China as Described in a Manuscript of the Second Century B.C." (1987) is the first published philological study of a Chinese sexology text in English. Although his considerable scholarly talents are unleashed on but a single paragraph of one text, the Ma Wang tui "Uniting Yin and Yang," he gives a comprehensive review of Western and Japanese scholarship in the field and provides complete bibliographic data. His literary, medical, and philosophical tools all are equally sharp and allow him not only to dissect problems in the text itself, but to bring his new findings to bear on previously obscure references in early literary texts. There are few blindspots in his analysis, and it is exceptionally free of axe grinding. However, his use of parallels in the later sexual literature begins and ends with the *Ishimpō*, and he fails to mention obvious similarities between the sexual journey metaphors in the "Uniting Yin and Yang" passage he translates and instructions for ritual touching sequences in the *Shang-ch'ing huang-shu kuo-tu i.*

My only serious quarrel with Harper's translations, apart from their awkward, overly literal style, involves his interpretation of the *shih-i* 十巳 passage in the "Uniting Yin and Yang," which he renders "the ten intermissions." He concludes, "Similarly, I have found nothing comparable to the 'ten intermissions' in later sexual literature. . . . Judging from this section, the ten intermissions refer

to ten stages of transformation of the woman's sexual essence during intercourse. . . . The description suggests female orgasm." Close parallels, including instances of exact wording, in fact do exist in the *Classic of Su Nü* (*wu-shang* 五傷), *Prescriptions of Su Nü* (*ch'i-shang* 七傷), *Wondrous Discourse* (*wu-shang* 五傷), and *Chu-ping yüan-hou lun* (*ch'i-shang* 七傷), based on which it is safe to conclude that the *shih-i* (which I translate as "ten exhaustions") refer to ten abnormal qualities of male ejaculate seen as symptoms of pathology. The *shih-i* also appear in the "Highest Tao under Heaven" in the same paragraph and immediately following the *san-chih* 三至 (three stages of arousal of the penis), a context strongly suggesting continuity of subject.

We now leave four scholars—Maspero, van Gulik, Needham, and Harper—whose integrity and linguistic skills were equal to their tasks, for two teams of collaborators, Ishihara and Levy (*The Tao of Sex*) and Hsia, Veith, and Geertsma (*The Essentials of Medicine in Ancient China and Japan*). The concept of collaborative translation, which at its best is synergistic and helps "keep everyone honest," results here in much less than could be expected from one competent translator. As I have devoted several hundred footnotes to indicating specific shortcomings in their translations from *Ishimpō*, let me confine myself here to a more general pattern of problems. All of the deficiencies may be traced to three basic areas: first, an allergy to handling dictionaries; second, an insufficient command of the usages of classical Chinese; third, an inadequate grasp of the theory and practice of medicine, meditation, and sexual practice itself. Both books have the trappings of scholarship—footnotes, bibliographies, handsome hardcover binding—however, they fall far short of the standard of accuracy achieved by Maspero, van Gulik, and Needham, and indeed show no evidence of having profited from the work that preceded them. Needham referred to Ishihara and Levy's translation as "inelegant," a polite way of saying that too often the translators, not knowing what they were looking at, lapse into awkward word-for-word renderings, which constantly call attention to the plight of the translators rather than the sense of the text. Another unscrupulous practice engaged in by both teams is preemptory excision of difficult passages, while promising the reader a complete and unabridged translation.

Another category of Western publications in the field of Chinese sexology I will call, for lack of a better word, "popular." They eschew strict scholarly protocols, are unabashedly subjective, and richly garnished with reproductions or line drawings based on original Chinese erotic art. Charles Humana and Wang Wu's *The Chinese Way of Love* attempts to duplicate van Gulik's survey of sex life in China in a more accessible package and with a more obvious appeal to interest in exotic erotica. Even the scholar will appreciate the publication of rare artifacts from private collections, some of the curious anecdotal information, and quotations from the byways of Chinese and Western literature, but the large number of gross factual errors and misquotations from primary sources are disappointing and eminently avoidable. The authors warn us in the introduction of their "free translation" practices, and that "interpretation rather than the exact terminology has been considered of more importance." My response is that when fact is stranger than fiction, there can be absolutely no rationale for tampering with the letter in the name of the spirit. This license to alter the original is arbitrary and masks a basic incomprehension of the texts, rather than a "wish to communicate the spirit and the wider meaning." Among the book's many fabrications, let me cite just one for the sake of comic relief. A long quotation is offered from a work entitled, "*Ways of Sex*, published in 1927 by Yeh Te-hui." First, the significance of the date, "1927," lies soley in its being the year of Yeh's demise; and second, there is no such book. Throughout, the emphasis is on the worldly and exotic aspects of sexual life in China with nary a word on sexual yoga. Nevertheless, there are some rewarding art re-

productions and some interesting observations on the Chinese mind, sexual phenomena, and attitudes in various contemporary Chinese communities.

The text of Marc de Smedt's *Chinese Eroticism* may appear to the casual reader to be merely an adornment to an art book on Chinese erotic painting, but for the fact that it actually consists of original translations from the *Ishimpō* material. Considering the total lack of scholarly amenities (footnotes, bibliographies, and so on) the quality of the translation is no less than that of Ishihara and Levy or Hsia, Veith, Geertsma, and on the whole surpasses them for sheer accuracy.

Nik Douglas and Penny Slinger's *Sexual Secrets* covers the whole range of Hindu, Buddhist, Middle Eastern, Japanese, and Chinese sexual yoga. The scholarship will not satisfy the scholar; the art will not satisfy the art historian; and the practical instructions will not satisfy the serious practitioner. Having said this, however, it should be noted that the book rests on a fairly solid foundation of secondary and presumably primary Sanskrit and Tibetan sources and provides an adequate introduction for beginning practice. The novel design and organization of the book, which makes use of mainly Hindu mythic archetypes, helps create an integrated thematic journey rather than a series of stops at exotic ports of call—altogether a monumental and seductive resource. The authors' voice comes through as an authentic teacher and tour guide, both sane and inspirational. Their translations from the Chinese are remakes of van Gulik's, but fortunately they had the good sense to stay away from Ishihara and Levy. Although making no original contributions to the field of Chinese sexology, their practical background prevent them from straying too far from the essence even while relying on secondary sources.

Jolan Chang's *The Tao of Love and Sex* and its sequel, *The Tao of the Loving Couple*, is more a panegyric on the pleasures of love and the author's personal prowess than either a scholarly study or technical manual. More than any other account, this book is aimed at the general public and seeks to convince the whole

Western world of the benefits of Chinese sex techniques. The author weaves quotations from the classics with Western sexological studies and personal anecdotes to construct a convincing argument for a daily regimen of love making without emission. As a kind of sexual ambassador, he offers the gift of Chinese sexual yoga to the West in the hopes that barbarians will learn to make love more poetically. His guidance and role modeling should be particularly inspiring to older adults wishing to maintain active sex lives. His first book sets out the basic argument for Chinese *coitus reservatus*, and the sequel presents a number of case studies of individuals and couples who were rescued from various sexual predicaments by adopting Chinese attitudes and techniques.

Another logical pair of publications is Étiemble's *Yun Yu: An Essay on Eroticism and Love in Ancient China* and Wonchan Cheng's *Érotologie Chinoise*. Apart from both being published in French, the most obvious similarity is that both are the work of qualified scholars who temporarily put aside their caps and gowns for pajamas to share their very personal and enraptured accounts of Chinese eroticism. Both are content to draw uncritically on the original scholarship of van Gulik, and both are extraordinarily generous with the color plates. Étiemble reveals the stages of his own sexual awakening, beginning with a conservative Catholic upbringing and leading up to his transformative encounter with what he considers the freer atmosphere of Chinese sexual culture. The author's delight in his discovery and the cornucopia of beautiful art reproductions compensates in some degree for the absence of index, bibliography, or even table of contents. In sum, the strength of this highly subjective essay lies in its use of literary sources, though it has almost nothing to offer in the area of sexual yoga.

Cheng frankly acknowledges his debt to van Gulik and, like many others, faithfully reproduces him warts and all. Happily the warts are few, and he makes the virtues of his model all the more apparent to the general reader by adopt-

ing a thematic rather than chronological exposition. One might be tempted to say, in fact, that *Érotologie Chinoise* actually is an illustrated version of van Gulik's *Sexual Life in Ancient China*, for it indeed is lavishly illustrated and beautifully designed. One regrets that the author, being a native Chinese, did not check the original sources and correct at least some of the more obvious errors in previous translations, but his goals are more sumptuary than scholarly, and these are admirably achieved. In the last section of the book, the author, writing in a more autobiographical vein, does contribute some firsthand observations of sex life in the foreign concessions before World War II.

Mantak Chia's impact on the importation of Chinese sexual yoga into the West goes well beyond the two books, *Taoist Secrets of Love* and *Cultivating Female Sexual Energy*, which I propose to review. No one to date has published such a detailed system of Taoist sexual yoga or personally propagated it so widely. Chia's stance is one of a modern day master who addresses his readers as potential disciples. Because the pair of books represents two sides of the same coin, and much of the information in the first is duplicated in the second, I will treat them as one in my discussion.

In the introduction to his first book, Chia tells us that his teachings are a synthesis of practices he learned from four masters in Thailand and Hong Kong. Although his teachings accord in the main with those found in the present anthology, Chia's books show no evidence of his having studied the ancient texts in the original. The only title ever mentioned is the *Classic of Su Nü*, which is quoted at the head of various chapters, but invariably from the Ishihara and Levy translation, and one passage containing a gross error is quoted in both books. All of this by way of speculation that what he offers seems largely to be the product of oral transmission and in fact contains much of value not found as such in any of the published documents in this collection.

Judged against the background of the present anthology, Chia borrows broadly   *63* but selectively from traditional teachings, making an important contribution to adapting these to the modern social and scientific setting. For example, the concept of mutual absorption, which plays a minor role in the tradition, becomes the centerpiece of Chia's system. Chia ensures a balanced trade partnership by requiring that both practitioners be schooled in the techniques of microcosmic orbit meditation and absorption of sexual energy. Introducing Western notions of love and monogamy makes his message more palatable to modern couples, but his strict construction of *coitus reservatus* and suspension of menses proves that he is not merely watering the potion for the current marketplace. As radical as Chia's message is in regard to ejaculation for procreation only, the pleasure principle and romantic love have by no means been banished from his system. By accentuating the healing properties of pleasure still apparent in the early classical texts and combining this with the later phases of sexual alchemy, he promises unimaginable ecstasies far surpassing exoteric orgasm. Chia seems willing to allow his students to focus on the immediacy of pleasurable sensation and, by enforcing a strict code of nonejaculation, trusts the health benefits to follow as a matter of course.

Although Chia's conclusions regarding the role of sex in spiritual practice spring directly from Chinese roots, he also is the product of cross-cultural influences and uses Western scientific theories extensively to support and even to express his own teachings. Chinese and Western medical models are woven so tightly together in his system that acupuncture points and endocrine glands constantly jostle each other in the same sentence. Purists might protest his eclecticism, and scholars might find some loose ends in his synthesis, but most readers will sense that Chia is simply availing himself of an expanding palate of language to communicate authentic experience. However, although borrowing freely from Western physiology for his own purposes, Chia is not impressed with modern sex therapy's emphasis on orgasm or techniques like

Karezza that build heat and tension in the prostate without teaching the upward cycling of sexual energy. Like many observers of the West, Chia finds that sexuality is the chief obsession of our culture, but comes to the original conclusion that because of this perhaps only sex itself can serve as a vehicle for the spiritual awakening of the masses. To attempt another path in such a sexually charged culture, he fears, can only lead to repression and all of its distortions of personality and society. The advanced stages of Chia's system, again following traditional lines, demonstrate that sex may not be the ultimate experience of the union of *yin* and *yang*, but it is the safest and surest place to start.

Chia's writings throw considerable light on the critical process of "refining the *ching* into *ch'i* and the *ch'i* into spirit." Arguing that the *ch'i* available from food and air is too gross to be absorbable in large amounts, we must turn to *ching*, a more highly refined and concentrated source of *ch'i* simply waiting to be transmuted through sexual alchemy. His belief that *ching* energy is the fuel of creativity, spirituality, and even kindness and compassion is reminiscent of the classical Western conception of eros. If conserved, he says, the *yang* fire in the *ching* burns up negativity, whereas *ching* loss engenders physical lassitude and dries up the very "will to enlightenment." Giving an egalitarian twist to the tradition, he states that a law of sexual practices prevents one from absorbing the partner's power without giving freely of one's own.

Chia's concept of "Valley Orgasm" or "Beyond Orgasm," though perhaps implied in some traditional texts, is elaborated in great detail in his two books. He says: "No technique can guarantee it will happen. . . . It is a state of prolonged orgasm that generally occurs during the plateau phase when *yin* and *yang* energies come into an exquisitely delicate balance. It is a fusion of opposites, a meltdown. . . . The valley orgasm actually is a fusion of ching, chi and shien in the two lovers." Dismissing genital orgasm as merely "itch relief," he emphasizes the necessity of properly channeling sexual energy, for once aroused it can travel either up or down, but travel it must. The process of channeling this energy requires mastery of two techniques: the "Big Draw," or puboccoccygeal pump; and "microcosmic orbit meditation" to circulate the energy and share it with the glands, organs, and finally the brain. One feels simultaneously satisfied and revitalized after releasing the sexual energy from the semen. As the "Valley Orgasm" rises from the lower *tan-t'ien* to engulf the middle and upper *tan-t'ien*, it permeates all the organs and fuses *ching*, *ch'i*, and spirit. Finally Chia offers a glimpse of what in the present anthology is called, "intercourse of the spirit without physical contact," and beyond this, cessation of semen production and direct absorption of cosmic energy. This breatharian state also is in keeping with traditional teachings and considered the next thing to immortality.

Meeting possible objections to his system of sexual yoga, Chia marshals most of his defenses on the Chinese front. Perhaps with more than 2,000 years of experience, China has had more opportunity to judge these techniques than the West, whose only educated response is to dismiss nonejaculation as neurosis. Chia disarms criticisms of the exploitative aspects of traditional sexual practices by placing the arrangement on a strictly egalitarian footing and by asserting that most of the energy gained is from one's own store of *ching*. As for the "pure practices" objection that the sexual path easily leads one astray and rarely conducts one safely to the gates of heaven, Chia counters by stating that one must master sexual energy or be mastered by it and that it is not, after all, an end in itself. Although he teaches a version of injaculation as a preliminary practice, he is mute when it comes to addressing traditional objections that the semen ends up in the bladder rather than the brain and that, even if it is forced back into the prostate, it already has "left the palace" and become "corrupt *ching*."

To summarize, Chia's books contain a wealth of authentic teachings and original synthesis, incorporating Western science, Tantric concepts, and the author's own experience. They are the richest documents for researching the continuity of Chinese sexual practices in the modern era and for the process of their acculturation in the West. The detail of his discussion of genital calisthenics simply has no parallel in the published traditional texts and marks the debut of large quantities of oral transmission in print. The books perhaps are a bit too commercial in their design, style, and format to attract the notice of the scholarly community, and it is certainly not helpful that nearly every citation from Chinese history or primary sources reveals conspicuous factual errors. For example, the Manchu dynasty, actually founded in the seventeenth century, we are told belongs to the "Eighth Century A.D.", and the Yellow Emperor, who belongs to the legendary period prior to 2000 B.C. is plunked down smack in the middle of the Han dynasty in the "Second Century B.C." The titles of Ko Hung and Sun Ssu-miao's great works are badly mauled in translation. These and the indiscriminate mixing of standard Mandarin Wade-Giles transliteration with nonstandard Cantonese renderings is disconcerting to even amateur sinologists. The seriousness and value of the subject deserves a slightly better treatment in some of these formal areas, if only to avoid giving skeptics a pretext for rejecting the work out of hand.

Stephen Chang's *The Tao of Sexology*, like Mantak Chia's works, is part of the author's series introducing every major aspect of Taoist macrobiotic practices, including dietetics, herbology, acupuncture, meditation, and *ch'i-kung*. As a practicing M.D. and the great grandson (on his mother's side) of a personal physician to the Dowager Empress, one is not surprised at the frequent packaging of Chinese pills in Western bottles. So developed, in fact, are his powers of synthesis that all boundaries of culture and even chronology collapse before our eyes. Readers may be able to bear with characterizations of the sympathetic nervous system or positive ions as "yang," but statements such as, "Throughout the centuries, Taoists understood that the

65

body's Seven Glands were the energy centers responsible for regulating the flow of energy with the various systems of the body," seem to put words in the mouths of the sages. The "Seven Glands" in question, or endocrine system, did not exist as such for traditional anatomists, who were far more likely to understand these functions in terms of *ch'i* than hormones. This revisionist interpretation of Taoism rewards us with some fascinating parallels if we are willing to separate the ingredients of influence for ourselves, though one cannot help but regret the facile homogenization, which blurs many important distinctions in the two systems. Similarly, much terminology of his own invention is represented as literal translation from the Taoist or medical traditions, where no actual Chinese antecedents exist.

Chang's biography tells us that he also holds doctorates in philosphy and theology as well as two law degrees. Many readers will find his syncretism of Taoism and Christian theology even more arresting than his mixing of Chinese and Western medicine. For example, "By following the Tao of Sexology, mankind will eventually incarnate God's nature to its fullest." Particularly startling is his Taoist interpretation of the quest for life everlasting in Christianity: "With the appearance of Jesus, immortality assumed unprecedented importance in the West. In the Old Testament, except for a few references to Enoch and Elijah, immortality was not mentioned. Jesus may have acquired an interest in immortality during his travels to India and China." Similarly his warnings to avoid certain negative attitudes or practices are couched as "the principle of Satan" or "Disintegration into Evil."

At the heart of Chang's system are two practices: the "Deer Exercise" and "Valley Orgasm." Like Chia, Chang teaches "Injaculation" as a preliminary exercise, claiming a 50 percent saving in energy and resulting in the semen being "recycled into the bloodstream." Outlining the benefits of the "Deer Exercise," or anal sphincter contraction for men, he lists the following: tones sex organs,

pumps energy up the chain of endocrine glands, increases abdominal circulation, stimulates prostate to secrete endorphins, and cures premature ejaculation, low sex hormones, infection in the testes, wet dreams, and impotence. For women, when practiced together with breast and vaginal massage, the "Deer Exercise" provides redirection of blood from uterine walls to sex glands, stimulation of estrogen production, improvement in vaginal tone, and elimination of premenstrual syndrome, fibroid tumors in the uterus, and breast lumps. Reverting to Chinese categories, however, he tells us that the two most important benefits, when all is said and done, are the raising of energy from the sex center to the brain in the male and the cessation of menses in the female.

Cessation of menses, analogous to nonejaculation in the male, is perfectly safe, he assures us, and occurs naturally during pregnancy, lactation, and menopause. Beyond this, when the "Deer Exercise" and breast massage succeed in halting the menstrual cycle, biological aging also ceases and one's appearance remains unchanged indefinitely. Moreover, it is also a safe and effective method of birth control. Chang's teachings on women's practice correspond closely with Mantak Chia's, and both of them accord with the traditional texts in this anthology.

When the "Deer Exercise" is practiced by both partners during intercourse, the combined effect may be called "Valley Orgasm," or "Superior Orgasm," as he says he now prefers to call it. As the arousal level rises, the man applies the "Hold Back" technique of sphincter contraction to pump the sexual energy out of the prostate until he drops to 60 to 70 percent of arousal and then soars back to 99 percent. By synchronizing inhalation and exhalation with withdrawal and penetration, he may stay at 99 percent indefinitely. This also permits the man to urge his partner to the summit of a nine-tier ascent he calls the "Nine Levels of Female Orgasm." His presentation here is very confusing for readers familiar with the *Classic of Su Nü*'s theory of the "nine *ch'i*" on which it is loosely based. For one thing, the "nine *ch'i*" described in the *Classic*, as well as in the *Wondrous Discourse of Su Nü*, are nine levels of preliminary arousal and not nine levels of orgasm. The *Classic*'s "five signs" and "ten movements" trace the progress from foreplay to climax, but the "nine *ch'i*" really are all prelude . For another thing, at level "four," where the original says only, "she becomes slippery," Chang interpolates, "Women experience a series of vaginal spasms at this time and secretions begin to flow." He concludes by saying that most women confuse this sensation with "complete orgasm," or "coming together," and settling for this, never see the five peaks beyond. This may be a valid theory, but the unsuspecting classics should not have been hijacked as its vehicle.

Chang's book contains a host of fascinating curiosities randomly distributed throughout the text. For example, buried in the very back in a catch-all miscellany called "Supplements" is a practice he calls "Extractive Techniques," which demonstrates the survival of the "corrupt *ching*" theory of the *Exposition of Cultivating the True Essence*. Here the "Hold back" technique is used repeatedly until the store of "nutrients, hormones, and energy—the essences of semen" are extracted and absorbed by the system to nourish the endocrine chain, culminating with the seat of enlightenment in the pineal gland. The semen now is considered a "residue" that may be ejaculated without loss to the system. Chang advocates anal and vaginal hygiene and the need for frequent internal cleansings, but strongly condemns as unnatural circumcision, intrauterine devices, hysterectomy, tubal ligation, visualizations during meditation, or fantasies during sex. He also presents a complete theory of penile and vaginal reflexology; exercises for enlarging, shaping, and desensitizing the penis; and prostate massage. Also outside the classical record are two diagnostic techniques for determining biological age keyed to sexual function: one is based on measuring the angle of the erect penis and the other a formula applied to the number of days for the male to reach unbearable sexual longing. Drawing on Buddhist lore, he explains the phenomenon of "*she-li-tzu*," or gemlike stones reportedly found among the ashes of enlightened monks after cremation, as "the semen replaces the other cells in the body," and becoming imperishable are enshrined in pagodas where they can be seen "emitting flashes of light at night." This is introduced unflinchingly as absolute fact. Mysteriously, the linking of *coitus reservatus* and microcosmic orbit meditation, which marks the culmination of traditional sexual practice and constitutes the core of Mantak Chia's system, appears but briefly and without fanfare in one inconspicuous paragraph of *The Tao of Sexology*.

Most scholarly approaches to Chinese sexual beliefs and practices have been undertaken by sinologists, whose studies have been largely descriptive. But what of the brave new sciences of anthropology and psychology? Attempts by Western anthropologists and psychologists to account for the Chinese model of sufficiency-deficiency in sexuality have been prompted mainly by a fascination with the phenomenon of "*koro*" (*suoyang* 縮陽), a mental disorder characterized by hysterical fears of shrinking penis. One exception to this is John Weakland's "Orality in Chinese Conceptions of Male Genital Sexuality," published in *Psychiatry* (1956), which attempts to understand the very core of Chinese sexual beliefs by applying Freud's theory of the oral, anal, and genital phases of human psychological development.

Using data gathered from van Gulik's translations of the classical texts, folkloric and literary material, as well as native informants, Weakland concludes: "In sum, it is clear that one very basic and powerful Chinese conception of sexual intercourse is an oral relationship of feeding and eating, like that of mother and infant, but reciprocal." He also cites the work of Warner Muensterberger and Virginia Heyer, whose studies emphasize the Chinese ideal of marriage as replicating the mother-son relationship, in which the wife plays the role of unde-manding nurturer. Weakland finds ample evidence in van Gulik's translations for conceptions of the penis and vagina as consumer and object of consumption. Though not yet discovered at the time, passages such as the following from the Ma Wang tui "Shih wen" would have been music to Weakland's ears, "Give breath to the penis; give food and drink to the penis. Feed it as if nourishing a child." Weakland advances his explana-tion of Chinese sexual beliefs as an alternative to Muensterberger's earlier theory that the oral fixation in Chinese sexuality might be due to oral indulgence and a failure to master oral renunciation, which he traces to long and liberal breast feeding, the general cultural obsession with food and feasting, and castration threats in the genital phase. Focusing on the same critical mother-son relationship, Weakland comes to a different conclu-sion:

> The sexual ideas examined show fears of being drained, connected with the notion of someone *actively desiring and taking*. Chinese mothers are concerned about in-dependent motor activity in babies, and babies' hands are symbolically tied. That this tying occurs only during the first month or few months, when sucking is the child's main form of activity, suggests that the mother may primarily be anxious about active oral rather than manual "grasp-ing. . . ." It seems likely that the Chinese infant initially is less "dependent" psycho-logically than biologically, and wants satis-faction of both "passive" and "active" oral desires—to be fed but also to express as in sucking. Presumably, the satisfaction of both needs would be conducive to optimal development, including the development of "realistic" and "rational" thought. . . .
> The data presented earlier, however, that the child cannot satisfy both needs because the mother is afraid of active demands, although she will meet the passive-receptive oral needs abundantly if the child restricts his activity and autonomy. . . .
> The end result might well be the develop-ment of such highly polarized and orality-filled fantasies about genital sexuality.

Though ignored by the sinological community, Weakland has brought an entirely new set of analytical tools to bear on the question of Chinese sexual beliefs and should be congratulated for opening a new dimension to the inquiry. Rather than responding in psychological terms, however, let me point out what seem to be a number of fundamental intellectual problems in his approach. Weakland was not unaware of some of the difficulties in-volved in psychoanalyzing another cul-ture, but he did not sufficiently overcome the tendency to assume that the normal, the natural, or the ideal either is manifest within or can be glimpsed only by mem-bers of one's own culture. This underlies his fundamental assumption of irrational-ity or mental disorder in Chinese sexual beliefs. This response does not allow for the possibility of a rational basis for Chinese claims of greater health, plea-sure, or compatibility and, though pre-sumably pronounced in the name of "sci-ence," arrives with no epidemiological or clinical data or hint of experimentation. To grant even a shred of rationality to the Chinese side, of course, would involve admitting the possibility that one has been making love the wrong way lo these many years, a degree of objectivity not many can muster. There also is an impli-cit denial of the possibility of an alterna-tive esthetic in an area that contains, after all, such an important esthetic compo-nent. Many Western intellectuals have developed a taste for the Chinese esthetic in the literary and visual arts, but the sancti-ty of genital orgasm has been a powerful deterent to a fair hearing for even the theory of the "art of the bedchamber."

Finally, there is a built-in circularity to psychological explanations of cultural phenomena based on early childhood ex-perience. It is tempting to look to this formative period for fundamental deter-minants of beliefs and behavior, but ways of relating to children in turn are deter-mined by the culture at large. This is like looking for the roots of Chinese feu-dalism or the patriarchy in childrearing practices. Causality is very difficult to establish, and somehow early childhood development and adult sex life both par-ticipate in a greater cultural gestalt that eludes us. Moreover, Chinese sexual practices are embedded in the wider context of medicine, yoga, and cosmology, all of which then must be explained in terms of arrested orality. This is a lot to bite off. Perhaps sociologists could make something of Lu Hsün's characterization of all of traditional Chinese society as "man eating" (*ch'ih jen* 吃人), although it is interesting that the imagery in the sexual literature is not of hunter and prey, but of a very domesticated food source. Or, in Freudian terms again, could one not also make an argument for *coitus reservatus* as a sexual manifestation of anal retentiveness? To some Freudians, then, the Chinese male may look "orally arrested," but it is worth remembering that to many Chinese, the Western male looks hopelessly addicted to the adolescent thrill of genital orgasm. It is a two-way street. Although beyond the scope of Weakland's article, Freud's emphasis on the sublimation of eros as the basis for civilization and creativity bears comparison with China's channeling of sexual energy for health and transcendence.

If Freudians are appalled by the concept of *coitus reservatus*, one can imagine the reaction of Reichians. Unfortunately, imagination is all we have, as no such studies exist; however, the striking similarites and contrasts between Reich's ideas and Chinese sexual practices make a little imagining well worth the effort. As outlined in *The Function of Orgasm* and other writings, Reich's theory of "sexual energy" and "orgone" in many ways answers to the Chinese concepts of *ching* and *ch'i*. Taoist meditation, yoga, and sexual practices are aimed at breaking

down what Reich called "muscular armour." Reich's opposition to monogamy, of course, sets well with the Chinese custom of polygamy and the insistence in sexual practice on multiple partners. Both Reich and the Chinese share a common fear of sexual repression and belief in the importance of sexual contact for maintaining psychological health. However, Reich's vision of social revolution through sexual liberation and China's pursuit of health and immortality through sexual yoga diverge in the interpretation of orgasm. For Reich, the function of orgasm is to discharge sexual tension, and full orgasmic potency is characterized by "involuntary muscular contractions" and "the clouding of consciousness." The feeling of pleasure is derived from the decline in tension and the return to equilibrium. This to the Chinese makes a narcotic of sex. For them, contact and arousal are the most fundamental biological needs, not orgasm. The energy discharged during sex should not be drained from the body, but shared with the organism as a whole, and particularly the brain. This results in a state of "spiritual illumination" (*shen-ming* 神明), which may be said to be diametrically opposed to Reich's "clouding of consciousness." The spiritual "irrigation" experienced by the Chinese sexual yogis is a far cry from the Western "waters of oblivion." Finally, although Reich's "sexual politics" is completely beyond the purview of Chinese sexual yoga, the coupling of sex and salvation in the Taoist church, and its association with antifeudal liberation struggles, would undoubtedly have caught Reich's fancy.

VII. CONCLUSION

A number of details in the Ma Wang tui medical corpus make it likely that some of these works predate the *Su wen* and *Ling shu*, long considered our earliest

medical texts and dated late Chou. For example, although the *Su wen* describes nine kinds of metal acupuncture needles, the Ma Wang tui texts mention only stone needles. The Ma Wang tui medical texts indeed may represent a more primitive stage of the development of medical science than we have previously known. However, more remarkable for the history of sexology is that from a purely empirical point of view, the level of development of the "Uniting Yin and Yang" and "Highest Tao under Heaven" was not significantly surpassed by the *Ishimpō* or later sexual literature. We can tentatively suggest, then, that sexual practices had reached the height of their scientific development prior to the introduction of metal needles in acupuncture, or even before meridian theory reached its classical "twelve meridian" (*shih-erh cheng-ching* 十二正經) formulation. Although the medical aspect of sexual practices appear to have reached nearly full-blown proportions by the early Han, we also catch glimpses in the Ma Wang tui texts of the sexual ritual and elixir traditions. The opening verse passage of the "Uniting Yin and Yang" may be a link between an earlier shamanistic tradition and the sexual rituals of late Han religious Taoism, while other passages in this work prefigure the sexual elixir school of inner alchemy.

The importance of sex in Chinese conceptions of health can be documented by the unrivaled sexual literature. The ancient physicians analyzed human sexual response with the same keen interest and precision with which they approached the influence of foods, herbs, emotions, and environment. The works in this collection represent an age when physiological phenomena were treated as susceptible to rational analysis and control, but were also capable of inspiring wonder, an age when the mythopoetic imagination was as active in probing the human body as in interpreting the heavens and human personality. For the sexual school of physicians, no activity poses as great a threat to health as coitus improperly practiced or offers such benefits if carried out properly to stimulate without taxing. Traditional Chinese medicine takes the "three treasures," *yin* and *yang*, the organs, and *ch'i* channels as its essential working principles. Sexual

activity strengthens the *ching*, *ch'i*, and spirit, balances *yin* and *yang*, tonifies the organs, and circulates positive *ch'i* throughout all the meridians. Whether expressed as "heart and kidneys" or "fire and water" in medicine, or "*Li* and *K'an*," "mercury and lead," or "dragon and tiger" in meditation, body-mind harmony is recognized as the very foundation of health. Once body-mind harmony became the goal, the integrative power of sexuality was difficult to overlook; once the battle lines were drawn between positive (*cheng* 正) and negative (*hsieh* 邪) *ch'i*, the healing power of sexuality became irresistible. The physicians of old fully exploited the health-giving potential of the bedchamber, possibly the only arena of athletic endeavor for the Confucian literati and their sequestered wives.

The absence of any Western analogue to Chinese sexual yoga is perhaps the most telling indicator of fundamental divergence in the two culture's approaches to sexuality. Joseph Needham and Alan Watts have made very learned attempts to account for some of these differences, and their work may serve as useful points of departure for concluding this study with a brief foray into East-West comparison. Professor Needham in his sermon appended to Jolan Chang's *The Tao of Love and Sex* laments the "Manichean" takeover of Christianity and the resulting separation of "love charnall" and "love seriphick." He looks forward to a time when the Victorian influence will disappear, and the West, like China, will accept human sexuality as continuous with "cosmic libido." Anyone who considers the subject even superficially must conclude that sex, as much as eating, is rooted in biology, but is also a creature of culture, and in no society is it not the arena for social etiquette and religious values. The Christian (or "Manichean") influence on Western sexuality has been to keep us focused on the business of biology and alienate sex from pleasure and love. For the Christian, sex is for procreation; for the Chinese orgasm is for procreation, but sex is for pleasure, therapy and salvation. All pleasures of the flesh are deemed sinful in the Christian view, and sex as an expression of love ranks a poor third behind love of God and brotherly love. For the majority of Chinese, the sacred resides within nature, and sexuality as a part of nature belongs to the fundamental design of the universe. Nature is not only sacred but the source of "medicine"; one becomes holy by becoming healthy. Sex, being a natural function, also is seen as a source of bioenergetic medicine. However, it is interesting that the later Taoists—the alchemists, inner alchemists, and sexual alchemists—took a path that very much resembles the Western tendency. If Western thinking arrived at a dualism of "God the father" and "Mother Earth," Chinese elixirists strove to transcend the *yin* materiality of earth and rise to the *yang* spirituality of heaven. The drive for transcendence is one for Christian and Taoist, but for the Christian it was an act of faith backed up by will and mental concentration, whereas for the later Taoists the substance of the body itself could be transmuted.

In his *Man, Woman and Nature*, Alan Watts presents a masterful analysis of Christian, Hindu, Buddhist, and early Taoist attitudes towards sex. Curiously, however, he has omitted the perspectives of Tantrism and Chinese sexual practices, which are really a special case. Nevertheless, his discussion may be said to epitomize the enlightened contemporary Western view, and as such, bears quoting at length to highlight critical East-West contrasts:

> Sexuality will remain a problem so long as it continues to be the isolated area in which the individual transcends himself and experiences spontaneity. He must first allow himself to be spontaneous in the whole play of inner feeling and of sensory response to the everyday world. Only as the senses in general can learn to accept without grasping, or to be conscious without straining, can the special sensations of sex be free from the grasping of abstract lust and its inseparable twin, the inhibition of abstract or "spiritual" disgust. . . . For when sexual activity is sought in the abstract its disappointments are proportionate to its exaggerated expectations, asso-
> ciating themselves with the swift transition from extreme excitement to the lassitude which accompanies detumescence. The aftermath of intercourse, which should be a state of fulfilled tranquility, is for the prude the depression of guilt and for the libertine the depression of ennui. . . . But when the mounting excitement is accepted rather than grasped, it becomes a full realization of spontaneity, and the resulting orgasm is not the sudden end but the bursting in upon us of peace. . . . The experience of sexual love is therefore no longer to be sought as the repetition of a familiar ecstacy prejudiced by the expectation of what we already know. It will be the exploration of a relationship with an ever-changing ever unknown partner, unknown because he or she is not in truth the abstract role or person. . . . All these are *maya*, and the love of these is an endlessly frustrating love of fantasy.

Some will recognize Watts's analysis as essentially a Zen critique of mental meddling in sexuality, and others will recognize in it the position of progressive modern psychotherapy. Prude and libertine are exposed as two sides of the same false coin, and interpersonal communion is held out as the ultimate sexual reality. The personalities that come together for sexual experience, however, must have achieved a perfect state of mental health through Zen therapy so as to be free of grasping and illusions. It is interesting that T'an Ssu-t'ung, writing a century earlier, promised that this enlightened attitude would give sex "the taste of wax." The Chinese are certainly guilty, for the most part, of depersonalizing sexual relations and making sex a vehicle for pursuing what Watts calls "abstract" goals, granting for the moment that health is abstract in the same sense that "spontaneity and transcendence" are. However, Watts's perfect orgasm, "the bursting in upon us of peace," from the point of view of Chinese sexual practices is what the Roman historian called "creating a desert and calling it peace." From the Chinese perspective, relaxation should not be achieved at the price of depletion: relaxation is achieved by relaxing. The function of sex is to send a charge of bioenergetic *ching* electricity through a conductor whose resistance has been lowered by relaxation.

The Chinese have made an art, a yoga, a ritual, a therapy, and a meditation of sex. Watts, and the West in general, have left all of these possibilities completely out of the discussion. After clearing all illusions away, is there not still a need for art, even a Zen art? Modern Occidentals, very much like the early Taoists, are suspicious that technique compromises spontaneity and sincerity, and in many cases the fear is justified. However, to banish technique from the bedroom is to fail to recognize that sex is a form of heightened expression in the same way that singing and dancing are. The artist learns to expand his or her range of expression through technique, and to wring themselves to the depths without self-destructing. Watts seemingly has not considered that a bit of art or yoga may actually enhance the interpersonal goals he has in mind, that without art and a mastery of internal energy, spontaneity may be only the spasm of a few seconds, and that the anticipated human communion may become an exercise in frustration.

In assessing East-West differences with respect to sexual attitudes, cross-cultural comparatists such as Watts and Needham have focused on the role of religion as the most important normative influence. Another area, more difficult to document but perhaps equally influential, is esthetics. In the West, the relationship of esthetics to the senses is such that the arts of sight, sound, and the written word are considered "high," whereas gastronomy and sexuality are considered "low," or no arts at all. Dance falls somewhere in between. In China, and the East in general, it is safe to say that gastronomy and sexuality have been the domains of greater esthetic attention and refinement.

Because of the onus of sin laid on sexuality by religion, Western sexuality has taken on an esthetic of "forbidden fruit," heightening the thrill of abstinence for the prude and of conquest for the libertine. However, the Chinese sexual practitioner is neither prude nor libertine. In China, the medical emphasis on *ching* conservation led to an epicurean esthetic that maximizes pleasure by moderating the price—truly a strategy for "having one's cake and eating it too." For Chinese esthetes, orgasm as an esthetic experience is like peach blossoms, something painful in its transience, which must be transformed by art into a more durable form. Impermanence, the arch theme of Chinese poetry, is experienced most poignantly and viscerally in the act of sex—the "little death." Chinese sexual practices attempt to seize the prize of immortality from the jaws of impermanence, to separate the desire for "release" from the experience of loss and transform orgasm into rebirth.

Western esthetics as a discipline focuses on the characteristics of the "objet d'art"; much of Chinese esthetics focuses on the subjective state of the artist as a preliminary to producing esthetic objects, or even as an end in itself. Art and literary criticism often read like a form of graphology or *ch'i* diagnosis. The ability to simultaneously relax and mobilize *ch'i* sets the stage for inspiration, while technique channels the energy and ensures that it is not dissipated. Similarly, the art of the bedchamber seeks to elevate and refine energy. This is an esthetic of happy endings rather than climax and catharsis, of long volleys rather than smash and point, of riding the swells and avoiding the breaking waves.

The exportation of Western religious, political, and scientific ideas to the East has been spectacular; the importation of Eastern culture to the West has been less pervasive but a no less interesting sociological phenomenon. The past two decades have seen major breakthroughs in the acceptance of Chinese medicine, meditation, and martial arts in the West. Each breakthrough required a radical paradigm shift, but just as Indian yoga has proven to be more than a passing fad, Chinese health practices, too, are likely to remain as naturalized citizens of the West. If medicine, meditation, and martial arts are here to stay, can sexual practices be far behind? Entering the world of Chinese sexual yoga requires a similar paradigm shift, the initial threshold of which is the disassociation of sexual satisfaction from genital orgasm. The traditional Chinese meal has little meat and no dessert, hence culinary interest and satisfaction are shifted to the grain and vegetables. For Westerners sampling Chinese cuisine or sexual techniques, some will find them a coming home and others an acquired taste; some will adopt them as a steady diet and others as a change of pace.

Just as the suppression of discursive thought in meditation requires sacrificing a habitual pattern, but results in opening new dimensions of consciousness, so Chinese sexual techniques open new dimensions of energy sharing and the possibility of tasting the nectar of inner orgasm without emptying the cup. Rather than squandering the gold coin of sexual energy, it is pounded thin enough to guild the entire body in a coat of shining armor. Methods that evolved in a polygamous society can be adapted to combating monotony within the four corners of modern monogamy. These techniques may contribute greatly to the forging of a truly egalitarian sexual covenant, offering as they do enhanced sensitivity and control and providing a greatly enriched vocabulary for sensual communication. On an elementary level at least, is Chinese sexual yoga so different from Western social dance or African religious rites, both of which aim straight for the sex center, but channel libido into a sustainable "all night" form? The Chinese perfected in the bedroom what the West does in the ballroom. "One *yin* and one *yang*" make the world go round.

PART TWO

THE CHINESE SEXUAL
YOGA CLASSICS

VIII. The Han Classics Rediscovered

Introduction

The Ma Wang tui sexology classics are the long lost ancestors of the Sui-T'ang texts which Yeh Te-hui rediscovered in the *Ishimpō*. The 1973 unearthing of these second century B.C. manuscripts in tomb three at Ma Wang tui in Changsha, Hunan, confirms Yeh's faith that the *Ishimpō* fragments preserved the Han tradition. Donald Harper says of these, "Two texts, both written on bamboo slips, bear a particularly close resemblance to the later sex manuals in style and content. . . . I judge them to be the oldest extant Chinese sex manuals and to represent the textual antecedents of the sex manuals that circulated in the later Han and Six Dynasties period." The two texts in question are the "Ho yin yang" (Uniting *yin* and *yang*) and the "T'ien-hsia chih-tao t'an" (Discourse on the highest *tao* under heaven); two others, the "Shih wen" (Ten questions) and "Yang-sheng fang" (Prescriptions for nurturing life) contain significant passages relating to sexual cultivation. The original manuscripts were discovered untitled, and the titles used here are those assigned by the editors of the *Ma Wang tui Han-mu po-shu* (Silk manuscripts from the Han tomb of King Ma), published by Wen-wu Press in 1985.

Placing all the received sexual texts after Ma Wang tui on an evolutionary continuum, the "Uniting Yin and Yang" and "Highest Tao" fit rather nicely into a predictable retrogression. That is, the further back one goes chronologically in the sexual literature the greater is the preponderance of empirical material and the lesser the symbolic or ritual. Elements in the *Ishimpō* and thereafter that strike the modern reader as superstitious or sexist are almost entirely absent from Ma Wang tui. There are no calendrical, astrological, or physiological prohibitions on the time of intercourse or prescriptions for the age or physical traits of the woman. There is nearly no sense of one-sided exploitation, and references to absorbing the woman's *ching* carry no hint of this being at the woman's expense. Although the concept of mutuality is largely subtextual, the "Yang-sheng fang" says, "He asked how man and woman might achieve simultaneous arousal and mutual harmony and avoid harm to the body," and the "Uniting Yin and Yang" says, "I nourish the woman's *ching* with my *ching*." There is no mention of loss of female sexual energy through menses, pregnancy, or orgasm, or even the need for men to frequently change partners. What the Ma Wang tui sexual corpus shares with its descendents in later centuries is the importance of *ching* conservation as a theoretical base and the codification of the stages and signs of sexual arousal, the postures and methods of love making, and the benefits and ills of sex.

Credit for preservation of the *Ishimpō* classics belongs to conscientious Japanese collectors and copyists. Given the fragmentary nature of these sixth to ninth century texts, who could have expected originals to surface from the early Han? After Ma Wang tui, dare we now hope that buried somewhere in China are sexual texts of the late Chou?

Uniting *Yin* and *Yang*

Ho yin yang

This is the method for uniting *yin* and *yang*:

> Clasp her hands[1] and cross over to the outside of her wrists;[2]
> Stroke the "elbow chambers";[3]
> Go beside the armpits;
> Move up to the "stove frame";[4]
> Go to the "neck region";
> Stroke the "receiving basket";[5]
> Cover the "encircling ring";[6]
> Descend to the "broken basin";[7]
> Pass over the "sweet wine ford";[8]
> Cross the "Bounding Sea";[9]
> Ascend "Mount Constancy";[10]
> Enter the "dark gate";[11]
> And mount the "coital sinew."

By sucking her "*ching* spirit"[12] upward, one can live forever and be coeval with heaven and earth. The "coital sinew"[13] is the "coital channel" within the "dark gate." If one is able to lay hold of and stroke it, this causes both bodies to be pleasurably nourished and joyfully radiant in a wonderful way.[14] Although full of passion do not act. Exchanging exhalations and embraces, carry out the *tao* of dalliance step by step.[15] This is the *tao* of dalliance:

> First, when her *ch'i* rises and her face becomes flushed, slowly exhale.
> Second, when her nipples become hard and her nose perspires, slowly embrace her.
> Third, when her tongue spreads[16] and becomes lubricious, slowly press her.
> Fourth, when secretions appear below and her thighs are damp, slowly take hold of her.
> Fifth, when her throat is dry and she swallows saliva, slowly agitate her.

These are called the "signs of the five desires." When all of the signs manifest then mount her. Stab upward, but do not penetrate, in order to stimulate its *ch'i*. When the *ch'i* arrives, penetrate deeply and thrust upward in order to distribute the heat. Now once again withdraw so as not to cause its *ch'i* to dissipate and for her to become exhausted. Afterward, practice the "ten movements," unite according to the "ten postures," and combine the "ten refinements." Uniting bodies after sunset,[17] the *ch'i* extends to the "ancestral gate."[18] Now observe the "eight movements;" listen to the "five sounds"; and examine the signs of the "ten exhaustions."

The "ten arousals"[19] begin with ten, then twenty, thirty, forty, fifty, sixty, seventy, eighty, ninety, and one hundred. Move in and out without reaching orgasm.

> One arousal without orgasm makes the ears and eyes sharp and bright.
> Two and the voice is clear.
> Three and the skin is radiant.
> Four and the back and flanks are strong.
> Five and the buttocks and thighs become muscular.[20]
> Six and the "water course"[21] flows.
> Seven and one becomes sturdy and strong.
> Eight and the pores are lustrous.
> Nine and one achieves spiritual illumination.
> Ten and the body endures.

These are the "ten movements":

> The first is "roaming tiger."
> The second is "cicada clinging."
> The third is "measuring worm."
> The fourth is "roe deer butting."
> The fifth is "locust spreading."
> The sixth is "monkey's squat."
> The seventh is "toad in the moon."
> The eighth is "rabbit bolts."

The ninth is "dragonflies."
The tenth is "fishes gobbling."

The "ten refinements" are:

The first is up.
The second is down.
The third is to the left.
The fourth is to the right.
The fifth is rapidly.
The six is slowly.
The seventh is sparingly.
The eighth is frequently.
The nineth is shallow.
The tenth is deep.

The "eight movements" are:

The first is "clasping hands."
The second is "straightening elbows."
The third is "extending heels."
The fourth is "hooking from the side."
The fifth is "hooking from above."
The sixth is "entwining thighs."
The seventh is "calming the movement."
The eighth is "quivering."

"Clasping hands" means that she desires contact with her belly. "Straightening the elbows" means that she desires her upper body to be rubbed and scratched. "Extending heels" means that penetration is insufficient. "Hooking from the side" means that she wants her side rubbed. "Hooking from above" means that she wants her lower body rubbed. "Entwining thighs" means that penetration is excessive. "Calming the movement" means that she desires shallow penetration. "Quivering" means that she wants to be held for a long time.

When she holds her breath, it means that she is experiencing inner urgency. When she pants it means that she feels intense joy. When she moans it means that the "jade pod"[22] has penetrated and the pleasure[23] begins. When she exhales it means that the sweetness[24] is intense. When she grinds her teeth and her body quivers it means that she wants the man to continue for a long time.

In the evening the man's *ching* is strong; in the morning the woman's *ching* is concentrated. Using my *ching* to nourish the woman's *ching*, the anterior channels are all activated; and the skin, *ch'i*, and blood are stimulated. This opens closures and unblocks obstructions. The "central treasury"[25] benefits from the circulation and becomes full.

The symptoms of the "ten exhaustions"[26] are:

With the first exhaustion [the semen] is transparent and cold when emitted.
With the second exhaustion it has the odor of burnt bones.
With the third exhaustion it is dry.
With the fourth exhaustion it is congealed.
With the fifth exhaustion it is fatty.
With the sixth exhaustion it is slimy.
With the seventh exhaustion it is slow.
With the eighth exhaustion it is oily.
With the ninth exhaustion it is sticky.
With the tenth exhaustion it is corrupt.

When you reach the "corrupt" exhaustion it once again becomes slimy and clear on emission. This is called "great violence."[27] The symptoms of "great violence" are perspiration about the nose, white lips, involuntary movements of the arms and legs, and buttocks lifting off the mat. Death itself approaches.[28] If instead, when the *ch'i* begins to well up in the "central extremity,"[29] one conceals the spirit, then spiritual illumination is attained.

Discourse on the Highest Tao under Heaven

T'ien-hsia chih-tao t'an

Huang Shen[1] addressed a question to Tso Shen[2] saying: "The penis[3] is born together with the 'nine orifices'[4] and 'twelve segments,'[5] but why does it die first?"[6] Tso Shen replied: "Do not overexert yourself; do not indulge in excessive sorrow or joy; do not overeat or drink to excess. Its location is extremely *yin* and it is not exposed to *yang*. If it is employed abruptly and violently without waiting for it to be strong or for both parties to be fully aroused, there will be immediate injury. Avoid calling its name and conceal its form. It is because of excessive violence and lack of propriety that, although it is born together with the body, it is first to die."

If [the penis] is enraged but not large, the flesh has not yet been aroused. If it is large but not stiff, the sinews have not yet been aroused. If it is stiff but not hot, the *ch'i* has not been aroused. If [the penis] is employed before the flesh is aroused, it becomes flaccid. If it is employed before the *ch'i* is aroused, it hides. When the three are all aroused, this is called "the three levels of arousal."

Discourse on the highest tao under heaven

Like the obscurity of water or the *ch'i* of spring and autumn, if what passes is not seen, we cannot receive its contribution; if what comes in the future is not seen, I feast on its gifts. Oh, be careful, indeed! The matter of achieving spiritual illumination consists of locking. If one carefully holds the "jade" in check, spiritual illumination will he achieved. The art of managing the body takes *ching* conservation as its first task. When the *ching* is full it inevitably escapes; when it is dificient it must be strengthened.[7] The process of supplementing loss must address itself to the deficiency. Carry this out by first sitting down together. The hips, buttocks, nose, and mouth each play their part in turn. Moving back and forth, how can I stop the *ching* when it is about to escape? There is a fixed law governing deficiency and repletion. Engage wisely and never be careless. If you do not harass and do not exhaust it, the sinews and bones will be swift and strong. Arouse[8] the "jade spring"[9] and nourish yourself with her fragrance. Withdraw slightly and penetrate slightly; wait for fullness, this is the rule. When the three harmonious *ch'i* are aroused, [the penis] is sturdy and strong. Wishing to regulate this, one must be guarded[10] in one's speech, and then by locking the "jade" during arousal, one can become an immortal.

> One arousal [without orgasm] and the ears and eyes are sharp and bright.
> Two arousals and the voice becomes clear.
> Three arousals and the skin becomes radiant.
> Four arousals and the backbone becomes strong.
> Five arousals and the buttocks become muscular.
> Six arousals and the "water course" flows.
> Seven arousals and one becomes stout and strong.
> Eight arousals and the will is magnified and expanded.
> Nine arousals and one follows the glory of heaven.
> Ten arousals and one manifests spiritual illumination.

There are "eight benefits" to the *ch'i* and also "seven ills." Those who are unable to use the "eight benefits" to rid themselves of the "seven ills" find that at forty their sexual *ch'i* is reduced by half, at fifty their mobility is impaired, at sixty the ears and eyes no longer are sharp and clear, and at seventy they are dried up below and withered above. Not exercising their sexual *ch'i*, tears flow ceaselessly.[11] There is a *tao* for regaining one's strength. Eliminate the "seven ills" to revive from illness; use the "eight benefits" to increase the *ch'i*. The old regain their strength, and the strong do not decline. The gentleman dwells in peace and contentment, eating, drinking, and indulging his desires. The pores of his skin are fine and dense; the *ch'i* and blood are full and abundant; and the body is light and agile. However, when disease menifests within, it cannot be controlled. He becomes sick, perspires, and pants. He suffers internally and his *ch'i* is out of order; the condition is incurable. Suffering internal heat, he drinks herbal infusions and applies moxibustion to improve his *ch'i*; he takes tonic medicines to help his exterior. However, if he is excessive in sex, illness cannot be controlled and boils and swellings appear. If the *ch'i* and blood are full and abundant, but the "nine orifices" are not regulated and above and below not exercised, then boils and ulcers appear. Therefore, by skillfully employing the "eight benefits" to eliminate the "seven ills," the "five illnesses" cannot manifest.

These are the "eight benefits":

> The first is "regulating the *ch'i*."
> The second is "promoting saliva."

The third is "understanding the proper time."
The fourth is "storing *ch'i*."
The fifth is "harmonizing the saliva."
The sixth is "stealing *ch'i*."
The seventh is "waiting for abundance."
The eighth is "stabilizing imbalance."

These are the "seven ills":

The first is "blockage."
The second is "leakage."
The third is "exhaustion."
The fourth is "absence."
The fifth is "affliction."
The sixth is "termination."
The seventh is "waste."

This is the method for practicing the "eight benefits":

Arise in the morning and sit up; straightening the spine, open and contract[12] the buttocks, pressing down.[13] This is called "regulating the ch'i."
While eating and drinking, relax the buttocks; straighening the spine, contract the buttocks and open the *ch'i*. This is called "promoting the saliva."
First dally for your mutual pleasure, doing anything your heart desires. This is called "knowing the proper time."
Engage in the act while losening the spine, contracting the buttocks, and pressing down. This is called "storing *ch'i*."
Engage in the act without haste or rapidity, moving in and out harmoniously. This is called "harmonizing the saliva."
Withdraw, lie down, and have your partner raise it. When it is enraged it should be let go of. This is called "storing the *ch'i*."
Just before finishing, penetrate from the rear, but do not move; absorb *ch'i*, press down, and still the body waiting patiently. This is called "waiting for abundance."
Washing it when finished and resting when enraged is called "stabilizing imbalance."

The preceeding are called the "eight benefits."

These are the "seven ills":

Suffering pain during the act is called "internal blockage."
Perspiring during the act is called "external leakage."
Engaging in the act without stopping is called "exhaustion."

Passion without potency is called "incompetence."
Panting and internal disorder during the act is called "affliction."
Forcing oneself to engage in the act when there is no desire is called "termination."
Performing the act in haste is called "waste."

These are the "seven ills." Thus those who are skilled at using the "eight benefits" to overcome the "seven ills" will find that the ears and eyes become sharp and clear, the body light and agile, and the *ch'i* of the sexual organs stronger. One enjoys length of years and lives in constant happiness.

There are two things that human beings fail to study: the first is breath and the second is food. Failing these two, the remedy is none other than study and practice. Therefore, that which increases life is food and that which decreases life is sex. For this reason, the sage follows correct principles in the matter of sexual union. Thus,

The first is "tiger roaming."
The second is "cicada clinging."
Beyond this, the third is "inch worm."
The fourth is "roe deer butting."
The fifth is "locusts spreading." Rest from penetration.
The sixth is "monkey squat."
Beyond this, the seventh is "toad in the moon."
The eighth is "rabbit bolts."
The ninth is "dragonflies."
Beyond this, the tenth is "fishes gobbling."

The preceeding are called the "ten postures."

The first [refinement] is "promoting the *ch'i*."
The second is "establishing the taste."
The third is "regulating the joints."
The fourth is "encouraging prosperity."
The fifth is "proper timing."
The sixth is "perfection of talent."
The seventh is "slight movement."
The eighth is "waiting for fullness."
The ninth is "ordering life."
The tenth is "resting the body."

The preceeding are called the "ten refinements."

The first [of the "eight ways"] is called "rising high."
The second is called "lowering."
The third is called "going to the left."
The fourth is called "going to the right."
The fifth is called "deep penetration."
The sixth is called "shallow penetration."
The seventh is called "moving rapidly."
The eighth is called "moving slowly."

The preceeding are the "eight ways."

The "ten refinements" are now complete, the "ten postures" displayed, and the "eight ways" combined. Make physical contact after sunset so that the perspiration does not escape. The *ch'i* extends to the "blood gate"; suck and swallow, swaying in front. This opens the channels and loosens the sinews. Now observe the "eight movements" to determine the location of her *ch'i*; understand the "five sounds," which is later and which earlier.

These are the "eight movements":

The first is "joining hands."
The second is "straightening the elbows."
The third is "calming the movement."
The fourth is "extending the heels."
The fifth is "entwining thighs."
The sixth is "quivering."
The seventh is "hooking from the side."
The eighth is "hooking from above."

These are the "five sounds":

The first is breathing from the throat.
The second is panting.
The third is moaning.
The fourth is exhaling air.
The fifth is biting.

Observe the "five sounds" to know her heart; observe the "eight movements" to know her pleasure and openness.

"Joining hands" means that she desires contact with her belly. "Straightening her elbows" means that she desires her upper body to be rubbed and scratched. "Hooking from the side" means that she desires her sides to be rubbed. "Entwining thighs" means that penetration is too deep. "Extending her heels" means that penetration is not deep enough. "Hooking from above" means that stimulation from below has not yet reached her heart. "Calming the movement" means that she desires shallow penetration. "Quivering" means that she has achieved the greatest joy. These are called the "eight observations."

When the *ch'i* rises and her face becomes hot, gently murmur to her. When her nipples become hard and she perspires, slowly embrace her. When her tongue spreads and becomes lubricious, slowly press her. When secretions moisten her thighs below, slowly hold her. When her throat becomes dry and she swallows saliva, slowly agitate her. These are called the "five signs" and the "five desires." When all the signs appear you may mount her.

If [the penis] is enraged but not large, it means that the skin is not yet aroused. If it is large but not hard, it means that the sinews are not yet aroused. If it is hard but not hot, it means that the *ch'i* is not yet aroused. When the "three arousals" have manifested you may penetrate. The first exhaustion is when the [*ching*] emitted is transparent and cold. The second exhaustion is when it has the odor of rotten bones. The third exhaustion is when it is dry. The fourth exhaustion is when it is congealed. The fifth exhaustion is when it is dry. The sixth exhaustion is when the *ching* is like millet or sorghum. The seventh exhaution is when it is obstructed. The eighth exhaustion is when it is oily. The ninth exhaustion is when it is slimy. With the tenth exhaustion it is brackish.[14] When brackish, it once again becomes slippery and may [spontaneously] be emitted in the early morning.

The first [part of the female genitalia] is called "hairpin channel."
The second is called "sealing net rope."
The third is called "(?) gourd."
The fourth is called "rat wife."
The fifth is called "grain seed."
The sixth is called "wheat teeth."
The seventh is called "baby girl."
The eighth is called "going back."
The ninth is called "what dwelling."
The tenth is called "red (?)."
The eleventh is called "red (?)."
The twelfth is called "(?) rock."[15]

Those who obtain this and refuse to let it

go only hasten the approach of death. The pores become coarse; the waist and heart are destroyed; the lips become completely white; and the perspiration flows all the way to the feet. The afflictions of sexual exhaustion are legion.

Among the skills possessed by men, a knowlege of women is indispensible. When one does have a woman, only the skillful are equal to the task. Do not be too generous nor too controlling; do not be too taxing nor too apprehensive. One must be slow and patient; one must be gentle and sustained. If one acts as if finished but not finished, the woman will be greatly pleased. When she breathes from her throat it means that being stimulated below she emits *yin* and is full of *yang*. When she pants it means that her *ch'i* is rising and her countenance naturally opens. When she moans it means that her buttocks are sore and she moves her "sealing net rope." When she exhales it means that the voluptuous sweetness is intense and she is beginning to experience pleasure. Whe she bites and her body quivers it means that she wishes not to be abandoned but continue for a long time. Therefore, the male belongs to *yang* that is external and the female belongs to *yin* that is internal. The male should be rubbed on the outside and the female should be rubbed on the inside. This is called the art of *yin* and *yang*, or the principle of male and female. If one practices this without success, the fault lies in insufficient mastery of the art. The essence of dalliance is slowness. If one proceeds slowly and patiently, the woman will be exceedingly joyful. She will adore you like a brother and love you like a parent. One who has mastered this *tao* deserves to be called a heavenly gentleman.

IX. The Sui-T'ang Classics Reconstructed

Introduction

With the exception of *The Prescriptions of Su Nü*, all the works in this section are translated from reconstructions based on fragments preserved in a Japanese compendium of Chinese medical literature, the *Ishimpō*, compiled by Tamba Yasuyori between 982 and 984. The late Ch'ing-early Republican scholar Yeh Te-hui (1864–1927) made the exciting discovery that titles in the twenty-eighth section of the *Ishimpō*, "Fang-nei" (Art of the bedchamber), closely corresponded to those listed in the *History of the Sui* bibliography, and concluded that these represented the survival of sexology classics long since lost in China from the Han to the T'ang. Yeh included his reconstructions of the *Ishimpō* sexology classics in a collection of rare works he saw published in 1903, entitled *Shuang-mei ching-an ts'ung-shu* (Shadow of the double plum tree collection).

The *Tung Hsüan tzu* is not listed in either the Han or Sui dynastic histories, first appearing in that of the T'ang, but it shows every sign of being one of the most intact texts in the *Ishimpō*. Maspero attributes the authorship to the seventh century physician, Li Tung-hsüan, but van Gulik argues that the style and content belong to the Six Dynasties Period (third–sixth centuries). *The Prescriptions of Su Nü*, by contrast, is listed in the Sui bibliography but is not found in the *Ishimpō* fragments. Yeh's text of the *Prescriptions* is taken from Sun Hsing-yen's *Ping-chin kuan ts'ung-shu*, which in turn is based on the T'ang work *Wai-t'ai pi-yao fang* by Wang T'ao, who cites Chen Ch'uan's *Ku-chin lu-yen* as his source. Yeh supplements the five sections in Sun Hsing-yen's text with two from Sun Ssu-miao's (601–682) *Ch'ien-chin yao-fang* (Priceless prescriptions) to bring the total to seven, the number he feels represents the state of the original.

Another work published by Yeh, but not translated in the present anthology, is the "Ta le fu" (Prose-poem on the supreme joy), discovered in the Tun-huang material. The text bears the name of Po Hsing-chien (died 826), younger brother of the famous poet, Po Chü-i, but because of its genre and the excessive number of errata and lacunae, it did not make a good candidate for translation. Stylistically, it is closest to the *Tung Hsüan tzu*, even sharing some expressions and parallel passages, but in the end it is more a poetical essay than an instructional manual.

Yeh Te-hui's motivation and methodology have been touched on briefly elsewhere in this study, but the Preface to his reconstruction of the *Classic of Su Nü* reveals his purpose most plainly:

> Today Western authorities on health and hygiene are exceedingly thorough in their study of all matters relating to diet and sex. Many new books have been translated detailing the human sex organs, sexual intercourse and new theories on marital relations. The most ignorant fellow can become an instant expert. But they do not realize that the descendants of China's holy emperors and divine rulers already developed this art four thousand years ago.

Methodologically, Yeh assumed that the thirty thematic headings in the "Art of the Bedchamber" section of the *Ishimpō* represented the standard order of appearance of topics in the original texts, and that dialogues involving the goddesses Hsüan Nü and Ts'ai Nü originally belonged to a single classic. He is guided consistently by Tamba's emendations, rejecting only the most speculative ones. His explanation for the relatively small number of passages directly attributed to the *Classic of Su Nü* and his rationale for borrowing from other texts, especially the *Secrets of the Jade Chamber*, to flesh

out his own reconstruction of the *Classic* are best stated in his Preface:

> The language of the *Classic of Su Nü* is often used in the opening passages of the *Secrets of the Jade Chamber*, the *Essentials of the Jade Chamber*, the *Classic of Physiognomy*, and the *Classic of Obstetrics*. Thus the *Classic of Su Nü* is the progenitor of the art of the bedchamber and all others draw upon it. Since this knowledge was so readily available, there was no need for the independent transmission of the *Classic of Su Nü*.

Looking at the *Classic of Su Nü* and *Secrets of the Jade Chamber* in light of the Ma Wang tui sexual texts, we may say that from the point of view of content the *Classic* and *Secrets* very closely parallel the recently discovered Han texts, but from the point of view of form, neither the goddess Su Nü nor any female initiatress appears in the earlier works.

By the tenth century, Tamba Yasuyori was able to obtain only fragments of the texts in this section; and no originals, whole or fragmentary, yet have come to light from this period. In style and content the *Ishimpō* fragments clearly are the textual descendents of the Ma Wang tui manuscripts. Traces of their transmission up to the Ming, when the *Wondrous Discourse* was written in apparent imitation of the *Classic of Su Nü*, are glimpsed but fleetingly in official bibliographies and passing literary references. Nothing survives from the Sung, whose official history still lists a few sexual titles, whereas a number of important manuals have come down to us from the Ming, whose history lists none. There is a gap of more than a thousand years between the burial at Ma Wang tui and Tamba's compilation of the *Ishimpō*, yet they represent a direct line of descent, and another five hundred years between the *Ishimpō* and *Wondrous Discourse*. These may be considered the main trunk of the transmission whose branches include the sexual connoisseurship of the *Tung Hsüan tzu*, the yoga and alchemy of Chang San-feng, and the ritual of the *Shang-ch'ing huang-shu kuo-tu i*.

The Classic of Su Nü

Su Nü ching

The Yellow Emperor[1] addressed a question to Su Nü[2] saying, "My *ch'i*[3] is weak and out of harmony. There is no joy in my heart and I live in constant fear.[4] What is to be done?" Su Nü answered:

All debility in man is due to violation of the *tao*[5] of intercourse between *yin* and *yang*.[6] Women are superior to men in the same way that water is superior to fire.[7] This knowledge is like the ability to blend the "five flavors"[8] in a pot to make delicious soup. Those who know the *tao* of *yin* and *yang* can fully realize the "five pleasures";[9] those who do not will die before their time without ever knowing this joy.[10] Can you afford not to view this with the utmost seriousness?

Su Nü continued:[11] "There is one called Ts'ai Nü[12] who has a wondrous knowledge of the arts of the *tao*. The King[13] sent Ts'ai Nü to inquire of P'eng Tsu[14] into the methods of attaining longevity and P'eng Tsu replied:[15]

By treasuring his *ching*,[16] cultivating his spirit, and consuming herbs[17] a man may indeed attain long life. However, if he is ignorant of the *tao* of intercourse, the taking of herbs will be of no benefit. The mutual fulfillment of man and woman is like the mutual dependence of heaven and earth.[18] Because heaven and earth have attained the *tao* of union,[19] they are eternal; because mankind has lost the *tao* of intercourse, he suffers the onset of early death. If we could but avoid those things that gradually injure our bodies and learn the art of *yin* and *yang*, this would truly be the *tao* of immortality.

Ts'ai Nü bowed twice[20] and said: "Will you instruct me in the essential teachings?" P'eng Tsu answered:

This *tao* is easily understood; it is just that men fail to practice it faithfully. Today the Emperor controls the complex machinery of rulership and cannot be a master of all the arts.[21] However, his responsibilities in the seraglio are many and it is important that he know the proper method of intercourse.[22] Its essence lies in frequently mounting young girls but only rarely ejaculating.[23] This makes a man's body light and eliminates the hundred ailments.

Su Nü said:

In engaging the enemy[24] a man should regard her as so much tiles or stone and himself as gold or jade. When his *ching* is aroused, he should immediately withdraw from her territory. One should mount[25] a woman as if riding a galloping horse with rotten reins or as if fearful of falling into a deep pit lined with knife blades. If you treasure your *ching*, your life will have no limit.[26]

The Yellow Emperor addressed a question to Su Nü saying: "If I were to refrain for a long time[27] from intercourse, what would be the result?" Su Nü answered:

That would be a grave mistake. Heaven and earth have their opening and closing, and *yin* and *yang* their activities and transformations. Man must conform to *yin* and *yang* and follow the four seasons. If you were to abstain from intercourse, your spirit[28] would have no opportunity for expansiveness, and *yin* and *yang* would be blocked and cut off from one another. How could you thus strengthen yourself? You must cultivate your *ch'i* through frequent practice[29] and "eliminate the old while absorbing the new"[30] to improve yourself. If the "jade stalk" does not stir, it dies in its lair.[31] So you must engage frequently in intercourse as a way of exercising the body.[32] To be aroused[33] but not ejaculate is what is called "returning the *ching*." When the *ching* is returned to benefit the body, then the *tao* of life[34] has been realized.[35]

The Yellow Emperor said: "How then should man and woman regulate their sexual relations?" Su Nü answered:

The *tao* of intercourse has definite characteristics[36] that enable man to preserve his health and woman to be free of all illness. They will be happy in their hearts and the power of their *ch'i* will be strong. Those who are ignorant of its practice will gradually grow weaker. If you wish to know this *tao*, it consists in settling the *ch'i*, calming the mind, and harmonizing the

85

emotions.[37] When the "three *ch'i*"[38] are awakened and the spirit is focused, then when you are neither cold nor hot, neither hungry nor full, completely settle the whole body.[39] Now relax, penetrate shallowly, and move slowly with infrequent thrusts and withdrawals. In this way the woman will be satisfied and the man retain his vigor. These are the principles by which to regulate one's sexual relations.

The Yellow Emperor addressed a question to Hsüan Nü saying: "I have received Su Nü's teachings on *yin* and *yang* and begin to have a grasp of its principles. Will you instruct me further so that I may fully understand its *tao*?" Hsüan Nü replied:

All movement in the world results from the interaction of *yin* and *yang*. When *yang* unites with *yin*, *yang* is transformed; when *yin* unites with *yang*, *yin* becomes open. *Yin* and *yang* are mutually dependent in their operations. Therefore, when man is roused, [his penis] becomes hard and strong, and when woman is moved [her vagina] becomes open and enlarged. When the two *ch'i* (*yin* and *yang*) mingle their *ching*, then their fluids are exchanged.[40] For the man there are "eight divisions" and for the woman "nine palaces."[41] If these are violated, the man will suffer carbuncles and the woman's menses will be afflicted. A hundred ailments will appear and life will waste away. To know this *tao* is to be joyful and strong. The span of life will be lengthened and one's countenance will become beautiful and radiant.

The Yellow Emperor asked: "What is the *tao* of intercourse between *yin* and *yang*?" Su Nü answered:

There are definite characteristics to the *tao* of intercourse by which man develops his *ch'i* and woman eliminates all illness. The heart is gladdened and the *ch'i* strengthened. Those who are ignorant of this *tao* will be subject to decline. If you wish to know this *tao*, it consists in calming the mind, harmonizing the emotions, and concentrating the spirit.[42] Neither cold nor hot, neither full nor hungry, you should settle the body and compose your thoughts.[43] Then, with a relaxed attitude, penetrate deeply and move slowly. Thrusts and withdrawals should be sparing. If you observe these principles and are careful not

to violate them, then woman will be joyful and man will not decline.

The Yellow Emperor said: "Now when I try to force[44] myself to have intercourse, my 'jade stalk' will not rise, I blush and feel embarrassed and beads of sweat the size of pearls stand out.[45] Still, there is passionate desire in my heart and I force myself with the aid of my hand. How can I regain my strength? Please instruct me in the *tao*." Su Nü replied:

What Your Majesty inquires about is a common condition. Whenever you wish to have intercourse with a woman there is a prescribed order of things. You must first harmonize your *ch'i*[46] with that of your partner before the "jade stalk" will rise. Act in accord with your "five constancies"[47] and concentrate on the arousal of her "nine parts."[48] The woman manifests "five colors"[49] by which to assess her satisfaction. Gather her overflowing *ching* and take the liquid from her mouth.[50] The *ching-ch'i*[51] will be returned[52] and transformed in your own body, filling the brain.[53] Avoid the prohibitions of the "seven ills," employ the *tao* of the "eight benefits," and do not violate the "five constancies." In this way the body may be preserved. When filled with healthy *ch'i*,[54] what illness will not disappear? When the internal organs are at peace, one will appear radiant and glossy. Every time you have intercourse there will be immediate erection[55] and your strength will increase a hundredfold. When your enemy pays homage to you, what need is there for shame?

The Yellow Emperor said: "Sometimes during intercourse the woman is not happy, she is not moved to passion,[56] and her secretions do not flow. The 'jade stalk' is not strong, but small and impotent.[57] What is the reason for this?" Hsüan Nü answered:

Yin and *yang* respond to each other's influence. *Yang* without *yin* is unhappy; *yin* without *yang* will not rise.[58] When the man desires intercourse but the woman is not pleased, or if the woman desires intercourse but the man is not desirous, their hearts are not in harmony and their *ching-ch'i* is not aroused. If you move up and down suddenly and violently,[59] the joy of love will not be shared. But when the man is desirous of the woman and the woman is desirous of the man, and their emotions are as one, then they will both be happy in their hearts. The woman is stirred to the quick and the man's "stalk" is full of vigor. In full possession of his virility,[60] the man presses[61] her *yü-shu*[62] as her secretions overflow. The "jade stalk" moves freely, now slowly and now fast, while the "jade gate" opens and closes. Working but not wearying oneself, one routs the mighty enemy. Absorbing her *ching* and drawing in her *ch'i*, the "red chamber" is irrigated.[63] Now allow me to elaborate the eight[64] possibilities that encompass all methods. These are extension and contraction, lying face down or face up,[65] advancing and withdrawing, flexing and folding.[66] I hope Your Majesty will faithfully carry out these precepts and never be guilty of violating them.[67]

The Yellow Emperor asked: "Is it important that one follow certain methods in the art of *yin* and *yang*?" Su Nü answered:

When you are preparing to mount[68] a woman, first have her recline comfortably[69] and bend her knees. The man positions himself between them, kissing her mouth and sucking her tongue. Brandishing[70] his "jade stalk," he attacks the east and west sides of her "gate." After carrying on in this manner for a short time, he inserts the "jade stalk." Those with large [penises] should penetrate to a depth of one and a half inches,[71] those whose [penises] are small an inch. Without agitating, slowly withdraw and then penetrate again. This cures a hundred ailments. Do not allow her secretions to spill forth from the four sides.[72] When the "jade stalk" enters the "jade gate," it naturally becomes hot and excited. The woman's body naturally will undulate upward to join the man's. Now penetrate deeply, and every ailment of man and woman will disappear. Withdrawing to a shallow depth, stab her "zither strings,"[73] and then penetrate three and a half inches. You should keep your mouth closed while piercing her and count one, two, three, four, five, six, seven, eight, nine.[74] Now penetrate all the way to the sides of the "rock of *k'un*"[75] and move back and forth. With your mouth opposite hers, inhale her *ch'i*, practicing the method of nine times nine. This then is the conclusion.

The Yellow Emperor asked: "What is meant by the five constancies?" Su Nü answered:

The "jade stalk" does indeed possess the *tao* of the "five constancies."[76] Dwelling in deep seclusion, restrained and self-controlled, cherishing the highest virtue and carrying out its work unstintingly,[77] the "jade stalk" desires to give of itself. This is "benevolence." The middle being empty is "righteousness." The joint at the extremity is "propriety." To rise when desirous and to rest when not, this is "good faith." Approaching the act, it fluctuates between high and low.[78] This is "intelligence." Therefore the man of true wisdom[79] relies on the "five constancies" and exercises restraint. Although in his "benevolence" he desires to give of himself, his *ching* will suffer if it is not maintained intact.[80] In "righteousness" he preserves its emptiness, for clearly one must not permit it to be overly full.[81] This is the path of prohibition, but when it is appropriate to give of oneself, then doing so with "propriety" shows restraint. Carrying this out with sincerity demonstrates one's "good faith." Thus one must understand the *tao* of intercourse. If one succeeds in following the "five constancies," one will achieve longevity.

The Yellow Emperor asked: "How can I tell if the woman is experiencing pleasure?" Su Nü answered:

There are "five signs,"[82] "five desires," and also "ten movements" by which you may observe her transformations and understand their causes. These are the stages of arousal represented by the "five signs." First, when her face is flushed, slowly press her to you. Second, when her breasts are hard and perspiration appears on her nose, slowly enter her. Third, when her throat is dry and she swallows saliva, slowly begin to move inside her. Fourth, when her private parts are well lubricated, slowly penetrate her more deeply. Fifth, when her secretions spread out over her buttocks, then slowly withdraw.[83]

Su Nü continued:

These are the "five desires" by which you may know her responses. First, if there is desire in her mind for union, she will hold her breath.[84] Second, when her private parts desire contact,[85] her nostrils and mouth will widen. Third, when her *ching* desires to be excited,[86] she will quake, quiver, and embrace the man. Fourth, when her heart desires complete satisfaction,[87] perspiration will soak her garments. Fifth, when her desire for orgasm reaches the greatest intensity, her body will go straight and her eyes close.

Su Nü said:

The effects represented by the "ten movements" are, first, when she embraces the man with both arms, she desires their bodies to be close and their private parts to come together. Second, when she stretches out her legs, rub the upper portion [of her vulva]. Third, when she distends her belly, it means that she desires shallow penetration.[88] Fourth, when she moves her buttocks, it means that she is experiencing great pleasure. Fifth, when she raises her legs to encircle him, it means that she desires him to penetrate more deeply. Sixth, when she presses her thighs together, it means that her internal sensations are becoming overwhelming. Seventh, when she moves from side to side, it means that she desires deep thrusts to the left and right. Eighth, when she arches her body against the man's, it means that her sexual pleasure has reached its peak. Ninth, when she stretches out and relaxes, it means that pleasure fills her entire body. Tenth, when her secretions are copious, it means that her *ching* has been released. By observing these effects you may know the degrees of her pleasure.[89]

The Yellow Emperor said: "I am desirous of intercourse, but my 'jade stalk' will not rise. Should I force myself to perform or not?" Hsüan Nü answered: "Absolutely not! According to the *tao* of desiring intercourse, the man manifests[90] 'four levels'[91] that in turn bring about the woman's 'nine *ch'i*.'" The Yellow Emperor asked: "What are the 'four levels?'" Hsüan Nü answered:

If the "jade stalk" is not aroused, it means that the "*ch'i* of harmony"[92] has not yet arrived. If it is aroused but not large, it means that the "flesh *ch'i*"[93] has not yet arrived. If it is large but not stiff, it means that the "bone *ch'i*" has not yet arrived. If it is stiff but not hot, it means that the "spirit *ch'i*" has not yet arrived. Therefore.

arousal is the dawn of the *ching*; largeness is the threshold of the *ching*; stiffness is the portal of the *ching*; and hotness is the door of the *ching*.[94] When the four *ch'i* have arrived, and they are regulated by means of the *tao*,[95] then one will not foolishly release the mechanism nor shed the *ching*.[96]

The Yellow Emperor said: "How wonderful! But how can one come to recognize the woman's 'nine *ch'i*?'" Hsüan Nü answered:

You may recognize the "nine *ch'i*" by observing[97] them. When a woman breathes heavily and swallows her saliva, the "lung *ch'i*" has arrived. When she makes sounds[98] and kisses the man, it means that her "heart *ch'i*" has arrived. When she embraces and holds the man, it means that her "spleen *ch'i*" has arrived. When her "*yin* gate" becomes slippery and wet, it means that her "kidney *ch'i*"[99] has arrived. When in the throes of passion she bites the man, it means that her "bone *ch'i*" has arrived. When she entwines her feet around the man, it means that her "sinew *ch'i*" has arrived. When she strokes the "jade stalk," it means that her "blood *ch'i*" has arrived. When she fondles the man's nipples, it means that her "flesh *ch'i*" has arrived.[100] Having intercourse for a long time,[101] you may play with her "seed"[102] to stimulate her desire, and all of the "nine *ch'i*" will arrive. If they fail to arrive, then one may suffer harm.[103] One should then carry out the appropriate number[104] to remedy it.

The Yellow Emperor said: "I have never heard an explanation of the so-called 'nine methods.' Could you set them forth and analyze their significance[105] so that I might treasure them as in a vault of stone and practice them?" Hsüan Nü replied:

The first of the "nine methods" is called "flying dragon."[106] Have the woman lie flat on her back facing up, while the man lies face down on top of her with his thighs buried in the bed. The woman should raise her private parts to receive the "jade stalk." The man should stab her "grain seed" and attack the upper part [of her vulva]. Now undulate slowly according to the method of "eight shallow and two deep" and "thrust dead and withdraw live."[107] In this way your power[108] will be robust and strong and the woman will be beside herself[109] and wild with joy.[110] Lock yourself securely[111] and a hundred ailments will disappear.

The second posture is called "tiger stance."[112] Have the woman lie on her stomach with buttocks raised and head facing down. The man kneels behind her and embraces her belly. Then he inserts the "jade stalk" and stabs her innermost center. It is important to be deep and intimate. Move in and out, pressing tightly together. Carry on for a count of five times eight,[113] and when the proper degree is reached, the woman's private parts will close and open by turns and her *ching* secretions overflow. Now you may stop and rest. This prevents a hundred ailments and increases a man's virility.

The third posture is called "monkey's attack." Have the woman lie on her back. The man uses his shoulders to push her thighs and knees back beyond her chest[114] until both buttocks and back are elevated. He now inserts the "jade stalk" and stabs her "odiferous mouse."[115] The woman, intensely excited,[116] begins to move as her *ching* secretions pour forth like rain. The man should press deeply with great strength, as if enraged. When the woman has reached orgasm, stop, and a hundred ailments will be cured.

The fourth posture is called "cicada clinging." Have the woman lie flat on her stomach with her body stretched out long. The man lies on top of her, face down, and deeply inserts the "jade stalk." He raises her buttocks slightly to press her "red pearl"[117] and continues for a count of six times nine. When she is in the throes of passion her *ching* will flow. The interior of her private parts pulses urgently, while the exterior opens and relaxes. After she has reached orgasm you may stop. The "seven injuries"[118] will naturally disappear.

The fifth posture is called "turtle rising."[119] Have the woman lie flat on her back with both knees bent. The man then pushes them until her feet reach her breasts. Penetrate deeply with the "jade stalk" and stab her "baby girl."[120] Alternate deep and shallow to the proper measure. Strike her "seed" squarely[121] and the woman will experience great joy. Her body will naturally writhe and undulate as her *ching* secretions pour forth. Now penetrate to her innermost depth. When she reaches orgasm, stop. In carrying out this method be sure not to lose your *ching*

and your strength will increase a hundred-fold.

The sixth posture is called "phoenix soaring." Have the woman lie flat on her back and raise her legs. The man kneels between her thighs supporting himself with both hands on the mat. Penetrate deeply with the "jade stalk" and stab her "rock of *k'un*." Stiff and hot, he should stick inside her,[122] while she moves her body for a count of three times eight.[123] As their buttocks press tightly together and her private parts open up, she naturally emits her *ching* secretions. When the woman has reached orgasm, stop, and a hundred ailments will cease.

The seventh posture is called "rabbit licking its fur." The man lies flat on his back and stretches out his legs. The woman straddles him with her knees on the outside, her back to his head and facing his feet. She inclines her head forward while supporting herself with her hands on the mat. Now he should insert his "jade stalk" and stab her "zither strings." When the woman reaches orgasm,[124] her *ching* secretions will gush forth like a spring. Joy and happiness move her body and soul.[125] When she has reached orgasm, stop, and a hundred ailments will never appear.

The eighth posture is called "fishes touching their scales together." The man lies on his back while the woman straddles him with her two thighs facing forward. Enter slowly, and after slight penetration, stop and go no deeper, like a child sucking the breast. The woman alone should move, and they should stay this way for a long time. When the woman reaches orgasm, the man should withdraw, and all conditions of stagnation and accumulation[126] will be cured.

The ninth posture is called "cranes with necks entwined."[127] The man sits in "winnowing basket" pose,[128] and the woman straddles his thighs with her arms around his neck. Insert the "jade stalk" and stab her "wheat teeth,"[129] being sure to strike her "seed." The man should embrace the woman's buttocks to aid her undulations. When the woman feels satisfied, her *ching* secretions will overflow. After the woman reaches orgasm, stop, and the "seven injuries" will naturally be cured.

Su Nü said: "In uniting *yin* and *yang* there are 'seven ills' and 'eight benefits.'"[130]

The first of the benefits is called "strengthening the *ching*." Have the woman lie on her side with her thighs spread open. The man lies on his side between them and carries out a count of two times nine strokes.[131] When the count is finished, stop. This strengthens the man's *ching* and cures bleeding in women. Practice this twice daily for fifteen days and one will be cured.

The second benefit is called "calming the *ch'i*." Have the woman lie on her back with her head resting on a high pillow. She should spread her thighs while the man kneels between them and stabs her. Carry out a count of three times nine strokes and, when finished, stop. This harmonizes the man's *ch'i* and cures coldness of the female "gate." Practice this three times daily for twenty days and one will be cured.

The third benefit is called "profiting the internal organs."[132] Have the woman lie on her side and draw up her thighs. The man lies transversely and stabs her. Carry out a count of four times nine strokes and then stop. This harmonizes the man's *ch'i* and also cures coldness of the female "gate." Practice this four times daily for twenty days and one will be cured.

The fourth benefit is called "strengthening the bones." Have the woman lie on her side, bend her left knee, and stretch out her right thigh. The man lies on top and stabs her. Carry out five times nine strokes and, when the count is finished, stop. This regulates the joints of the man's body and cures blocked menses in women. Practice this five times daily for ten days and one will be cured.

The fifth benefit is called "regulating the circulation."[133] Have the woman lie on her side, bend her right knee, and stretch out her left thigh. The man supports himself on the ground and stabs her. Carry out six times nine strokes and, when the count is complete, stop. This opens and promotes the man's blood circulation and also cures cramps in the woman's "gate."[134] Practice this six times daily for twenty days and one will be cured.

The sixth benefit is called "nurturing the blood." The man lies flat on his back and has the woman raise her buttocks and kneel on top of him, taking his "stalk" deeply inside her. Have the woman carry out seven times nine strokes and, when the count is finished, stop. This makes a man strong and cures irregular menses in women. Practice this seven times daily for ten days and one will be cured.

The seventh benefit is called "increasing the fluids." Have the woman lie face down and raise her posterior. The man mounts her and carries out eight times nine strokes. When the count is finished, stop. This fills the bones.

The eighth benefit is called "regulating the whole body."[135] Have the woman lie on her back and bend her thighs so that her feet touch beneath her buttocks. The man makes use of his thighs and ribs to stab her.[136] He carries out nine time nine strokes and, when the count is finished, stop. This causes the man's bones to be full and cures malodorousness of the female's private parts. Practice nine times daily for nine days and one will be cured.

Su Nü said:

The first of the "seven ills" is called "exhaustion of the *ch'i*."[137] Those who suffer from "exhaustion of the *ch'i*" lack desire. When they force themselves to perform, they perspire[138] and feel weak. This condition causes heat in the heart and blurred vision. The cure is to have the woman lie flat on her back while the man supports her two thighs on his shoulders[139] and deeply penetrates her. Have the woman execute the movements herself[140] and, when the *ching* comes forth, stop. The man should refrain from orgasm.[141] Practice this nine times daily for ten days and one will be cured.

The second ill is called "overflow of *ching*." Those who suffer from "overflow of *ching*" are greedy and perform the act before *yin* and *yang* have been properly harmonized. In this way, the *ching* overflows in mid-course. Another cause is intercourse during intoxication.[142] When one is panting and the *ch'i* is upset, the lungs are harmed. This can cause gasping cough and "emaciation-thirst"[143] symptoms. There may also be [excessive] joy or anger, or depression, parched mouth, fever, and difficulty in standing for a long time. To remedy this, have the woman lie on her back, bend her knees, and take the man between them. The man should shallowly insert his "jade stalk" to a depth of an inch and a half and have the woman perform the movements herself. When the woman's *ching* comes forth, stop. The man should refrain from orgasm. Practice this nine times daily for ten days and one will be cured.

The third ill is called "weak pulse."[144] Those who suffer "weak pulse" force themselves to perform, and although the private part is not hard, they force themselves to ejaculate in mid-course. If one engages in intercourse when the *ch'i* is exhausted or one is full from eating, this injures the spleen and causes digestive problems, impotence, and insufficiency of *ching*. To remedy this, have the woman lie on her back and wrap her legs around the man's thighs. The man supports himself on the mat[145] and penetrates her. Have the woman perform the movements herself and, when her *ching* comes forth, stop. The man should refrain from orgasm. Practice this nine times daily for ten days and one will be cured.

The fourth ill is called "*ch'i* leakage." "*Ch'i* leakage" results when one engages in sexual intercourse in a condition of fatigue and before perspiration has dried. This causes heat in the abdomen and parched lips. To cure this have the man lie on his back with the woman astride him and facing his feet. The woman supports herself on the mat[146] and shallowly takes the "jade stalk" into her. Have the woman perform the movements, and when her *ching* comes forth, stop. The man should not reach orgasm. Practice this nine times daily for ten days and one will be cured.

The fifth ill is called "injury to the joints."[147] This results from forcing oneself to have sex immediately after urination or moving the bowels when the body is not yet settled. This injures the liver. Another cause is hurried and violent relations and unregulated pace.[148] Unregulated pace wearies the sinews and bones, causes blurred vision, and both carbuncles and ulcers appear. There is a general failure of the circulatory system and, if the condition persists, a tendency to withering of the body and impotence. To remedy this have the man lie flat on his back with the woman straddling his thighs. She kneels forward and slowly presses him into her. Do not allow the woman to move herself.[149] When the woman's *ching* comes forth, the man should refrain from orgasm. Practice this nine times daily for ten days and one will be cured.

The sixth ill is called the "hundred blockages."[150] The "hundred blockages" result when one has overindulged in sex with women,[151] spending oneself without restraint. Repeated intercourse without the proper measure exhausts the *ching-ch'i*. When one forces oneself to ejaculate, but the *ching* is exhausted and does not come forth, a hundred ailments all appear together. One suffers "emaciation-thirst" symptoms and blurred vision. The remedy is to have the man lie flat on his back, while the woman straddles him and, inclining forward, supports herself on the mat. Have the woman insert the "jade stalk" and move herself.[152] When her *ching* comes forth, stop. The man should refrain from orgasm. Practice this nine times daily for ten days and one will be cured.

The seventh ill is called "exhaustion of the blood." "Exhaustion of the blood" is the result of union while perspiring from the effort of physical exertion or walking in haste. After both are finished one lies back and continues to press to the very root with violence and passion.[153] From this comes serious illness. Repeated ejaculation without rest results in drying up of the blood and exhaustion of the *ch'i*. This causes deficiency and drawing of the skin, pain in the "stalk," dampness in the scrotum, and blood in the semen. To remedy this have the woman lie on her back, raise her buttocks high and spread her thighs. The man kneels between them and deeply penetrates her. Have the woman move herself, and when her *ching* comes forth, stop. The man should refrain from orgasm. Practice this nine times daily for ten days and one will be cured.

Ts'ai Nü asked: "The pleasure of intercourse lies in ejaculation. Now if a man locks himself and refrains from emission, where is the pleasure?" P'eng Tsu answered:

When *ching* is emitted the whole body feels weary. One suffers buzzing in the ears and drowsiness in the eyes; the throat is parched and the joints heavy. Although there is brief pleasure,[154] in the end there is discomfort. If, however, one engages in sex without emission, then the strength of our *ch'i* will be more than sufficient and our bodies at ease. One's hearing will be acute and vision clear. Although exercising self-control and calming the passion, love actually increases, and one remains unsatiated. How can this be considered unpleasurable?

The Yellow Emperor said: "I wish to hear of the advantages of sex without emission." Su Nü replied:

One act without emission makes the *ch'i* strong. Two acts without emission makes the hearing acute and the vision clear. Three acts without emission makes all ailments disappear. Four acts without emission and the "five spirits"[155] are all at peace. Five acts without emission makes the pulse full and relaxed. Six acts without emission strengthens the waist and back. Seven acts without emission gives power to the buttocks and thigh. Eight acts without emission causes the whole body to be radiant. Nine acts without emission and one will enjoy unlimited longevity. Ten acts without emission and one attains the realm of the immortals.

The Yellow Emperor addressed a question to Su Nü saying: "The essential teaching is to refrain from losing *ching* and to treasure one's fluids. However, if we desire to have children, how should we go about ejaculating?"[156] Su Nü replied:

Men differ in respect to strength and weakness, old age and youth. Each must act according to the strength of his *ch'i* and never force orgasm. Forcing orgasm brings about injury. Therefore, a strong lad of fifteen may ejaculate twice in one day and a weak one once a day. A strong man of twenty may also ejaculate twice in one day and a weak one once a day. Strong men of thirty may ejaculate once a day and weak ones once in two days. Strong men of forty may ejaculate once in three days and weak ones once in four. Strong men of fifty may ejaculate once in five days and weak ones once in ten. Strong men of sixty may ejaculate once in ten days and weak ones once in twenty. Strong men of seventy may ejaculate once in thirty days but weak ones should refrain from ejaculating altogether.
The method of Su Nü allows men of twenty to ejaculate once in four days, thirty year olds once in eight days, forty year olds once in sixteen days, and fifty year olds once in twenty-one days. Those who have reached sixty should stop altogether, lock their *ching*, and refrain from further ejaculation. However, if they are still strong in body, they may ejaculate once a month. Men whose *ch'i* is exceptionally strong must not repress themselves too long and refrain from ejaculating, lest they develop carbuncles and ulcers. Those past sixty, who after several weeks[157] without intercourse remain mentally at peace, may lock their *ching* and refrain from ejaculating.[158]

Ts'ai Nü said: "What are the signs by which we may judge a man's strength or weakness?" P'eng Tsu replied:

When a man's *yang*[159] is flourishing and he is full of *ch'i*, the "jade stalk" will be hot and the *yang-ching* thick and concentrated. There are five signs of a man's decline. The first is the inability to restrain ejaculation. This indicates that the *ch'i* has been injured. The second is transparency and scarcity of the *ching*, which indicates that the flesh has been injured. The third is a turning of the *ching* so that it is foul smelling, which indicates injury to the sinews. The fourth is failure of the *ching* to be ejaculated with force, which means that the bones have been injured. The fifth is weakness and impotence of the private parts,[160] which indicates injury to the whole body. All of these injuries result from failure to have intercourse slowly and ejaculating in haste and violence. The remedy is to mount without emission. Within a hundred days the strength of one's *ch'i* will develop a hundredfold.

The Yellow Emperor said:

Human life begins with the union of *yin* and *yang* in the womb. At the moment of this union one must be careful to avoid the "nine misfortunes." The first is children conceived during daylight, who are prone to vomiting. The second is children conceived at midnight when the interaction of heaven and earth is obstructed who, if not born mute, are either deaf or blind. The third is children conceived during eclipses of the sun, who will suffer physical deformity and injury.[161] The fourth is children conceived during thunder and lightning when heaven is angry and threatening. These will easily succumb to insanity. The fifth is children conceived during eclipses of the moon, who will come to misfortune along with their mothers.[162] The sixth is children conceived during a rainbow, who will meet with misfortune in whatever they do.[163] The seventh is children conceived at the winter or summer solstice, whose birth will bring harm to their fathers and mothers. The eighth is children conceived on the nights of the first and last quarters of the moon, or the full moon,[164] who will become bandits and wildly reckless.[165] The ninth is children conceived after intoxication or overeating, who will be afflicted with insanity, ulcers, hemorrhoids, and sores.

Su Nü said:

There is an established method[166] for obtaining children. Purify the heart and banish all cares, compose your girdle and gown,[167] maintain humility[168] and an attitude of solemnity.[169] Then on the third day following the cessation of menses, after midnight and before cockcrow, begin to engage in foreplay until she is fully aroused. Now go with her, adapting to her ways and sharing her joy. Withdraw[170] the body slightly and ejaculate, being sure not to penetrate too deeply, but only to the "wheat teeth."[171] Further than this and one will have passed the "child's gate"[172] and will fail to enter the "child's door."[173] If one follows the proper methods, the children begotten will be virtuous[174] and long lived.

Su Nü said:

In uniting *yin* and *yang* one must avoid certain taboos. Partners who take advantage of the time when the *ch'i* is most vigorous[175] will bear long-lived offspring. If man and wife are both advanced in age, although they may be able to conceive, the resulting children will be short lived.

The Yellow Emperor said: "What are the physical traits by which a man may recognize a woman suitable for intercourse?" Su Nü answered:

Women possessing the appropriate traits are by nature gentle and soft spoken. Their silky hair should be jet black, their flesh tender, and bones fine. They should be neither too tall nor too short, neither too fat nor too slight. Their "bore hole" should be elevated[176] and the private parts without hair.[177] Their *ching* secretions should be copious. They should be between twenty-five and thirty years[178] of age and never have borne children. While having intercourse with them, their secretions should flow generously and they should move with abandon. Their perspiration should flow freely and they should follow the movements of the man. If a man can

find this kind of woman, even if he does not practice the prescribed methods, it will do him no harm.

The following are taboo days of the bedchamber: the last and first days of the moon, the first and last quarters of the moon, the six *ting* or six *ping* days of the sexegenary cycle,[179] the "*p'o* days,"[180] the twenty-eighth of the month, eclipses of the sun and moon,[181] high winds, heavy rains, earthquakes, resounding thunder and lightning, great cold or heat,[182] and the five days of "bidding farewell and welcoming"[183] of each of the four seasons. These taboos should be most strictly observed during one's Terrestrial Branch year.[184] One must not unite *yin* and *yang* on the sexegenary cycle days *ping-tzu* and *ting-ch'ou* following the summer solstice and *keng-shen* and *hsin-yu* following the winter solstice,[185] as well as when one has just washed the hair or completed a long trip, when tired, overjoyed, or enraged. Men in their declining years should not foolishly[186] shed their *ching*.

Su Nü continued her discourse:

One must not have intercourse on the sixteenth day of the fifth lunar month when heaven and earth are mating.[187] To transgress this brings sure death within three years. How can this be verified? On the eve of this day simply hang a one-foot piece of new cloth from an eastern wall. Look at it on the following day and it will be stained the color of blood. This should be strictly avoided.

Ts'ai Nü asked: "How is it that some suffer the illness of intercourse with ghosts?" P'eng Tsu answered:

This occurs when *yin* and *yang* do not have an opportunity to interact, and one's desire becomes overwhelming. Then ghosts and demons assume human appearance and engage in intercourse with them. In the art of intercourse they are superior to human beings. Those who indulge in this for a long time become deranged. They keep it secret and hide it from the world, not daring to tell others. Considering this something sublime,[188] they thus end up dying by themselves without anyone knowing the cause. If one is afflicted with this condition, the remedy is simply to have the man or woman engage in intercourse for a whole day and night without the man ejaculating. Sufferers[189] will surely be cured within seven days. If one is physically too ex-hausted to engage in active sex,[190] then simply penetrate deeply and do not move. This also is beneficial. If untreated, one will be dead within a few years. If you want to verify the truth of this, go out in the spring or autumn to a place deep in the mountains or great marshes. Say and do nothing,[191] but simply stare off into the dis-tance, concentrating your thoughts exclu-sively on sexual relations. After three days and three nights, the body will become hot and cold by turns, the mind will become troubled and the vision blurred. A woman will then appear to a man or a man to a woman. When they engage in intercourse, the pleasure will exceed that enjoyed with ordinary human beings. However, one will become ill of a disease most difficult to cure. This is a result of the evil influence of resentment for being without a mate curs-ing later generations.[192] In the case of vir-gins or women of high position who suffer restrictions on having sexual relations with men, the remedy is to burn several *liang*[193] of sulphur,[194] and use this to fumigate the woman's body below her private parts. She should also take a "square-inch spoon-ful"[195] of powdered deer horn and she will be cured. You will behold the ghost weep-ing as it departs. Another prescription[196] is to take one "square-inch spoonful" of deer horn for three days, adjusting dosage to progress of the cure.[197]

Ts'ai Nü said: "I have heard you speak on the matter of intercourse. May I now venture to ask about taking drugs and which are effective?" P'eng Tsu answered:

To make a man strong and youthful, pro-tect him from loss of strength in the bed-room, and help him retain his color, nothing surpasses deer horn.[198] The method of preparation is to shave ten *liang* of powder from the antler and combine it with one raw eight-point aconite root. Take a "square-inch spoonful" three times daily. The effect is very good. One can also[199] simmer[200] the deer horn until it turns slightly yellow and take this by itself. This also helps to preserve youth, but the effect is slower and not as good as combin-ing it with aconite root. Take this for twen-ty days and one will feel a great effect. One can also add[201] to the deer horn an equal amount of Lung-hsi[202] tuckahoe root pounded and sieved. Take one "square-

inch spoonful" three times daily. This gives a man long life and prevents declining vigor in the bedroom.

The Yellow Emperor asked Su Nü a question and she replied:

A woman of twenty-eight or nine may appear like twenty-three or four. She is full of *yin-ch'i* and uncontrollably desirous of a man. Food has lost its taste, there are pal-pitations in her pulse and on testing, her "*ching* pulse" is full. Secretions stain her garments and parasites resembling horse-tails three-inches long appear in her private parts. Those with red heads are sluggish, while those with black heads cause froth-ing. The remedy is to form wheat dough into the shape of a "jade stalk" of any de-sired length or size. Apply soy sauce and wrap with two lengths of cotton cloth. In-sert it into the private parts and when the worms appear, withdraw it and then rein-sert. This is as effective as if one had se-cured the services of the imperial physi-cian. The maximum number of worms is thirty and the minimum twenty.

Prescriptions of Su Nü
Su Nü fang

The Yellow Emperor addressed a ques-tion to Su Nü saying:

Men are endowed with equal amounts of *yin* and *yang ch'i*. However, often in the exercise of his *yang*, a man first suffers affliction in the ears and eyes.[1] Although it is something he is very fond of, he may fail to achieve erection, his strength may de-cline, and he may be unable to maintain robust health. May I venture to ask what is the remedy?

Su Nü answered:

What Your Majesty asks about is some-thing that affects all people. The interplay of *yin* and *yang* in the body is determined by one's relationship with women. Because of the danger of shortening one's life, a man must practice self-control and not think only of lust for women. Those who violate this principle will exhaust their strength. One must not fail to be mindful of the conditions producing the "seven ills." To be constantly aware and vigilant is the *tao* of long life. If illness and disease appear, they must be addressed with medicines. The violations I have mentioned are seven.[2] The first set of taboos relate to the last or first days of the moon, the first or last quarters of the moon, the full moon, and the six *ting* days of the sexegenary cycle.[3] Intercourse on these days will damage the *ching* of one's offspring,[4] make a man impotent in the face of the enemy,[5] cause frequent spontaneous erections,[6] red or yellow coloration of the urine, spermatorrhea, and early death. The second set of taboos relates to thunder and lightning and wind and rain, for these are times when *yin* and *yang* are obscure, heaven and earth tremble, and the sun and moon are without luster. Intercourse at these times will produce children who are mad, deaf, blind, mute, absent minded or forgetful, emotionally disturbed, alternately happy and anxious, or depressed. The third set of taboos relates to immediately after eating and drinking when the energy of the food has not yet been distributed, the stomach is full, and the Five Viscera sensitive. To have intercourse at these times will result in injury to the Six Bowels; red, white, or yellow coloration of the urine; pain in the lower back and stiffness in the head and back of the neck; or swelling and distension of the chest and abdomen. This destruction of the body and early death accord perfectly with the laws of nature. The fourth set of taboos relates to the time just after urination when the *ching-ch'i* is weak, the "nutritive *ch'i*"[7] is unstable, and the "defensive *ch'i*"[8] not yet deployed. To have intercourse at this time makes a man suffer deficiency syndrome, blockage of *yin* and *yang-ch'i*, and loss of appetite. The abdomen will feel bloated and full of knots, and one will be uneasy, absent minded, or subject to inappropriate joy and anger as if mad. The fifth set of taboos relates to the times after work or a long journey on foot when the body is weary, the "nutritive *ch'i*" is not yet settled, and the "defensive *ch'i*" not yet deployed. If one has intercourse at these times, the *ch'i* of the internal organs will interfere with each other. It causes deficiency of *ch'i*, shortness of breath, dryness of the lips and mouth, perspiration, indigestion, distension in the chest and abdomen, soreness in a hundred places, and restlessness. The sixth set of taboos relates to the times immediately after bathing when the head,

body, and hair are wet, or after heavy work when the sweat pours down like rain. To have intercourse at these times will surely bring harm if there is a cold wind. The lower abdomen will become acutely painful, the lower back aching and stiff, the four limbs sore and painful, and the Five Viscera sensitive. It may rise up to attack the head and face or cause discharge below. The seventh taboo relates to sudden erection of the "jade stalk" while speaking with a woman. To have intercourse at this time, without benefit of propriety to guard your *ch'i*, causes the pores to open and pain and injury to the inside of the "stalk." Externally, it disturbs the body's musculature and internally injures the Bowels and Viscera. If this happens on the first night of marriage, it may stop up the ears and cause the vision to become blurred. One may become fearful and subject to fits of joy and forgetfulness. One will feel as if there is a pestle pounding in the diaphragm and begin coughing. The internal organs will be severely damaged. This is also extremely weakening to the woman. One must not fail to guard against this. The results of transgressing these seven taboos have already been graphically described. However, heaven has provided marvelous medicines and there are remedies to cure them.

The Yellow Emperor addressed a question to Kao-yang Fu[9] saying:

I know that Su Nü clearly understands the meridians, Viscera, and Bowels and conditions of deficiency and excess. She understands the "five ills"[10] and "seven injuries" of the male, and blockages of *yin* and *yang*, red or white vaginal discharge, and infertility in the female. Men are endowed with equal amounts of *yin* and *yang ch'i*; what then are the causes of their illnesses? I would like to inquire and request an explanation.

He replied: "This is a profound question! The diseases associated with the 'five ills,' 'six exhaustions,'[11] and 'seven injuries' of the male all have their root causes and symptoms." The Emperor said: "Wonderful! I would like to hear all about the illnesses associated with the 'seven injuries.'" He replied: "The first is perspiration of the private parts. The second is weakness of the private parts. The third is transparency of the *ching*. 95

The fourth is scarcity of the *ching*. The fifth is dampness and itching below the private parts. The sixth is infrequent urination. The seventh is impotence and inability to successfully perform the sex act. These are the symptoms associated with the 'seven injuries.'" The Yellow Emperor said: "If these are the 'seven injuries,' what is their cure?" He answered:

There is a marvelous medicine suitable for all four seasons which is called *fu-ling* (tuckahoe root). Whether spring, autumn, winter, or summer, the cure should follow the conditions of the illness. If the illness is "cold" add "hot" herbs; if the illness is "warm," use some "cool" liquid.[12] If one suffers from "wind,"[13] then add some anti-wind medicine. Medicines should be added according to color and pulse diagnosis of the illness as set forth in this classic.[14]

During the three months of spring one should take "rejuvenation pills."[15] This cures a man of the "five ills" and "seven injuries," weakness and contraction of the private parts, sores beneath the scrotum, pain in the lower back preventing one from bending and rising, a frequent sensation of heat and itching in the knees during cold weather, or periodic swelling and difficulty in walking, tearing in the wind, nearsightedness, coughing, weakness and sallowness of the whole body, tightness around the navel with pain extending to the bladder, blood in the urine, pain and injury to the "stalk" with occasional discharge, perspiration that stains the garments red or yellow, or nightmares, dry mouth and stiff tongue, thirst, irregular eating or insufficient strength, and a frequent "reversal of *ch'i*."[16] If one violates the "seven taboos" and thus suffers the "ills" or "injuries," the following medicine has proven extremely effective:

苻苓   *Sclerotium poriae cocos (tuckahoe root), 4 fen*. If one suffers difficulty in digestion, increase by one-third.

菖蒲   *Rhizoma acori graminei (sweetflag rhizome), 4 fen*. If one suffers deafness, increase by one-third.

山茱萸   *Fructus corni officinalis (fruit of Asiatic cornelian cherry), 4 fen*. If the body itches, increase by one-third.

栝樓根   *Radix trichosanthis, 4 fen*. If one suffers fever and thirst, increase by one-third.

兔絲子   *Semen Cuscutae (dodder seeds), 4 fen*. If one suffers impotence or premature ejaculation, increase by half.

牛膝   *Radix achyranthis bidentatae, 4 fen*. If the joints are stiff, double.

赤石脂   *Halloysitum rubrum, 4 fen*. If one suffers internal pathology, increase by one-third.

乾地黃   *Radix rehmanniae glutinosae (dried Chinese foxglove root), 7 fen*. If one suffers fever accompanied by irritability or oppression, increase by one-third.

細辛   *Herba asari cum radice (Chinese wild ginger), 4 fen*. If one suffers unclear vision, increase by one third.

防風   *Radix ledebouriellae sesloidis, 4 fen*. If one suffers "wind" syndrome, increase by one third.

薯蕷   *Radix dioscoreae oppositae, 4 fen*. If the genitals are clammy and itchy, increase by one-third.

續斷   *Radix dipsaci (Japanese teasel root), 4 fen*. If one suffers hemorrhoids, double.

蛇牀子   *Semen cnidii monnieri, 4 fen*. If one suffers deficiency of *ch'i*, increase by one third.

柏實   *Semen biotae orientalis (arborvitae seeds), 4 fen*. If one's strength is deficient, double.

巴戟天   *Radix morindae officinalis, 4 fen*. If one suffers debility and weakness, increase by one-third.

天雄   *Radix cynanchi, 4 fen, quick fry*. If one suffers "wind" syndrome, increase by one-third.

遠志皮   *Radix polygalae tenuifoliae (root of Chinese senega), 4 fen*. If one is fearful and anxious, increase by one-third.

石斛   *Herba dendrobii (dendrobium stem), 4 fen*. If the body is in pain, double.

杜仲   *Cortex eucommiae ulmoidis (eucommia bark), 4 fen*. If the *yang* is exhausted and there is pain in the waist, increase by one-third.

菩蓉   *Herba cistanches (stem of broomrape), 4 fen. If one is cold and debilitated, double.*

The preceding twenty herbs should be pounded, sieved, and formed with honey into pills the size of dryandra seeds.[17] First take three pills, and thereafter three daily. If there is no perceptible effect, gradually increase the dosage using your own judgment. This prescription also may be taken in powder form with plain rice congee. Take one "square-inch spoonful." The effects will be felt after seven days, and one will be cured after ten. After thirty days, the remaining negative *ch'i* will return to normal. If one takes this for a long time, even the old will become youthful again. While taking it, avoid pork, mutton, malt sugar, cold water, raw vegetables, fermented elm seed[18] preparation, and so forth.

The Yellow Emperor asked another question: "What is the best prescription for the three months of summer? I would consider myself very fortunate to hear your answer." [Kao-yang Fu] replied:

One should take "kidney-strengthening tuckahoe pills" to cure male internal deficiency syndrome,[19] loss of appetite, fits of elation and forgetfulness, depression, uncontrolled rage, bloating of the body, red or yellow coloration of the urine, spermatorrhea, painful constrictions in the bladder, pain and numbness in the calves making it difficult to stretch them out and walk, thirst, and swelling in the chest and abdomen. All of these symptoms are the result of violating the "seven taboos" that have been explained earlier. The cure should be appropriate to the condition. The following prescription may be used:

茯苓   *Sclerotium poriae cocus (tuckahoe root), 2 liang. If one suffers difficulty in digestion, double.*

附子   *Radix aconiti carmichaeli praeparata (prepared accessory root of Szechuan aconite), 2 liang, quick-fried. If one suffers "wind" syndrome, increase by one-third.*

山茱萸   *Fructus corni officinalis (fruit of Asiatic cornelia cherry), 3 liang. If the body itches, increase by one-third.*

杜仲   *Cortex eucommiae ulmoidis (eucommia bark), 2 liang. If one suffers pain in the waist, increase by one-third.*

牡丹   *Cortex moutan radicis (cortex of tree peony root), 2 liang. If there is ch'i circulating in the abdomen, increase by one-third.*

澤瀉   *Rhizoma alismatis plantago-aquaticae (water plantain rhizome), 3 liang. If one suffers "water ch'i" [edema], increase by one-third.*

薯蕷   *Radix dioscoreae oppositae, 3 liang. If there is "wind" in the head, double.*

桂心   *Cortex cinnamomi cassiae (inner bark of Saigon cinnamon), 6 liang. If one's color is insufficient, increase by one-third.*

細辛   *Herba asari cum radice (Chinese wild ginger), 3 liang. If one suffers unclear vision, increase by one-third.*

石斛   *Herba dendrobii (dendrobium stem), 2 liang. If the genitals are clammy and itching, increase by one-third.*

菩蓉   *Herba cistanches (stem of broomrape), 3 liang. If the body is debilitated, increase by one-third.*

黃耆   *Radix astragali (milk-vetch root), 4 liang. If the body suffers pain, increase by one-third.*

The preceding twelve herbs should be pounded, sieved, and formed with honey into pills the size of dryandra seeds First take seven pills, and thereafter two a day. Avoid raw scallions, raw vegetables, pork, cold water, vinegar, parsley, and so forth.

Again the Yellow Emperor asked: "Now that I have learned of the excellent remedies for the ills of spring and summer, what is the prescription for the three months of autumn?" [Kao-yang Fu] answered:

One should use "kidney-strengthening tuckahoe pills"[20] to cure male kidney deficiency and coldness, internal injury of the Five Viscera, and sensitivity to cold wind causing a feeling of clamminess and itching over the entire body. One also may become distracted and oblivious while walking, suffer loss of appetite, or blurred vision. The body feels constrained and anxious and the lower back is sore and stiff. One becomes unable to eat and daily thinner and more emaciated. There is a stifling feeling in the breast and one is subject to coughing. Help is required to turn over and support to stand up. Acupuncture, moxibustion, and drugs can offer only a slight improvement. Some are afflicted by wind when riding horseback; some fail to cover themselves indoors or to observe the proper measure in eating and drinking; and some overexert themselves. Some experience dryness of the mouth and parched tongue, or drooling, nocturnal emissions, blood in the urine or urinary incontinence, itchiness and dampness beneath the private parts, a feeling of uneasiness and palpitations, tension in the lower abdomen, soreness and pain in the four limbs, labored breathing, swelling of the body, or *ch'i* rising to the chest and ribs. Physicians who fail to recognize these symptoms mistakenly prescribe superfluous remedies. The appropriate prescription is as follows:

茯苓   *Sclerotium poriae cocos (tuckahoe root), 3 liang.*

防風   *Radix ledebouriellae sealoidis, 2 liang.*

桂心   *Cortex cinnamomi cassiae (inner bark of Saigon cinnamon), 2 liang.*

白朮   *Rhizoma atractylodia macrocephalae, 2 liang.*

細辛   *Herba asari cum radice (Chinese wild ginger), 2 liang.*

山茱萸   *Fructus corni officinalis (fruit of Asiatic cornelian cherry), 2 liang.*

薯蕷   *Radix dioscroeae oppositae, 2 liang.*

澤瀉   *Rhizoma aliamatis plantagoaquaticae (water plantain rhizome), 2 liang.*

附子   *Radix aconiti carmichaeli praeparata (prepared accessory root of Szechwan aconite), 2 liang, quick fried.*

乾地黃   *Radix rehmanniae glutinosae (dried Chinese foxglove root), 2 liang.*

紫菀   *Radix asteris tatarici (purple aster root), 2 liang.*

牛膝   *Radix achyranthis bidentatae, 3 liang.*

芍藥   *Radix paeoniae lactiflorae (peony root), 2 liang.*

丹參   *Radix salviae miltiorrhizae, 2 liang.*

黃耆   *Radix astragali (milk-vetch root), 2 liang.*

沙參   *Radix glehniae littoralis (root of beech silver-top), 2 liang.*

蓯蓉   *Herba cistanches (stem of broomrape), 2 liang.*

乾薑   *Rhizoma zingiberis officinalis (dried ginger rhizome), 2 liang.*

玄參   *Radix scrophulariae ningpoensis (Ningpo figwort root), 2 liang.*

人參   *Radix ginseng, 2 liang.*

苦參   *Radix sophorae flavescentis, 2 liang.*

獨活   *Radix duhuo, 2 liang.*

The preceding twenty-two ingredients should be pounded, sieved, and formed with honey into pills the size of dryandra seeds. Take five pills before eating, using wine to wash them down. Avoid sour pickles, raw scallions, peaches and plums, sparrow meat, raw vegetables, pork, fermented elm seed preparation, and so forth.

Again the Yellow Emperor asked: "There are excellent prescriptions for the spring, summer, and autumn seasons. What then is the remedy for the three months of winter?" [Kao-yang Fu] replied:

"Life-saving tuckahoe pills" are the cure for the male's "five ills" and "seven injuries," blurred vision, tearing in the wind, stiffness in the head and neck preventing it from turning, a feeling of pressure in the heart and belly extending up to the chest and ribs and down to the lower back, pain in both the exterior and interior of the body, difficulty in breathing, coughing up of food, sallowness of countenance, urinary incontinence, transparency of the *ching* and spermatorrhea, impotence and inability to perform the sex act, or soreness and pain in the feet and calves. Some experience mental oppression and irritation, bloating of the body, profuse perspiration, muscle spasms in the four limbs that are sometimes moderate and sometimes acute, nightmares, shortness of breath, dry mouth and parched tongue resembling "emaciation-thirst disease," fits of joy and forgetfulness, or depression and choked sobbing. The following medicine addresses these conditions and strengthens all deficiencies. It makes a man stout and healthy and doubles his strength. If taken regularly this prescription cures the hundred ailments:

茯苓	*Sclerotium poriae cocos (tuckahoe root), 2 liang.*
白朮	*Rhizoma atractylodis macrocephalae,*[21] *2 liang.*
澤瀉	*Rhizoma alismatis plantago-aquaticae (water plantain rhizome), 2 liang.*
牡蒙	*Radix salviae miltiorrhizae, 2 liang.*
桂心	*Cortex cinnamomi cassiae (inner bark of Saigon cinnamon), 2 liang.*
牡蠣	*Concha ostreae (oyster shell), 2 liang.*
牡荆子	*Fructus viticis cannabifoliae, 2 liang.*
薯蕷	*Radix dioscoreae oppositae, 2 liang.*
杜仲	*Cortex eucommiae ulmoidis (eucommia bark), 2 liang.*
天雄	*Radix cynanchi, 2 liang, quick fried.*
人參	*Radix ginseng, 2 liang.*
石長生	*Herba pteridis, 2 liang.*
附子	*Radix aconti carmichaeli praeparata (prepared accessory root of Szechwan aconite), 2 liang.*
乾薑	*Rhizoma zingiberis officinalis (dried ginger rhizome), 2 liang.*
菟絲子	*Semen cuscutae (dodder seeds), 2 liang.*
巴戟天	*Radix morindae officinalis, 2 liang.*
蓯蓉	*Herba cistanches (stem of broomrape), 2 liang.*
山茱萸	*Fructus corni officinalis (fruit of Asiatic cornelian cherry), 2 liang.*
甘草	*Radix glycyrrhizae uralensis (licorice root), 2 liang, roasted.*
天門冬	*Tuber asparagi cochinchinesis (tuber of Chinese asparagus), 2 liang, remove the heart.*

The preceding twenty ingredients should be pounded, sieved, and formed with honey into pills the size of dryandra seeds. First eat five pills, or take with a bit of wine. Avoid seaweed, cabbage, carp, raw scallions, pork, vinegar, and so forth.

Again the Yellow Emperor asked: "I have now learned of the medicines for the four seasons. Is there a medicine that can be taken all year round?" [Kao-yang Fu] answered:

There is a powder for all four seasons that is called "tuckahoe powder." You need not observe seasonal prohibitions of cold or hot. If taken over a long period, it will lengthen one's years and restore strength to the aged. The prescription is as follows:

茯苓	*Sclerotium poriae cocos (tuckahoe root).*
鍾乳	*Stalactitum (stalactite), ground.*
雲母粉	*Mica, powder.*
石斛	*Herba dendrobii (dendrobium stem).*
菖蒲	*Rhizoma acori graminei (sweetflag rhizome).*
柏子人	*Semen biotae orientalis (arborvitae seeds).*
菟絲子	*Semen cuscutae (dodder seeds).*
續斷	*Radix dipsaci (Japanese teasel root.)*
杜仲	*Cortex eucommiae ulmoidis (eucommia bark).*
天門冬	*Tuber asparagi cochinchinesis (tuber of Chinese asparagus).*
牛膝	*Radix achyranthis bidentatae.*
五味子	*Fructus schisandrae chinesis (schisandra fruit).*
澤瀉	*Rhizoma alismatis plantago-aquaticae (water plantain rhizome).*
遠志	*Radix polygalae tenuifoliae (root of Chinese senega).*
甘菊花	*Flos chrysanthemi morifolii (chrysanthemum flower).*
蛇床子	*Semen cnidii monnieri.*
薯蕷	*Radix dioscoreae oppositae.*
山茱萸	*Fructus corni officinalis (fruit of Asiatic cornelian cherry).*
天雄	*Radix cynanchi.*
石韋	*Folium pyrrosiae.*
乾地黃	*Radix rehmanniae glutinosae.*
蓯蓉	*Herba cistanches (stem of broomrape).*

The preceding twenty-two ingredients should be pounded and sieved into a powder. Take one "square-inch spoonful" with wine twice daily. There will be perceptible effect after twenty days and complete recovery after thirty. After 100 days, one's *ch'i* will be healthy and strong. If taken over a long period, at eighty or ninety an old gentleman will be like a youth. Avoid sour pickles, mutton, malt sugar, carp, pork, fermented elm seed preparation, and so forth.

Kao-yang Fu said:

All of the prescriptions in this classic were created by the immortals. Their ability to cure illness already has been thoroughly discussed. One must follow these instructions, for from the beginning of time they have never failed to cure an illness or save a life.

"Tuckahoe rescue remedy":

苻苓	*Sclerotium poriae cocos (tuckahoe root), Boil 5 chin in lye ten times, boil the liquid ten times, and the clear water ten times.*
松脂	*Colophony (rosin), Boil 5 chin using the same method as for the tuckahoe root. At each stage boil forty times.*
天門冬	*Tuber asparagi cochinchinesis (tuber of Chinese asparagus), 5 chin, remove hearts and skin, dry in the sun and powder.*
牛酥	*Butter, 3 chin, clarified thirty times.*
白蜜	*White honey, 3 chin, heated until the froth disappears.*
蠟	*Bees wax, 3 chin, clarified thirty times.*

The preceding six ingredients should each be pounded and sieved. Fill a copper vessel with hot water. First add the butter,[22] then the wax, and then the honey. When they have melted, add the herbs and stir rapidly without interruption, making sure that all the ingredients are thoroughly blended. Place in a crock and seal tightly so that no *ch'i* escapes. First do not eat for one day. Even if the desire to eat arises, do not eat. Then eat an especially good meal until you are very full, after which stop eating and take two *liang*. After twenty days take four *liang*, and after another twenty days take eight *liang*. Form into tiny pills and take as many as can be swallowed at one time as a single dose. For the second round take four *liang* at first, after twenty days eight *liang*, and then after another twenty days two *liang*. For the third round, begin with eight *liang*, after twenty days two, and after twenty more four. At the end of this one hundred and eight day period the dose is complete. Following this, take three pills as a supplement. Even if one no longer takes the medicine, continue the butter and honey to regulate the condition. Best

results are obtained when this medicine is taken with a *sheng* of fine wine. In compounding this prescription, select the "monarchial and ministerial days" and strictly avoid the days designated *hsing* 刑, *sha* 煞, and *yen* 厭 of the almanac, as well as the inauspicious days of the four seasons.[23]

"Tuckahoe paste":

苻苓	*Sclerotium poriae cocos (tuckahoe root), clean and remove skin.*
松脂	*Colophony (rosin), 24 chin.*
松子人	*Pine nuts, 12 chin.*
柏子人	*Semen biotae orientalis (arborvitae seeds), 12 chin.*

The preceding four ingredients should be simmered according to the proper method. Do not simmer the pine and cypress kernels, but pound and sieve them. Place two *tou* and four *sheng* of white honey in a copper vessel, add water and decoct over a low flame for a day and a night. Add the herbs one at a time and stir so that they blend together. Continue to decoct for seven days and seven nights over a low flame. After this, form into pills the size of small dates and take seven pills three times a day. When you feel like giving up food, take the whole dose all at once so that you are full. Immediately you will feel light in body, clear sighted, and youthful.

Essentials of the Jade Chamber

Yü-fang chih-yao

P'eng Tsu said:

The Yellow Emperor mounted 1,200 women and thus achieved immortality, whereas the ordinary man cuts down his life with just one. Is there not a great gap between knowledge and ignorance? Those who know the *tao* regret only having too few opportunities for mounting. It is not always necessary to have those who are beautiful, but simply those who are young, who have not yet borne children,[1] and who are amply covered with flesh. If one can secure but seven or eight such women, it will be of great benefit.

P'eng Tsu said:

There is no mystery to the *tao* of intercourse. It is simply to be free and unhurried and to value harmony above all. Fondle her *tan-t'ien*[2] and "seek to fill her mouth."[3] Press deeply into her and move ever so slightly to induce her *ch'i*.[4] When the woman feels the influence of *yang* there are subtle signs. Her ears become hot as if she had drunk good wine. Her breasts swell[5] and fill the whole hand when held. She moves her neck repeatedly while her feet agitate. Becoming passionate and alluring[6] she suddenly clasps the man's body. At this moment, draw back slightly and penetrate her shallowly. The *yang* will then gain *ch'i* at the expense of the *yin*. Also the secretions of the Five Viscera are released at the tongue, or what Ch'ih Sung tzu[7] called, "the 'jade liquid' that allows one to go without food." When having intercourse one should imbibe much of her tongue secretions and saliva. This produces a feeling of openness[8] in the stomach as if one has just been instantly cured of "emaciation-thirst disease" with a draught of herbal tea. Rising *ch'i* sinks to its proper level, the skin becomes glossy and one has the air of a maiden. The *tao* is not far to seek; it is just that ordinary people do not recognize it.

Ts'ai Nü said: "To gain years of life without going against the grain of natural human impulses, is this not a great joy?" Taoist Liu Ching[9] said:

The *tao* of mounting women is first to engage in slow foreplay so as to harmonize your spirits and arouse her desire,[10] and only after a long time to unite. Penetrate when soft and quickly withdraw when hard, making the intervals between advancing and withdrawing relaxed and slow. Furthermore, do not throw yourself into it as from a great height, for this overturns the Five Viscera and injures the collateral meridians,[11] leading to a hundred ailments. But if one can have intercourse without ejaculating and engage several tens of times in one day and night without losing *ching*, all illnesses will be greatly improved and one's lifespan will daily increase.[12]

Even greater benefits are reaped by frequently changing female partners. To change partners more than ten times in one night is especially good.[13]

The classics on immortality[14] say that the *tao* of "returning the *ching* to nourish the brain" is to wait during intercourse until the *ching* is greatly aroused and on the point of emission, and then, using the two middle fingers of the left hand, press just between the scrotum and anus. Press down with considerable force and expel a long breath while gnashing the teeth several tens of times, but without holding the breath.[15] Then allow yourself to ejaculate. The *ching*, however, will not be able to issue forth and instead will travel from the "jade stalk" upward and enter the brain. This method has been transmitted among the immortals who are sworn to secrecy by blood pact. They dared not communicate it carelessly for fear of bringing misfortune on themselves.

If one desires to derive benefit from mounting women, but finds that the *ching* is overly aroused,[16] then quickly lift the head, open the eyes wide and gaze to the left and right, up and down. Contract the lower parts, hold the breath and the *ching* will naturally be stilled. Do not carelessly transmit this to others. Those who succeed in shedding their *ching* but twice a month,[17] or twenty-four times in one year, will all gain long life, and at 100 or 200 years will be full of color and without illness.[18]

The following prescription strengthens the male in the bedchamber and enables him to perform more than ten times without intermission:

蛇床   *Semen cnidi monnieri.*
遠志   *Radix polygalae tenuifoliae (root of Chinese senega).*
續繼   *Radix dipsaci (Japanese teasel root).*
縱容   *Herba cistanches (stem of broom-rape).*

The preceding four ingredients should be powdered in equal amounts and a "square inch spoonful" taken three times daily. Duke Ts'ao took this and had intercourse with seventy women in one night.

Prescription for enlarging the male member:

柏子仁   *Semen biotae orientalis (arbor-vitae seeds), 5 fen.*
白斂   *Radix ampelopsis, 4 fen.*
白朮   *Rhizoma atractylodis macrocephalae, 7 fen.*
桂心   *Cortex cinnamomi cassiae (inner bark of Saigon cinnamon), 3 fen.*
附子   *Radix aconiti carmichaeli praeparata (prepared root of aconite), 2 fen.*

The preceding five ingredients should be powdered and a "square-inch spoonful" taken twice daily after eating. Within ten or twenty days there will be enlargement.

Prescription for shrinking the woman's "jade gate":

硫黃   *Sulphur, 4 fen.*
遠志   *Radix polygalae tenuifoliae (root of Chinese senega), 2 fen.*

These should be powdered and placed in a silk pouch that is inserted in the "jade gate."

If one is in a great hurry, another prescription calls for:

硫黃   *Sulphur, 2 fen.*
蒲華   *Pollen typhae (cattail pollen), 2 fen.*

These should be powdered and three pinches added to a *sheng* of hot water. Wash the "jade gate" with this solution for twenty days and she will be like an unmarried girl.

Secrets of the Jade Chamber

Yü-fang pi-chüeh

Ch'ung Ho tzu[1] said:

One *yin* and one *yang* are called the *tao*;[2] intercourse and procreation are its function.[3] Is this principle not far reaching? The guiding principles are contained in the Yellow Emperor's questions to Su Nü and in P'eng K'eng's[4] responses[5] to the King of Yin.

Ch'ung Ho tzu said:

Those who would cultivate their *yang*[6] must not allow women to steal glimpses of this art. Not only is this of no benefit to one's *yang*, but it may even lead to injury or illness. This is what is called, "Lend a man your sword and when the time comes to roll up sleeves for a fight, you cannot win."[7]

P'eng Tsu said:

If a man wishes to derive the greatest benefit, it is best to find a woman who has no knowledge of this *tao*. If he chooses young maidens for mounting, his complexion too will become like a maiden's.[8] When it comes to women, one should be vexed only by their not being young.[9] If one can obtain those between fourteen or fifteen and eighteen or nineteen, this is the best.[10] In

any event, they should not exceed thirty. Those not yet thirty but who have given birth are of no benefit. My late master handed down this *tao* and lived for 3,000 years. If combined with drugs one can attain immortality.

Those who seek to practice the *tao* of uniting *yin* and *yang* for the purpose of gaining *ch'i* and cultivating life must not limit themselves to just one woman. You should get three or nine or eleven; the more the better. Absorb her *ching* secretions by mounting the "vast spring" and "returning the *ching*."[11] Your skin will become glossy, your body light, your eyes bright, and your *ch'i* so strong that you will be able to overcome all your enemies. Old men will feel like twenty and young men will feel their strength increased a hundredfold.

When having intercourse with women, as soon as you feel yourself aroused, change partners. By changing partners you can lengthen your life. If you return habitually to the same woman, her *yin-ch'i* will become progressively weaker and this will be of little benefit to you.

Taoist priest Ch'ing Niu said:

To frequently change female partners brings increased benefit. More than ten partners in one night is especially good. If one constantly has intercourse with the same woman, her *ching-ch'i* will become weak, and this is not only of no great benefit to the man, but will cause her to become thin and emaciated.

Ch'ung Ho tzu said:

It is not only *yang* that can be cultivated, but *yin* too. The Queen Mother of the West cultivated her *yin* and attained the *tao*. As soon as she had intercourse with a man he would immediately take sick, while her complexion would become radiant without the use of rouge or powder. She always ate curds and plucked the "five stringed lute" thereby harmonizing her heart, concentrating her mind, and was without any other desire.

The Queen Mother had no husband but was fond of intercourse with young boys. Therefore, this cannot be an orthodox teaching; but can the Queen Mother be alone in this?[12]

When having intercourse with men, you must calm the heart and still the mind. If the man is not yet fully aroused,[13] you must wait for his *ch'i* to arrive and slightly restrain your emotion to attune yourself to him.[14] Do not move or become agitated lest your *yin-ching* become exhausted first. If your *yin-ching* becomes exhausted first, this leaves one in a deficient state and susceptible to cold wind illnesses. Some women become jealous and vexed when they hear their husbands having intercourse with another woman. Their *yin-ching* becomes aroused, they sit up indignantly,[15] and their *ching* secretions come forth spontaneously. Wanness and premature aging result from this. One must exercise restraint and be extremely careful.

If a woman knows the way of cultivating her *yin* and causing the two *ch'i* to unite harmoniously, then it may be transformed into a male child.[16] If she is not having intercourse for the sake of offspring, she can divert the fluids[17] to flow back into the hundred vessels. By using *yang* to nourish *yin*, the hundred ailments disappear, one's color becomes radiant and the flesh fine. One can enjoy long life and be forever like a youth. If a woman is able to master this *tao* and have frequent intercourse with men, she can fast for nine days without knowing hunger. Those who are sick and have sexual relations with ghosts are able to fast but become emaciated. How much more can we expect from intercourse with men?[18]

A man of twenty, as a rule, may ejaculate once in two days, at thirty once in three days, at forty once in four days, and at fifty once in five days. After sixty one should refrain from ejaculating altogether.

Ch'ung Ho tzu said:

If one indulges in emotional extremes and unbridled passion, one surely will suffer harmful illnesses. This is obvious to those with experience in sexual relations. Because one may become ill from this, one may also be cured by it. To cure a hangover by means of wine is an apt comparison.

If one has intercourse with the eyes open,[19] gazing upon each other's bodies, or lights a fire to look at illustrated books, one will be afflicted with drowsiness of the eyes or blindness.[20] The remedy is to have intercourse at night with the eyes closed.

If during intercourse you place the enemy upon your belly and raise your waist from below to join her, then you may suffer pain in the waist, tension in the lower abdomen, cramped feet and crooking of the back.[21] The remedy is to turn over so that you are on top, straighten your body and play with her leisurely.

When having intercourse by approaching the enemy from the side, and lifting her buttocks with your hands, one may suffer pain in the ribs. The remedy is to lie straight and play leisurely.

When having intercourse with the head lowered and throat stretched out, one will suffer heaviness of the head and stiffness in the back of the neck. The remedy is to place one's head upon the enemy's forehead and not lower it.

"Intercourse when overly full" refers to sexual play at midnight when the meal has not yet been digested. As a result, one will suffer chest pains with fullness of *ch'i*, a pulling sensation beneath the ribs, and rending within the breast. There will be a loss of appetite, knotting and blockage beneath the heart,[22] frequent vomiting of green and yellow matter,[23] fullness of stomach *ch'i*, and slow and irregular pulse. Some experience nose bleeds, or hardness and pain beneath the ribs and sores on the face. The remedy is to have intercourse after midnight and close to the approach of dawn.

"Intercourse under the influence of wine" refers to becoming ill as a result of intercourse while intoxicated and recklessly using force to penetrate to the extreme. This brings on "yellow jaundice" or "black jaundice"[24] and pain with *ch'i* beneath the ribs. If one continues in this way, there is a feeling between the thighs as if the scrotum is full of water and this extends up to the shoulders and arms.[25] In extreme cases there is pain in the chest and back, coughing and spitting up of blood and rising *ch'i*. The remedy is to abstain from wine's influence and have intercourse close to the approach of dawn, dallying leisurely and relaxing the body.

Having intercourse when overdue for urination produces urinary incontinence, *ch'i* pressure in the lower abdomen, and difficulty in urinating. One feels pain inside the "stalk" and a frequent urge to grip it with the hand. After a moment one feels like urinating. The remedy is to first urinate and then lie down and settle yourself. After a short time have intercourse leisurely and you will be cured.

To have intercourse when overdue to move the bowels will cause one to suffer piles and difficulty in defecating. After a time there will be dripping pus and blood, and sores will appear around the anus resembling bee hives. Straining at stool, the bowels do not move in timely fashion. Though suffering pain and bloating, one finds no rest in lying down. To cure this by means of the *tao*, first arise at cockcrow and go to the toilet. Then return to bed, settle yourself and slowly engage in playful dalliance. When your whole body has a feeling of relaxation, cause your partner to be slippery with secretions[26] and then withdraw. The illness will be cured in a miraculous way.[27] This also cures female maladies.

If you exceed the proper measure in intercourse, resulting in beads of sweat the size of pearls, then your thrashing about produces wind beneath the coverlets,[28] and in the condition of deficient *ching* and exhausted *ch'i*, wind pathogens are able to penetrate your body and sickness follows. Gradual weakening of the body leads to lameness and an inability to raise the hand to the head.[29] The remedy is to nourish the spirit and take a decoction of foxglove.

Wu Tzu-tu[30] said:

The *tao* for achieving clear vision is to wait for the impulse to ejaculate and then raise the head, hold the breath, and expel the air with a loud sound,[31] gazing to the left and right. Contract the abdomen and "return the *ching-ch'i*"[32] so that it enters the hundred vessels.

The method for preventing deafness is to wait for the impulse to ejaculate and then inhale deeply, clench the teeth, and hold the breath. Produce a humming sound in the ears, and then contract the abdomen, concentrate the *ch'i*, and circulate it throughout the body until it becomes very strong. Even in old age you will not become deaf.[33]

The *tao* of regulating the Five Viscera, facilitating digestion, and curing the hundred ills is to wait for the approach of ejaculation and then expand the belly and use the mind to internalize *ch'i*. After contracting,[34] the *ching* will disperse and return to the hundred vessels. Practice nine shallow and one deep strokes between the "zither strings" and "wheat teeth." Your positive *ch'i* will return and the negative *ch'i* depart. The method for preventing pain in the lower back is to stand against a wall and stretch out the waist without letting the head incline either too far forward or too far back. Level all those places where the lower back does not make contact with the wall. During the sex act you should strive for circulation. To supplement deficiency, nourish your body, and cure disease, you must refrain from ejaculating when the desire arises and recirculate it. The whole circulation will then experience a warming effect.[35]

The *tao* of *yin* and *yang* is to treasure the semen. If one can cherish it, one's life may be preserved. Whenever you ejaculate you must absorb the woman's *ch'i* to supplement your own. The process of "reestablishment by nine" means practicing the inner breath nine times.[36] "Pressing the one" refers to applying pressure with the left hand[37] beneath the private parts to return the *ching* and restore the fluid. "Absorbing the woman's *ch'i*" is accomplished by "nine shallow and one deep" strokes. Position your mouth opposite the enemy's mouth and exhale through the mouth. Now inhale, subtly drawing in the two primary vitalities,[38] swallow them and direct the *ch'i* with the mind down to the abdomen, thereby giving strength to the penis. Repeat this three times and then insert the penis to a shallow depth. Execute nine shallow and one deep strokes nine times nine, which is eighty-one, the completion of the *yang* number. When the "jade stalk" erects withdraw it; when it weakens insert it. This is the idea of "entering weak and withdrawing strong." The harmony of *yin* and *yang* is found between the "zither strings" and "wheat teeth." *Yang* is in peril[39] beneath the "rock of *k'un*"; *yin* is in peril among the "wheat teeth." At a shallow depth one gets *ch'i*, but too deep and the *ch'i* disperses. If one penetrates to the "grain seed," the liver is harmed, the eyes tear when facing the wind, and there are extra drops of urine on emptying the bladder. If one penetrates to the "odiferous mouse," the intestines[40] and lungs are harmed, and there is coughing and pain in the lower back. If penetration reaches the "rock of *k'un*," the spleen is harmed, the belly feels bloated, there is a fetid odor, frequent[41] diarrhea, and pain in the thighs. The hundred ailments arise in the "rock of *k'un*," and therefore one may indeed be harmed by intercourse. So when engaging in intercourse, do not seek to penetrate deeply.[42]

The Yellow Emperor said: "If one transgresses these prohibitions, what is the remedy?" Tzu-tu replied:

One must use a woman to restore oneself to health. The method is to have the woman lie straight on her back with her thighs nine inches apart. The man follows her, first drinking of her "jade fluid." After a long time begin to play with her "vast spring" and then slowly insert the "jade stalk," controlling it with your hand so that it reaches only as far as the area between the "zither strings" and "wheat teeth." When the enemy is writhing with passion and she is beside herself with excitement, always restrain yourself and do not ejaculate. Remain hard and strong for a count of thirty breaths and then slowly penetrate to the "rock of *k'un*." When you have reached the greatest depth and maximum size,[43] then withdraw. Rest for a moment until you become limp[44] and then insert it again. If you frequently practice entering weak and withdrawing strong, within ten days you will be as hard as iron and as hot as fire. In a hundred battles you will never be in peril.

In the union of *yin* and *yang* there are "seven taboos." The first taboo forbids intercourse on the last or first days of the moon and the first and last quarters of the moon, which are harmful to the *ch'i*. If one conceives at these times, the offspring will surely suffer corporal punishment. You should be extremely cautious of this.

The second taboo forbids intercourse during lightning storms or earthquakes when the pulse is bounding. If one conceives at these times, the offspring will surely suffer painful abscesses.

The third taboo forbids intercourse when one has just drunk wine or eaten, before the *ch'i* of the food has been distributed. The belly will become swollen[45] and the urine milky or turbid. Children conceived at these times will surely be insane.

The fourth taboo forbids intercourse after one has just urinated, when the *ching-ch'i* is exhausted. The channels of circulation become irregular, and if one conceives at this time, the offspring will be subject to evil influences.[46]

The fifth taboo forbids intercourse when one is weary from shouldering heavy burdens and one's mind is not yet calm. One will suffer pain in the sinews and waist, and if children are conceived, they will be short lived.

The sixth taboo forbids intercourse when one has just taken a bath and the hair and skin are not yet dry. This causes a man to suffer shortness of breath, and if a child is conceived at this time, it will not be whole.

The seventh taboo forbids intercourse when one's weapon is hard and fully enraged, but there is pain in the channel of the "stalk."[47] One should not then have intercourse,[48] for this results in internal injury and illness. These then are the "seven injuries."[49]

Those born deaf and dumb are the children of the last night of the last month of the lunar year, for at this time the hundred demons assemble and do not rest the entire night. The superior man observes abstinence, but the inferior secretly indulges in intercourse. The children of these unions surely will be deaf and dumb.

Those born to injury and death are called the "children of fire." If one has intercourse before the candle is extinguished, the offspring will suffer injury or death in the midst of the marketplace.[50]

Those who are born insane are the children of thunder and lightning. During the fourth and fifth lunar months when there are great rains and crashing thunder, the superior man observes abstinence, whereas the inferior secretly indulges in intercourse. Children conceived at this time will surely be insane.

Children devoured by tigers or wolves[51] are children of deep mourning. Filial sons wear clothes of hemp and abstain from meat. The superior man becomes wan and weary, whereas the inferior secretly indulges in intercourse. If a child is thus conceived, it will surely be eaten by tigers and wolves.

Children who drown die because their father and mother have committed an error.[52] They place the placenta in a copper vessel, cover, and bury it beneath a shady wall at a depth of seven feet.[53] This is called "the young child enclosed within" and ultimately it dies of drowning in water.

Children conceived during great winds are afflicted with multiple illnesses. Children conceived during thunder and lightning will become insane. Children conceived during extreme inebriation will surely be idiots or mad. Children conceived during great fatigue will suffer early death or injury. Children conceived during menses will die as soldiers. Children conceived during twilight will suffer much turmoil.[54] Children conceived in the middle of the night when everyone is resting will either be deaf or dumb. Children conceived at sunset will suffer misfortune from verbal disputes.[55] Children conceived at noon will be insane. Children conceived during the late afternoon will bring injury upon themselves.

P'eng Tsu said:

The method for obtaining children is to store and cultivate *ching-ch'i* and to not frequently shed it. If one has intercourse on the third or fifth day[56] after the conclusion of menses when the woman is clean and pure, the male offspring will be intelligent, talented, long lived, and honored; and the female pure, virtuous, and a worthy mate for a man of position.

To engage in the union of *yin* and *yang* during the hour of the approach of morning is beneficial and soothing to the body and one's radiance will be magnified. If children are conceived at this time, they will be rich, honored, and long lived.

If a man of full 100 years sires offspring, most will not be long lived. If a man of eighty is capable of mounting women of fifteen to eighteen and does not transgress any of the taboos, the children will all be long lived. An old woman of fifty who obtains a young husband may also have children.

On the *wu-tzu* (twenty-fifth) day of the sexagenary cycle, if a pregnant woman before the end of her first trimester takes the tassel of a man's cap, burns it, and drinks the ashes in wine, the child will be wealthy, honored, intelligent, and eminent. Keep this strictly secret!

If a woman is childless, have her hold fourteen[57] small beans in her left hand and with her right guide the tip of the man's private parts into her "gate." She should place the beans in her mouth simultaneous with the man's penetration. When she hears that the man's *ching* is coming down, she should swallow the beans. This is efficacious to the point of not 1 failure in 10,000. When the woman hears that the man's *ching* is coming, she must not miss the exact moment.

Ch'ung Ho tzu said:

To be pleasant and agreeable, virtuous and prudent, this is the beauty of the feminine nature. When the ample and the delicate are in perfect proportion, and the long and the short in harmonious measure, this is not only pleasing to the heart and eye, but can actually increase longevity.

If the *yang-ching* predominates, a male child will be born; if the *yin-ching* predominates, a female child will be born. *Yang-ching* becomes bone and *yin-ching* becomes flesh.

Wishing to have intercourse with

women, one must choose young girls who have not yet borne children and who are amply covered with flesh. They should have silken hair and small eyes with the whites and pupils clearly defined. The face and body should be moist and glossy. The sound of her speech should be harmonious and low. The bones of the four limbs and hundred joints should be buried in ample flesh, and the bones should not be prominent. Her private parts and underarms should be free of hair, but if hair is present, it should be fine and glossy.

The traits of women unsuitable as partners are tangled hair, a fearful countenance,[58] malletlike neck,[59] prominent Adam's apple, irregular teeth,[60] husky voice, large mouth, high nose bridge, lack of clarity in the eyes, long hairs about the mouth and chin resembling whiskers, prominent large joints, yellowish hair, scant flesh, and pubic hair that is copious, coarse, and growing contrariwise.[61] To consort with these types of women can only rob a man and do him harm.

You should not mount a woman whose flesh and skin are coarse or a woman whose body is too thin. Do not mount a woman who habitually prefers the superior position.[62] Do not mount a woman who has a manly voice and is assertive.[63] Do not mount women whose lower legs and thighs have hair. Do not mount those who are prone to jealousy. Do not mount those whose private parts are cold. Do not mount those who do not have good dispositions.[64] Do not mount those who overindulge in food. Do not mount those past forty.[65] Do not mount those whose hearts and bellies are out of order. Do not mount those whose hair grows contrariwise. Do not mount those whose bodies are always cold. Do not mount those whose bodies are strong and firm. Do not mount those whose hair is curly or whose Adam's apple is prominent. Do not mount those whose armpits are inclined to be malodorous. Do not mount women who have [spontaneous] vaginal secretions.[66]

Ch'ung Ho tzu said:

In the *I ching* it says: "Heaven reveals signs by which we may know fortune good or bad. The sage conducts himself accordingly."[67] The *Book of Rites* says: "When thunder is about to resound, if one conceives children contrary to the taboo, calamity will surely follow." Thus the sages have issued a warning that we must

not fail to heed. Heavenly changes manifest above and earthly disasters take place
below. How can man dwelling between the
two not be awed and respectful, especially
in the matter of uniting *yin* and *yang*? This
then is the great taboo of reverence and
awe.

P'eng Tsu said:

It is important to be wary of conditions of
change.[68] Avoid great cold, great heat,
great winds, and great rains, solar and
lunar eclipses, earthquakes, and lightning,
for these are the taboos of heaven. Intoxication, over eating, [excessive] joy, anger,
anxiety, sorrow, fear, and apprehension,
these are the taboos of man. Mountains,
rivers, the gods of heaven and earth, the
altars of earth and grain,[69] wells and kitch-
en stoves,[70] these are the taboos of earth.
One must avoid these three taboos. Those
who transgress them will fall ill and their
children will be short lived.

All those who engage in intercourse
while taking medicine, in a weakened condition, or not yet fully recovered from an
illness will suffer harm.

One must not have intercourse on the
almanac day designated as *yüeh-sha*.

One must not have intercourse on the
almanac days designated as *chien*, *p'o*,
chih, and *ting*, as well as the "blood taboo"
days, for this is injurious to a man.

P'eng Tsu said:

Short life owing to lust and licentiousness is
not necessarily the work of ghosts and
gods. Some place powders in the private
parts or use male "stalks" fashioned of
ivory. This robs one of years of life, causes
premature aging and hastens death.

To cure male impotence, weak erection, and lack of enthusiasm, all of which
are caused by lack of *yang-ch'i* and weakness in the "kidney source,"[71] use the following prescription:

縱容	*Herba cistanches (stem of broomrape)*, 2 fen.
五味	*Fructus schisandrae chinensis (schisandra fruit)*, 2 fen.
蛇床子	*Semen cnidii*, 4 fen.
兔床子	*Semen cuscutae (dodder seeds)*, 4 fen.
枳實	*Fructus citri seu ponciri immaturus*, 4 fen.

The preceding five ingredients should be
pounded, sieved, and taken with wine in
the amount of one "square-inch spoonful"

three times daily. A prefectural magistrate
in Szechwan began to have children again
after the age of seventy.

Here is another prescription:

雄蛾	*Male moth*,[72] *not yet mated, dried*, 3 fen.
細辛	*Herba asari cum radice (Chinese wild ginger)*, 3 fen.
蛇床子	*Semen cnidii monnieri*, 3 fen.

Pound, sieve, and form with sparrow egg[73]
into pills the size of dryandra seeds. Take
one just before intercourse. If the erection
will not subside, wash the member with
water.

Prescription for enlarging the male
member:

蜀椒	*Fructus zanthosyli bungeani (fruit of Szechwan pepper)*.
細辛	*Herba asari cum radice (Chinese wild ginger)*.
肉縱容	*Herba cistanches (stem of broomrape)*.

Equal measure of these three ingredients
should be sieved and inserted into the gall
bladder of a dog and this hung up in one's
living quarters for thirty days. If this is
rubbed on the member it will elongate
one inch.

Prescription for curing women's pain
that persists for several days following
defloration.

甘草	*Radix glycyrrhizae uralensis (licorice root)*, 2 fen.
芍藥	*Radix paeoniae lactiflorae (peony root)*, 2 fen.
生薑	*Rhizoma zingiberis officinalis recens (fresh ginger rhizome)*, 3 fen.
桂心	*Cortex cinnamomi cassiae (inner bark of Saigon cinnamon)*, 10 fen.
水	*Water*, 3 sheng.

Prescription for women who have been injured by their husbands due to sexual excess and whose private parts are swollen
and painful:

桑根白皮	*Cortex mori albae radicis (bark of mulberry root)*, 1/2 sheng, sliced.
干薑	*Rhizoma zingiberis officinalis (dried ginger rhizome)*, 1 liang.
桂心	*Cortex cinnamomi cassiae (inner bark of Saigon cinnamon)*, 1 liang.
棗	*Fructus ziziphi jujubae (jujube fruit)*, 20 dates.

107

Boil three times in one *tou* of wine and drink one *sheng*. Avoid perspiring when exposed to wind. One also may boil in water.

Tung Hsüan Tzu

Tung Hsüan tzu said:

Heaven gave birth to the 10,000 things, but of all of these man is noblest. Of that which man holds dear,[1] nothing exceeds the desires of the bedroom. One must imitate heaven and pattern oneself on earth, take *yin* as compass and *yang* as square. By understanding these principles, one may nourish one's nature and lengthen one's years. Failing to respect these natural truths, one suffers injury to the spirit and early death. As for the methods of Hsüan Nü, these have been handed down from ancient times and the broad outline has been set forth. However the subtle details have not yet been fully expounded. Perusing its precepts, I thought to supplement its omissions, to review old customs and compile this new classic. Although I have not exhausted the finer points, I have nevertheless collected the fundamental ones. [Herein may be found] the forms of sitting and reclining, stretching out and curling up, the postures prone and supine, open and spread, the methods of approaching from the side, back, advancing, and retreating, the rules for withdrawing and entering, shallow and deep. These also are combined with the principle of *yin* and *yang* and harmonized with the order of the Five Phases. Those who follow this are able to preserve their lives, but those who violate it fall into danger and death. Being of such benefit to all people, how should it not be handed down for 10,000 generations?

Tung Hsüan tzu said:

Heaven revolves to the left and earth rotates to the right. Spring and summer depart and autumn and winter take their places. Man sings and woman harmonizes. What is above acts and what is below follows. This is the eternal law of all things. If the man stirs but the woman does not respond, or if the woman moves but the man does not follow, this is not only harmful to the man but can also be injurious to the woman. These result from violations of *yin* and *yang* or transgressions of above and below. To come together in this way is not beneficial to either party. Therefore, the man must rotate to the left, and the woman must revolve to the right. Man thrusts downward from above, and woman receives him from below. To come together in this way is called "heavenly peace and earthly fulfillment."[2]

The principles of deep and shallow, slow and fast, thrusting and twisting, and east and west do not follow a single path, but have 10,000 strands. For example, there is slow thrusting like a gold carp toying with the hook, or the tense urgency of a flock of birds facing a stiff wind. Advancing and retreating, pulling in and drawing out,[3] up and down, following and receiving, left and right, going forth and returning, withdrawing and entering, separation and closeness,[4] all need to be orchestrated and properly adjusted. One must not forever sing the same old tune in every circumstance.[5]

When first coming together for the purpose of intercourse, the man should sit on the woman's left and the woman on the man's right. The man, sitting in "winnowing basket" pose, embraces the woman to his bosom. He clasps her slender waist and caresses her jade body. Expressing their joy and speaking of deep attachment, of one heart and one mind, they now embrace and then clasp, their two bodies beating against each other and their mouths pressed together. The man sucks the woman's lower lip and the woman sucks the man's upper lip. Then simultaneously sucking, they feed on each other's juices. They may slowly bite each other's tongues, or gently nibble each other's lips; they may cradle each other's heads, or urgently pinch the ears. Caressing above and patting below, kissing to the east and nibbling[6] to the west, a thousand charms are revealed and a hundred cares forgotten. Then let the woman take the man's "jade stalk" in her left hand, while the man caresses her "jade gate" with his right. At this moment, the man senses her *yin-ch'i* and his "jade stalk" is aroused like a solitary peak reaching up to the Milky Way. The woman senses the man's *yang-ch'i* and liquid flows from her "cinnabar hole" like the trickling down of a secluded spring spilling from a deep valley. This is the result of *yin* and *yang* stimulating each other and not the product of human effort. When conditions reach this stage, then intercourse is possible. If the man is not aroused or the woman is without copious secretions,[7] this is a manifestation of internal illness.[8]

Tung Hsüan tzu said:

When having intercourse one should begin first by sitting and then proceed to reclining. The woman should be on the left and the man on the right. After reclining have the woman lie straight out on her back, spreading her feet and opening her arms. The man lies upon her, kneeling between her thighs and drawing his erect "jade stalk" to the mouth of her "jade gate," luxuriant[9] like a canopied pine at the entrance of a deep valley cave. Then they clasp each other tightly,[10] moaning and sucking tongues. One may gaze up at her jade countenance or look down at her "golden gully,"[11] patting the region between belly and breasts and stroking the sides of her "jade terrace."[12] When the man is entranced and the woman enraptured, then with his "*yang* sword tip" he attacks in all directions. He may thrust down at her "jade veins,"[13] or ram the "golden gully" above,[14] stabbing at the sides of her "imperial college"[15] or resting on the right of her "jade terrace."[16] When the woman's sexual secretions fill the "cinnabar hole," he then plunges his "*yang* sword tip" into her "children's palace,"[17] as she ecstatically releases her *ching*[18] secretions, watering her "sacred fields"[19] above and irrigating her "secluded vale"[20] below. He moves in and out wildly attacking, advancing and retreating, rubbing and grinding. The woman begs for death, she begs for life,[21] pleading for her very existence. Then after wiping with a silk cloth, he plunges the "jade stalk" deeply into the "cinnabar hole" all the way to the "*yang* terrace,"[22] towering steeply like a great rock blocking a deep mountain stream. He then executes the method of "nine shallow and one deep," now leaning forward on his staff and now prodding sideways with his pole, pulling on one side and uprooting on the other, suddenly slow and suddenly fast, now deep and now shallow. For a count of twenty-one breaths observe the *ch'i* as it moves in and out.[23] When the woman is on the point of orgasm, the man quickly stabs and rapidly attacks, raising her high. Observe the woman's movements and adapt to her pace. Then with your "*yang* sword tip" attack her "grain seed," pur-suing all the way to the "children's palace" and grinding left and right. Without becoming excited,[24] carefully pull out.[25] When the woman's secretions overflow, retreat, for one must not withdraw dead but return alive. It is very harmful to the man if he withdraws dead. One must pay special heed to this.

Tung Hsüan tzu said:

If we study the postures of intercourse, there are no more than thirty methods. Among these are ways that feature bending and extending, facing up and facing down, withdrawing and entering, and shallow and deep. The similarities are great and the differences minor. It may be said that herein all is complete, collected without any omissions. I have described the postures and recorded their names, delineated their forms and given them designations. My fellow gentlemen, may you fully appreciate the marvels of their meaning.

1. *Expressions of Attachment.*
2. *Declarations of Inseparability.* Not parting.
3. *Fish with Gills Exposed.*
4. *Unicorn's Horn.* The external foreplay of these four postures is all part of the first stage.[26]
5. *Silkworms Tenderly Entwined.*[27] The woman lies face up, and extending her arms, embraces the man's neck and entwines her feet around his back. From above, the man embraces the woman's neck, kneeling between her thighs and inserting his "jade stalk."
6. *Twisting Dragon.*[28] The woman lies face up and bends her legs. The man kneels between her thighs and with his left hand pushes her two feet forward all the way past her breasts. With his right hand he inserts the "jade stalk" into the "jade gate."
7. *Fishes Eye-to-Eye.* The man and woman lie down together. The woman places one leg over the man's body. Facing each other they kiss and suck tongues. The man opens his legs and with his hand supports the woman's raised leg, advancing his "jade stalk."
8. *Swallows with Hearts United.* Have the woman lie face up and spread her legs. The man rides the woman, lying on top of her belly and embracing her neck with his two hands. The woman

109

clasps his waist with her hands, while he inserts the "jade stalk" into the "cinnabar hole."

9. *Kingfishers Entwined.*[29] Have the woman lie face up and bend her legs. The man assumes the "barbarian squat" with his feet apart and sits between the woman's thighs. Embracing her waist with his two hands, he advances his "jade stalk" between her "zither strings."

10. *Mandarin Ducks United.* Have the woman lie on her side and bend both legs, resting [one] on the man's thigh. From behind the woman's back the man rides on top of her bottom leg and raises his knee, placing her elevated thigh on top of it. He then inserts the "jade stalk."[30]

11. *Butterflies Fluttering in the Air.*[31] The man lies on his back and spreads his legs. The woman sits on top of the man, facing him, with her legs resting on the bed. Then using her hand to assist him, the "*yang* sword tip" is advanced into the "jade gate."

12. *Wild Ducks Flying with Backs to Each Other.*[32] The man lies face up and spreads his legs. The woman sits on top of him with her back to his face and her feet resting on the bed. She lowers her head, and embracing his "jade stalk," inserts it into the "cinnabar hole."

13. *Reclining Canopy Pine.* Have the woman cross her feet and point them upward.[33] The man embraces her waist with both hands, while she embraces his waist. The "jade stalk" is inserted into the "jade gate."

14. *Bamboos Bordering the Terrace.*[34] The man and woman stand facing each other, kissing and embracing at the "cinnabar cave." He drives[35] the "*yang* sword tip" deeply into the "cinnabar cave," burying it up to the "*yang* terrace."[36]

15. *Dance of the Paired Female Phoenixes.* There is a man and [two] women, one lying face up and the other on her stomach. The woman lying face up bends her legs and the one facing down rides on top of her so that their two private parts face each other. The man sits in "winnowing basket" pose, and wielding his "jade member," attacks alternately above and below.[37]

16. *Female Phoenix Tends Her Fledgling.*

A large fat woman uses a boy in conjunction to have intercourse.[38] What a great pleasure!

17. *Soaring Seagulls.* The man approaches the edge of the bed and lifts up the woman's legs so as to elevate them. With his "jade stalk" the man enters the "children's palace."

18. *Wild Horses Leaping.* Have the woman lie face up. The man lifts the woman's legs and places them on his [left][39] and right shoulders, inserting his "jade stalk" deeply into her "jade gate."

19. *Galloping Horse Hooves.* Have the woman lie on her back. The man squats and with his left hand supports her neck, while the right hand raises her leg. He then inserts his "jade stalk" into her "children's palace."[40]

20. *Horse Shaking Its Hooves.* Have the woman lie face up. The man lifts one of her legs and rests it on his shoulder, while she pulls the other leg toward her. The "jade stalk" is inserted deeply into the "cinnabar hole." What a great pleasure!

21. *White Tiger Pounces.* Have the woman kneel on her knees face down. The man kneels behind her and embraces her waist with his two hands, inserting his "jade stalk" into her "children's palace."

22. *Dark Cicada Clinging.* Have the woman lie face down and spread her legs. The man positions himself between her thighs, and bending his legs, embraces her neck with both hands. He then inserts the "jade stalk" into her "jade gate" from behind.

23. *Goat Faces a Tree.*[41] The man sits in "winnowing basket" pose[42] and has the woman sit on top with her back to him. The woman lowers her head in order to see and inserts the "jade stalk." The man passionately embraces the woman's waist and clasps her tightly.

24. *Fowl Approach the Field.*[43] The man assumes the "barbarian squat"[44] on the bed and has a young girl take the "jade stalk" and insert it into the [other] woman's "jade gate." Another girl pulls the [other] woman's girdle and skirt from behind to give her complete satisfaction. What a great pleasure![45]

25. *Phoenix Frolics at Cinnabar Hole.*

Have the woman lie face up and raise her feet with both hands. The man kneels behind, and supporting himself on the bed, inserts the "jade stalk" into the "cinnabar hole." How supremely pleasurable!

26. *Roc Soars over Dark Sea.*[46] Have the woman lie face up. The man takes the woman's two legs, places them on his left and right upper arms, and reaches down with his hands to embrace her waist, inserting the "jade stalk."

27. *Moaning Monkey Clings to Tree.* The man sits in "winnowing basket"[47] pose while the woman rides on his thighs and embraces him with both hands. Using one hand, the man supports the woman's buttocks, inserts the "jade stalk," and with the other hand leans on the bed.

28. *Cat and Mouse Share the Same Hole.* One man lies face up and spreads his legs. The woman lies on top of him and deeply inserts his "jade stalk." Another man lies on the woman's back and with his "jade stalk" attacks the "jade gate."[48]

29. *Donkeys of the Three Months of Spring.*[49] The woman supports herself with both hands and both feet on the bed. The man stands behind her and embraces her waist with his two hands. He then inserts his "jade stalk" into the "jade gate." How exceedingly pleasurable, indeed!

30. *The Dogs of Autumn.*[50] Man and woman, back to back, each place both hands and feet upon the bed and lean their buttocks together. The man lowers his head and with one hand pushes the "jade member" into the "jade gate."

Tung Hsüan tzu said:

The "jade stalk" sometimes attacks left and right like a fierce general breaking through the enemy's ranks. This is the first style. Sometimes it rises and suddenly plunges like a wild horse that has jumped into a mountain stream.[51] This is the second style. Sometimes it may appear and disappear like a flock of seagulls on the waves.[52] This is the third style. Sometimes it pounds deeply or pecks shallowly like a sparrow's beak in a crow's nest.[53] This is the fourth style. Sometimes it thrusts deeply or stabs shallowly like a great stone thrown into the sea.[54] This is the fifth style. Sometimes it rises slowly and pushes deliberately like a freezing snake entering its hole. This is the sixth style. Sometimes it charges quickly and stabs urgently like a frightened mouse rushing into its hole. This is the seventh style. Sometimes it raises its head and flexes its claws like a hawk dragging a crafty hare.[55] This is the eighth style. Sometimes it is carried up and then suddenly plunges down like a great sailboat in a wild wind.[56] This is the ninth style.

Tung Hsüan tzu said:

When having intercourse, one may sometimes press down with the "jade stalk," moving in and out sawing her "jade veins." This attack is like prying open an oyster shell and taking the shining pearl. This is the first attack. Sometimes one may raise the "jade veins" below or thrust at the "golden gully" above.[57] This attack is like splitting a rock looking for beautiful jade. This is the second attack. Sometimes one may pound the "jade terrace" with the "yang sword tip." This attack is like an iron pestle plunging into the medicine mortar. This is the third attack. Sometimes one may move in and out, attacking the "imperial college" to the left and right. This attack is like five hammers tempering iron.[58] This is the fourth attack. Sometimes one may move in and out with the "yang sword tip," grinding and plowing amid the "sacred fields" and "secluded valley." This attack is like a farmer turning over the earth in autumn. This is the fifth attack. Sometimes one may allow the "dark garden" and "heavenly court" to rub and pound together. This attack is like two collapsing cliffs bowing to each other.[59] This is the sixth attack.

Tung Hsüan tzu said:

Whenever one desires to ejaculate, one must await the woman's orgasm and then bestow the *ching*, ejaculating at the same time.[60] The man should withdraw to a shallow depth and play between the "zither strings" and "wheat teeth." The "yang sword tip" moves deep and shallow like an infant sucking the breast. Then one closes the eyes and turns one's thoughts inward. As the tongue is pressed against the lower palate,[61] arch the back, stretch out the head, dilate the nostrils, hunch the shoulders, close the mouth and inhale, and the *ching* will rise of itself.[62] The degree of control is always dependent on the individual. One should only ejaculate two or three times in ten.

Tung Hsüan tzu said:

If one desires children, wait for the cessation of the woman's menses, and if intercourse takes place on the first or third days thereafter, it will be a son, and on the fourth or fifth a daughter. After the fifth day it simply does harm to the strength of one's *ching* without any benefit.[63] When having intercourse with emission, wait for the approach of the woman's orgasm and ejaculate together with her. In ejaculating, one must do so completely. First have the woman lie straight and face up. She should rectify her mind and concentrate her thoughts, close her eyes and direct her thoughts inwardly as she receives the *ching-ch'i*. Therefore Lao tzu said: "Children conceived at midnight will achieve the greatest longevity, those before midnight medium longevity, and those after midnight the least."[64]

After a woman has become pregnant, she should engage in good works, see no evil, hear no evil, control her sexual desire, refrain from cursing and reviling, avoid fright, fatigue, loose talk, and worry, and abstain from eating raw, cold, vinegary, oily, or hot foods. Do not ride in a carriage or on horseback. Do not ascend great heights or approach great depths. Do not descend slopes or go too fast. Do not take drugs[65] or submit to acupuncture or moxibustion. You should at all times rectify your heart and correct your thoughts and listen often to the reading of the classics. In this way your sons and daughters will be intelligent and wise, loyal and true. This is what is called "educating the unborn."

Tung Hsüan tzu said:

If a man is twice the age of the woman, this is harmful to the woman; if the woman is twice the man's age, this is harmful to the man.

There are directions to face during intercourse and auspicious times. Benefit and harm follow the time. Conforming to this brings great success.

In spring the head should point east, in summer south, in autumn west, and in winter north.[66]

Yang days are beneficial [odd days]; *yin* days are harmful [even days]. *Yang* times are beneficial [the period after 11:00 PM to 1:00 AM and before 11:00 AM to 1:00 PM]; *yin* times are harmful [the period after 11:00 AM to 1:00 PM and before 11:00 PM to 1:00 AM].

Spring: Sexegenary cycle days beginning with *chia* and *i*.
Summer: Sexegenary cycle days beginning with *ping* and *ting*.
Autumn: Sexegenary cycle days beginning with *keng* and *hsin*.
Winter: Sexegenary cycle days beginning with *jen* and *kuei*.[67]

Bald Hen Powder cures the "five ills" and "seven injuries," impotence, and inability to perform. The magistrate of a prefecture in Szechwan, Lü Ching-ta,[68] took this medicine at the age of seventy and sired three sons. After taking it for a long time his wife developed skin eruptions[69] of the "jade gate" and was not able to sit or lie down. She threw the medicine into the courtyard, whereupon the rooster ate it and immediately mounted the hen. He did not dismount for many days and pecked the hen's head bald. This is why it has come to be called "Bald Hen Powder" or "Bald Hen Pills." The prescription is as follows:

縱容	*Herba cistanches (stem of broom rape), 3 fen.*
五味子	*Fructus schisandrae chinesis (schisandra fruit), 3 fen.*
兔絲子	*Semen cuscutae (dodder seeds), 3 fen.*
遠志	*Radix polygalae tenuifoliae (root of Chinese senega), 3 fen.*
蛇床子	*Semen cnidii monieri, 4 fen.*

The preceding five ingredients should be pounded and sieved into powder. Take one "square-inch spoonful" two or three times daily on an empty stomach with a bit of wine. This should not be taken if one has no "enemies."[70] After sixty days one will be able to mount forty women. It also can be prepared with white honey[71] and formed into pills the size of dryandra seeds. Take five pills twice daily and thereafter be guided by your own judgment of its effects.[72]

Deer Horn Powder cures the male's "five ills" and "seven injuries," impotence, approaching a woman in haste and inability to consummate the act, loss of erection in mid-course, uncontrolled emission, leakage of extra drops after urination, and pain and coldness in the lower back. The prescription is as follows:

鹿角	*Cornu cervi (deer horn).*
柏子仁	*Semen biota orientalis (arborvitae seeds).*
兔絲子	*Semen cuscutae (dodder seeds).*
蛇床子	*Semen cnidii monnieri.*
車前子	*Semen plantaginis (plantago seeds).*
遠志	*Radix polygalae tenuifoliae (root of Chinese senega).*
五味子	*Fructus schisandrae chinesis (schisandra fruit).*
縱容	*Herba cistanches (stem of broomrape), 4 fen of each of the preceding.*[73]

The preceding should be pounded and sieved into powder. Take half a "square-inch spoonful"[74] after meals three times daily. If you do not feel any effect, increase dosage to one "square-inch spoonful."

Prescription for lengthening the private parts:

肉縱容	*Herba cistanches (stem of broomrape), 3 fen.*
海藻	*Herba sargassii (seaweed), 2 fen.*

The preceding should be pounded and sieved into powder and mixed with the bile of a white dog born during the first month of the [lunar] year.[75] Apply this three times to the penis and wash it off with fresh well-water at dawn. It will lengthen three inches. This prescription is extremely efficacious.

Prescription for curing slackness and coldness of the woman's private parts that immediately shrinks it[76] and gives great pleasure in intercourse:

石硫黃	*Sulphur, 2 fen.*
青木香	*Radix aristolochiae (root of birthwort), 2 fen.*
山茱萸	*Fructus corni officinalis (fruit of Asiatic cornelian cherry), 2 fen.*
蛇床子	*Semen cnidii monnieri, 2 fen.*

The preceding four ingredients should be pounded and sieved into powder. Just before intercourse insert a bit in the "jade gate," but not too much lest it close altogether.

Another prescription is to add three pinches of powdered sulphur to one *sheng* of hot water. If this is used to wash the private parts, one will immediately become like a girl of twelve or thirteen.

X. MEDICAL MANUALS AND HANDBOOKS FOR HOUSEHOLDERS

Introduction

The works in this section are the most difficult to date. We know, for example, that the texts in the first group cannot be later than 984, the date of their preservation in Japan; and it is reasonable to assume, based on citations in earlier sources, that the contents reflect the state of sexology from as early as the Han. The logic of the organization of this section, however, has less to do with chronology than genre and content. The first work, "Health Benefits of the Bedchamber," consists of Chapter 83 of the great T'ang physician Sun Ssu-miao's *Priceless Prescriptions.* The text was printed and reprinted during the Sung, Yüan, and Ming, and my translation is based on the copy provided in van Gulik's *Erotic Colour Prints of the Ming.* "The Dangers and Benefits of Intercourse with Women" also is extracted from a longer work, the *Yang-hsing yen-ming lu* (Record of nourishing nature and extending life), preserved in the *Tao tsang,* and bearing the names of both T'ao Hung-ching (sixth century) and Sun Ssu-miao. Needham insists that the work cannot be earlier than the Sung, but acknowledges that "some passages and expressions in it may well be." The "Dangers and Benefits" indeed does share some language, concepts, and even parallel passages with Sun's "Health Benefits," but contains none of the cosmological and alchemical elements distinguishing post-Sung works.

Of *The Wondrous Discourse of Su Nü*, van Gulik says: "This is, as far as I know, the most complete bona-fide handbook of sex of the Ming period that has been preserved. Some day it should be translated in its entirety." Van Gulik's text, on which the present translation is based, was copied from two Japanese versions of the sixteenth and nineteenth centuries. The preface and colophon, both dated mid-sixteenth century and signed with pen names, are not able to shed any light on the original authorship. Both the form and content of the *Wondrous Discourse* look back to the early classics, with some original features already discussed in detail in this Introduction. Although the text appears to be "re-written and arranged . . . from fragments of older handbooks," as van Gulik says, it is surprising that it does not contain the phrase "return the *ching* to nourish the brain," or even the concept of raising and transmuting the *ching*.

The full title of the *True Classic* contains the honorific name of the Sung Immortal, Lü Yen (Tung-pin). The commentary was contributed by a certain Teng Hsi-hsien who identifies himself only as a disciple of Master Lü. The work is unique for its extended military metaphor, a stylistic device functionally equivalent to the mythical dialogue form of other classics. It and the *Exposition* were published together in one volume in Japan, probably in the late nineteenth century. Van Gulik found it identical to a Chinese blockprint of the late Ming. I agree with his opinion that the main text, "points to the T'ang period, or perhaps even earlier," but that the commentary, so essential to deciphering the text, belongs to the Ming.

The Preface to the *Exposition of Cultivating the True Essence*, signed by Teng Hsi-hsien, attributes the text to Wu Hsien, whom van Gulik feels the author confused with Wu Yen mentioned in an *Ishimpō* fragment (not included in Yeh's

reconstruction of the *Classic of Su Nü*) as tutor in sexual matters to Emperor Wu of the Han. Van Gulik's copy is based on four texts preserved in Japan. The work contains much that appeals to the general householder, but its detailed treatment of the process of absorption would be of interest only to the serious adept. The *Exposition* also contains the rudiments of microcosmic orbit meditation expressed in straightforward physiological terms. In my view, this text lays out one of the most complete programs of sexual practice and, by virtue of including nearly all the theoretical elements of both the householder and elixer traditions, occupies a uniquely central position in the evolution of sexology.

Health Benefits of the Bedchamber

Fang-chung pu-i

from Sun Ssu-miao's *Priceless Prescriptions (Ch'ien-chin yao-fang)*, Chapter 83

I

It has been said that before the age of forty men give free rein to their passions, but after forty suddenly become aware that their strength is declining. As soon as decline sets in, countless illnesses come swarming. If this persists unchecked for a long time, it will become incurable. Therefore, P'eng Tsu said: "To use one human being to cure another, this is the true way." Therefore, when a man reaches forty, he must become familiar with the art of the bedchamber.

II

The *tao* of the bedchamber art is within easy reach, yet none is able to practice it. The method is to have intercourse with ten women but to remain securely locked oneself. This is the sum of the art of the bedchamber. If combined with tonic supplements taken faithfully throughout the four seasons, the strength of one's *ch'i* will increase a hundredfold and one's intelligence will be daily renewed. However, the practice of this art has nothing to do with the pursuit of illicit gratification or the shameful quest for pleasure. Rather, one should maintain self-control to promote the cultivation of life. It does not involve the shameless desire to strengthen one's body to engage in womanizing or wantonness. Instead, one's concern should be with improving health to banish illness. This is the subtle principle of the bedchamber.

III

Therefore, partaking of aphrodisiacs during the years before forty is precisely calculated to hasten disaster. Be extremely careful of this! For this reason, it is useless to discuss the affairs of the bedchamber with a man who is not yet forty, for his lust is not yet stilled. If he consumes tonic medicines, his redoubled strength will be wasted, and before half a year his *ching* and marrow will be exhausted. This is simply to court the approach of death. Young men must be especially careful of this. After forty, a man must constantly strengthen his *ching*, nourish and not waste it. In this way he can avoid aging. Consuming mica[1] also can cure illness and lengthen one's years. After forty, refrain from taking purgatives and consume tonic supplements often. This is the best course. Long ago, the Yellow Emperor had intercourse with 1,200 women and ascended into the realm of the immortals, whereas the ordinary man cuts down his life with only one woman. How far apart indeed are knowledge and ignorance. Those who understand the *tao* regret only having too few women to mount.

IV

In selecting women it is not necessary that they be fair and beautiful, but simply that they be young, have not yet given birth[2] and are amply covered with flesh. These are beneficial to one's health. If one's financial resources are sufficient,

one may choose those with fine hair, clearly defined whites and pupils of the eye, supple bodies, and soft bones. Their skin should be fine and glossy and their speech harmonious. The joints of their four limbs should be sufficiently covered with flesh and the bones should not be large. The entire body, including the armpits, should be free of hair, but if there is hair it should be soft and fine. One must not be too demanding in the area of appearance, but the following traits are unacceptable: unruly hair and hideous faces, malletlike necks and bulging Adam's apples,[3] manly voices and large mouths, high noses and "wheat teeth," dull pupils, hair about the mouth and chin, prominent joints, yellow hair and scant flesh, pubic hair that is stiff and coarse, and also hair growing in the wrong direction. Intercourse with these types of women will rob you of life and shorten your years.

V

In practicing the *tao* of mounting women, do not unite before the *ch'i* is aroused; that is, when the *yang-ch'i* is still weak. One must first slowly develop harmony, causing the spirit to be harmonious and the will to be stirred, and then after a long time one may obtain the *yin-ch'i*. If the *yin-ch'i* is encouraged, in a short time it will become strong of itself. This is what is called "inserting soft and withdrawing hard." The pace of advancing and retreating should be very slow and, when passions are aroused, rest. Do not throw yourself into it with abandon, for this upsets the Five Viscera, damages the *ching* channels, and leads to a hundred illnesses. Have intercourse frequently, but take care to be on your guard.[4] In this way, all illnesses will be cured, and one's lifespan will increase daily. This is not far then from immortality.

VI

It is not necessary to proceed according to the numbers nine and one or three and five. Those who are able to make contact a hundred times without ejaculating will gain long life. By mounting many women

115

one can absorb their *ch'i*. The *tao* of absorbing *ch'i* is to make deep contact without becoming aroused. After a long time, the *ch'i* rises and the face becomes hot. Pressing your mouths together, take in the woman's *ch'i* and swallow it. You may slowly enter and withdraw, but as soon as your passion is aroused, rest. Slow the breath, close the eyes, lie on your back and guide the *ch'i* internally. Your body will become strong and you will be able to have intercourse with another woman. Frequently changing partners increases the benefit. Constant intercourse with the same woman results in a weakening of her *yin-ch'i*, and the benefits will be little. The *tao* of *yang* imitates fire; the followers of *yin* imitate water. If one persists in this manner, the *yin-ch'i* becomes increasingly *yang*, while *yang*, on the contrary, suffers loss.[5] What is gained cannot compensate for what is lost. If one is able to mount just twelve women without ejaculating, this makes a man youthful and handsome. If one can have intercourse with ninety-three women and remain locked, one will live for 10,000 years.

VII

Whenever the *ching* becomes insufficient, one will become ill; when it is totally exhausted one dies. One must not fail to consider this seriously or to be very cautious. If one has frequent intercourse and ejaculates only once, then the *ching-ch'i* increases accordingly and there is no risk of the man becoming deficient. However, if one does not have frequent intercourse, but ejaculates each time one does, then there is no benefit. After ejaculating, the *ching-ch'i* naturally increases again, but it is slower and less powerful than when there is frequent intercourse, making contact without ejaculation.[6]

VIII

When practicing sexual union, one should take in a great amount of *ch'i* through the nose and exhale lightly through the mouth. In this way there will be natural benefit. After finishing intercourse there will be a feeling of steam heat. This means that one has obtained *ch'i*. Take three *fen* of sweetflag rhizome powder and white millet flour, mill, and dry them. This both makes a man strong and prevents damp sores.

IX

When one feels the impulse to ejaculate, close the mouth and open the eyes wide, hold the breath and clench the fists.[7] Move the hands to the left and right, up and down. Contract the nose and take in *ch'i*. Also constrict the anus, suck in the abdomen,[8] and lie on the back. Now quickly press the *p'ing-i* point[9] with the two middle fingers of the left hand. Exhale a long breath and at the same time gnash the teeth a thousand times. In this way the *ching* will ascend to nourish the brain, causing one to gain longevity. Foolishly shedding *ching* injures the spirit. The classics on immortality say that to live long and remain youthful one must first play with a woman and drink her "jade fluid." "Jade fluid" is the secretion within the mouth. When both man and woman are aroused, he should grasp [the penis][10] in his left hand and imagine that there is "red *ch'i*" in the *tan-t'ien* which is yellow within and white without.[11] This then becomes transformed into the sun and moon that move about in the *tan-t'ien* and enters the *ni-yüan*[12] point where the two halves reunite as one. One should then hold the breath and penetrate deeply without moving in and out, but absorbing *ch'i* above and below. When one becomes emotionally aroused and feels the impulse to ejaculate, immediately withdraw. Only the superior gentleman of keen intelligence will be able to carry this out . The *tan-t'ien* is located three inches below the navel and the *ni-yüan* is located in the center of the head opposite the two eyes and straight back. In imagining the sun and moon, one should think of them as approximately three inches in diameter. The two halves lose their separate forms and become one. This is called "sun and moon in conjunction." Even as you move in and out, continue to think of the imagined objects and do not let go of them. This is a wonderful practice.

X

It is also said that the *tao* of mutual immortality for both men and women is deep penetration without arousing the *ching*. Imagine a red color within the navel the size of a hen's egg. Slowly move in and out, but when your emotions are aroused, withdraw. If executed several tens of times in a day and night, it increases a man's years.

XI

The method of mounting women is to ejaculate twice a month or twenty-four times in one full year. Those who practice this live for 200 years, maintain their youthful color, and are without illness. If one supplements this with tonic medicines, one can live indefinitely. At twenty years of age a man may ejaculate once in four days, at thirty once in eight, at forty once in sixteen, at fifty once in twenty, and at sixty one should lock the *ching* and not ejaculate. However, if one's body is still strong, a man may ejaculate once per month.

XII

There are those whose strength is naturally great and surpasses other men's.[13] They must not repress themselves and go long without ejaculating for this leads to boils and ulcers. If one is still strong after sixty, and though without opportunity for intercourse for several weeks yet maintains mental equilibrium, one may naturally lock the *ching*. Some time ago during the beginning of the Chen-kuan reign (627–649) of Emperor T'ai Tsung of the T'ang dynasty, there was an old peasant of over seventy who came to me for advice saying, "For the past several days my *yang-ch'i* has been unusually strong and I feel like sleeping with my old wife in broad daylight. In fact, I am able to consummate the act without fail. I do not know if this is common in old age. Should I consider it good or bad?" I answered him saying: "This is a very bad sign. Is it

possible you have not heard of the oil lamp? Just before the lamp is about to burn out, it first becomes dark and then bright. When the brightness is over it dies out. You, Sir, have reached an advanced age and should long ago have locked your *ching* and stilled your desire. Now suddenly your sexual longing burns fiercely. Is this not something highly abnormal? I fear for you and advise great care." Four weeks later he took sick and died. This is because he failed to be careful. This case is not unique, but I simply relate the story of one man for the edification of future generations.

XIII

Therefore, those who excel at cultivating life, whenever they feel a particularly strong urge in the *yang* matter should be careful and hold it in check, for one must not rob oneself through wantonness. Each time one is able to exercise control it is like adding oil to a flame that is about to go out. If one is unable to control it and wantonly ejaculates, this is like taking oil away from a lamp that is about to burn out. Is this not the tragedy of failing to protect oneself? In their youth men do not understand this *tao*, and even those who do are not able to practice it faithfully. Upon reaching old age they come to understand, but it already is late and the error is difficult to correct. Those who are able to guard themselves in old age still can gain long life and length of years. However, those who are able to practice the *tao* while young and strong quickly join the immortals.

XIV

Someone asked: "If a man not yet sixty locks his *ching* and holds fast to the One, is this permissible?" I answered: "No. Man must not be without woman, and woman must not be without man. Without woman, a man's mind will be disturbed; when the mind is disturbed, the spirit is wearied. When the spirit is weary, one's life is shortened. To keep the mind always on the True and to be without cares, this is ideal, and long life follows. However, there is not 1 in 10,000 who succeeds in this. Forced repression is difficult to maintain and easily lost. It causes repletion of the *ching* and turns the urine turbid. It may even lead to the illness of copulation with ghosts. In this state one loss is equal to a hundred."

XV

In practicing the methods of mounting women, one must avoid those days in the sexegenary cycle beginning with the Celestial Stems *ping* and *ting*, as well as quarter and full moons, the last and first days of each moon, and days when there are great winds, rain, fog, cold or heat, thunder, lightning, and sudden thunderclaps, darkness over heaven and earth, solar and lunar eclipses, rainbows, and earthquakes. To mount at these times injures a man's spirit and is inauspicious. It harms men a hundredfold and causes women to become ill. Children conceived at these times will be mad, foolish, perverse, or stupid; mute, deaf or dim visioned; crooked, crippled, blind, or sightless in one eye; sickly or short lived; unfilial and malevolent. One should also avoid the glare of the sun, moon, and stars; the interior of shrines to the gods; proximity to Buddhist temples, wells, kitchen stoves, and privies; and the vicinity of graves and coffins. All of these are forbidden.

XVI

If one has intercourse in the correct manner, the womb will be blessed with offspring who are fortunate, virtuous, wise, and good. This will cause the dispositions and ways of mother and father to be harmonious and all of their actions to be congenial. The *tao* of the family will become daily more prosperous and good omens will crowd about them. If one does not follow the correct methods, the womb will be visited by offspring who are unfortunate, stupid, and evil. This will cause the dispositions and ways of the father and mother to be cruel and malicious. Whatever they do will be unsuccessful and the *tao* of the family daily will become more ill-fated. Disasters and mis-

fortunes will arrive in droves. Although they grow to maturity, the family and nation will perish. Disaster and fortune are effects that return to us just as shadow and echo. This is an inescapable principle. Does this not warrant careful thought?

XVII

If one desires children, simply wait for the first, third, or fifth days after the cessation of the woman's menses. Select the "monarchial and ministerial" days and those days when the moon is in "auspicious mansions." If you ejaculate after midnight, the time when the *ch'i* is born, all of your offspring will be male. They will be long lived, wise, and honored. If you use the second, fourth, or sixth days after the cessation of menses to ejaculate, the offspring surely will be female. After the sixth day, do not ejaculate. Not only will you fail to be blessed with children, but if they are born, they will be short lived.

The "monarchial and ministerial" days are:

> *Spring*: Those beginning with Celestial Stems *chia* and *i*.
> *Summer*: Those beginning with Celestial Stems *ping* and *ting*.
> *Autumn*: Those beginning with Celestial Stems *keng* and *hsin*.
> *Winter*: Those beginning with Celestial Stems *jen* and *kuei*.

The "lunar mansion" days are:

> *First lunar month*: First, sixth, ninth, tenth, eleventh, twelfth, fourteenth, twenty-first, twenty-fourth, twenty-ninth.
> *Second lunar month*: Fourth, seventh, eighth, ninth, tenth, twelfth, fourteenth, nineteenth, twenty-second, twenty-seventh.
> *Third lunar month*: First, second, fifth, sixth, seventh, eighth, tenth, seventeenth, twentieth, twenty-fifth.
> *Fourth lunar month*: Third, fifth, eighth, tenth, twelfth, fifteenth, sixteenth, eighteenth, twenty-second, twenty-eighth.
> *Fifth lunar month*: First, second, third, fourth, fifth, sixth, twelfth, fifteenth.
> *Sixth lunar month*: First, third, tenth, thirteenth, eighteenth, twenty-third, twenty-

sixth, twenty-seventh, twenty-eighth, twenty-ninth.

Seventh lunar month: First, eighth, eleventh, sixteenth, twenty- first, twenty-fourth, twenty-fifth, twenty-sixth, twenty-seventh, twenty-ninth.

Eighth lunar month: Fifth, eighth, tenth, thirteenth, eighteenth twenty-first, twenty-second, twenty-third, twenty-fourth, twenty-fifth, twenty-sixth.

Ninth lunar month: Second, sixth, eleventh, sixteenth, nineteenth, twentieth, twenty-first, twenty-second.

Tenth lunar month: First, fourth, ninth, tenth, fourteenth, seventeenth, eighteenth, nineteenth, twentieth, twenty-second, twenty-third, twenty-ninth.

Eleventh lunar month: First, sixth, eleventh, fourteenth, fifteenth, sixteenth, seventeenth, nineteenth, twenty-sixth, twenty-ninth.

Twelfth lunar month: Fourth, ninth, twelfth, thirteenth, fourteenth, fifteenth, seventeenth, twenty-fourth.

If one combines the following days with the earlier "lunar mansion days," the results will be even more beneficial:

Spring: *Chia-yin* and *i-mao*.
Summer: *Ping-wu* and *ting-chi*.
Autumn: *Keng-shen* and *hsin-yu*.
Winter: *Jen-tzu* and *kuei-hai*.

XVIII

The miscellaneous taboos of the Yellow Emperor state that to have intercourse when one is angry and the blood *ch'i* is unsettled gives a man carbuncles. Also to have intercourse when one needs to urinate gives a man urinary problems, pain in the "stalk," and loss of ruddy complexion. Beyond this, to enter the bedchamber for the purpose of intercourse when one is weary from a long journey will result in the "five ills," deficiency syndrome, and few offspring. Moreover, to have intercourse with a woman before the cessation of her menses causes a man to fall ill and develop vitiligo. Mercury should not be allowed to come close to a man's private parts, for this causes them to wither and contract. The same is true for the fat of deer or swine, for this causes impotence.

The Dangers and Benefits of Intercourse with Women

Yü nü sun i

from *Record of Nourishing Nature and Lengthening Life* (*Yang-hsing yen-ming lu*), Chapter 6

Attributed to T'ao Hung-ching or Sun Ssu-miao

The *tao* [of longevity] takes *ching* as its treasure. To expend it is to give birth to another human being; to conserve it is to give life to one's own body. If one cultivates the life of the body then one may aspire to immortality; if one gives birth to a human being then one gains merit at the expense of the body. When merit is gained at the expense of the body, then one falls headlong into the realm of desire. How much more so as a result of foolishly shedding it and abandoning one's life! Failing to realize the extent of loss, one grows increasingly weary as life declines.

Between heaven and earth there is *yin* and *yang*. *Yin* and *yang* is what men most value. Valuing it, one should unite them according to the *tao*. This consists simply in being cautious and not wasteful. P'eng Tsu said: "The superior man sleeps by himself in a separate bed; the average sleeps under a different quilt. Consuming a thousand packets of medicine is not as good as sleeping alone." Colors blind the eye, sounds deafen the ear, and flavors spoil the palate.[1]

The "one day taboo" means that one must not overeat in the evening. (Going to sleep at night on a full stomach causes one to lose one day of life.) The "one month taboo" means that one should not drink to intoxication in the evening. (Going to bed drunk at night causes one to lose a month of life.) In the evening one should keep distant from one's wife. (A single act of intercourse causes one to lose a year of life, which cannot be regained by any amount of self-cultivation.) The "lifelong taboo" means that in the evening one should protect one's *ch'i*. (When lying down in the evening one should acquire the habit of keeping the mouth closed. By keeping the mouth open, one loses *ch'i* and allows evil influences to enter by the mouth.)

Ts'ai Nü addressed a question to P'eng Tsu saying: "Is it correct for a man when he reaches sixty years of age to lock his *ching* and maintain the One?"[2]

P'eng Tsu replied:

Certainly not. A man does not wish to be without a woman. If he is without a woman, his mind will be agitated. When the mind is agitated, the spirit becomes weary. When the spirit is weary, one's lifespan suffers. If one's thoughts are correct and one can be without cares, this is ideal. However, there is not 1 such man in 10,000. To lock the *ching* by repression is a practice difficult to maintain and easy to lose. Furthermore, it causes a man to lose *ching* through leakage and for his urine to be turbid. It may even lead to the illness of copulation with ghosts. Also, by seeking to prevent the *ch'i* from becoming excited, they weaken their *yang* principle. Those who desire to have intercourse with women should first become aroused and cause [the penis] to rise up strong. Slowly engage her and absorb her *yin-ch'i*. Circulate the *yin-ch'i* and after a moment you will become strong. When strong, employ it, being certain to move slowly and in a relaxed manner. When your *ching* becomes aroused, stop.[3] Lock the *ching* and slow the breath. Close the eyes, lie on the back and circulate your internal energy. When the body returns to normal, one may have intercourse with another woman. As soon as one feels aroused, immediately change partners. By changing partners one lengthens life. If one has intercourse with just one woman, her *yin-ch'i* becomes weak and is of little benefit.

The *tao* of *yang* takes after fire; the *tao* of *yin* takes after water. Water is able to control fire just as *yin* is able to extinguish *yang*. If one persists in this manner, the *yin-ch'i* absorbs the *yang*, and the *yang* suffers as a result. What one gains does not compensate for what is lost. However, if one is able to have intercourse with twelve women without ejaculating, one will retain a beautiful countenance in old age. If one has intercourse with ninety-three[4] women without ejaculating, one will attain the age of 10,000 years. When the *ching* is insufficient, illness ensues; when the *ching* is ex-

hausted one dies. One cannot but forebear; one cannot but beware. If one has frequent intercourse, but only occasionally ejaculates, the *ch'i* will increase again, and this cannot cause a man deficiency or harm. If one has frequent intercourse with ejaculation, the *ching* will not be able to increase and will become exhausted. Those who have frequent intercourse at home regain the *ching* of one emission for every time they achieve arousal without ejaculation. If one is unable to have frequent intercourse, then simply reckon two ejaculations per month. In this case, the *ching-ch'i* will also naturally rise again, but slowly and weakly. It cannot rise as rapidly as when there is frequent intercourse without ejaculation.

(Ts'ai Nü acquired this art when very young and understood how to nourish one's nature. At the age of one hundred and seventy she appeared as if fifteen. During the period when she served the King of Yin, she asked P'eng Tsu about this art.)

P'eng Tsu replied:

Licentiousness shortening a man's lifespan is not the work of ghosts or gods, but the result of base and vulgar impulses. When they feel the *ching* aroused and the urge to ejaculate, they try to please their partners. They expend all their strength insatiably. This does not promote their mutual health, but rather engenders harm. Some are shocked into insanity or experience "emaciation-thirst" disease. Some lose their minds or suffer malignant sores. This is the result of *ching* loss. When emission does occur, one should circulate energy internally to supplement the loss in that area. Otherwise, the blood vessels and brain daily will suffer more harm. When wind and dampness attack them they take ill. This is because common people do not understand the necessity of supplementing what is lost in ejaculation.

P'eng Tsu said:

Man cannot be without woman, and woman cannot be without man. To be solitary but long for intercourse shortens a man's life and allows a hundred ailments to appear. Ghosts and demons take advantage of this to copulate with them. *Ching* lost once in this way is equal to a hundred times in the normal way.

If one desires to bear offspring who are long lived, virtuous, intelligent, wealthy, and honored, then it is best to choose the "lunar mansion" days to bestow the *ching*. The "lunar mansion" days are recorded later.

T'ien Lao[5] said:

At birth all men possess the "five constant virtues," and this is no less true of their physical forms. However, there are distinctions of high and low, respected and reviled. All of this is the result of father and mother uniting their "eight stars" and *yin* and *yang*. If *yin* and *yang* are not united at the proper time, the offspring will be average. If the stars are not united, but the time is proper, the offspring will be average to superior. If both stars and time are improper, then the offspring will be common. To have intercourse in harmony with the stars, even if wealthy and honored offspring are not produced, is still beneficial to oneself. This is a very auspicious sign. (The "eight stars" are: *shih* 室, *ts'an* 參, *ching* 井, *kuei* 鬼, *liu* 柳, *chang* 張, *hsin* 心, tou 斗. When the moon is in these stars one may unite *yin* and *yang* and seek offspring.) The second, third, fifth, ninth, and twentieth days of the [lunar] month are the "monarchial and ministerial" days when the *ch'i* is most vital. Intercourse at these times is fivefold as auspicious, and vitality will suffer no harm. This enables a man to be without illness. Making use of the "monarchial and ministerial" days, choose the hour after midnight and before cockcrow. Now slowly play with her "jade spring" and drink her "jade sap," dallying with her. If one combines the *chia-yin* and *i-mao* days of spring, the *ping-wu* and *ting-wei* days of summer, the *keng-shen* and *hsin-yu* days of winter with the "lunar mansion days" just mentioned, it is especially good. If you wish to seek offspring, wait for the first, third, and fifth days after the cessation of the woman's menses. Select the hour after midnight on the "monarchial and ministerial" days when the *ch'i* is most vital. Then if *ching* is shed and children conceived, they will all be male and surely long lived, virtuous, and intelligent. The "monarchial and ministerial" days refer to those beginning with Celestial Stem characters *chia* and *i* in the spring, *ping* and *ting* in the summer, *keng* and *hsin* in the autumn, and *jen* and *kuei* in the winter.

The essential principle of cultivating life lies in cherishing the *ching*. If one can ejaculate only twice a month, or once for each of the "twenty-four climatic periods" of the year, longevity of 120 years is assured. If, in addition, one takes tonic supplements, one can live a very long time. The tragedy is that either men do not know this in their youth or, if they do, they are unable to faithfully practice it. To begin to grasp this *tao* in one's old age is very late, and illnesses are difficult to cure. However, although late, by protecting oneself, one can still lengthen one's lifespan. If one is able to begin practicing this *tao* when young and strong, there is hope of achieving immortality.

The classics on immortality state that the *tao* of man and woman achieving immortality together is to use deep penetration without allowing the *ching* to be aroused. Imagine something red in color and the size of an egg in the middle of the navel. Then slowly move in and out, withdrawing when the *ching* becomes aroused. By doing this several tens of times in the morning and in the evening, one may increase the lifespan. Man and woman should both calm their minds and maintain their concentration. They need only remember the words of Taoist Liu Ching: "In the spring one may shed *ching* once in three days, in the summer and autumn twice a month, but in the winter lock the *ching* and do not ejaculate. The *tao* of heaven is to store its *yang* in the winter. If man can emulate this, he can live a long time. One emission in the winter equals a hundred in the spring." The Taoist K'uai said: "When a man reaches sixty he ought completely to avoid the bedroom. If, however, he is able to have contact without ejaculation, then he may emulate women. If he is not able to control himself, then it is better to keep distant from them. To take a hundred kinds of medicine is not as important as this one thing. One thus can gain long life."

Tao Lin said:

The source of destiny is the root of life. The determining factor lies in this *tao*. Those who take the "great elixir," engage in breathing exercises and internal circulation, and have thoroughly practiced 10,000 *tao*, but do not know the root of life, are like trees who have ample branches and luxuriant leaves but are without roots. They cannot live long. The root of life is in *121* the business of the bedroom. Therefore the sages have said: "If one desires long life, one must proceed from that which gives life." The business of the bedroom can give life to a man but can also kill him. We may compare this to water and fire. Those who know how to use them can thereby nourish life, but those who do not may suffer immediate death.

When having intercourse, it is especially important to avoid intoxication and satiety, for otherwise one will be harmed a hundredfold. If one feels the need to urinate, but withholds it and has intercourse, this causes urinary problems, difficulty in urinating, pain in the penis, and tightness in the lower abdomen. Intercourse following great anger causes carbuncles. The taboos of the *tao* of the bedchamber include the last and first days of each moon, the first and last quarters of the moon, solar and lunar eclipses, great winds or excessive rain, earthquakes or lightning and thunder, great heat or cold, and the five days when spring, summer, autumn, and winter are changing and are being sent off and welcomed. During these times one must not carry out the union of *yin* and *yang*. The taboos of month and day are especially important during one's Terrestrial Branch birth year. (One must not unite sexually when *yin* and *yang* are crossing, for this injures one's vitality and causes one to expel the healthy and absorb the foul influences. This particularly injures the positive *ch'i* and should be carefully avoided.) One must not engage in the affair of the bedroom when one has just washed the hair, is fatigued from travel, or when feeling great joy or anger.

P'eng Tsu said:

One must not fail to understand conditions of change. Avoid great cold and great heat, great wind, great rain and great snow, eclipses of the sun and moon, earthquakes and thunder. These are the taboos of heaven. Intoxication and satiety, joy and anger, depression, sorrow, and fear are the taboos of man. The environs of mountains and rivers, altars to the gods of heaven and earth, wells, and stoves are the taboos of earth. In addition to avoiding these three taboos, there also are auspicious days, which are those beginning with Celestial Stem characters *chia* and *i* in the spring, *ping* and *ting* in the summer, *keng* and *shen* in the autumn, and *jen* and *kuei* in the

winter. Throughout the entire year, days beginning with Stems *wu* and *chi* all are "monarchial and ministerial" days. It is appropriate to make use of these favorable opportunities, for they confer long life, and likewise benefit one's offspring. If one transgresses these taboos, one not only will suffer illness oneself, but the children begotten will be subject to evil influences and short lives. Lao tzu said: "If one returns the *ching* to nourish the brain, one will never grow old."[6] The *Tzu Tu ching* says: "The proper method of emission requires that one enter weak and withdraw strong." (What is the meaning of "enter weak and withdraw strong?" Insert the "jade stalk" to a depth between the "zither strings" and "wheat teeth." When it becomes very large, withdraw it, and when weak insert it. This is what is meant by "enter weak and withdraw strong." Continue in this fashion for a count of eighty movements and then the *yang* number is complete.[7] This is marvelous, indeed!) Lao tzu said: "One who enters weak and withdraws strong knows the art of life. One who enters strong and withdraws weak, even if blessed with a favorable destiny, will die."[8] This is our meaning.

The Wondrous Discourse of Su Nü

Su Nü miao lun

Anonymous
Ed. by Ch'üan T'ien-chan

Preface

The techniques of sexual alchemy through absorption and supplementation are attributed to the goddess Su Nü (Immaculate Woman). The word "Immaculate" (*Su*) is an epithet for uncontaminated. To put contaminated words in the mouth of one whose essential nature is uncontaminated is intended as a warning against licentiousness. The "nine times" refined elixir uses the dragon and tiger to play the roles of *yin* and *yang* and lead and mercury to represent male and female. What these illustrate is not the *tao* of pleasure for man and woman, for the human body naturally contains within itself *yin* and *yang*, *ch'i* and blood, exterior and interior. If one is able to quiet the mind and sit in stillness, alchemically refining the elixir of immortality in one's own body, then male and female unite in harmony, water and fire complement each other, and heart and kidneys mutually interact. This is the essential teaching of the "Three Pure Ones"[1] and the mystery of the "golden chest."[2] One need only seek it in solitude to gain enlightenment and then, by investigating the principles of "yellow and white,"[3] one will surely lay hold of the dragon's whisker at Lake Ting[4] and hear the cocks and dogs among the clouds.[5] However, it is precisely its purity which is easily corrupted and difficult to communicate in writing. Therefore, if one is able to guard one's purity and not lose one's innocence, then those inclined toward study will reach the gate of Tsou and Lu,[6] and those who cultivate the *tao* will attain the pure realm of the immortals.

I do not know who is the author of this work. Some say it was transmitted by a Taoist priest of Mount Mao. The two chapters entitled, "The Nine Postures" and "Shallow and Deep" both describe the forms of breath control and sexual alchemy. These must not be discussed in a vulgar way and surely are not without their health benefits. (Note by Master of the Yin-yüeh Monastery: There is an omission or error in this sentence.) If this is taken as the secret of carnal relations with creatures of red rouge behind the bedcurtains, then one will surely suffer the disaster of adding fuel to the fire while reducing the oil.

Sexegenary cycle year *ping-yin*(1566),
eleventh lunar month,
Master of the Chai-hung Pavilion

Chapter 1. Origins

Long ago the Yellow Emperor addressed a question to Su Nü saying:

> I have heard that the sages of high antiquity lived to 1,000, 800, or 200 years. The sages of middle antiquity lived for 120 years. Today some people die at thirty or twenty, some at five or seven, or even two or three years of age. There are few who enjoy peace and contentment and many who suffer disease. What is the reason for this? Please enlighten me and withhold nothing of importance.

Su Nü answered him saying:

> All people are conceived of father's *ching* and mother's blood and formed of the combining of the "four elements."[7] Therefore the causes of longevity or early demise are many. Death at two or three years of age, five or seven, or up to twelve or thirteen is invariably the result of conception without observing the taboos. This is why the children are not long lived. Those who die at twenty or thirty are inherently deficient in their "four elements." They lack sturdy constitutions and fail to study the arts of self-cultivation. Upon reaching manhood, when the vitality is strong, they lose themselves in amorous pursuits and squander their *ching-ch'i*. Many illnesses arise, and they do not know the means to cure them. Having cut themselves off at the root, how can they hope to attain long life?

The Emperor asked:

> When *T'ai-chi* (the Great Ultimate) split apart, this was the beginning of the division of *yin* and *yang*. The light and the pure became heaven; the turbid and impure became earth. The way of *Ch'ien* became man and the way of *K'un* became woman. Man stands in the midst of this and the myriad things are born therein. How could they be without *yin* and *yang*? If heaven was without *yin* and *yang*, the sun and moon would have no brightness. If earth was without *yin* and *yang*, the myriad things would not be born. If man was without *yin* and *yang*, the *tao* of human relations would be severed. There cannot be a single day without the interaction of *yin* and *yang*. However, there are still some things I do not understand about what you have said. I beg you to speak in detail of the essentials of intercourse between man and woman and the methods of curing illness so as to promote longevity.

Su Nü replied:

> Splendid! Splendid! The union of man and woman is the *tao* of "one *yin* and one *yang*."[8] Therefore there is *yang* within *yin* and *yin* within *yang*. Yin and yang, man

and woman, this is the *tao* of heaven and earth. However, if one misses its significance, then sickness and disease arise. It is also said that "we embrace *yin* in our arms and carry *yang* on our backs,"[9] Thus when *yang* reaches its peak, *yin* is born, and when *yin* reaches its peak *yang* begins to sprout. Within the woman's private parts there naturally exists both *yin* and *yang*, and therein the firm and the yielding each possesses the potential for pleasure.

The Emperor asked:

I have now learned of the *tao* of mutual interaction between man and wife, but have not yet grasped its essence. Can you explain why man and wife sometimes fail to enjoy a feeling of pleasure from their intimacy when they engage in sexual intercourse?

Su Nü replied:

If one seeks to achieve the *tao* of union between man and woman, together with the methods for supplementing the *ching* and gathering *ch'i*, the principles of massage and exercises for *ch'i* circulation, "reverting to the root and returning to the source," "deepening the root and firming the stalk," and long lasting love between partners, but neglects to include the method of gathering *yin*, then one simply grows weary from intercourse and misses its pleasure. One languishes forever in the dark, unable to comprehend its joy. This is because people are unable to respect this *tao*. If one practices these methods, they are truly the secret of cultivating life. When man and woman unite in intercourse, the secret of pleasure is naturally contained within the woman's private parts, but those who know its charm are very few. Therefore, to be full of love but end in feelings of unhappiness for both partners is to unite in vain and without pleasure. Moreover, if the woman's *ching* secretions have not yet issued forth and her private parts are dry, but the man forces his way, then the "jade stalk" simply pierces in vain and it is a useless waste of spirit. Sometimes the fire of desire in the woman has already been stirred, but the man's "jade stalk" is not hard when the *ching* fluid leaves his body and the feeling of comfort has not yet been realized. The woman is without joy or satisfaction in her heart and will be resentful for a lifetime.

Chapter 2. The Nine Postures

The Emperor asked: "Relations between man and woman represent the great desire of humanity and is the source of life for the myriad things. How is it that nowadays there are those who neglect this and fail to grasp its significance?" Su Nü replied:

This must be spoken of with great care and subtlety. The ignorant regard this as indecent, but it is not a teaching that encourages lust or leads people to desire. In reality it is the marvelous art of cultivating life. The secret of intercourse includes nine methods. Their names are as follows: (1) Dragon Flying, (2) Tiger Stance, (3) Monkey's Attack, (4) Clinging Cicada, (5) Turtle Rising, (6) Phoenix Soaring, (7) Rabbit Licking, (8) Fishes Nibbling, (9) Cranes Entwined.

The Emperor asked: "I have now heard the names of the 'nine postures.' Is there a method to their practice?" Su Nü replied:

Every posture has its own method, and they imitate the likeness of creatures. Therefore the list of names is called the 'nine postures.'

1. Dragon Flying. Have the woman lie face up with her feet pointing to the sky. The man lies upon her, resting on her thighs and sucking her tongue. The woman raises her "female gate" and receives the "jade stalk" as it pierces the door of the "mysterious feminine." Withdraw and tap her "gate." Raise your body and undulate, carrying out the method of eight deep and six shallow. In this way her private parts will be firm and hot, and his *yang* member will be hard and strong. The man will be happy and the woman joyful. Both will experience emotional delight, and the hundred ills will disappear. This method resembles the form of a dragon rousing from hibernation and mounting into the clouds.

2. Tiger Stance. Have the woman assume the "barbarian squat" and lower her head. The man squats behind her, embraces her waist and inserts his "jade stalk" into the "feminine gate," carrying out the method of five shallow and six deep. He withdraws a hundred times, and as her "jade pincers" open up, *ching* juices gush forth. Water and fire are in complementary interaction, and the marvels of elixir and cauldron are fully realized. Vexations are all eliminated and the blood vessels flow freely. It fortifies the heart and strengthens the will. This method resembles a tiger or leopard emerging from the jungle and roaring into the wind.

3. *Monkey's Attack.* Have the woman spread her thighs and sit on the man's legs. When her "feminine gate" is open and well lubricated, he inserts the "jade hammer" and repeatedly taps the "*yin* door." He then carries out the method of nine shallow and five deep. When the woman whispers ceaselessly and her secretions overflow, the man firmly secures his "*yang* treasure chest" and does not ejaculate. The hundred ills suddenly disappear, the *ch'i* is increased, life extended, and hunger banished. This method resembles a monkey clinging to a branch and plucking a fruit. Its secret lies in agility.

4. *Cicada Clinging.* Have the woman stretch out her left thigh straight and bend her right thigh. The man squats behind her and, drawing his "jade scepter,"[10] freely knocks at her "red pearl." Carry out the method of seven deep and eight shallow, as her "red ball"[11] opens wide. Ecstatic and lively, one fully enjoys the pleasure of this activity. It opens the body's joints and channels and over a long period is very beneficial. This method resembles a golden cicada embracing a tree, sipping dew, and chirping with a clear voice. It conceals its prize within and does not spew it forth.

5. *Turtle Rising.* Have the woman lie face up. She should be contented and vacant as if unaffected by emotion. The man uses the fingers of both hands to support her legs and lifts them up past her breasts. Extending the head, he suddenly enters her "red gate," deeply thrusting at her "grain seed." Suddenly retracting and suddenly extending, it imitates the movements of a turtle head. This is capable of eliminating retained heat and expelling the pathogenic *ch'i* in the Five Viscera. This method resembles a dark turtle swimming up from the deep. It protects itself with a hard shell, drags its tail in the mud, and preserves its purity.[12]

6. *Soaring Phoenix.* Have the woman lie face up with her body across the bed and raise her thighs with her hands. The man tightly embraces her waist with both hands and inserts the "golden hammer" into the "jade gate." He attacks wildly to the left and right until her private parts are very

hot and her body moves supply. Carry out the nine shallow and eight deep method, and the woman will be satisfied and pant lightly, while her slippery liquid boils over. This supplements all deficiencies, fortifies the *ching* and marrow, and makes the body light. It lengthens the lifespan and arrests aging. This method resembles the auspicious phoenix of Mount Tan that beats its wings, sways, and soars over the world.

7. *Rabbit Licking.* First the man lies face up on the bed and stretches both legs straight out. Now have the woman mount backwards astride the man's thighs. With her hand she grasps his "middle member" and probes for her "house gate." As he pierces her "zither strings," she feels the "jade stick" become firm and hard. He then carries out the method of shallow and deep. This nourishes the blood and activates the *ch'i*, and eliminates soreness and pain in the four limbs. This method resembles the joy of a jade rabbit leaping about, now crouching and now jumping, appearing and disappearing unpredictably. Because it never loses its natural purity, it is able to catch the moon in the highest heavens.

8. *Fishes Nibbling.*[13] Have two women, one face up and one face down, clasp each other as if having intercourse. Their "feminine gates" should be pressed together, and by rubbing themselves, their "fish mouths" will naturally open like fish swimming about nibbling duckweed. The man sits in "winnowing basket" pose beside them and waits until the "red tide" pulses forth. First, with his hand, he probes where the two mouths are joined and places his "stalk" between them. Then, above and below as he pleases, he penetrates both parties in joyous union. This greatly strengthens the sinews and bones and doubles the strength of one's *ch'i*. It warms the interior and cures the "five ills" and "seven injuries." This method resembles fish swimming and playing among the seaweed. The essential thing is to consume the pure and expel the foul.

9. *Cranes Entwined.* Have the woman embrace the man's neck and place her right foot on the bed. With his right hand he raises the woman's left thigh and supports it on his shoulder. Their two bodies press tightly together. He slightly withdraws his "jade stalk" to peek at her "water caltrop teeth."[14] He slowly thrusts at her "grain seed," and undulating lightly and leisurely,

carries out the method of nine shallow and one deep. Suddenly the heart of the flower opens and her scented secretions seep forth. Guard your center and preserve your spirit. This aids digestion and stimulates the appetite. It cures a hundred ills and confers long life and resistance to hunger. This method resembles the red crane circling back. It spreads its long feathers and does not fold them until it reaches the land of marvels.

Chapter 3. Shallow and Deep

The Emperor asked: "Understanding the stages of arousal and shallow and deep are essential for refining the elixir. However, if one fails to regulate them correctly, can these be dangerous?"

Su Nü replied: "To be shallow and insufficient is perverse; to be deep and go too far is malicious. There are also the methods of the 'thirty-six varieties' and the 'seventy-two kinds,' which are capable of harmonizing sweet emotions and intensifying the feeling of joy. However, its principles are very profound."

The Emperor asked: "The *tao* of intercourse between man and woman is such that if one recklessly performs the methods of shallow and deep, the result will be much injury and little benefit. I have heard of the secret of 'gathering and supplementing' to promote one's own longevity. Would you reveal its details?"

Su Nü replied:

The man must observe the woman's emotional state and at the same time carefully guard his own "precious substance" and not shed it. First rub your two hands together until they are hot and then firmly grasp the "jade stalk." Next use the method of withdrawing shallow and entering deep. Having the patience for protracted war enhances the sublime pleasure. One must not be too hasty nor too slow. Also avoid straining to penetrate deeply, for excessive depth will cause injury. Stab her "zither strings" and attack her "water caltrop teeth." When she reaches the height of ecstasy, she will unconsciously close her teeth. Perspiring fragrantly, she pants and sighs. Her eyes close and her face becomes hot. Her scented flower bud opens and the slippery liquid overflows. This is the height of pleasure. Now there are eight names for the inside of the woman's private parts. The first is called "zither strings" at a depth of one inch. The second is called "water caltrop teeth" at a depth of two inches. The third is called "peaceful valley" at a depth of three inches. The fourth is called "dark pearl" at a depth of four inches. The fifth is called "valley seed" at a depth of five inches. The sixth is called "palace of delight" at a depth of six inches. The seventh is called "gate of posterity"[15] at a depth of seven inches. The eighth is called "north pole" at a depth of eight inches.

The Emperor asked: "What are the illnesses that arise from the injuries of intercourse?"

Su Nü replied:

It is critically important in intercourse to avoid excessively deep penetration. Too great depth injures the Five Viscera. If penetration reaches the "valley seed," it injures the liver, and one will be afflicted with clouded vision, caked tears, and discomfort in the four limbs. If penetration reaches the "palace of delight," then the lungs are injured and one is afflicted with nausea, belching, asthma, and dizziness. If penetration reaches the "gate of posterity," then the spleen will be injured and one will suffer sallowness of complexion, distension of the abdomen, depression, and cold dysentery. If penetration reaches the "north pole," then the kidneys will be injured and one will suffer weakness in the waist and feet, "steaming of the bones,"[16] and "tidal fever."[17] If penetration is suddenly shallow and suddenly deep, this injures the heart and the person will experience heat in the face, coughing due to deficiency, nightmares, and nocturnal emissions. Therefore, in intercourse, penetration must not be too deep. The woman's "*tan* point" is located three inches below the navel. Be careful not to injure it. Also, one must not be too hasty or too slow. If one is too hasty, this injures the blood; and, if too slow, this harms the *ch'i*. There is only harm and no benefit in this.

The Emperor asked: "Understanding the stages of arousal is the essential factor in regulating shallow and deep. This much already has been examined and understood. The principles of injury and harm must also not be overlooked. However, there remains the influence of the prohibitions and taboos that I hope you will discuss without sparing any details."

Su Nü replied:

In refining the elixir, if one transgresses the taboos, then in the case of major offenses, heaven and earth will take away their allotted spans and ghosts and gods will afflict their bodies. The "three internal parasites"[18] will seek to invade them and they will harbor sickness and suffer evil. If children are born they will be short lived. They will be dull and unworthy, or stupid and evil. They will bring harm to father and mother. How can one fail to be cautious? One should not have intercourse when heaven and earth are dark and trembling, when there is swift lightning, violent winds, and heavy rain, nor during the first and last quarter of the moon, half and full moons, bitter cold and intense heat, eclipses of the sun and moon, the birthdays of the gods, the sexegenary cycle days *keng-shen* and *chia-tzu*, one's own birthday, the "three commencements"[19] and "eight festivals,"[20] the fifth day of the fifth lunar month, the inauspicious days of the almanac *yüeh-sha* and *yüeh-p'o*,[21] the period of mourning, and "red slaughter" days all must not be transgressed. Furthermore, geographical settings such as the "five sacred peaks"[22] and great rivers; the environs of shrines and altars; temples to the gods; the presence of all images of gods and ghosts; the proximity of wells, kitchen stoves, eaves, and toilets all are harmful and bring on early death. Some as a result may give birth to deformed offspring. There also are taboos for the time of intercourse. One must not transgress those times when one is hungry, full, and drunk; mentally exhausted and physically fatigued; distressed and anxiety ridden; recently recovered from an illness; in mourning, or during the woman's menses.

Chapter 4. The Five Desires and Five Injuries

The Emperor asked:

If the young and strong overexert themselves, they suffer decline. Extreme joy inevitably brings much sorrow. The sage regulates himself by means of the *tao*. Therefore, it is said that if a man mounts a hundred women, his longevity will equal that of heaven and earth. However, people today suffer weak sinews and slack flesh before they reach fifty. The element of fire

rages while the water dries up.[23] Why is it that in the end they come to ruin?

Su Nü replied:

All people are subject to the various conditions summarized in the "five desires," "five injuries," and "ten movements." If these are properly observed there is contentment and satisfaction. If not, each brings injury.

The signs of the five desires:

1. When the woman's face is flushed and moist, it means that she feels longing. First insert the "jade stalk" and leisurely undulate. Slowly withdraw, and remaining outside the "gate," examine her state.
2. When she pants from her nostrils, it means that the fire of passion is slightly aroused. First pierce the "*yin* gate" with the "jade stalk" and stab her "valley seed,"[24] but do not go too deep and wait for the next stage of arousal.
3. When her throat becomes dry and hoarse, it means that her emotions are stirred and her fire is ablaze. Now withdraw the "jade stalk" and wait for her eyes to close and tongue to emerge. When she pants audibly you may move in and out as you please and you will gradually arrive at the realm of the sublime.
4. When the "red ball" becomes lubricous, it means that the fire of the heart is at full strength. Stab her and the slippery wetness overflows to the outside. Gently penetrate to the "water caltrop teeth" and move left or right, slowly or rapidly, using whatever method pleases.
5. When she raises her "golden lilies"[25] and encircles the man, it means that she has reached the stage of complete satisfaction and is moved to wrap her feet around his waist and embrace his shoulders and back with her hands. When her tongue emerges and does not retract, you may stab her "palace of delight." Now joy permeates her four limbs.

The signs of the five injuries:

1. When the "*yin* gate" is still closed and not yet open, one should not penetrate it. To penetrate it at this stage injures her lungs. If the lungs are injured this will result in asthma and loud wheezing.

127

2. If the "golden stalk" is soft and weak when her passion reaches its peak and intercourse takes place after it has past, this injures the heart. If the heart is injured, then her menses will become irregular.

3. When a young woman and an old man come together, the fire of his passion burns in a vacuum and not having her desires satisfied injures the liver. When the liver is injured, the mind becomes confused and the vision unclear.

4. When desires are satisfied and emotions fulfilled, but the *yang* arousal does not subside, this injures the kidneys. When the kidneys are injured this causes vaginal bleeding.

5. When intercourse is forced before the end of the "monthly affliction," the spleen is injured. When the spleen is injured, the countenance becomes sallow.

The stages of the ten movements:

1. With her jade hands she embraces the man's back and her lower body moves of itself. She thrusts out her tongue and presses him tightly to stir his emotions. This is the stage of arousal.

2. When her scented body reclines, and she stretches out her hands and feet without moving, panting lightly from the nose, it means that she has reached the stage of desiring penetration and withdrawal.

3. When she extends her wrists and opens her palms, grasps the sleeping "jade hammer" and rotates her body, this is the "mouth watering" stage.

4. When her speech becomes playful and chattering, her eyes roll alluringly, and she makes frequent moaning sounds, this means that she has reached the stage of the height of desire.

5. When she embraces her own "golden lilies" with her hands and exposes the gate of her "mysterious feminine," it means that she has reached the stage of emotional fulfillment and bliss.

6. When she takes the "jade scepter" in her mouth and appears at once blissful, drunk, and drowsy, and the inside of her private parts longs for stimulation, then this is the stage of desiring wild thrusts shallow and deep.

7. When she stretches out her "golden lilies" and pulls his "jade hammer" as if advancing and retreating, while emitting a low moaning sound, this is the stage of the running of her *yin* tide.

8. When suddenly she realizes her desire and slightly turns her waist, her fragrant perspiration not yet dry and her smile constant, then this is the stage of fearing that his *yang-ch'i* may be spent and his emotional interest exhausted.

9. When the sweet emotion has arrived and the supreme joy gradually increases, her *ching* secretions have been released, and she clutches him ever so tightly, this is the stage of incomplete satisfaction.

10. When her body is hot and she is soaked with perspiration, her feet become languorous and her hands inert, this then is the stage of peak emotion and complete satisfaction.

Chapter 5. The Supreme Human Relationship

The Emperor asked: "The supreme human relationship consists of a man and a wife, and then children and grandchildren. Is it not true that we must be discriminating in respect to a woman's virtue and appearance?"

Su Nü replied:

A woman's virtue is her inner beauty; her appearance is her outer beauty. First observe her skin and then observe her inner qualities. If a woman's hair is burnt black, her bones large, or her flesh coarse; if she is disproportionately fat or thin, exceptionally tall or short or of an unsuitable age, then she will be barren, manly of speech, or violent and abrupt in her actions. Her private parts will be dry and her womb cold. She will leak red or white discharge and have a savage odor. This is extremely harmful to one's *yang-ch'i*.

The Emperor asked: "I have now heard your explanation of how one's *yang-ch'i* may be harmed. What do you think of those who use drugs and special foods as tonic supplements?"

Su Nü replied:

Intercourse between man and woman should not be for the purpose of lustful pleasure. People today do not understand the meaning of self-cultivation. They force themselves to perform the act and therefore most often harm their *ching* and damage their *ch'i*. Sicknesses arise one after another from this. Some mistakenly consume medicines that are harmful to their lives. Is this not a great pity!

The Emperor asked: "The *tao* of man and wife is an arrangement for children and grandchildren, but today why is it that there are those without offspring?"
Su Nü replied:

There are three reasons why women are childless and three why men are without offspring. Men whose *ching* is cold and slippery; men who are exhausted from excessive lust; and men who suffer fear and shrinking in approaching the "enemy" are all without offspring. Women who are licentious by nature and sexually aroused at the mere sight of the object; women whose "treasury of heirs" is deficient and cold and whose "treasury gate" does not open; and those where there is no harmony between husband and wife and the fire of jealousy rages, these are all without children.

The Emperor asked: "By what techniques may the childless obtain children?"
Su Nü replied:

The method for seeking children is based on calculating the correspondences of *yin* and *yang*. Use yellow gauze, yellow damask, and yellow silk to make clothing, coverlet, curtains, and bedding. Choose an auspicious day and write the hour, day, month, and year of birth on a peach tree[26] branch and place this within the bedroom. Also on the third day of the ninth [lunar] month one may take a peach branch growing in an easterly direction, write one's name upon it, and insert it in the bed. It is necessary to observe when the woman's menses has ceased for three or four days, then each partner must bathe, burn incense, pray to the spirits of heaven and earth, and then enter the bed curtains for intercourse. At this time, her "palace of heirs" has not yet closed, and so conception can take place. As for the method of mounting, follow the correct methods for entering and withdrawing. Cleanse the heart and free the mind from anxiety. Do

not play or act foolishly; do not use aphrodisiacs; and do not look at books with erotic illustrations. If one transgresses these, it is harmful to the parents and disadvantageous for conception.

The Emperor asked: "Why is it that the *tao* of *yin* and *yang* is called 'intercourse?'"
Su Nü replied:

In the union of *yin* and *yang*, the man bestows and the woman receives, therefore it is called "intercourse." Within the woman's private parts there is naturally a clear sign. First stab her "zither strings" and then penetrate to the "water caltrop teeth." When the sublime joy has reached its peak, then the true treasure is released. If the *yin* blood surrounds the *yang-ching*, then a male child is born. If the *yang-ching* surrounds the *yin* blood, a female child is born. This is what is called the *tao* of intercourse between *yin* and *yang*.

The Emperor asked: "Intercourse is the source of human relationships, but why is it that there are those who are not harmonious and happy?"
Su Nü replied:

The reason is that the woman is not able to determine her husband's desires, and the husband does not understand the nature of women. Thus they fail to realize the *tao* of human relations or the principles of producing descendants. Each is perverted and licentious, each harbors dissatisfaction, and both are filled with anger. Some abandon their wives and concubines and have relations with kept mistresses. Some betray their husbands and engage in illicit affairs and deceitful lust. There also are men who are impotent and unable to fulfill their desires, and others who rush in with reckless abandon and do not let up. Later they feel disgust for the rest of their lives.

The Emperor asked: "Between man and wife, closeness and intimacy, mutual respect and love are the constants of human relationships. But where do respect and love come from?"
Su Nü replied:

The hexagram "After Completion" represents concord; the hexagram "Before Completion" represents conflict. When the couple's "eight characters"[27] are in accord and young and vigorous partners come together at the proper time, then this is concord; when the "eight characters" do not agree and old and young partners do not meet at the proper time, then this is conflict. When both are talented and comely, and emotionally compatible, this is concord. When their stupidity and ugliness makes them repulsive and they are cruel and quarrelsome, this is conflict. However, when kindness and love are in accord, then there is respect. With respect comes wealth, honor, and long life; moreover, children and grandchildren will be numerous.

Chapter 6. Large and Small, Long and Short

The Emperor asked: "Why is it that among men's 'precious things,' there are distinctions of large and small, long and short, and hard and soft?"

Su Nü replied:

Physical endowments differ just as men's countenances. Distinctions of large and small, long and short, hard and soft are all matters of natural endowment. Thus there are short men with heroic members and also sturdy men with short members. Some men are weak and thin, but possessed of members that are fat and hard; some men are fat and large, but possessed of members that are soft and retracted. Some members are like express carts, some are highly ambitious, and still others have enraged flesh and bursting veins. None of these, however, are detrimental to the essence of intercourse.

The Emperor asked: "In respect to the 'middle member,'[28] there are distinctions of large and small, long and short, and hard and soft. However, are there also differences in the pleasure derived from intercourse?"

Su Nü replied: "There indeed are distinctions in physical endowment. Large and small, long and short, and physical differences are matters of external appearance. Deriving pleasure from sexual intercourse is a matter of inner emotion. If first you bind them with love and respect and press them with true sentiments, then of what relevance are large and small, long and short?"

The Emperor asked: "Are there not also distinctions of hard and soft?"

Su Nü replied: "Long and large, but weak and soft, does not compare to short and small, but firm and hard. Firm and hard, but rough and violent is not as good as soft and weak, but gentle and refined. If one can achieve the "Doctrine of the Mean," then it may be said that beauty and goodness have both been realized."

The Emperor asked: "Taoist priests make use of medicinal substances to enable the short and small to become long and large, and the soft and weak to become firm and hard. Is there danger of disastrous side effects, or do they offer strengthening and opening benefits?"

Su Nü replied:

When two hearts are in harmony and the *ch'i* flows freely throughout the body, then the short and the small naturally become longer and larger, the soft and the weak naturally firm and hard. Gentlemen of the *tao* who possess this ability have intercourse with a hundred women without softening. Possessing the techniques of self-cultivation, one can make use of *yin* to benefit *yang*. By regulating the breath and "borrowing water to control fire," one can strengthen the "true treasure" and go the whole night without ejaculating. After long practice one can achieve greater longevity and be free of illness. However, if one uses "five stones"[29] *yang* strengthening medicine or prescriptions based on seal penis and testes, which increase the body's fire, the flame burning unchecked in the midst of deficiency causes one's true *yang* to be exhausted. The damage will not be inconsiderable.

The Emperor asked: "Are there then not restrictions for those who possess the art of self-cultivation?"

Su Nü replied:

The *ch'i* circulation flows throughout the body. Partners come together for sexual union and at the appropriate time they stop. One must measure one's own strength and ejaculate accordingly. Anything else is simply force and foolishness. In this way, even a cultivated gentleman may come to decay and ruin. To take medicine for three mornings is not as good as sleeping alone for one night. This was the teaching of the wise men of old.

Chapter 7. Cultivating Life

The Emperor asked: "What is the root of the *tao* of cultivating life?"
Su Nü replied:

Ch'i is the root of the *tao* of cultivating life. *Ch'i* is able to circulate the blood. Blood can be transformed into *ching*, and *ching* can nourish the spirit. As long as the spirit survives there is life. When the spirit dissipates there is death. *Ch'i*, then, is the root of spirit. Those who train their *ch'i* can walk through fire without being burned and submerge themselves in water without drowning. If one can protect the *ching* and not allow it to be dissipated, then one can have intercourse the whole night without ejaculating. If one is unable to guard the *ching* and spirit, and wildly and foolishly does whatever one pleases, one surely will sacrifice one's spirit and lose one's *ch'i*. This is called "the axe that snatches away life."

The Emperor asked: "If a man devotes himself exclusively to the *tao* of nourishing life, but does not practice the rites of man and wife within the bed curtains, will not the principle of human relationships be destroyed and the line of descendants suspended?"
Su Nü replied:

When people are young, their vitality is not yet sufficient and they must observe moderation in sex. They must not indulge in excessive lust or extravagant ejaculation. When one reaches manhood, the *ching-ch'i* is full to overflowing, and if one locks the *ching* and represses desire, then strange illnesses will appear. Therefore one must not abstain from ejaculation altogether, but it must be neither excessive nor too little.

The Emperor asked: "What about frequent ejaculation for the sake of amusement or completely locking one's *ching* for the sake of nourishing the spirit?"
Su Nü replied: "This is inadvisable. Frequent ejaculation, but occasionally refraining from leakage, on the contrary produces abscesses. If one usually locks, but occasionally ejaculates, then one will suffer the effects of sudden deficiency. Both are harmful to the *tao* of cultivating life."

The Emperor asked: "How does one know when a man's *ching* and blood are full and his spirit and *ch'i* sufficient?"
Su Nü replied:

A boy reaches puberty at sixteen, but his vitality is not yet sufficient and his mind not yet stable. He therefore must observe abstinence. When he reaches the age of twenty, his vitality is becoming stronger, and the *ching* is concentrated in the intestines and stomach. One may then ejaculate once in thirty days. At thirty, the vitality is strong and abundant, and the *ching* is in the thighs. One may ejaculate once in five days. At forty, the *ching* is concentrated in the lower back, and one may ejaculate once in seven days. At fifty, the vitality begins to decline, and the *ching* is concentrated in the spine. One may then ejaculate once in half a month. When one reaches sixty-four years of age, the period of one's potency is finished and the cycle of hexagrams complete. The vitality is weak and the *ching* secretions exhausted. If one can preserve one's remaining *ch'i* after sixty, then those who are vigorous may still ejaculate. When one reaches seventy one must not let the emotions run wild.

The Emperor asked: "There are ignorant and shameless men who relying on their physical strength ejaculate three times or even five times in one day. What of this?"
Su Nü replied: "Those who ejaculate excessively suffer drastic deficiency. They will later become weak and disabled. To ejaculate ceaselessly is to invite an early death."
The Emperor asked: "Why is it that in the middle of the night a man's *yang-ch'i* vigorously rises and is powerfully aroused?"
Su Nü replied:

Dawn, daytime, sunset, and night: these are the four seasons of one day. Thus, *yang-ch'i* is born during the *tzu* period [11:00 PM to 1:00 AM] and is represented by the hexagram *Fu* (Return). During the *ch'ou* period [1:00 to 3:00 AM], two *yang* lines are born in the lowest position, and this is represented by the hexagram *Lin* (Approach). During the *yin* period [3:00 to 5:00 AM], the three *yang* lines are complete, and this is represented by the hexagram *T'ai* (Peace). If a man ejaculates

131

excessively at midnight, his *yang-ch'i* will dry up and be lost. Before the age of fifty, he will surely suffer dizziness, pain in the bowels, blurred vision, and hearing impairment. There are also "five injuries." The first is when a man and woman have intercourse and the *ching* ejaculated is very scant. This indicates injury to the *ch'i*. The second is when the *ching* emitted is copious. This indicates injury to the flesh. The third is when there is pain on ejaculation. This indicates injury to the sinews. The fourth is when the *ching* is emitted but roughly. This indicates injury to the bones. The fifth is when one approaches the "gate" but suddenly goes limp and drools *ching*. This indicates injury to the blood. In every case the cause is excessive ejaculation and exhaustion of the *ching*. How can one not be cautious!

Chapter 8. The Four Levels and Nine Stages

The Emperor asked: "When a man and woman are a perfect match,[30] they understand each other's feelings without saying a word. This is something subtle and secretive. By what method may one gauge and arouse her interest?"
Su Nü replied

When a man wishes to discover a woman's private feelings, he must first use words to playfully joke with and excite her interest. One should use gestures to stimulate her feelings. Man exhibits the "four levels" and woman the "nine stages." If one has intercourse when the "four" have not yet been achieved or the "nine" attained, there will, certainly be a disastrous outcome.

The Emperor asked: "What are the 'four levels' of the male?"
Su Nü replied:

If the "jade stalk" is not strong, it means that the *yang-ch'i* has not yet arrived. If it is hard and strong but does not move, it means that the muscle *ch'i* has not yet arrived. If it trembles but is not "enraged," it means that the bone *ch'i* has not yet arrived. If it is "enraged" but not long lived, it means that the kidney *ch'i* has not yet arrived. If just one of these has not yet arrived and a man transgresses it, there will surely be harm and injury.

The Emperor asked: "What are the 'nine stages' of the female?"
Su Nü replied:

If a woman is lethargic and yawning, drowsy and hazy, it means that her lung *ch'i* has not yet arrived. If her "gate" is not moist and she bends her thighs without opening them, it means that her heart *ch'i* has not yet arrived. If her eyes do not swim and her movements are not joyful, it means that her spleen *ch'i* has not yet arrived. When she feels the "jade stalk" with her hand, but without emotional pleasure, it means that her blood *ch'i* has not yet arrived. When her hands are limp and her feet slow, and she lies across the bed without moving, it means that her sinew *ch'i* has not yet arrived. When you fondle her breasts, but she shows no interest, it means that her bone *ch'i* has not yet arrived. When there is only a slight ripple of movement in her eyes and her delicate mouth is not open, it means that her liver *ch'i* has not yet arrived. When she raises her body and inclines toward the man, but her peachlike cheeks have no blush, it means that her kidney *ch'i* has not yet arrived. When her "jade pass" is barely moist, but her mouth is not yet parched, it means that the *ch'i* of her secretions has not yet arrived. When the "nine signs" have all arrived and one practices the method of nine shallow and one deep, then *yin* and *yang* are in harmony and their emotions romantically entwined. This strengthens the *yang-ch'i* and restores the damage of deficiency.

The Emperor asked: "What is the method of 'nine shallow and one deep?'"
Su Nü replied:

It means shallow insertion nine times and deep stabbing once. Each time use inhalation and exhalation, or one breath, as your measure. This is what is meant by the method of "nine shallow and one deep." From the "zither strings" to the "dark pearl" is shallow; from the "peaceful valley" to the "valley seed" is deep. When one is too shallow, there is no pleasure, and when too deep, there is injury.

The Emperor asked:

I already have heard your description of the marvels of inner alchemy, the painstaking stages of refinement, and the complementary relationship of water and fire as in the hexagram "After Completion." But there still remain some mysteries whose principles I wish to fully understand. These include universal love, salvation from early death, and ridding the world of the sorrow of sickness and barrenness.

Su Nü replied:

"Heaven and earth combine prosperously"[31] and *yin* and *yang* cooperate generously. First examine her state of emotional excitement and then observe whether the stages of *ch'i* arousal have reached their peaks or not. Energetically withdrawing and inserting, one realizes the marvel of "adding charcoal." This secures and strengthens one's own "*yang* coffers." Enjoying scented kisses and pressing closely together, absorb her *yin-ching* to supplement your *yang-ch'i*. Draw in the *ch'i* of her nostrils to fortify your spine marrow. Swallow her saliva to nourish your *tan-t'ien*. Cause the hot *ch'i* to penetrate the *ni-wan* point and permeate the four limbs. As it overflows, it strengthens the *ch'i* and blood, preserves the complexion, and prevents aging.

The Emperor said: "Self-cultivation through absorption and supplementation is the first principle of refining the inner elixir. The wise must not fail to grasp this idea."

Su Nü replied:

It is just as Your Majesty has said. This indeed is the secret of lengthening one's years and increasing the lifespan. Heaven is deficient in the northwest, therefore a man is more than sufficient in *yang-ch'i*, but deficient in blood. Earth is deficient in the southeast, therefore a woman is ample in *yin* blood, but deficient in *yang-ch'i*.[32] Those who are able to comprehend this subtle mystery use repletion to supplement deficiency. Even if one reaches a hundred years, the pleasure will be the same. Contentment and happiness will know no limit. Enjoying a long life, one's longevity will match that of heaven and earth. It will deserve to be inscribed in metal and stone and transmitted for generations to come. The beneficial influence of one's virtue will not be insignificant.

The Emperor observed the rules of self-purification and bathed. Then using these methods, he refined the inner elixir for eighty-one days. When he reached the age of 120 years, the alchemical preparation was complete and he cast a cauldron by the side of the lake. Divine dragons descended to receive him, and in broad daylight together with Su Nü, he ascended into heaven.

All-Merciful Savior Lord Ch'un-yang's True Classic of Perfect Union

Ch'un-yang yen-cheng fu-yu ti-chün chi-chi chen-ching by Lü Yen (Tung-pin)

Annotated by the Disciple, Teng Hsi-hsien, Great Immortal of the Purple-Gold Splendor

Preface

Perfect Union (After Completion) is the name of a hexagram in the *I ching*. The upper trigram is *K'an* and the lower *Li*. *Li* represents the male. Its empty middle is true *yin*, therefore the male is *yang* on the outside and *yin* on the inside. *K'an* is the trigram that represents the female. Its full middle is true *yang*, therefore the female is *yin* on the outside and *yang* on the inside. When *K'an* and *Li* have intercourse,[1] it is possible to absorb the true *yin* to supplement the true *yang* and thus become pure *yang*. Therefore, the term "Perfect Union" has been used in entitling this work. I, Hsi-hsien, longed for the *tao* for many years but groped blindly without results. Then I chanced to meet the Immortal Master Lü Ch'un-yang [Tung-pin] and became a devoted follower. I stayed with him for many years and noticed that the more intimate he was with women, the higher his spirits. I was very surprised and said: "I have heard that seekers of the True nourish their *ching*, refine their *ch'i*, and revert to the root, but I was not aware that this was involved." Master Lü laughing said: "To supplement oneself by means of another

133

allows a man to be called an adept. Are you not familiar with this method?" Hearing my question he drew out the *Classic of Perfect Union* and secretly revealed the aphorisms. In a burst of clarity I realized that the *tao* was close at hand. The *Classic* consists of some hundred verses that explain things by use of metaphor. I, therefore, most humbly attempted to explicate its profundity. I hope that seekers of the True will be able to fully realize it.

> The superior general in engaging the
> enemy
> Must be skilled in fondling, sucking, and
> inhaling.
> His mind must be detached and his body
> entrusted to heaven and earth.
> He should close his eyes as if lost to him-
> self.

"Superior general" is a metaphor for the adept. "To engage" means to perform the act. "The enemy" is the woman. When he first enters the bedchamber, a man "fondles" the woman's "*yin* gate" with his hand, and with his tongue he "sucks" her tongue. He fondles her breasts and with his nose "inhales" the pure *ch'i* from her nose to move her heart. I must restrain myself and "detach my mind" to roam freely above the heavens, while "entrusting my body" to the land of nonbeing. I close my eyes and seeing nothing lose myself, not allowing my heart to be stirred.

> Feeling a desire to attack, I must not
> attack,
> But withdraw my forces and avoid the
> enemy.
> Sharpening my spears and lances,
> I seem to join the battle, but then again am
> fearful.
> I wait for my opponent to grow weary,
> While cultivating my own comfort.

"Desiring to attack" the opponent means desiring to move. "Sharpening" means that the opponent's hands approach to rub and fondle me. "Seeming to join the battle" describes my attitude. The opponent desires that I move, but I refuse to move and retreat to avoid her. If the opponent does not rub and

fondle my *yang* member, I give the appearance of joining the battle, and then again pretend to be fearful. I wait for my opponent to grow weary, while cultivating my own comfort.

> The bandits rise up with a show of bold-
> ness,
> Their fiendish forces arrayed like the
> spines of a hedgehog.
> My side slowly rises and with banners and
> war gongs sets forth from its camp.
> When lances are crossed, I do not contend,
> But enter a state of mental abstraction.
> The opponent seeks to take up arms
> To breech my stronghold,
> But with deep trenches and high ramparts,
> I rest secure in my fastness.
> From time to time I provoke a battle,
> And the enemy's forces come out to accept
> the challenge,
> But I seem not to respond,
> Withdraw my forces and move slowly.

"Bandits" refers to the opponent. When the opponent's passions are fully aroused, her power is that of "fiendish forces"[2] arising on all sides. I must respond slowly and engage without "contending." "Contending" means to move. "Entering a state of mental abstraction" means that I lie in wait serenely and do not allow my mind to be stirred. When the opponent attempts to contend, but without success, she will initiate movements from below to shake me above. I should close my eyes and hold my breath as if restraining urine or a bowel movement, inhale and contract without being startled. After a long time, I then "provoke" her. "Provoke" means that I move. She then will be greatly aroused and respond, but I must immediately retreat, just leaving an inch or so within her.

> The enemy brandishes her might in all
> directions,
> Pressing me with her advancing forces.
> I enter and then retreat again to lay an
> ambush.
> The enemy will then attack,
> But I inform her
> I will now occupy the low ground,
> While she may take the high.
> The one on top becomes complacent,

And, though the opponent harasses me, I
   maintain my concentration,
And am ever victorious.

"Victorious" means that I am victorious over my opponent. When the enemy's passion is aroused, she will "press me with her advancing forces." I have no choice but to respond and so "enter" the "gate of *K'un*." Soon, however, I once again retreat to the outside, turn over, and lie on my back as stiff as a corpse. The opponent's desire increases and again she returns to the attack. I am now in the lower position, and, encouraging her to occupy the upper, I entice her to perform the movements. In this way I "remain concentrated" and victory is assured.

As the enemy occupies the higher ground,
She must approach from above.
My forces maintain strict discipline,
Keeping a tight rein on the horses.
The turtle retracts and the dragon inhales;
The serpent swallows and the tiger trembles.
I shake her two armies
And give the opponent no rest.
Sensing alarm in my forces,
I order them to hold to the heights,
Without descending and without contending.
I wait for her storm,
And in a short time
Her forces are transformed into water.
The enemy comes to me to surrender,
But my magnanimity and reasonableness
Causes her to sincerely capitulate.
Giving up her treasure to me,
She lays down her arms and puts away her
   siege walls.

The preceding is the most important secret verse. The emphasis is on the eight words: "Turtle retracts, dragon inhales, serpent swallows, tiger trembles." Close your eyes and shut your mouth. Withdraw your hands and retract your feet. Pinch closed the anus[3] and concentrate the mind. This is what is meant by "turtle retracts." Inhale her "true fluid" in a reverse direction so that it flows upward from your *wei-lü* point, creating a continuous circuit and directly entering the *ni-wan*. This is the "inhaling" of the dra-

gon. The serpent in "swallowing" things gently holds them in its mouth, waits for them to experience difficulty, and then swallows them down, refusing to let go. The tiger in stalking its prey "trembles" lest they become aware, conceals its body, and watches in silence. In the end, it inevitably seizes and catches it. By using these four methods, the opponent surely will tire, and I then may employ my hands to "shake the opponent's armies." "Shake" means to toy with; the "two armies" are her breasts, and this causes them to become intensely excited. I do not go in for the kill but maintain my vigilance. Raising my body to a high position, I refrain from moving or coming down, waiting for the opponent's true *ching* to descend. The opponent then feels loathe to stir, but I continue to tease her in a good-natured way, and she surrenders with complete sincerity. Having captured her "treasure," I gather it up and cache it securely.

Again I suck her provisions,
And again dip into her grain stores.
Sucking her grain-stores and dipping into
   her secret parts,
The short weapon enters again.

This is the second time one performs the act. "Provisions" refers to her tongue, and "grain-stores" to her breasts. "Secret parts" is the "jade gate." "Short weapon" means that when retracted it becomes shortened. "Entering again" means re-entering the "jade gate" to arouse it.

When the enemy's forces join the battle
   again,
Their spirit will be high,
But again I lie face up, stiff as a corpse,
Waiting for her forces to arrive.
Using my stiff straightness to block the
   opponent,
Her storm rages more furiously.
My seeming to be helpless
Makes the enemy more determined.
I warn her to halt,
And our two armies face each other
Less than a foot apart.
I address the enemy,
Neither attacking nor laying down my
   arms,
But sitting and biding my time,

135

Waiting for her *ch'i* to subside,
While my heart is dead as ashes.
With words as warm as sweet wine
I adopt an attitude of deliberateness,
Slowing down to observe the opponent.

"More determined" means that the opponent moves without resting. But I "warn her to halt and not to move." The opponent being on top and I below is referred to as "the two armies." Being "less than a foot apart" means that I leave just one inch inside and the rest outside. Again I address her, neither moving nor giving up. "Sitting and biding" means that I have the woman support herself on hands and feet while waiting out the period before her *ch'i-ching*[4] comes down. At the same time, my heart becomes even more like "dead ashes," although my speech must be "sweet and warm" to heighten the opponent's passion. I, however, slow down and wait for her.

I am slow, but the opponent is hurried,
As the struggle once again intensifies.
When swords are crossed,
I enter and then once again retreat.
Again I suck her provisions,
And dip into her grain stores.
The turtle, tiger, serpent, and dragon
Retract, tremble, swallow, and inhale.
The opponent certainly will throw down
    her arms,
While I gather up the spoils of battle.
This is called "After Completion,"[5]
And brings about a generation of peace.
Withdrawing from the battlefield and dis-
    charging the troops,
I relax and take a breather,
Returning it to the arsenal and raising it to
    the highest point.

"Intensifies" means that the passion is rising. When her passion reaches the level of "After Completion," I must "enter" her again and execute deep and shallow thrusts according to the proper method. After an interval, I once again "withdraw" slightly, suck her tongue, fondle her breasts, and continue in the preceding manner. In this way, the opponent's true *ching* will be completely released, and I then "gather" it up. "After Completion" means that I already have obtained her true *yang*. "One genera-

tion" indicates a period of twelve years. With one coition, if a man is able to obtain the true *yang*, his lifespan may be increased by twelve years. The "arsenal" is the brain[6] and the "highest point" is the *ni-wan*. When the battle is over one dismounts from horseback and lies down on the back to catch the breath. Stretch the waist and move with an undulating motion so that [the true *yang*] "rises" up to the *ni-wan*, thereby returning to the primal source. In this way, one avoids illness and achieves longevity.

Building a mountain of nine *jen*[7]
Begins with one basket of earth.
This cannot be transmitted to one who
    lacks virtue,
But if the spirit is fully realized, one will
    grasp its meaning.

"Building a mountain of nine *jen*" refers to becoming an Immortal of the Nine Heavens. "One basket of earth" means one gathering of the true *yang*. One gathering lengthens the lifespan by "twelve years," thus long life begins with one gathering. However, this art must not be transmitted to those without virtue, for only the virtuous will be fully realized in spirit. When the spirit is realized, the mind is at peace and therefore able to grasp the meaning and practice it.

Exposition of Cultivating the True Essence by the Great Immortal of the Purple Gold Splendor
Tzu-chin kuang-yao ta-hsien hsiu-chen yen-i

Preface

In the third year of the Yüan-feng reign [108 B.C.] of the Han dynasty, Wu Hsien presented the *Record of Cultivating the True Essence* (*Hsiu-chen yü-lu*) to the Emperor Wu. Alas, the Emperor was not able to make use of it. However, the book has been handed down to later generations. Those who are able to practice even a fraction of this art will achieve strength of body and long life. If applied to the begetting of children, the offspring will be intelligent and easy to raise. However, there are some things that must be avoided and some that are taboo. Only after understanding what is to be avoided and what is taboo can one progress step by step in this discipline. I have set forth its principles in twenty chapters. Various practices have been explained and a sequence established, basing the practices on a graded sequence. The order must not be altered in any way or the practices incompletely performed. In this way, seekers of the True will naturally gain what they desire.

By Teng Hsi-hsien

Chapter 1. Essentials of the Avoidances and Taboos

When mounting women one must first have a clear understanding of the "five avoidances." Women who have manly voices and coarse skin, yellow hair and violent dispositions, and are sneaky and jealous constitute the first avoidance. Those with evil appearances and unhealthy countenances, bald heads and underarm odor, hunched backs and jutting chests, and who hop like sparrows or slither like snakes constitute the second avoidance. Those who are sallow, thin, frail, and weak, cold of body and deficient of *ch'i*, and whose channels of circulation are out of harmony constitute the third avoidance. Women who are mad, deaf, or dumb, who are lame or blind in one eye, who have scabies, scars, or are insane, who are too fat or too thin, or whose pubic hair is coarse and dense constitute the fourth avoidance. Women who are over forty, have borne many children and whose *yin* is weak, whose skin is loose and breasts are slack, these are harmful and confer no benefit. This is the fifth avoidance.

There are certain times suitable for intercourse, and therefore one must know the "five taboos." The fifteenth day of the first, seventh, and tenth lunar months, the *chia-tzu* day of the sexegenary cycle, the Stem and Branch of one's birth year, the "mating of heaven and earth,"[1] solar and lunar eclipses, the last and first days of each [lunar] month, quarter and full moons, great winds and great rains, thunderclaps and lightning bolts, and exposure to the sun, moon, and stars all constitute the first taboo. Mountain woods or the vicinities of garden ponds, Taoist sanctuaries or Buddhist temples, pagodas or shrines to the gods, and the Yangtze, Huai, Yellow, and Chi Rivers constitute the second taboo. Great cold or heat, great hunger or satiety, great happiness or intoxication; when one urgently needs to move the bowels or urinate; or when one's *ch'i* is either overactive or when one is disinterested constitute the third taboo. Continuous intoxication over a period of days, recent recovery from a long illness, or fatigue from a long journey constitute the fourth taboo. After giving birth and before the woman completes the period of forty-nine days when impurities still exist constitutes the fifth taboo. One must learn to shun these "five avoidances" and "five taboos." Those who violate them not only harm themselves, but their offspring often will be defective, diseased, and imperfect. This is the result of defects in the offspring's natural endowments.

Chapter 2. Cultivating the Subtle Ch'i

Concerning the *tao* of regulating one's health, what is most valuable is a study of its methods. Diminishing lustful desires is the means to cultivating the *ching-ch'i*. Reducing rich foods is the means to cultivating the blood *ch'i*. Swallowing saliva is the means to cultivating the lung *ch'i*. Guarding against anger is the means to cultivating the liver *ch'i*. Moderation in eating and drinking is the means to cultivating the stomach *ch'i*. Having few worries is the means to cultivating the heart *ch'i*. Self-realization is the means to cultivating the flesh *ch'i*. If one proceeds with due respect for these principles, the *ch'i* will be strong and the spirit more than sufficient. When one passes middle age, the time of declining *yin* and waning *yang*, one should not go to sleep drunk and sated, for this can lead to blockages of the hundred vessels and stiffness and pain in the joints. At this stage one should first guide the flow through the "four channels,"[2] and then stretch the hands and feet to invigorate the body's *ch'i* function. In this way, the "nutritive" and "defensive" *ch'i* flow freely, *yin* and *yang* become harmonious, the *ching* becomes strong and the spirit whole, pathogenic *ch'i* cannot invade us nor cold and heat attack us. This then is the *tao* of cultivating health.

Chapter 3. The Miraculous Elixir of the Bedchamber

The secret transmissions state that, by using one human being to supplement another, one naturally obtains the true essence. In the *tao* of *yin* and *yang*, *ching* and marrow are the treasures. By moving and circulating it, one achieves long life. The bed chamber can kill a man, but it also can nourish him. Those who use it nourish life; those who abuse it bring an end to life. Those who grasp the art of the bedchamber open the joints, circulate the *ch'i*, mobilize the *ching* and supplement the marrow. Therefore they are able to achieve longevity.

Chapter 4. The Precious Crucible Within the Stove

The "crucible" is a vessel for refining the sacred elixir, a "wine jar" for warming the true essence and cultivating the *ch'i*. The requirements for true crucibles are women who have not yet given birth, who are clean and pure, and who are without bad breath or body odor. Making use of them confers great health benefits. As with the "five avoidances" earlier, all but these are unsuitable for use.

Chapter 5. Observation of the Male's Four Levels of Arousal

If the man's "jade stalk" is not aroused, it means that the *yang-ch'i* has not yet arrived. If it is aroused but not yet enlarged, it means that the muscle *ch'i* has not yet arrived. If it is enlarged but not yet hard, it means that the bone *ch'i* has not yet arrived. If it is hard but not yet

hot, it means that the *ch'i* of the spirit has not yet arrived. When having intercourse, one must first observe the "four levels" of arousal, and only then carry out the act accordingly.

Chapter 6. Examination of the Female's Eight Stages of Arousal

When a woman silently swallows her saliva, it means that her blood *ch'i* has arrived. When she presses her body against the man, it means that her stomach *ch'i* has arrived. When she touches the man with strength, it means that her sinew *ch'i* has arrived. When she plays with the man's breast, it means that her flesh *ch'i* has arrived. When her brows are knit with a melancholy mien, it means that her liver *ch'i* has arrived. When she grasps and fondles the "jade stalk," it means that her blood *ch'i* has arrived. When she sucks the saliva from the man's tongue, it means that her lung *ch'i* has arrived. When her slippery secretions flow forth, it means that her spleen *ch'i* has arrived. When all of the *ch'i* have arrived, then one may have intercourse.

Chapter 7. Foreplay and Dallying

When one desires to have intercourse, first concentrate the spirit and settle the temper. Embrace the woman and gently play with her. Suck her lips and tongue and twirl her breasts with your fingers. Have the woman grasp and fondle the "jade stalk" to move her heart. Then seek the "*yin* gate" with your hand, and if there is a slight slippery secretion, one may enter the "wine jar." Continue to slowly carry out your methods, and the woman will surely experience bliss and be first to go down in defeat.

Chapter 8. Arousing Her Emotions

A woman's emotions are deep and hidden. How then may they be stirred, and how can one be aware of their arousal? Desiring to arouse them, if the woman is fond of wine, offer her fine fragrant wine; if she is highly romantic, seduce her with sweet words; if she is greedy for material things, give her gifts of money and silk; and if she is lustful, please her with your mighty member. A woman's heart has no fixed master. They respond emotionally to whatever scene presents itself and are easily moved. If one wishes to become aware of the state of their arousal, then observe that some pant and utter sounds unceasingly in a quaking voice. Some close their eyes, open their nostrils and are unable to speak. Some stare with a fixed gaze. Some have red ears, blush, and the tip of their tongue becomes slightly cold. Some develop hot hands, warm bellies, and confused speech. Some become mentally scattered, physically weak, and lose control of their limbs. Some experience drying of the saliva beneath the tongue and press their bodies tightly against the man. Others manifest such signs as palpitations of the blood vessels in the "*yin* hole" and an overflow of slippery secretions. All of these are evidence of emotional arousal. At this point, the man must not be hasty, but slowly practice absorption to obtain the "true *yang*."

Chapter 9. Tempering the Sword Tip and Cultivating Sharpness

When having intercourse, if the man's "jade stalk" is both long and large and fills the "*yin* gate," then the woman easily is made ecstatic. There is a method to developing the "stalk." An old saying goes, "If one wants to do a good piece of work, first sharpen the implements." One must not fail to understand this. Every day after the *tzu* and before the *wu* hour, when *yin* is waning and *yang* is waxing, one should sit quietly in one's room, loosen the garments, and sit with erect posture facing the east. Concentrate the spirit and banish all cares. The stomach should not be full, for satiety bottles up the *ch'i* and blocks the blood. But one also must not be famished, for then the blood *ch'i* races about. Expel the stale *ch'i* through the mouth and inhale the pure *ch'i* through the nose. Gather the saliva in the mouth, swallow, and direct it to the lower *tan-t'ien*, and then circulate it into the "jade stalk." This should be practiced seven, fourteen, twenty-one, or even forty-nine times. Rub the two hands together until

they are as hot as fire. With the right hand hold the scrotum, allowing the "jade stalk" to relax freely. With the left massage the area below the navel eighty-one times to the left. Then exchange hands and with the right hand massage below the navel eighty-one times to the right. Now extend the right hand to the *wei-lü* and raise the root of the "jade stalk" upward. Then grasping it firmly, slap the "stalk" against the left and right legs. It is not necessary to keep count. Now embrace the woman and slowly insert the "jade stalk" into the "*yin* gate." Gather the woman's saliva and inhale the *ch'i* from her nostrils. Swallow, directing it to the "jade stalk" to nourish it. After this, use both hands as if twisting rope to rub it an indeterminate number of times. After a long time one will feel an enlargement. To practice the "battle of absorption," first use a silk band to firmly encircle the root of the "stalk," and then together with the scrotum, use the two hands, one above and one below, to raise it up. Gather your saliva and inhale *ch'i*, swallowing it to the *tan-t'ien*. Then raise the *wei-lü* up to make contact, as if seeking to unite above and below. This helps to strengthen the power of *yang*. Afterward one may engage in sexual intercourse.

Chapter 10. Mock Maneuvers for Training the Troops

At the beginning of one's career, one should strive to eliminate lustful thoughts. First practice with a "stove" that is loose and ugly. As your passion mounts, do not allow yourself to become overly excited or reach the point of intense ecstasy, and then it will be easy to control yourself in intercourse. One must perform the act slowly, entering soft and withdrawing hard. Execute three shallow and one deep thrusts eighty-one times as one round. If the *ching* becomes slightly aroused, immediately stop and retreat. When resting, allow an inch or so to remain inside, and after the heart's fire has calmed, continue the procedure as earlier. Now execute the five shallow and one deep method, and finally nine shal- *139* low and one deep. Strictly avoid haste and impatience. If one practices in this way for half a month, one's skill will be complete.

Chapter 11. The Marvelous Method for Winning Victory

When a man finds a truly beautiful crucible, he will surely love her with all his heart. However, during intercourse he must force himself to detest her. One should settle the mind and move slowly back and forth within the stove. Some practice this for one round, and some for two or three rounds. Rest, quiet the mind, and after a moment proceed again according to the method. When the opponent's ecstasy become intense and she feels it difficult to control, then be even more loving and she will surely be first to reach orgasm. At this point, one may proceed to attack and capture the spoils according to the proper method. If you feel yourself about to ejaculate, quickly withdraw the "jade stalk" and execute the locking technique. When your power has subsided and your *ch'i* is settled and even, then use the proper method to attack once again. In doing battle do not be afraid to go slow; in gathering the spoils do not be afraid to be gradual. If one proceeds with due care, all will be well.

Chapter 12. Locking the Mysterious Mechanism

"Locking" is the method of applying the hand so as to arrest the flow of the "Yellow River." Hot tempered people will have to practice for twenty days before they can master the technique of locking, but mild-tempered individuals can acquire it in ten or so days. If one is diligent for a whole month, the "golden pass" will forever be secure and the "jade portal" always bolted. One can then participate freely in the act without leaking. This method is marvelously effective. Moreover, if during intercourse the "jade stalk" slowly enters and withdraws, carrying out three shallow and one deep, and one closes the eyes and shuts the mouth, breathing gently only through the nose,

then one will never become overexcited. If you feel a slight impulse to ejaculate, quickly lift your waist and body, withdraw the "jade stalk" an inch or two, and do not move. Inhale a breath and raise it to the upper *tan-t'ien*. It rises up the spine past the ribs, beginning at the *wei-lü* point. Herein lies the supremely precious *ching-ch'i* that must not be allowed to slip away. Now inhale a breath of pure *ch'i* and swallow it all at once. After a moment when your energy has settled, continue your techniques slowly as before. When there is a slight cessation of pleasure, once again withdraw, inhale, and settle the spirit. Contract, concentrate the mind, and one will thus succeed in preventing ejaculation. Moreover, the body's channels of *ch'i* circulation will flow freely from top to bottom. If control is not exercised early enough and one permits oneself to become ecstatic, the fire of passion will be difficult to check. This results in the *ch'i* being drawn out and the *ching* issuing forth and causes great harm to oneself. If one attempts to forcibly lock it, then the corrupt *ching* will ooze into the urinary bladder and scrotum. This may give rise to the production of pathogenic *ch'i* in the small intestines and urinary bladder and coldness, swelling, and pain in the kidneys. As a rule, before the first sign of passion, one should perform the raising and withdrawing, and repeatedly calm the temper. Thus the "jade stalk" will never collapse, and the strength of one's sinews will be more than sufficient. When one has bestowed 5,000 thrusts,[3] only then may one ejaculate the corrupt *ching*, while the "original *yang*" and "true *ch'i*" remain in the *tan-t'ien* to nourish the spirit. If one is truly able to practice this for a long time, one can take on ten enemies in a single night. Therefore it is said: "lock the mysterious mechanism."[4]

Chapter 13. The Great Medicine of the Three Peaks

The uppermost is called "red lotus peak;" its medicine is named "jade spring," "jade liquid," or "sweet wine spring," and it issues from the two openings beneath the woman's tongue. Its color is emerald green, and it is the *ching* of the saliva. The man should suck it up with his tongue. The spring bubbles forth from the "flowery pool." It should be sucked and swallowed down the "storied pavilion" to be deposited in the *tan-t'ien*. It has the ability to irrigate the Five Viscera. On the one hand, it fills the "mysterious gate," and on the other, strengthens the *tan-t'ien*. It generates *ch'i* and blood. The middle peak is called "twin water chestnuts;" its medicine is named the "peach of immortality," "white snow," or "jade juice," and it issues from the woman's two breasts. Its color is white and its flavor sweet and fine. When a man sucks, imbibes, and deposits it in the *tan-t'ien*, it has the ability to nourish the spleen and stomach and strengthen the spirit. Sucking it also opens all of the woman's meridians and relaxes her body and mind. It penetrates up to the "flowery pool" and stimulates the "mysterious gate" below, causing the body's fluids and *ch'i* to be full to overflowing. Of the three objects of absorption, this one is your first duty. A woman who has never borne children and is without milk in her breasts confers the greatest tonic benefit when tapped. The lower peak is called the "peak of purple fungus," "cave of the white tiger," or "mysterious gate." Its medicine is called "black lead" or "moon flower," and it is located at the woman's "*yin* palace." Its fluid is slippery and its gate normally is closed. When intercourse takes place, the woman's emotions are voluptuous, her face red, and voice trembling. At this time her "gate" opens up, her *ch'i* is released, and her secretions overflow. If the man withdraws his "jade stalk" an inch or so, and assumes the posture of "giving and receiving," he then accepts her *ch'i* and absorbs her secretions, thereby strengthening his "primal *yang*" and nourishing his spirit. This is the "Great Medicine of the Three Peaks." Only one who understands the *tao* is able to suppress emotion in the presence of the object and be dispassionate in the midst of passion. He surely will achieve the goal. In this way, white hair turns black again, old age is reversed and youth returns, and one achieves long life.

Chapter 14. The Five Character Teaching

The five characters are: concentrate, contract, absorb, inhale, and lock. "Concentrate" refers to the consciousness. During the act of intercourse, if one feels the impulse to ejaculate, quickly withdraw the "jade stalk," shut the mouth and close the eyes, and concentrate the consciousness below the *chia-chi* in the *wei-lü* point. The *ming-men* point is the locus of the *ching-ch'i* that is one's most precious possession and should not be allowed to slip away. One should relate only with the body and not with the spirit, just as if paying no attention at all. Concentrate the consciousness as prescribed, and even if by chance one should ejaculate, these times will not be many and will not deplete your strength. If this is practiced for a long time, one will be able to eliminate leakage altogether. This is the meaning of "concentrate."

"Contract" means to contract in fear and not dare to advance. When you feel the impulse to ejaculate, quickly draw back and retreat, lifting out the "jade stalk." Inhale a breath and raise it to the upper *tan-t'ien*. Draw back and lift the *wei-lü*. Now contract the lowest point in the body and do not allow the *ch'i* to descend, as if restraining the urge to urinate or move the bowels. Settle the breath and concentrate the consciousness. Do not move, and in a moment your energy will subside. Expel a breath from the mouth and embrace the woman with both arms. Suck the woman's tongue, gather her saliva and swallow it five or six times, sending it to the lower *tan-t'ien*. One can then commence intercourse again without tiring. However, at the very outset, one must strictly avoid hasty entry and direct penetration, for as soon as one becomes greatly excited it is difficult to control. However, if forcibly locked, the corrupt *ching* having no means of dispersal will give rise to other illnesses. As a rule, one should repeatedly lift out and withdraw without giving free rein to the passions. *141*

In this way, it will be easy to control one-self during intercourse. This is the meaning of the word "contract." When the work of the two words, "concentration" and "contraction," is carried out together without distinction of prior or latter, this then is the male method for locking the *ching*.

"Absorb" means to appropriate. During intercourse, when the woman becomes ecstatic, she will always pant and her voice will quaver. The man should close his mouth and slowly execute soft entry and hard retreat. One must avoid hasty, deep penetration, but advance just half a step, and with one's own nose draw in the *ch'i* from the woman's nose, inhaling it to the abdomen. One must not inhale with the mouth for this injures the brain. One inhalation and one absorption: this is what is known as "inhaling her *ch'i* above and absorbing her secretions below." After a moment, one's *ch'i* will be in sympathetic response above and below, and the *yang* member will naturally become firm and hard. If there is a slight feeling of loss of self-control, immediately withdraw and continue the method of "concentrating the consciousness." In this way one can avoid loss of semen almost entirely. This is the meaning of the word "absorb."

"Inhale" means to gather in. After the woman has released her *ching*, the man should withdraw the "jade stalk" an inch or so and adopt a posture of half engagement, inhaling her nostril *ch'i* above and her slippery secretions below. The nostrils are the "gate of heaven" and below is the "gate of life" (*ming-men*). The "gate of heaven" occupies the "upper source" and the "gate of life" the "lower source." If the "wonderful handle" absorbs alone, then water and fire will fail to reach the proper balance. However, if one simultaneously inhales from the "gate of heaven" with one's nose, then with one absorption and one inhalation, above and below in sympathetic response, it is like drawing water up through a bamboo tube that flows upward against gravity. If one succeeds in following this method, it greatly increases the *ching* and strengthens the *yang*. The spirit then is naturally steadfast. However, if

practiced too long, one will suffer injury, so wait for the woman to rest for a while, and then mount her again. This is the meaning of the word "inhale." By "absorbing" and "inhaling," withdrawing and entering, above and below become open and interconnected. When there is absorption within inhalation, and the two are practiced together, this then is the method used by the man to gather the woman's secretions.

"Locking" means to close the mouth. During engagement in battle, one should close the eyes and shut the mouth without allowing any outflow. Using only the nose, gradually guide [the breath] so that [above and below] are in sympathetic response. One must not allow oneself to reach the point of panting. If one fails to lock, the "gate of man" then connects with the "gate of heaven" and the "gate of heaven" connects with the "gate of life." If the kidneys and "gate of heaven" are not secure, and there is escape from above, then the *ching* secretions of the "primal *yang*" inevitably will be ejaculated from below. If the "gate of man" is securely locked, then the *ch'i* of the brain descends to the kidneys and flows into the "jade terrace."[5] There now being complete circulation from top to bottom, the *ching-ch'i* is in harmony and one will never leak. This is the meaning of the word "lock." The word "lock" functions in the midst of the other four. At the outset of intercourse, one must cherish one's own body and seal in the *ch'i*, never letting go of it for a moment. In this way, the word "lock" always operates in conjunction with the work of the other four words.

Chapter 15. The Sequence of Absorbing and Refining

The *Hsien ko* (Song of the immortals) says:

> A woman's passion is infinite.
> First rouse her emotions,
> Then slowly engage her in battle.
> The superior general surely will be
>   victorious.

Desiring to have intercourse, one must first embrace the crucible, fondle her two breasts, and suck her lips and tongue. After arousing her passion, one may then insert the *yang* in the *yin* and slowly unite. Carry out nine times nine strokes with eyes closed and mouth shut; repeatedly pull out and the "golden spear" will never topple. In this way, one first absorbs from the lower peak. When the lower absorption has reached great intensity, the woman's *ch'i* becomes expansive and stimulates the middle peak above. I slowly embrace her, suck the juices from the left and right [breasts], and swallow them. After obtaining their wonderful essence, one may stop. This then is absorption from the "middle peak." When absorption from the "middle peak" has reached great intensity, the woman's *ch'i* expands again and penetrates all the way to the "upper peak." I allow my tongue to explore freely beneath the opponent's tongue. Probing the two openings there, I suck the secretions, swallowing again and again. This then is the "upper peak" of the "three absorptions." When the upper absorption is complete, the woman will be at the height of ecstasy and the "true *ch'i*" of her private parts will be released. At this time, one should withdraw the "wonderful handle" an inch or so and elevate the body like a turtle, raising a breath of *ch'i* directly to the upper *tan-t'ien*. Take in the opponent's *ch'i* and absorb her secretions, circulating them throughout your body. At this point, the three absorptions are complete. The woman, too, is thoroughly satisfied from top to bottom; and her channels of *ch'i* open up and flow freely. Now exhale a breath or two of *ch'i* and have the woman inhale and swallow it to calm her spirit. When this art is thoroughly mastered, and when the "true essence" released by the partner is obtained and one's own unshed *ching* "returned," then this is of little harm to the woman and of great benefit to oneself . When *yin* and *yang* obtain each other and water and fire are in "perfect union," this then is the marvelous benefit of mounting women.

Chapter 16. The Time for Inner Circulation

When the woman has released her *ching*, she will invariably manifest such signs as panting and trembling voice. At this mo-

ment one must still the heart and calm the *ch'i*, embrace the woman and absorb from the "jade spring" above, the "peach of immortality" in the middle, and the "moon flower" below. Refine and receive it, circulating it upward from the *wei lü*, ascending the two "white channels,"[6] passing through the *chia-chi*, penetrating the *k'un-lun*, entering the *ni-wan*, and flowing into the mouth. Here it is transformed into "jade juice," which should be swallowed down the "storied pavilion" until it reaches all the way to the *tan-t'ien*. This is called the "reverse flow of the Yellow River," and has the ability to augment the *ching* and supplement the marrow, increase longevity and lengthen the years. The secret verse for summarizing this process is "Raise the *ch'i*, swallow the *ch'i*, and concentrate the consciousness in the meridians." This also is what is meant by, "Wherever the spirit goes, *ch'i* goes, and wherever the *ch'i* goes, the *ching* goes."

Chapter 17. Fulfilling the Significance and Completing the Relationship

In human life, there is first the distinction of male and female, and then that of husband and wife. Husband and wife are the beginning of human relationships. Without sexual intercourse there would be no means of achieving harmony of the heart and oneness of spirit, which would be a perversion of human relationships. However, man belongs to *yang*. *Yang* is easily aroused and easily stilled. Woman belongs to *yin*. *Yin* is difficult to arouse and difficult to still. Nowadays, people engage in sexual intercourse without understanding the art, allowing themselves to become excited and ejaculating in a moment, thus often leaving the woman unsatisfied. However, if one proceeds according to the method of the "battle of absorption," then when entering the "stove" one very slowly penetrates without any haste. Slowness facilitates control; haste makes halting difficult. Furthermore, do not allow the woman to pat the small of one's back. Advance and withdraw for a long time, engaging in the "battle of absorption" according to the method. This not only is beneficial to the body, but causes the woman to feel great love. The man experiences great comfort and the woman feels lovely. There is a mutual balance of benefit. This then is the *tao* of "fulfilling the significance" and the business of "completing the relationship."

Chapter 18. Rejuvenation through Grafting

Man's cultivating the True[7] and nourishing life is like an old tree flourishing again through grafting. Supplementing one human being by means of another is precisely the same principle as grafting a branch onto a tree. The *Hsien ko* says:

> Those who fail to understand the principle
> of longevity,
> Need only look at the grafting of pear in
> the midst of mulberry.

Anyone who desires to engage in this work must obtain a perfect precious crucible whose age is above fifteen but no more than thirty. Women of fourteen represent the "minor *yin*," those of twenty-one the "abundant *yin*," and those of twenty-eight the "strong *yin*." The "minor *yin*" nourishes the body and the "abundant *yin*" increases the lifespan. You should obtain one and raise her gently. Wait until her "red tide"[8] converges, and then allowing neither excess nor insufficiency, employ her with profit to yourself. If absorption and cultivation are practiced for a long time, one's physical form may remain in the world. When a woman reaches thirty-five, this is the phase of "declining *yin*." Forty-two is called "major *yin*," and forty-nine is "exhausted *yin*." One must realize the importance of avoiding these. It is especially important to avoid those who are too fat, for it is difficult for their vessels to flow freely. Those who are too thin have too little flesh and fluids. Those who are weary have too little spirit and *ch'i*. Those who are weak will actually harm a man's *yang*. Those who are weary in spirit have cold *yin*. Those who are ill have poison in their *yin*.[9] All of these are called "*yin* thieves" and should be avoided. More-

over, absorbing and supplementing is a matter of my own mind. One must empty the mind, calm all cares, understand the taboos, and observe the signs of arousal. Withdraw and fill her again slowly; dally and toy with her deliberately. Enter weak and exit hard. Pay careful attention to the point when one feels the urge to ejaculate, but has not yet ejaculated. Withdraw and withhold it. Clearly distinguish the point between imminent arousal and full arousal. Remember that a ship is steered with a rudder of but one foot, and a crossbow shot with a trigger of but one inch. Gentlemen of intelligence can use their minds to reverse it.

Chapter 19. Returning to the Source and Reverting to the Root

"Returning to the source" refers to the method of retrieval. The "true *yin*" represented by the middle line in the trigram *Li* is formless but reveals a sign. Its fire tends to rise upward. If employed in the ordinary way, conception occurs and a human being is born. If the process is reversed, a precious pearl is formed. This is known as the "Yellow River turns back its waves." It is pulled back to its source until it returns to the "gate of heaven." When absorbing and refining, use mental concentration and contraction to lock[10] it; use absorption and inhalation to gather it. If one does not follow the correct method in "dismounting," how can one expect to "revert and return," distributing it [throughout the body]? After finishing the act, one must lie flat on the back, extending the arms straight out, and relaxing the feet, with the head resting on the pillow and the heels making contact with the bed. The body should feel as if suspended in space. Hold the breath with all your might and shake your body several times, finally letting the air escape from the nose. Execute this in a smooth and even manner. If one feels heat in the face, this is because the *ching-ch'i* already has ascended to the *ni-wan*. At this moment, one should use both hands to massage the skin of the face and cause the heat to disperse. Now close the lips and stop breathing. With the tongue, stir about in the "flowery pool" and swallow the "holy water" to the *tan-t'ien*. In this way one is able to circulate the *ching-ch'i* throughout the body and it becomes a very useful thing. If practiced for a long time, one may wander freely in the Milky Way and feast in the "yellow court."[11]

Chapter 20. Conception and Prevention of Miscarriage

By practicing "absorption" during intercourse, men and women gain longevity, but by ejaculating, the womb is calmed and conception results. There is a saying: "There are three things that are most unfilial, but the worst is to fail to produce descendants." Therefore, conceiving offspring is one of life's most urgent duties. The man must first supplement his *ching* and strengthen his kidneys to invigorate his *yang-ch'i*. The woman must regulate her menses and nourish her blood, and then the womb will be congenial and warm. Wait for the "monthly affair" to be past and the "red flow" to be finished. Precisely when the womb is open is the most suitable time for intercourse. On the first day one will conceive males and on the second females, based on the principle of *yang* corresponding to odd numbers and *yin* to even. If one proceeds according to the proper method, the children will be endowed with virtue and intelligence. They will be free of illness and easy to raise. After the fifth day, the "yin gate" closes and it is a waste to have intercourse. When having intercourse it is essential that both partners be emotionally aroused, for only then will there be a successful response. If the woman is still unmoved when the man is already aroused and his *ching* arrives, then she will not be able to accept the *ching*. If the woman is aroused first and her passion is already past, although the man's passion has not yet subsided, then the *ching* will arrive late and also will not be accepted by her. It is possible only when the two are both ecstatic. The man penetrates deeply with the "jade stalk" and ejaculates as the woman raises her waist to receive it into her womb. They rest together for a short time and then separate. Have the woman lie straight with her face up. With 100 attempts there will be 100 successes. Also the *tzu* and *wu* are the time of "*yang* major" and intercourse then will produce sons. The *mao* and *yu* hours belong to "*yin* major" and intercourse then will produce daughters. Furthermore, if the *yin* blood arrives first and the *yang-ching* bursts through later, then the blood opens and envelops the *ching*. The *ching* penetrates, becoming the bones, and a male is formed. If the *yang-ching* arrives first and the *yin* blood joins it later, then the *ching* opens and surrounds the blood. The blood then is in the interior and a woman is formed. If the *ching* and blood arrive simultaneously, twins result. This is the basic principle and it thus is appended here.

Colophon

During the reign of Emperor Shih-tsung [Ming dynasty, 1522–1566] I served at the Imperial Court in Peking. At that time the Taoist adept T'ao enjoyed imperial favor because of his magical powers. If we trace his accomplishments, however, they were nothing but illusion and fantasy without legitimacy. However, his mastery of the art of "absorption and supplementation" was indeed genuine. Therefore, the Emperor's enjoying a ripe old age was entirely due to this. I very much admired his art and, bribing a close attendant, was able to purchase some of the secret transmissions preserved there, including two works, the classic of Master Lü Tung-pin and the exposition of his disciple. I practiced accordingly but found it difficult at first to gain control. After a long time, however, it came quite naturally. Thus, during a period of sixty years, I had intercourse with more than 100 women and reared 17 sons. I have lived through five emperors and personally seen five reigns. Although I am very old, I am still not weary of the bedchamber, and when on occasion I have intercourse, I always manage to vanquish several women. Although heaven has blessed me with years, the contribution of the art of "absorption and supplementation" cannot be denied. There is a saying that goes,

"Those who monopolize their skill will come to misfortune." Moreover, a man's lifespan is less than a hundred years. I cannot bear the thought that when I die these two books might be lost. For this reason, I had them printed to spread the influence of the great Immortal's virtue and offer it to the men of my generation that they might reach the age of P'eng Tsu. To say that this is nonsense and un-founded is simply to throw away years of one's life. Of what concern is that to me?

Written in the first lunar month of the cyclical year *chia-wu* [1594] of the Wan Li reign by the ninety-five year old native of Chekiang Province in the Purple Fungus of Immortality Studio on T'ien-t'ai Mountain.

XI. THE ELIXIR LITERATURE OF SEXUAL ALCHEMY

Introduction

With this section we sail out of van Gulik's sights into waters charted only by Joseph Needham. Ko Hung announced the existence of a sexual elixir school in his fourth century *Pao P'u tzu*, and Tseng Tsao's tenth century *Tao shu* outlined its theory. Our earliest complete texts in this tradition, however, are not until the Ming. It is difficult to say whether this low survival rate should be attributed to the secrecy surrounding all methods for attaining immortality or to the sexual nature of the practice. Certainly, were it not for Japanese interest in collecting Chinese medical texts we might have lost the householder manuals of the same period. Nevertheless, the five texts in this section span the middle to late Ming, and possibly the Ch'ing, and represent the advanced stage of sexual alchemy.

Lu Hsi-hsing (1520–1601?), founder of the so called Eastern Branch (*tung-p'ai*) of Ming Taoists noted for their sexual teachings, is the author of the *Chin-tan chiu-cheng p'ien* (Seeking instruction on the golden elixir), which bears a preface dated 1564, and was included in his *Fang-hu wai-shih* (Unofficial history of the Fang-hu Paradise). Sun Ju-chung's *Chin-tan chen-chuan* (True transmission of the golden elixir) is also blessed with an author's preface, dated 1615, which simplifies the problem of chronology. The three texts attributed to Chang San-feng, however, are beset with formidable obstacles to determining both date and authorship. The *Chin-tan chieh-yao* (Summary of the golden elixir), *Ts'ai-chen chi-yao* (Secrets of gathering the true essence), and *Wu-ken shu* (Rootless tree) all appear in Fu Chin-ch'üan's *Cheng-tao pi-shu shih-chung* (Ten kinds of secret treatises on verification of the *tao*), a collection which may be approximately dated early nineteenth century.

Of the three texts attributed by Fu Chin-ch'üan to Chang San-feng, the *Summary* and *Secrets* are unmistakably sexual, "The Rootless Tree" poems more metaphorically so. Ignoring for the moment that Ming and Ch'ing biographies of Chang San-feng variously place him in the Sung, Chin, Yüan or Ming and putting aside efforts to distinguish several historical figures sharing the same or homophonous names, it should be noted that the *Summary* and *Secrets* are absent from Li Hsi-yüeh's (1795–1850?) *Chang San-feng ch'üan-chi* (Complete works of Chang San-feng), while "The Rootless Tree" is included in the *Complete Works* with two distinctly anti-sexual commentaries. The twenty-four "Rootless Tree" poems, with preface dated 1802, appear in Liu Wu-yüan's *Tao-shu shih-erh chung*

(Twelve kinds of Taoist works) published in 1913. Liu's notes to the verses are adopted by Li Hsi-yüeh, who also adds his own commentary. Although Liu interprets the central image of the "rootless tree" as symbolizing the fragility of the human body, and Li takes it as the *ch'i* which supports life as an invisible root system, nevertheless Liu and Li make common cause in opposing a sexual reading of the verses. The first edition of the *Complete Works* was published in 1844, but the extant printing is that included in the *Tao-tsang chi-yao* (Essence of the *Tao tsang*) published in 1906. A preface to "The Rootless Tree" by Ho Hsi-fu is dated 1847, and thus the poems must have been added during the interval between 1847 and 1906. Another compilation of writings attributed to Chang San-feng, the *Chang San-feng t'ai-chi lien-tan pi-chüeh* (Secret transmissions of Chang San-feng on the Great Ultimate cultivation of the elixir) is of unknown editorship but may be approximately dated late Ch'ing. It contains the "Rootless Tree," but not the *Summary* and *Secrets* as such. Oddly though, six chapters of the *Summary* are reproduced in the *Chang San-feng t'ai-chi lien-tan pi-chüeh*, a clue which may some day lead us to the origins of all these works.

Several other factors further confuse the picture of the three texts attributed to Chang San-feng. First, Li Hsi-yüeh is at great pains to distinguish "his" Chang San-feng from another Chang San-feng whom he describes as an exponent of sexual disciplines during the Liu Sung dynasty (420–77). In at least six sections of the *Complete Works* Li takes the opportunity to attack the general theory of sexual cultivation, and one wonders why he did not spare himself the trouble of explaining away the sexual implications of "The Rootless Tree" by simply attributing it to the "other" Chang San-feng and tossing it out. It may be that the poem was considered a hot property and that the sexual and solo schools both desired to appropriate it. If the sexual implications of the text are less than nakedly transparent, a number of contemporary scholars have nevertheless managed to

decode its metaphors. Anna Seidel reports in a note to her article, "A Taoist Immortal of the Ming Dynasty, Chang San-feng," that she was alerted to the sexual meaning of "The Rootless Tree" by Liu Ts'un-yan in personal communication. Huang Chao-han makes this point even more directly when he says in his book *Ming-tai tao-shih Chang San-feng k'ao* (A study of the Ming dynasty Taoist, Chang San-feng): "What is the real nature of the language of 'The Rootless Tree?' Does it really have nothing to do with sexual practice as stated by Liu Wu-yüan and Li Hsi-yüeh . . . ? The poem very obviously describes 'paired cultivation' and to claim that it does not is very difficult to believe." Reading "The Rootless Tree" alongside the sexual literature of the Ming, and especially the *Summary* and *Secrets*, one cannot help but be struck by such parallel phrases as, "Graft peach branches onto willow and pear onto mulberry," "An unfertilized egg produces no chicks," "Practicing only solitary meditation, the *ch'i* dries up," "*K'un* is a human being," "The lead flowers appear when the *kuei* is over," and "Repress your feelings as you confront the scene." Seen in this context, "The Rootless Tree" appears to be a rendering of the theme of sexual cultivation in a literary form. Needham dates these works "1410 (if genuine)," and I am inclined to agree with Huang Chao-han's 1976 Ph.D. thesis, "On the Cult of Chang San-feng and the Authenticity of his Works," which concludes that the "Rootless Tree" was written "by someone else during the early Ch'ing dynasty." I feel that the *Summary* and *Secrets* also reached their present form during the Ch'ing, perhaps even by the same hand.

Just as the names P'eng Tsu, Su Nü and Jung Ch'eng were synonymous with sexual practices in their day, so Chang San-feng symbolized the sexual school from the Ming forward. Taoist solo practitioners have spared no effort to distinguish the Chang San-feng 張三峯 (whose name recalls the "Three Peaks" of the *Exposition of Cultivating the True Essence*) from the Chang San-feng 張三豐   *147*

who is revered as a patriarch of numerous sects of religious Taoism, as a god of riches, as the creator of the internal school of pugilism, and so forth. Even fellow "paired" practitioner, Lu Hsi-hsing, felt obliged to disassociate himself from the infamous Chang when he says in the preface to his *Seeking Instruction*: "When I foolishly asked him [Lü Tung-pin] about the teachings of Chang San-feng, he rejected them." As for the legendary Lü Tung-pin, mentioned by Lu Hsi-hsing as his teacher, his association with sexual disciplines appears as early as the *Tao shu*, where Tseng Tsao portrays him as an innocent dupe of the sexual doctrines of Ts'ui Hsi-fan's *Ju-yao ching*. The *True Classic of Perfect Union* is also attributed to Lü Tung-pin, as is the women's practices text, *Queen Mother of the West's Ten Precepts*. Both Chang and Lü have been so encrusted with legend that it is nearly impossible to uncover a core of historicity, although in the popular imagination Lü remained an appealing figure, while the sexual Chang seems to have gained the reputation as a bit of a de Sade.

A common thread in Teng Hsi-hsien's preface to the *True Classic* and the prefaces of Lu and Sun is the fruitless search for immortality through solo practices, their fateful meetings with sexual masters, and subsequent conversions. Just as Chen Luan described his turning away from Taoist sexual practices to Buddhism, so Sun Ju-chung in a short essay entitled *Hsiu-chen ju-men* (Introduction to cultivating the true essence) outlines the argument for embracing sexual practices:

> When it comes to strengthening the *ch'i*, there are two theories: some advocate strengthening it through "purity" and others by "*yin* and *yang* . . . ." However, for those who have already experienced seminal leakage, rapid strengthening is difficult to achieve [using "pure" methods] and it is not easy to rein in the mind that already is scattered. This is not as effective as the mutual strengthening of *yin* and *yang*, for here there is something concrete to work with. This method does not tax the spirit and is easy for beginners. One must employ the "crucibles." First open the "passes" and

"orifices," and then strengthen the *ch'i* and blood. What are the "crucibles?" The *Wu-chen p'ien* calls them "the divine father and holy mother." When carrying out this practice, there is intercourse of the spirit but not of the bodies; intercourse of the *ch'i* but not of the physical form. The man does not loosen his garments nor the woman her girdle. They respect each other as divine beings and love one another as father and mother.

Revealing the role of temperament in scholarly debate, it is interesting here that Sun expresses impatience with the slowness of "pure" meditative methods and the difficulty of controlling the restless mind, while "pure" criticisms of sexual cultivation often emphasize their undue complexity and the difficulty of controlling the excited *ching*.

What distinguishes the texts of sexual alchemy from the other categories in this anthology? Above all, it is that the theme of immortality is no longer a literary convention but a literal and exclusive obsession. Questions of emotional harmonization, sexual synchronization, eugenics, and therapies for sexual dysfunction have become completely irrelevant. The adept enters a state of meditative abstraction in which sexual arousal has been vitually divorced from personalized passion and in which the partner has been reduced to mere "medicine." The emphasis on timing has shifted away from macrocosmic "avoidances and taboos" to the precise microcosmic moment when the *yang* essence ripening within the female reproductive system is ready for "gathering," a moment having more to do with a primitive concept of ovulation than orgasm. Finally, the *yang* extract, collected under controlled laboratory conditions from the woman, is centrifuged within the body of the adept by a process of microcosmis orbit circulation, which is indistinguishable from solo inner alchemy meditation. What sets the works attributed to Chang San-feng somewhat apart from the relatively chaste tone of Lu and Sun is his explicitness regarding matters of patronage and procurement, the details of coaxing the essence from female donors, and the yogic techniques of absorption. Liu Ts'un-yan in an article entitled "Taoist Self-Cultivation in Ming Thought" collected in Wm. Theodore de Bary's *Self and Society in Ming Thought* draws a distinction between the bedchamber art and sexual alchemy in these terms:

> The cultivation of the internal pill, though easily confused with the idea of dual cultivation in its sexual aspects, should not be interpreted as being identical with the study of the 'bedchamber art' (*fang-chung*). The *fang-chung* scholars of the Former Han, during the Northern and Southern dynasties, and of the T'ang mainly concerned themselves with hygienic arrangements in Chinese family life, and to some extent they also made contributions to the Chinese pharmacopoeia. But they did not often recommend the cultivation of the *ch'i*.

I cannot entirely endorse this analysis, and even less its conclusion. While there is surely a distinction in emphasis between the "bedroom art" and sexual alchemy, the former more aligned with the medical tradition and the latter with the meditative, it is the cultivation of *ch'i* which unites rather than separates them and has been the most consistent theme underlying the diverse developments within the sexual school for more than two thousand years.

Seeking Instruction on the Golden Elixir

Chin-tan chiu-cheng p'ien

by Lu Hsi-hsing (Ch'ien- hsü)

Preface

I have perused countless works on the elixir of immortality, and all insist that the great medicine of longevity requires the primordial undifferentiated true *ch'i*. If one asks from whence comes this *ch'i*, the answer is that it can be found in the "other." We cannot find this *ch'i* in our own bodies, but those who believe it can be found in others are rare while skeptics are many. From an early age I sought to

understand this *tao*; however, because of my own dullness and lack of talent, I was not able to fathom its principles. Turning to the *Ts'an-t'ung ch'i* and *Wu-chen p'ien*, I found the path thorny and progress impossible. As first explained to me by Master Yü Yen, these works taught the *tao* of purity and non-action. All practice external to one's own body was condemned as heterodox, and everything to do with "golden crucibles" and "fire charms" he considered alchemy. Steadfastly maintaining this view he could not be shaken. Alas! If purity is truly so incomprehensible, why is it ridiculed by so-called "inferior scholars,"[1] and why have critics continued to arise? At that point in my studies, I could not help being skeptical. In the year 1547 of the Chia-ching reign of the Ming dynasty, I chanced to meet Master Lü [Tung-pin] at his hut in Shantung. He encouraged me to stay and treated me most graciously. He offered fine black millet wine and exhorted me with words of wisdom. Only once in three lifetimes or a thousand years does an opportunity so rare present itself. He encouraged those of my generation to follow the highest *tao*. When I foolishly asked him about the teachings of Chang San-feng, he rejected them. In the meantime, he transmitted the "Song of Forming the Fetus" and the principles of entering the chamber. The subtle words and deep doctrines could fill volumes, and although I recorded and preserved them, my understanding was very superficial. Thus for twenty years I failed to live up to my teacher's kindness. In the last month of the year 1564, retiring to the countryside, I gazed into the mirror and was saddened by the sight of gray hair encroaching on my temples. I deeply regretted the failure to realize my goal. Just as I was feeling that time was running out, I was visited by Master in a dream and determined to change my ways. After this great inspiration, I searched my memory for his words and was able to recollect 80 to 90 percent. I also brought in all the classics and treatises that explain this over and over. One night, while in a state between sleep and wakefulness, I felt suddenly enlightened and wrote down this work. Confucius said: "Review the old and grasp the new." Today, what I review is indeed old, and what I have grasped is new. My words are but the inspiration of a moment, and I would not dare impose upon those who have truly realized the *tao*. Nevertheless, they are not far from the ideas of my Master.

Preface written on the first day
of the last quarter of the moon,
last month of the year, 1564,
by [Lu] Ch'ien-hsü.

Chapter One

Someone asked Master Ch'ien-hsü: "What is meant by the words in the elixir classics that the primordial undifferentiated *ch'i* must be sought among one's own species?" I replied:

I have heard my Master say that the *tao* of the golden elixir is based on the union of *yin* and *yang*. *Yin* and *yang* means one man and one woman, one *Li* and one *K'an*, one lead and one mercury. This is the medicine of the great elixir. The true *ch'i* of *K'an* is called *lead*, and the true *ching* of *Li* is called *mercury*. I store my own prenatal *ching*, while borrowing my partner's prenatal *ch'i*. How is this so? My partner is *K'an*, which is *yin* on the outside and *yang* on the inside. This is symbolized by water and the moon. In the human species, it is female. I am *Li*, which is *yang* on the outside and *yin* on the inside. This is symbolized by fire and the sun. In the human species, it is male. Thus, following the normal course of the *tao* of man and woman, or *yin* and *yang*, produces offspring, but reversing it produces the elixir. The principle is the same.

The question was asked: "As explained in the *I ching*, *K'an* is the middle son and *Li* the middle daughter. You, however, say that I, a male, am represented by *Li*. What is the meaning?" I replied:

This refers to the primordial configuration. Master Shao [Yung][2] said that the *ching* of *yin* and *yang* is concealed within each other's domain. Thus, T'ai-chi divided into the "two aspects," and the "two aspects" became the "four images," and from the "four images," the "eight trigrams." In

this way, *Li* belongs to *Ch'ien* [The Creative] and *K'an* belongs to *K'un* [The Receptive]. In man and woman, when *yin* and *yang* have intercourse, a material being is formed. Therefore, when *Ch'ien* and *K'un* have intercourse, *Ch'ien* inevitably becomes empty in the middle and is transformed into *Li*; *K'un* inevitably becomes full and is transformed into *K'an*. When male and female have intercourse, *yin* cannot but embrace *yang*, and *yang* cannot but be rooted in *yin*. This is the difference between *K'an* and *Li*, other and self.

"Now if I understand you correctly, in the middle of *Li* is *yin-ching*, and in the middle of *K'an* is *yang-ch'i*. Why do I not possess *ching* and *ch'i* within my own body and must borrow it from a partner?" I replied:

You do possess them, but I have not yet completed my explanation. I used to be mired in the theories of Old Yü Wu, but now I have finally discovered the truth. Please listen to me and I will attempt to explain it. I heard my Master say that when *yin* and *yang*, the two fives, unite and coalesce, a human being is born. At its conception, it is like an uncarved block, a perfect body of undifferentiated T'ai-chi. Lao tzu said: "The highest power is like the infant. Though knowing nothing of the union of male and female, yet its penis erects. This is the height of *ching*. It cries all day without becoming hoarse. This is the height of harmony."[3] Here then is the purity of *yin* and *yang*. At this stage, the prenatal body is homogeneous and perfect. What need is there to borrow or supplement? What can possibly be added to the power of nonaction? However, at the onset of puberty, *yin* and *yang* begin to interact and the prenatal *ch'i* flees to the middle of *K'un*. As a result, the three lines of the pure *Ch'ien* are ruptured and it becomes *Li*. *Li* is the sun, corresponding to the departure of the setting sun in the West, or advanced old age. Can one survive in this condition very long? Therefore, the elixir method borrows from *K'an* to repair the broken *Ch'ien*, supplement its empty line, and restore its pure *yang* body. This is the theory of the returning elixir of immortality.

"Because of the flight of my middle *yang* line I am represented by *Li*. Before the flight of her middle line the female partner is *K'un*. How does she become *K'an*?" I replied:

This is an excellent question! During the stage of undifferentiated unity, she certainly is a *K'un* body, but at fourteen the *yang* begins to stir. In the middle of pure *K'un*, *yang* stirs. Is this not *K'an*. Therefore *K'an* is *yang* within *yin*. When T'ai-chi reaches the height of stillness, movement naturally manifests. This is called primordial. Heaven, represented by the number one, gives birth to water that is the true unitary *ch'i* concealed in the middle of *K'an*. A mother conceals her fetus, gold within water. Wishing to produce the golden elixir, our method must be to borrow from *K'an*. This is the source of the medicine and the key to attaining immortality. The *yang* in the midst of *yin* is ruled by movement. Therefore, to determine the proper time for borrowing from *K'an*, one must observe its movement. The *yin* in the midst of *yang* is ruled by stillness. Therefore, after supplementing *Li*, one must cultivate it in stillness. Only the sage is able to understand movement and stillness without missing the proper time. The sage observes the *tao* of heaven and grasps heaven's movement. Thus the waxing and waning of the moon is like the age or freshness of the medicine; the dawn and dusk of each day is like the ebb and flow of the firing time. When fire and medicine meet, the elixir forms. When the elixir forms, the fetus emerges and immortality is realized.

"What you have discussed relates only to the postnatal realm. Can you explain the prenatal?" I replied:

I searched for this in the *I ching* and found, "*Ching* and *ch'i* produce all things; the release of the soul brings about change."[4] The *yang* within *yin* is called *ch'i*; the *yin* within *yang* is called *ching*. When the two interact things are born. Following the natural course, when the *ching* arrives first and the *ch'i* later, *yin* is surrounded by *yang* and becomes a girl. When the *ch'i* first stirs, and the *ching* follows after, *yang* is surrounded by *yin* and becomes a boy.[5] Nevertheless, the distinction between *Li* the male and *K'an* the female does not depend on the material realm, but already is prefigured at their inception. Moreover, the *tao* of the golden elixir comes about through the union of *yin* and *yang*. The *tao* of man follows the normal course by be-

stowing; the *tao* of immortality reverses the normal course by borrowing. It is simply a matter of borrowing the medicine from *K'an* to prepare the elixir in *Li*. Is there any room left for doubt?

Chapter Two

Someone asked me: "The 'four elements' in the body all are classified as *yin*, but sometimes they are in motion. In this case, do they not belong to *yang*?" I replied:

Li is fire and sun. Although movement belongs to *yang*, in reality, it is rooted in *yin*. Therefore, it may be said that fire, which is *yang*, is rooted in *yin*. Behold the flash of spiritual light that nothing can restrain. Just so is the *yang* within one's body. Therefore, we frequently suffer its escape. The sages, understanding this, borrowed the true unitary water from within *K'an* to help control it. Therefore passion blazing on the inside and *ching* escaping to the outside is like fire burning below a pot of boiling water. Borrowing the partner's prenatal true unitary *ch'i* to subdue my restless *ching* is like using a jar of spring water to rescue the boiling pot. This never fails to save the day.

"Can you tell me about the method of borrowing from *K'an*?" I replied: "Heaven's secret is tightly guarded. Without the instructions of a master, who would dare to speak rashly? Please reveal a clue to enlighten us."

In the *I ching*, thunder from within the earth is the hexagram *Fu* (Return). From within the many *yin* lines of the earth, suddenly *yang* stirs. This is the root of the cosmic process of creation and the pivot of all living things. When Confucius came to this hexagram, he said with a sigh: "Does the hexagram *Fu* not reveal the mind of heaven and earth?"[6] The [*Ts'an-t'ung*] *ch'i* also refers to this when it says: "Therefore the *I ching* encompasses the mind of heaven. The hexagram *Fu* establishes the beginning of things."[7] It also says: "In words and deeds we must follow the proper time and not violate the movement of the lines."[8] This pertains to our subject. Therefore, understanding that *Fu* consists of thunder within the earth, we realize that *yang* is born in the midst of *yin*, and that true unitary *ch'i* is hidden within the female partner. How can we avoid speaking of this and illustrating it with examples?

Someone asked: "In speaking of the medicine, the elixir classics always say, 'On the third day it appears in the West.' Can you explain this?" I replied:

K'an is the moon. The moon is Yin Major (*t'ai-yin*). It receives the light of the sun and shines forth. "On the third day it appears in the west" means that the *yang* begins to grow just as in the hexagram *Fu*. The eighth day is the first quarter. This is represented by the hexagram *Lin* (Approach), which has two *yang* lines at the bottom. When there is fullness in the east, the three *yang* lines at the bottom represent *T'ai* (Peace). By the last quarter, *yang* is in decline, and by the last day of the lunar month, *yang* is exhausted. *Po* (Splitting Apart) and *Fu* (Return) pursue each other, round and round, without beginning or end. Therefore, on the third day there is rebirth. The biological processes within the female partner are no different. The elixir method symbolizes this by observing the age or freshness of the medicine.

"How is this applied?" I replied:

The golden elixir is formed of the prenatal true unitary *ch'i*. The prenatal *ch'i* is light, pure and formless—*yang* within *yang*. Its beginning is most subtle and its mystery unfathomable. Therefore it must be gathered quickly at the very beginning of the menses and used as the charm of an instant. A moment too late and it becomes dregs, falling into the postnatal realm. This is the transition from *yang* to *yin*. The verse in the *Wu-chen* [*p'ien*] says: "When it becomes visible it is useless." This means it is too old. "In a split second of fire and smoke the immortal appears." This expresses its speed. Alas! Can the wonder of creative process be understood by any but the sage? And who but the sage can put it into practice?

Someone asked: "You have said that the mystery of the cosmic process of creation can be mastered only by the sage, but today there are no sages. If one seeks to practice this, what are the essentials?" I replied:

Did not the Master say that the "true earth" captures the "true lead," and that the "true lead" controls the "true mercury"? What is the "true earth"? It is the "*chi* earth." If those who would gather the medicine fail to cultivate the "*chi* earth," the subtle mercury easily will escape and one's training will come to naught but suffering and shame. The classics speak of "establishing the foundation" and "refining the self." This is what they mean. As a specific entity, the "self" in man is his consciousness. It is also called "self-nature," because it functions everywhere amidst the "four images"[9] and has no fixed locus. For this reason it is called "earth." From beginning to end, the golden elixir relies on this. Therefore, in refining the medicine and seeking the lead, it is the self that receives it; in preparing the fire and filling the crucible, it is the self that sends it; in heating the ingredients and resting, it is the self that guards them; and in incubating and rebirthing, it is the self that brings the process to completion. Rectify the mind and be sincere in one's intentions. In this way the self will be cultivated, the nation ordered, and the world at peace. This is the key to refining the elixir. The [*Ts'an-t'ung*] *ch'i* says: "To turn the wheel align the axle."[10] It also says: "The highest point in the heavens rules from the center."[11] The ancient immortals handed down their teachings full of commandments and warnings. Moreover, it is from the parent's passion that we are born, and therefore by nature out contact with the world gives rise to feeling. Now if we have not succeeded in "refining the self" and the "six senses" are not under control, upon entering the chamber we will be overwhelmed. Our spirit will be agitated, our passions flare up, and the "beautiful maiden"[12] will escape. How can we expect to quickly capture the pearl from the jaws of the black dragon. It is said that if one explores the tiger's lair and plucks his whiskers, it will be difficult to avoid the tiger's jaws. How dangerous indeed! Only one of great wisdom can emerge victorious. Only one of great power can win the day. My Master has said: "The mirror of preliminary practice is one's own mind. If the mind is not empty, the scene reflected will not be true." Ah! The key to emptying the mind is simply the principle of "refining the self." The *Ch'ing-ching ching* says: "Look within to find the mind, and the mind does not exist; look without to find the body, and the body does not exist; look beyond to find the world, and the world does not exist. When one realizes these three truths, then all is void. When even the void does not exist, then nonexistence not existing also does not exist." This is what is meant by emptying the mind. This is the great liberation of "refining the self," the great peace. Therefore, later in the text it continues: "Eternal stillness and eternal response." Alas, is "eternal stillness" not the experience of "refining the self," and is "eternal response" not the practice of seeking the lead? My Master instructed me saying that the fifteenth of the eighth lunar month is the medicine within the stove. He bade me answer him, but I was confused and could find no response. Then he answered himself saying that wind and flowers are like dust on a chair. Those who are enchanted with beautiful scenery consider wind, flowers, snow, and moon to be the four most impressive elements. The emotional response to the beautiful scene is totally absorbing, but the Master compared it to dust on a chair. Does this not require forgetting the self, forgetting the world, and forgetting forgetfulness? Master instructed me in the "medicine gathering charm" and the essentials of "refining the self." Formerly I grasped the essential meaning of his words, but now I thoroughly understand them. Someone hearing this teaching lept to his feet and exclaimed: "Were it not for your words I might never have learned of the principles of the great *tao*. Please excuse me. I must go and practice 'refining the self.'"

True Transmission of the Golden Elixir

Chin-tan chen-chuan

by Sun Ju-chung

Author's Preface

I wrote the *True Transmission of the Golden Elixir* as an elaboration of the ideas of my Father Master. My master was my father, and so I refer to him as Father Master. Father Master's family had lived for generations in Teng-huang County, Shantung. He was born in the seventeenth year of the Hung-chih reign [Ming dynasty, 1505], sexegenary cycle year *chia-tzu*. In his youth he was a lover of the *tao* and visited all the famous moun-

tain retreats. He practiced breathing exercises and *ch'i* circulation. As a young man he received Ch'in Yeh-ho's methods for "holding the center," "gathering the medicine," "forming the fetus," and "emergence of the spirit." He later encountered Wang Yün-ku's teachings on the "fetal breath," the "gate of the mystery," "embracing the One," and "nonaction." As a result, he became a seeker of the elixir of immortality along with Li Jo-hai. He sat in seclusion for more than a year and was approaching a state of perfect enlightenment. At the stage just before the culmination of the *tao*, he was as radiant as a burning candle. Jo-hai believed that the *tao* had been realized, but Father Master felt that this was not the *tao* of the *yang* spirit that rushes upward.

He then traveled over land and water for six years until he met the Taoist adept, Master Shih Ku, who gave him the secrets of the "fire and tally of the golden crucible," "jade liquid for refining the self," and "golden liquid for refining the body." He then returned to Jo-hai's hut and once again prepared the seclusion room. He spared no effort in his practice, but yet failed to attain the highest level. He was painfully aware that falling short by the thickness of one sheet of paper was the same as missing by a thousand mountains.

One day Master An came by leaning on his cane. His body was withered but his spirit was lively. He said to Father Master, "What a pity, Sir, that you are so determined in the pursuit of your practices, but in the end will never succeed." Father Master was taken aback and said, "What is the great *tao* that transcends life and death?" Master An slowly replied, "It is the 'golden liquid returning elixir.' To become an immortal or a Buddha, this is the one and only principle. You must first clearly understand the concepts of the 'true *yin* and true *yang*,' the 'true lead and true mercury,' and that 'going contrary to what is normal brings gain, while going in accord with it causes loss.' Only then can we dare to speak of the *tao* of the 'nine revolutions golden liquid' and 'returning the elixir.'"

Father Master asked him to fully explain these ideas, and Master An answered, "If creatures were not divided into *yin* and *yang*, how could one conceive offspring by itself? When a hen produces an egg by itself, the chick does not form. By nature I am *yang* on the outside and *yin* on the inside, which may be represented by the trigram *Li* or mercury. If I fail to obtain the true lead from a partner, absorbing it upstream to join the mercury, how can I form the holy fetus and become a Buddha or an immortal? The opposite sex is by nature *yin* on the outside and *yang* on the inside, represented by the trigram *K'an* or lead. If she fails to obtain my true mercury, and going downstream combine it with lead, how could she form the mundane fetus and give birth to sons or daughters? Therefore, going in accord with what is normal results in a human being, while going contrary to it results in the elixir. These indeed are guiding principles! The classics on the cultivation of the elixir invariably expound on this. The elixir is obtained in the bedroom, but has nothing to do with 'mounting the maiden and engaging in the battle of stealing essences.' Every family naturally has the wherewithal, yet it is not that one's own body possesses the raw materials or 'crucible and stove.'" He spoke also of such things as the "crimson county," "sacred district," "external protector," "sacred ground," "companions," "yellow dame," and so forth. However, Father Master still did not grasp his meaning.

One day he remembered having visited Mount Hua,[1] where he chanced to meet a mendicant monk who was a marvelous diviner and asked, "When will I meet my true master and receive instruction in the *tao*?" The monk answered, "Your teacher is Master An." He asked three times and the answer was always the same. He also added, "It is easy for a master to find disciples, but difficult for a disciple to find a master." Today with Master An's arrival, the diviner's words had come true. Thereupon he and Jo-hai respectfully and sincerely agreed to carry out the secret transmissions. The master said, "Wonderful! If you can be faithful to me, I will hold nothing back but reveal to you the nine stages of cultivating immortality. The first is 'establishing the foundation'; the second, 'obtaining the medicine'; the third, 'forming the fetus'; the fourth, 'refining the self'; the fifth, 'returning the elixir'; the sixth, 'incubation'; the seventh, 'becoming a disembodied immortal'; the eighth, 'obtaining the mysterious pearl'; and the ninth, 'proceeding to the Jade Pool Heaven of the Immortals.' The first three stages enable one to become a 'human immortal,' the middle three stages to become an 'earthly immortal,' and the last three stages a 'heavenly immortal.'" He generally explained the "three stages" and "three passes," and elucidated the secrets of the "three levels of immortality." [He introduced the] "nine zithers," "nine swords," and the method for carrying out the work of the "nine revolutions." It therefore is called the "nine revolutions elixir of immortality." However, if the stage of "establishing the foundation" is not completed, one dare not "obtain the medicine." If the process of "refining the self" is not ready, one dare not "return the elixir." If one's practice is not complete, one will not obtain the "mysterious pearl." One by one he fully explained everything and gave him instructions on the "elixir medicine," "firing time," "weights and measures for gauging one's progress," "age or freshness," and "floating or sinking."

Father Master then suddenly achieved perfect understanding and, along with Jo-hai, performed the rites of discipleship and vowed to realize their goal. Withdrawing, he compared Master An's words with the classics on cultivating the elixir and found that they corresponded perfectly. Therefore, he quickly set up an "elixir chamber," "vessels," "tiger and dragon," and "zither and sword." Bowing to Master An, he entered the chamber. Jo-hai was concerned about the insufficiency of "elixir material," and so brought in his friend Tao Hsüan Ch'en tzu to help when needed. Within five months his physical appearance changed, in nine months he obtained the medicine, and in two years the work of "refining the self," "returning the elixir," and "incubation" were complete. Master An then took his leave and departed.

Father Master remained in a state of abstraction and tranquility for twenty years without finding like-minded comrades. At the age of sixty he went to Lu-an[2] and had great success using the first stage of practice to cure deathbed cases of illness. As a result, he was restrained by the local officials and prevented from leaving. At the age of sixty-eight he had no alternative but to take my mother as his wife, and in his seventieth year she gave birth to me. At seventy-three he sired my younger brother and at eighty-eight my younger sister. However, because he was simply absorbing postnatal *ch'i* for the purpose of longevity and was not able to obtain external help, he failed to get the "great medicine."

How could he bear that this *tao* fall into obscurity? Therefore, he summoned me to him and commanded me saying, "This *tao* may be transmitted only from father to son, for fear that it fall into the wrong hands. Now you my son are good material, and we must not allow this *tao* to become extinct." He gave orders for an auspicious day to be divined, incense to be burned, and oaths sworn to the gods. Then he completely transmitted the art to me. Each time he taught me a section he would weep and shed tears, for he realized that he himself had not been able to achieve it. Then he said to me, "Will you suffer the same fate in relation to me as I did with Master An?" I felt as if I had just come from an audience with the Duke of Chou.[3]

I discussed this enterprise with old Sheng An-pai, and he introduced me to officials in the capital such as Chih Yüe-ho and Ts'ang Heng-wang who provided assistance when needed. A modest effort was made to provide crucible and stove, zither and sword. Before my practices proceeded very far, my physical appearance suddenly changed and my spirit became progressively more enlightened. Buoyantly floating, I experienced the pleasure of transcending the dust of the world.

When Father Master reached the age of 106 years he grew weary of the chaos of the world and longed to transcend the mundane realm. But I together with my brother and sister begged him to remain with us, and he did stay another few months. Then he summoned me to him and revealed the details of the teaching, bidding me to pursue it with courage. Sighing, he said, "Today I am leaving you for a long journey. The dream that I was not able to fulfill I entrust to you. This art must not be lightly revealed to anyone. Is it possible that your destiny outweighs even that of the ancient immortal masters? You must take a lesson from P'ing-shu who thrice met with heaven's reproach." Thereupon he departed this world. At the moment of his death he was sitting in meditation on a low couch when a kind of white *ch'i* appeared at the top of his head. Its radiance floated in space, and an extraordinary fragrance permeated everything. The local officials and common people were all amazed and paid their respects.

I closed my door and mourned his passing for three years. However, I did not want Father Master's teachings to remain secrets confined to Anhui and Hupeh provinces alone, and so I traveled north to the capital[4] and searched far and wide for fellow seekers. I was able to make contact with five or six who were interested in using the *tao* to achieve physical health, but after succeeding in this, they all quickly took off in pursuit of fame and fortune. In the end, there was not one who was devoted to the art of immortality.

I went to Kaifeng[5] in sexagenary cycle year *jen-tzu* [1552] and in a bookstore saw the *Yü-tung ts'ung-shu*. I traced the author and discovered that this work was written by Li Ch'u-yü. I later chanced to meet him in the office of Fan Shih, but because our meeting was without prior introduction, he shyly demurred. I bowed and asked him, "Among the immortals are there differences in level?" He answered, "Yes, there are. First there are the 'human immortals,' then the 'earthly immortals' and finally, the 'heavenly immortals.' The 'human immortals' are the foundation for the 'earthly immortals,' and it is from them that the 'heavenly immortals' spring." I said, "May I ask, how should one practice to become a 'human immortal?'" He answered, "First strengthen the *ch'i* and blood, then create the 'Ch'ien body,'[6] and finally obtain external medicines to aid in forming the internal elixir. This is the 'human immortal.' Gather the lead and refine the mercury until it crystallizes to form cinnabar. The 'true *yang*' comes from without and the 'holy fetus' molts. This then is the 'earthly immortal.' The mysterious throne floats in space, and there hangs a single pearl. Swallowing it one becomes an immortal and ascends to the 'golden gate.' This then is the 'heavenly immortal.' However, 'forming the elixir' and 'returning the elixir' are not the same: lead belonging to the Celestial Stem *kuei* and lead belonging to the Celestial Stem *jen* are not the same.[7] The method of forming the elixir relies on myself and not another; the work of returning the elixir depends on a partner and not on myself. When it comes to medicine we speak of *kuei* and *jen*. It is the *jen* that must be gathered and not the *kuei*. The elixir is divided according to two and four.[8] Two is for obtaining the elixir and four for combining it. Lead and mercury represent the two participants. Half is my partner and half is myself. Female and male are two swords: one a crouching tiger and the other a descending dragon. This is the analysis of the elixir medicine."

At that time, old Heng Lu-chang invited me to stay in his official residence and every day together with Ch'u Yü we compiled this book. When the work of explaining the nine stages of practice was nearly completed, Ch'u Yü requested that we reveal the author's name to make it plain to all the world. I was concerned that, as my *tao* was not yet fully realized, it was an embarrassment to disclose it publicly. As a result I relate the *tao* that my Father Master received from beginning to end. At the head I place the title *True Transmission of the Golden Elixir*, inviting corrections from men of wisdom. May my Father Master's teachings, like the call of the phoenix or mist and vapor, spread to all people.

Forty-third year of the Wan-li reign [1616], *i-mao*, fourth lunar month, sons Ju-chung and Ju-hsia touch the ground with their heads and dedicate this book.

Chapter 1. Establishing the Foundation

If one asks about the first stage of establishing the foundation,
Then one must understand the bellows and the gate of the mystery.
Chasing the partner's *ch'i* and blood over to my *tan-t'ien*
Is precisely the meaning of supplementing *Li* by taking from *K'an*.
When speaking of the blood, we must analyze the lines of the hexagrams and fractions of ounces, the old and the fresh;
When speaking of *ch'i* we must understand *tzu* and *wu*, absorbing and augmenting.
This practice may be completed in 100 days when the body becomes pure *Ch'ien*.
At this point we are not far from becoming a human immortal.

Notes: "Establishing the foundation" means that the body is the "foundation" for the elixir, and "establishing" means to strengthen it. The "bellows" is the instrument for establishing the foundation. This is the same as the ancient saying: "To establish the foundation we must first understand the 'bellows'; in 'refining the self' one must use the 'true lead.'" The "gate of the mystery" is the entrance of the elixir. The blood belongs to *yin* and the *ch'i* to *yang*. Both come from the outside and must be captured so that they pass over to the *tan-t'ien*. The trigram *Li* represents oneself. The center line in *Li* is empty and represents *yin*. The partner is represented by *K'an*. *K'an*'s middle line is full and represents *yang*. Chasing the partner's *ch'i* and blood into my *tan-t'ien* is what is meant by "supplementing *Li* by taking from *K'an*." The "age or freshness" of the blood depends on the time. Therefore, one must analyze the "lines of the hexagrams and fractions of ounces." In "absorbing and augmenting" the *ch'i*, one must guard against cold and dry. Therefore, "one must understand *tzu* and *wu*." "Completing the practice in 100 days" means that *Li* has obtained the middle line from *K'an*, that it is full, and has become pure *Ch'ien*. This then is the work of becoming a "human immortal."

Commentary: A human being is endowed with the father's *ching* and mother's blood, and from this the body is formed. After a process of combination and gestation, it gradually reaches the stage of manifesting as physical form. The father's *ching* is stored in the kidneys; the mother's blood is stored in the heart. The heart and kidneys are connected by a channel, and following the mother's breathing, the *ching* and blood are produced together. After they have accumulated for ten months, there is one *liang* of *ching*, and the blood being distributed throughout the entire body, it can separate from the mother's belly. After it is born, it sucks the mother's breast. The breast responds to the menses and carries the *ch'i* upward. Red is converted to white, and thus *yin* becomes *yang*. The breasts contain the *ching* of *yin* and *yang*, and as the infant sucks them, its *ching* increases and its *yang* develops, its blood increases and its *yin* develops. When accumulation proceeds for one year, it reaches two *liang* of *ching*, three *liang* at two years, and one *chin* at fifteen. Now the *tao* of the male is complete. At this moment, the *ching-ch'i* is replete and the state of pure *Ch'ien* is realized. This is called the "highest power." If he receives enlightening instruction from an adept, then his foundation may be secured by itself, and there will be no need to engage in such exercises as "strengthening the *ch'i*," "strengthening the blood," "obtaining the medicine," or "returning the elixir." He will naturally exist as if hanging suspended between heaven and earth, controlling *yin* and *yang*, harmonizing his heart with the *ch'i*, the *ch'i* with spirit, and spirit with the void. His lifespan equals heaven and earth and has no end. The *Ts'an-t'ung ch'i* says: "The highest power is nonaction. Seek not by deliberate pursuit." However, at this stage in a man's life knowledge arises and emotions are born. When the *ching* is full one is unable to control oneself; when the spirit is complete one cannot remain stable. They take error as habit and suffering as happiness. They are busy by day

and active at night, all of which harms the *ching* and damages the blood. As a result our pure bodies become corrupt. When the middle line of *Ch'ien* departs and enters the "palace of *K'un*," it leaves a void and is now *Li*. This then is called the "lower power." Being empty it is necessary to supplement it to make it full. Having escaped, it is necessary to pursue it and make it return. Therefore, one must employ methods for repairing and returning. Only then can one regain the condition of the *Ch'ien* body. Set up the elixir foundation as the root of cultivating immortality. However, repairing and returning are two separate matters. The *Ts'an-t'ung ch'i* says: "The lower power engages in deliberate action and must be employed continually." Therefore, to strengthen *yang* one must use *yin*, and to strengthen *yin* one must use *yang*. If bamboo breaks, bamboo is used to mend it; if a human being suffers injury, another human being may be used to repair the damage. That is, each takes from its own kind. Therefore, the *Ts'an-t'ung ch'i* says: "With one of similar kind, it is easier to carry out one's practices; with other than one's own kind, it is difficult to achieve marvelous results." "Repairing" means to strengthen the *ch'i* and strengthen the blood. The blood and *ch'i* originally were not two separate entities. The *ch'i* diffuses throughout the body providing a nutritive and defensive function. Flowing everywhere it becomes blood. When the blood travels through the vessels of the womb, it once again vaporizes and becomes *ch'i*. When the *ch'i* is harmed it is unable to produce blood, and when the blood is harmed it is unable to produce *ch'i*. This is why it is necessary to carry out strengthening. Further, the circulation of the *ch'i*, being insubstantial, follows the inhalation and exhalation of the breath in passing in and out. Therefore, exercises for strengthening the *ch'i* should be many. The circulation of the blood, being substantial, once it has entered does not issue forth again. Therefore, exercises for strengthening the blood should be few. One should strengthen the *ch'i* first on account of its insubstantiality and cause it to be sufficient, and only then strengthen the blood's substantiality, giving it a place to revert to. If the *ch'i* has not been strengthened, it is impossible to strengthen the blood. Without strengthening the *ch'i* and the blood, it is impossible to complete the foundation. The *ch'i* is the prenatal *ch'i* produced in the postnatal crucible. For strengthening purposes there is a "zither" and a "sword." One must understand the correct day and hour, the "tally" and the "fire." The blood may be the prenatal within the crucible or it may be the postnatal within the crucible that descends by itself. To strengthen it there is also the zither and the sword. It is necessary to distinguish the "old" and the "fresh," the "lines of the hexagrams," and the "fractions of a *liang*." When strengthening them, the spirit engages in intercourse but the body does not; the *ch'i* engages in intercourse but the body does not. Although one is engaged in intercourse, it is as if one was not. This is a matter of taking the partner's blood *ch'i* and employing methods to combine it with my own *ching* spirit so that the two coalesce as one. In this way, the empty is no longer empty and the injured no longer injured. The elixir foundation is now strong so that one may obtain the medicine. This is the first task in cultivating immortality.

Chapter 2. Obtaining the Medicine

If one asks how the medicine is obtained,
It is by gathering the lead to subdue the
 yin-ching.
The yellow dame and companions should
 be of one heart.
Then one may arrange the stove and set up
 the crucible.
When the tiger sits on the mountain top
 there is a response,
But the dragon sleeps silently at the bottom of the sea.
The lead pearl rolling on traverses Mount
 K'un-lun.
At this point it is called the root of the
 elixir.

Notes: "Obtaining the medicine" means the prenatal external medicine produced in the postnatal crucible. The lead is the medicine obtained. The *yin-ching* is difficult to make secure and

strong and so requires the lead to control it. The "yellow dame" refers to the external "yellow dame." The "companions" refer to three like-minded persons. The "stove" is the other party and I am the "crucible." The "tiger" is by nature difficult to subdue. As in the hexagram *Lü* (Treading) from the *I ching*, if one treads [on the tiger's tail] without the proper *tao* it will bite you. The one "seated" is controlled by the dragon. The *I ching* says [of the hexagram *T'ung-jen* (Fellowship with Men)] that "first the like-minded weep aloud, but later they laugh." [The "Great Commentary" of the *I ching* says:] "When two people are of like mind, their strength can break even metal." The "tiger sitting on top of the mountain" refers to the male tiger that howls on top of the magnificent mountain. "Response" is the response of heaven to the stars and is the moment of production of the medicine. The "dragon" is a creature capable of infinite transformation. "Sleep" is the idea of the peace of meditation. "The bottom of the sea" is what the [*Ts'an-t'ung*] *ch'i* calls the "deep abyss," or what the [*Wu-chen*] *p'ien* calls the "bottom of the pool." "Silently" means that the exchange takes place without words. The "rolling of the lead pearl" describes the condition of the medicine. "Mount K'un-lun" is the highest point on the human body. It is not the same as the note to the *Wu-chen* [*p'ien*] that indicates that the summit of the "lower peak" is called "Mount K'un-lun." The "root" means that the elixir must be rooted in this before it forms.

Commentary: At the very beginning of conception one derives substance from father and mother for there to be life. After training, one's substance is derived from the "true mother" to obtain the medicine. The "medicine" is the external medicine produced in the postnatal crucible. "Obtaining the medicine" refers to gathering the postnatal crucible's external medicine, taking it into my body and combining it with the *ch'i* and blood that I have finished refining to control the *yin-ching* and transform it into "true mercury." After this, the body and spirit are both whole. When the primal source of life is strong and secure, this then is the ladder that leads by degrees to immortality or Buddhahood. Therefore it is said that to gather the prenatal essence within the prenatal enables one to become an immortal or a sage. To gather the prenatal essence within the postnatal enables one to increase longevity and lengthen years. However, the prenatal within the postnatal includes both *jen* and *kuei*. The *kuei* is the *yin* within *yin* and is not suitable as medicine; the *jen* is the *yang* within *yin*, and this alone may be considered medicine. Therefore, when we speak of "gathering medicine," we do not take the *kuei* but rather the *jen*. Now why is it that the crucible for obtaining the medicine is designated "postnatal," whereas the medicine itself belongs to the "prenatal"? Although the Great Ultimate (*T'ai-chi*) divides, *yin* and *yang* have not yet paired and remain in a state of primal homogeneity. Because the *kuei* is unusable, we first eliminate it with the masculine sword; the *jen* is usable and must be gathered with the masculine sword. However, if one has not prepared the "yellow dame" and set up the "zither and sword," what will one do when the medicine is produced? It therefore is said that if one desires to catch fish, one must first weave nets and not merely sigh longingly by the water's edge. Now the true medicine that comes to us from outside belongs by nature to the prenatal *ching*, a bit of original *ch'i* that is completely pure and whole and has never experienced excitement. I, for my part, use my postnatal substance to quickly receive this prenatal medicine. *Yin* is chased by *yang*; *yang* is harassed by *yin*. *Yin* seeks to retire, but is enclosed by form and is not able to escape control. *Yang* seeks to assert itself, but is still immature and soft and not able to rest secure. Therefore, that which desires to decrease is not able to do so at that moment, and that which desires to increase is also not able to do so at that moment. With tarrying and lingering, with passion and ardor, the whole body from top to bottom is as if drunk or bewitched. Without the support of the "companions" and "yellow dame," how could one circulate the "*yin* tally" and

mobilize the "*yang* fire"? Subduing the *yin* mercury depends wholly on this stage of the practice. After obtaining this several times, the "three *tan-t'ien*" are full of treasure and the elixir foundation will be firm and substantial. At this point, even if one has not yet succeeded in "returning the elixir," one will still enjoy long life and earn the title of "Immortal Among Men." This then is the second task in cultivating immortality.

Chapter 3. Forming the Elixir

If one asks how the elixir forms,
It is when the six gates are fast secured and the spirit concentrated.
Now cause the true earth to sit in the yellow court,
And carefully guard the original *yang* as one dreams in sleep.
The wood nature and metal condition should be harmonized.
Water rises and fire descends unceasingly.
To remain in the world in a lively state and preserve one's true form,
It is necessary to wait for the complete disappearance of the *yin* tally.

Notes: "Forming the elixir" means gathering the external medicine, concentrating my "true *ch'i*," and their combining to become the elixir. It does not refer to "returning the elixir" or "forming the holy fetus." The "fast securing of the six gates" refers to the "three treasures"—ears, eyes, and mouth—and their "securing" so that nothing escapes. "Concentrating the spirit" means "embracing the Source," "holding to the One," and "incubating the inner elixir." The "true earth" is one's own mercury. The "yellow court" is the treasury where the *ching* is stored. "Sitting" means not stirring. "Sitting in the yellow court" means that after obtaining the external medicine and transforming the *ching* into mercury, it reverts to the "yellow court." "Guarding the original *yang*" means guarding against leakage of the *yang*, being careful of nocturnal emissions, eliminating mental confusion, being sparing in one's speech, avoiding foolish notions, and regulating the breath so that it is slow and continuous. "Wood" is associated with the direction east and the trigram *Chen*; 159

"metal" is associated with the west and the trigram *Tui*. "Nature" has to do with myself and belongs to the category of wood; "condition" has to do with my partner and belongs to the category of metal. Their "harmonizing" means that wood by nature loves metal, is obedient and righteous; metal by predilection cherishes wood, is kind and benevolent. "Water," which originally flows downward, is carried upward by the rising *ch'i*; "fire," which originally flames upward, meets water and descends downward. "Unceasingly" means that the "water wheel" turns without rest. "The complete disappearance of the *yin* tally" means that after the elixir forms, the *yin-ch'i* gradually and naturally disappears. This together with the previous two chapters concludes the work of attaining "human immortality."

Commentary: My body's *ch'i* originally is scattered and chaotic; it does not accept control and is not willing to coalesce. This is called *yin-ching*. Only when the external medicine absorbed into my body unites with this bit of my own *yin-ching* does it become concentrated and not disperse. This is called "forming the elixir." There is a specific location for the formation of the elixir. One of its names is the "sea of *ch'i*" and another is the "lower *tan-t'ien*." In relation to the navel, it measures two fingers above and two below with one inch and two-tenths in the middle. Open and clear, it is empty. It is the place to which water reverts and *ch'i* converges. The ancient immortals said: "When the *ch'i* reverts to the 'original sea,' one's life becomes infinite." Now how does the elixir form? It is by borrowing this external medicine, capturing and controlling the *ch'i* of the Five Viscera and preventing it from dispersing so that it may unify and become the elixir. Therefore, when the "elixir foundation" is newly established and has not yet been refined, it is necessary to guard against leakage, be careful of nocturnal emissions, eliminate unclear thinking, and be sparing in speech. Before the *tzu* hour "advance the fire" and after the *wu* hour "withdraw the tally." At other times, regulate the breath so that it is

slow and continuous, so that it seems to exist and yet seems not to exist. "Eliminate foolish notions" and appear as if stupid or slow of speech, like a hen brooding over its eggs. The warm *ch'i* is inexhaustible, like a dragon cultivating a pearl and hibernating motionlessly. When the fire function is sufficient, the inner elixir naturally forms. A point of subtle brilliance like a red tangerine forms in the *tan-t'ien* giving off a glorious effulgence. At this point, the blood is transformed into *ching* and the *ching* into mercury. The "original nature" now is perfect and brilliant, and the "truth" shines forth forever. The *yin* demons have retreated completely and all that remains is half a *chin* of active "true mercury." This is called the "inner elixir." Therefore we say that the "inner elixir" becomes and the "external elixir" approaches. The "inner elixir" is one's own "true mercury" and is called the "*chi* earth." The external elixir is one's partner's "true lead" and is called the "*wu* earth." After the elixir has formed, one immediately becomes a "human immortal." This chapter has described the practices for cultivating one's nature and establishing life. It is not yet the *tao* of "returning the elixir" and "forming the fetus." This then is the third task in the process of attaining immortality.

Chapter 4. Refining the Self

If one asks about refining the self,
It is when crucible, stove, zither, and
  sword are without blemish.
Before and after the quarters of the moon
  gather the golden flower.
To regulate the fire use the hexagrams
  After Completion and Before
  Completion.
Nine and six are the stages of the cosmic
  orbit.
The dragon's head and tiger's tail must be
  held tightly.
Use lead to cook the mercury so that cinnabar is formed,
And then we may speak of the process of
  returning the elixir.

Notes: "Refining the self" means refining the mercury contained in one's own body, causing it to be transformed and become cinnabar. The "crucible, stove, zither, and sword" are not the same as those in the previous chapter on "obtaining the medicine," nor the following on "returning the elixir." "Without blemish" means that in the midst of desire one is without desire, that in the midst of the "dust of the world" one transcends it. "Before and after the quarters of the moon" are stages in the emergence of the "golden flower." In refining one's own "fire," one uses the two hexagrams "After Completion" and "Before Completion" to divide the hours *tzu* and *wu* and distinguish "old and fresh," relying on the "companions" to regulate the clepsydra. "Nine and six" represent the *yin* and *yang* lines of the hexagrams in the *I ching*. "The stages of the cosmic orbit" are the stages in the process of "refining the self." The "dragon's head and tiger's tail" are the gate and entrance for delivering the lead fire. "Holding tightly" means securing it and not allowing it to escape, taking from the other and not losing one's own; that is, taking the quicksilver in one's own body and refining it into a lump of dry mercury. This is why we speak of its "becoming cinnabar." When one's practice has reached this level, then it is possible to "return the elixir."

Commentary: "Refining the self" means refining the "true mercury" within one's own body until it becomes cinnabar.[9] Although one employs "crucible, stove, zither, sword, partner, and yellow dame," one must remain proper and dignified. One must be as reverential as of the gods and as loving as of one's own father and mother. Cherish it with virtue and treat it kindly with benevolence. When the mind is without random thoughts and foolish notions have been eliminated, only then does one receive the proper results from crucible and stove and satisfy the requirements for "refining the self." Now when the elixir chamber already has been set up, stove, crucible, vessels, and receptacles respond to each other perfectly and the elixir of immortality naturally forms. If but one thought is slightly "blemished," the "medicine demons" arise in legions and the stove, crucible, vessels, and receptacles all be-

come useless. It therefore is said that "returning the elixir" is easy, but "refining the self" is most difficult. One must not fail to be cautious. It is necessary in the midst of desire to suspend desire and, dwelling in the dust of the world, to transcend the world. Cleanse the altar, arrange the zither and sword, observe the "flowers of lead," and carry out the process of alchemical firing. Entrust the "yellow dame" to determine the floating and sinking; rely on the companions to regulate the clepsydra. Follow the hours *tzu* and *wu* to prepare for absorption and supplementation and employ the "miraculous flying sword" to gather lead from the "tiger's tail." With the "sword that reaches to heaven" deliver fire to the head of the dragon. Pursue the "higher *hun* soul" and control the "lower *p'o* soul" according to the proper methods. Rely on the craftsman's hand to capture the mist and grasp the clouds, causing spirit to propel the *ch'i* and *ch'i* the body so that one's whole being is permeated. Fire refines the lead and lead refines the mercury. Harmonize the "three elements," beat back the "three maggots" and "nine thieves," and crush the "six desires" and "seven emotions." When a drop of *ching* fluid and blood are transformed into "jade paste," not even half a drop of saliva, snivel, sweat, or tears is produced in the orifices. When the blood turns to white marrow, the "true mercury" and bone *ch'i* are both "golden *ching*," and flesh and skin turn to jade substance. Then the process of "refining the self" is perfected and these effects manifest. This cannot be accomplished in a single step. Only at this stage may one seek to "return the elixir." This then is the fourth task in cultivating immortality.

Chapter 5. Returning the Elixir

If one asks about the process of returning the elixir,
It is necessary to understand the prenatal aspect of the *yang*.
During the last or first days of the moon when there is no extreme tendency,
Steal a bit of golden *ching*.
During the [first] two stages of practice the responsibility is with the partner,

And in the [second] four I employ my own control mechanism.
Just as the infant and beautiful maiden are uniting,
Outside the door Master Ting is giving a war cry.

Notes: "Returning the elixir" means returning the gold of the prenatal true *yang* and causing it to revert to the "palace of *Ch'ien*." This has nothing to do with "forming the elixir" or the "millet-sized pearl." The prenatal element within the *yang* is the prenatal element within the prenatal. We do not call it lead, but call it *yang*, and therefore is the idea that *yang* is produced from lead. "During the last or first days of the moon" is the time when sun and moon mate; that is, precisely during the two days that are the last day of one lunar month and the first of the following. They join bodies in progression, and their emerging and waning together represents the inseparability of *yin* and *yang*. The "golden *ching*" is the *ching* of the golden fluid that appears at sixteen years of age, or the prenatal true *ch'i*. Therefore we speak of "one drop." The "two stages" have to do with the function of the external elixir; that is, the period of obtaining the elixir. Its operation rests with the partner and not with oneself. The "four stages" is the function of the internal elixir, or the period of uniting the elixirs. Its operation rests with myself and not with my partner. The "infant" is the true lead; the "beautiful maiden" is the true mercury. "Uniting" is the idea of harmonious combination. "Master Ting" is the true fire. This is the fire used in refining the elixir. If the fire is too low, the elixir will not form; and if too high, there is danger of damaging the elixir. The fire comes from without and reaches my body. In a process analogous to smoking or steaming, it penetrates everywhere. With the release there is a sound, clearly resonating without end. Therefore, the text says: "Outside the door Master Ting is giving a war cry."

Commentary: The elixir is the prenatal bit of true *yang* gold. It is not the medicine obtained from without and also is not the *jen* within *kuei*. It therefore is said that lead is born after the advent of *kuei*, and *yang* is produced in the midst of lead. "Returning the elixir" means returning the gold of the prenatal true *yang* and causing it to revert to the "palace of *Ch'ien*." It therefore is said that one must rely on the partner who represents *K'un* to give birth to the perfected body planted in the *Ch'ien* party's "palace of mutual interaction." Thus, at the obscure beginning of creation, before the division of the Great Ultimate (*T'ai-chi*), this prenatal *yang* gold originally belonged to *Ch'ien*, and so we call it "*Ch'ien* gold." *Ch'ien* interacts with *K'un* and then flees into the "palace of *K'un*." Therefore, it is called "gold within *K'un*." When *K'un* receives this gold, its middle becomes full, and thereupon it assumes the form of *K'an*. *K'an* dwells in the north, the land of the *kuei* water. When gold is concealed within water it is called "gold in water." This gold is the prenatal treasure and cannot dwell for long in the postprimordial *K'an*, so it is transformed into *Tui*. *Tui* emerges from the gate of *K'an* and dwells in the west of the Western Heaven. This is also called "*Tui* gold." If one seeks this gold, do not look for it in *Ch'ien*, or in *K'un*, or in *K'an*. Seek for it only in *Tui*. *Tui* and the moon of *K'un* are of one kind, and therefore it is able to stand for *K'un* in carrying out its mission. Moreover, *K'un* is the mate of *Ch'ien*. *Tui* is the daughter of *K'un* and of one species with *Ch'ien*. The *Ts'an-t'ung ch'i* says: "With the same species it is easy to carry out one's practice, but with unrelated kinds it is difficult to achieve marvelous results." This is the meaning. Thus the *yang* gold of *Ch'ien* revolves and reverts to *Tui*. In this way, gold once again reverts to *Ch'ien*, and *Ch'ien* can return this original gold as the elixir. Therefore, we speak of "returning the elixir." "Forming the elixir" means gathering and returning the medicine that comes from without, controlling my own body's *ch'i* to prevent it from becoming scattered, and concentrating it until it becomes manifest and forms the inner elixir. "Returning the elixir" means that when the partner's "true *yang*" is stirred, we mobilize a bit of our own mercury to welcome it. There is external contact and internal excitement, producing a visible reaction; there is internal contact and external sensation, producing an invisible spiritual awakening like the attraction of loadstone for iron, drawing it to the *tan-t'ien* and returning the external elixir. The elixir is born of the moon. The moon embodies the idea of fullness. On the fifteenth of the eighth lunar month during the *tzu* hour in the middle of the night, the inferior *yin* soul completely disappears and the superior *yang* soul is completely full. This is called "pure *Ch'ien*." It corresponds precisely with the quantity one *chin* and is exactly the time for gathering and collecting. It therefore is said that the concept of the fullness of the moon is preserved in the oral verses and the marvelous effect of the *tzu* hour is found in secret transmissions. The inferior *yin* soul belongs to water; the superior *yang* soul belongs to metal. On the eve of the eighth of the month, the *yang* soul is half full and the *yin* soul has half disappeared. This is called the first quarter. This *yang* within *yin* produces eight *liang* of metal within water. On the night of the twenty-third, the *yang* soul has half waned and the *yin* soul is half full. This is called the last quarter. *Yang* within *yin* produces half a *chin* of water within metal. The first quarter is the period when the *K'un* of the last and first days of the moon undergoes change and becomes the *Chen* of the third day of the month. Changing again it becomes the *Tui* of the eighth of the month. *Tui* is the youngest daughter and has the responsibility of representing *K'un*. The last quarter is the period when the *Ch'ien* of the fifteenth undergoes a change and becomes the *Hsün* of the sixteenth. Changing again, it becomes the *Ken* of the twenty-third. *Ken* is the youngest son and has the responsibility of managing *Ch'ien*. If one uses the period after the last quarter and before the first quarter, then *yang* and *yang* combine together, higher soul and higher soul unite. This is twice eight that equals one *chin*. This is the full moon. This is pure *yang* and the fulfillment of the *tao* of the

elixir. It therefore is said that eight *liang* of lead and half a *chin* of mercury combine to form one lump of purple gold elixir. The Immortal [Chang] Tzu-yang said: "When *yin* and *yang* find partners of their own kind and come together in mutual intercourse, the two eights match each other and unite in perfect intimacy." This is the meaning. When "returning the elixir" it is necessary to understand the discourse of Yin Chen-chün. He said: "If one desires to cultivate this art, one must borrow raw materials, for without them it will be impossible to refine the golden elixir." It also is necessary to have three "companions," for only then can one carry out the practices. These are the three friends whose hearts are of one will. Secretly, on the evening of the full moon of the eighth lunar month when *yang* first stirs, the host should solemnly mount the altar with the dragon on his left hand and the tiger on his right. Carefully adjust the proper time and calculate according to the movement of Jupiter; match *yin* and *yang* and regulate them by the clepsydra. In this way, one achieves the union of metal and water, and dragon wood becomes pregnant with glory. One "companion" sits inside a tent and skillfully records the activities from beginning to end without the slightest error. Therefore Hsien Weng has said: "Everything depends upon the power of one's practice, for with the slightest error the elixir fails." Another companion secretly inspects the clepsydra, minutely adjusting the process of absorption and supplementation, and directs the firing work without confusing the correct degrees. If the proper time or favorable moment is exceeded, it will be difficult for the elixir to form. Thus it is said that to seek it without missing the proper moment, one must surely possess the destiny of an immortal. At this stage, the man becomes pregnant and the holy fetus forms. This then is the fifth task in cultivating immortality.

Chapter 6. Incubation

If one asks about incubation,
During *Chun* and *Meng*, one absorbs and
   supplements, using water and fire.

During *yin* and *shen*, *tzu* and *wu*, one must
be on guard.

When *mao* and *yu* approach, desist from
practice,

And let all revert to the purple palace.

When the demons arrive, the sword of wisdom always must be raised.

The elixir forms and in ten months the holy
fetus is complete.

Now naturally the immortal appears.

Note: "Incubating" means that the fire
ch'i should not be too cold nor too hot,
but nurtured sensitively. The hexagrams
Chun and *Meng* represent the succession
of morning and evening. "Absorption
and supplementation" contain the idea of
"advancing the *yang* fire and withdrawing
the *yin* tally." "*Yin* and *shen*" are the regions of flourishing metal and fire; *tzu*
and *wu* are the periods of the advent of
yin and *yang*. It is necessary to "be on
guard" to prevent the loss of *ch'i*, lest any
portion of the holy elixir be diminished.
Calculating "*mao* and *yu*" refers to the
gates of *yin* and *yang*. These two periods
represent stages of rest, and one should
suspend the exercises; for if fuel is added
to the fire at this point, one actually
courts disaster. It therefore is said, "desist from practice." The "purple palace"
is the place to which the "true *ch'i*" reverts and is stored. The "sword of wisdom" is our enlightened mind. The
"formation of the elixir in ten months"
and the "appearance of the immortal"
means that the *yang* spirit has emerged
from the gate.

Commentary: "Warming" means
neither cold nor hot. If it is too cold the
fire cools and the elixir will not gel. If it is
too hot the fire scorches and the elixir
easily melts away. Therefore, it is necessary to be neither cold nor hot, like cultivating cinnabar and mercury. This is what
is called "incubation." Nurture it in a relaxed manner and wait for it to be transformed of itself, just as heaven nourishes
all creatures. Rain and clear weather
alternate at the proper time. A mother in
gestating her child regulates her eating
and sleeping, and thus it naturally forms
and is born. This is what is meant by nurturing. There is an ancient saying that,
"Gathering the lead lasts for but a mo-

ment, but combining it with mercury lasts
for ten months." "A moment" refers to
the period when one "understands the
feminine but keeps to the masculine,"[10]
and "before the four stages, obtain the
elixir during the first two." The "ten
months" refers to the period during
which one "understands the white but
keeps to the black,"[11] or the period of
one year during which one completes the
"nine revolutions." Therefore, during
the period of incubation it is necessary to
employ crucible and stove and distinguish
Chun and *Meng*. In the morning, advance
the fire of *yang* as the hexagram *Chun*
comes to the fore; in the evening withdraw the *yin* tally as the hexagram *Meng*
comes to the fore. The hexagram *Chun* is
composed of the trigrams *Chen* below
and *K'an* above. The middle line in *K'an*
represents the elixir that is returned . The
first line in *Chen* represents the fire advanced. This may be described as the elixir
above that is approached by the *yang* fire
below to warm it. The hexagram *Meng*
has the trigram *K'an* below and *Ken*
above. *Ken*'s third line is the withdrawing
tally and means that the elixir is below,
while the tally approaches from above to
nourish it. There are twelve [Chinese]
hours in a day and 30 [hexagram] lines
in an hour, which, when multiplied by
the twelve hours, produces the sum of
360 lines. *Chun*, the morning, and *Meng*,
the evening, represent the method of
"advancing the fire and withdrawing the
tally." Carrying out this activity during a
twelve-hour period combines to produce
the sum of 360. "Morning" is called
"advancing the fire." Morning belongs to
yang, and *yang* rules advance. Therefore,
to the number thirty advance and add six.
From *tzu* to *ssu*, for each thirty add six,
and combine them for the sum of 216.
The hexagrams [in the cycle] correspond
to *Fu* (Return), *Lin* (Approach), *T'ai*
(Peace), *Chuang* (Power of the Great),
Kuai (Breakthrough), and *Ch'ien* (The
Creative). Evening means the period of
"withdrawing the tally." Evening belongs
to *yin* and *yin* rules withdrawing. Therefore, to the number thirty withdraw and
subtract six. From *wu* to *hai* subtract six
from each thirty. Adding these together

produces a total of 144. The hexagrams correspond to *Kou* (Coming to Meet), *Tun* (Retreat), *P'i* (Standstill), *Kuan* (Contemplation), *Po* (Splitting Apart), and *K'un* (The Receptive). *Yang* is born at the *tzu* hour, and the fire should be advanced during *tzu*. However, it is not at the *tzu* hour but rather the *yin*, for fire is born at the *yin* hour. Therefore, advancing the fire takes advantage of the time of fresh power. *Yin* is born at the *wu* hour, and the "*yin* tally" should be withdrawn during *wu*. However, it is not at the *wu* hour but rather the *hsü*, for the "storehouse of fire", dwells in *hsü*. Therefore, "withdrawing the tally" waits for the time of storing, and thus it is that the time of "advancing the fire and withdrawing the tally" includes a period of rest within it. "Rest" means halting the fire, ceasing work, cleansing the heart, and washing away cares to guard against danger and be mindful of peril. The time of "flourishing wood" comes in the *mao* period. *Mao* begins with the first "climatic period" of the second lunar month. After "flourishing wood"[12] comes "fire advent."[13] The process of "advancing the fire" should rest during the second month. Therefore, on the fifteenth of the first month, one ought to know when to stop. The first lunar month belongs to the hexagram *T'ai* (Peace), which is three *yang* lines below and three *yin* lines above. This represents *yin* and *yang* poised at the balance point, like the half image of the first quarter of the moon that is metal within water. Metal flourishes during *yu*. *Yu* begins with the first "climatic period" of the eighth lunar month.[14] After reaching the period of "flourishing metal," the fire is sufficient. "Withdrawing the *yin* tally" should rest during the eighth month. Thus, on the fifteenth of the seventh [lunar] month, one ought to be aware of guarding one's gains. The seventh month belongs to the hexagram *P'i* (Standstill), which is three *yin* lines below three *yang* lines. This is *yin* and *yang* poised at the balance point like the half image of the last quarter of the moon, which is water within metal. The *Tu-jen ching* says: "The astrolabe and sextant cease their revolutions for a mo-

ment. This is called "rest." The work of incubation originally is ten months, but after subtracting two months for rest, that leaves only eight months of actual incubation. Therefore, it requires one year of work to fulfill the ten months for the holy fetus to form and the infant to appear. Old [Chang] Tzu-yang[15] said: "The infant contains the true *ch'i*. After ten months the fetus is complete and the foundation is established." He also said: "Sons born within the year all will ride the crane of immortality." This is the meaning. Gentlemen who seek to cultivate the True, in circulating the fire and mobilizing the *yin* element, must be finely attuned to the natural world when they set the Big Dipper in motion. They must follow the processes of *yin* and *yang*, the four seasons, and the cycles of renewal. They must understand the principles of heaven and earth, the Five Phases, and mutual creation and destruction. Our exhalation should be silent and our breathing slow and continuous. Chuang tzu said: "The common man breathes from the throat, whereas the adept breathes from the heels." This illustrates our meaning. The Old Immortal Yü Ch'an said: "When closure is extreme one suffers from urgency; when there is complete abandon one suffers from wantonness." Chen I tzu said: "Regulate the clepsydra, adjust the sundial, assemble the gods and ghosts of *yin* and *yang*, gather the positive *ch'i* of the 360, return the vital passages of the seventy-two stages, advance the *yin* tally of the sixty-four hexagrams, and stir up the *yang* fire of the twenty-four climatic periods. The 'heavenly gate' is in the hand and the 'earthly axis' proceeds from the heart. Heaven and earth must not conceal the secret of creative power; *yin* and *yang* must not harbor the root of stasis and stagnation. One must achieve the level of boundless spirit and pure creative power." Wu Ming tzu said: "If there are errors in the stages of refining or failures in the timing, the cinnabar and mercury in the 'golden palace' will not sprout and moth larvae breed in the 'jade crucible.' In serious cases, mountains collapse and the earth crumbles. The 'metal tiger' and 'wood dragon' soar into space. In less serious cases, rains beat and winds blow, and the *K'un* male and *Li* female[16] run off together. Be extremely careful!" This then is the sixth task in the cultivation of immortality.

Chapter 7. Parturition

If one asks about the creative process of parturition,
Who can understand this phenomenon?
For how long has it dwelled in the crimson palace?
It then travels to the *ni-wan* where after three days,
Suddenly, in the gate of the crown, there is a peal of thunder,
And one clutches the infant to one's breast.
Legions of heavenly soldiers arrive to protect it,
And your name is already known to the Lord on High.

Notes: "Parturition" is something rare among men. Impregnation of the normal womb takes place by following the natural course of things, and therefore parturition takes place from below. The holy womb is impregnated contrary to the natural course of things, and therefore parturition takes place from above. Impregnation of the "lower *tan-t'ien*" is equally easy for both men and women. However, when it comes to the "crimson palace,"[17] it is very narrow, and the *ni-wan* is even narrower . How is it then that they can be "dwelled in" and "travelled to"? "Spirit" is a way of speaking of that which is without bounds and without substance. It is capable of penetrating even metal or stone, so what difficulty is there in "dwelling in the 'crimson palace'" or "travelling to the *ni-wan*"? When the "gate of the crown" bursts open, this then is the time of the dragon's offspring emerging from the womb. The *yang* spirit now appears and one has earned the title of "Immortal." Now the *yin* demons of the dark and ghost bandits are transformed into the "three protectors of the Law"; the "eight realms" are sanctified, and the "36,000 radiances" are transformed into divine warriors. Your name will be removed from the "black list" and inscribed in the "book of the elixir." How

could the Lord on High overlook your name? This together with the two preceding chapters concludes the work of becoming an "earthly immortal."

Commentary: Within the great cosmic process, the two *ch'i—Ch'ien* the father and *K'un* the mother—blend harmoniously and give birth to all creation. Therefore, it is said that in all creation only man is also thus. Man possesses a prenatal and postnatal nature. The prenatal is the spiritual father and divine mother; the postnatal is the mundane father and mundane mother. When the mundane father and mother have intercourse, the mercury arrives and is projected into the lead. When *yang* bestows and *yin* receives, this is called "the natural course." When the natural course is followed, then the human fetus is formed and sons and daughters are born. When the spiritual father and mother have intercourse, the lead arrives and is projected into the mercury. When *yin* bestows and *yang* receives, this is called "contrary to the natural course." If carried out contrary to the natural course, the holy fetus forms and birth is given to Buddhas and immortals. The principle of forming the holy and the human fetus is one and without distinction. The difference is simply one of following the natural course or going against it. After ten months the fetus is complete and with a "peal of thunder" the "gate of the crown" bursts open. After the "infant" appears, there is an additional stage of work to harmonize the spirit, and only then does the *yang* spirit emerge three to five steps before withdrawing again. Then it ventures half a [Chinese] mile or a mile and returns again, and then two or three miles and back again. Each time it fears that it will become lost and unable to find its way back. After a long time, this is thoroughly mastered, and 1,000 miles or 10,000 miles are like stretching out the arm. This then is the work of harmonizing the spirit. "Spirit" is the term for "infinite transformations."[18] When thoroughly harmonized, it becomes concentrated and naturally takes on the nature of existence. Not being exclusively of the nature of existence, it disperses and takes on the nature of nonexistence, but it also is not exclusively nonexistent. Not being exclusively existent, the *yang* is not sufficient to contain it, and it transcends the *yang*; not being exclusively nonexistent, the *yin* is not sufficient to limit it, and it transcends the *yin*. When *yin* and *yang* are both transcendent and existence and nonexistence are without limit, then 1 is transformed and becomes 10, 10 is transformed and becomes 100, 100 is transformed and becomes 1,000, and 10,000 roam everywhere throughout the "three realms,"[19] coming and going with perfect freedom. The *Ta-tung ching* says: "The 10,000 *ch'i* all attain immortality." This is the meaning. When one's training has reached this level, one deserves to be called an "earthly immortal." This then is the seventh task in cultivating immortality.

Chapter 8. The Mysterious Pearl

If one asks about the wonder of the
  mysterious pearl.
It is that the immortal once again becomes
  immortal.
He spreads his virtue far and wide among
  the realm of man,
Handing down the Golden Book and Jade
  Decree.
When the precious pearl of the mystery is
  swallowed,
One sprouts feathers and flies swiftly.
With a gust of wind, one disappears from
  Mount Wu-i
And soars to the Blessed Isles of P'eng-lai
  and the Holy Land of Lang- yüan.

Note: The "mysterious pearl" is the precious pearl that sits suspended in the void five *chang* above the earth, the size of a millet grain, exquisite and glittering. This is what the Buddhists call "the precious pearl of peace" offered by the Dragon King's daughter to the Buddha. The "immortal once again becomes immortal" means that one advances from "earthly immortal" to "heavenly immortal." It is imperative that not a single thought remain and that the tiniest speck of dust be transformed. There must be no perceived distinction of self and other; enmity and kindness must be seen as one; far and near, intimate and distant must be united as one body; birds and beasts, insects and fish are all of the same *ch'i*. One's lofty *tao* and weighty *te* are equal to heaven's. Following this, in the midst of obscurity and utter silence, the blessing is received and the "mysterious pearl" presented in all its splendor and brilliance, more precious than words can tell. When the "pearl" is consumed, the body sprouts feathered wings, and "disappearing from Mount Wu-i"[20] flies to the paradise of the immortals. P'eng-lai is as far away as the 3,000 mile course of the River Jo; Lang-yüan is located in Hsi-ying, 20,000 miles from China. Both are regions inhabited by the immortals.

Commentary: The "mysterious pearl" is not the prenatal medicine in the midst of the post-natal; neither is it the prenatal lead in the midst of the prenatal. Receiving the "mysterious pearl" is not a matter of gathering the *jen* after the *kuei*; neither is it a matter of obtaining *yang* from the midst of lead. Rather it is the millet-sized pearl produced in the prenatal crucible over a period of 5,048 days without error. It is difficult to find one or two such crucibles among the millions or meet more than one in over a century. Given the difficulty of meeting such a marvelous crucible, how can even those followers of the *tao* who are devoted to the "mysterious pearl" succeed in consuming it? Therefore, the pearl is bestowed by heaven and received by man. It requires the completion of 3,000 practices and the perfection of 800 exercises . Possessed of lofty *tao* and weighty *te*, one enjoys a state of purity and peace. Heaven above accompanies the Jade Emperor; earth below accompanies the beggar. This then is the true man in the world. Following this, in "total obscurity and utter silence," the summons is heeded and the "Dragon's daughter" appears. It should be noted that the period of 5,048 days precisely corresponds to the number required for one reading of the *Buddhist Canon*. The essences (*ching*) of heaven and earth, sun and moon come together at this time; the quintessences of *yin* and *yang* and the Five Phases now unite. In a spiritual and auspicious atmosphere the "precious pearl" forms and manifests suspended in space. Splendid and brilliant, its value is beyond words. The *Tu-jen ching* says:

"Mysteriously floating in space hangs a 'precious pearl,' the size of a millet grain, which is variously called the 'great Mahayana prajna (wisdom of the Great Vehicle),' the 'nine-storied pagoda,' the 'Buddha body,' 'cintamani (talisman-pearl),' 'saddharma (wonderful law),' or the 'marvelous Muni pearl.'" When the adept consumes it, his body sprouts wings and he joins the ranks of the immortals. The "jade lady" attends him before and the "golden lad" conducts him from the side. He eats the provisions of the "heavenly cook" and disdains the delicacies of the human realm. He dons the "six pearl garment" and scorns the silk robes of the world. He drives the chariot of the wind and rides the fabulous bird of immortality. This is the culmination of the "heavenly immortal." This then is the eighth task in cultivating immortality.

Chapter 9. Proceeding to the Jade Pool of the Immortals

If one asks about the happiness of the
   Jade Pool of the Immortals,
It is enjoyment without end.
Above, one faces the Imperial Palace on
   Jade Capital Mountain.
Coming and going in the roc car and
   phoenix carriage,
One eats the delicacies of the immortals
   from the heavenly kitchen.
Floating about, one wears the six pearl
   feathered garment,
And all of the immortals arrive together to
   congratulate the new immortal.
Now one will know eternal contentment.

Notes: The "Jade Pool" is the garden of K'un-lun and the park of Lang-feng Mountain. These are the haunts of the Queen Mother of the West. The "Imperial Palace" is the Brilliant Palace of the Jade Emperor. The "Jade Capital Mountain" is called Hsiao-t'ai. The "roc car and phoenix carriage" are the "wind car" and "feather wheels." The "delicacies of the immortals from the heavenly kitchen and "six pearl feathered garment" are food and clothing that occur naturally. These are what is known as the

"delicacies of the immortals from the five Kitchens" and "seamless clothing." "Eternal contentment" is the time that Shang-yang refers to as "when merit is achieved and fame follows."

Commentary: The "Jade Pool" is the garden of K'un-lun and the park of Lang-feng. This is the realm inhabited by the Queen Mother. At the beginning of heaven and earth, before the existence of man, the wood *ch'i* of the east coalesced to form a heavenly immortal. Its name was the Duke of Wood. The metal *ch'i* of the west coalesced to form a heavenly immortal. Its name was the Mother of Metal. After the two immortals descended, they gave birth to twenty-eight daughters. It is from these that humankind multiplied and mortal and immortal came to be distinguished. These two immortals are the eternal mother and father of man and of all creatures. After finishing 3,000 practices and completing 800 exercises, those who aspire to immortality are selected by the Great Emperor of the East and chosen by the Lord of Fang-chu. Upon reaching the Jade Pool, one is presented with a banquet and given an audience with the Mother of Metal who bestows the Heavenly Mandate. One then goes before the Jade Emperor to accept the post of Immortal, to oversee the creative processes of heaven, and to be a true minister to the Lord of Heaven. When merit is accomplished fame follows, and the mission of the great man's life is complete. Those trifling official posts in the world of men are mere sparks from flint, lightning flashes, or floating bubbles. How are they worthy of envy, and why do the jealous sigh with regret? Although the Jade Pool cannot be reached by ordinary men, after all, the Buddha did not bubble up from the earth, nor did Kuang Ch'eng and Lao tzu fall out of the sky. The common householder, husband and wife, are endowed with *ch'i*, blood, *ching* and spirit, and are not different from the great *tao*. Each and every one of them is capable of perfection. The blazing "golden elixir" can be consumed by any man. The only obstacle is failure of will or, if having the will, not being steadfast. Those with determination must find true teachers to instruct them on the "three stages" and "three gates"; transmit the "nine zithers" and "nine swords"; explain the order of "obtaining the medicine," the "elixir," and the "mysterious pearl"; and detail the attainments of the "earthly and heavenly immortals." For these, the "feathered wheels" are not needed to convey them to the Jade Pool 20,000 miles distant, for it is just feet away. One need not mount the celestial winds to the brilliance of the "ninefold heaven." Suddenly opening my eyes, the Immortals Chang, Ko, Chung, and Lü[21] become my comrades, and the serenity of heaven is my home. This then is the ninth task in the cultivation of immortality.

Summary of the Golden Elixir

Chin-tan chieh-yao

by Chang San-feng

Preface

The *tao* unfolds in three stages[1] as one advances step by step from the first. Leaving the world behind, there are five degrees[2] of immortality. One begins with "establishing the foundation" and "refining the self" and ends with "obtaining the medicine" for "absorption and supplementation." Even if one fails to form the fetus of immortality, one will at least lengthen one's lifespan and remain in the world. This *tao* has been handed down for a long time. Only if practiced from beginning to end is there hope of attaining results. The likes of "achieving *nirvana* while sitting or standing" or "reincarnation by entering the bodies of young corpses" are as far from the greatness of this *tao* as clouds and earth. Truly they cannot be spoken of in the same breath. Moreover, this illustrious *tao* of mysterious heaven precedes the emergence of the 10,000 phenomena. Taking heaven as warp and earth as woof, it originates from the Single Source. Therefore, if a man can fully realize this art. entering upon the path with sincerity, maintaining it in silence, using it with gentleness, and

practicing it with faithfulness, he can then be restored to life and revived from death, revert to the state of primal unity, enter sagehood and transcend the mundane, seize the sun and moon, and recover the luster of lost beauty. Oh, its glory extends from ancient times to the present! It is hidden and unfathomable, but there is nothing that does not possess it and no time when it is not present. The *tao* is such that we can never depart from it. If it can be departed from, it is not the *tao*. In ancient times the venerable Yellow Emperor cast nine cauldrons and ascended into heaven.

Lord Tung Hua[3] refined the "three glorious essences"[4] and realized the *tao*. Although its sects are divided into northern and southern and the teaching revealed as eastern and western, those who have ascended into heaven are more than 10,000, and whole families that have achieved immortality are more than 800. The names of those who have transformed their physical bodies are unrecorded, and those who have left their bodies behind and gained immortality are innumerable. These practices are absolutely orthodox and enlightened, for one may not ascend to the True by heterodox paths. Without the teachings of a master, how could one realize such wonders of body and spirit? I have studied all of the classics on refining the elixir of immortality, but this *tao* of the "golden elixir" truly is the method of the heavenly immortals and foremost in all the world. However, in later generations it was rarely heard of. Students who are able to grasp the mysteries of this art already have developed the necessary attributes and affinities. There are those who obtain some of "their own kind,"[5] and easily realize the goal, and others who fail for lack of raw material for preparing the elixir. Can seekers of the elixir not be extremely cautious? Today we are most fortunate to receive the teachings of an enlightened master and should quickly set about the task. We should advance with sincere dedication and strong purpose to accumulate both inner virtue and correct action through simultaneous practice. From the lowest to the highest, becoming greater and greater, gradually progress and courageously advance and success is assured. Although we possess only a limited physical body (*rupakaya*), we have also an infinite spiritual body (*dharmakaya*). Oh, how beautiful indeed! This art already is inherent and perfect in each of us. If today we are able to firmly grasp *yin* and *yang*, tomorrow it will be easy to match heaven and earth in longevity. Thus, if one comes to this study in the spirit of high-minded fellowship and absolute sincerity, the teaching will not be in vain. Therefore, it is expressed here in plain language for the edification of the followers of this way and to explain the subtle mystery of the true *tao*. It has been gathered together in a book of seven chapters and entitled *Summary of the Golden Elixir*. Taken in order, the various topics are all included. Students should thoroughly study and savor it to get to the bottom of its mysterious principles. When suddenly one day it is completely comprehended and there is a full realization, then the faculty of reason becomes clear, the heart transformed, the emotions calm and the spirit harmonious. When it is attained at last, it is attained forever, and the *tao* of immortality is realized. However, if one is careless for just one breath, 10,000 things can go astray. If one seeks to forcibly realize this *tao* and attain immortality, it will be extremely difficult. One must exercise great care from beginning to end, and only then is success certain.

Chapter 1. Breathing from the Heels and Refining the Ch'i

How great indeed is the primordial monadal *ch'i*! The "mysterious feminine" in its midst is called the "great bellows." Its origin is The Infinite (*wu-chi*). How supreme indeed are the Two Aspects![6] All of the various species of living things had no means of multiplying and came in the end to possess desire. Heaven and man were as one, but the states of mortal and immortal became two paths. The years and months flowed on, and in a short time the dark and light became permanently separated. Alas, heterodox

shortcuts are easily trodden, but the true path is difficult to travel. If the *tao* of man is not practiced, the *tao* of immortality will be far indeed. To gain the truth, one must proceed from disciplined practice. Its marvelous methods should be carried out during the period of transition between day and night. Eat only a little, loosen the garments, and sit within a quiet room. The hands are brought together in the attitude of meditation and the heels are pressed against the "gate of earth."[7] The tongue supports the hard palate and the lips and teeth are closed. Regulate your "heel breathing" so that it is slow and continuous and harmonize inhalation and exhalation. Calm your body and mind in perfect silence so that you are at peace within and undisturbed without. Concentrate your mind and dismiss the 10,000 attachments. Close the "four gates"[8] to the outside and direct the gaze of the eyes inwardly. Imagine a beautiful pearl that acts as ruler of the "yellow court."[9] Then maintain the "sun of your intrinsic nature" in the *ni-wan* and place the "moon of your life" in the *tan-fu*.[10] Hovering between existence and nonexistence, the spirit is focused and the *ch'i* concentrated. Sustain this for some time, resting in a natural way. Then slowly swallow and the true *ch'i* will gradually enter the *tan-t'ien*. It excites the "life source" and following the *Tu* meridian passes through the *wei-lü* and ascends to the *ni-wan*. Pursuing its course, it activates the "intrinsic nature source," is guided into the *Jen* meridian, projected through the *ming-t'ang*,[11] and descends again to the lower *tan-fu*. The "three sources"[12] above and below rotate like wheels as [the *ch'i*] ascends up the back and descends along the front in a continuous circuit. The heart becomes like water, still and clear, and the body like an ice pitcher. Lightly raise the anus as the "heel breath"[13] slowly circulates. If the *ch'i* becomes agitated, slowly swallow it. If the spirit becomes faint, then make an effort to concentrate your thoughts. Beginning with one breath, multiply this by a hundred and a thousand to make a complete "cosmic orbit,"[14] and in this way one will see marvelous results. Seekers of the True should begin with this discipline. If one is unable to practice "heel breathing" and be at peace with the world, then all is done in vain. This is the first difficult task in cultivating this art.

Chapter 2. Accumulating Ch'i and Opening the Passes

The purpose of this phase is similar to the previous exercise. Assume the meditation *mudra* known as "inserting the golden spade"[15] and with one mind return to the "king's treasury."[16] Unify your spirit and concentrate your *ch'i*. If disturbed, return to a state of tranquility and abstraction. Now begin by concentrating on your *ch'i* and, starting with the "bubbling spring"[17] of the left foot, proceed to the knee and calf, slowly ascending to the "three passes" and finally to the *ni-wan*. It then gently descends to the "sea of the source."[18] Now from the right "bubbling spring" cause it to rise and fall along the right side just as on the left. Execute four circulations each on the left and right, and then one ascent from the [two "bubbling springs"] simultaneously for a total of nine revolutions. This then is one round. Now exercise the anus by gently raising it, and practice the "heel breathing" for nine rounds, with nine revolutions each, for a total of eighty-one as a complete set. The *ch'i* then will naturally flow unimpeded throughout the body and the passes will be completely open. If they are not yet open, add some martial exercises, performing them in the proper sequence. First, practice the exercise, "lion sitting upside down," opening the eyes and taking three breaths, so that the *ch'i* traverses the "lower pass." Then the "golden *ching*" flies up the back, and as one raises the shoulders a number of times, it naturally rises to the *ni-wan* and the "great water wheel" turns. Now shake "Mount K'un-lun," rub the belly and massage the waist eighty-one times. Grind the hands together and massage the face twenty-four times. Pat the top of the head, rotate the eyes twenty-four times and then rest. Concentrate the spirit and knock the teeth together twenty-four times. When doing this exercise always constrict the anus and hold the breath. Each time you finish the exercise, clear the throat and swallow three times, stand up and shake the body, and then twist to the left and right nine times.[19] This is the "moving method" that can be used in conjunction with the sitting exercises over and over endlessly. If one proceeds in this way without lapse, success will follow. The superior man will experience an opening of the "passes" in three days and nights; the average will experience a breakthrough in two weeks; and those below average will experience an opening after a month. Those who are lax in their practice may take a hundred days for the opening to occur. If there is pain in the joints, proceed with the practice more slowly; and if the eyes become hot, add some rotations. If one is dedicated and unstinting in practice, no illness will be able to attack. At this time, there will be a stirring of wind in the *ni-wan* as the kidney *ch'i* begins to rise. In a moment, there is a wonderful sensation at the "magpie bridge" and the "sweet dew" begins to fall. For seekers of the elixir, anything but this is error. If one does not embark on the path in this way, how would it be possible to effect the upward and downward movement [of *ch'i*] and combine this with "refining the self."

Chapter 3. Jade Liquid and Refining the Self

The jade liquid returning elixir is even
  more mysterious.
All depends upon the golden liquid and
  the refining of base lead.
One must also cast the sword[20] and graft
  the branch[21]
To win eternal youth and a lifespan of
  10,000 years.

The method involves selecting three to five "precious crucibles." Each should weigh sixteen or seventeen *liang*. Those of fourteen are even better, and they should be shiny and lustrous.[22] Having obtained a "flower," do not hesitate to use it, and there is no variety that is unsuitable. Dwell together in a quiet room within the bedcurtains. There are no limitations as to day or night. As two bodies sit facing each other, two sights reveal their forms. First "strike the bamboo" and raise it, then "strum the zither" to harmonize the sound. Execute each three times to bring about emotional communion. Even if the urge to go in for the kill arises, do not give free rein to your desires. Instead, slowly chase the "dragon" into his "cave" and then gently withdraw the "sword," bringing home the "successful candidate."[23] Advance one inch, keeping three to five inches outside. Now immediately raise the anus, adjust the waist, elevate the shoulders, and retract the neck, silently concentrating your mind. Located between the kidneys are two kinds of *ch'i*, one red and one white, that slowly rise to the space within the "great void"[24] and are transformed into a single sun, the brilliant "mysterious feminine."[25] Close the eyes and guard your inner concentration, allowing the yellow light within to shine upon the "gate of heaven."[26] Gaze upward, glaring as if angry, to the "mysterious valley."[27] Self and other are both forgotten; emotion and environment both disappear. Withhold the "sweet dew" and send it down to the *tan-t'ien*. In this way one experiences [what the *I ching* calls] "silently and without moving, one senses and apprehends all." This is intercourse of the physical body without intercourse of the spirit, the union of dragon and tiger. It is "preparing the stove and setting up the crucible." Blending the ingredients in the "great cauldron" is harmonizing *yin* and *yang*. In this way the two strands entwine. The four exercises, moving and sitting, constitute one phase of the "cosmic orbit." Practice them diligently in order over and over. Be sure that the "three passes" are completely warm and that the "two *ch'i*"[28] are in harmony. This is intercourse of the spirit without intercourse of the body. Activate the "great bellows," moving in and out, while always guarding the mind within. Fan continually and drum slowly. Move up and down like a gentle penetrating wind, rising and falling at will. When advancing, slowly exhale; when withdrawing, inhale fiercely. First fan her thirty-six times and then stop and calm

yourself. Now continue for a count of twenty-four. Harmonize yourself internally and gently raise [the anus]. Then you can take a deep swallow of *ch'i*. Now continue to contract your abdomen sixteen times. Practice this cycle three times, using six repetitions as a complete round. Sometimes one may choose the normal position and sometimes enjoy the wonder of reversing roles. After each practice session carry out your sitting meditation exercises. Or afterward, one may revolve the "three sources" nine times. If one is afraid that the *ch'i* still has not ascended, then add the three martial techniques. Approach the "stove"[29] and engage in joint training. Practice the four exercises day and night, quietly activating the mechanism. Frequent practice is especially effective. As the "time of the tide"[30] approaches and the "moon rises in the west,"[31] then one may arouse her. Achieving the [transmutation] of base lead is not the work of a moment, but, if accomplished three or five times, it can extend one's life to 200 or 300 years. While carrying out these exercises, there are some other marvelous techniques. Drink often of the "wine of the immortals,"[32] but do not pluck the "flower that is just about to fall";[33] leisurely stroke the "zither without strings,"[34] and slowly blow on the "flute without holes."[35] These techniques reach the height of mystery and wonder. However, if carried out with tension and haste, they produce only harm and no benefit. In the great *tao* of the "golden elixir," the gold is found during physical intercourse in the mystery of the "jade liquid." There is no other method so marvelous. Therefore it is said that "gathering the medicine" is easy, but "refining the self" is difficult. Be sure to keep your intrinsic nature sensitive and your spirit open. The heart must be still and the mind settled. The work may be accomplished in a hundred days, and the "cosmic orbit" marvelously attained. The *tao* of "returning the elixir" is none other than this; the work of "grafting [the new on the old]" is simply this. With courage it is attained easily, but with laxness it is difficult to accomplish. Truly this is the central principle of "the jade liquid and refining the self" and the critical concept of "the water of metal and casting the sword."

Chapter 4. Choosing Resources to Aid in Pursuit of the Tao

It is important to obtain righteous resources. One must put by a sufficient store without any shortfall. Ill-gotten resources will bring evil consequences. Be very careful in your selection.

Chapter 5. Choosing a Location to Establish the Foundation

One must live in the commercial district of a city and rely on a family with position and financial power. If the family has position but not financial power, there will be no way of meeting the tremendous expenses. If it has financial power but not position, there will be no means of controlling the myriad outside disasters. Some prefer to live in the countryside. The earth should be red or yellow and without ancient grave sites. There should be a sweet spring in its midst and good neighbors nearby. It should not be close to buffalo, buffalo swimming holes, or manure pits. A place where the mountains and rivers are pure and beautiful is auspicious indeed. Otherwise I am afraid it will not be suitable for your needs. This is why one must be selective with respect to location.

Chapter 6. Choosing Comrades to Assist in Practice

One must choose like-minded comrades for a relationship of deep commitment. They should be by nature poised, loyal, filial, friendly, and fraternal. When you are borne into the "elixir chamber," they must be able to sustain the rigors without tiring and be on guard both day and night lest you err in approaching the "stove." At the moment of obtaining the elixir, one is as if drunk or without reason. Everything then depends upon the careful nurturance of the "comrades" and "yellow dame." Otherwise, the impulse to go in for the kill rises like a sharp temper.

Chapter 7. Setting up the Elixir Platform

What is meant by "entering the chamber"? The chamber is the elixir room for refining the "true essence." Altogether there are three levels of chambers. In the front there is a great hall and facing it an open space with rooms to the left and right of the main gate. The second level is the central hall with three side rooms on the left and right, respectively. There should be kitchens on the left and storerooms on the right. In the very center one should store wealth for future use. In the kitchen one should provide a tablet to the Heavenly General of the Altar. In the centermost chamber one should provide an altar in honor of the Founding Masters, the Five Patriarchs,[36] Seven Adepts,[37] and Sixteen Heavenly Generals. The altar table should include pure water, incense, candles, flowers, and vases. Arrange the ancient ritual implements and a clock so as to know the precise time, together with a complete set of the classics. One should worship here both morning and evening. To the left and right of the central chamber are apartments for carrying out one's practice in safety. These should be cut off from the outside save for an opening of approximately one square foot through which to convey food and drink. The rear halls should include three chambers with three siderooms to the left and right and three in the center. Of these, the one on the east is the "chamber of the green dragon," and the one on the west is the "chamber of the white tiger." In the center is the altar for making offerings at the tablet of the Founding Master. Due north (*tzu*) and south (*wu*) should be precisely aligned. On the left is the "elixir chamber" and on the right the "spirit chamber." The windows should be clear and the tables clean. The four sides should be surrounded by high walls to prevent people from peeking in. Fences and barriers ensure peace and seclusion. Plant flowers and shrubs and raise cranes and deer to provide an area for the gentlewoman to relax.

Chapter 8. Choosing the Crucible

The "crucibles" are the "true dragon" and "true tiger." First choose a beautiful tiger with clear eyebrows and lovely eyes. You must find one with red lips and white teeth. There are three grades of crucibles. The lowest are twenty-five, twenty-four, or twenty-one. Although they belong to the "postnatal,"[38] they may be employed in "practicing fire work" "nourishing the weak dragon," "adding oil to supplement the lamp," and "enriching the nation and ordering the people." Those of the middle grade are twenty, eighteen, or sixteen who have never engaged in intercourse, but already have had their first menses. Because they have never given birth, their placenta[39] has never been broken; and they may be used to extend life and achieve "human immortality." The highest grade are "medicine material" of fourteen. Their condition precedes the division of "primal unity" and corresponds to the *keng* moon based on the number seven.[40] These are called the "true white tigers."[41] A "*Ch'ien* dragon" of sixteen who has never lost his "true *ching*" is a "true green dragon." Although the crucibles are of three grades, the principle of selection remains the same. One wants those whose four limbs are without blemish and whose "five facial features"[42] are in perfect proportion. Those who are of a harmonious disposition, respectful of the gods of heaven and earth, and not jealous or envious are the best. Those who are abnormal or violate the "ten taboos" are all unsuitable.

Chapter 9. Appraising the Crucible

There are three grades of crucibles. The first is metal, the second fire, and the third water. What is meant by the "metal crucible"? It refers to the metal of a fourteen-year-old girl represented by the trigram *Tui*. When she has reached 5,048 days, this corresponds with fourteen years, or what the Buddhists call one "collection."[43] At this time her menses is about to commence and her "yellow path"[44] regularly opens. A woman's first menses is the "true metal" and is a price-less treasure. The *Chen-ching ko* says: "There is not one word in this classic that can save all sentient beings and enable them to reach the highest heaven." The *Ch'iao-yao ko* says: "Fourteen is the white tiger and sixteen the green dragon." This is our meaning. A "*Ch'ien* crucible" must obtain the services of a virtuous partner, instruct her morning and evening in filiality, and help her perfect the correct path and be without evil thoughts. The "*K'un* crucible" must have faith in the direction of the "yellow dame." This is the great medicine of the internal and external and the waxing and waning half moons. It is no mere trifle, for if collected and refined, before half a [Chinese] hour, one will immediately become a "heavenly immortal." What is meant by "fire crucible"? This refers to beautiful tigers of eighteen or sixteen. If the medicine is obtained two or three times from a compatible partner of fifteen, one can extend the lifespan several hundred years, attain the immortality of the Yellow Emperor, and live forever in the world as an "immortal among men." What is meant by a "water crucible"? It refers to those of approximately twenty-one, twenty-six, twenty-five, or twenty-seven who have had the experience of "green dragon plays in water," but never given birth, or young girls whose "placentas already are broken." These may strengthen one's *ch'i*, build one's foundation, and aid in the work of "gold in water" and "casting the sword." One must absolutely avoid those with the "five imperfections" or "ten taboos," for these will only cause harm.

The "five imperfections" are *luo*, *wen*, *ku*, *chiao*, and *mai*.[45] The *luo* are those with prominent pubic bones, which makes it inconvenient to gather the medicine. The *wen* are malodorous of both body and menstrual flow. The *ku* are virgins whose private parts are absent and have never had menses. The *chiao* are those with masculine voices, rough skin, black faces, and yellow hair. They are impatient and cruel, and their *ch'i* and blood are impure. The *mai* are those with malaria and irregular menses.

Among "*Ch'ien* crucibles" there also

are "five imperfections": *sheng, tai, hu, pan,* and *tu.*[46] The *sheng* are those with small penises and whose testicles are not raised. The *tai* are impatient, reckless, violent, and intractable. The *hu* are precocious and already have shed their "true *ching.*" The *pan* are not men and not women, or what are popularly called "hermaphrodites." The *tu* have yellow hair and bulging eyes, body odor and sores, and are frequently ill or dishonest in their conduct.

In choosing a crucible look for one with well-defined eyebrows, lovely eyes, and harmonious disposition. The year, month, and day of her birth should be in favorable correspondence to one's own. Avoid those whose birth dates are antagonistic, such as those who violate the taboos of *hsing* 刑, *chung* 冲, *ch'uan* 穿, and *p'o* 破. It is recorded that those born during the Terrestrial Branch year *shen* should employ women born during a *ssu* year, and *hai* men should seek *yin* women. Furthermore, the "*K'un* crucible's" beauty or lack of it is obvious to all, but how can one know the quality of her internal medicine. The method is to use one *ch'ien*[47] of pure gold and pound it into the form of a gold coin. Now take the finest silver and pound it too into the form of a coin. The two coins should then be placed together and strung with a silk thread. Now place these within the "mouth of the crucible"[48] and stay together with her for one night. The following morning remove and examine it. If the gold coin is vermilion and the silver coin is red, this is the highest of the high. If the gold coin is red and the silver vermilion, this is second best, but still serviceable. That which has flowers and seeds and medicine and fire is the second highest crucible. If the gold coin turns pale red and the silver turns black, this is the lowest of the low. That which has no flowers or seeds, and upon "gathering the medicine" is without fire, is the second lowest crucible. This is not up to the level of the "fire crucible" and unlike the great method of the "metal crucible." Soak a piece of cotton paper in a solution of alum and water and dry it in the sun. Now take a piece the size of a coin and place it

on your navel. Seeking her tongue with your tongue, arouse her passion. Now have the "crucible" sit on your navel as if straddling a horse. After a moment remove the "crucible" and observe the paper. If the paper is damp and has fluid, this is a "broken crucible." Another method is to take a water bucket filled with clean ashes and have the partner sit on it for a while. Now remove the "crucible" and see if there is a depression on the surface of the ashes. If so, this is also a "broken crucible" and not usable. The status of the "water crucible" once again is completely different. Ask your partner on what day and what hour her menses began during the previous month and whether it is possible to meet at this time. Have the "yellow dame" examine it, and if the color is purple or black, or if she is early or late, these all indicate unhealthy conditions, and she should not be used. If she is regular and the color fresh red, this is very good.

Chapter 10. Refining the Self and Establishing the Foundation

Immortals and Taoist priests do not have the aid of the gods. They achieve the "True" by saving *ching* and accumulating *ch'i.* Saving *ching* means saving one's own *ching*; accumulating *ch'i* means accumulating your partner's *ch'i.* The *tao* is the essence (*t'i*) and the method the practice (*yung*). Cultivating both simultaneously, one is able to imitate the rise and fall of heaven and earth and transform both mind and matter. Effortlessly the "feelings" (*ch'ing*) arise and naturally revert to "intrinsic nature" (*hsing*). This is what is meant by "the body naturally possesses true *yin* and *yang*, and true husband and wife begin with [the mundane] husband and wife." However, if one does not first "establish the foundation" and "refine the self," how can one enter the chamber and enjoy the benefits of the medicine? We must respectfully proceed from the teachings of the Buddhist sects that hold that all phenomena are of the same essence as the noumenon (*hsing-tsung*) and only then can we gain the Truth (*chen-ju*). Then gathering the medicine is as simple as turning over the palm.

Chapter 11. Accumulating Ch'i and Opening the Passes

The human body has "three passes" and "nine orifices." The "three passes" are the *wei-lü*, *chia-chi*, and *yü-chen*. When the "true *ch'i*" accumulates for a long time, the "passes" and "orifices" naturally open. Moreover, if one regularly practices a great deal, the "water wheel" turns, rising up the back and descending along the front, removing the impure elements from the whole body. This is what is known as opening all "three passes" and "nine orifices" together.

Chapter 12. The Jade Liquid and Lengthening Life

The prenatal elixir is the "medicine of ascending heaven";
The postnatal medicine is the "elixir of lengthening life."
After the full moon has passed, the last day of the month approaches.
The gentleman should take note of the quarters of the moon.
After fifteen days there is another fifteen.
Fifty-eight and sixty- two.
Count them on your fingers and they equal 120.
Precisely twenty-two and a half days,
This is the "firing time," the true "waxing and waning."
Everything depends on the careful calculations of the "yellow dame."
On the fifteenth, the "metal *ch'i*" is at the height of its power,
And the "water source" a bit more than 20 percent.
With a piece of thin white silk test her color and *ch'i*.
When the color is like clear water, then seize the moment,
And with one hand embrace her shoulder and with the other her back.
When she exhales, I inhale, preserving the "true essence."
Face to face with her I remain free of emotion, while lead refines mercury.
The "magpie bridge" is sealed awaiting a propitious moment.
At this point, although engaged, one is as if unengaged.

At a depth of one and three-tenths inches do very little,
But have your partner move very slightly three to five times.
One's mental state is neither attached nor vacuous, but perfectly calm.
The "tiger's eye" opens wide like a flower bud spewing jade;
The "dragon's head" rears erect and drinks from the "tiny spoon."[49]
At first use four inches of the incense stick as your marker.
The second time add an inch of stick or so,
And the third and fourth an inch again.
When the "golden flowers" have completely fallen, invite her to depart.
When the "sword tip" is like fire, the medicine has passed to me.
Circulate it up to the "yellow court" and install it in the palace.
If you want the gold to return and match the *ch'i* and blood,
Then do not tarry in "mounting up to heaven" and completing the cycle of eighty-one.
When the fire burns fiercely, count to 150,
And if you proceed properly the fire will subside.
Now begins what is called "the method of advancing the water."
When water and fire achieve the complementary relationship "After Completion," the elixir foundation is established.
Three hundred [Chinese] hours is altogether twenty-five [days].
This is the life-lengthening art of the immortals.
Every word and every sentence is a spiritual teaching.
How could one leak the secrets of heaven for a thousand pieces of gold?

Chapter 13. Water of Metal and Casting the Sword[50]

My partner dwells in the palace with the water of metal, while I keep company with the fire of wood. The tiger is born in the direction of water; the dragon emerges from fire. An invisible sword secretly accompanies us to slay the demons and a visible sword is offered to the "green dragon" to stir up the "marvelous lead." In the course of practice the *ching* is aroused, but only when it does not move or shake can one approach the "stove" and participate in the act. Now heat the stove and cast the sword to de-

Chapter 14. The Golden Liquid Great Returning Elixir

When the "elixir chamber" is ready and the "crucibles" complete, make offerings in the central hall to all of the immortals, the God of Lightning, and the heavenly officials and generals. Three days after the sign of the termination of the menstrual period in the west, the two "crucibles," male and female, grasp each other's shoulders with both hands. The man is above and the woman below. The man should not loosen his garments nor the woman unfasten her girdle. The "yellow dame" harmonizes them, "strumming the zither" and "beating the bamboo," "calling the female phoenix" and "summoning the turtle." Now heaven mounts earth as in the hexagram *P'i* (Stagnation). The "*K'un* crucible" uses the "fire dates of immortality"[51] to ascertain the readiness of the "*Ch'ien* gold." When the tongue is like water, the medicine is about to arrive; when the dates are like fire, the medicine is nearly ready. Now quickly carry out the method of gathering it. Closely examine the space between the eyebrows, and at the moment when "the planet Venus crosses the heavens," the "white tiger" will squeeze out a bit of "*kuei* water."[52] When the *kuei* is finished the *jen* is pure.[53] Now observe the formation of the "pearl."[54] When "light shines through the curtains,"[55] the "*jen* water" emerges in waves, and the "good omens" fall like drops, the "tiger's" lower garments are then removed along with those of the adept. Have your partner sit on the "three-legged crescent moon chair" and assume the position "earth over heaven" as in the hexagram *T'ai* (Peace). Activate the "great bellows," being careful to lock the "three treasures." Reflect inwardly upon the mind, [realizing that] the mind is without mind; reflect outwardly upon the body, [realizing that] the body is without body. One should apprehend only emptiness. If one does not realize "emptiness," I am afraid one will become

The Elixir Literature of Sexual Alchemy

attached to appearances. Carefully guard against dangers and do not let yourself go even the slightest. Wait for her "true water" to arrive at the level of two parts, and then use the kidneys at the point near the anus to mobilize a drop of "true mercury" to meet her lead. One should effect the "gathering" in a motionless state. Now order a "thought messenger" to issue a "fire charm"[56] from the "gate of the mystery"[57] that rises from the *wei-lü* to the *ni-wan*, and, crossing the "golden bridge," enters the "yellow court." With your whole mind reflect inwardly like a hen brooding over its egg, or a dragon nurturing a pearl. One must not let go of it for even a moment. As soon as the adept has obtained the medicine, he should respectfully withdraw.

The adept repeatedly toasts the "Holy Mother," drinking several mouthfuls of the "peach wine of immortality," which quickly cools the fire. Feeling intoxicated and fatuous, he remains confused and senseless for seven days. Everything depends on the cooperation and support of the "yellow dame" and "comrades." Having reached this point one is now an immortal.[58] However, when first the "one ch'i" returns and the "holy fetus" forms, it easily disperses or breaks if startled or touched. Be even more careful to treasure and guard it.

Chapter 15. The Cosmic Orbit and Determining the Time

"Time" is not the time calculated by year, month, and day, but rather the prenatal "hour of the living *tzu*."[59] Gentlemen engaging in spiritual cultivation who seek to "return the elixir" must determine the proper time. One must choose a crucible of from fifteen to forty-two. Begin your calculations from the time of her birth. There are twelve [Chinese] hours in the day, thirty days in each month, and twelve months in a year. Do not fail to include the intercalary month in your calculations. Take the first of twelve years of age as the Terrestrial Branch *tzu*, the second as *ch'ou*, the third as *yin*, the fourth as *mao*, the fifth as *ch'en*, the sixth as *chi*, the seventh as *wu*, the eighth as

177

wei, the ninth as *shen*, the tenth as *yu*, the eleventh as *hsü*, and the twelfth as *hai*. This is a complete cycle of years. To regulate the complete cycle of months, take the first month of the thirteenth year of age as *tzu* and continue to the twelfth month as *hai*. This is the complete cycle of months. Now we come to the cycle of days. Beginning with the first day of the fourteenth year of age, take the thirty hours of every two and a half days as one month and calculate thirty days. Altogether 360 hours equal twelve months. This is the complete cycle of days. Now as for the cycle of hours, take the *tzu* hour of the first day of the *ch'ou* month of the *ch'ou* year as the starting point and the *chi* hour of the third day as the end for a total of twelve hours. This is the complete cycle of hours. This is what is meant by, "On the third day the moon rises in the west." Although on the third day the moon rises in the west, this is still not the true transmission. To take the third day as the time for gathering the medicine fails to consider the mating of the "true dragon." If the third day arrives and the time of the medicine has passed and substance is produced, this may be compared to the last day of the lunar month, which is called *hui*, and the first day of the next month, which is called *shuo*. At the juncture of the last and first days of the lunar month, the *ching* of the sun and moon shoot their *ch'i* at each other. Thus the moon responds to the *yang* rays of the sun and becomes pregnant. If it were the second day, the moon and sun come up at the same time and set at the same time. On the third day, when the sun sets, the moon appears like the mark of a moth's antennae in *keng* (the west). *Keng* is the metal of the trigram *Tui*; that is, the metal of the trigram *Ch'ien* that already is returning to the house of the youngest daughter, *Tui*, of *K'un* in the southwest. If one seeks the "great medicine," it should be the "two later stages" during the "living *hai* hour" (9:00–11:00 PM) of the evening of the "living thirtieth day" and the "four later stages" before the "living *tzu* hour" (11:00 PM–1:00 AM) of the "living first day."[60] Within the "six stages" one may obtain the "medicine" and obtain the "elixir." At the beginning of the "four earlier stages" observe whether the "crucible's" lips are purple and her face is red, and if between her eyebrows it is radiant and glossy. When the *kuei* is over and the *jen* is pure, this is the time when the medicine is born. The *Classic* says: "Carefully observe that of five parts she has just reached two, and [her juices pour forth] like fish-scale waves or drops of water, for this is the beginning of the auspicious moment."

Secret Principles of Gathering the True Essence

Ts'ai-chen chi-yao

by Chang San-feng
annotated by Chi Yi tzu
(Fu Chin-ch'üan)

Establishing the Foundation

To lock the *yin-ching* is to establish the foundation.
Establishing the foundation consists of maintaining the feminine.
By maintaining the feminine without shaking, the lock is secure.
To lock the *yin-ching* is to establish the foundation.

To establish the foundation it is most important to maintain the feminine attitude and not the masculine. If one is able to maintain the feminine, this is called "locking the *yin-ching*". In this way we can say with certainty that the foundation will be established. Hey! Do you not know? When the wind rises, the sail must be lowered; when the jar is set upright, the water returns full.

Gathering the Medicine

When the foundation is securely locked, one can study immortality.
To study immortality one must find the true lead.
When the true lead has been gathered, lock the foundation.
When the foundation is securely locked, one can study immortality.

The "foundation" is the *tan-t'ien*. If the "true mercury" is not wasted, one may seek the "true lead." When one has obtained the "true lead," only then can one hope for immortality. It is first necessary to establish the foundation, and then gather the medicine. The medicine does not come of itself, but depends upon our effort. Ha! Do not talk foolishness! When there is wine, what a pity not to invite guests. Without money how can one be a merchant?

Knowing the Proper Time

One must know the time when the medicine is produced.
Only after knowing this can east and west be matched.
Before east and west are matched, it is difficult to produce the medicine.
One must know the time when the medicine is produced.

"Producing the medicine" means producing the "lead." The medicine is produced at a specific time, and only if one knows the true time can one obtain the true medicine. Absorb your partner's lead to augment your own mercury. When east and west are in complementary rapport, the elixir is naturally formed. Otherwise one runs the risk of excessive *yin* or excessive *yang*. Ha! Wait for the right time! The moon will come out and the "golden flowers" appear. When the tide comes in the water covers all.

Strumming the Zither

Beat the bamboo until it opens, and then strum the zither.
Strumming the zither and beating the bamboo brings out the pure sound.
If the pure sound has not yet arrived, the bamboo must be beaten.
Beat the bamboo until it opens, and then strum the zither.

"Beating the bamboo" empties my mind; "strumming the zither" excites my partner's "thing." I use myself to excite my partner. When her "thing" arrives, the "pure sound" will be loud and clear. Ha! Do you know? When the string is slack no arrow flies. When the wind moves, one can then set sail.[1]

Approaching the Enemy

In doing battle one must make the opponent furious.
Though the opponent is furious, I do not play the hero.
If I do not renounce heroism, there will be contention.
In doing battle, one must make the opponent furious.

"Doing battle" means approaching the battlefield. I counsel you gentlemen, in approaching the battlefield do not underestimate the enemy. This expresses the idea that, when having intercourse, you must allow your partner to move on her own, while refraining from movement yourself. If I were to move but once, I would lose my invaluable treasure. Ha! Stop going wild! Cheating others is cheating oneself; losing to oneself is losing to others.

Upside Down

Carrying out the act upside down results in inversion.
Only when upside down do the two things achieve completion.
Completion depends on carrying out the act upside down.
Carrying out the act upside down results in inversion.

"Upside down" means earth over heaven. Upside down means going against the normal course. The common method goes with the normal course, but the path of immortality lies in going against it. Following the normal course leads to the fire of hell; going against it one becomes a "golden immortal." Upside down, upside down; only then is there completion. Hey! You ought to know this! By her occupying the superior position, west has come to east.

Utmost Sincerity

The desire for sagehood and the true lead requires utmost sincerity.
Utmost sincerity requires that we use mercury for the meeting.

If, in meeting, one fails to converge, it is
vain to hope for sagehood.
The desire for sagehood and the true lead
requires utmost sincerity.

The "desire for sagehood" refers to
the heart's fondest hope. The "true lead"
is the prenatal monadal true *ch'i*. Desiring that this primordial monadal true *ch'i*
come to us requires absolute seriousness,
extreme care, and utmost sincerity.[2] It is
especially important that one mobilize a
bit of "true mercury" in the region of
one's own anus to welcome it. Moreover,
this must be done just right. Hey! Be
careful! The dragon must not seek the
tiger, but the tiger must find the green
dragon herself.

The Water Wheel

Capturing the *yang-ching* is called obtaining the lead.
After obtaining the lead, it immediately
ascends to heaven.
Having ascended to heaven for a count of
nine times nine, it is securely captured.
Capturing the *yang-ching* is called obtaining the lead.

"Capturing" means that it cannot
escape again. "*Yang-ching*" is the prenatal true singular *ch'i*, the gold within water. To obtain this is to obtain the lead.
Carry out the practice of ascending up the
back and descending down the front. Rising to the *ni-wan* is called "ascending to
heaven." After nine times nine revolutions, the golden elixir naturally forms.
Hey! One needs the secret transmissions!
To ascend to heaven one must start the
wheel. Only then can the water rise.

The Sign Gate

The top of the head clearly bears the sign
gate.
When the sign arrives at the fontanel, there
is perfect freedom.
There is freedom when water and fire join
on the dragon's head.
The top of the head clearly bears the sign
gate.

The "dragon" is oneself. The "sign" is
the stage of progress. When the tide
reaches the highest point there is a sign.
The "pearl" of the "red water" must

traverse this gate and then descend. Hey!
At this point, a "column of jade"[3] flows
within the nose, while on top of the head
one balances the "golden pearl."

With and Against the Normal Course

Heaven over earth will become earth over
heaven.
Only when earth surmounts heaven can
one become an immortal.
The immortals equal heaven and earth in
their longevity.
Heaven over earth will become earth over
heaven.

Heaven over earth is called *P'i* (Standstill); earth over heaven is called *T'ai*
(Peace). *P'i* represents the normal course
and *T'ai* the reverse. The normal gives
rise to the common and the reverse to
sagehood. Without earth surmounting
heaven, how can one become an immortal? After gaining immortality, one's
years are as long as heaven's. Ha! When
you come face to face, this truth illumin-
ates heaven and earth, but very few in the
past or present have spoken of it.

Lock up the *yin-ching*; do not let it wander.
Sit erect in meditation and after ten
[Chinese] weeks stop.
Sleeping neither night nor day, maintain
your practice with constancy.
One wins freedom when the heart and kid-
neys interact.
When the *ch'i* and blood circulate every-
where there is a beautiful feeling.
When body and spirit both reach a marve-
lous state this is truly wonderful.
The *yü-chen* and *ni-wan* transmit a mes-
sage in the void,
While in the *chia-chi* and double passes the
spring runs early.
It is most important to learn to stop the
breath,
And just here it is necessary to [contract
the anus] as if restraining a bowel movement.
In this way one begins to build the foundation.
Now wait for the proper time and match
the male and female.

Notes: This describes the process of
establishing the foundation and waiting
for the proper time. Do you understand?

When the wind rises, the sail must be lowered; when the jar is upright, the water returns to full. If I am able to lock in the *yin-ching*, this is the body's treasure. Living in seclusion in a quiet room is the practice of a hundred days. Refrain from sleeping night and day, and without realizing it, there will be an interaction between heart and kidneys. The water rises and the fire descends. It is first necessary to raise it and "transmit a message in the void," but in preparation one must pull and then inhale the "spring." Holding the breath comes first and then "restraining the bowels." For "the spirit to emerge" is not extraordinary; to "leave the body" is not exceptional. When one has completed the work described in the verse and has not lost the marvelous eight *liang* of "true mercury," it then is possible to begin to gather the "lead" and obtain the medicine. Altogether it equals one *chin*. Because the pure wine remains in my keeping, I drink alone by West Pond.[4] This is precisely the idea of, "When one has wine, one may invite guests. Without money, how can one be a merchant?" When one realizes that the measure is sufficient, then wait for the proper time. If I am able to carefully guard the "true mercury" without losing it, this is the "foundation." The most important thing is to maintain the female role and not the male. Those who would be Immortals must not only preserve the "true mercury," but, above all, they must find the "true lead." If one is not yet able to gather the "true lead," it is first necessary to "establish the foundation." When this is completed, one then may gather and obtain the lead. The work of studying immortality is simply this.

> The flute without holes must not be transverse;
> Simply blow it and the *ch'i* flows freely.
> Cause it to fill with something,
> And wind naturally rises up in the *ni-wan* at the crown of the head.

Notes: For the purpose of "tiger blows flute" one should employ a woman. Sit properly opposite each other. The instructions that follow all call for a beautiful woman. If the flute is not blown, the *ch'i* will not enter, and if the *ch'i* does not enter; the path will not open. If the path is not open, the elixir will not pass. Because one cannot blow it oneself, one has a partner blow it, causing the path of *ch'i* to open and the elixir to pass. Only then can it be refined. When you feel wind rising in the fontanel and *ch'i* penetrating the *ni-wan*, then this is the effect of "blowing the flute."

Appended: Song of Blowing the Flute

> One three, two fives, and three sevens.
> Four nines are carried out, then fifty-one.
> Sixty-three and seventy-five.
> Eighty-one and nine nine seven.
> The tenth returns again to seven.[5]

Altogether there are seventeen verses on the secret principles.

Number One

> Pressing breasts together and entwining thighs moves her heart.
> Leaning together and embracing shoulders, the true pleasure is near.
> These are the wondrous tidings of the strummed zither.
> No need to pluck with fingers to produce the pure sound.

Notes: The "dragon" strums the "tiger's zither." "Pressing breasts together and entwining thighs" excites her emotions. "Leaning together and embracing shoulder's" stimulates her true pleasure. When the emotions are aroused, the "pure sound" comes; when the pleasure arises, the marvelous truth arrives. This is what is known as the "pure sound" that comes from within the "stringless zither." Having obtained the pleasure from within the "zither," why bother with the sound of the strings? Beating the bamboo causes my thing to dance; strumming the zither excites my partner's thing. Having made my thing dance and excited her thing, the "pure sound" comes forth naturally. Therefore, we say that if the pure sound has not yet arrived, one ought to beat the bamboo. When beating the bamboo opens it up, and the zither is well strummed, then this is not necessary. When the string is slack, do not unloose the arrow; when the wind stirs, one can launch the boat.

Number Two

The dragon first seizes the tiger, and the
  tiger seizes the dragon.
Dragon and tiger entwine together, and
  the true pleasure grows intense.
However, one must use the methods handed down through oral teachings and personal instruction.
With oral teachings and personal instruction, one must faithfully carry out the
  practice.

Notes: When the "dragon and tiger entwine together," the dragon is on top and the tiger below. This is the method of "installing the stove" and "setting up the crucible." She uses her two arms to "seize" me, and I use mine to seize her. This is precisely the coming together of the two "sevens"[6] and the leaning together of the two partners. The previous chapter cannot compare with this. The oral transmission may be found in the next chapter.

Number Three

The oral transmissions must be passed
  from mouth to mouth,
And, relying on them, the path opens to
  the mystery.
When one comes to know the issuing of fire
  and the penetration of the subtle light,
Then is revealed the green dragon who
  excites the marvelous lead.

Notes: In the art of the dragon and the tiger, it is taught that within the body the heart is ruler. The small intestines and tip of the tongue rule the heart, and therefore when tongue licks tongue, the fire of the heart burns strong. When the fire of the heart burns strong, the small intestines are strong. When the small intestines are strong, we know that the prenatal "true lead" is about to arrive. When the true lead arrives, then the wonderful aphorisms of the oral transmissions and personal instructions have been realized.

Number Four

When the green dragon appears, it excites
  the black turtle;

When the brilliance of the light flashes intensely, it penetrates the curtain.
If the head of the green dragon does not
  reveal itself,
How could the Gate of Heaven[7] resound
  with earthly thunder?

Notes: The "fire dragon" captures the tiger. The "Gate of Heaven" is the northwest. "Earthly thunder" (earth over thunder) is the hexagram *Fu* (Return). When one *yang* is born in the northwest, it is then the proper time for the "green dragon" to appear and excite the "black turtle." This is what is known as, "When the one *yang* begins to stir, then the mercury leaks at midnight. Warm the lead crucible and light will penetrate the curtain."

Number Five

When the dragon reveals himself and
  seizes the tiger, the two unite.
Now is the moment for earth to play the
  role of heaven.
Wishing to gain the marvel of role reversal
  in the mystery,
The true secret approaches the tongue.

Notes: Earth the tiger and heaven the dragon reverse positions. The "dragon reveals himself and seizes the tiger" involves the methods for exciting the partner. Upside down and downside up both express the idea of longing. Desiring the true fire to reach the top of the dragon's head, one must still look for the "true secret" beside the tiger's tongue. Continue to study the oral transmissions for [the secret of] the pure sound. With earth over heaven, experiment with tongue and heart. When fire has been transformed into water, it is time to begin. The dragon occupies the tiger's cave, and the tiger seeks the dragon. The tiger stirs and the dragon welcomes her. When the tongue is like fire, the tide runs; when it is like ice, then *yang* is born. This demonstrates the importance of the practice of the "tiger's lair."

Number Six

When dragon occupies the tiger's lair,
  intrinsic nature and emotion are one.
At this moment one must play dead.

In the upside down position, have your
partner move,
And, after a short time, one drop arrives at
my east.

Notes: "When dragon occupies the tiger's lair" means that the dragon is on top
and the tiger below. The dragon enters
the tiger's gate. When the tiger acts as
guest of the dragon, this is the same as
the worldly method. When the dragon
acts as guest of the tiger, this is the direction of the *tao*. However, one must act
dead to the world and be completely passive, allowing the partner to take the
initiative, while we circulate the "living
tzu."[8] If one does not carry out this kind
of work, how can one expect to obtain
that kind of transforming effect?

Number Seven

Although my partner's passion has become
intense, I am oblivious.
With trusting sincerity, she reveals her
secret, as I wait for the right moment.
When she lowers her head and closes her
eyes, the true lead has arrived.
Over a long distance, it comes flying like
racing fire.

Notes: The dragon asks the tiger about
her condition, for I am unable to know
the level of her pleasure. Only when I ask
her does she tell me. If she "lowers her
head and closes her eyes," I inhale, and
through my nose, communicate with the
mystery. Who can understand or comprehend this sort of work? The effect[9] is like
fire or a pearl.

Number Eight

The white tiger of the west receives the
green dragon.
Unexpectedly, the eastern road already is
open.
After inhaling, do not let it return to the
white tiger.
It would seem that this is all there is to the
extraordinary art.

Notes: The tiger leaps, the dragon
dives deep, and again they turn upside
down. The tiger receives the "green dragon," and the dragon receives the tiger.
First, open the path through the back,
and then inhale through the nose. When

the lead comes like a "fire pearl," use the
raft for ascending to heaven. Without the
instructions of a master, how dare one
recklessly embark? However, those who
receive the true transmission all gain results without exception.

Number Nine

When the east arrives, then push and pull.
Failing to push and pull, it leaves the pass.
If now your practice is perfected,
Then naturally it will traverse the *wei-lü*
pass.

Notes: When the tiger arrives, the dragon points his feet toward heaven and,
holding his two bent knees with his
hands, uses strength to "push and pull."
This passage involves more details than a
dragon tapestry. If at this point there are
additional discoveries, see above for matters of "refining the self." In reality, it is
all here, including how to effect circulation of the whole body and achieve the
marvel of swallowing [the elixir].

Number Ten

Firmly they believe that man and woman
are real,
And adamantly insist that *K'an* and *Li* are
false.
Although belonging to *yin*, the woman's
body becomes the male body;
The man, though originally the *yang* body,
becomes the female body.[10]
Do not be alarmed that guest plays *Ch'ien*
the host,
For you must teach yourself temporarily to
play the guest.
Heaven, though above, turns over now to
play the part of earth;
K'un, though formerly below, reverses
roles to play the part of *Ch'ien*.
When partners alternate styles, they are
naturally joyful and adoring.
Yin and *yang* must never be passive.
Though free in spirit and content, one must
be strictly conscientious.
In an elegant and spotless chamber one
must be totally sincere.
Going in the gate we know that delicacy
and tact are appropriate,
And entering the door requires lingering
and tarrying.
At this moment, then, there is no danger,   *183*

And conditions are favorable for the pre-servation of *yin* and *yang*.

Notes: This is precisely the work of begin-ning the process. The completion of the act is a matter of man and woman. For the sake of discussion we consider them *K'an* and *Li*. I am fundamentally *yang*, but contain within me the height of *yin*; she is fundamentally *yin*, but conceals within her the most marvelous "true ess-ence." I take my body as a woman's body and pretend that the woman's body is a man's. The work is simply a matter of turning things upside down. Perfectly at ease, I guard my *ching*, but am never idle and lazy. Enter the hole in a leisurely way, withdraw with an attitude of sincere respect, and enter again slowly. But whatever you do, do not be tardy in with-drawing.

Number Eleven

If one asks about the arrangements, it is
  not difficult.
The work takes only a brief moment.
The body reclines while the mind contem-
  plates.
The two knees are pulled up to the chest,
  as the hands pull down.
The path of the elixir is opened, not allow-
  ing blocks;
The water wheel rotates without permit-
  ting gaps.
Ascending to heaven with a count of
  nine times nine, do not be lazy,
And the thing will circulate through the
  pass.
Circulating through and turning back, the
  path is long.
Now quickly sit up straight in a pose of
  strength.
It is essential that the buttocks contract as
  if restraining the bowels,
And most important that the hands are
  placed upon the waist.
Inhale *ch'i* through the nose to open the
  chia-chi,
And enclose your teeth with the lips as you
  pull up *yin* and *yang*.
If the entire body does not exert strength,
How can one expect the delicious morsel to
  enter one's mouth to taste?

Notes: This explains that in the begin-ning when we are preparing to obtain the lead, our minds must reflect and our

bodies recline. The hands "pull" the two knees until they press against the chest. "Ascending to heaven for a count of nine times nine" allows us to maintain posses-sion. Capturing the *yang-ching* is what is called "obtaining the lead." First I laugh at her, and then she laughs at me. As the path opens for the elixir medicine, put irrelevant thoughts aside. The "water wheel" moves the stream with an im-pressive force, powerfully raising it and maintaining a continuous flow. Hey! "Ascend to heaven" and heaven must rise; mobilize the water with the wheel and the water becomes circular. When you realize that it has made the turn, then quickly sit up straight. Now, maintain-ing a dignified demeanor, restrain the bowels[11] and place the hands on the waist without allowing it to move downward. If you want to "open the *chia-chi*," open the nose: if you want to "lift up *yin* and *yang*," lift up the lips. When the medicine reaches the mouth, then with impressive confidence slowly and gently elevate it. When you have reached this stage, clap your hands and laugh with a great ho, ho!

Number Twelve

When lead arrives in the east, at first one is
  not aware,
But realizes as it enters like a speeding fire
  pearl.
Rapidly reverting to my body, it must first
  leave hers.
Now having left her body, I quickly commence my work.
Make believe that the elixir really exists,
And although there is no concrete thing,
  pretend to raise it.[12]
Before raising it up, we must first know if
  the west has come.
Now when it comes to the east, I quickly
  pull down the knees.
Gently, nine times five and three times
  three, raise it up;
Over and over, nine times nine and three
  times three, elevate it.
First, passing through the *wei-lü*, it
  traverses the *chia-chi*;
Next, it approaches the *yü-chen* and then
  reaches the *ni-wan*.
When finally it has been transported to the
  ni-wan peak,
How does it then descend the storied pavilion?

Swallow mucus in the throat, repeatedly
   encouraging it to fall,
And plant scallions in the nose to temporarily draw it open.
In a moment, without acting, it arrives at
   the mouth;
In an instant, without moving, it naturally
   approaches the cheeks.
It trickles down the throat to the *tan-t'ien*,
And with ten months of careful tending,
   the holy fetus forms.

Notes: When the chance meeting takes
place, carry out the method of "pounding
the chest." After "ascending to heaven,"
quickly perform the folded-leg exercise.
Gently, nine times nine, pull it up in the
front and repeatedly, three times three,
raise it in the rear. Ah, who is capable of
viewing this ascent? Only oneself knows.
It is easy to travel on water, but difficult
to cross mountain peaks. At the crown of
the head is the fontanel. When you have
gathered your partner's "sign," you must
transport it to this gate and then send it
down the "storied pavilion." Therefore,
it is said that even when it has reached the
ni-wan, this is not yet the heavenly pleasure, but when it stays in the "storied
pavilion," this is the joy of the immortals. Wishing to send it down to the *tan-
t'ien*, it must descend from the *ni-wan*.
When it travels to the *tan-fu*, then it
naturally circulates in the body's orifices.
Now the "jade column" flows in the nose
and the "golden pearl" balances on top of
the head. Encourage and swallow mucus
in the throat. Draw it down, "planting
scallions" in the nose. Now behold in the
brain a gradual feeling of pleasure. As
the time approaches, it arrives at the
mouth. Proceed with the utmost attention. Following its progression, do not
move when it nears the cheeks. The work
of gathering in the front only uses a moment of time, but advancing and withdrawing the fire and tally in the back requires an additional ten months.

Number Thirteen

Three tigers face the dragon for the prac-
   tice of irrigation.
Always keep two tigers to act the roles of
   Chun and *Meng*.
The two hexagrams, *Chun* and *Meng*,

should be put to use morning and
   evening,
For we must guard against just one tiger
   who monthly menstruates.

Notes: "Three tigers face the dragon"
means that while one tiger has her
menses, the other two play the roles of
Chun (Difficulty at the Beginning) and
Meng (Youthful Folly). They have not
yet had their periods and still possess
their original *yang*. In this way, the crucible rests on three legs. In the morning use
this one and in the evening the other.
When menses comes and the "flower
opens," then once again use the other.
Begin with *Chun* and *Meng* and end with
Chi Chi (After Completion) and *Wei Chi*
(Before Completion). After ten months,
the fire is sufficient and the 600 hexagrams complete.

Number Fourteen

Every month the red opens and every
   month there is gold.
However, one must prepare in advance to
   capture the gold.
When the golden flower already has fallen,
   how can it compare to jade?
When jade flowers are first born, this is the
   true classic.

Notes: When the time of gathering
arrives, this means watering and cultivating. We must come to know the
time of the production of the medicine.
Only knowing this can we match east and
west. If perhaps one fails to be aware,
then there is danger of the onset of
menses. Observe the movement of the
"tide" and the appearance of the "golden
flower." When the "tide" comes in, the
water overflows. Do not pluck[13] the "golden flower" already fallen, but pick instead the "jade bud" newly born. They
are sweet as a spring and congealed like
ointment. Observe the arrival of the
menses that is just like the brilliance and
fullness of a clear moon. Watch the
rounding of the moon that is just like the
coming of menses in human beings. This
requires that, although it is traceless and
formless, we nevertheless know and
sense it.

Number Fifteen

One now begins to understand how to seize
one's own life destiny,
And the necessity of pursuing the process
of watering and cultivating.
From now on, continue to blow the flute
without holes;
Likewise, beginning today, pluck the
stringless zither.
When the zither strings become excited,
withdraw into your own belly.
And with fear and trepidation guard your
heart.
The myriad affairs of the world should all
be put aside,
And all of our thoughts should be concentrated on the yellow gold.

Notes: It may not be said that having
obtained it, one's work is finished. After
obtaining the one, plant mercury in the
lead pond. From above, repeatedly cover
it with leaking and dripping; from below,
repeatedly use the civil and the martial
[fires] to transport it. Because this is
carried out month after month, it is called
"watering and cultivating." After ten
months, take your leave of the crucible.
It thus can be seen that the method of cultivating the elixir requires this kind of
plan. Simply blowing the "flute without
holes" is not bad; simply strumming the
"stringless zither" is not foolish. Go with
the wind in blowing the fire; follow the
water in pushing the boat. It should be
hidden in the belly, and one should be
diligent every day. Guard it in the heart
and be constantly cautious.

Number Sixteen

From the beginning, the process of watering takes 600 chapters;
Every chapter, each the same, consists of
gathering the true lead.
At the *tzu* hour advance the *yang* fire,
practicing the upside-down position;
At the *wu* hour withdraw the *yin* tally,[14]
turning downside up.
When it touches the ground then wind produces fire,
And it seems to mount up the back and descend down the front.
Proceed in this way for ten months and the
work will be complete;
Face the wall and sit majestically for nine
years.

Notes: The "process of watering"
means incubating for ten months, or what
is referred to as "watering the infant."
"Six hundred chapters" means using the
two hexagrams, *Chun* and *Meng*, every
day. In ten months there are 300 days, so
in the end we arrive at a total of 600 hexagrams. One must advance at the *tzu* hour
and withdraw at the *wu*. Now fire is born
during the Terrestrial Branch *yin* and
stored during *hsü*.[15] Is it possible that one
need only practice during *tzu* and *wu*?
Between morning and evening one employs the methods of *yin* and *yang*, never
forgetting the technique of "upside
down." During the "living *tzu*, *wu*, *mao*,
and *yu* hours"[16] apply the civil and martial fires[17] gently and subtly. Do not dare
to make foolish interpretations, but wait
for the master's instructions. Ha! Although most people in the world ridicule me, I laugh at their stupidity.

This is the method of twelve dragons
and tigers having intercourse. First have
the woman "blow the flute" so that the
ch'i enters and the "mysterious path"
opens. Then press your breasts together
and entwine your thighs. Incline toward
each other and embrace shoulders. Excite her emotions so that they become intense. Alternate playing passive and pursuing. Using tongue to suck tongue, stir
up the fire of her heart and the blaze of
her desire. When pleasure is felt in her
very innards, and her whole face shines
with a rosy glow, then she offers up her
"pearl." Excite her and excite her again.
When at last the one *yang*[18] is set in
motion and the "true lead" is about to
arrive, then turn bottom over top, use
tongue to lick the heart of tongue, and
dragon to explore the tiger's cave. Finally,
when the tiger's tongue is like ice and the
dragon's head is like fire, have your partner carry out the movements. I, however,
do not move. If I were to move, I could
not overcome her in battle. Therefore,
my late teacher has said: "In doing battle,
one must know how to allow the opponent to be aggressive. While the opponent is aggressive, I do not attempt to
play the hero." Finally, when the partner
becomes excited to the point that she can-

not contain herself, she is moved to her innermost part. As the "hour of the living *tzu*" arrives, she lowers her head and closes her eyes, and "sweet dew" fills her mouth. Now, when she probes my mouth with her tongue, I inhale through my nose, causing the path of the spine to open. Once again, inhaling through the nose, the lead comes racing like a fire pearl. The thing is warm within the stove, and the dragon's head is ablaze with fire. Now, with both feet facing heaven, grasp the crooks of the knees with the hands, and using strength, hoist them up and then pull them down again until they are even with the chest. At first, be gentle and later a bit heavier. Have her remove herself from contact with your body. Capture the "true lead" as it flies through the *wei-lü*. Now quickly sit upright and restrain the bowels. Placing the hands on the waist, inhale through the nose, press the lips together, and gently raise it eighty-one times. Once again circulate it eighty-one times. When it traverses the "double-passes" and *yü-chen* and reaches the *ni-wan*, then quickly "plant scallions" with the nose, swallow mucus with the throat, and imagine that the brain produces secretions which on reaching the mouth should be deliberately swallowed. The two things mix as they come together in the "central extremity."[19] Then sit in meditation, practicing ascending and descending; internalize the *ching* and swallow the *ch'i* until spirit and *ch'i* merge.

Number Seventeen

Seeking sagehood and the true lead, one must strive for utmost sincerity,
And with the utmost sincerity I should welcome it with my own mercury.
If the two fail to meet, it is vain to hope for sagehood.
Seeking sagehood and the true lead, one must strive for utmost sincerity.

Notes: The passing of the primordial true lead to my body, in reality, is accomplished by means of the "utmost sincerity." Because utmost sincerity is employed, one must mobilize a drop of "true mercury" from the region of the

anus to meet it. The time of the meeting must be precisely the right moment. If it is not the precise moment, it is useless to seek sagehood. Hey, be a little bit careful! The dragon should now refrain from seeking the white tiger, while the tiger seeks the green dragon herself. Gentlemen who pursue the True should first sit in meditation and regulate their breathing, circulate their *ch'i* and lock the *ching* to cause the *ch'i* and blood to circulate throughout the body and the mind to be at peace. Therefore, after perfecting the practice of breath retention, restraining the bowels, hoisting up and pulling down [the knees], ascending and descending, and so forth, for 100 days in a secluded chamber the passes and orifices will open. However, for the time being, do not be hasty. Before one has carried out the gathering for 5,048 [days], first gather for thirty [Chinese] hours, using this to refine the heart, the intrinsic nature, the *ching-ch'i*, and the "divine sword," to supplement the water, the fire, the bodily fluids, the *ch'i* and blood, and to learn raising and lowering, transporting and lifting, and swallowing and sending. When all are operational, engage in the act at the proper time, "beating the bamboo" and "strumming the zither." Harmonize one with the other, as earth over heaven commune after the fashion of the hexagram *T'ai*. As the "white tiger's tail" moves and twists, the "green dragon's head" continually rises erect; as the "moon cave" closes and opens, the "heavenly root" is repeatedly excited.[20] Because of the continuous closing of the "moon cave," the "heavenly root" is constantly excited. Through constant excitation, the *wei-lü* too will be repeatedly excited and thus repeatedly pinch tight. As the *wei-lü* experiences this repeated pinching, the "sea of *ching*" cannot fail to be aroused nor *yin* secretions fail to flow. It is almost as if one is inundated by a rising wave of pleasure, like swift waters against sand banks. Now by all means gnash and grind the teeth, stop the ears and close the eyes, shut the mouth and inhale through the nose, restrain the bowels and halt the breath.

Above and below, the gates are securely locked. Caress the tiger's thighs, squeeze the tiger's breasts, suck the tiger's tongue, embrace the tiger's waist, and plant the tiger's knees upright. Pinch the dragon's door, advance the dragon's fire, use the dragon's will, and concentrate the dragon's mind. Stimulate the tiger's lead, allow the tiger to move, permit the tiger to twist, and cause the tiger to leak. The tiger is female, and when her passion reaches the peak of intensity, the "gold" naturally floats up. When you see the tiger tightly embrace the dragon's waist, when her head is lowered and her eyes closed, then the water already has descended. The tiger's tongue is as cold as ice and the "sweet dew" bubbles forth like spring water. Now do not let her swallow it, but continually take it into your own mouth. When the tiger's tongue is as hot as fire and the boiling water in the stove is scalding, then have her separate from the dragon's body and quickly withdraw your sword. Now return [to the supine position] with the feet straight up. Grasp the crooks of the knees and "ascend to heaven" for a count of nine times nine. The nose inhales and the tongue sucks, the shoulders are raised and the *ch'i* returns. Mobilize the consciousness and focus it in the "mysterious gate." Maintain the mind on the medicine. The head should be erect and the back straight supporting it. As it passes through the *wei-lü*, sit upright and place the hands on the waist. Inhale once through the nose and the medicine will rise one level. It should be as if contracting the nose to punch a hole. At the same time hunch the back and it will naturally traverse the "three passes." Then with one beat of the head and one pulling up of the lips, it passes through the *yü-chen*. Now, lower the head, and continuing to pull up the lips and "plant scallions" in the nose, it naturally arrives at the *ni-wan* in the crown of the head. Contract the nose and forcefully roar in a downward direction. Then as if swallowing mucus in the throat, cause it to travel from the palate to the cheeks. Having transported this drop of "true mercury," effortlessly and with a sincere heart and tranquil

mind, send it down the "storied pavilion" to meet the "golden liquid" that was swallowed first. When it reaches the "central extremity," continue to sit in meditation, raising and lowering it. Take in *ch'i* and swallow saliva, causing the spirit and *ch'i* to merge. From "refining the self" to the stage of "watering and cultivating," this is the one and only method. Only during periods of rest and withdrawing the "*yin* tally" does one stop temporarily. Carry out gentle cultivation and spiritual exercises, emphasizing attention to the minutest subtlety. If those whose destiny it is to read this book will but cultivate this secret virtue, they will have no difficulty attaining the highest *tao*.

The Rootless Tree

Wu-ken shu

by Chang San-feng

1. The rootless tree,
   Its flowers secluded.
   Who among those attached to the red
     dust of the world would cultivate it?
   The affairs of this floating life;
   A ship on a sea of bitterness.
   Driven hither and thither, out of control.
   No sight of land or shore, how difficult
     to find safe mooring.
   We drift forever in a region of cruel
     sea monsters.
   If you will but turn your head,
   And look back at this shore.
   Do not wait for the wind and waves to
     wreck your ship.

2. The rootless tree,
   Its flowers so fragile.
   When the tree grows old, graft tender
     young branches.
   Graft peach onto willow
   And pear onto mulberry.[1]
   We may take these as models of cultivating the true essence.
   This grafting method of the ancient
     immortals
   Is the original cure for old age.
   Seek out an enlightened master
   And inquire into the technique.

To practice in great haste is as bad as
practicing too late.

3. The rootless tree,
Its flowers so fresh.
From ancient times, flowers and wine
have been the companions of the
immortals
Houses of pleasure;
Feasts of wine and meat.
Do not be guilty of flesh eating or lust.
To be guilty of lust is to lose the trea-
sure of long life.
Wine and meat pass through the intes-
tines, but the *tao* is in the heart.
Open your door;
Let me tell you:
Without wine or flowers, the *tao* can-
not be realized.

4. The rootless tree,
Its flowers so solitary.
Let me ask if *yin* and *yang* have found
their mates?
An unfertilized egg produces no
chicks,
For this violates[2] the creative process
of *yin* and *yang*.
A woman without a husband becomes
resentful;
A man without a wife becomes embit-
tered.
Alas, those deluded souls
Are lost in a daze.
Practicing only solitary meditation, the
ch'i dries up.

5. The rootless tree,
Its flowers inclined.
Departing from *yin* and *yang* the *tao* is
incomplete.
If metal is separated from wood
Or mercury from lead,
Lone *yang* and solitary *yin* become iso-
lated from each other.
In this world *yin* and *yang* express
themselves as the mating of man and
woman,
And children and grandchildren con-
tinue the generations.
Going with this process is the common
way;
Going against it is the way of the im-
mortals.
It is all a matter of turning things up-
side down.

6. The rootless tree,
Its flowers so new.

Production is with *K'un*, and *K'un* is a
human being.
Pluck the flower's cap;
Pick the flower's heart.
The flower bud conceals layer upon
layer of spring's beauty.
People today fail to understand the
principle contained in the flower.
One transmission of heaven's secret is
worth ten thousand pieces of gold.
We borrow the flower's name
To explain the flower's form.
Every line and every verse is solemn
truth.

7. The rootless tree,
Its flowers profuse.
Beautiful, elegant and as adorable as a
rice cake.
Guard against [thoughts as wild as]
monkeys and horses,
So unworthy and foolish.
Put on the iron-faced countenance of a
stern mother,
And bring out the green dragon, the
true precious sword.
Gather all the fresh flowers from the
top of the wall.
Take advantage of favorable winds,
And return with a full load.
How could one travel for nothing to a
mountain of treasures.

8. The rootless tree,
Its flowers in flight.
There is a fixed time for retiring and
reopening.
The lead flowers appear
When the *kuei* is over.
As always, flowers cover all the
branches in the Western Garden.
Go out gathering under the moon,
And mend your robe in the morning
sun.
This subtle mystery
Is known by very few.
One must commune with the immor-
tals and carefully study.

9. The rootless tree,
Its flowers are open.
Plucking them from the crescent moon
stove,[3]
One may lengthen the years
And eliminate illness and disaster.
Make good friends to prepare tech-
niques and resources.
From this point, one may become a
treasure of heaven,

Though those dwelling in delusion
  may ridicule our foolishness.
Encourage those of worth and talent,
And do not engage in trouble making.
Without an enlightened teacher do not
  try to guess the answer.

10. The rootless tree,
  Its flowers so round.
  When you harvest the fruit, the flavor
    is perfect.
  Red oragnges
  As round as pellets.
  Be protective and watchful, without
    allowing idleness.
  Learn a bit of the head retraction tech-
    nique of plants,
  So that one may restore life, revert to
    the root, and return to the original
    source.
  Choose a spiritual location
  To establish your meditation cell.
  Combine the primordial essences and
    complete the great circulation.

11. The rootless tree,
  Its flowers so prosperous.
  Although we speak of rootlessness, it
    does have roots.
  The three powers points;
  And two fives essence.
  When heaven and earth mate, all
    things are born.
  When sun and moon mate, cold and
    heat alternate at suitable times.
  When man and woman mate, preg-
    nancy ensues.
  In great detail,
  I set this forth,
  Fearing only that receiving these
    teachings you not seriously practice.

12. The rootless tree,
  Its flowers so fine.
  Repress your feelings as you confront
    the scene and play with the moon's
    halo.
  The splendor of the golden essence
    dazzles the eyes.
  Do not pick the wrong flowers from
    the garden.
  The five metals and eight minerals
    are all false;
  The ten thousand herbs and thousand
    prescriptions are all worthless.
  The golden toad;
  And jade crow.
  Those who understand the true lead
    will be accomplished adepts.

13. The rootless tree,
  Its flowers so numerous.
  When the whole earth is in bloom,
    keep distant from the river of love.
  What a pity if one falls into de-
    bauchery!
  Step carefully as if in a dragon or ti-
    ger's lair;
  Pluck the yellow flower and return to
    the cave.
  Your name will be inscribed in the
    Purple Palace, never to be effaced.
  Laugh, ha ha,
  As white clouds gather.
  Prepare the heavenly ladder and
    ascend to the celestial sphere.

14. The rootless tree,
  Its flowers so fragrant.
  The head, now warm, reveals its
    precious light.
  From atop the golden bridge,
  Gaze at the winding river.
  Within the moon, so clearly, see the
    blazing sun.
  Consume the crow's liver with the
    rabbit's marrow
  And remove every speck of filth from
    the old belly and guts.
  The realm of fame and fortune;
  And the land of love and kindness.
  Never look back again at the vanity of
    life.

15. The rootless tree,
  Its flowers so fresh.
  The tally fire heats the mercury and
    lead.
  When you approach the stove,
  The scene appears before you.
  While gathering the medicine, rely on
    the ship of salvation,
  Handling the rudder with skill and
    firmness.
  Now let the great waves roll from the
    bottom of the sea.
  Traverse the three passes
  And penetrate the *ni-wan*
  As it passes through the nine orifices
    of the entire body.

16. The rootless tree,
  Its flowers intense.
  Identify the true lead as the real pre-
    cursor.
  Ching, *ch'i* and spirit
  Are heated together in the crucible.
  A woman can become a man and the
    old revert to youth.

Capture the white tiger from the west,
But first subdue the dragon of the east.
Each according to its own kind,
Work with diligence.
When the external medicine pene-
trates, so does the internal.

17. The rootless tree,
Its flowers so delicate.
Stars respond in Heaven,
And the tides on earth.
The dragon slaying sword;
And tiger tying cord.
Mobilize the Big Dipper, turning its
handle,
And refine the true sun and moon in
the stove.
Sweep out all of the three thousand six
hundred items.
Stroll in the heavens,
Wandering freely and easily.
All sins and worldly defilements dis-
appear in a single stroke.

18. The rootless tree,
Its flowers so tall.
The waves of the sea fill the sky, while
the moon toys with the tides.
The path of the Milky Way
Pierces the most distant space.
The raft's shadow traverses the
heavens and moors at the Dipper's
handle.
Touch the Weaving Maid's loom
stone,
Walk about the Herd Boy, and drive
across the Magpie Bridge.
Meeting ranks of immortals
One's courage soars.
Steal the Queen Mother of the West's
peach of immortality from the Jade
Pool Paradise.

19. The rootless tree,
Its flowers are paired.
Dragon and tiger enter the lists to en-
gage in battle.
Lead is cast into mercury;
Yin is matched with *yang*.
The mysterious pearl of the phe-
nomenal world is a priceless gift.
These are the true seeds of the back-
yard garden.
Reverse aging, return to youth, and
enjoy long life.
Mount to heaven;
The way of supreme happiness.
Avoid the wheel of reincarnation and
meeting the King of Hades.

20. The rootless tree,
Its flowers extraordinary.
Plant them in the moon for a moment.
Take the cloud hands;
Climb the cloud ladder.
Pluck the first primordial branch,
Drinking the wine and carrying off the
flowers in high spirits.
Laughing himself to death, the immor-
tal seems to be in a drunken stupor.
Entrust yourself to close companions,
Who carefully help and support you.
Fear only that the first stage of the
essence escape from the stove.

21. The rootless tree,
Its flowers so yellow.
Production is in the central region of
Celestial Stems *wu* and *chi*.
The partner of the east becomes a girl,
And the partner of the west becomes a
boy.
Matching husband and wife, enter the
nuptial chamber.
The Yellow Dame invites them to
drink the wine of true wisdom.
Daily heat the wedding wine and drink
a bout.
The formula of the immortals
Is a liquer that revives the soul.
Rising from death and returning to
life, this is the king of medicines.

22. The rootless tree,
Its flowers so bright.
The dark side of the moon and Pole
Star press the brightness of the sun.
Marrow of the golden flower;
Ching of the jade rabbit.
Capture the two and cook them
together.
The *yang* fire and *yin* tally are divided
by Terrestrial Branches *tzu* and *wu*.
Now rest as you approach the gates of
Branches *mao* and *yu*.
Concentrate on the yellow court;
And cultivate the valley spirit.
A man becomes pregnant and laughs
himself to death.

23. The rootless tree,
Its flowers so red.
Pick all the red flowers till the tree is
empty.
Shunyata is *samsara*;
Samsara is *shunyata*.[4]
Know that the true *shunyata* is found
in the midst of *samsara*;
And when one fully understands the

191

nature of *shunyata*, *samsara* disappears.
The *dharma* lives forever, never falling
into emptiness.
This is called perfect enlightenment,
And one deserves the title of great
hero.
The ninth patriarch achieves salvation
and ascends to heaven.

24. The rootless tree,
Its flowers disappeared.
Without trace or form, impossible to
represent its image.

It is without name,
But responds to the call.
Capture and place it in the transforma-
tion stove.
Circulate the fire of *samadhi* one
cosmic orbit.
Strive for the true emptiness and
return to the great void.
Received in the paradise of the
immortals,
Accept the heavenly tally.
Now one is truly a great man.

XII. WOMEN'S PRACTICES

Introduction

These works on women's meditation
have been included in this anthology of
sexology classics for a number of reasons.
First, although some of the literature on
"paired practices" has been translated
and studied before, this is the first
attempt to make available in translation
a significant body of works on women's
solo practice. Second, these texts show
the continuation of theories of immortality for women glimpsed in the
Ishimpō fragments as they reemerge a
thousand years later in the very different
context of women's solo self-cultivation.
And finally, the existence of a special
branch of women's inner alchemy, paral-
leling the male "pure practices" school,
underscores the critical role of sexual
energy in Chinese meditation.

The *Ten Precepts* and *Precious Raft*
both were edited by Min I-te in the early
nineteenth century, and this translation is
based on copies in a collection entitled
Ku-shu yin-lou ts'ang-shu. Original authorship of the *Ten Precepts* is attributed
to the T'ang Immortal, Lü Tung-pin, with
editorial contributions by Female Immortal Sun, wife of Ma Tan-yang, one
of the Seven Patriarchs of the Northern
School. The *Precious Raft* is attributed to
the Taoist Patriarch, Li Ni-wan, with

transcription and commentary by Shen I-
ping. *The Essentials* and *Correct Methods*
both are translated from the *Tao-tsang
ching-hua.* The former was edited by the
prolific late Ch'ing Taoist scholar, Fu
Chin-ch'üan, who points out in his
Preface that, although men require nine
years to attain immortality and women
only three, nevertheless, women are
handicapped by their confinement to the
home and the difficulty of seeking out
true masters. The text of the *Essentials*
actually is a patchwork of passages
relating to women's practice from a
variety of sources. The *Correct Methods*
was first published in 1945, edited by
Ch'en Ying-ning, who excerpted chapters
from a work entitled *Tseng-pu chin-hua
chih-chih nü-kung cheng-fa* (Expanded
instructions of the golden flower on the
correct methods of women's practice),
attributed to Lü Tung-pin and his female
disciple, Ho Hsien-ku. An introduction,
dated 1881, also is attributed to Master
Lü. Ch'en Ying-ning informs us that in
editing the text, he sought to eliminate
the interpolations, exaggerations, and in-
elegance of style that he felt characterized the original.

All the texts in this section show the
confluence of traditional gynecology,
Taoist meditation, and Buddhist terminology. The distinctive Buddhist influ-

ence is due perhaps in part to the relatively late date of these texts and to the development of many of these techniques within Buddhist convents. Nevertheless, the playing out of the familiar law of "conservation" in the environment of female physiology rests on a solid foundation of traditional Taoist theory.

Queen Mother of the West's Ten Precepts on the True Path of Women's Practice

Hsi Wang Mu nü-hsiu cheng-t'u shih tse

Expounded by Master Lü Yen [Tung-pin]
Transmitted by Taoist Abbot Shen I-ping, T'ai-hsü Weng
Edited by Female Immortal Sun
Annotated by the disciple Min I-te

It is said that spiritual practice for women is subject to nine disciplines. The code of discipline states that, if maintained without fail, there will be great benefit. When the fruits of discipline are realized, one passes not through the tribulations of hell, but meets in life with the "ten virtuous friends."[1] One's name mounts up to the "purple palace"[2] and one takes one's place in the ranks of the immortals. Now in promulgating this *True Path of Women's Practice*, the "nine disciplines" are the first precept. The text says: Be filial, respectful, yielding, and gentle; be cautious in speech and avoid jealousy; be chaste and restrained; shun all wanton ways and love all living things; be compassionate and refrain from killing; recite with decorum and be diligent and careful; abstain from meat and wine; dress simply and without ornamentation; regulate the disposition; do not let yourself become troubled; do not go frequently to religious feasts; do not mistreat slaves and servants; do not conceal the virtues and expose the faults in others. One who is able to observe these nine disciplines is worthy to receive and uphold the true path. What has been promulgated here is supremely precious and valuable. To teach without adherence to these disciplines is to make a mockery of heavenly treasures. Both teacher and student will be punished. It is best to be cautious and serious.

Note on the Entire Work: Every section begins with the words, "It is said." This text is the product of oral transmission and represents pronouncements from the golden lips of the Queen Mother of the West. The words of the scribe here are similar to "Thus have I heard" in Buddhist scriptures and "The *tao* says" in Taoist classics.

Another Note: The masters of old placed these "nine disciplines" at the head of the first precept. It consists of passages on purifying the body, speech, altar, and so forth. In expounding this text, Master Lü placed the disciplines with explanation in the first precept. The idea that the *tao* should not be transmitted lightly thus is as clear as opening the door and beholding a mountain.

It is said that this is the second precept in the true path of women's practice. Its title is "One's Own Life," and it speaks of the *yin* nature of women and the moon as their symbol. At the age of thirteen, fourteen, or fifteen, her "original *ch'i*" is complete and her "true blood" full. This is *yang* in the midst of *yin*, and the light of the moon becomes resplendent. At the moment the menses descends, her "original *ch'i*" is broken and her "true blood" leaks. Following marriage and the birth of children, the "original *ch'i*" gradually is weakened and the "true blood" progressively destroyed. Although every month the menstrual flow regenerates, in reality, it every month is reinjured. Herein lies the difficulty in cultivating a woman's life. If a woman desires to preserve her life and return to the original state, she must seek out the transmissions on self-cultivation. If she practices according to the transmissions, the work will be completed quickly. The reason this chapter is entitled "One's Own Life" is that a woman's life is bound up with her menses. If the menses is not transformed, how can her life be preserved? Because it is impossible to predict exactly when a woman will succeed in returning to the state of original purity, nothing is more important than beginning these practices. Therefore, the "nine disciplines" are considered the first precept and "one's own life" the second. This is in accordance with the principle of putting "intrinsic nature" first and then life. Following this precept, the text continues with "the source of intrinsic nature," and thus it is said that the effect of cultivating "intrinsic nature" is precisely to preserve one's life.

Note on the Entire Work: With the exception of the first precept, which was compiled by Master Lü, numbers two through nine were all edited and compiled by [Sun] Pu Erh Yüan Chün, and then personally corrected by Master Lü. Because his purpose was to be as clear as possible, the style is intentionally accessible, lest the words obscure the meaning and later generations be misled. Readers must not make the mistake of doubting that this is the work of the immortals from a lack of antique elegance in the style. The whole classic, from the beginning through the tenth precept, was compiled by Master Lü. After being submitted for approval, additions were made according to his meaning.

It is said that this is the third precept in women's practice. Its title is "The Source of Intrinsic Nature," and it speaks of women's nature as water and her substance as flowers. When she is young but already aware of things, she must be reserved and neither playful nor wild. At this point, the first evidence of menses will appear within her "inner feminine," like a star or a pearl. This is the prenatal treasure hidden above the *K'un* abdomen and located in the middle of the central yellow region. At this time, if the woman knows how to maintain the purity of her "intrinsic nature," refrains from looking upon lewd play and from listening to lewd speech; if she is retiring and tranquil in her daily routine, follows the rules for

womanly behavior and is at ease in her stillness, then this one thing will remain close to its heavenly nature and revert to primal unity. It will not be converted into "red pearls" nor be transformed into menses. But unfortunately the common girl is ignorant, childish, and fond of action. She is given to pursuing games and wild careening. Invariably her *ch'i* is agitated and her mind unsteady. Her spirit becomes confused and her "true *ch'i*" unstable. Thus, this starlike heavenly treasure wells up and melts. As hot as fire, it seizes the gate and descends, bursting through the door as it emerges. The world now calls this "menses". After this event, even if one maintains chastity and does not marry, one is still a common woman. This is simply a failure to recognize the "origin of intrinsic nature." If one is determined to cultivate return [to the primal state], begin with the next precept.

Note on the "Inner Feminine": This refers to the "gate of the feminine." Below, it is called either the "fountain gate" or the "gate of the feminine." Therefore, as the gate of the "yellow center," it is called the "inner feminine."

Another Note: The first menses is life's great treasure. If one knows how to cultivate it, one may remain close to one's heavenly nature and be transformed into primal unity. Among the holy women of antiquity were those who practiced this. The great Empress of Heaven is clear proof. There is no lack of gifted women, but unfortunately they are without wise fathers and mothers or sage teachers. Of a thousand gifts, a thousand are wasted. What a great pity!

It is said that this is the fourth precept in the true path of women's practice. It is entitled "Cultivating the Menses." After the menses has already descended, the "true *ch'i*" is broken and the "true blood" injured. If one does not devote oneself to cultivating the menses, the "true blood" will be diminished daily and the "true *ch'i*" destroyed daily. Even if one practices intensively, what is the benefit? Works on inner alchemy say that "when bamboo breaks, bamboo must be used to repair it." What is the meaning of this aphorism? Those who have already experienced menses must first slay the "red dragon"; those whose menses has ceased must first cause it to resume and then "slay" it. The first step is to use the method of "microcosmic orbit." At the two hours, *tzu* and *wu*, one "straddles the crane." The 10,000 cares should be put aside. Knock the teeth together seventy-two times to open the two lung *shu* points.[3] Next inhale and exhale softly through the nostrils thirty-six times to open all the blood vessels in the body. At this moment, there is danger of the *ch'i* escaping from below, so one must be more diligent in "riding the crane" and not allow oneself to be lax. The two hands should be applied to either side of the area below the navel and above the "gate." Now with the mind, send it to the rear and upward. Do this for about thirty-six breaths, and then "push the sky" with the palms of the two hands. Now maintain the mind in the *wei-lü*. Following this, one may relax the hands, placing them on the sides of the waist, and elevating the shoulders in a shrugging gesture thirty-six times. One then will feel *ch'i* begin to stir and rise in the *chia-chi*, "double passes," and lung *shu* points. If there are still blockages, practice clenching the teeth while maintaining the mind in the back of the neck and raising the *ch'i* thirty-six times. One will then feel the *yü-chen* and *ni-wan* open. After this, embrace the upper lip with the lower lip, gently exerting pressure. One then feels the *ch'i* of the *ni-wan* descend to the bottom of the nasal cavity. Now without any force, simply use the tongue to form the "heavenly bridge." Maintain the mind at the point where the tongue bridges and the "sweet dew" will descend naturally. Then with a slight contraction of the nasal passage, use the mind to dispatch the "dew" and swallow it all the way to the heart. Maintain it there for a moment and then guide it with the mind down and to the rear. Now dividing it left and right, it should arrive and remain at the two sides of the waist, revolving internally thirty-six times on each side. After this, direct it with the mind to the "navel wheel," revolving it thirty-six times to the left and thirty-six to the right. One will then feel that the whole belly is open and relaxed. At this point, the hands should be placed below the navel and above the "gate." Use the mind to separately guide it to the left and right simultaneously. Raising them together thirty-six times, one will feel that there is a tiny bit that enters the uterus. Now, neither consciously nor unconsciously, be aware of this for a brief moment. This is the general idea of "cultivating the menses." There also is a technique called the "incomparable rejuvenation method" that cannot be discussed at this point, but it is none other than what is meant by the phrase, "awareness within stillness."

Note on Points within the Body: The uterus is the "inner feminine." It is analogous to the "mysterious orifice" in the male. Works on inner alchemy state that the *yang* is called "mysterious" and the *yin* "feminine." Combining them gives us what Lao tzu called the "gate of the mysterious feminine," or what the *Huang Ti yin-fu ching* records as the "miraculous instrument." Although there are four names—"miraculous instrument," "mysterious orifice," "feminine gate," and "palace of children"—in terms of location, there is but one point.

Note on the Expression, "Palace of Children," in This Precept: This can be illustrated from our everyday experience, for we can see it is here that both the "holy fetus" and the human fetus are formed.

Note on the Phrase, "It Is None Other Than.": This means that one should proceed only on the basis of inner experience and not simply vague notions.

When one feels a rush of warm *ch'i* circling in the uterus, it is most important to securely lock the "gate of the spring" and not allow it to relax. If there is a sensation of pleasure, it is critical that random thoughts do not arise. There may be a slight longing for love, leading to a feeling of voluptuousness throughout the entire body. If one does not immediately subdue the emotions, then it is here that the immortal and the common part ways.

One must not be casual in speaking of

the requirement to "lock securely." If in locking the "gate," one relaxes ever so slightly, then the "true *ch'i*" will escape. The text then goes on to describe an even greater danger, for at this time there will be an extraordinary tickle within the "gate," and after raising and locking, there will be an unusual sensation of pleasure in the "feminine." If one fails to subdue the emotions, it will lead to a voluptuous feeling through the entire body, and one will slip into the "sea of emotion." At this point, even if one attempts to subdue them, it will be too late. Therefore it is said that this is where the immortal and the common part ways. Master T'ai-hsü has said that the true way is difficult to sustain. If this feeling is not subdued, the "gate" will open like the mouth of a cave and the *ching* spill forth like a stream. What a great pity! At this point, it is necessary to rest the mind for a while and quietly wait for the "palace of children" to regain calm. This then is what Female Immortal Wei[4] called, "the treasure reverts to the 'north sea' where it rests securely." However, this is merely "yellow leaves curing a child's cough"[5] and should not be mistaken for the formation of the fetus.

Note: The "sea of sensation" is the "south sea" and the "palace of children" is the "north sea," located north of the "central extremity" and the "central yellow." This then is the *I ching*'s "comprehending all truth from the yellow center."[6] "North" and "south" apply to front and back, not to above and below. Is this not proven by Female Immortal Wei's statement? Therefore one must quietly wait for the "palace of children" to regain calm before ending one's exercises.

Allow me to comment on this precept. In carrying out such practices as "cultivating the red dragon" and "slaying the red dragon," it is very important to maintain the body in a state of calmness, for one rash move and the work is ruined. It therefore is said that "from here the immortal and the common part ways."

Another Note to This Precept: This is the "full moon," or what is called "returning to the primal source and reverting

to the root." When the "formation of the fetus" has been achieved, then the "state of mystery" is realized. However, this precept's taking heaven and earth and the Five Phases within the body and refining them into the supreme treasure of "returning and reverting" still is considered merely "small return and small reversion." This is achieved easily through daily and constant practice and is what works on inner alchemy mean by "grain by grain, this becomes the highest treasure." Therefore, this precept must be understood as "yellow leaves." However, as for collecting aphorisms for training, reverting to tranquility, and so forth, these relate exclusively to the "great return" and "state of mystery"; and it is imperative to grasp them without negligence.

It is said that this is the fifth precept in the true path of women's practice. Its title is "Returning Again." Among the women of the world there are those who reach old age, but whose bodies are not yet "clean," and those of only forty-five whose "dragon" already is suspended. Both must practice until they succeed in "returning to the primal state" and becoming like virgins. This exercise and method are those of the first four precepts. However, from here on, instead of raising it up the back, one must allow it to descend down the front and flow back to the "stream sea."[7] One should swallow the "sweet dew," but only as far as the "palace",[8] and do not send it all the way down. Now use the hands to massage the "breast stream" thirty-six revolutions to the left and thirty-six to the right. When you feel an expansive pleasure in the "palace" and "stream," then once again separately massage the two breasts, thirty-six times slowly and thirty-six times rapidly. Now gently massage each thirty-six times, and then forcefully thirty-six times. Altogether, this equals 144 times. When you feel the "true *ch'i*" rising like mist in the breasts and "stream," there will be a cool liquid like a spring, which emerges from the "double passes" and, overflowing, reverts to the "south sea." Calmly wait for it, but do not allow it to divide behind the heart and penetrate the two sides of the waist. Abandon all cares in the "central palace," and without using deliberate effort to circulate it, simply allow it to disperse of its own. When you feel that your entire body has reached a state of perfect purity and harmony, maintain this for a whole day without interruption. Gradually, the weak will grow strong and the feeble robust. The old will become young again. They will develop the complexion of flowers and their breasts will shrink to the size of a maiden's, with the center gradually forming like walnuts.[9] If carried out for 100 days, this is sufficient to reduce the color of the menses to rouge water. After three days, practice the internal exercises described in the fourth precept, neither adding nor changing the slightest detail, and the "red dragon" automatically will be slain. When one becomes aware of the sun and moon appearing as a pair of discs, then the true victory has been won.

Note on the Taoist Classics Speaking of Old Women Still Having Their Menses: This is not menstrual flow but fluids derived from food and drink that are formed from the drying effect of the "popular" and "ministerial"[10] fires and do not revert to the liver and spleen. It may take the form of "intestinal blood,"[11] "red vaginal discharge,"[12] or "reverse menses."[13] All of these are derived from this same substance, and the conditions are the result of "exhaustion." Therefore, just as with restoring the menses after menopause, one must first return to the virgin state and then apply oneself to "slaying the dragon."

A Note on the Word "Aware" (*chien* 見) *in the expression* "Becoming Aware": It should be pronounced as if it were the character *hsien* 現. "Aware" then means manifesting a sign. Only when the mind silently intuits can one become aware. Manifesting as something apparent, one then becomes intuitively aware. Commenting on these two characters, their meaning has many levels, and one must not read them carelessly.

It is said that this is the sixth precept in the true path of women's practice. Its title is "The Breast." The breasts connect with the fluids of the heart and lungs above and with the "true juice" of the "sea of blood" below. When, through training, the breasts become like those of a virgin or a child, then a woman's body is transformed into a man's. The training methods simply are those described in precepts four and five. For women, blood is the most basic element, and the key to this precept is refining the red so that it returns to white. However, fearing that the basic element become exhausted, one must first refine the fluids and transform them into blood. In transforming the fluids into blood, nothing is superior to maintaining the "dew" in the "palace" and focusing the mind in the "double passes." The long-accumulated congealed fluid in the "passes" melts and reverts to the "stream sea."[14] When the blood reverts it necessarily is in a flourishing state. The subtle principle involved can be found in the fifth precept. Desiring to transform the blood and cause it to return to white, nothing surpasses concentrating the mind in the "stream" and breasts. Firmly clench the teeth, still mental activity, and the *ch'i* will naturally revert to the "stream" and extend to the breasts. Use the palms of the hands to rub the breasts, first slowly and then rapidly, first lightly and then heavily, altogether 144 times. As the *ch'i* accumulates, it becomes doubly abundant. Using the mind, withdraw it to the two sides of the waist and then with the power of vision lead the *ch'i*, revolving it to the left and right a total of seventy-two breaths. In this way, the *ch'i* is heated as if by moxibustion. Now without counting, guide it with the mind to circle about the "wheel," and there will be a sensation of boiling at the body's lowest extremity. The red thus is transformed into white. The transformed *ch'i* passes through the *wei-lü* and ascends to the *chia-chi*; it traverses the *yü-chen* and penetrates the "valley." At this point, though the scene that appears to one's inner vision is unrivaled by even the "three islands"[15] and "mysterious garden,"[16] one must quickly practice forgetfulness. If suddenly all becomes as dark as night, one must guard it in silence, and after a long time, one will surely be visited by a bolt of lightning and crash of thunder. The "dew" flows like a stream and the "flowery pool" is so full one can hardly keep up with swallowing. Overflowing, it descends to the "palace" and then reaches the navel. The whole body feels pure and harmonious. One must continue to observe all of this in a state of perfect composure. If maintained for a hundred days without interruption, those with mature breasts will become as flat as a young girl's, and those with empty breasts will become like walnuts. One first becomes like a maiden and then finally like a young girl. It is from the successful transformation into white that one regains the state of maidenhood. Not a few in our school have completed the work of transforming the red. In this connection there is a poem entitled "Phoenix Maiden," which we offer as evidence:

> Sun on the left and moon on the right—a *yin* and *yang*.
> Closing the nose and circulating internally is called turning the Dipper.
> If one desires *yin* and *yang* to revert to sun and moon,
> Then with true fire in the hands massage the breasts.
> Those who receive this teaching must strive to realize it.

Note on the "Double Passes": They are located in front of the *chia-chi* and behind the "crimson palace." Within the "passes" are two points that are the seat of the "congealed fluids" in the body. The left is called *gao* and the right *huang*.[17] It cannot be reached by the power of medicine, and the "true *ch'i*" does not extend to it. When congealed fluids become lodged here, it brings harm to the whole body. In creating humankind, nature established a "pass" to aid the heart, and therefore this site is called the "double passes." We say that the fluid is "congealed" because it seems like fluid but actually is not. Originally, these are "thin fluids,"[18] which are transformed from food and drink. Borne by the *ch'i*, they reach the lungs and are distributed throughout the body to lubricate the meridians. When the body's "true *ch'i*" is

flourishing, this substance is transformed in its course and becomes infinitely beneficial. However, if the "true *ch'i*" is weak, then it fails to be transformed and flows into the organs and meridians. It is not actually harmful here, except if it is influenced by extremely *yin yin-ch'i*, at which point it becomes "congealed fluid." This seems to be *ching* but is not, and it blocks the *ch'i* pathways. The site of greatest accumulation is the lower extremity of the "double passes." The damage is greatest in the "double passes" because, being inaccessible to the "true *ch'i*," it accumulates here. This accumulation is like snow and ice on the shady side of the K'un-lun Mountains, which does not melt even after the summer solstice.[19] Although one has the "*chi* earth" and "heart dipper"[20] to guard and protect it, only if the spirit is flourishing is all well. However, if the spirit is weak there is damage. Understanding this, the wise transmitted an aphorism that says, "concentrate the spirit and heat the passes," though few in the world have heard it. Among practitioners who have been recorded in poetry, there is only the "Phoenix Immortal." This is why it was presented as a case in point. However, if one wishes to emulate the "Phoenix Immortal" through practice, one must return to the starting point and first devote oneself to "stilling the mind." Only after "stilling the mind" can one accomplish reversion of the spirit and flourishing *ch'i*. When the exercises for focusing on the "stream" and massaging the breasts are added to this, then the "congealed fluid" melts and issues from the passes. When it reaches the "sea" and is refined, the marvelous effect of the complementary balance of existence and nonexistence can be enjoyed.

Another Note: The left breast is connected with the liver and the right with the lungs. The "stream" is connected with the heart, kidneys, and spleen. Therefore, one must focus on them constantly. Normally, however, one need only maintain this with an attitude that is neither attentive nor inattentive. The heart is the root of a woman's life and is signified by the reception of the middle line in *K'un* to form the trigram *Li* that conceals the "true fire." However, blood is generated under cool conditions, and when the blood flourishes, the spirit is at peace. It therefore is essential to be doubly serene. This is the most important requirement for curing illness, cultivating health, returning to the "primal state," and realizing the *tao*. However, one must practice according to the *Ch'ing-ching ching* (Classic of purity and stillness) to realize the marvel of the "three contemplations" meditation method.[21]

It is said that this is the seventh precept in the true path of women's practice. It is entitled "Jade Liquid." Men begin their practice from purity and peace. When one's training is perfected, the circulation of the "water wheel" is complete. When the "true *ching*" is safe and sufficient, it does not leak from the "mysterious gate," but flows upward to the crown of the head and waters the "heavenly vale." Then descending copiously to the "flowery pool," it is known as the "jade liquid." When the *yin* spirit appears, the *yang* soul (*hun*) travels to the "jade mansion", while the *yin* soul (*p'o*) pays court to the Imperial Immortal. An aura encircles the crown of the head, a tide rises in the "mysterious sea," and reverberations penetrate the "realm of jade purity."[22] This then is the return of the elixir of "true jade liquid." The ancient immortals referred to this as "wisdom like clarified butter irrigates the crown of the head." As for women's "jade liquid," it is the "red dragon" liquid transformed into "white phoenix" marrow. When the marrow is replete, one can commence the process of reversing the flow without deceiving oneself. Although the training methods do not depart from what has been indicated in the fourth precept, realization of its subtle significance must follow the sixth. Only when one accomplishes this is the benefit truly infinite. This is what the wise men of old called "grain by grain." How could its functioning ever be exhausted? After receiving the "true seeds:"[23] one must continue to exert oneself. However, the source of fulfillment and accomplishment

ultimately depends on the ability to still the mind. Those who receive this teaching should strive to achieve it.

Note: For this precept, we shall quote the words of Ts'ui O Hsien tzu by way of commentary. She has said: "Formerly I devoted myself to 'returning the elixir.' At the outset, the method I used was 'forgetting oneself and forgetting the method.' In due course I was able to perfect it to the point that I forgot my own identity and proceeded solely from 'this now and this tomorrow.' ('Now' means today, and 'tomorrow' means the next day. 'This' means the great task of 'returning the elixir.') I was able to forget what day it was and what time. Suddenly heaven and earth also disappeared. After a long time, I awoke as if enlightened and simply listened and observed in total silence. Finally I forgot everything and felt only something like heat or burning, and then in the back something like fat or oil. (The 'back' refers to the back of the 'north pole.' 'Like fat or oil' is the liquid of the 'red dragon' that has been transformed into the marrow of the 'white phoenix.') I experienced no limits and no boundaries, as if there was sound and as if there was silence. It flowed and stopped; it splashed and spewed. Sometimes I felt suspended like a cascade, white as silk; sometimes I felt pure as a frozen lake. There was not one time nor one place. Vision was not confused nor spirit weary. Suddenly my perception and hearing became as if enchanted, but I warned myself saying, 'Do not be seduced by appearances.' Suddenly I had another revelation and said, 'Time like a river passes by, never to return.'[24] I felt omnipotent and was about to test it when suddenly I had another revelation and said, 'Heaven and earth are as one body with me.'[25] I reflected on this and concluded that it was thus with my own body. Whatever principles apply to the external world also apply to the inner, and whatever is true of the inner applies to the outer. Thereupon, I reflected and discovered that I was without self. After a long period of stillness my self manifested. However, when I sought to reflect more deeply, there was no passage. As   *199* if in a dream, I felt that there was a burning sensation within my body like moxibustion, extending from the middle to the lowest point, and a sound like thunder. The sound of wind and tide rose up in the midst of this. Suddenly penetrating the *wei-lü*, it rose up to the *chia-chi*, passed through the *yü-chen* and reached the "vale".[26] Like a stream, the 'sweet dew' dripped down from the nose, and the 'flowery pool' became so full that I could hardly swallow it. Before long the liquid bubbled up from the 'southern sea,' flowed into the waist, and circled the navel. By melting and fusing, I became one with heaven and earth. Truly, inner and outer were as one. At this moment, everything followed the normal course; the training was complete and I withdrew. . . ," and so forth. What Hsien tzu has described essentially is transformation training. Normally, one should devote oneself first to attaining stillness and then to forgetfulness. I [I-te] therefore have quoted this to verify this technique.

It is said that this is the eighth precept in the true path of women's practice. It is entitled "Fetal Breathing." The "fetal breath" is the culmination of the *tao* and the ladder to heaven. After the woman "returns the elixir," her *ching-ch'i* is replete and her body like a man's. Without employing the fetal breath, "returning to the void" is highly uncertain. The efficacy of this breath is infinite and its practice supremely simple. However, not all achieve the same results, and there are many levels of accomplishment. This is not something that nature controls, for nature relies on creatures to create themselves. When one seeks this breath with stillness, then there is no thought or worry focused in the nose itself. If practiced morning and night, one day the "ancestral orifice" will be discovered and it naturally opens wide. Neither seeking nor resisting it, the breath and nose unite in harmony. Vast it is, without margin; boundless it is, and unfathomable. Unawares, the ancestor is myself and I am the ancestor. The inhalation and exhalation of the nose is what the wise men of old called the "fetal breath." *Yin* and *yang*, the Five Phases, heaven, earth, humankind, and creatures all are born of this orifice. The breath is influenced by the subtle mechanism, and the subtle mechanism in turn responds to it. This naturally gives rise to the six ranks of immortals: heavenly, watery, earthly, human, godly, and ghostly. The teaching consists simply of achieving perfect stillness. When practice proceeds from the union of virtue and the "true One," this is the heavenly immortal. When practice proceeds from the union of virtue and the "mysterious one," this is the watery immortal. When practice proceeds from the union of virtue and the "pure One," this is the earthly immortal. When practice proceeds from the union of virtue and the "essential One," this is the human immortal. The two lowest ranks result when practice proceeds from the union of virtue and the "emotional One." If one favors the *yang*, the results are godly; if one favors the *yin*, they are ghostly. The fruits of the good person alone do not qualify one for immortality. The origin of these various ranks lies in the influence and response of the subtle mechanism. Although it is said that this is a gift of heaven, is it not really won through our own efforts? Those who receive this teaching must strive to achieve it.

Carefully considering the content of this precept, the practice of the "fetal breath" is truly the culmination of the *tao* and the ladder to heaven. Can one dare be less than diligent?

It is said that this is the ninth precept in the true path of women's practice. It is entitled "Namo."[27] Its realization is unlike the difficult path of Kuan-yin. The power to become a Buddha or a bodhisattva is in the two words *nan-wu* (*namo*). Within these two words is concealed the mystery. One must preserve the truth that this body is the Buddha, like a crystalline seven-story pagoda established on the summit of Mount Potala. Before the pagoda is a "red child,"[28] which is the mental leader. When the Bodhisattva allows one to seek spiritual guidance in the east and west and one has consulted all the "fifty-three wise ones," then one holds the Buddha and comprehends all the *koans*.[29] After this, the "mysterious pearl" of perfect peace is offered by the daughter of the Dragon King, and one lives apart in the "purple bamboo grove."[30] Before long, the "white parrot"[31] flutters freely up and down. The hand, holding the pure vase, inserts the willow branch. Collect the natural "sweet dew" liquid. Sit unshakably atop Mount Patola, practicing the "Tara method"[32] and placing the syllable *Om* in the realm of truth. When the highest treasure is claimed, it is placed in the "fish basket."[33] Reciting *chia-lo-ta-to* all the cares of the world are released in the "southern sea." As a result of this, the waves of the sea roll on and on. I am enlightened, knowing only enlightenment. The internal exercises of the fourth precept are indispensable in this great method. It is especially important to follow the preceding precept precisely, for one will then naturally return step by step to the true void and the true stillness. When one's training is complete and practice perfected, one then shares a glance with the Bodhisattva and smiles, perfectly at ease and relaxed. Those who receive this teaching should strive to achieve it.

Note to This Precept: It is only through transformation training that one masters the secret of transformation. One may understand it only within one's own mind and should not talk about it glibly. It is necessary only to be diligent and sincere in one's own commitment. Hold to the realization that this body is the Buddha, and one will be full of vitality and without spatial limitations.

It is said that this is the tenth precept in the true path of women's practice. It is entitled "Caution at the End." Women represent the virtue of *K'un*. If the *tao* of earth is not yet realized, persistence will bring it to completion. One thus must carry out the process of assisting nature's operations in broad daylight. Here, too, the training begins with stillness. Without spending a penny or wasting an ounce of effort, one achieves it by merely sitting. Without another soul being aware, our power rivals that of nature itself. Thus it is that with our own selves we save the whole world. Yet the method is simply to harmonize the mind and rest in stillness. When harmony reaches the level of total purity and calm, then there is peace in the heavenly capital. When harmony reaches the level that the *K'un* abdomen is open and comfortable, then the "village gate" is prosperous and populous. When harmony reaches the level wherein the four limbs are open and free, then the "four barbarian tribes" are pacified. As the body is harmonized, the world is ordered. This is the fruit of cause and effect. Therefore, if one is able to achieve a moment of purity and harmony, this is a moment of true power. Although the result is not visible, it nevertheless exists. One need guard against only a lack of sincerity in study or failure of the "three *tan-t'ien*" to be connected. Moreover, there has never been one who was not himself saved who could save the world. The teaching consists simply of practicing day and night. "What others do once, I do a hundred times, and what they do ten times, I do a thousand." Even the ignorant can comprehend this. Those who receive this teaching should strive to achieve it.

Note to This Precept: This was authoritatively handed down by the Queen Mother of the West. Pu Erh Yüan Chün followed the Holy Mother of Jade Purity's oral instructions for the great *tao* of world salvation. The last precepts of former transmissions were collected and revised to serve as the final word for this precept. Truly, from the beginning of time, there has never been a more matchless classic. Master Lü considered it a great blessing for universal creation; Pu Erh Yüan Chün considered that it would surely promote the evolution of the *tao*. We thus can see their profound hope for future generations of students. (Min I-te says:) Those who are interested in reading this work should encourage each other to strive to realize its teachings.

Essentials of the Golden Elixir Method for Women

Nü chin-tan fa-yao

Compiled by Chi Yi Tzu (Fu Chin-ch'üan)

Master Lü's "Tz'u Poem in the Meter 'Strolling under the Moon'" says:

> The trigrams *K'an* and *Li*, *Chen* and *Tui* are divided according to the Terrestrial Branches, *tzu* and *wu*.
> You must realize that this is taken from the family ancestors.
> When thunder shakes the earth, there is rain on the mountain
> That washes the yellow sprouts[1] which emerge from *K'un*, the earth.
> When you have captured the golden *ching*, then lock it securely.
> To practice the art of longevity, you must give birth to dragon and tiger.
> If they ask who is the transmitter of this,
> Simply say that the gentleman's name is Lü.

In the *Shang-yao ling-ching*, the chapter entitled "Three Lives" says: "The subtle mystery of life is difficult to describe. The process of waxing and waning undergoes 1,000 changes and 10,000 transformations. Man's navel is called the 'gate of life.'[2] In the center of the body is the 'yellow court,' located behind the 'secluded pass,'[3] above the *kuan-yüan*[4] and below the 'sea of *ch'i*.' On the left is the sun and on the right the moon, and these are both light. Life has three kinds of light. The yellow light is the *tan-t'ien*, the white light is the 'embryo source,' and the purple light is the 'blood source.' The 'blood source' is the breasts. The one and two-tenths of an inch between them is not the breasts. A man's life is in the *tan-t'ien*. The *tan-t'ien* is the 'true earth' that gives birth to the elixir. A woman's life is in the breasts. The breasts are the original *ching* of the mother's *ch'i*. The 'embryo source' forms the embryo, the 'blood source' produces the blood, and the *tan-t'ien* produces the elixir. One's practice should be carried out during the *tzu* and *wu* hours. Maintain mental concentration in the "empty orifice"[5] of the breasts.

Breathe slowly, exhaling little and inhaling much. Wait for the 'monthly signal'[6] and move it up from the *tan-t'ien* to the breasts. 'Monthly signal' does not refer to the arrival of the menses. The word 'signal' is comparable to letters written home when traveling abroad that arrive before one does oneself. The day that the 'signal' is about to arrive is known to the woman. It may be that she experiences pain in her waist or legs, a feeling of uneasiness in her head and eyes, or loss of appetite. The 'signal' that arrives and becomes blood is *ch'i*. Two and a half days before this, concentrate on your exercises. After the menses begins to flow, the 'red dragon's' *yin-ching* cannot be seized. Reckless practice at this point has killed not a few people. You must now wait for two and a half days after the menses and cover [the private parts] with a piece of fine white silk. When the color appears golden yellow, this is a sign that the menses is over and you must use the method described earlier to mobilize it upward and cut it off. If you practice in this way for several months, the menses turns yellow, the yellow turns to white, and the white is transformed and becomes nothing. We can see, then, that this is the *tao* of existence reverting to nonexistence. A woman's blood acts as her *shen* organ, and thus it opens to the outside. After forty-nine, the 'waist' dries up and the blood is exhausted. There is no more life-giving potential. However, after long self-cultivation, one may rejuvenate the 'blood source' and be like a virgin again. This, then, is the marvel of existence arising out of non-existence. When you see it appear, then with one cut, it is transformed, and life is reborn. At this point, carry out the exercises for cultivating both 'intrinsic nature and life,' just as for men. When wind is born in the region of the navel, thunder sounds, and lightning strikes, this signals the transformation of the 'original spirit.' When clouds rise and mists drift, flowers laugh and birds fly, the 'highest source' is born. Who can comprehend this mystery?"

Taoist Master Lan said: "How is it that there are three [important centers] in a woman's life? These are the upper, middle, and lower. The upper is the '*yang* point,' the middle is the 'yellow house,' and the lower is the *tan-t'ien*. When young, a woman is ruled by the upper, in her later years by the middle, and in her middle years by the lower. Also a woman's interior is *yang* and her exterior *yin*. She must 'slay the red dragon' to preserve her body. In this way, *K'an* may be transformed into *Ch'ien*. After this, use the male exercises that, if practiced for one year, will bring success. This is because the 'golden elixir' is within her."

The *T'ai-yin hsiu-lien fa* says: "The '*yin* major' methods of training the physical body have much in common with those of the '*yang* major.' At the very beginning, close the eyes and concentrate the spirit, completely resting for a while to calm the heart and regulate the breathing. Then concentrate the spirit and focus it in the *ch'i-hsüeh* (between the two breasts and just above the solar plexus).[7] Cross the hands and hold the breasts, gently massaging 360 times. Gently inhale the *ch'i* upward from the *tan-t'ien* 24 times. Continuing to hold the breasts, reflect inwardly, and regulate the breathing. After a long time, the 'true breath' will move in and out naturally, opening and closing. This nourishes the body to the outermost reaches. The spirit and *ch'i* become full and the 'true *yang*' naturally abundant. The menses naturally ceases and the breasts shrink so that they resemble a man's. This is called 'slaying the red dragon.' If this practice is maintained for a long time, one no longer needs to hold the breasts and inhale *ch'i*. One need only concentrate the spirit in the *ch'i-hsüeh*, return the light and reflect inwardly. This is called the 'gate of the mysterious feminine.' The 'true breath' moves freely and easily; the mind is completely empty and one experiences profound peace. As the *yang-ch'i* streams upward, the 'water-wheel' turns backward, 10,000 purple clouds face the 'Jade Heaven,'[8] and 1,000 'white channels' converge on the *ni-wan*. One will sense a subtle light, neither internal nor external, that rises from the 'lower field' to the 'crimson palace' and *ni-wan*, and then descends the 'storied pavilion,' returning

to the 'sacred chamber of the golden embryo.' After ten months of labor, the *yang* spirit appears just as with a man. At the outset, there is no difference between the two."

The *Hsien-t'ien hsüan-wei* says: "Before the birth of a girl, when the mother and father have intercourse, the father's *ching* arrives first and the mother's blood thereafter. The blood surrounds the *ching* and a female body is formed.[9] At the moment of conception a female receives one *liang* of the mother's lead *ch'i*. First the right kidney is generated. A strand of silk is pulled from above, and the two eyes are generated; a strand of silk is attached from below, and the 'golden elixir' is generated. Following this, one *chu*[10] of menstrual fluid is generated within 12 days, and within 180 days, one *liang*. Thereafter, every fifteen days another *chu* is generated, and after every year another *liang*. At fourteen years of age, fourteen *liang* of menstrual fluid have accumulated in the 'sea of blood' that, together with the two *liang* carried over from the woman's fetal stage, makes the sum of one *chin*. Three hundred and eighty-four *chu* correspond to the 384 degrees of a complete cosmic cycle. There are 384 days in one year, and the lines of the hexagrams in the *I ching* also number 384, or the number of heaven and earth. When *yin* reaches its peak, *yang* is born. When the menses is complete the lead appears, and therefore at fourteen the menses descends. After the menses descends at fourteen, within twenty-six months seven and a half days, one *liang* of menstrual fluid is expended. At forty-nine years of age the expenditure is complete. Herein are contained secret transmissions which are difficult to fully explain."

In the *Hsiu-chen pien-nan* someone asks: "What is the difference between men and women when it comes to the first stage of training?" The answer: "For men, the most important thing at the outset is training the *ch'i*; for women, the most important thing is training the physical body. Training the *ch'i* means causing it to lie in hiding. In causing it to lie in hiding, one should seek to make it substantial and return it. When it is returned, one reaches the height of emptiness and total peace. By 'reverting to the root and returning to life,' the 'white tiger'[11] descends. Training the physical body means concealing the body. In concealing the body, one should seek to obliterate it. When the body is obliterated, the 'four elements' are all experienced as void. When the body has been totally stripped away, the 'red dragon' is slain. In men, after the 'white tiger' descends, they are transformed into the body of a youth, and the postnatal *ching* is not shed. In this way, they are able to form the elixir and lengthen their lives. In women, when the 'red channel' is cut, she is transformed into the body of a man and the impure blood naturally ceases to flow. She can escape from death and enter life. Therefore, a man's training is described as '*yang* major trains the *ch'i*,' and women's training is described as '*yin* major trains the body.'"

There is another question: "In training the physical body, does the woman not cause the *ch'i* to lie in hiding?" The answer: "Women are *yin* by nature and their *ch'i* is easily subdued, but the 'red channel' is most injurious to the *tao*. That is why the emphasis is on this. Therefore, at the outset, force is applied to the critical point. When the 'red channel' is cut, the *ch'i* is naturally obedient. It is not like a man who is by nature *yang* and whose *ch'i* is difficult to subdue. For example, if it takes a man three years to subdue his *ch'i*, then a woman can accomplish it in one. If a woman of great ability receives the secret teachings of a master and practices the '*yin* major' methods for training the body, within three to five years, she can realize the *tao*, and with less effort than a man. However, women of great ability are most difficult to find. What is difficult to find are those whose strength and courage are a hundred times that of a man, for only that will do. If their power is simply equal to a man's, there is absolutely no possibility of attainment."

There is another question: "If it is true that the 'great *tao*' makes no distinctions between man and woman, how is it that there are differences here?" The answer:

"The *tao* is the same but the practice is different. It is because their natures are different and their bodies dissimilar that the practices are so very different, even though there is but one *tao* of life."

It is asked: "How does one go about cutting down the 'red channel'?" The answer: "The 'red channel' is a transformation of the body's postnatal *yin-ch'i*. When the *yin-ch'i* is excited, the impure blood flows. If one wishes to transform the blood, first train the *ch'i*. When the *ch'i* is transformed, the blood returns upward and enters the breasts, where the red changes to white and circulates throughout the entire body. One is then free of the inflammatory influence of the fire of desire. When the fire of desire is extinguished, the 'true fire' manifests. From this point, everything is settled and proper, even and smooth. To then protect one's life and preserve one's body naturally presents no difficulty."

Master Li Ni-wan's Precious Raft of Women's Dual Practice

Ni-wan Li Tsu-shih nü-tsung shuang-hsiu pao-fa

Recorded and annotated by the Old Man of the Great Void, Master Shen Edited by the disciple, Min I-te

Chapter One

Ni-wan said: "The sequence of women's practice involves first stilling the thoughts and harmonizing the mind. When the thoughts are stilled and the mind harmonized, one can then begin the work of massage. The prohibitions of this method are to avoid heat in favor of cold. For women, blood is the basic element. Their natures incline to the *yin*, and *yin* by nature loves cold. If one does not employ massage to subtly activate the *ch'i* function, then one easily falls into pure *yin*. *Yin* is cold and cold is icelike. If one does not engage in exercise, this may produce phlegm congestion and blood obstructions, making it very difficult to carry out one's practice. One therefore must begin with stilling the thoughts and harmonizing the mind. Woman belongs to *K'un*, and *K'un* conceals the 'true fire.' When the fire lies in wait, there is prosperity, but when it flares up, it can melt metal. If one engages in exercises without harmonizing the mind, then metal encounters the encroaching fire, and one experiences the phenomenon known as 'cock's crow rises to heaven.'[1] Therefore, teachings on women's practice must begin from stilling the thoughts and harmonizing the mind. One should not hesitate to practice this often and long, for within stillness there is movement."

T'ai-hsü said: "When the thoughts are stilled the *ch'i* is pure; when the mind is regulated the *ch'i* is harmonious. If, following this, one practices massage, then there is the potential for generating *yang*. However, there is danger that the potential become depressed and impatience arises. Therefore, once again a warning is given. Moreover, women by nature incline to the cold and shun the hot, but when they first achieve stillness and harmony, and experience the pleasure of peace, some actually become depressed and impatient. This inevitably gives rise to thoughts of watering the 'true *yin*' and causes turbulence or stagnation of the pure *yin*. If one remains passive, the *yin* congeals, and if one does not move, the *yang* becomes depressed. This error is inevitable at the beginning of training, and one will not be able to get to the root cause of impatience and anxiety. It is an error to seek temporary coolness and comfort. Instead, one must step up one's practice, using the method of mobilizing the body's *ch'i* function. When the *ch'i* is set in motion, impatience naturally dissolves. To pursue the benefits of practice while failing to understand this can only exacerbate the error. This again becomes the cause of phlegm congestion and blood obstruction. Therefore, one must be strictly warned against this. The method is simply to apply massage to prevent the problem of obstruction. Also as a result of the natural tendency to be overzealous in practice and eager for progress, some engage in excessively aggressive massage. When the earth fire flares up, the common fire follows, resulting in the problem of melting the metal. Therefore, we are warned of the danger of 'cock's crow rising to heaven.' The 'cock's crow' represents a *yu* 酉 creature[2] that, if hard pressed, flies upward. Consequently, the marvel of stilling the thoughts and harmonizing the mind is emphasized again. Thus, from beginning to end, this precept represents the essential teachings of women's practice."

Chapter Two

Ni-wan said: "Women's practice begins with increasing the *yang* and ends with diminishing the *yin*. This method is highly secret, and those who understand it very few. Those who are deluded follow the teachings for men; those who are wise incline toward Ch'an Buddhism. From the fruits of practice one gains enlightenment. The ignorant fall into fiendish pleasures and stray far from the *tao*. For women, blood is the most fundamental element. When the blood flourishes, the *ching* is full; when the mind is cool, then blood is generated. The ancients said that when the fluids and blood are refined and the blood and *ching* transformed, the spirit is restored and becomes clear. When the blood is without fluid transformation and the fluid loses the spirit's heat, the fluid congeals and forms phlegm that flows into the spleen and stomach, rises as gas to the lungs and diffuses into the meridians. A hundred illnesses then arise like porcupine quills. The Five Viscera suffer calamity and the Six Bowels disaster. Therefore ancient teachings on the elixir say that one must first calm the mind, for when the mind is calm, the spirit becomes clear. Now the mind is cool. Therefore, one must wait for the mind to be cool and the fluids flowing. After this, concentrate on the 'breast stream,' massaging in a circular motion with the hands and fully activating the '*ch'i* function.' Now simply wait for the 'mist' to circulate throughout, and one will feel warm *ch'i* burning in the back. When there is smoke and flame in the 'double passes,' the power penetrates the passes. All of the congealed fluids in the passes flow into the 'breast stream' like a bubbling spring. After a short time, guide the 'true mind' to the 'south sea,' maintaining it there silently for approximately thirty-six breaths. Maintaining an attitude of relaxation, one feels at this point that it descends copiously and flows into the two sides of the waist, spinning left and right for approximately thirty-six breaths. Now concentrate on drawing it to the depths of the navel, revolving slowly eighteen times and rapidly forty-nine times. Observe warm *ch'i* in the *wei-lü* penetrating up the back. If the force is slow, one may use the technique of lifting and contracting the muscles that control the two functions of elimination and it will naturally pass through the *wei-lü* and ascend to the *chia-chi*. Rising to the head, it flows into the *ni-wan*. When one feels the *ni-wan* as expansive as the sea, one may pause to nourish it. Following this, it descends to the 'flowery pool' and 'crimson palace.' The 'isle of Jambudvipa'[3] is sprinkled with pearls. One becomes oblivious and experiences unconsciousness. Neither exhaling nor inhaling, neither inhaling nor exhaling, without consciously raising, one naturally raises, and without consciously swallowing, one naturally swallows. While remaining in this state, one experiences a taste both sweet and fragrant. The *ch'i* and spirit are full and harmonious, and the 'three *tan-t'ien*' are connected. When the whole world dissolves into obscurity, one must immediately look within and let go of all attachments. In a short time, one feels as if the whole body is empty and that the earth has disappeared. One is subtly invaded by cool *ch'i* as mist fills the four quarters of the world. Now suddenly, once again, the mist disperses and the clouds withdraw. Below appears the 'sea of intrinsic nature'[4] with clear waves of green. One should remain in a state free of all thoughts, oblivious to surroundings or feelings. Suddenly golden light is everywhere and a fine rain like pearls. Following the light as it flows downward, revolve it to the left and right until it is transformed into a pure white moon, which floats and sinks into a crystalline sea. Suddenly one awakens as from a dream." Ni-wan says: "At this point one must immediately reflect upon this body. Now the *ch'i* is refreshed, the spirit pure, and the whole body is harmonious and comfortable. When this is accomplished, the entire body is fused for a moment. By directing the mind to the 'feminine,' one experiences a feeling of peace and comfort. Now once again rub the hands and face and circulate the spirit around the abdomen. Raise the 'windlasses,'[5] putting each into motion for forty-nine breaths. Slowly rotate the waist and shake the knees and legs. Touch the tips of the toes in a sitting position for a count of twenty-four breaths and then stop. Practice this three times daily for a hundred days without interruption. In this way the foundation for becoming a heavenly immortal will be established."

T'ai-hsü said: "The general outline of this chapter is what the ancients called 'ascending the heavenly ladder.' Herein are the elixir teachings of the great *tao*. Other than this, there are no great works on the subject.[6] Students should study until every word is fully grasped, comprehending the meaning in silence and serenity. After reading it ten or a hundred times a day, when one comes to practice the exercises, it will be like entering upon a familiar path, and one will not lose the way. Even if what one actually experiences is somewhat different, with repetition everything will fall into place. Students must strictly avoid reading this as if it were the novel *Hsi yu chi* (*Journey to the West*).[7] Elixir classics for men come by the cartload and are piled to the rafters, but those for women could hardly fill a single volume. If one is able to obtain such works as the *Chin-hua chih-chih i-shih-pa tse* (Eighteen precepts on the golden flower insturctions),[8] this may indeed be considered a secret transmission. By combining such a guide with this work, we may say that the secret teachings of the *tao* of immortality thus are complete. If one is able to obtain only the *Chin-hua chih-chih*, this is merely the way of the earthly and human immortals."

Chapter Three

Ni-wan said: "'Dual practice' for men does not employ a crucible. Those who use the crucible never succeed in achieving the *tao*. 'Augmenting the oil' is a minor method and not a true teaching. The true teaching is that the 'three powers'[9] are all within the body. It is the same with women's 'dual practice.' Without all three, the chances of developing the elixir are as one grain in a granary. When it is thoroughly cooked in the great stove of nature, then one may eat." He also said: "We may know that the 'quinquennial assembly'[10] exists in the world and that from the beginning 'seeds'[11] fill the universe. Borrow an altar as stove and crucible. When the stove is eliminated, the true transmission is lost." He also said: "This chant of mine will startle each of the eight classes of divine beings.'[12] I might be accused of hollow cant and expose myself to divine retribution, but I must state that I have received the imperial decree of the Jade Pure Holy Mother who, regretting the disappearance of the great *tao*, ordered Pu Erh Sheng Ku to solemnly proclaim and orally transmit it to me. Her intent was to reveal it directly without the use of pseudonym and thus avoid confusing future generations." She said: "How could those who have realized a body beyond the body and who have forgotten their physical forms stoop to the likes of 'Solitary practice is not the highest *tao*,' and 'Those of the same species need one of their own kind?'" Her teachings state: "The *Ch'ien* essence[13] is obtained from the 'summit';[14] the *K'un* essence[15] is lost through the 'feminine';[16] and the human essence fills the universe. The 'three essences' are all under the command of one mind. This means simply that the mind is still and the body is without blockages. Movement and stillness unite with the 'eternal reality.'[17] When the self disappears, the 'essences' naturally fuse. When the 'essences' fuse, the One does also. The one 'essence' consists of emotion and intrinsic nature. Emotion is the essence of intrinsic nature. Intrinsic nature is talent and natural endowment. If one can be without the 'essences,' one can attain the whole of the truth and naturally ascend to the highest rank. This then is the proclamation of the Jade Pure Holy Mother transmitted by Pu Erh Sheng Ku. May those who are able follow it."

T'ai-hsü said: "'Those of the same species need one of their own kind' is the principle of T'ai-chi [the Great Ultimate]. This is what is meant by the essence of the two fives[18] marvelously uniting and fusing together. The inner and outer chapters of the *Wu-chen p'ien* and the entire *Ts'an-t'ung ch'i* describe nothing but this principle. Because it has been misinterpreted, we have the shameful practices of [Chang] San feng. Having now received the instructions of the master, the spiritual transmissions of countless generations are clearly revealed. How fortunate I, Ping, am to have received them! ('Ping' is T'ai-hsü's sect name.) How fortunate is the world to be thus enlightened! This is the final great work for both men and women. However, without great intelligence, few will be able to realize it. As I, Ping, understand its fundamental principle, the method is simply to be without attachment to the illusion of self or material things. When things and self are both forgotten, then the true One manifests. After the true One manifests, if we are able to follow and maintain it, then the One naturally dissolves, and transformation and creation proceeds as if without end. Within this great *tao*, nothing compares to the 'great quinquennial Buddhist assembly,' or what the Taoist elixir books call 'the living dragon and tiger fill all of space.' As I understand the concept of this 'assembly,' it is necessary to follow the ancient system, for only then will there be no regrets. The significance of the 'assembly' is most secret, but the signs are most obvious. Do not misunderstand this. What is meant by 'secret' refers to the secret in the mind. The success or failure cannot be known by any other. What is meant by 'obvious' is that it is as obvious as a marketplace. Not a single activity can be concealed. Only by following the prescribed method can one avoid the world's censure. Alas, how painstaking the wise ones were and how farsighted."

Chapter Four

Ni-wan said: "Yes, the sages of old had a saying that until all substance is transformed the *tao* cannot be fulfilled, and until one's practice is perfected the attainment of the goal is impossible. To progress by skipping levels only proves the error of the path. Attainment before perfection is a lesser level, a lesser fruit. Students must take seriously this compassionate advice. One must first refine the 'dharma-body'[19] so that it is strong and secure, and only then is the foundation laid for receiving training. If this foundation is not established, the previous chapter remains meaningless. The previous chapter was devoted solely to the work of transformation, which proceeds step by step beginning with the physical body. That is, the insubstantial resides within the substantial, or the process of reaching the insubstantial from the substantial. This then is the training method of the heavenly immortal."

T'ai-hsü said: "The 'dharma-body' is the body beyond the body. This body is not obtained by concentration nor brought about through training. The secret teaching lies in cultivation of the 'true.' What is cultivated is none other than the physical body, and the teaching is simply to train the physical body. Within and without are chaste and pure. It is a body, but is not a body; it is not a body, but is a body. This is what is meant by the body not existing during practice but existing again when practice ceases. When the body ceases to exist, then all sensations of cold and heat, pain or irritation are not experienced as one's own. This is what is known as experience without attachment. How is this attained? The method is simply for the spirit to dwell in voidness. When the body is not a body it is mastered. When the true One is apprehended, then apart from the One

all is illusion. This is even greater mastery. When one's practice reaches the level that there is neither far nor near, inner nor outer, this is even more advanced. When one's practice reaches the level that there is no going and no coming, no entering and no emerging, then far and near, inner and outer are eliminated. Beyond this, if one can practice to the point of eliminating origination and destruction, movement and stillness, then one is truly without going and coming, emerging and entering. This then is the pure realm of the 'dharma-body,' but it is not found outside of the 'physical body.'"[20]

Chapter Five

Ni-wan said: "Chen-yang's words are true indeed. (Chen-yang is the name given to T'ai-hsü by Ni-wan.) If one practices diligently in this way, the 'dharma-body' naturally will be complete. If one perseveres without retreating, there will be a body beyond the body. You must understand that the wise ones of old rely upon the writings of later generations to fulfill the *tao*. These are simply shortcuts to fulfilling the *tao*. However, the 'true *yin*' and 'true *yang*' in one body are limited. To apply oneself to refining them is to simultaneously train the postnatal and the prenatal. If one faithfully practices this teaching, one will surely see the cumulative effect of days and months. What a pity, though, that the body's postnatal mundane accretions also are subject to gradual increase. Even if one is dauntless in carrying out one's practice, throughout the ages, there have been many who have met with misfortune. What a great pity! The 'true prenatal' within the body can be calculated, but the 'false postnatal' increases without measure. How much more so when training does not begin from the 'prepubescent true,' but from the stained and defiled. Few can avoid this. On this account, one may have great fears for the world."

T'ai-hsü said: "When drinking water or soup, you yourself can tell whether it is cold or hot. When the 'dharma-body' is complete, there is no need to ask others concerning the 'teaching on tending and protecting' and the 'timing of reining in and relaxing.' Surely one's own experience is sufficient. Even if the 'dharmabody' is not complete, the teaching and the timing are appropriate only for adjusting the waxing and waning within one body. It is simply a matter of obstruction and openness, rising and falling, cold and warm, and dry and moist. In carrying out these practices, is there anything to it but opening the obstructions, warming the cold, and moistening the dry, round and round exchanging positions? The main principle is concentration and softness and not to be seduced by worldly things. Harmonize the mind *ch'i* and unify the body's *ch'i* function. Know that this is a borrowed instrument. As for employing such techniques as massage, raising and constricting, and concentration, these simply activate the *ch'i* function. When the *ch'i* function is activated, the method is based on concentrating [the *ch'i*] and [developing] softness. As soon as a thought arises, it is transformed immediately, and as soon as it is restrained, it ceases. Be careful to avoid 'riding an ox to go in search of an ox.' To exercise restraint without understanding cessation is called 'mounting a head on top of the head.'[21] This is like empty and full, rising and falling, warm and cool, flat and embellished, which are known by one's own experience. In all things, avoid impediment and obstruction; just as in restraint, one must understand cessation. Taking this as a standard for self-cultivation, there need be no worry over whether one will escape death or not. This is my opinion."

Chapter Six

Ni-wan said: "Yes, your words are quite true. The flight of the woman's spirit and the congealing of the man's *ching* are both caused by 'mounting[22] a head on top of the head.' What the spirit adores is *ching*. When the spirit is concentrated and the *ching* unruffled, there is peace. When the *ching* is dry and the spirit isolated then it flies. The ignorant take this for liberation. What a great pity! Thus we

may know the disadvantage of excessive massage and concentration. What is the reason? The woman is *yin* on the inside and *yang* on the outside.[23] In relation to the trigrams, she belongs to *Li*[24] and her 'true *yin*' is constantly lost through the 'monthly signal.' Therefore, when tranquility surpasses activity, she enjoys good fortune, but when activity surpasses tranquility, there is disaster. For man, *ching* is the root, and for woman, blood. *Ching* flourishes when warm, and blood is generated when cool. Knowing this, one knows how to cultivate them. There are two reasons why women's practice must not forsake massage and concentration. The first is that it opens the *ch'i* function, and thus allows free flow in the meridians. The second is that by refining the fluids, it prevents them from becoming blocked and converting into phlegm. In this way, the fluids are transformed into blood. There also are two reasons why the wise ones of old took tranquility and concentration as their first principles. When the ruler is at peace, his subjects all will be at peace. Therefore, when the spirit is clear, it does not fly away. Furthermore, wisdom is born of tranquility, and when one is not disturbed by passions, life may be securely guarded. This, then, is the teaching of the 'dual cultivation' of one individual. When the *ch'i* function is open and the mind pure, and fullness and harmony are added to this, then with the passage of not days but months of continued devotion, one day the whole body will be as if empty, the 'three elixir fields' will be connected, and one will feel only that every limb, every joint, and every orifice is bright and shining. When one's practice reaches this level, the body beyond the body will be prepared. If one persists without backsliding, the spirit will be sufficient and the *ch'i* full, the thoughts will not run wild and the spirit will not follow the thoughts. The blood will be produced in abundance, and the 'true *yin*' will be sufficient. The *ch'i* and *ching* naturally fill heaven and earth. However, if following the thoughts they fly away, one then falls into the second rank. This is what the elixir books call, 'the spirit escaping its shell.' 209

Students must not fail to be on guard against this."

T'ai-hsü said: "I have heard from the masters that the spirit is the spirit of the mind. Holding steadily and not flying away means that it cherishes the *ching* and holds steadily. As soon as the *ching* is exhausted, the spirit flies away. The *ching* is the *ching* of the kidneys. The noncongealing of the *ching* is accomplished through the control of the spirit. The congealed *ching* is not the 'original *ching*,' but belongs to the category of fluids, or blood that is not yet perfected. As soon as the 'true spirit' departs, this *ching* congeals. The *I ching* says: 'One *yin* and one *yang* is called the *tao*.' The chant says: 'Half a *chin* and eight *liang* are the beginning of the true essence.' It also is said that *yin* alone cannot live, and *yang* alone cannot survive. The trigrams *Ch'ien*, *K'un*, *K'an*, *Li*, *Chen*, *Hsün*, *Tui*, and *Ken*; earth and heaven, sun and moon; intrinsic nature and life, man and woman; one *yin* and one *yang*; round and round, end and beginning—this is called the constant *tao*. If there is the slightest distortion[25] in our practice or the slightest imbalance in our influence, then the whole becomes a corrupt regime. In general, at the outset of practice, one should strive for complementary union within one's own body. However, there is a prescribed order in this. The first is called 'true' and the later 'false.' Originally, the false is begotten by the true, and the true is also called the false. When the false reverts to the true, it is called the 'primal source.' If in 'gathering the medicine' one misses the proper time or indulges in fantasies, one will fall into erroneous byways and suffer common delusions. Serious cases may result in personal disaster, but there still is hope of rescue. In more severe cases, nothing is worse than approaching the perfection of one's practice and entering the state of pure abstraction, only to have one thought go awry and the whole enterprise become skewed. Even if one attempts to halt the process, it will be too late. For a woman this will result in the spirit taking flight, and for a man in congealing of the *ching*. Can one afford to be less than cautious! Alas, we must understand that Ts'ui [Hsi-fan's] *Ju yao ching* emphasizes 'intrinsic nature' and 'life,' not spirit and *ch'i*. To speak of spirit and *ching* is like using "yellow leaves" to cure a child's crying. Without understanding the 'true gold,' how can one distinguish the 'yellow leaves.' Chung Tsu has said: "The 'four elements' in the body all belong to *yin*, but we do not know what is that thing called '*yang-ching*.' If one is fated to meet an enlightened teacher, then realizing the *tao* and gaining immortality lies simply in serving the body." He also said: "Existence and nonexistence interpenetrate and form the basis of the elixir; the hidden and the revealed support each other, becoming the gold in water. Do not insist on clinging to the body in speaking of this *tao*, for cultivating only one thing leads to isolated *yin*." Combining these instructions of the master, we may ask if the "true seeds" are present. Thus it is not to be found outside of this body. How profound this principle!

Chapter Seven

Ni-wan said: "Quite so. The *Tao te ching* says: 'There is something that comes into being from the primal chaos. It is born before heaven and earth. Silent and rarified, it stands alone, immutable. It travels in endless cycles without wearying and may serve as mother of the world. I do not know its name, but if name it I must, I call it *tao*.'[26] It also says: 'Though obscure and indistinct, there is something there; though invisible and imperceptible, there is a subtle essence. This essence is supremely true and the reality at the center of things.'[27] Now this one 'thing' is locked in the mountain of physical form. The ancients had a saying, 'Seek it not in the body, neither gather it outside the body.' Dimly and obscurely, it seems to exist in the midst of the empty and invisible. However, it is not outside the orifice of the 'mysterious pass.' This orifice is so vast that nothing is beyond it and so small that nothing is within it. You cannot grasp it with the mind or open it by circulation. The method is simply to wait for the body to reach a state of emptiness and all cares are laid to rest. In the midst of the void, forget the void; in the midst of stillness, forget stillness. The spirit naturally enters the shell and the *ch'i* emerges from within. The *ch'i* mass, as amorphous as mist, is without head or tail. This is the first appearance of the 'thing' and the first sign of the body beyond the body. Without opening this orifice, even if one is able to 'slay the dragon' and become divine, it is no more than the illusion of 'yellow leaves.' How can this be called 'forming the fetus'? How can this be called 'entering the gate'? What has been described in preceding chapters still is merely 'yellow leaves' and not the 'true gold.'"

T'ai-hsü said: "Even if massage is carried out improperly, to abandon it would result in a failure to activate the *ch'i* function. Even if concentration is carried out mistakenly, to abandon it would result in insufficient *ch'i* and *ching*. Pursuing our practice further, even reaching the level of understanding that the material world exists yet does not exist is still not considered the final goal by the Master, for it still is merely a matter of 'this side.' Nevertheless, when the matter of 'this side' is complete, then 'that side' is easily opened. If 'that side' is not open, then the *ch'i* function is many mountains away. Its opening is accomplished by guiding it with the mind, and then it naturally rushes in from all sides. Therefore, although separated by mountains and lakes, as soon as the *ch'i* function is opened, it is like meeting face to face. What is the method for achieving this?" Hearing this the Master said: 'Projecting the light to attract it, concentrating the mind to wait for the proper moment, descending when it rises and returning when it retreats—this is merely cultivated ability and confers no benefit. The method is simply to be perfectly still in the midst of chaos, to maintain an attitude of emptiness and receptivity. As soon as the *ch'i* function is activated, one feels a pleasurable sensation. Now continue to remain motionless and make a mental effort to secure it, harboring and refining it internally. From the trigram *K'un* (The Receptive) one reaches *Ken* (Keeping Still).

Boarding the raft and entering the Milky Way, one senses a golden light like a flash of lightning and cool *ch'i* spreading in space like clouds or mist that encircle the whole body. At this point, avoid all human judgments, whether of admiration or doubt. As soon as a thought arises, discard it. One will feel as if there is a kind of *ch'i* function that fills one completely, so that there is no inner and outer and no boundaries. Suddenly a host of transformations appear, too numerous to count. They are indescribable and inexplicable. However, there also are those who experience total silence without flashes of light, as if plunged in lacquer black night. All these are called 'mysterious manifestations.' They also are called the 'signs of perfection of the other shore.'[28] In reality, these are also images of the perfection of the enlightened self.' It is called the 'three realms of the Avatamsaka, Surangama, and Lotus Sutras'[29] and the mysterious lands of the 'three isles'[30] and 'ten regions.'[31] In reality, this is the 'transformation *ch'i* function' of the self of the other shore. The 'other shore' is not actually another shore, but at the same time this is actually proof of the other shore. The Master said: "Someone once asked Yüan-chün about perfect purity, and Yüan-chün answered: 'This is it; this is it!'" She also said: "Is not men's practice just the same?"

Chapter Eight

Ni-wan said: "There is a verse that goes, 'Upside down and downside up, this is the work of *Ch'ien* and *K'un*. The two *ch'i* exchange *ching*, combining *Ken* and metal.'" He also said: "The eagle catches the sparrow and the hawk gets the cold crow. The fine within the fine; the wonder within the wonder. This is none other than knowing the white, but keeping to the black; knowing the male, but playing the female. What is this but maintaining nonexistence and preserving existence?"

T'ai-hsü said: "Though women may not be able to daily recite the *Lao tzu* and *Chuang tzu*, nevertheless, the *Ch'ing-ching ching* should be thoroughly studied. The household rules for women should be respected, but is there nothing beyond this save the two classics, *K'un-ning* and *Chen-i*? However, if one's 'intrinsic nature' is not thoroughly developed, one's life will be difficult to preserve, and if one's discipline is not strict, one's work will not be serious. The Master's meaning in quoting these verses is most esoteric and profound. Can this be easy to fathom? Even if one was to reveal the highest method, how could the common woman comprehend it? Many are those for whom it would be utterly unattainable. Thus containing the whole of the *Huo chi*,[32] thoroughly study the *Huang Ti yin-fu* [*ching*], the *Ts'an-t'ung* [*ch'i*], and *Wu-chen* [*p'ien*]. Only then can one begin to discuss what is set forth in this chapter. Let me generally reveal some clues. Upside down and downside up, round and round it goes. Perceiving the one within the one and apprehending the one before us, everything that strikes us is simply the two *ch'i*. When their essences interact, myriad manifestations are produced, and there is nothing that does not appear to us. This is able to contain the whole universe.[33] The manifestations of the universe are brilliant and resplendent. Brilliance and splendor are the beginning of the 'other shore,' but do not be led astray by the beginning. The original beginning is my beginning. The beginning of the beginning is not one and one. One and one and one are not complete. How can one say that stillness and immobility represents an inferior level of achievement? The small swallow takes after the great swallow; the cold crow suffers the cold. If one is not hungry, it is because the time has not come, but when the time comes then one may eat. This is the wonder within the wonder, and the mystery within the mystery. Knowing the white, one holds to the black. Through total forgetfulness one gains perfect completeness. If we ask him what is gained, it is that absolute nothingness is absolute possession. This then is the Master's subtle meaning. Thus, existence and nonexistence are mutually dependent; both taking and giving up must follow the One. If the material body is not transformed, there is no hope for success."

Chapter Nine

Ni-wan said: "How wonderful are your words! It is said that wishing to transcend the mundane, one must first purify the mundane mind. Then one must come to see the 'three realms'[34] as void, but without violating the duties of a woman. Do not flatter the ghosts and gods. Be filial and benevolent, never offending one's elders. Be obedient and proper, never violating the *tao* of *K'un*. Follow reason in your activities and be like a Buddha in your stillness. While wielding the dustpan and broom, dwell in the mystery of the *tao*. While managing the stove and cooking fire, realize the spiritual 'firing time.' The *Odes* say: 'As majestic and magnificent as great mountains or the Yellow River, but how unfortunate she was, and what is to be done?'[35] Is this not a warning to later generations?"

T'ai-hsü said: "The principles contained in this chapter are most subtle. Among Taoists and Buddhists, few are those who adhere to the duties of womanhood; and few are those who understanding the true dharma-nature of reality[36] are able to serve their masters and elders with gentleness and obedience. For the most part, they are envious and cruel, and violate the norms of propriety. Disciples and masters have no respect for morality, and thereby cast themselves into the deepest hell. Is this not a pity!"

Correct Methods for Women's Practice

Nü-kung cheng-fa

by Ling Yang Tao Jen (Ho Hsien-ku)
Edited by Ch'en Ying-ning

Introduction

At sixteen a man's *ching* becomes functional. When the *ching* is full it is shed. At fourteen a women's menses becomes operational. When the menses is full it overflows. If people wish to avoid shedding and overflowing, they must understand wind and fire. Fire is the "original spirit," and wind is the "true breath." Bringing the spirit and breath into complementary balance is accomplished by inner awareness. The method is to direct the gaze from the "mysterious orifice" in the eye to the *ch'i-hsüeh*. The concentration of the *ch'i* and spirit comes from the act of mental absorption. When the natural wind and fire interact continuously, it transforms the *ching* and increases the *ch'i*, transforms the *ch'i* and increases the spirit. When the spirit has been perfected and the body transformed, then there is a body beyond the body.

The aphorism says:

If one can but keep the spirit and breath in
  constant mutual gaze,
Then the body will be changed and the
  "jade liquid" flow.
Relying solely on the "Cave of Life Everlasting," We refine the *yang* spirit that
  manifests at the "Gate of the Highest."
We must understand that all creatures that
  live must die,
But we must know that when the "original
  spirit" dies it is born again.
If we can cause the "spirit of the mind" to
  dwell within the *ch'i*,
Then the "infant" will be securely
  nourished and success is assured.
If one practices in this way,
What danger that the inner elixir fail?

The method is to burst open the *Jen* and *Tu* channels. The circulation is within and without the "middle pass." It is just that here women's practice is a little different. The exercises begin at the breast, or "upper pass," proceed to the navel, or "middle pass," and end by returning to the womb, or "lower pass." Later the middle and lower are transformed into one point. A man refines his *ching*. This is called "*yang* major refines the *ch'i*." The woman refines her blood. This is called "*yin* major refines the body."

The secret of fire and wind is knowing the appropriate use of "civil and martial." The "martial" is employed in the middle and the "civil" at the beginning and end. While practicing "cosmic orbit" circulation, do not forget both "observation and stillness." In one day there are

twelve [Chinese] hours. Whatever the mind conceives can be accomplished. Whoever can grasp both the prenatal and the postnatal *ch'i* will feel as if intoxicated the whole day.

Common women in the world are too deeply stained by custom. They covet flesh foods and are easily prey to lustful thoughts. They spy someone and are given in marriage, but in their hearts they have regrets. In the spring they are moved to love, but in the autumn they are wounded, even to the point of suffering consumption. They indulge in raw and cold foods, which bring on irregular menses. Added to this, they are easily led astray, so that both their bodies and reputations are destroyed. They spend the whole day harboring hatred. People should take a lesson from this and not create negative *karma*. Those who forbear know peace within themselves; those who repent know happiness within themselves. The mind is content and the heart like still water. One should constantly emulate the golden statue with mouth sealed and tongue hidden. In movement or stillness, in words and deeds, maintain fidelity and preserve decorum. Break down the barrier of the emotions and leap out of the sea of desires. In the human body, puberty is the wellspring for the cultivation of life. By urgently seeking the proper training methods, this may be transformed through refinement into the "true essence." When practices are performed over a long period in this world, the spirit returns to heaven above. You seekers of the way should each motivate yourselves.

*Chapter 1. Understanding the
Foundation and Purifying the Heart*

If you wish to understand the foundation, you must first purify the heart. When not a speck of dust remains to pollute us, we will never go astray in the world. When the heart is empty and the desires purified, there naturally is a sense of peace and tranquility. With the clarity of a mirror or the transparency of water, the heart is now pure. We may now speak of understanding the foundation. Woman   *213* belongs by nature to the *K'un* principle. Her back is *yin* and her front *yang*. The breasts are the external orifices, and the "breast stream" the internal point. The point is located six-and-a-half-tenths of an inch on the sixth story of the "storied pavilion," facing the "palace gate towers" of the tenth story. In sitting, first "straddle the crane," with legs and knees placed one upon the other. Tightly lock the "lower pass" (the "fountain gate") to secure the primal *ch'i*. Move the "upper pass" (the "breast stream") and avoid leakage from the lower. The "middle pass" is one and three-tenths of an inch within the navel.

If one desires to avoid the "five leakages," one must guard the "three passes."[1] The senses of hearing and vision should be constantly directed within, and the mouth closed without speech. The *ch'i* should be concentrated in the "breast stream" and the spirit focused in the "golden chamber."[2] One's "intrinsic nature" is settled in the "sea of enlightenment,"[3] and the consciousness fixed in the "palace of the elixir."[4] Revert to the One and concentrate the mind. The "Golden Mother"[5] focuses the attention in the heart, Lao tzu in the "orifices," and the Buddha on the end of the nose. The end is the "tail of the nose," which is called the "root of the mountain"[6] and it is located between the two eyes. The sages have considered this the point at which to practice stillness. If one can faithfully maintain this, it is the locus of the highest good.

When [a boy] is sixteen, observe the term just before the onset [of puberty]. The "seven emotions" are absent and the "five *skandas*"[7] void. The heart is always content, and one is sprightly and full of life, like my teacher, Master Lü. When the "*tao* source" is jade pure, concentrate the spirit at the *ch'i-hsüeh*, focusing on the "lower *tan-t'ien*." Consciousness issues from between the eyes and is drawn down to the *ch'i-hsüeh*. The prenatal *ch'i* arrives, and the postnatal *ch'i* enters. Painstakingly preserve them.

The woman's "breast stream" is her upper elixir point. The location behind the navel and in front of the kidneys is the "middle pass." The "feminine gate" is the "lower pass." The womb is the crucible. Now draw the consciousness down from between the eyes to the "breast stream" and then to the navel and the womb, creating a single connecting channel. The "primordial seeds" are the source of life. The man's original *ching* is the highest *yang-ch'i*; the woman's true blood is the highest *yin-ching*. These are the treasures that give life to the body and are the root of the myriad transformations. The man stores it in the *ming-men*, that is, the *ch'i-hsüeh*; the woman stores it in the "feminine gate," that is, within the womb. When passion stirs, it is difficult to preserve them, but when the heart is still, they may be protected. However, one needs both wind and fire to refine and transform them so that they are forever preserved.

Chapter 2. Cultivating the Menses

At fourteen a woman's menses begins and her blood becomes deficient. Although every month the menstrual flow is replenished, in reality, every month brings injury and waste. Postmenopausal women who desire to cultivate the menses through refinement and transformation must first cause it to return again. Refrain from eating raw or cold foods to avoid stagnation of the blood. However, because the menstrual flow is the very foundation of life, the method for beginning to refine it seems to involve deliberate action. It transforms and increases the blood and *ch'i* so that there will be no further injury. Existence is the beginning[8] of nonexistence; nonexistence is the end of existence.

Where there is a specific point, use effort so that the postnatal *ch'i* can flow freely; where there is no specific point, use the mind so that the prenatal *ch'i* becomes full. Wherever the mind goes the eye follows, and the spirit and breath are coordinated. It transforms the blood and increases the *ch'i*, refines the *ch'i* and nourishes the spirit. Begin with the "middle pass" and deliberately raise it straight up thirty-six times. Raising it to the "upper pass," cause it to revolve thirty-six times each to the left and right. Now direct it to the breasts and revolve it thirty-six times each to the left and right. If the "vale of heaven" is not hot, the *ch'i* has not yet risen. If the "earth fountain" is not hot, the *ch'i* has not yet descended. The mind should direct the eye to focus on the "upper and lower passes." Interlace the fingers of the two hands and place them over the area below the navel and above the "fountain." Now, as if using conscious effort, raise it directly up thirty-six times. Bring it up to the "breast stream" and then to the inside of the external orifice of the breasts. Revolve to the left and right each thirty-six times.

Chapter 3. Training Methods for Slaying the Dragon

The secret method for "slaying the dragon" involves deliberate action. At the *tzu* and *wu* hours sit as if "riding the crane" and knock the teeth together seventy-two times to open the "lung *shu*" points. Using your postnatal *ch'i*, breathe through the nose naturally for a count of thirty-six, and the meridians of the whole body will open. The heel should firmly press against the "gate of the fountain." Interlace the fingers and place them under the navel. Now deliberately raise [the *ch'i*] straight up thirty-six times. Bringing it to the "upper pass," use the imagination to revolve it in each direction thirty-six times. Now extend it to the "middle pass" and revolve it with the imagination in each direction thirty-six times. The hands press up against heaven in a relaxed manner thirty-six times and likewise in an urgent manner thirty-six times.

When there is a sudden movement in the *wei-lü*, place the two hands on the sides of the waist, gnash the teeth tightly, and raise the shoulders straight up. When the *chia-chi*, "double passes," and lung *shu* points all feel moved, then deliberately straighten the head and back, and raise [the *ch'i*] to the *yü-chen*, and then all the way to the *ni-wan*. Now press the lower lip tightly against the upper lip,

while consciously sending the true *ch'i* up to the *ni-wan* and down to the nasal orifice.

When the tongue touches the "bridge of heaven," the "sweet dew" comes naturally. With one contraction of the nose, the saliva is deliberately swallowed and directed down to the area below the navel. Place the hand on the female part, and with the idea of using effort, [press] all the way to the womb thirty-six times. When the "sweet dew" enters the crucible, the hot *ch'i* begins to circle about. The heel of the foot should be pressed tightly, and body and mind should both be calm. The womb is now settled and peaceful. As Wei Yüan-chün said: "When the treasure returns to the 'north sea,'[9] then one is at peace and everything is in its proper place."

Chapter 4. Training the Breasts and Returning to Youth

The breasts connect with the heart and lungs above and reach down to the "sea of *ch'i*" below. If one wishes to train the breasts so that they acquire the form of a young girl's, the work consists of "slaying the dragon." Increase and direct the "sweet dew" straight to the "crimson palace." Focus the mind on the two breasts and revolve to the left and right thirty-six times each. The lips [are pressed together] above and below, the teeth are clamped together tightly, and the nostrils are closed. Use internal breathing.

Apply the palms of the two hands to the breasts, massaging each in a circular motion to the left and right seventy-two times. First relaxed and then harder; first light and then heavy. In 100 days your training will be complete and they will resemble the form of walnuts. Long ago Feng Hsien Ku's *Lien ju chüeh* (Secret transmission on training the breasts) said:

> The left is the sun and the right the moon:
>   a *yin* and *yang*.
> The internal circulation of the nasal breath
>   is called "turning the Big Dipper."
> If you want *yin* and *yang* to revert to the
>   sun and moon,
> The true fire must be cultivated in the two
>   palms.[10]

Chapter 5. Setting up the Crucible and Forming the Fetus

For men, the "lower, middle, and upper *tan-t'ien*" are the crucibles. For women, the "womb, navel, and breast stream" are the crucibles. The womb is one and three-tenths inches from the lower *tan-t'ien* and two and eight-tenths inches from the navel. It is also located below the "upper pass," or breasts. Above is the "breast stream," in the middle is the navel, and below the womb. Its position extends from the exterior to the interior, but its function is from the interior to the exterior. The male is without womb and instead takes the *tan-t'ien* as the great crucible. This is why although the name is the same, what they point to is different.

Master Lü's *Chin-hua chi* says that the two eyes "return the light." From the point between the eyes concentrate the mind and focus it on the lower *tan-t'ien*. After the woman has carried out the training methods for "slaying the dragon," she should relax for a few moments and then "return the light" from the point between the eyes and deliberately direct it to the "breast stream" thirty-six times. Then direct it in turn to the navel and lower *tan-t'ien*, or womb, each thirty-six times. Use the mind to draw the water of the "flowery pool" to the upper crucible, and draw the secretions of the heart and lungs there as well. Consciously direct the "true gold from the middle of the sea" to the upper crucible. After this, deliberately direct it down to the middle crucible, and then to the great crucible, where it is revolved eighteen times. When it is hot within, the fire rises; when the crucible has been established, the fetus begins to form.

Chapter 6. Natural Regulation of the Fetal Breath

If you are able to avoid such errors in breathing as panting, roughness, and shallowness, then the nasal breath will become regulated. When every breath reverts to the root, this then is the fetal breath. As long as the breath moves, there is pulse in the blood vessels, but when the breath is stationary, the pulse stops. Ancient texts declare: "Consuming *ch'i* does not lead to long life, one must subdue the *ch'i*." When the true breath circulates, one can then subdue the *ch'i*. After practicing "slaying the dragon," rest for a while. When the "seven emotions" no longer manifest and random thoughts no longer arise, then press the foot against the "gate of the fountain," bring the lips together to conceal the teeth, and let the mind follow the vision in focusing on the three and eight-tenths of an inch that separate the heart and kidneys. Spin [the *ch'i*] to the left and revolve it to the right for forty-nine breaths. When the "sweet dew" comes naturally, imagine swallowing and raising [the *ch'i*]. "Raising" means causing it to revert to the navel. The *ch'i* then becomes concentrated and after a long time turns into the "fetal breath." By not attempting to exhale, the exhalation comes naturally; by not attempting to inhale, the inhalation comes naturally; and by not attempting to raise anything, the ascent comes naturally. Within the "gate of the feminine" is a natural opening and closing. Naturally and gently, the elixir comes into being of itself.

Chapter 7. Return of the Fluid and Formation of the Fetus

When a man practices the "water wheel," the spirit is fire and the breath is wind. What he daily gathers is returned to the stove, where it is refined into the "lesser medicine." When the *ch'i* is abundant and the spirit perfected, the "greater medicine" forms. When the "five dragons serve the sage"[11] and the circulation becomes natural, then move from the lower to the middle [*tan-t'ien*]; as the *ch'i* increases and the spirit is nourished, now shift to the "upper *tan-t'ien*." First penetrating the "gate of the highest," the "jade liquid returning elixir" like clarified butter irrigates the crown of the head. When the *yang* spirit has been thoroughly tempered, this then is called becoming an immortal.

If one asks what is the woman's "jade liquid returning elixir," it is the "red dragon" that has been transformed into the "white phoenix." When it fills the "lower field," it is like gestating a fetus. After one's practice is complete, the *ch'i* is transformed and the spirit becomes luminous and rounded to perfection. As it passes through the "gate of the highest," it approaches the state of *yang* spirit. The "jade liquid returning elixir" like clarified butter irrigates the crown of the head. Never departing from the practice above, one must emulate the Bodhisattva Kuan-yin atop Mount Potala.[12]

Chapter 8. Refining and Transforming the Yang Spirit

First transforming the *ching* and increasing the *ch'i*, then refining the *ch'i* into spirit: this is the man's inner elixir. First transforming the blood and increasing the *ch'i*, then refining the *ch'i* into spirit: this is the woman's inner elixir. Both use fire and wind. As for the woman "slaying the dragon," it consists of transforming the blood into *ch'i*. It also is said that one must regulate the breath and transform the *ch'i* into spirit. If the *ch'i* is not refined, the spirit will not be sufficient, and the body too will not be healthy. If one serves only the *yin* spirit, the *yang* spirit will not come into being. The method consists of entering the stillness of meditation and using the "Six Character Secret Transmission."[13] Mentally mobilize the sound *an*, arising in the navel, and fix it in the "middle *tan-t'ien*." Now revolve it to the left and right, each thirty-six times. Mentally mobilize the sound *ma* and place it to the east in the liver. Now revolve it to the left and right each thirty-six times. Mentally mobilize the sound *ne*, and place it to the south in the heart. Revolve it to the left and right each thirty-six times. Mentally mobilize the sound *pa*, and place it to the west in the lungs. Revolve it to the left and right each thirty-six times. Mentally mobilize the sound *mi*, and place it to the north in the kidneys. Revolve it to the left and right each thirty-six times. Mentally mobilize the sound *hung*, and extend it to the *ni-wan*. Revolve it to the left and right each thirty-six times. By concentrating the mind, the "*hun* spirit" and the "*p'o*

ch'i"[14] both revert to the highest point and are refined and transformed into *yang*. *Yin* dwells in the "great crucible," remaining still to guard the fetus. Now once again mentally mobilize the sound *an*[15] and direct it to the "central pass." After nine times your work will be complete. The *yin* rises and the *yang* descends, and they meet in the "central crucible." A halo surrounds the "gate of the highest" as the Bodhisattva Kuan-yin sits atop Mount Potala.

Chapter 9. The Yang Spirit Luminous and Perfect

During the stage of the "jade liquid returning elixir," the *yang* spirit is not yet pure, but when the "pearl" is received in the "southern sea," the *yang* spirit becomes luminous and perfect, like the Bodhisattva Kuan-yin atop Mount Potala. The mind like a dragonfly consults the "fifty-three wise ones"[16] and takes refuge in the Buddha. When the root of consciousness reverts to the primal source and the six senses are transcended, then the spirit becomes naturally perfect and clear. The virtuous[17] daughter of the Dragon King, holding the precious pearl in her hand, offers it as light fills the ten directions. When the heart and kidneys have interacted, the spirit and *ch'i* naturally harmonize. The true seed is formed, and the holy fetus is nourished. "Purple bamboos live apart" means that the nature of the liver is benevolent. "White parrot dances in flight" means that the condition of the lungs is righteous. The "combining of metal and wood" means that nature and condition are unified. "Tiger crouches and dragon descends" means that water and fire complement each other. The "pure precious vase" metaphorically expresses the secretions of the lungs. The "willow branches" represent the tail of the liver. The saliva of the "flowery pool" may be compared to "sweet dew." The *ni-wan* at the crown of the head sits unshakably as if atop Mount Potala. The method of salvation is to mentally mobilize the sound *an* and direct it to the place of the "true breath"; that is, the "great crucible." The monk Pao

An's basket[18] is projected into the navel, and the mouth seems to be reciting the mantra *chia-lo-fa-to*. The mind is concentrated and all is peace. Wisdom is now pervasive and perfect. Allow the waves of the "southern sea" to roll on and on. When the original *yang-ch'i* is abundant and the fire of the spirit luminous and perfect, then the great medicine bursts through the passes. One knows and contemplates only contentment. The heart is settled and the mind pure, and there is nothing but contemplation. This great method is the marvelous true secret. It is far superior to the method of "slaying the dragon." Carry this out for "nine revolutions" and one will gain the "seven returns." When the fruits of your practice revert to the navel, the *yang* spirit appears at the crown of the head. After the precious radiance has ascended, body and spirit both attain a wondrous state. One's meritorious achievement has reached perfection and the heavenly decree is about to arrive.

Chapter 10. Incubation and Enlightenment

When the "great crucible" has been established and the "great medicine" obtained, when the holy fetus has formed and the *yang* spirit has appeared, it is still necessary to incubate it. Suckle it for three years, and meditate facing the wall for nine. Settle the breath so that it is smooth and continuous, maintain undivided concentration, and coordinate the spirit and breath. For 3,000 days one should guard it as if protecting an infant. Never forget this for an instant. Close the eyes for two days, and light will follow wherever the mind focuses. Maintain it in the inner orifices, and with stillness it penetrates even deeper. The *ch'i* becomes warm as springtime and the "sweet dew" is produced copiously. *Ch'i* circulates throughout the entire body, beginning with the womb and then traveling up the back and down the front. The "water wheel" turns of itself, transforming the mundane body into our true form. When a man realizes enlightenment, white light penetrates the crown of the head, and then black, green, red, and finally gold. When a woman realizes enlightenment, black light penetrates the crown of her head, and then red, green, and gold. When one's training is complete, the light will be perfected and the five lights unite as one. Earth thunder naturally resounds, and the gates of heaven naturally open. The *yang* spirit goes forth and after doing so returns. At first it stays close by and later ventures further. Be on guard against getting lost, for at this juncture it is necessary to be very careful.

Chapter 11. Perfection of Training and Transcendence of the World

When the *yang* spirit is able to come and go freely and easily, then the true self travels comfortably at will. Still living in the world of men, one establishes great merit. When one's merit is profound and the moment of destiny arrives, the true master appears with final salvation and brings you into the presence of the Lord on High. One next visits all the heavens and finally the "jade pool," where after an audience with the "Golden Mother," one receives appointment as an immortal. This is transcendence of the world.

Appendix 1. First Cure the Menstrual Problems

Before pregnancy or following childbirth there may be blockage of the menses resulting in illness. In such cases, add waist massage to your practice, thirty-six times to the left and right; likewise for the shoulders, up and down and to the left and right each thirty-six times. To this add massage of the center of the navel. With the two hands interlaced, massage seventy-two times in each direction. When the interior of the body is warm, stop. If there is profuse bleeding between periods or vaginal discharge, then to the preceding exercises add the upside down "hanging tiger method." Hang upside down by your feet from a horizontal beam. The body takes the shape of a golden hook with the fingers supporting you on the ground. Mentally focusing on the area below the navel, make a complete orbit by circling to the left and right each 120 times. To cure blocked menses, stagnant blood, and swelling in the lower abdomen, add "right side up hanging sea tortoise" to the above exercise. Hang from a horizontal beam with the palms together and the toes touching the ground. With eyes closed and head lowered, contemplate the heart thirty-six times. The mind follows the eye's gaze as it is directed to the point six-tenths of an inch below the navel thirty-six times. The eyes then contemplate the afflicted area thirty-six times. This eliminates every kind of affliction. Secretly use the true fire of the mind's spirit to cure illness. This is the secret method of curing illness transmitted by Wei Yüan-chün, Ts'ui Feng, Sun Ma-t'uan, and Yü Ch'ou-pieh.

Appendix 2. Reestablishing Menses after Menopause

If the menstrual flow has already dried up, then it is first necessary to restore it. The method for mentally raising it employed in the practice of "slaying the dragon" should be reversed to send it forth. Revolving left and right should be changed to massaging left and right. In 100 days the menses will return. Now wait three days and then apply the previous practices. After another hundred days one's practice will be complete and [the dragon] will be "slain."

Notes

Abbreviations Used in Notes

CC	"Colloquial Chinese" translation and commentary on the *Ishimpō* fragments published anonymously under such titles as *Su Nü ching* (Hsiang-kang i-hsüeh-yüan yen-chiu-she) and *Su Nü ching ta-ch'üan* (Sheng-huo ch'u-pan-she)
Chang	*The Tao of Love and Sex*
CKYSTPS	*Chung-kuo yang-sheng ts'ai-pu shu*
CTCY	*Chin-tan chieh-yao*
CW	*Chung-wen ta tz'u-tien*
FCPI	*Fang-chung pu-i*
HCYI	*Hsiu-chen yen-i*
HMF	*Hsing mi-fang chih pai-ping*
Humana	*The Chinese Way of Love*
H.V.G.	*The Essentials of Medicine in Ancient China and Japan*, Vol. 2.
Levy	*The Tao of Sex*
Needham	*Science and Civilization in China*, Vols. 2, 5.
PS	*Ma Wang tui Han-mu po-shu*
PSN	*Prescriptions of Su Nü* (reconstructed)
SNC	*Su Nü ching* (reconstructed)
SNML	*Su Nü miao-lun*
de Smedt	*Chinese Eroticism*
TH	*Tz'u hai*
THT	*Tung Hsüan tzu* (reconstructed)
V.G.	*Erotic Colour Prints of the Ming Period* or *Sexual Life in Ancient China*
WMH	*Su Nü ching chin-chieh*
WHM	*Yü-fang pi-chüeh* (colloquial Chinese translation and commentary by Wu Hsiu-ming)
YFCY	*Yü-fang chih-yao* (reconstructed)
YFPC	*Yü-fang pi-chüeh* (reconstructed)
YNSI	*Yü-nü sun-i*

The Han Classics Rediscovered

Uniting Yin and Yang

1. The expression *wo shou* 握手 is more ambiguous than the *chieh shou* 接手 used elsewhere in the Ma Wang tui sexual texts to denote clasping of partner's hands. Contextual parallelism between the two, however, makes any interpretation other than "clasp her hands" unlikely. Harper favors this view, but also proposes an alternate reading based on the association of *wo shou* 握手 and *wo ku* 握固, which he suggests might indicate foreplay with fisted hands. There is no parallel for this practice anywhere in the sexual literature. The *Shang-ch'ing huang-shu kuo-tu i* uses the phrases *hsiang ch'ih ch'a shou* 相持叉手 and *hsiang ch'a ch'ih* 相叉持 for mutual hand clasping, and as here, it often is the prelude to prescribed touching sequences.

2. The PS editors read the graph *t'u* 土 as *tu* 度, whereas Harper interprets it as *t'u* 吐. I accept the former interpretation, though their case is weak, and reject the latter despite Harper's creative philology. In support of their reading PS cites only *Chou li*, "Tien jui," where 土 is taken by most commentators to mean "measure." Harper cites two precedents for his 吐 reading: one from the Tun-huang "Ta le fu" and the other from Ma Wang tui "Shih wen." The "Ta le fu" transcription from which Harper quotes, however, gives the characters *ching-ye* 精液, not renderable as "saliva" without considerable force. The V.G. transcription does give *chin-ye* 津液, but it is not clear whether this is his emendation or simply the state of the manuscript from which he copied. The "Shih wen" does indeed describe spitting on the hands, but it is in the context of automassage, not sex, and the graph is *t'o* 唾 not 吐. In the

221

absence of unequivocal parallel in the sexual literature for the practice of spitting on a partner's wrists, we must begin to look elsewhere for a plausable reading of 土. I propose to read 土 as 度 in the sense of "cross" or "pass over," partly by default and partly because it resonates sympathetically with the other verbs of journeying in the passage.

3. I concur with Harper's reading of *hsün* 揗 as "stroke," but not without much soul (and text) searching. The characters 揗 and 循 are interchangeable in ancient literature, and both can be made to work in this context. Pulling in the direction of 循, meaning to continue or follow along, are the use of travel metaphor in this passage and parallels in the medical literature, such as the Ma Wang tui *Tsu-pei shih-i mai chiu-ching* and *Su wen*, "Ku kung lun," where the verbs 循, 抵, 上, 下, 入, and even 環 appear in tight contexts describing sequences of meridian points. Pulling in the direction of the "stroke" interpretation are the *Shuo wen* definition of 揗 as *ma* 摩, the combination *ts'ao-hsün* 操揗 in the middle of this paragraph, the phrase 唾手循臂 in "Shih wen," and most of all, the closely parallel 操以循玉筴 in "Yang-sheng fang." The object of the verb, *chou-fang* 肘房, like most of the points in this topography, is unattested in the received literature. Like *ju-fang* 乳房, however, the metaphor being incomplete allows us reasonably certain identification.

4. Harper explores the possibilities for *tsao-kang* 竈綱 quite resourcefully, but in the end cannot definitively decipher the metaphor, let alone its referent. Because it lies somewhere between armpit and neck in our itinerary, Harper's "Perhaps *tsao kang* refers to the thorax or to some part thereof" seems a safe assumption. The use of the word 綱 in anatomical nomenclature can be seen in *yang-kang* 陽綱, an acupuncture point on the bladder meridian, and *mu-chih-kang* 目之綱, the ends of the eyelids.

5. The term *ch'eng-k'uang* 拯匡 is amply attested in such sources as the *I ching* and *Shih ching*, and its feminine associations are well argued by Harper. Its appearance in the "Ta le fu," however, gives us the best context from which to capture its sexual implications. I accept Harper's "the pelvic region, the 'osseous basket' which holds the sexual organs."

6. Harper feels that the character *fu* 覆 in the phrase 覆周環 instructs the man to "cover" the woman's body with his own and marks the "shift from foreplay to copulation . . . coinciding with the shift in rhyme."

Although Harper offers no parallel passages in the sexual literature to support this interpretation, they indeed are rare, and *fu t'i* 覆體 in the *Secrets of the Bedchamber* is the only example I know of. The verb *fu* 覆 is used frequently in the *Shang-ch'ing huang-shu kuo-tu i* to indicate placing of the hands over the partner's hands, but never body over body. One cannot avoid also noticing in the *Huang-shu* the frequent use of *fu* 復, *chou* 周, and *huan* 還, often in close proximity, meaning again, all over, and return. Harper associates *chou-huan* 周環 with 周圍 and 周圓 to reinforce its reading as a noun, but unlike other points or place names in this passage, it is too generic and lacks specificity of reference. In fact, it is better attested as a verb, meaning to circle, as in *Han shu*, "Chiao-ssu chi-hsia," Fan Yüeh's "She chih fu," and in inverted form in *Su wen*, "Chü t'ung lun." We perhaps should not entirely rule out the possibility that the phrase may mean something like "repeat the circuit again."

7. According to references and commentaries in the *Shih chi*, "Tsang Kung chuan," the *ch'üeh-p'en* 缺盆 is the "bone above the breast." The *Su wen*, "Ch'i fu lun" defines it as an acupuncture point in the "well of the clavicle," the sense in which it still is used today.

8. The expression *li-chin* 醴津 is reminiscent of *li-ch'uan* 醴泉 (see *Huang-t'ing ching* and HCYI), which denotes the secretions of the "jade pool" under the tongue. Harper acknowledges these associations, as well as the apparent linear progression of points from breast bone to vagina, but he spares no philological footwork in shifting the source south to the "vicinity of the receiving canister." I think it is possible that "sweet wine ford" refers to the breasts or cleavage. HCYI calls the breast essence *ch'iung-chiang* 瓊漿, a term mentioned as early as the *Ch'u tz'u*, indicating drink of the highest quality. We might also summon *ju-hsi* 乳溪, "breast stream," from the literature of women's cultivation in support of this interpretation. Is it possible that there is a double-entendre involving the character 津, meaning both a ford in a stream and bodily secretions?

9. Harper points out the occurence of the term *p'o-hai* 勃海 in Chinese geography as the body of water into which the Yellow River empties. In *Chuang tzu*, "Ch'iu-shui," we are told that the 勃海 at its eastern extremity pours into the *wei-lü* 尾閭, a term of known physiological significance denoting the anal area at the base of the spine. Unfortunately, the physiological significance of 勃海 is not

similarly attested, though its extrapolated position in the present sequence of points and its resonance with *ch'i-hai* 氣海, *yüan-hai* 元海, and *pei-hai* 北海 make it a likely cover for the *tan-t'ien*. Harper asks, "could the Spurting Sea refer, then, to a region below the navel and above the genitals?"

10. The PS editors identify 常山 as 恒山, the northern of the Five Holy Peaks of China. Harper considers its anatomical referent to be "the rise of the female genitals, the *pudendum femininum*." I feel that *mons Veneris*, or prominence of the pubic symphysis, may be more accurate. The pudendum refers to the vulva itself, which then makes *hsüan-men* 玄門 redundant.

11. Harper traces the term *hsüan-men* 玄門, undeniably vagina, to *Lao tzu* 玄牝之門 and the "Hsiang erh" 想爾 commentary's definition as *yin-k'ung* 陰孔. It is interesting that 玄門 also is used to designate Taoism itself, based on *Lao tzu* 玄之又玄衆妙之門. Perhaps most telling in the present context is the parallel *hsüan-kuan* 玄關 in HCYI, where it represents the "lower peak."

12. There are a number of perplexing ambiguities in the phrase *shang ho ching shen* 上歘精神. Is 精神 a fused semantic unit or coordinate complements? If fused, is 精 the dominant aspect or 神; in other words, is it the *ching*-like *shen* or the *shen* of the *ching*? Lastly, is the 精神 the man's, the woman's, or a blend of the two? Harper's "the essence and spirit" indicates a spearate but equal interpretation of the two characters, but his "the" leaves the source of these entities in doubt. I cannot produce a single unequivocal example of the two characters as coodinate complements in either the earlier or later literature. Casting about for parallel passages, we find another instance of 精神 at the very end of this text, where I believe the male is the subject; and the sentient rather than the energetic aspect of the combination is emphasized. An approximate parallel exists in SNML, Chapter 7, 保守精神, where again it seems to indicate "the spirit." The phrase 精神泉益 in "Shih wen" also shows the same tendency. Three dialogues in "Shih wen" end with mutually parallel phrases using the term *shen-ch'i* 神氣 to denote sexual energy. By the time of the *Ishimpō* texts, one would normally expect to see the combination 精氣 wherever there was a question of absorbing or circulating sexual energy. The term 精氣 appears only twice, however, in the Ma Wang tui *yang-shen* texts, both times in "Shih wen," where once it refers to the "spirit" of grain in wine and later, in a general way, to male virility. The clearest ex-

amples of absorbing female sexual energy in Ma Wang tui exist outside of the two texts translated here. Found chiefly in "Shih wen," absorption most often is expressed with the verbs *shih* 食, *yin-shih* 飲食, or *ju* 入. We sometimes find *ching* 精 alone as the object of absorption, but never *shen* 神 alone. I believe that 精神 here is the functional equivalent of 精氣, and that it denotes the energetic aspect of the *ching*. My translation, "*ching* spirit," is intended to indicate the uniqueness of the original compound; however, the sense should be understood as essentially sexual energy.

13. The term *chiao-chin* 交筋, translated rather stiffly here as "coital sinew" (a more colloquial rendering might be "love muscle"), though not attested in the literature, is defined later in this paragraph as *chiao-mai* 交脈, "coital channel." It is not one of the twelve vaginal points enumerated in the "Highest Tao" and it is difficult to determine if it refers to a structual locus or an energetic pathway. Harper calls it "the duct (*mo*) inside the vagina that triggers orgasm." Unfortunately the term 莖脈, which appears once in YFPC and nowhere else in the sexual literature, is equally mysterious. The verbs *tsao hsün* 操揗 are highly suggestive of digital manipulation, but whether the object is the clitoris, the vaginal tract as a whole, or some third concept is problematic. Surveying this entire passage, the metaphoric terminology most closely resembles that of the *Tung Hsüan tzu*, and the ritualistic tone resonates with the *Shang-ch'ing huang-shu kuo-tu i*. At the same time, the various anatomical points seem to represent a coherent sequence based on medical theory. Comparison with current acupuncture meridians, however, is inconclusive. Stephen Chang's *Tao of Sexology* describes a sequence of foreplay involving a two-stage stimulation of various acupoints beginning with the stomach meridian and ending with the kidney meridian. Although Chang does not reveal the source of his sequence, nor is it a perfect match with the present passage, an interesting similarity is that both patterns begin at the extremities and end at the genitals.

14. There are a number of problems in the phrase 使體皆樂養說澤以好. I stand with Harper's rejection of PS reading of 癢 for 養 and 懌 for 澤. Without providing corroborative parallels, PS emends all instances of 養 to 癢, regardless of whether the context calls for pleasure or irritation. *The Wondrous Discourse*, Chapter 4, does contain the phrase 陰中隱癢者, where the meaning of 癢 is unmistakably positive. The question remains, however, as to whether 養 denotes pleasure,

223

forming a synonym compound with *le* 樂, or retains its more standard meaning of nourishment. Both interpretations work satisfactorily here, but unfortunately 說澤 cannot act as a decisive tie-breaker, being itself encumbered with ambiguity. PS 悅懌 would result in a synonym compound meaning joyous, and interpretting 養 as pleasure would give us four characters in a row with nearly identical semantic values. The terms 悅澤 and 悅懌 are both attested combinations, but 悅澤 is dominant in *yang-sheng* texts; for example, *Ts'an-t'ung ch'i* and YFPC. Parallelism therefore would require us to translate 養 as nourishment, but here it is clearly the "nourishment" derived from pleasure.

15. I concur in Harper's rejection of PS reading *tzu* 恣 for *tz'u* 次 in the phrase 以次 戲道. Although there are examples of this loan in Ma Wang tui, 次 here precisely describes the orderly sequence of foreplay and congress, as against 恣, which denotes abandon and loss of self-control.

16. The PS editors suggest 薄 for 溥, though the combination is unattested, except perhaps for the expression 尖嘴薄舌. The *Shuo wen t'ung-hsün ting-sheng* lists 薄 as a loan for 敷, and the PS editors give 敷 for 蒲 in the "Shih wen." Because the expression is not found in the later literature and the image is less than transparent, I consider my translation somewhat tentative.

17. I side with Harper's translation of 沒 as "sunset" in the passage 接刑已沒 based on parallelism with 桵刑以昏 in "The Highest Tao" and resonance with the expression 日沒. Yamada Keiji's "finish" seems very forced to me.

18. Harper translates the unattested term *tsung-men* 宗門 as "progenitive gate." The parallel passage in "The Highest Tao" gives *hsüeh-men* 血門, which also is unattested. Harper speculates that the 宗門 may be the *ming-men* 命門 or *ching-she* 精舍, indicating "a recepticale for storing sexual essences following successful intercourse." Before attempting to identify the 宗門, it is critical to determine whether the *ch'i* is concentrated here at this time because of the activity of intercourse or because of the time of day. According to traditional Chinese medicine's theory of the "body clock," the *ch'i* is most active in the *shen* (urogenital system) at 7:00–9:00 PM. It is possible to use such medical expressions as *tsung-chin* 宗筋, *tsung-ch'i* 宗氣, *tsung-mai* 宗脉, or *ch'i-men* 氣門 as points of departure, but I can derive nothing definitive. How this passage relates to the statement later

in this text that the man's *ching* is at its peak in the evening and the woman's concentrated in the morning, or to advice in the later literature to seek conception after midnight is unclear.

19. Parallel passages may be found in "The Highest Tao," "Shih wen," and SNC (*Ishimpō*, YFPC). What is unique in the present formulation is the apparent definition of one *tung* 動 as ten thrusts, giving a kind of quantitative analysis to the phenomenon of arousal. The "Shih wen" version substitutes the word *chih* 至, which is the more familiar designation for level of arousal.

20. My translation of *fang* 方 here as "muscular" is tentative. The parallel passage in "Shih wen" 尻脾能方 contributes little to our understanding, and PS suggestion of *cheng* 正 is uninspiring. My interpretation is based on an unusual but nevertheless attested loan of 方 for 旁 in the sense of *ta* 大, "large." From this I derive the meaning of fullness or amplitude. I believe that the parallel passage in YFPC reinforces my reading.

21. Although very rare in the later medical literature, the term *shui-tao* 水道 does appear in *Su wen*, "Ling-lan mi-tien lun," which says: "The triple-heater governs the breaching of ditches and is the point of emergence of the 'water-course' 水道." Though I can find no specific gloss, the term perhaps indicates in a general way the movement and transformations of the water element in the human body, much as *ku-tao* 穀道 indicates the alimentary tract.

22. The PS editors, here and elsewhere in the Ma Wang tui *yang-sheng* texts, interpret *yü-chia* 玉莢 as *yü-ts'e* 玉策. Both combinations are unattested in the sexual literature, and 玉莢 is unattested anywhere. The term 玉策 appears in historical annals, metaphorically or actually, as "jade documents" or "a jade whip." The term 莢 is a standard variant of 策, and 莢 easily may be a scribal error for 莢. Because both terms are unattested, we must choose on the basis of metaphoric credibility. The term 玉莢, "jade pod," resonates with its vegetable relative 玉莖, "jade stalk," while 玉策 is reminiscent of 玉如意, a man-made implement. Going out on a limb a bit, I must opt for "jade pod."

23. Here is a good example of why the *Kuang ya* 廣雅 defines 養 as *le* 樂, "pleasure."

24. The combination 鹽甘 is unattested and somewhat mystifying, although the general meaning seems inevitable from context. The ordinary meaning of 鹽, "salt," juxtaposed with 甘, "sweet," can throw one off the scent

a bit. Two other leads that might be followed center on the attested loan of 鹽 for 豔 (*Li chi*, "Chiao t'e-sheng") and 鹽 for 嗜 (*Tso chuan*, "Hsi Kung"). The former interpretation might translate "voluptuous sweetness" and the latter, "gorging on sweetness." My translation, then, does not represent a solution to this problem, but a temporary palliative.

25. The unattested combination *chung-fu* 中府 I take as synonymous with *wang-fu* 王府, which also is rare but appears in the *Summary of the Golden Elixir* as "lower *tan-t'ien*," and *chung-chi* 中極, which appears later in this text.

26. I am in fundamental disagreement with Harper's interpretation of this whole paragraph. He states: "Similarly, I have found nothing comparable to the 'ten intermissions' (line 38) in later sexual literature. . . . Judging from this section, the ten intermissions refer to ten stages of transformation of the woman's sexual essence during intercourse. . . . The description suggests female orgasm." The passage as it appears in "Uniting Yin and Yang" is contexually isolated, but its parallel in "The Highest Tao" is embedded in a section devoted to the stages of male sexual arousal and diagnosis of sexual dysfunction. In "The Highest Tao" version, the use of *ching* 精 in the sixth exhaustion and the allusion to nocturnal emissions in the last line further point to a male subject. Beyond Ma Wang tui, there are close parallels in the theory of *wu-shang* 五傷, "five injuries," in SNC and SNML and the *ch'i-shang* 七傷, "seven injuries," in SNF and *Chu-ping yüan-hou lun*, "Hsü-lao hou." The abundance and closeness of parallels leaves little room for doubt that the subject of the present paragraph is male ejaculation and the properties of the ejaculate as indicators of sexual excess.

27. Harper's translation, "great completion," for *ta tsu* 大卒 flows from his interpretation of the whole process described here as female orgasm. I acknowledge the possibility that 卒 may mean end-point in the sense of termination or death, but choose instead to interpet it not as 卒 but 猝. The phrase 萃而暴用 appears in "The Highest Tao" and the paragraph describing the "five injuries" in the SNC concludes: 凡此衆傷皆由不徐交接而卒暴施寫之所致也.

28. Harper relates the phrase 成死爲簿 here to *Tung Hsüan tzu* 求生求死 to establish support for the metaphor of death and female orgasm. I am more convinced by the phrase 成死有薄 in "The Highest Tao" in an unequivocal context describing the threat to

male health of sex addiction, even including parallel symptoms of sexual exhaustion.

29. In keeping with his general interpretation of this paragraph, Harper relates the term *chung-chi* 中極 to the womb or vagina. The term appears in medical, sexual, and yogic texts and applies equally to both men and women. The *Su wen*, "Ku k'ung lun," says, "The *jen* meridian begins just below the 'central extremity' 中極." Most medical texts list it as the third point on the *Jen* meridian, and there it appears on contemporary acupuncture charts. The text and diagram of the *Hsing-ming kuei-chih* show the 中極 as a point just below the *tan-t'ien* where the *Jen* meridian originates. The *Ten Precepts* in the present anthology says, "The uterus is the 'northern sea' located to the north of the 'central extremity' 中極 and the 'central yellow.'" Interpretations of the term *tzu-kung* 子宮, "uterus," must be keyed carefully to context. Two alternates of *kuan-yüan* 關元, the fourth point on the *Jen* meridian, are *ta-chung-chi* 大中極 and *tzu-kung* 子宮. Therefore even a term as seemingly gender specific as 子宮 may serve as the name of a general acupuncture point. The use of 中極 in SNC, "nine postures," "tiger stance," indicates the depth of penetration and is not a synonym for the vagina itself as Harper implies. The term 中極 appears in TCCY, Chapter 16, in the present anthology as a cover for the *tan-t'ien*, where the captured sexual essence is concentrated and cultivated. I believe, then, that 中極 refers here to the male sex center at the base of the body.

Discourse on the Highest Tao under Heaven

1. According to the *Wen hsüan* commentary to Pan Ku's "Yu-t'ung fu," the name Huang Shen 黃神 refers to the Yellow Emperor.

2. Tso Shen 左神 is a god in the Taoist pantheon.

3. I accept PS emendation of *yin-yang* 陰陽 to *yin yü* 陰與, based on the parallel passage in "Shih wen."

4. The term *chiu-ch'iao* 九竅 appears in works as varied as the *Chou Li*, *Su wen*, *Chuang tzu*, *Lü lan*, *Kuan tzu*, *Shih chi*, *Huai Nan tzu*, and *T'ai-hsüan ching*, where it is either stated or interpreted by commentators to refer to the seven openings of the head (eyes, ears, nostrils, and mouth) and the two of the lower body (genitals and anus). The *Nan ching* version, which substitutes tongue and throat for the last two, probably is not

operative here, nor is the model of the same name in the later inner alchemy tradition, where it stands for nine points on the microcosmic orbit.

5. The *Su wen*, "Sheng-ch'i t'ung-t'ien lun," features the terms 九竅 and *shih-erh chieh* 十二節, "twelve segments," in a single passage. The commentary relates the "twelve heavenly *ch'i*" to the "twelve meridians of the body." In view of the parallelism between the present passage and that of the *Su wen*, it perhaps is more likely that the "twelve segments" here refer to the "twelve meridians" than to the other medical definition of the same term, which denotes the twelve major joints of the limbs.

6. This passage, unusual for its anthropomorphic conception of the penis, parallels two passages in the "Shih wen," where instead of *ssu* 死 we find the verbs *lao* 老 and *ch'ü* 去. It also resonates with SNF, "Men are endowed with equal amounts of *yin* and *yang ch'i*. However, often in the exercise of his *yang*, a man first suffers affliction in the ears and eyes."

7. The parallel passage in "Shih wen," 務在積精精盈必寫精出必補補寫之時於臥爲之, makes it difficult to interpret *she* 舍 as anything but 捨. The PS editors provide a parenthetical 瀉 for 寫 in the "Shih wen" passage, but fail to provide a parenthetical 捨 here. There are some examples of 舍 in the sense of lodge or secure in these texts, but that interpretation is not arguable in the present context.

8. The graph 蝩 appears twelve times in the last half of this paragraph. The PS editors read the first two as 踵 and the remaining as 動. Apart from instinctive discomfort with divergent interpretations of the some graph in a single narrative context, a consistent reading of 動 seems perfectly appropriate, whereas 踵 requires considerable force and ingenuity.

9. The "Shih wen" provides a clear passage from which to identify the *yü-ch'üan* 玉泉: 玉閉堅精必使玉泉毋頃. That the term refers to a seminal spring or resevoir is confirmed by Porkert, who lists it as an alternate of 中極.

10. I accept PS suggested reading of 害 for 審, although the sense remains somewhat obscure. Is there a possible relationship with the phrase 諱其名 in "Shih wen"?

11. This passage closely parallels *Su wen*, "Yin-yang ying-hsiang ta-lun": "At forty, the *yin-ch'i* is reduced by half and one's activities become sluggish. At fifty, the body is heavy and the ears and eyes no longer sharp and clear. At sixty, one becomes impotent, the

ch'i greatly declines, the 'nine orifices' are weak, the lower portion of the body is deficient and the upper excessive, and tears and snivel come forth."

12. I interpret *hsi chou* 翕州, "contract the buttocks" in the sense of 縮, 提, 撮, and 挾 in the later literature, indicating contraction of the anal sphincter. The combination *so chou* 縮州 actually appears in "Shih wen."

13. The sense of the three appearances of *i hsia chih* 印下之 in this paragraph leaves some room for ambiguity. The character *chih* 之 in this text, when acting as a pronoun, usually refers either to the penis or the sex act. In two of the three cases in this paragraph it follows directly after *hsi chou* 翕州, and it is grammatically possible that anus is the object of pressure. The verb 抑, in fact, is used to express just this procedure in YFCY. The third instance in this paragraph where *hsi ch'i* 翕氣 rather than 翕州 precedes 印下之 makes one think that the object may be penis, although the notion of pressing the penis down makes no sense here and corresponds to nothing in the later literature. The term 抑 appears frequently in *Ishimpō* either alone or in such combinations as 自抑, where the meaning is "control oneself," though this is probably not relevant in the present case.

14. PS interprets the character *hsi* 澌 here as *ch'i* 迄, but without explanation. I find no suggestion that 澌 is related to 迄, though a variant of 迄 indeed is 愺. I can find no definition of 迄 or 愺 that seems relevant here. The preceding nine items describe the properties of a liquid, and as 澌, too, relates to the watery realm, I find no reason to reject it for so uncertain a substitute. According to the *Chi yün*, 澌 refers to a salt pond or the process of mixing fresh and salt water to make salt. My translation, "brackish," however, is impressionistic and tentative.

15. This list appears without any contextual frame, but items 5, 6, and 7 (穀實, 麥齒, and 嬰女), being identical with the vaginal vocabulary of the later literature, makes the general drift virtually certain. The clustering of these three known entities in the middle of the pack roughly parallels their position in SNC, YFPC, and SNML, though with some inversions. Three other terms have one character in common with counterparts in the later literature: *shu-fu* 鼠婦 shares a *shu* 鼠 with *yü-shu* 俞鼠 and *hsiu-shu* 臭鼠; *ch'ih-tou* 赤毁 and *ch'ih*-(?) 赤繳 share a *ch'ih* 赤 with *ch'ih-chu* 赤珠; (?)-*shih* 磌石 shares a *shih* 石 with *k'un-shih* 昆石. Three items, 調瓠, 赤繳, and 磌石, contain characters, 調, 繳, and 磌, that are unattested, unlisted, or undefined in the re-

ceived literature or lexicons. Only one of these terms, 封紀, appears outside this list in the body of "The Highest Tao," but unfortunately not in a context that allows more definitive identification. At the end of the reasonably intact portion of the "Yang-sheng fang" is a diagram of the female genitalia with the following eight labels as reconstructed by PS: [弄]光, [臭]鼠, □□, 麥齒, 穀實, 赤朱, [琴]絃, 付□. The condition of the original scroll makes anatomical judgments difficult, but the appearance of [琴]絃 here demonstrates the antiquity of this familiar term. Whether any of these terms is descriptive of specific physical features or merely conventional designations for degrees of vaginal depth is another open question. I tentatively accept the PS reading of *mai* 脈 for *kuang* 光 in 弄光; however, *chu* 珠 for *tou* 豉 in 赤豉 seems remote from the point of view of both orthography and phonetics. It could be argued with equal cogency that the appearance of 赤朱 in "Yang-sheng fang" makes the loan here more likely or less likely.

The Sui-T'ang Classics Reconstructed

The Classic of Su Nü

1. The Yellow Emperor is the third of five mythical emperors who ruled during the prehistoric period (third millennium B.C.) of Chinese history. His name first appears in the *I ching*, *Shih chi*, and *Huai Nan tzu*, and later, coupled with that of Lao *tzu*, is associated with the Taoist sciences of self-cultivation. Classical medical and sexological texts often are framed as dialogues between the Yellow Emperor and specialist advisors.

2. Su Nü 素女 appears as goddess and sex initiatress in sexological works from the Sui to the Ming. Her name does not figure in the title of works on sexology listed in the bibliographic section of the *Ch'ien Han shu* but does in those of the *Sui shu*. Prior to this, she was portrayed as a divine singer and musician during the time of the Yellow Emperor as noted in the *Shih chi*, *Ch'u tz'u*, Yang Hsiung's "T'ai-hsüan fu," Chang Heng's "Ssu hsüan fu" and "T'ung sheng ko," and Tso Ssu's "Wu-tu fu." Su Nü is mentioned in the Han work *Wu Yüeh ch'un-ch'iu* by Chao Ye as "one who understands *yin* and *yang* and the *tao* of heaven." In a commentary to the *Shan-hai ching*, her name is linked with that of Hou Chi, god of grain, and hence the cult of fertility. The Ming *Sou shen chi* casts Su Nü in the

role of a river goddess, who assumes the form of a shell to help poor but virtuous people. Apart from the *Su Nü mi-tao ching* and *Su Nü fang* listed in the *Sui shu* bibliography, Su Nü also is alluded to as sex initiatress in Chang Heng's "Yüeh fu," Hsü Ling's "Ta Chou ch'u-shih shih," and in the biography of Nü Chi in the *Lieh hsien chuan*. I have chosen to render the name "Su Nü" in transliteration out of both prudence and a distaste for translating personal names. Maspero and Étiemble's "Fille de Simplesse," V.G.'s "Plain Girl," Schipper's "Lady Bright," Levy's "Woman Plain," Humana's "Forthright Female," H.V.G.'s "Plain-Speaking Woman," Stephen Chang's "White Madame," and Needham's "Immaculate Girl" demonstrate the difficulty of achieving agreement even on the meaning of *Su*. The only interpretation internal to these texts appears in the Preface to the SNML where the word is glossed as "pure" or "immaculate." I can accept the idea of purity as the dominant association with the goddess's name, but not candor or frankness as implied in the translations of H.V.G. and Humana. Chang and de Smedt concur with my preference for transliteration.

3. Maspero translates *ch'i* 氣 as "Souffle," V.G. as "spirit," H.V.G. and de Smedt as "energy," and Levy as "life-force." By now it is safe to say that *ch'i*, like *tao* before it, has passed into the English language as a loan word, due mainly to the propagation in the West of Chinese martial arts, medicine, and meditation. Acceptance in transliteration, however, does not entirely obviate the need for definition and clarification in the present context. In sexological texts, *ch'i* is used very much as it is in writings on medicine or meditation. In this opening sentence of the SNC it refers to homeostasis, health, or the general energy level of the body. Elsewhere in these texts, *ch'i* may refer to the breath, to the physiological functioning of various organs or organ systems in the body, to the energy circulating within the meridians, or to atmospheric or celestial influences.

4. In the line 身常恐危, all previous translations correctly take 身 as "I," meaning oneself, with the exception of Levy and H.V.G. who render it "body." The concept of oneself subsumes that of body; and it is properly the person, or "I," that experiences the state of "fear" expressed in the verb. Moreover the use of 身 in the sense of "I" is by no means rare in literary Chinese.

5. *Tao* 道 is used in several different senses in the sexual literature. It may mean way, art, method, or the entire body of natural law and

universal principles. When used for way, art, or method, the *tao* always implies the correct or natural manner, though specific prescriptions may vary from text to text.

6. The *yin/yang* paradigm describes the complementary waxing and waning phases of cyclical processes or the dominant aspects or qualities of things. At the highest level of abstraction they approximate our concepts of positive and negative, creative and receptive, or active and passive. In the phenomenal realm they correspond to light and dark, heat and cold, firm and yielding, and opening and closing. On the macrocosmic level they stand for heaven and earth, sun and moon; and on the microcosmic, male and female. In the immediate environment they express themselves as day and night, the four seasons, and all organic processes of growth and decay. In traditional medical theory the human body is seen as internally, ventrally, and in its lower parts *yin*, and externally, dorsally, and in its upper parts *yang*. Physiologically, the Five Viscera are *yin* and the Six Bowels *yang*; structive and storing functions are *yin*, active and defensive are *yang*. Pathologically, deficiency is *yin* and excess *yang*. Numerologically, even numbers are *yin* and odd numbers *yang*. In sexology specifically, *yang* may refer to the male gender, the male member, or virility, whereas *yin* may refer to the female gender or the private parts of both sexes. In this sentence, *yin* and *yang* refer to man and woman, but also carry all the other correspondences and associations, thus reinforcing the larger context in which intercourse takes place.

7. In the line 夫女之勝男猶水之滅火, Yeh has emended Tamba's 滅 to 勝, apparently on the basis of stylistic sensitivity as the meaning is not altered.

8. The "five flavors" as distinguished in both gastronomy and pharmacology are acrid (pungent), sweet, sour, bitter, and salty.

9. According to the *Ch'ün-i lun t'an-yao chi*, the "five pleasures" are those associated with the five sense: eyes, ears, nose, tongue, and body (touch). The term also is used in Buddhist texts for the five negative sense attachments.

10. The original line 何得歡樂 might be more literally translated: "What joy thus is obtained?" Among all translations, Levy's "What pleasures and joys to be gotten!" stands alone in rotating the original meaning a full 180 degrees.

11. Yeh has emended the character 云 in the *Ishimpō* phrase 素女云 to 曰. This is based, we can assume, on the almost exclusive (we

find only one exception) use of 云 for introducing quotations from works and 曰 for introducing dialogue. The possibility of interpolating the character 經, and thus preserving the 云, is precluded by the appearance of 素女經云 later in the section. The thirty sections of this twenty-eighth chapter of the *Ishimpō* group the collected fragments by source. Generally, after the title of the work and the initial paragraph, subsequent paragraphs from the same source follow either without heading or with the characters 又云, "it is also stated." In the former case it seems we can infer that the two paragraphs follow directly in the original without break, and in the latter, 又云 indicates a lacuna in the text.

12. Ts'ai Nü 采女 appears in these early sexology classics as one of a trio of sex initiatresses. Many references in the *Hou Han shu* mention "ts'ai-nü" as women chosen for the emperor's harem. A passage in Ko Hung's *Shen-hsien chuan* re-creates a dialogue between Ts'ai Nü and P'eng Tsu during which he gives advice on sexual matters. Although I favor transliteration over translation, V.G.'s "Elected Girl" and Maspero's "La Fille Choisie" at least make grammatical sense, whereas Levy's "Woman Selective" leaves one wondering if Ts'ai Nü is the subject or object of selection.

13. Most translators and commentators have taken "King" 王 in the passage as a reference to the Yellow Emperor, but H.V.G. calls him "reigning monarch of the Yin dynasty." Looking at the *Ishimpō* text, the name 殷王 does indeed appear on the same page preceding the passage under consideration. This apparently led H.V.G., who assumed that this passage belonged to the YFPC, to conclude that the second "King" refers to the first. Levy, however, also working from the *Ishimpō* text, tells us in a translator's parenthesis that "King" is none other than the Yellow Emperor. V.G., while purporting to translate excerpts from the *Ishimpō*, follows Yeh's practice of attributing all passages in Su Nü–Yellow Emperor dialogue form to the SNC, although Tamba's format would seem clearly to forbid this. Additionally, I cannot find another instance in this twenty-eighth chapter of the *Ishimpō* where the Yellow Emperor is referred to as "King" 王, but always as "Emperor" 帝. The earlier passage on the same page of *Ishimpō* text links the Yellow Emperor with Su Nü and P'eng Tsu with the "King of Yin" 殷王. This association is confirmed by an interlinear commentary in the "Dangers and Benefits of Intercourse with Women," which recounts the story of Ts'ai Nü, the "King of Yin," and her interview with

P'eng Tsu. Flaws in logic and continuity that will be discussed in note 15 also point to embarrassments in the "Yellow Emperor" theory. In fact, surveying the whole of the *Ishimpō* fragments, the Yellow Emperor and Ts'ai Nü always are strictly segregated, as if not contemporaries. Wherever the original text appears to link the name of the Yellow Emperor with that of Hsüan Nü 玄女, the third of the divine initiatresses, Tamba provides an interlinear emendation changing her identity to Su Nü. The appearance of the two characters 君王 later in the paragraph fails to influence the outcome of the case. The passage is unique in several other respects. First, there is no other example of Su Nü playing the role of narrator or introducing the circumstances surrounding an exchange; and second, there is no example of the Yellow Emperor (if we accept this interpretation for the moment) dispatching someone to interview a third party. The fourth sex manual listed in the *Ch'ien Han shu* bibliography, *T'ang Pan Keng yin-tao*, attributes authorship to Kings T'ang and Pan Keng of the Yin dynasty. The *Lieh hsien ch'üan-chuan* has King Mu of the Western Chou sending Ts'ai Nü to P'eng Tsu, whereas the *Shih-i chi* casts the Queen Mother of the West in the role of King Mu's tutor. Perhaps the most conclusive evidence pointing to the "King of Yin" interpretation is *Pao P'u tzu*, Chapter 13, which says, "The King of Yin sent Ts'ai Nü to [P'eng Tsu] to learn the art of the bedchamber."

14. In sources such as the *Shih chi*, *Huai Nan tzu*, *Chuang tzu*, *Pao P'u tzu* and *Lieh hsien chuan*, P'eng Tsu is described as a Taoist adept born during the Hsia who lived 700 or 800 years and was still flourishing at the end of the Yin. The Yin king offered him an official post, but he declined on the pretext of illness. In another version, the Yin king solicits his instruction, and then after verifying its efficacy, seeks to kill him to terminate the transmission. The historical association of P'eng Tsu and the King of Yin in the transmission of the secrets of longevity thus is very strong and not weakened by the device here of Ts'ai Nü as intermediary.

15. A number of punctuation possibilities result from the uncertainties described in the previous three notes. Tamba's arrangement suggests that the four paragraphs listed under YFPC appear consecutively in his original copy, and he reproduces them without 又云. Levy and CC explicitly take "King" as the Yellow Emperor; H.V.G. opt for "King of the Yin dynasty;" and V.G. remains neutral in simply rendering "King" without comment. These differences have led to slight variations in punctuation, but the most radical departure belongs to CC and de Smedt, who preserve the continuity of dialogue, but end Su Nü's remarks with 道術, and complete the line as if by third person narrator. This does no violence to the grammar, but there is no precedent for a narrator interrupting a character's speech in the YFPC.

16. For an extended discussion of *ching* 精 see the Introduction to this book. Here, perhaps, it is worth repeating briefly that the word "*ching*" alone in sexology texts generally combines the aspects of semen (or sexual secretions in women) and sexual energy, though in specific contexts one aspect may be dominant. Still less common in transliteration at the time of this translation than *tao* or *ch'i*, *ching* fares much better in transliteration than such one-dimensional translations as "sperm," or even such contextual rendering as V.G. and H.V.G.'s "semen" and "vital essence," Levy's "semen" and "essence," and de Smedt's "sperm" and "quintessence." Maspero's "l'Essence" parallels his translation of *ch'i* as "le Souffle" and typifies the efforts of a more innocent age. The *Shuo wen* tells us simply that *ching* means "to select," by implication to select the finest. The *Su wen* says, "The *ching* is the body's root," and the *Ling shu*, "The *ching* forms before the birth of the human being." Tai Yüan-ch'ang's *Tao-hsüeh tz'u-tien* (Dictionary of Taoist studies) contains a somewhat apocryphal but typical Taoist interpretation: "The character *ching* 精 features the rice 米 radical, belonging to grass, and on the right the element *ch'ing* 青, indicating the east and belonging to wood. Because it derives from the essence of that which man consumes from the vegetable kingdom, it is one of the body's treasures. Grass and trees are born of water during the *tzu* period, and thus *tzu* belongs to water. The kidneys, too, belong to water and may be called the 'treasury of water,' whose location is the north as designated by the Terrestrial Branch *tzu*. Therefore *ching* also is born in the *tzu* position. It is supplemented through the food we eat such that every seven mouthfuls of food becomes one drop of blood, and seven drops of blood become one drop of *ching*. Seven drops of *ching* become one drop of *ch'i*, and seven drops of *ch'i* become one drop of spirit. By wasting one drop of *ching* we forfeit one drop of *ch'i*, and thus the spirit has no means of strengthening itself. Therefore it may be observed that those who suffer from nocturnal emissions, spermatorrhea, or promiscuity appear feeble and unsanguine."

17. V.G.'s translation of the phrase 服食 衆藥 as "dieting and taking various drugs"   *229*

raises some questions. All other translators simply take 服食 as a compound verb and 眾藥 as its object. This is supported by the appearance several lines later of the construction 服藥 and by the author's effort to maintain four-character lines. Ignoring for the moment the unhappy coincidence that for the contemporary English speaker the word "dieting" implies a restricted regimen of food intake for weight control, we may grant that what he probably means is the consumption of foods conducive to health and longevity. Although it is true that, in Chinese medicine and culture in general, the medicinal properties of food are much discussed, nevertheless a distinction exists between food and medicines consumed for specific effects. I believe clearly medicine alone is intended here.

18. The line 男女相成猶天地相生也 summarizes in rhymed verse the cosmic significance of the sexual union of man and woman. These ten characters, seemingly so lucid and individually still so common in contemporary colloquial speech, have inspired very different translations. V.G: "The union of man and woman is like the mating of heaven and earth." Levy: "The producing of man and woman is like the begetting of Heaven and earth." De Smedt: "Men and women are like the earth and the heavens, they are destined to unite and are also eternal." H.V.G.: "The mutual fulfillment of male and female resembles the mutual creation of the heavens and the earth." V.G. makes unambiguous sense in English, but is not, I believe, the precise meaning of the original. De Smedt's translation is an impressionistic paraphrase, while Levy and H.V.G. leave us wondering if man and woman and heaven and earth are doing the "producing" and "begetting" or being produced and begotten. I feel that my colleagues have been somewhat misled by the verbs 成 and 生, and that what is emphasized is not the act of creating or producing, but of existing in complementary synergy and mutual dependence. The CC colloquial rendering shows general agreement with this interpretation. The phrase 不以相生反以相害 in the "Dangers and Benefits of Intercourse with Women" illustrates my understanding of the combination 相生 here, which is not to beget each other but to support ech other.

19. Yeh gives 交絕 for 交接 in the *Ishimpō* text. Undoubtedly a typographical error.

20. Levy's "second obeisance" and de Smedt's "bowed many times" are surely incorrect. CW gives no fewer than eight citations for 再拜 to support the "bowed twice" interpretation.

21. V.G. misses the character 不 in the text and thus mistranslates this phrase as a command, "he must familiarize himself with all the disciplines of Tao."

22. Tamba provides an interlinear 幸 beside the character 事 in the line 事多後宮宜知交接之法 that Yeh accepts as an emendation. The line makes perfect sense to me as is, though 事 and 幸 easily could be confused in cursive script. If 幸 indeed was the intended word, it admits of two interpretations: "fortunately" or "imperial sexual favor." If the emendation were to be accepted, I feel the latter would be the obvious choice, but Levy and H.V.G. both translate it as "fortunately." Only V.G. agrees with my preference for the original. For me the question turns on the relationship of 事 or 幸 to 宜. I find greater cohesiveness to the logic of "many responsibilities" in the harem "requiring" a knowledge of the *tao* of intercourse than "fortunately" he has many concubines and therefore "must" acquire this knowledge. In the second case, I simply cannot make "must" follow from "fortunately." The English translations do not resolve the gap in logic, but the CC paraphrase translation explains at length that what is "fortunate" about "many concubines" is that, once the art of intercourse is mastered, one then has an opportunity to supplement what is lost through the wear and tear of public life.

23. The phrase 莫數瀉精 is not unambiguous. The character 數 contains the possibility of "many," "a few," or "times." De Smedt and HMF opt for the last, thus translating it as "never ejaculate." V.G.'s "emitting semen only on rare occasions" and Levy's "emitting semen infrequently" take 數 as "many" and, combining it with the negative 莫, agree with my interpretation. Maspero's "san jamais émettre l'Essence plusiers fois" takes the phrase in another and unwarranted direction. The meaning of the original surely is not that one should avoid multiple orgasms on a given occasion, as this has never entered the discussion. The phrases 數數易之 and 數交而一瀉 in Sections 6 and 7 of the FCPI support my interpretation, as does "Uniting Yin and Yang," 數之 "frequently."

24. There is a double pun in the phrase 御敵. In the military sense, 御 means to resist and, in the sexual sense, to have intercourse; 敵 means both enemy and sex partner.

25. The term 御 also means to drive or mount when applied to horse-drawn vehicles. It is the most frequently used transitive verb in these texts for male initiated sexual intercourse with women. I feel that rather than

such neutral translations as "make love" or "have intercourse," "mount" better conveys the concrete origins of the word and the nature of the subject-object roles it connotes.

26. H.V.G. translates 窮 as "impoverished or limited." Poverty and limitation indeed are two of the meanings of the character, but we cannot have it both ways in this context. The chief concern here, of course, is longevity and not financial status.

27. The character 長 in the phrase 長不交接 has evoked a variety of interpretations. V.G.: "refrain entirely"; Levy: "a long time"; Chang: "any more"; de Smedt: "abstain"; CC: "temporarily abstain and then resume"; and H.V.G.: "abstain completely." My sympathies here lie with Levy and CC because the Yellow Emperor is seeking a prescription for a temporary state of debility and not inquiring about abstinence as a lifelong regimen. WHM alone takes 強助以手 in the next phrase as "aided by the woman's hand." The sense is not unreasonable but for the grammar of the original.

28. CW gives the following definitions of 神氣: (1) miraculous *ch'i*, (2) subtle *ch'i* of the Five Phases, and (3) spirit. Needham's "the *shen* and the *ch'i*" indicates that he is reading the two characters independently. I agree with Porkert's interpretation, "composite synonym of *shen*," and V.G. and Levy's translations, "spirit" and "life spirit."

29. Needham translates the expression 練氣 as "recast the *ch'i*." Both *Ishimpō* and Yeh give 練, originally meaning to boil raw silk to make it pliable, and by extension to practice, train, or exercise. Its interchangeable homophones 鍊 and 煉 mean to smelt, refine, or temper, but in view of the use of 練 in the original text and the fact that "recast the *ch'i*" is incomprehensible in English, something more like "cultivate the *ch'i*" would be more appropriate for an expression, after all, that still is in common use today. H.V.G. mispunctuate the line, running it on with the next and resulting in a translation of 練氣數行 as "drill the movements" instead of "frequent practice."

30. This is a standard expression in ancient texts for breathing exercises, meaning that one exhales "the old" and inhales "the new."

31. Through faulty punctuation, Levy has grouped the four characters 其舍所以 together in one phrase, though no translator before or since has made that mistake. The result of splicing the last two characters of one phrase with the first two of the next produces the incongruous and highly forced translation,

"Reject all reasoning about sex."

32. Needham's interpretation of the line 所以常行以當導引 is both unique among translations and commentaries and extraordinarily misleading. He translates: "Therefore (if you insist on refraining from women) you should regularly exercise it (the Jade Stalk) by masturbation." Needham's habit of finding masturbation under every bed in these texts is discussed as a general proposition in my Introduction, but let me demonstrate here how a key translation error contributes to the skewing of a crucial theoretical issue. First, by severing this line from the rest of the passage (which he himself quotes earlier), he not only deprives the reader of the essential context, but apparently erases his own memory of Su Nü's flat rejection of abstention from contact with women. Furthermore, the words in parenthesis are purely his own and in no way are justified by either the logic or intent of the paragraph as a whole. The paragraph contains three common expressions, 練氣, 去故納新, and 導引, all of which refer to the Taoist curriculum of cultural exercises for health and longevity. In all of the voluminous literature on Taoist yoga, one finds no text, commentary, or gloss that supports the interpretation of 導引 as "masturbation." The term 導引 appears as early as the *Su wen* and *Chuang tzu*, interpreted by commentators in the narrow sense of moving exercises, or more broadly to include breathing and self-massage. Needham himself translates the term no fewer than ten times as "gymnastic exercise" in his chapters on physiological alchemy, though he takes great pains to insist that "what it really came to designate is that part of them which involves self-massage." This narrowing of his own focus may have provided the mental stepping stone whereby he stumbled unconsciously from "self-massage" to "masturbation." In fact, in all of these sexology texts we find no references to solitary practices for men, except those specifically intended to strengthen or elongate the penis. Finally, the critical four characters 以當導引 actually appear in the biography of the famous physician, Hua T'o, in the *Hou Han shu*, where he is made to describe the benefits of the exercise form, "The Play of the Five Animals" 五禽戲. Proceeding to other translators, V.G. takes "Jade Stalk" as the subject of the verb, which he then translates literally as "controlled and guided," apparently unaware that 導引 is simply the ancient term for what is now more commonly known as *ch'i-kung* 氣功. Levy's "special gymnastics" suffers from the wrong associations in English and fails to express the

inner aspect of movement implied in 導引 through coordinating calisthenics and breathing to circulate the *ch'i*. H.V.G.'s "breathing exercises and massage" conjures up exclusively stationary practices and misses Su Nü's point, which is precisely that intercourse itself is a highly beneficial kind of yoga. Very much to the point in all of this is the parallel passage in the YNSI "Close the eyes, lie on the back, and circulate your internal energy 導引." Schipper's "This is why one must exercise it regularly," is not far.

33. The word 動 occurs with great frequency throughout all of the sexology texts. A survey of its appearances in all contexts reveals two basic meanings: (1) movement in the physical sense, and (2) sexual arousal. Needham translates the line, "If you can erect it (in orgasm) and yet have no ejaculation," thereby forcing 動 to play the role of erection, for which there is no precedent, and supporting his thesis of injaculatory masturbation. V.G.'s "copulate," Levy's "move," de Smedt's "motion," Chang's "make love," and H.V.G.'s "movement" all fail to appreciate the vital link between "arousal" of the sexual energy and "returning the *ching*" in the next line, which refers to raising this energy to the brain. Very clear examples from other texts could be cited on this behalf, but drawing just from the work at hand, four paragraphs later we find, "Sometimes the woman is not happy. Her passions are not aroused (動)." It then goes on to explain the factors that bring both partners into harmonization, concluding, "Thereupon the woman's passions are aroused (振感)," using a synonym that precisely defines the sense in which 動 was intended. Later, too, 動 and 感 are used in parallel couplets proving the same point.

34. The expression 生道 first appears in *Mencius*, "Chin hsin," Part 1.

35. Following Tamba's note, Yeh emends 乃者 in *Ishimpō* to 乃箸. The former is actually a standard combination, but wholly inappropriate here, and I therefore accept the emendation.

36. Levy takes the four characters 故有形狀 as "From the first there has been a fixed order," but it is difficult to know if by "order" he means sequence or configuration. H.V.G.'s "shapes and forms" clearly is too literal, and what is meant, I believe, is rather features or characteristics. The expression actually appears again two paragraphs later where it comes very close to meaning method.

37. I take 志 in the expression 和志 in the sense in which it is used in the medical term 五志, the "Five Emotions" (joy, anger, sorrow, anxiety, and fear). The term 志 has many shades of meaning including will, ambition, intention, aspiration, and desire, but none of these work with what precedes it or as the object of 和. Levy's "harmonizing the will" makes little sense in English, and Chang's "achieve an accord of the wills" makes both partners the subject of the verb and is not supported by the syntax of the text itself. De Smedt's "strengthen the will" attempts to make sense of 志 as "will" by totally misconstruing the verb. CC's "mental relaxation" comes closest to my interpretation.

38. Levy's "the three phenomena" and H.V.G.'s "these three forces" are an apparent attempt to relate 三氣 to the three conditions stated in the previous line, but flies in the face of both logic and grammar. Actually, the line is essentially identical with one in the *Huang-t'ing ching*, where the commentary explains 三氣 as the three primordial *ch'i* that converge at conception to produce the upper, middle, and lower portions of the body.

39. Among standard dictionary definitions of 亭, based on passages in the *Shih chi*, *Han shu*, and *Huai Nan t'zu*, are 平 and 定. H.V.G.'s rendering of "erect" for 亭 thus is untenable.

40. This interpretation follows a four-character line punctuation of the passage, although it is grammatically possible to break the phrase in another way as CC has done.

41. This is the unique appearance of the terms 八節 and 九宮. Levy's "eight sequential progressions . . . nine reactions" is guesswork, and de Smedt's "eight stages . . . eight [sic] palaces" is literal. Both are without gloss. CC takes them as "rules and precepts," whereas H.V.G. give us "eight sections . . . nine compartments," adding in a note that the latter are "nine labyrinthine compartments inside the female genitalia" and providing specific anatomical equivalents. This analysis was made possible, we are told, on the basis of two premodern Japanese medical works that I have not had an opportunity to examine. They also suggest in note 14 that 九宮 "may be interpreted as an alternative term for 九部." Unfortunately this also is the sole occurrence of 九部, which is not defined either explicitly or by context. Does 八節 mean something like 五常, which are anatomically based, or 四至, which are physiologically based? Does 九宮 mean something like 九部, which is undefined but looks to be anatomically based, or 九氣, which combines anatomical points and physiological re-

sponses? The two terms appear in the *Ling shu* but with definitions unrelated to the present context. The 九宮 in Taoist meditation lore, which refer to nine points and corresponding spirits in the head, likewise seems irrelevant. The 十節 in the "Uniting Yin and Yang" parallel the 十勢 in the "Highest Tao" and refer to postures of coition.

42. The phrase 精神統歸 is translated by H.V.G. as "the essence and vigor of life will be fully restored"; and Levy, even further from the mark, "the spirit reverts to a death state." There is no reason to take 精神 as anything but "spirit," nor 統歸 as anything but "concentration" (literally, unified reversion). Actually, the expression is common in meditation texts, where it invariably refers to concentrating the mind and eliminating random thoughts. CC agrees with my reading.

43. I take everything following 在於, "it consists in," as describing the preconditions for successful coition. Levy, de Smedt, and H.V.G. break the line, taking half as preconditions and half as results. What may have confused them is that "neither cold nor hot; neither sated nor hungry" sounds reminiscent of phrases used to describe the attainments of Taoist adepts who become impervious to discomfort and desires. The telling difference, apart from syntax, is the use of 不飽 along with 不飢. CC agrees with my reading. A parallel passage in the SNML leaves no room for ambiguity: 大飢勿犯大飽勿犯.

44. Only Levy's translation, "forced," of the character 強 fully accords with my own. It is supported by the second appearance of 強 in this passage and its use again in the same sense later in the section on the "four levels." All other translator's have either diluted or ignored it altogether.

45. Levy's "I am embarrassed to my face and ashamed in my heart, and I perspire like a bead" both misreads the Chinese line and falls short of coherent English.

46. The two characters 和氣 have been variously rendered: V.G., "the man must harmonize his mood with that of the woman"; Levy, "harmonize the life force"; Humana, "a harmonious spirit"; Chang, "harmonize the atmosphere"; H.V.G., "the energy must be harmonized"; and CC, "calm mind and harmonious *ch'i*." *Ch'i*, I feel, is used here in the broadest possible sense of everything pertaining to one's mental, emotional, and physical state, but the question remains as to whether the author refers to the mutual harmonization of both parties or of an enhancement of the man's condition alone. CW and

TH provide many persuasive examples of the expression 和氣 describing the relationship of two parties, and the passage in question also deals with the sexual responses of both man and woman. However, the popular *ch'i-kung* exercise set known as 和氣功 shows the viability of harmonization in the solo mode.

47. The term 五常 is defined later in this text as the five Confucian virtues applied to the penis: benevolence, righteousness, propriety, trustworthiness, and intelligence. Ignoring this, Chang calls them "his five organs."

48. As mentioned in note 41, the term 九部 is not defined here nor does it appear again. One guess is that it may be associated with the nine locations outlined later in the text that are successively aroused during lovemaking and manifest the "nine *ch'i*."

49. According to *Su wen*, "Mai-yao ching-wei lun," the condition of the *ch'i* may be determined by observing the color (green, red, yellow, white, or black) of the face, especially about the eyes. The term 五色 here may simply refer in a more general way to the manifestation of a woman's mood in her face.

50. This text operates within a theoretical framework that holds that *ching* is possessed by both man and woman. Over and over in unequivocal contexts, *ching* is used for female sexual energy, secretions, and reproductive potential. One must be disabused of the modern colloquial bias that reads "semen" for every mention of *ching*. Levy and Chang err precisely on this account, whereas de Smedt and Humana simply throw the line out. The next four characters 取液於口 admit of several interpretations. If 液 is taken as standing for the liquid aspect of *ching* in the previous line, then the line would translate, "Take the secretions into your mouth." However, because no mention is made in any of these texts of oral absorption of vaginal secretions and because simultaneous absorption by mouth above and penis below occurs in later texts, then oral absorption of the female partner's salivary secretions is the obvious choice. Failure to appreciate the niceties of both these lines leads to the textual torture of Levy's, "By gathering in your overflowing semen and by taking the fluid into your mouth. . . ."

51. There are two possible readings of *ching-ch'i*: either *ching* modifies *ch'i*, or *ching* and *ch'i* function as coordinate complements. The latter is extremely rare, and I believe never occurs in these sexology texts, so there is every reason to interpret *ching-ch'i* as the subtle energy of the *ching*. For this reason I must take exception to H.V.G.'s "essence and

233

energy," which stands alone in interpreting the term here as a case of coordinate complements.

52. The verb 還, rendered "return" in this translation, denotes the process of raising the *ching* energy from its center at the base of the body up the back to the brain.

53. The second character in the term 髓腦 (same in Tamba and Yeh) is a variant of 腦. The combination, similar to 髓海, means brain. De Smedt's "marrow" and H.V.G.'s "the bone marrow and the bloodstream" not only miss the mark in this instance, but ignore the watchword of the entire enterprise, "return the *ching* to fortify the brain."

54. All previous translations have failed to realize that 正氣 is a technical term in Chinese medicine denoting the positive health-giving *ch'i*, which constantly does battle with the negative pathogenic *ch'i* 邪氣. Levy's rendering of the line, "If your orthodox life force is moribund within every illness will disappear," shows the unfortunate result of misreading 充 as 死.

55. H.V.G. take 氣 as the subject of the verb 起, translating, "Arising right after each intercourse, Your Majesty's energy will increase a hundredfold." The term 起 rarely if ever is used to signify elevation of energy level, whereas it nearly always is the verb of choice where penile erection is concerned. Levy is guilty of the same error, but Chang, Humana, and CC are not deceived.

56. The line 其質不動 presents an unusual use of 質, which more often means something like substance or nature. Here the word clearly refers to the woman's core, quick, innermost being, or very soul; and its use in this sense is unique to this text among those in this collection. Most previous translations have interpreted it correctly, but H.V.G.'s "No motion is felt in her" seems to have missed the point.

57. The character 勢 in *Ishimpō* is reproduced in Yeh's reconstruction. Throughout Tamba's copy there is some confusion of the characters 熱 (熱, hot) and 勢 (power or strategic position). Here 熱 actually might be more typical in the phrase, and in some passages noted later, Yeh has overridden the Tamba text and emended 熱 to 勢.

58. I have translated the line 故陽不得陰則不喜陰不得陽則不起 just as it appears in both *Ishimpō* and Yeh, though it is highly unusual and suspicious. Over and over throughout the text, the female sexual response is described as "joy" (快, 喜, 歡) and the male as "erection, vigor, health, or strength"

(起, 盛, 和, 强). This is the only example of a complete reversal. All other translations attempt to render 起 in some way as applicable to the woman's response, except for CC who simply translates as if the more normal expectation were in fact the text.

59. Only Levy takes this line in the psychological sense, translating, "go up unexpectedly or go down suddenly (in emotion)." All others agree with the concrete interpretation of rough motion.

60. The *Ishimpō* gives 男熱營, but Yeh emends 熱 to 勢 with ample justification. The penis is often described as "hot," but never the whole man. The "Penal Code" of the *Official History of the Chin* (*Chin shu*) states: "Those guilty of sex crimes will be castrated." "Castrated" is expressed as 割勢 "cut off their testicles." The term 勢, then, in this line may be interpreted as power located in the testicles, or virility. As for 營, standard dictionaries fail to yield relevant definitions, but by a train of associations from its medical usage denoting energy derived from food and its interchangeability in that context with 榮, whose general meaning is flourishing, I arrive at "in full possession of his virility." CW cites an instance of 勢榮 in the *Hsün tzu*.

61. Contextual comparison of all appearances of 扣 in these texts strongly suggests that the unstated subject of the verb is the man's hand and not the penis as some translators have been led to believe in some instances. In two cases the objects of the verb 扣 are 俞鼠 and 赤珠. These terms do not appear in any of the several expositions of degrees of vaginal depth but belong, I feel, to the external genitalia, making them particularly strong candidates for manual "pressure." In Taoist yoga manuals 扣 is one of several verbs used to denote the compression of the perineum with the middle two fingers of the hand.

62. The term 俞鼠 (*yü-shu* or possibly *shu-shu*) is highly problematic. The term 俞 alone has several specific meanings in Chinese medicine, none of which seem to have any relevance here. Taking the first character at face value, then, the only promising definition would seem to be "dugout canoe." The image of a mouse in a canoe could be descriptive of the clitoris. This, indeed, is the conclusion of Levy and H.V.G.'s glossaries of female genital terminology, although V.G. is more reserved in his assessment of our ability to make definitive judgments based on extant sources. The term is absent from the SNML list. H.V.G. adds in a note that 俞鼠 actually

should be 龥齒 without explaining the basis. We have never seen this combination either in dictionaries or the literature, and it brings us no closer to making sense. Looking for a moment at the word 鼠, it appears in the YFPC in the combination 臭鼠, referring to one of the points of greatest depth in the vagina and in the "Highest Tao" in 鼠婦 as the fourth of twelve degrees. In general anatomy, the "groin" sometimes is denoted by the term 鼠蹊 , literally "rat path." The only thing that is perfectly clear from context is that the term 龥鼠 refers to something quite specific; however, in the absence of unequivocal evidence, anything but transliteration would be rash.

63. The term 朱室 does not appear in CW or V.G.'s appendix on terminology. H.V.G. call it a synonym for 子宮, uterus. Levy likewise interprets it as uterus, but his "he irrigates her red chamber," implies that the "irrigation" is the result of the man's seminal emission. CC takes the four characters 灌溉朱室 as "in order to augment his physical strength," thus identifying the "red chamber" with the male side. From the flow of the sentence as a whole, this actually seems the greater likelihood, but for the difficulty of the precise location. At this point, regrettably, I can do no better than literal translation.

64. The *Ishimpō* gives 九, nine, and Levy and H.V.G. follow suit. I accept Yeh's emendation in view of the list of eight items in four pairs.

65. Levy's "looking up and down" shows the disastrous results of relying on colloquial associations with such familiar words as 俯仰, or not looking past the first few dictionary definitions, and especially of ignoring its specific use in sexology texts.

66. H.V.G.'s translation of the last pair 屈折 as "and the like" can hardly be considered adequate. It is true that this pair sounds more like synonyms than the first three, which are clearly antonyms, but that need not deter us altogether from translating them literally.

67. Real, but for the most part surmountable, difficulties in the second half of this paragraph cause all of my fellow translators to delete and interpolate so frequently that it is impossible to point out every transgression.

68. The term 御 that appears on nearly every page of these early texts and is rendered in the present translation as "mount" is variously handled here by Levy, de Smedt, and H.V.G. as "control," "make love," and "ride." "Control" and "ride" are infelicitous and show a lack of initiative in discovering a

word with the associative resonance of 御 but that also works in English. "Make love" is too contemporary in its ring for an ancient text. I chose "mount" both because it actually was used in Elizabethan times to denote the sex act and because it preserves the equestrian flavor of the original. The absence of this usage from CW's list of no fewer than thirty-five definitions of 御 is indicative of the modesty of standard dictionaries in matters of sexology.

69. The expression 放平, which seems so obviously to mean lie flat, Levy and H.V.G. translate as "slacken the hands" and "relax the hands." The answer to this paradox can be found only in a misreading of the character 平 as 手 in the handwritten *Ishimpō* text.

70. The verb here 柎搏 is somewhat unusual. At first glance, both characters, which can mean "pat," look like a synonym compound. This, however, leaves us with the great warrior "patting" his penis, which seems too weak a prelude for the "attack" that follows. From two passages in the *Book of Rites*, 柎搏 appears to have been a kind of drum in ancient times and the verb-object combination 柎鼓 does mean to beat a drum, or to drum. Transferring this image to the present context, does the penis then become the drum or the drumstick? Closer perhaps to the martial atmosphere of this passage is the combination 柎劍, which means to place the left hand on the hilt of a sword or to hold a sword. Some of these possibilities are apparent in the earlier translations: Levy, "pats and guides"; de Smedt, "touches"; CC, "using his hand to tease the penis"; and H.V.G., "let the jade stem advance." My "brandishing" derives from the conviction that the possessor of the penis is wielding it in the manner of a drumstick or sword.

71. The Chinese "inch" is defined for medical purposes as the distance between the folds formed at the second and third joints of the middle finger when its tip and that of the thumb are brought together closing a circle. It also may be determined by the width of the index finger at the second knuckle.

72. CC consistently attributes to the male partner every act associated with the words 精, 洩, or 施, regardless of the real subject. Here the result produces the untenable anomaly of the male ejaculating at the commencement of penetration and then proceeding as if nothing happened. Again the error may be traced to the narrowness of contemporary usage and a failure to "stay in character" or embrace the linguistic ethos of an earlier period.

73. The term 琴絃 appears consistently throughout these texts in association with shallow penetration. It is absent from the "Highest Tao's" list, but 弦 preceded by lacuna appears in the diagram. Levy and H.V.G., following Japanese studies, define it as "frenulum clitoridis." CC agrees. A gloss to the T'ang "Ta le fu" defines it as "one inch within the vagina" and the Ming SNML concurs. All previous translations have rendered 琴 as "lute." The word is used in Chinese in two ways. Originally it referred to the very ancient musical instrument already in existence during Chou times consisting of an elongated horizontal sound box with five or seven strings running its full length and movable bridges. Later it was prefixed by various characters to denote everything from the Chinese violin 胡琴 and "moon lute" 月琴 to instruments of Western origin, including the entire classical string family, piano, organ, and humble harmonica. There is no reason to believe that early Chinese sexologists had anything else in mind than the classical Chinese *ch'in* in creating their nomenclature. The closest Western relative by structure, if not role, is the zither. V.G. suggests the "lesser labia," whose position reinforces the image of the classical *ch'in* and which makes sense in every appearance. Schipper's "Lute strings (Labia minora)" agrees. Surveying every context surrounding the term, there is no basis for assigning a location with the degree of specificity of "frenulum clitoridis." V.G. sees a contradiction between these oldest texts, which seem to refer to the labia minor, and later texts, which assign it to a depth of one inch, but this may well be a matter of where one begins measuring. The phrase "advance the 'jade stalk' between the 'zither strings'" 進玉莖於琴絃 in THT, "Posture 9," obviously denotes penetration of the vagina. "Frenulum clitoridis" would put the penis on the wrong trajectory.

74. All translations take this numerical series as indicating a mental count of one to nine, except de Smedt who gives us, "Insert the Jade Stalk . . . nine times." Grammatically and logically both are possible. My reason for siding with the majority is that I feel the only explanation for writing out the whole series number by number is to slow down the rhythm of the text and thus evoke a mood of suspension. If nine thrusts was the intended meaning, it could have been expressed more economically in another way. "Nine" itself, of course, is the highest odd number before ten and represents here, as in the *I ching* and elsewhere, the penultimate *yang* force.

75. Not surprisingly, the combination 昆石 does not appear in any dictionary. Yeh changes the character 昆 in *Ishimpō* to 崑 here, but later is inconsistent. Perhaps this emendation indicates his belief that 昆 refers to the K'un-lun Mountains. Other meanings of 昆 include multitudinous, posterity, and elder brother. Because all of the descriptive terms for female parts are based on concrete images, usually natural but a few architectural, one would like to make this fit the pattern. We know from an adequate sample of contexts that 昆石 always indicates a considerable depth in the vagina. The SNML ranks it seven on a scale of one to eight; that is, if we accept that its 昆戶 and the present 昆石 are one and the same. The difference could easily be explained by a scribal error given the form of the characters. On the other hand, if the earlier text proves to be corrupt on this point and the SNML turns out to be the true-transmission, 昆戶 could quite nicely be interpreted as "gate of posterity." This is unlikely, however, in view of the "Highest Tao's" 磏石 indicating early use of stone metaphor. V.G.'s translation, "Elder Brother Stone," shows he is prepared to put aside his normal caution and hitch his wagon to what for me is a highly improbable choice. Levy translates the term as "mixed rock" and defines it as "vestibular glands." H.V.G.'s "*k'un* stone" combines transliteration and translation, but they agree with the location, as does CC. I cannot reconcile this interpretation with the texts. The vestibular or Bartolin's glands are located at either side of the vaginal opening; that is, less than one inch in depth, although every indication in the texts cries out for maximum, or nearly maximum depth (see especially YFPC and SNML). Its position on the SNML scale would indicate a correct observation of proportions, and the SNC in its discussion of conception advises against maximum penetration to avoid passing the "gate of children" 子門. This seems to show an awareness of the os of the uterus, and my best guess for *k'un-shih* would be cervix, though more evidence would be needed to induce me to venture beyond the safety of transliteration at this point. A better understanding of the "Highest Tao's" twelve vaginal terms in which 磏石 is the very last, may someday yield an answer.

76. The *locus classicus* for 五常, "five constancies" or "five virtues," on which this genital version is based, is *Analects*, Chapter 2.

77. The two characters in *Ishimpō* 無行, seem an obvious scribal error and are deleted by Yeh. Levy and H.V.G.'s heroic efforts to

make sense of the original are not successful. What remains is not without ambiguity, however. It is impossible to determine from the handwritten Tamba text whether the combination intended is 無己 or 無已. Both have precedents in the classics and both can be made to work here: one meaning ceaselessly or unstintingly, and the other selflessly. Yeh takes it as 已 and I concur.

78. The four characters 臨事低仰 occasion very different interpretations among previous translators. The term 臨事 is common in literary usage, appears in every dictionary, and is used in virtually every sexology text in the sense of "approaching the act." This, unfortunately, has escaped every translator with the exception of CC. De Smedt even strays so far as to render it "after the act." The last two characters, on the other hand, are a genuine problem. The simple definition is "up and down, fluctuating between high and low." Applied to the penis, this would mean alternating between erect and flaccid. Why, however, does this constitute "wisdom"? My colleagues are not much help: Levy, "To approach the matter of lowering and raising is wisdom"; de Smedt, "droops"; and H.V.G., "moves sometimes up and sometimes down." My best guess finally is that "rising and falling" expresses the kind of trepidation that bespeaks restraint or prudence. CW gives the combination, but cites no *locus classicus* to support an idiomatic interpretation. CC's "calmly contemplates the methods of intercourse" seems more a case of bending the text to a preconceived and comfortable conclusion than of deciphering the idiom.

79. There is no universally accepted English translation for 真人. "Sage" has more or less settled in for 聖人, and "immortal" for 仙人, but 真人 still elicits such diverse efforts as Levy's "man of Verity," de Smedt's "a real man," and H.V.G.'s "Immortal." In practice, 真人 is broadly used as an honorific form of address for those who have realized the *tao*.

80. The four characters 精苦不固 should be clear to anyone with a background in Chinese sexology or even general medical theory. The character 苦 means to suffer the effects of such and such a cause and is defined as equivalent to 患 or 困. The characters 不固 should resonate with the familiar expression in Chinese medicine 固精, meaning to strengthen the *ching* in the sense of making it stable and resistant to leakage. The expression 不固 then denotes unstable, insecure, or weak. By missing these technical niceties, my fellow translators have failed to sharply focus the

contradiction posed by the exercise of "benevolence" and the physiological deficit of semen loss. No one is further from this understanding than H.V.G. who give us, "in order to preserve the semen it should never become too firm."

81. Most of my fellow translators get the drift here, but once again H.V.G. are not in striking distance: "Righteousness implies an appreciation that, although it should not be exposed to open daylight, its abstinence according to the *Tao* is in reality intended to promote giving."

82. The character 候 in the phrase 夫五徵之候 is ignored by all previous translations with the exception of Levy, who mistranslates it as "waiting." As used in works on sexology, or medicine and meditation in general, the word 候 has four different possible meanings: (1) to wait, (2) to observe, (3) sign or symptom, and (4) the condition of a thing within a dynamic process or stage of development. In the last two definitions it is instructive to recall the combinations 症候 and 火候. Here in this passage I feel that 候 partakes both of the senses of stage and sign.

83. When four translations vary as widely as V.G., "freely proceed with the act"; Levy, "leisurely draw (the fluid) out (from her)"; de Smedt, "penetrate and withdraw gently"; and H.V.G., "slowly pull," one should suspect wild guessing or misplaced literal straw clutching. Two of the more than forty definitions of 引 in CW are "withdraw from" and "pull out of." This may well be the appropriate meaning, especially in view of the terminal position of this passage in the sequence of sexual events.

84. Why there should be so much confusion over an expression that even pocket dictionaries define as "to hold the breath in apprehension" is a mystery. The four characters 屏息屏氣 are subjected to the following treatments: V.G., "breathing will become irregular"; Levy, "her breath is bated and her energy is withheld"; de Smedt, "she breathes rapidly"; Chang, "a change in the way she breathes"; and H.V.G., "breath becomes labored." Due to a fundamental misunderstanding of the grammar of this and the following four passages, Levy and de Smedt's translations are seriously flawed in phrasing and intelligibility. Only V.G. is sound on every count in this paragraph.

85. H.V.G. choose to ignore and not translate the co-verb 得 in this sentence. Levy translates 陰欲 as "sex awareness," demonstrating a fundamental lack of attunement to

the basic vocabulary of Chinese sexology. The actual meaning here of 陰, vagina, escaped no other translators, including those who preceded him.

86. The term 煩 is used often in these early texts to express excitement, stimulation, "hot and bothered." De Smedt and H.V.G. simply throw the verb out.

87. The sense of 心欲滿者 is not H.V.G.'s "her mind is full of desire," but closer to V.G.'s "her heart desires to be satisfied."

88. Yeh gives 洩 for *Ishimpō* 淺. Levy and CC translate the error, ignoring the logical progression of the paragraph and nonejaculation as the central tenet of Chinese sexology.

89. Most translators agree in the main, but Levy's misreading of the grammar and key usages in this paragraph cause his whole translation to be seriously skewed.

90. The character written 注 in *Ishimpō* does not appear elsewhere in the text or as such in CW. Because of its similarity to a cursive variant of 往, V.G., Levy, and H.V.G. have all translated it as "pass through." However, elsewhere in Tamba, where 往 unquestionably is the character intended, it is written 往. Yeh does not read it as 往, but instead gives us 候, though it in no way resembles the real 候 elsewhere in the text. Reviewing standard variants of 候 and the interpretations of various noted calligraphers, I have not found one that resembles the character in *Ishimpō*. Accordingly, my translation represents only an interpretation of the intended sense and not a claim of positive identification.

91. Cf. three levels of arousal in the male and five in the female in "The Highest Tao" and *Fu-k'o yü-ch'ih.*

92. This second appearance of 和氣 gives us an opportunity to examine the expression in another context. It occurs here at the head of a list of male responses to sexual arousal. Though the last three levels are expressed in terms of concrete loci, this first is a state rather than a locus. Again, the question arises as to whether it refers exclusively to the male participant or to a harmonious rapport of both partners. Here the context points more clearly to the male point of view, but, I would contend, it is the experience of mutual harmony recorded from one side.

93. For the character 肌 V.G. gives "skin," Levy "fatness," de Smedt "muscular," and H.V.G. "muscles." The word in its broadest sense encompasses all of these, and I think the meaning here is intended to be just that general. Accordingly, my translation, "flesh," aims to avoid misleading partiality.

94. Given the Chinese penchant for parallelism, the character 明 at the beginning of a series including 關, 戶, and 門 is disconcerting. V.G. translates, "stirred . . . concentrating . . . inner door . . . outer door"; Levy, 'dawning . . . beginning . . . shutting off . . . gate"; de Smedt omits the last of the four and deals with the rest by resorting to transliteration and parenthetical translation; and H.V.G., "indication . . . opening . . . pathway . . . gateway." CC falls back on explication rather than translation, and HMF simply quotes the original. Clearly, there is much floundering. In approaching this passage I make two assumptions: the four key characters function as the same part of speech, and they represent some sort of progression. Ignoring for a moment the rest of this text, the rest of the works in this collection, and the rest of classical Chinese literature, and focusing just on this paragraph, we find that 怒, 大, 堅, and 熱 are all parallel verbs, and that 和氣, 肌氣, 骨氣, and 神氣 are all parallel nouns. Now the last two, 戶 and 門 clearly are nouns and can function only as nouns. The character 關 can go several ways, but is perfectly comfortable here as a noun. That leaves 明, which not only normally is an adjective, but seemingly not of the same semantic family as the other three. Examining the similarity of certain cursive treatments of 明 and 門, one cannot entirely rule out the possibility of a scribal error involving some character with the 門 radical. However, making the best of the text as it stands, I have settled on "dawn" (with the blessing of CW) to keep the image concrete and to express the initial phase of a process. WHM agrees. Now, if the second term in each equation is a noun and the first is made nominal by the addition of 者, what does it mean to say, for example, that "stiffness is the gate of the *ching*"? The distinctions between even 關, 戶, and 門 are somewhat obscure, and it is difficult to derive a sense of stages. Finally, 開, the variant of 關 that appears in Tamba is obviously misread as 開 by H.V.G. who translate it as "opening."

95. Putting the syntactical cart before the horse, H.V.G. translates 節之以道 as "the *Tao* is controlled."

96. Levy takes the characters 開機 at the beginning of this sentence as "opening an opportunity." This is an obvious lapse into the wrong century and the wrong Chinese. I believe that V.G. has the right idea, even if his rendering is too explicit for my literary taste,

when he says, "The outlet of the seminal duct will not open." Out of the same two characters H.V.G. get all of, "the way made ready and [the gateway] opened." This paragraph needs to be carefully examined from the point of view of dramatic development. After a graphic analysis of the stages of male arousal, the climax, in keeping with the principles of Chinese sexology, must inevitably be anticlimax. If we think of 開 as "start the engine" rather than "open the throttle," then we have the basis for a subtle but real distinction between 開機 and 開精. Whether 機 here represents the whole machine or just the trigger mechanism is a relatively minor problem. If one clings to the translation of *ching* as "semen" as V.G., Levy, and H.V.G. have done, then what sense does it make to say, "open the semen without ejaculating"? Remembering that *ching* in these texts always carries the double meaning of semen and sexual energy, we may then take 開精不洩 as "activate the sexual energy without spilling [the semen]." The relationship of the last two four character phrases to the preceding sentence could be of the type, "If A then B" or "A and B," each of which will produce quite different results. Steering a safe course between a number of defensible alternatives, my interpretation is closest to CC's, "Do not get excited about sex and when having intercourse, do not recklessly ejaculate."

97. Only H.V.G. choose not to translate the verb 伺, "to observe or examine."

98. H.V.G. take 鳴 as 㗱, and thus translate "kiss." Later in the text the familiar combination 雞鳴 occurs where 鳴 is written just the same. Yeh and all translations concur in 鳴.

99. The translation here of 腎氣 as "kidney *ch'i*" is for convenience only, and the reader should remember that in Chinese medicine 腎 takes in all urogenital functions and is intimately connected with bone, marrow, and brain.

100. A note in the *Ishimpō* points out that one of the nine is missing.

101. The four characters 久與交接 admit of several interpretations: when you have been engaging in intercourse for a long time (on a given occasion); when you have long experience with intercourse; or if intercourse is to last for a long time. All of these possibilities have their partisans among previous translations. If my translation is somewhat circumspect, it is because I can see the good in all of them. Much of the ambiguity would be eliminated if we had a better handle on 實 in the next line.

102. Here is a good context from which to argue that 實 denotes glans clitoris, especially as it is the object of the verb 弄. Whether it is an abbreviation for 殼實 or an independent entity remains a problem.

103. H.V.G. translate 則容傷 as "the cause most likely lies in some injury," once again confusing cause and effect. No other translation makes this error.

104. My fellow translators have all greeted 數 as an old friend, addressing him as "number" and assuming perhaps a reference to "nine times nine" or "x shallow and y deep." Always wary of facile modern colloquial associations, it is instructive to remember that anciently 數 had over thirty meanings, including methods, techniques, and skills. Because of the preponderance of precedent in the text linking 數, the verb 行, and specific sets of numbers, one is virtually forced to lean in this direction. "Number" then should be understood to suggest the requisite combination and sequence of deep and shallow strokes, thus subsuming the concept of technique within number as most evident in the section on the "seven ills."

105. For 開其意 H.V.G. give "clear my mind" in complete violation of classical grammar. Fortunately, Levy's "reveal their intent" and CC's "explain in detail" offer a ray of hope.

106. V.G.'s "The Turning Dragon," Levy's "the dragon turns over," and H.V.G.'s "Upside-down Dragon" all show the limitations of colloquial intuition. The first definition in CW of 翻 is 飛, to fly (the radical, of course, is feather). Humana, whose "translation" normally is a tissue of pure fabrication, actually titles this posture "Dragon in Flight." The author of CC, though not about to reach for his dictionary, nevertheless did suspect that 翻 meant something other than "turn over" and thus explains, "Because the man's arms and legs are bent to support his body, he looks like a dragon. This is why it is called 龍翻. The character 翻, then, is the movement of the dragon." My final piece of supporting evidence is that the corresponding posture in the SNML is titled 龍飛, Flying Dragon. It is interesting that there is no "dragon" in the Ma Wang tui postures.

107. Fortunately only Levy fails to realize that 死往生返, meaning in practice "withdraw hard and penetrate soft," is one of the key slogans in the campaign against semen squandering. His "death goes and life returns" becomes totally meaningless.

108. The character in *Ishimpō* actually is 勢,   *239*

but it and 勢 are so frequently confused in the text, it is not surprising that Tamba and Yeh, joined by V.G. and Levy, take it as the latter. The character 熱 can be made to work both in terms of sense and grammar, but 勢 can function as a subject, and one feels the need of a stated subject at this point in the paragraph.

109. Again the failure to correctly interpret 煩 as intense excitation leads Levy to translate 煩悅 as "flustered and pleased" (obviously also mistaking 忦 for 悅). H.V.G.'s "anxiously pleased" shows the same compound error.

110. Although it is true that the character in the text 倡 is sometimes an alternate for 娼, hence Levy's "songstress" and H.V.G.'s "musical performer," it also is an alternate of 猖 meaning wild, frenzied, uncontrolled. The choice must work intimately with the next character 致 and with the whole phrase. One of the meanings of 致 in combination with other characters is mental state or condition, as in 興致. In this sense 猖 works well with 致 and reinforces the meaning of 煩悅. Finally, I know of no such conceit as the "happy hooker" in Chinese literature, and find the introduction here of the image of a sing-song girl singular and inappropriate.

111. The character 自閉 is one of the set phrases that echoes from one end of these texts to the other. Followed by 固 here, it simply means "restrain yourself" and refrain from ejaculating. H.V.G.'s, "This will effect a sustaining of the semen" is incomprehensible; and Levy's, "she naturally closes and firms" mistakenly identifies the gender of the subject.

112. Levy translates 虎步, "the tiger's tread"; V.G., "The Tiger's Tread"; and H.V.G., "Tiger's Step." The *Wondrous Discourse* interprets the posture in the following terms: "This method resembles a tiger or leopard emerging from the jungle and roaring into the wind." My translation, "stance," rather than "tread" or "step," is based on a nonambulatory interpretation of 步 as in such martial arts postures as 馬步.

113. One would not think there could be so many interpretations of so seemingly simple a phrase as 行五八之數. V.G. translates "alternating five shallow thrusts with one deep one"; and H.V.G., "counting to five times eight." I agree with CC and HMF's "forty times." Levy appears to be totally in the dark, and V.G. confuses this construction with those expressing the alternation of shallow and deep thrusts, such as 九淺一深.

114. H.V.G. omit to translate the phrase 還過胸. Levy once again presses the wrong

button on the time machine and translates 還 "still," as if the phrase had just been overheard on the street corner.

115. For 臭鼠 V.G. gives "Smelling Mouse," Levy "odiferous mouse," and H.V.G. "fragrant teeth" (taking 鼠 as an error for 齒). By "smelling mouse" I do not know if V.G. means mouse in the act of smelling or smelly mouse. Though 臭 is best known today in the sense of malodorous, there are numerous passages in the classics (e.g., *I ching*, "Its odor 臭 is like an orchid") where it undeniably means fragrant. Is it possible that the term is intended as a double-entendre, suggesting the sometimes fragrant sometimes pungent odor of the female parts? The character 臭 by itself occurs later in this text in a context where it certainly means malodorous. In view of its ambiguity, my translation is guardedly noncommittal. Turning then to its denotation, the situation is no less murky. H.V.G., CC, and HMF all favor "glans clitoris," but Levy translates, "vaginal secretion." The term is absent from the SNML list of eight depths. The YFPC uses it as just short of *k'un-shih*, the greatest depth. As the object of the verb 刺, it is highly unlikely that 臭鼠 could mean "vaginal secretions." Looking at the whole phrase, "Insert the 'jade stalk' and stab her 臭鼠," one would have to first withdraw again to "stab the clitoris," which seems like an unlikely procedure in view of the straightforward syntax. PS editors add a bracketed 臭 to the lone 鼠 on the diagram following "Yang-sheng fang."

116. The character in the Tamba text here is 煩, an old friend, which of course works perfectly. Yeh substitutes 還, however, which makes no sense and evidently is a typographical error.

117. The phrase 扣其赤珠 gives us an opportunity to see the verb 扣 at work within a well defined context. Our panel of experts seems to be unanimous as to the subject of the verb (penis understood), but variously interprets the action of the verb: V.G., "penetrate"; Levy, "tap"; H.V.G., "strike"; CC, "stab"; and HMF, "penetrate." All agree that the object of the verb is "labium minor." Reviewing for a moment the sequence of events, the woman is prone, the man approaches from the rear, penetrates deeply, and raises her buttocks. Would it be more likely that this was to facilitate his "penetrating," "tapping," or "striking" her labium minor with his penis or to enable him to reach beneath her with his hand to manipulate the "pearls"? I am also skeptical about the identity of "red pearl" or

"red pearls." Levy and H.V.G. render the term in the singular form, defining it as "labium minor pudendi," but I always understood this feature to come in pairs. Furthermore, the term 珠, literally pearl, has strong generic associations with anything spherical and glossy in appearance, including beads, drops, and so forth. Contemporary colloquial expressions for the clitoris include 陰珠 and 珠核, and an abnormally diminutive penis is 草裏珠, "pearl in the grass." The parallel passage in the SNML makes several significant changes: first, the woman prone posture is not specified, but rear entry is maintained; second, there is no separate verb for penetration; third, there is no mention of lifting the buttocks; fourth, the only operative verb is 叩 (cf. SNC 扣). This suggests that at least here in the SNML the subject is the penis, the verb 叩 denotes "knocking" as at a gate, and the object 赤珠 more likely indicates labium minor in this environment than clitoris. Once again, a better understanding of 赤朱 on the Ma Wang tui diagram would be invaluable.

118. None of our English translators have bothered to footnote the term 七傷, whereas our Chinese colleagues incorrectly define it as the seven internal pathogenic factors of Chinese medicine (joy, anger, melancholy, anxiety, sorrow, fear, and alarm). This list in fact is known as the 七情, and the term 七傷 refers in Chinese medicine to two distinct sets of etiological categories. The more relevant of the two outlines seven different manifestations of kidney (*shen*) weakness: cold genitalia, genital atrophy, impotence, spermatorrhea, thin semen, insufficiency of semen, dampness of genitalia, and incontinence. This list, quoted from the *T'an-ping yüan-hou lun*, published in 610, coincides very closely with the set of urogenital symptoms of the same name, "seven injuries," in the PSN included in this anthology.

119. The verb "to mount" in V.G.'s "The Mounting Turtle" and Levy's "the tortoise mounts" is ambiguous and may mean either to get up on or to ascend. In the present context, the choice of "mount" here suggests the image they have in mind is of the male mounting the female. I must object, if this is the case, that male turtles may very well approach the matter in this attitude, but that females certainly do not lie on their backs. Moreover, only rarely does the Chinese 騰 mean to ride on something, and I believe the image is actually of a turtle rising up from the deep, or if a fabulous specimen, soaring upward through the air. H.V.G.'s "Turtle Hopping" ignores the fact that in the fable of "the tortoise and the hare," it was the hare that did the hopping.

120. By deft splicing and inversion, H.V.G. manage to avoid dealing with the two central problems in this paragraph: 嬰女 and 令中其實. Although 嬰女 appears in their glossary, it is excised from the text here along with its verb 刺. Levy, H.V.G., and CC all define it as "vestibular glands," but there is no clue from other contexts to prove or disprove this. It cannot be found in either the SNML or YFPC lists. Levy and H.V.G. identify no fewer than three terms 嬰女, 陽臺, and 昆石 as vestibular glands, two bodies lying at the entrance of the vagina below the level of the vaginal wall and visible only on dissection. It is difficult to believe that a feature of so little prominence would have been given so much attention by ancient sexologists. It also is difficult to believe that "Penetrate deeply and stab her 'baby girl'" suggests anything but that the "baby girl" is located at a considerable depth. In fact, it is the seventh item in the "Highest Tao's" list of twelve vaginal terms.

121. V.G.'s "every thrust should be right in the middle" for 令中其實 stands alone against four translations on a theme of "hit the clitoris." Meeting it again in the ninth posture, he translates, "It is important to insert it deeply." Given the piston-cylinder configuration of components in intercourse, there is nowhere to thrust but in the "middle." I do not think 實 can be stretched to mean "deep" either, but I can sympathize with V.G.'s frustration at not knowing exactly what the word means and attempting to give it a vague rather than concrete locus. Levy's translation of "seed" and H.V.G.'s "fruit," offered without benefit of quotation marks or capitalization, can only leave the reader wondering why these foodstuffs have been left lying around the vagina. Once again, the precise interpretation of 實 turns on whether it is synonymous with 穀實, which seems from strong circumstantial evidence to be just past midway in depth, or is an independent term, perhaps clitoris. Why the special reminder to "hit" this spot (if spot it is) in postures five and nine does little to shed light on the subject.

122. The expression 內牽 is unusual if not unique and has been ignored, side-stepped, or misinterpreted by previous translations. V.G. reduces 堅熱內牽 to, "He moves his member vigorously"; Levy translates, "hot and hard he guides it in"; and H.V.G., "pressing inward firmly and warmly." Levy's "guides it in" overlooks the fact that penetration already has taken place; and H.V.G. mistake 堅熱 for

241

adverbs when they are standard adjectives for the erect penis. From the basic meaning of pull or drag, 牽 comes to mean involve, bring together, or match by force, as in the combination 牽合. I believe that 牽 operates here in the sense of the man "pulling" himself forward to "stick" inside the woman, while she carries out the movements.

123. All translators agree that it is the woman who has the major responsibility for moving at this point, except V.G., who because he persists in interpreting 三八 as "three shallow and eight deep," has no alternative but to render the whole phrase, "He moves his member vigorously, compelling the woman to respond to his movement." I feel, however, that it is this very context, where woman is the prime mover, that proves conclusively that all of the number combinations refer to sums or rhythms and not depths of penetration.

124. The verb 快 is used scores of times throughout these texts to express orgasm—female or male. H.V.G. suffer a temporary linguistic lapse here, translating it "quicken," but come to their senses when it appears for the second time in this paragraph, correctly translating, "climax."

125. H.V.G. is the only translation that agrees with my interpretation of 神形 as spirit plus physical form. The primary definition of the term in CW is "spirit and form," and the secondary is "form of a god." V.G. takes the phrase 動其神形 as "show on her face"; Levy, "move (her to a) divine appearance;" and CC "becomes visible in her appearance." The character 神 does mean appearance in such combinations as 神色, 神彩, and 神氣, but intuition tells me 動 would not be the verb of choice to express causation in change of countenance.

126. In Chinese medicine, the term 結聚 includes conditions such as constipation, congestion, blockages of the lymphatic system, and so on.

127. H.V.G.'s translation of 鶴交頸 as "Cranes Necking" cannot go unmentioned. The term 交頸 does mean literally to cross or entwine the necks, and Webster does offer "caress, pet" as a colloquial meaning of "neck." Nevertheless, given the strict distinction in the modern English speaker's mind between "necking" and sexual intercourse, it perhaps is best that the twain do not entwine in this context, despite the temptation of cross-linguistic punning.

128. The term 箕坐 should not be the problem that it is. The primary meaning of 箕 is

"winnowing basket," a triangular-shaped basket, wide in the front and narrow at the rear, used for throwing threshed grain into the air. The *locus classicus* for 箕坐 is the *Book of Rites*, where it says, "in standing do not lean; in sitting do not 箕." The commentary tells us that 箕 means to sit with legs open and outstretched in front of one, like the "tongue" of a winnowing basket. CW and TH give an impressive array of classical citations for 箕坐 and its close relative 箕踞. All commentators but one define it as sitting on the buttocks with legs outstretched, usually in the context of heaping insults on an enemy or general lack of decorum. The one exception says that the knees are bent. Our various translators contradict each other, and even themselves: V.G., "cross-legged"; Levy, "squatting" (illustration shows kneeling); H.V.G., "basket manner"; CC, "kneeling with the knees spread apart" (illustration coincides); HMF, "cross-legged" (photo shows kneeling); and WHM, "legs outstretched." Normally one would be swayed by the weight of classical opinion, which almost unanimously favors legs open and outstretched. However, other methods calling for this posture seem somewhat unlikely. Method 15 in the THT specifies the "winnowing basket" when calling for the man to alternately penetrate two women lying belly to belly. Here Levy translates "cross-legged," although his illustration shows kneeling. Method 23 in the THT features the man in "winnowing basket pose" and the woman on top with her back to him. Again V.G. translates "cross-legged," but Levy switches to "legs outspread" (illustration shows legs extended but not open). Number 27 in the same work has nearly identical instructions as "Cranes," but Levy now translates "legs outstretched," and V.G. is ever true to "cross-legged." The characters 跪, 胡跪, and 蹲 appear elsewhere in the text, so it seems that when kneel, squat, and some other version of squat were called for, the vocabulary was available. No commentator or dictionary suggests that 箕坐 meant "cross-legged," for which perfectly good terms exist in 盤坐 and 趺坐, though these combinations never appear in the texts. The only posture left unnamed, then, is that featuring outstretched legs (whether open or not might still be covered by 箕坐), a position for which there seems to be no ready English equivalent. A survey of hundreds of specimens of erotic art from the Ming and Ch'ing reveals two examples of cross-legged entry and approximately twenty with the man's legs outstretched. However, in view of certain still unreconciled contradictions in context, we offer a literal translation rather than locking the gate prematurely.

129. "Wheat teeth" is simply a literal rendering of 麥齒, which V.G., following Maspero's "l'Indentation en forme de grain de blé," calls "Wheat-shaped hole"; Levy "wheat buds"; H.V.G. "wheat tooth"; and CC and HMF "vagina." Levy and H.V.G.'s glossaries define the term as "labium minor." WHM inexplicably gives the characters 麥瞋. The YFPC and SNML list it as next in line after the 琴絃 "zither strings," or the second degree of depth. Actually, the very same term appears in a section on female typology, where it clearly indicates irregular teeth. Later in this text, during a discussion on conception, we are told that the optimum depth for ejaculation is the 麥齒, which would seem to indicate a level deeper than the "labium minor." The YFPC advises that the optimum depth for bringing about the harmony of *yin* and *yang* is between the "zither strings" and "wheat teeth," that is, neither too deep nor too shallow, again seeming to rule out the "labium minor" interpretation. It is number six of twelve vaginal terms in the "Highest Tao" and appears roughly in the middle of the "Yang-sheng fang" diagram.

130. The "Highest Tao's" system of "eight benefits" and "seven ills" differs from the present in significant details and is interesting for comparative purposes.

131. Here, although the construction is exactly the same as earlier, V.G. switches from "x shallow and y deep" to "eighteen strokes."

132. All but Levy realized that 藏 is an alternate for what is now commonly written 臟 and refers to the Five Viscera (heart, liver, spleen, lungs, and kidney.) He renders it "profitably hoarding."

133. V.G.'s "harmonizing the blood circulation" and H.V.G.'s "harmonizing the pulse" are acceptable, but Levy's "blending the conduits" communicates only confusion to the English-speaking reader.

134. The phrase 女門辟 evokes the following translations: V.G., "vaginal pains"; Levy, "excessive contraction"; H.V.G., "tightening of the female gate"; and CC, "spasm." The pack arrives in fairly tight formation, but I wish I knew the source of their certainty. CW gives over ten pronunciations and more than fifty definitions of 辟. The character does occur in the *Su wen* in a passage that by no means is transparent and does not relate to female afflictions, but is interpreted by commentators to denote cramps or tightness. I

thus tentatively side with the majority in the absence of a better alternative.

135. The title of the "benefit" 道體 is not a standard medical term, but among the nearly sixty definitions of 道 in CW, perhaps 導, 通, or 治 can be applied here. Everyone comes to the same conclusion, save Levy, who chooses the unlikely meaning of "speak, talk, or inform" for his "informing the body." "Regulate" is precisely the meaning of 道 in the "Highest Tao's" 疾使內不能道.

136. V.G., H.V.G., and CC choose not to translate the phrase 男以肫脅刺之. Levy opts for word-for-word literal translation: "The man stabs her with his thighs and ribs." The chief sources of confusion here are the two appearances of the character 肫 and the subject of the verb 刺, which one normally expects to be penis (stated or understood), but which here is "thighs and ribs." Without tracing every possible permutation, in the end, the strongest pull seems to come from the syntax itself, which in its simplest most direct sense means that the man throws his thighs and ribs forcefully into the act.

137. Although I do not favor translating *ch'i*, H.V.G.'s "exhaustion of energy" for 絕氣 certainly is preferable to Levy's "stopped air."

138. Fortunately, no one else save H.V.G. mistakes 汗泄 (literally "perspiration is emitted") for "release of semen."

139. The verb 擔 means to bear on the shoulders. It is highly specific and apropos in this phrase. Levy's "supports both her thighs" and H.V.G.'s "carries both of her thighs in his arms" miss the mark.

140. For 令女自搖精出 H.V.G. give us, "The woman shakes herself until she reaches orgasm," demonstrating an equal disregard for both Chinese and English. The character 搖 is used consistently in these texts as a verb denoting the undulations of lovemaking. One cannot simply run off with the first definition in a Chinese-English dictionary. Following "orgasm" in their translation, H.V.G. give the characters 溢精 instead of 出精, which appear in Tamba and Yeh.

141. The phrase 男勿快 appears here and in every succeeding "ill" in exactly the same position and exactly the same sense. Levy's, "The man is not to continue until he attains joyfulness" points the reader in precisely the opposite direction of the intended meaning.

142. *Ishimpō* gives just the character 醉 here, but Yeh interpolates a 飽 following it. Although 醉飽 is a common verb compound

in these texts, the original stands well enough on its own.

143. The expression 消渴 represents a set of symptoms usually associated with "diabetes" in Western medicine. H.V.G.'s "digestive thirst, *hsiao-k'o* (消渴) [diabetes]" is not only overloaded with transliteration, parenthesis, characters, and brackets, but due to faulty punctuation leads us to believe that there are actually two items involved. Moreover, the improvised "digestive thirst" ignores standard translations of the term and misinterprets 消 in this context for digestion instead of emaciation. The author of CC also is too proud to reach for his medical dictionary and explains in parenthesis that the two characters mean "parched throat and inability to urinate." Ironically, polyuria is probably the most common symptom of the condition actually indicated.

144. The first character in the combination 奪脈 is written 棄 in *Ishimpō*. Yeh takes it as 褋 (a variant of 雜) and H.V.G. and CC as 奪. Although I cannot find a specimen of calligraphy with the upper element written 六 instead of 大, Wang Hsi-chih does in one example write 木 at the bottom instead of 寸. Furthermore, I find no evidence of 雜脈 as a standard term in Chinese medicine, or of 雜 alone in any medical context that relates to this combination. The character 奪 by contrast is a standard equivalent for 傷 and 損, meaning harm, insult or exhaustion in such expressions as 奪血, 奪汗, and 奪氣.

145. H.V.G. translate 據席 as, "The man stands on the floor next to the bed." (Tamba gives now rare variants of both characters.) Nothing in the text suggests this interpretation, and the phrase occurs frequently in the text. Everyone else sees just what is there.

146. This time rather than struggle with the expression, H.V.G. simply throw it out.

147. The *Ishimpō* copyists use the convention 々 as ditto marks. In all of the "benefits" and "ills" in this section, the two character title is first introduced and then repeated in ditto marks as the subject of the first sentence. The Tamba text, which reads 機々關々厥々傷々, is confusing on a number of counts: first, the unorthodox use of ditto marks; second, the exceptional appearance of a four character title; third, the identity of the character written 開 in *Ishimpō* may be subject to varying interpretations; and fourth, regardless of whether we take 開 as 開 or 闓, there is no ready understanding of it in tandem with 機. H.V.G. take it as 開, but comparing it with unequivocal examples of 開 elsewhere in the text, they are not a perfect

match. Taking it 關, as Yeh and CC have done, the four characters seem to work well enough together grammatically, but we still do not know if the term is one of anatomy or physiology. By playing with the noun-verb roles, one can multiply the possibilities; and CC, with tacit approval from WHM, has come up with the novel entry, "what we mean by 機關 is 厥傷 (meaning a chronic disease of the internal organs)." CC seems to be reading 關 as a verb, meaning to "shut," and thus indicating a "shutting down" of the body's systems. This, then, is made to equal 厥傷, both of which are familiar characters in medical Chinese, although not together. The term 厥 has three distinct medical definitions, the most common of which is fainting, whereas 傷 is a general term for injury or insult to any part of the body or its functions. The two together could be coordinate complements or could indicate a 厥 type of 傷. The term 機關 does not appear in recent medical dictionaries, but the *Dictionary of Chinese Medicine* (*Chung-kuo i-hsüeh ta tz'u-tien*, Shanghai: Commercial Press, 1928), citing a passage in the *Su wen*, "Chüeh lun p'ien" defines 機關 as "joints" 關節. The "Chüeh lun p'ien" passage brings together the term 逆氣, abnormally rising *ch'i*, and 機關 in a context that can be hardly anything but joints. The combination appears twice in the SNF, once in a phrase precisely matching that in the *Su wen*: 機關不利.

148. H.V.G.'s translation of 遲疾 as "chronic diseases" instead of "slow and fast" (i.e., pace) is a sad day for Sinology.

149. The text here clearly says 勿令女人自搖, which cannot mean other than as we have rendered it. However, both H.V.G. and CC, exercising either editorial license or negligence, remove the negative imperative, thus diametrically altering the sense. Levy's "don't let the woman agitate herself" amounts to a pun and is too ambiguous for serious comment. There are many instances of 自搖 in these texts, but this is the sole appearance in the negative. Emendation might seem justified by a consistent pattern of usage and in view of the woman superior posture and absence of specific indications that the man initiate the movements. However, it was not sufficient cause for Yeh to emend it, and we likewise will demur. WHM accepts the text at face value, but acknowledging its exceptional nature, explains that the purpose is to avoid overstimulation of a weakened man.

150. The term 閉 represents a fundamental symptom complex in Chinese medicine. H.V.G.'s "closing out the hundred" seems

oblivious to this. The condition manifests during a sudden change in the course of an illness where the pathogenic influence gains the upper hand and becomes, as it were, "locked" in. Symptomatically, it can produce systemic dysfunction, coma, lockjaw, clenched fists, phlegm congestion, and so on. CC's "blockage of the pulse" is a wild guess, since ironically, 閉 syndrome is actually characterized by rapid pulse.

151. CC translates 淫佚於女 as "the woman's lust is uncontrolled," ignoring the norms of literary Chinese and the well-established pattern in these texts of all unstated subjects referring to the male.

152. An apparent erratum in Yeh gives 相搖 for Tamba's 自搖.

153. H.V.G. throws this sentence out of the text; and Levy, apparently not understanding its meaning, gives us a word-for-word literal translation that is devoid of sense in English.

154. Among the seven versions of the phrase 雖復暫快 surveyed, only CC and WHM render dissenting interpretations: "Although after a brief time it seems that one revives again" and "Although one quickly revives." CC, by misreading the intent of 復, and interpreting the "temporary pleasure" as referring to a second act of coition in one session of lovemaking, takes the whole thrust of the paragraph off on a tangent. I feel (and all other translators seem to agree) that the force of 復 implies that, on the many occasions one ejaculates, each time provides this transitory sensation, but that each time it ends in disappointment. The symptomology of *ching* deficiency described in this passage parallels *Su wen*, "Sheng-ch'i t'ung-t'ien lun:" 目盲不可以視耳閉不可以聽.

155. I agree with the notes of the various translators who take this as the "spirits" of the Five Viscera.

156. Levy's "how should one obtain leakage" shows total disregard for English idiom.

157. This refers to the traditional Chinese "week" 旬 of ten days.

158. Next to the characters 平平 in *Ishimpō* the Japanese commentator writes 午午. Yeh and H.V.G. do not accept the emendation, but Levy and CC do, resulting respectively in, "If the desire for intercourse rises up irregularly in his mind" and "frowning the whole day." The combination 午午 denotes the idea of multiplicity, but is exceedingly rare and, in the only example I can find, is applied to mountain peaks. Levy and CC's tortured efforts are even more mystifying in view of the perfect sense made by the original.

159. *Yang* is used in these early sexology texts to denote the male gender and male sexual energy. The words masculinity, virility, and potency come to mind in English. In later texts, other dimensions of *yang* become increasingly important, such as the "light" phases of the solar, lunar, and diurnal cycles and the "masculine" element within the female.

160. The expression 陰衰 is perfectly straightforward medical Chinese. The character 陰 refers to the genitalia and 衰 to a state of weakness or decline in function. H.V.G.'s "testicles sagging" would be laughable were it not so embarrassing to the profession of translation.

161. The four characters 體戚毀傷 pose a number of problems. The first two characters as they stand do not seem to be a standard medical, literary, or colloquial expression. The only definition of 戚 one can begin to work with is 憂 or 哀, but these refer only to distressed mental states. My translation thus is somewhat speculative here. The second pair 毀傷 appears in such familiar works as the *Classic of Filial Piety* and *Mencius*, where it means simply physical injury. V.G.'s "burned" and H.V.G.'s "injured by beating" are unnecessarily imaginative.

162. The four familiar characters 若作不祥 have elicited a number of very different interpretations. V.G., "will be exposed to ill-fortune"; Levy, "will perform an ill-omened (deed) in his youth"; and H.V.G., "will appear to be committed to do evil and unlucky things." If these translations seem to be English confessions obtained by torture from a Chinese suspect, it may be that the suspect is not altogether innocent. WHM agrees with my translation.

163. All are happily agreed that the meaning here implies misfortune for both mother and child, except for Levy, whose misreading of the syntax and key vocabulary results in the inappropriately oedipal "will commit evil with its mother."

164. H.V.G.'s "between the crescent and full moon" is flat wrong and, if taken literally, rules out twenty-seven days of the month. The first quarter occurs on approximately the eighth day of each lunar month, the last quarter on approximately the twenty-second, and the full moon on the fifteenth.

165. Again, six common characters 必為亂兵風盲 but many interpretations: Levy, "will initiate a troop rebellion and become blindly violent"; V.G., "will be killed in war or blinded by the wind"; and H.V.G., "will

side with rebel soldiers or be blinded by the wind." The two bones of contention, then, are whether 為 functions passively or actively and the meaning of 風盲. The next sentence also employs the phrase 必為, but in an unambiguous context, which precludes the possibility of passive voice. Thus in accordance with syntactical parallelism and the internal workings of the phrase itself, I feel that 為 must be functioning as an active verb. The two characters 風盲 as a combination cannot be found in any dictionary—general or medical—but must logically be either independent concepts or a single entity. The first alternative yields the meaning "insane and blind," where the character 風 is interpreted as an alternate of 瘋; and the second alternative, "wind blind," which could be a form of blindness inflicted by external atmospheric wind or the internal "wind syndrome." The interpretation adopted here instead is to take the whole phrase as generally descriptive of a state of blind recklessness associated with bandit behavior.

166. The meaning of this opening phrase, 求子法自有常體清心遠慮, is completely altered by Levy and CC through faulty punctuation. V.G. and H.V.G. correctly realized that 常體 is a combination (equivalent to 常理) and should not be divided. The term 清心 is an even more-familiar combination, and, likewise, must not be divided. By shifting the punctuation, all the other combinations line up incorrectly producing gibberish in Chinese and English.

167. There are many interpretations of 安定其衿袍. Levy, "settle the dress"; V.G., "sit quietly"; H.V.G., "neatly hang up the clothing"; and CC, "with garments in órder." I believe that the phrase conveys literally and ritually the proper decorum and attitude for conception. H.V.G.'s translation is misleading in its implication of premature disrobing and ignores the fact that the Chinese fold rather than "hang up" the clothes. WHM agrees with my interpretation.

168. The two characters 垂虛 do not seem to be a set compound, but by extrapolation from such expression as 虛心垂慮, 垂思, 垂念, and 虛心, I believe the meaning is to maintain an attitude of humility and reverence. H.V.G. choose not to translate it at all; V.G. and CC both render it "concentration"; and Levy's "transmit an emptiness" is both wrong and unintelligible. WHM agrees with my interpretation.

169. 齋戒 is a general term for abstinential self-purification. It has strong Buddhist asso-

ciations now, implying especially abstinence from flesh foods, but the combination appears as early as the *Book of Rites*, *Mencius*, *Moh tzu*, and *Chuang tzu*. As used in the *I ching*, it conveys the sense of an attitude of respectful solemnity, which I believe is the appropriate meaning here. V.G.'s "fasting" is narrow and misleading; Levy's "abstain" is inadequate; and H.V.G.'s "abstain from unclean meats and other vile things" is adequate to a fault.

170. I agree with Levy and CC's interpretation of 卻身 as "withdraw the body" (卻 does not seem to have been used for 但 before the Sung), but part company when it comes to the phrase 勿過遠. They take the "not too far" as referring to the withdrawal, whereas I feel that it advises moderate penetration. CC's reading seems grammatically plausible until he gets to the second 過, and then only by altering the text is he able to complete the sentence. It defies anatomy and logic to say that when ejaculating, the penis should not be withdrawn beyond the "labium minor" because it will then be in danger of "passing" the cervix. WHM makes the same error. For some reason V.G. translates 麥齒 as "half an inch," and then goes on to say, "if deeper he will have passed the opening of the uterus." First, both YFPC and SNML indicate a depth of two inches for 麥齒, and no source suggests "half an inch"; and second, one is more in danger of not reaching the "opening of the uterus" from such a shallow depth than of "passing" it. The phrase 淺則得氣遠則氣散 in YFPC supports my contention that the concept of "far" 遠 here means deep.

171. I take exception with every previous interpretation of the phrase 至麥齒, which I believe stands on its own and should not be aligned with either the preceding or following phrases. By following this reading (but not bending the original to a preconceived conclusion) the text corresponds perfectly with modern Western advice to ejaculate for conception from three-quarters depth to avoid overshooting the os of the cervix.

172. The term 子門 is still in use today in Chinese medicine for os of the cervix.

173. CW defines 子戶, citing a commentary to the *Su wen*, as 子宮, the more-familiar term today for uterus. H.V.G. reduce both 子門 and 子戶 to "birth portal" and then give us 子宮 in parenthesis as if this was the expression in the original text, which it is not.

174. The term 賢良 is a compound meaning "virtuous," and there is no need to translate the two characters separately as V.G., Levy, and H.V.G. have done.

175. The term 生氣 "the *ch'i* of life" may be used to characterize *ch'i* in any of its manifestations, from the natural world to artistic productions to man himself. If influenced by the preceding sentence, one would lean toward the external environment, but if by the following then toward the age of the partners. I am persuaded by the phrase in FCPI 以生氣時夜半後 that it refers to favorable macrocosmic conditions rather than age.

176. I take the four characters 鑿孔居高 as indicating a relatively anterior placement of the vulva, and especially the opening of the vagina. Levy and H.V.G. give us "high"; V.G., "the labia of the vulva should be well developed"; Humana, "the Jade Gate should be so placed that penetration is easy"; and CC, incomprehensibly, "her calves are strong."

177. In my mind there is some question as to whether 陰上 means above the genitalia, that is, the mons, or upon the genitalia, that is, the vulva.

178. This is much above the ideal age expressed in all other texts, which usually place it between puberty and twenty. Moreover, from everything we know of social customs, to be childless at twenty-five meant to be unmarried or barren, both of which were disasters.

179. The sexagenary (or sexagesimal) cycle is a very ancient system of reckoning days by which the Celestial Stems 天干 and Terrestrial Branches 地支 are continuously paired, like interlocking cogwheels of ten and twelve teeth, respectively, until they repeat again at sixty. During the Han, the system came to be employed for the year count as well.

180. The "*p'o* days" 破日 are the most consistently and thoroughly inauspicious of the cycle of twelve days in the Chinese almanac.

181. Levy and H.V.G. give us only "lunar eclipse," no doubt by associating 日 with 二十八 instead of 日月蝕. The FCPI offers 日月薄 in a passage that closely parallels this one, but admits of no ambiguous punctuation.

182. The phrase 大寒大暑 has two possible meanings: (1) the fifteen-day climatic period beginning January 20 or 21 and that beginning July 22 or 23; and (2) extreme cold or heat. Maspero's "les quinze jours qui précedent immediatement les deux équinoxes" cannot be correct because the equinoxes mark the beginning of spring and autumn. Only CKYSTPS takes it in the first sense, but I side with the majority opinion in view of parallel passages in other texts, especially the YFPC, where context positively precludes the "twenty-four climatic periods" interpretation.

183. Levy translates 春秋冬夏節氣日送迎五日之中 as "the five days before and after the start of spring, autumn, winter and summer"; and H.V.G., "The five day period before each of the twenty-four days of solar terms in the four seasons." The solar year is divided into twenty-four climatic periods, and those representing the beginning (立) of the four seasons were the occasion for special imperial rites known as 迎氣. My best guess is that 送迎 refers to the two days before, the day of, and the two days after the first day of each season. WHM concurs. Levy's "the five days before and after the start of spring, autumn, winter and summer" is ambiguous, admitting both the interpretation of a ten-day period of abstinence or of five days that straddle the first day. H.V.G.'s "The five day period before each of the twenty-four days of solar terms in the four seasons" produces a total of 120 days, or a prohibition extending to one-third of the entire year.

184. H.V.G. decline to translate the phrase 本命行年, but Levy's "your birthday and New Year's Day" and WHM's 本命或行年 over translates it. CW defines 本命年 as the year of one's birth in relation to the twelve Terrestrial Branches and 行年 as one's cumulative age.

185. Levy correctly recognizes 丙子丁丑 and 庚申辛酉 as four pairs of Stem-Branch combinations, but H.V.G. give eight independent transliterated entities without benefit of identification. Actually this whole paragraph as it appears in the *Ishimpō* is attributed to the 養生要集 (which Yeh renders 養生集要), and Tamba tells us in a note that YFPC gives 丙午丁未 for the postsummer solstice period, and the SNC 丙子丁丑 and 庚申辛酉. Yeh appropriates the whole paragraph for his reconstruction of the SNC, but for these taboo days he forsakes the 丙子丁未 version in favor of those noted by Tamba as belonging to the SNC. In their translations, Levy and H.V.G. mix elements from the various versions without noting the discrepancies.

186. I accept Yeh's emendation, following Tamba, of 妄 for 忌.

187. Although I cannot find the expression 天地牝牡 as such in other sources, I believe the meaning is the same as 天地合日, which occurs on the same day. V.G. and H.V.G. agree with my reading, but Levy's "heaven is female and earth is male (reversing the usual order of things)" errs by making too much of the fact that in the combination 天地 *yang* precedes *yin* whereas in 牝牡 *yin* precedes *yang*. If this were relevant, then what of 天地陰陽?

188. There is a lacuna in *Ishimpō* indicated   247

by a blank space the size of one character, which Yeh fills with two: 人, belonging to the end of the previous line; and 自, to the beginning of this. The text is intelligible with the lacuna, but Yeh's interpolation seems perfectly consistent with the intended sense. For Tamba's 以爲佳 (or Yeh's 自以爲佳), Levy translates "considering this beautiful" and V.G., "delight," which seem reasonably to the point; but H.V.G.'s "She never understands the seriousness [of this]" cannot be accounted for.

189. Beside the characters 用者 in *Ishimpō*, Tamba offers an interlinear emendation 困, which Yeh accepts. H.V.G. give "She" as the subject of this sentence, but all others realize that the condition applies equally to both sexes.

190. Previous translations are split between interpreting 若身體疲勞不能獨御者 as too tired from the cure or too tired from the affliction. I feel that the case in question is the affliction. Levy's rendering of the second half of the phrase as "can't control (your semen)" is another instance of misreading 御.

191. H.V.G. pretends the phrase 無所云爲 did not exist. V.G.'s "stay there in a condition of complete tranquility" is adequate, but Levy's "say and do nothing" can hardly be improved upon.

192. Three of our translators, V.G., CC, and de Smedt, who are obliged to offer only excerpts, elect to bail out just before the phrase   怨曠之氣爲邪所淩後世必當有此者, whereas Levy and H.V.G., who are forced to contend with it, give us, "there will always be such persons in later generations," and "in future generations this will happen again and again," respectively. Both seem to have missed the point that 曠 means, among other things, to be deprived of the opportunity to acquire a wife, and 怨, of course, means to harbor resentment. The focus of the phrase, then, is not to explain the future but the present.

193. Levy and H.V.G.'s translating the Chinese unit of weight, the *liang* 兩, as "ounce" is like translating meter as yard. The current ounce equals approximately 28 grams. According to historical tables in Wu Ch'eng-luo's *Chung-kuo tu-liang-heng shih*, the *liang* has been in use since the Chou dynasty. From the T'ang to the Ch'ing, a period of 1,300 years, it remained a constant 37.30 grams. The documents assembled by Tamba represent the Han, Sui, and T'ang, but these early sexology classics customarily are dated as Sui. At the beginning of the Sui (589) the *liang* had a value of 41.76 grams, but was revalued in 605 to 13.92 grams.

194. I accept Yeh's emendation of 硫 for *Ishimpō* 流.

195. A spoon or spatula measuring a "Chinese inch" on each side (i.e., 1 square inch) capable of holding approximately 2 grams of powdered mineral medicine or 1 gram of powdered botanicals. H.V.G.'s "cubic inch spoonful" is misleading.

196. The convention in Chinese medical texts of using 一方 to introduce alternative prescriptions is obscured by Levy's "If, on the other hand, you yourself take. . . ."

197. In the phrase 以差爲度, the word 差 is used, I believe, interchangeably with 瘥, which means to be cured. Levy obviously took it in the sense of to be sent on a mission and thus mistranslates, "you will attain the right level to dispatch the demon."

198. The species in question is 麋, or alces machlis.

199. Levy translates "one should also take" instead of "one may also take," which gives the mistaken impression that what follows is not an alternative method but a cumulative requirement.

200. H.V.G. and CC translate 熬 as "bake," and Levy as "heat." In medical terminology 熬 can mean either to simmer in water or to produce gels by boiling herbs in several changes of water, each time collecting and filtering the supernatant, condensing and solidifying it. Bake generally is 烘 or 焙, and even in culinary usage 熬 always means to boil in water. Levy's "heat" therefore is too vague, considering the high degree of specificity indicated in the preparation of Chinese herbal medicines; and "bake" cannot be supported by any stretch of 熬.

201. I accept Yeh's emendation of 用 for 內 in *Ishimpō*.

202. An area corresponding to the present southeast corner of Kansu Province famous for the production of medicinals.

Prescriptions of Su Nü

1. According to the "six extremes" 六極 theory of exhaustion in Chinese medicine, when the *ching* is severely deficient, it manifests as impaired vision and hearing.

2. De Smedt treats this whole passage with fanciful paraphrase, adding language such as, "intercourse with a woman who is advanced in years . . . , long abstinence from sex in the case of a man," which is simply not in the original.

3. De Smedt adds "eclipse of sun or moon" to this list, which is not in the original.

4. Translation of 傷子之精 presents two possibilities: (1) your own *ching*, or (2) the *ching* of your offspring. De Smedt's "weakening of the semen" shows an inclination for the former, and CC's "the *ching-ch'i* of your children" for the latter. Although 子 may function as a polite form of address in literary Chinese, for it to do so here in these texts would be a unique event and all the more unlikely in a dialogue with the emperor. Unfortunately, the formula for introducing the consequences to one's offspring of various sexual transgressions generally is 生子 rather than 子 alone. On balance, I must side with CC and interpret *ching* not so much in the sexual sense, but rather as 元精, or the hereditary aspect of the child's endowment.

5. "Enemy," here, of course, means sex partner.

6. De Smedt translates this and the preceding phrase as, "The man may also suffer from impotence with a woman even when his Jade Stalk erects." I cannot agree with this interpretation, but feel that CC does full justice to the line.

7. The 榮氣 is the energy derived from food that circulates in the blood.

8. The 衛氣 is *yang* energy circulating in the subcutaneous layer of the body, functioning as a first line of defense against external pathogens.

9. I can discover nothing about this figure, except that 高陽 appears to be a double surname.

10. The term 五勞 may be understood in two ways in Chinese medicine. The first denotes illnesses resulting from taxing the Five Viscera (heart, liver, spleen, lungs, and kidneys), and the second is summarized in the *Su wen*, "Hsüan-ming wu-ch'i p'ien:" "Using the eyes for a long time injures the blood; reclining for a long time injures the *ch'i*; sitting for a long time injures the flesh; standing for a long time injures the bones; and walking for a long time injures the sinews."

11. The 六極 represent exhaustion of the blood, sinews, flesh, *ch'i*, bones, and *ching*.

12. In Chinese herbology, herbs are classified according to the "four temperatures" 四氣 and "five flavors" 五味. "Cool, cold, warm, and hot" herbs generally are prescribed for symptoms according to the theory of opposites.

13. The word 風 has two meanings in Chinese medicine. First, it is the most important of the "six eternal pathogens," often combining with other factors such as heat, cold, or dampness to produce disease. Second, it is the 內風, or "internal wind," a symptom likened to wind in its abruptness and irregularity, but whose cause is an internal disorder. Because the emphasis here is on the effects of the four seasons, it must be the first meaning that is operative.

14. These represent two of the "four diagnostic techniques"; viz., inspection, auscultation and olfaction, interrogation, and pulse and palpation. The word 色, translated here as "color," belongs to the category of inspection and distinguishes five primary colors of the face and skin indicating various diseases. Pulse diagnosis involves three finger compression of the radial pulse at the carpal joint to assess its frequency, rhythm, fullness, smoothness, and amplitude. Classical diagnosis distinguishes twenty-eight pulse types, each indicating a specific syndrome.

15. In a note to 更生丸, the name of this prescription, Wang T'ao tells us that 更生 means 茯苓, tuckahoe, the first ingredient in all of these prescriptions. It is difficult to know if he means that 更生 is another name for 茯苓 or that it simply refers to it as a kind of epithet, "return to life." According to Li Shih-chen's *Materia Medica*, 更生 is another name for chrysanthemum.

16. "Reversal" indicates that the *ch'i* is moving in an abnormal direction, especially the *ch'i* of the lungs and stomach when rising. This manifests as panting or coughing in the case of the lungs or vomiting and hiccups in the case of the stomach.

17. The seeds of the *wu-t'ung* 梧桐 tree (*firmiana platanifolia*).

18. Li Shih-chen tells us that the seeds of the small variety of *wu-i* 蕪荑 are fermented as a strongly pungent condiment.

19. General state of weakness in the organs, *ch'i*, and blood, resulting in a decline of physiological function.

20. This is the same name as for the summer remedy.

21. Levy's "white glutinous millet" is a classic case of "faux amis."

22. Dictionary definitions of 牛酥 range from cheese, cream cheese, and koumiss to butter. Li Shih-chen tells us that it is made by bringing milk to a boil two or three times, removing it from the fire and placing it in a bowl to cool. The skin that forms on the surface is then heated until an oil emerges. The folk method involves churning the cream in a   *249*

leather bag or other vessel until the butter forms.

23. Yeh's 激 in the combination 四激, I believe is an error for 游.

Essentials of the Jade Chamber

1. Maspero translates the phrase 未生乳 as "les seins pas encore formés." I interpret the expression 生乳 as 生產, drawing on the SNC's 未在產者, the HCYI's 未生產, the CTCY's 未經產者, and "Shih wen" 新乳始沐 for support. To contend that the phrase denotes undeveloped breasts must explain the sentence just a few lines later which states, "Her breasts swell and fill the whole hand when held."

2. The term *tan-t'ien* 丹田, literally "elixir field," is used loosely here for the lower abdomen.

3. I feel that the line 求其口實, translated by H.V.G., "searching for her mouth and tongue," and Levy, "try to kiss her deeply," may be based on the words 自求口實 from hexagram 27 of the *I ching* (頤 The Corners of the Mouth). This may have been a refined expression for the act of kissing, or could carry the additional meaning of nourishment, which is associated with this hexagram.

4. Levy interprets the phrase 深按小搖 as continuing the theme of the preceding and thus mistranslates, "thrust forward with the tongue and lightly glide with it." Often the focus shifts very abruptly in these fast-paced texts, and the clues here are that the verb 按 always expresses the idea of penile penetration, and 搖 the undulations of intercourse.

5. I cannot locate the character 膎 anywhere, therefore my translation is based solely but confidently on context. I concur in Yeh's rejection of Tamba's suggested emendation to 暖.

6. Levy renders 淫衍窈窕 as "her licentious overflow appeals," and H.V.G., "happily and voluptuously." Failing to recognize the first two characters as a combination, Levy errs in translating them separately and literally. H.V.G.'s "happily" is too bland for an expression defined as unrestrained indulgence in pleasure.

7. The name 赤松子 first appears in the *Shih chi*, where according to one commentary, he was a "rain master" 雨師 during the time of Shen Nung, the god of agriculture. Some accounts identify him as a tutor of Ti K'u 帝嚳; and others state that there were two so named, one an immortal of the reign of Shen Nung and another of the Chin 晉 dynasty.

8. H.V.G.'s "comfort" and Levy's "purified" are not quite adequate translations of the expression 豁然. The basic meaning is to suddenly become open or disentangled, usually in the sense of sudden comprehension following a period of confusion. Used here, it expresses the sensation of relief or relaxation when something "hits the spot."

9. According to the *Ch'ien Han shu*, "Biographies of the Immortals," 劉京 was a Taoist of the Han, who at 130 years of age appeared like 30.

10. Both Levy and H.V.G. have created problems in the phrase 使神和意感 where none exist and ignored them where they do exist. Levy's "causing the spiritual (qualities) to harmonize and the intent to feel moved" and H.V.G.'s "harmonize the vigor and vitalize the ideas," when compared with V.G.'s "harmonize your mood with his and make her emotions respond," shows the difference between painful literalness and sensitive attunement. The very real problem involves the identity of the subject of the two verbs, which might be man, woman, both, or alternating. The flexible ambiguity of the Chinese language might intentionally allow us to look at the situation from multiple angles at once. Nevertheless, for the sake of translation, I feel that the "harmonization" emphasizes harmonization of her mood with his, and the "arousal" refers to the arousal of her desire.

11. Levy translates 絡脉 as, "life-energy conduits"; H.V.G., "veins and nerves"; and V.G., "blood circulation." In medical parlance the term has two rather distinct meanings. The first is secondary branches of the major meridians of *ch'i* circulation, and the second is veins. The *Ling shu* uses it in the former sense and the *Su wen* in the latter. My choice is sheer intuition.

12. The *Ishimpō* 日益 becomes in Yeh's version 自益 by way, I suspect, of typographical error.

13. For some reason both Levy and H.V.G. omit this passage, although it is in both Tamba and Yeh.

14. The characters 仙經 look at first glance to be the title of a book. Yeh transcribes Tamba's 又云仙經曰 as 仙經云, making it appear that he was convinced. V.G., Levy and de Smedt all treat it as a book title in their translations, however, Maspero's "A certain *Book of the Immortals* which is not designated with greater precision" and later, "A *Book of the Immortals* says," indicates that he was troubled by the identity of this work. The same term can be found in the "Health Benefits"

and "Dangers and Benefits" under similar contextual conditions. I find no bibliography listing this as the title of a specific work. The Ming *Tao tsang* contains many works with long titles, the last two characters of which are 仙經, but none of these, of course, is a sexual text. Pao Chao's "Fa Huai Nan Wang," Lü Yen's "Ch'i-yen ssu-shih-san shou," and the *Pao P'u tzu* (Chapter 8) all employ it as a generic term for works on immortality studies. The phrases 古仙經 in the *Yü-chi ch'i-chien* and 萬卷仙經 in the *Wu-chen p'ien* seem to me to clinch the point that 仙經 was used conventionally to introduce a summary or paraphrase of a general teaching when no specific work was cited. In this sense, it parallels the use of 古經, 舊經, or 仙歌 in the *Exposition*.

15. Levy misinterprets 勿閉氣 as "you won't shut off your energy." When 閉氣 appears again in the next paragraph, he translates, "cut off your life energy." The character 勿, of course, is a negative imperative, and 閉氣 means to hold the breath. V.G.'s "without holding your breath" shows that he understands all this perfectly well.

16. I take exception to Levy's "large and moving" for 大動.

17. Yeh's mistaking 日 here for *Ishimpō* 月 is quite misleading.

18. H.V.G. completely omit this passage and several others from the section.

Secrets of the Jade Chamber

1. I can discover nothing about the identity of this figure.

2. This line is from *I ching*, "Great Commentary," Part II, Chapter 5.

3. *I ching*, "Great Commentary," Part II, Chapter 5.

4. The character 鏗 is the given name attributed to P'eng Tsu.

5. H.V.G.'s "entertained" for 酬 is not correct. Following Tamba's note, Yeh reads 酬 for 酻 in *Ishimpō*, a character that I cannot locate in CW or lists of variants.

6. There are two interpretations of the character 家 in the phrase 養陽之家. Levy and H.V.G. favor "house" and V.G. and Needham "experts." Exercising the tie-breaking vote, I must side with the latter.

7. Levy reads 擬 in the phrase 莫擬也 as 疑, thus translating it "doubt." I agree with V.G.'s "one will not win" and Needham's "all your efforts will not avail," although I acknowledge that taking 莫擬 as 莫測 is another possibility.

8. Logically and grammatically there are the following possible interpretations of the last half of the phrase 又當御童女顏色亦當如童女: (1) young girls who look like young girls, (2) young girls or those who look like young girls, and (3) [you] will look like a young girl. Levy's "They also should initiate virgins (into sex) and their facial color will get to be like (the facial color of) virgins" leans awkwardly toward the third. The difficulty, of course, lies in identifying the subject of the second part of the line. The sense of the phrase in YFCY, "One's skin will become glossy and one will look like a maiden," and the structure of the familiar expression 老當益壯 influenced my final decision. Schipper's translation agrees.

9. This and the preceding sentence are omitted by H.V.G.

10. As it stands, the text considers those between fourteen and nineteen the most desirable, fourteen being the traditional age of puberty for women in China. This is perfectly consistent with the concept of maidenhood referred to earlier and the general attitude of Chinese sexual yoga. In view of this, Yeh's note following the phrase, which states that the text should read, "younger than thirteen or fourteen and older than eighteen or nineteen" is incomprehensible.

11. The difficulty in the phrase 採取其精液上鴻泉還精 is that an unfamiliar expression occurs in the midst of two familiar refrains. Does 上 mean to mount or to send up, and what is the 鴻泉? Both Levy and H.V.G.'s glossaries identify the 鴻泉 as "external urethral orifice," yet Levy translates, "He elects that his semen liquid revert to the Upper Vast Stream (of his brain cavity)," both turning his back on his own definition and misreading the verb in its modern colloquial sense. I agree with H.V.G.'s interpretation of the beginning and end of this sentence, but the middle, "sending it up to the great fountain" is incomprehensible in view of his reminder in a note that 鴻泉 refers to the urethral orifice. I can find no support for Levy's view that 鴻泉 means "brain cavity," but am influenced by the CW definition of 鴻溝 as "female genitalia" and the unequivocal use later in this text of the term in just this sense. Tamba admits that the term is problematic, but suggests "saliva" as its meaning. My reading takes the first five characters as theme, and the second five as recapitulation and variation, rather than linear progression.

12. The phrase 是以不可爲世教何必王母然哉 is one of the most variously translated in

this work. V.G., "The secret, however, must not be divulged, lest other women should imitate the Queen's methods"; Levy, "Therefore, even though it's not a part of the world's (commonly known) teachings, how could it have been (known to) the Queen Mother alone"; de Smedt, "Of course she set a bad example to mankind, but she was not the only depraved woman in the world"; H.V.G., "which cannot provide a model for education in this world—yet what is good for her is good for others too"; WHM, "She was an unusual character and unsuitable as a model of morality. The average woman should not attempt to emulate her, but perhaps she is not the only example of this type of woman"; and Schipper, "But it is expecially important not to publically reveal that this is the true nature of the Mother," (*Le Corps Taoïste*) and "But the common people must never learn why the Queen Mother did such things" ("Science, Magic and Mystique of the Body"). Without attempting to unravel all the variables in these six versions, the two critical touchstones are one's estimate of the author's attitude toward the Queen Mother and the reading of 何必. The contextual isolation of this fragment makes a difinitive judgment difficult, but there does seem to be an implied expression of ambivalence. A more concrete ambiguity surrounds the characters 何必, which should probably be interpreted as 何只 rather than its current colloquial usage, "Why is it necessary?"

13. I agree with Levy and H.V.G.'s "excited" and "ready," but V.G.'s "when the man has not yet reached orgasm" suffers a temporary lapse into the Western mind. De Smedt elects to discard the phrase altogether.

14. I agree with Levy and H.V.G.'s reading of 與之相應, but V.G. links it incorrectly with the following rather than the preceding phrase, thus deriving, "If she feels that she is going to respond." This tilting to the negative was prefigured in his interpretation of the previous line, which erroneously left the gentleman on the verge of climax.

15. The phrase 坐起悁恚 is simply excised by de Smedt and H.V.G. V.G. tackles it, but draws, I think, the wrong conclusion: "She will be afflicted with pain while sitting and standing." This interpretation interrupts the flow of the dramatic situation involving a jealous wife overhearing her husband making love to another wife, concubine, and so on. Although as early as the *Book of Rites* 坐起 meant sit and stand, by no later than the T'ang it could mean to sit up. The term 悁恚 has no-

thing to do with physical pain, but precisely describes an emotional state of resentment and anger. WHM offers: "Thereupon she sits up and reclines restlessly or feels unresolved resentment," which is close in spirit.

16. It is not surprising that 化爲男子 should evoke such divergent interpretations as V.G., "transformed into a man"; Levy, "convert this into a son"; de Smedt, "takes the form of child"; Needham, "she can transform herself into a man"; H.V.G., "conceive a male child"; WHM, "give birth to a son"; and Harper, "it will transform to become a boy." According to common practice in the *Ishimpō* texts, 男子 refers to mature males, 子 to offspring of unspecified gender, 男 to male, and 女 to female children. However, the self-transformation thesis cannot be reconciled with the example of the Queen Mother. Although Needham states in a note, "Changes of sex in man and animals were quite well known in ancient China." I believe this concept is foreign to the sexual literature at this period. *The Ten Precepts*, "in this way a woman may be converted to a man's body," and "The Rootless Tree's," "A woman becomes a man and the old young again" were written at least a thousand years later and show, I believe, the influence of Buddhist teachings. From a grammatical point of view, if we grant for the sake of argument the author's desire to lay equal emphasis on the notions of male and child, the use of 男 alone seems somehow inadequate in this phrase. The most pursuasive pull, for me, comes from the following phrase 若不爲子, where I believe the 子 in question refers back to the 男子.

17. Yeh takes the first character in *Ishimpō* 津液 as 精, although Tamba's 精 all look like standard 精, whereas 津 certainly does not. The Japanese scribe, in fact, simply has given us a cursive version of 津. Because 津液 and 精液 are both established compounds, the case for emendation would need to be exceptionally strong. Regardless of the outcome, there is still room for ambiguity as to the author of the substance, although there is an unequivocal example of 精液 referring to the feminine secretions earlier in this text and in the SNC. Turning, then, to 津液, it has two rather specific but not really relevant definitions in Chinese medicine, as well as being a collective term for all of the body's fluids. V.G.'s "vaginal secretions," Levy's "fluids," and H.V.G.'s "saliva-like fluid" reflect the various sides of the debate. When both interpretations can be made to work without undue coercion, the "beyond a shadow of

a doubt" doctrine would favor a decision of nonemendation.

18. V.G. and de Smedt elect to bail out just before this difficult last line: 況與人交乎. Levy and H.V.G. paraphrase the inevitable sense without showing a grasp of the grammar of the original, which hinges on the use of 況. Therefore, I have tried to render the original turn of phrase without sacrificing the sense.

19. Yeh gives us 閉目, "with eyes closed," but reminds us of Tamba's interlinear suggestion that the character be read 開. I join Levy and H.V.G. in accepting it as an emendation; based on the internal workings of this paragraph and parallelism with the many that follow in similar form.

20. The combination 目瞑 is a standard medical term describing the tendency for a patient's eyes to close as if too weary to keep them open. My guess is that 清盲 may refer to 青盲, a form of visual atrophy with a long course and without apparent organic defect. The cause in Chinese medicine usually is ascribed to deficiencies in the liver, kidney, spleen, or stomach. The first stage manifests as a lack of visual clarity and the second a blue, green, or reddish coloration of the perceptual field. Although we do not have a perfect match in terms of cause and progress, the condition of temporary blindness suggests a link.

21. I basically agree with Levy's interpretation of the phrase 兩腳拘背曲, which accepts Tamba's emendation of 物 to 拘, as "both legs are cramped and the back is bent," although 腳 is feet not "legs." H.V.G. attempt to read the whole phrase with a single subject, "misaligned arches on both feet," but apart from other reasons, 背 refers to the back or top, not the palm or sole, of the extremities.

22. Levy translates 結塞 as "obstructions accumulate in the stomach"; and H.V.G., "heart beating irregularly and extra systoles." H.V.G.'s interpretation seems to be based on the term 結脈 rather than what actually appears in the text. The term 結塞 is not a standard term for a single condition, but bearing in mind the cause and location, it is reasonable to consider it descriptive of fullness and indigestion.

23. For 嘔吐青黃 Levy gives us "vomit green and yellow matter," but H.V.G., "vomiting of blue and yellow stomach fluids." The problem, of course, is 青, which in different contexts may denote the colors blue, green, or black. H.V.G.'s "blue" seems a very unlikely choice.

24. Levy's "yellow and black ulcers" and H.V.G.'s "jaundice, dark depression" are both inadequate. The term 黃疸 is a standard term for what is called "jaundice" in Western medicine, but 黑癉, or as it is more commonly written now 黑疸, may not have a precise equivalent. Chinese medicine distinguishes two varieties, one induced by sexual indulgence and the other by alcohol. Symptoms of the former include black coloration of the forehead and gradually the whole body, tension in the bladder and frequent urination, black stools, and fullness of the abdomen as if bloated with water.

25. The 接接動手下髀裏若囊盛水撤齊上引肩膊 is highly problematic both from the point of view of punctuation and interpretation. Of the several logical variations, H.V.G.'s "swelling in the hands and feet which gradually extends upward to both shoulders," is riddled with sins of omission and commission, whereas Levy's "when you move your hands, there is a feeling in the buttocks below as if the scrotum were filled with water" is reasonable except for the first phrase. CKYSTPS "feels like a sack" inclines to the generic, but I cannot believe that the author would hazard such a metaphor so close to the neighborhood of *the* "sack." In interpreting this line, I have tried to tread a path that introduces the fewest possible one-of-a-kind novelties.

26. Levy's interpretation of 令滑澤 as "causing her to become slippery smooth" is correct in taking the woman as the object, but H.V.G.'s ambiguous, "the organ is well lubricated and then withdrawn" leaves the impression that the male "organ" is that "lubricated."

27. Levy's "and (you'll feel) godly" for 神良 and H.V.G's "also improves the man's vigor," both apply the force of the adjective to the patient rather than the cure. Based on the continuity of the passage and such familiar expressions as 良藥 and 神醫, I believe the words extol the efficacy of the cure.

28. H.V.G. catch the meaning of 屈伸轉側風生被裏, but Levy's, "elastic and turning aside, wind arises and is carried within," shows the unfortunate consequences of missing the concrete image.

29. Levy's interpretation of 跋蹇手不上頭 is basically sound, but H.V.G.'s "tender ankles and knees, or numb elbows which cannot be lifted to the head" is far more specific than the text will bear.

30. Levy interprets 巫 in the name 巫子都 as "Shaman," but I agree with V.G. and H.V.G., who take it as a surname. In a paragraph attributed to the YFPC by Tamba, but

253

not included in Yeh's reconstruction, Wu is identified as an official under Emperor Wu of the Han, who confesses under interrogation to gaining his longevity of more than 130 years through the bedroom arts. This chronology is difficult to reconcile with the passage later in this text where 子都 is portrayed in dialogue with the Yellow Emperor. V.G. says that 巫子都 is 巫炎, but I cannot find the source.

31. H.V.G.'s "yelling loudly" is closer for 大呼噴 than Levy's "take a great breath," which grossly misconstrues 呼 as inhalation.

32. The term 精氣 is by now so familiar an expression in these texts that H.V.G.'s "semen and energy" and Levy's "semen vapors" are inexcusable. Even V.G.'s "semen" is inadequate, as what is meant is "sexual energy," and semen is represented by 精液 or 精 alone.

33. H.V.G.'s translation of 至老不聾, "a man will have hearing difficulty until he is quite old," turns a deaf ear to the intended meaning.

34. Levy's "if you then shrink (your stomach)" and H.V.G.'s "contract the [muscles of the] anal area" show the two obvious possibilities for 縮後. Support for the adverbial interpretation may be drawn from the strong parallelism between 縮後精散而還歸百脉也 and 縮腹還精氣令入百脉中也 in the previous paragraph, together with 張腹 and 縮腹 as a logical pair. Only once in these early texts (SNC, the seventh "benefit") is 後 used in the sense of "rear" or "posterior," My decision was not made without giving due consideration to the possibility that 縮 here may be used in the sense of 退縮, "withdraw," as in the *Essentials* 小縮而淺之. WHM agrees with my translation.

35. The phrase 還流流中流中通熱, awkward enough in Chinese, has evoked some even more infelicitous translations: Levy, "the semen flows back centrally, and in the midst of the flow passes through heat"; and H.V.G., "the oozing flow returns to the stream, which circulates the heat energy." Despite the exceptionally inappropriate "oozing," on balance, H.V.G.'s attempt to simply render the sense is preferable to Levy's literal approach to each word. The chief difficulty in the line, of course, is the apparent but unaccustomed use of the character 流 as a noun.

36. I must side with H.V.G.'s "taking nine breaths" for 內息九也 against V.G.'s "pausing nine times" and Levy's "and (then) rest." Although the expression 內息 does not occur elsewhere in these texts, neither does 息 alone in the sense of "pause" or "rest." In light of

the very active role of the breath in the methods described in this paragraph and the absence of any suggestion of intermission, "inner breath" is the sole option. The expression 內息 is quite rare in the literature of Taoist yoga, but examples may be found in the *Huang-t'ing wai-ching ching* (Chapter 3) and *Yün-chi ch'i-ch'ien* (*chüan* 59), where in both cases it denotes inner circulation of the *ch'i*.

37. For some reason Levy translates 左手 as "left and right hand."

38. The expression 二无 that appears in *Ishimpō* is reproduced faithfully by Yeh, but remains a mystery as such. The two logical candidates for errata are 炁, which is never written in this form in these texts, and 元, which brings to mind the very common 三元 ("three primary vitalities"; viz., *ching*, *ch'i*, and spirit) and the very rare 咽元, which means to swallow the saliva. Backing up and extrapolating from 二, the "two" things one might possibly be swallowing are her *ch'i* and saliva or her *ch'i* and one's own. A roughly parallel passage in the FCPI, 以口相當引取女氣而吞之, would incline one to conclude that at the very least the woman's *ch'i* (breath) was in question, and the SNML's 引鼻氣以填脊髓含津液以養丹田 advanced me to the *ch'i* and saliva conclusion. V.G.'s translation of the whole passage shows uncharacteristic disregard for what is actually there: "Placing one's mouth over that of the 'enemy,' one inhales her breath and sucks her saliva. When swallowed it will descend into the stomach and there transform from Yin essence into Yang." Although exercising liberal interpretive license, he demonstrates a grasp of the structure of the original, which cannot be said for Levy's: "(The man) touches his adversary's mouth with his own and breathes through the mouth. (The woman) draws in her feminine breaths and (the man) doesn't swallow them. When he reaches her life force, he suppresses (his agitation). When (his suppression) reaches the inner organs, this assists (the excitement of) the woman, and her energy then becomes concentrated." H.V.G. take another tack, omitting the difficulties and translating only the most transparent portion: "Putting the mouth immediately against the partner's mouth, gently inhale through the mouth her exhaled breath, and swallow it. Complete this exercise in three cycles, using the mind to direct the intake of energy all the way to the abdomen to nourish the *Yin* and convert it into *Yin* energy." I agree with H.V.G.'s interpretation here of 陰 as "penis," but sympathize with the discomfort that prompted V.G. to read the second 陰

as 陽. The character 陰 is used in this same paragraph in the sense of male organ, but a scribal error involving the two characters cannot be summarily discounted.

39. H.V.G. correctly renders 困 as "incapacitated," whereas Levy's "fixed" seems to be influenced by 捆 or 綑.

40. Yeh omits the character 腸 in *Ishimpō*, though probably not intentionally.

41. I agree with H.V.G.'s interpretation of 時時 as "frequent," but not with Levy's "from time to time."

42. It bears emphasizing that this entire paragraph is exceptionally rich in summary material. After reviewing the three techniques—finger compression of the perineum, penile, and oral absorption—one would still like a clearer link between the two sets of "nine" and "one." The intriguing formulation 還精復液 raises more questions than it answers. Turning to the second half of the paragraph, its description of vaginal depths allows us to establish the following sequence of levels, beginning with the shallowest: "zither strings" 琴絃, "wheat teeth" 麥齒, "grain seed" 穀實, "scented mouse" 臭鼠, and *"k'un-shih"* 昆石. My reading of the very last phrase 合時不欲及遠 coincides exactly with H.V.G.'s, but Levy's, "when you unite, don't wish to unite what is distant" is indeed distant from the intended meaning.

43. Yeh emends 供 in the phrase 當極供大 to 洪, either by accident or design. 供 is interchangeable with 洪, but only in the sense of "great" or "large," which leaves Levy's "flood" out in the cold. Both Levy and H.V.G. take 供 as modifying the dimensions of the penis, whereas my version relates it to the arrival of the penis at the *k'un-shih* or greatest depth.

44. Levy's "the sickly and weak again insert it" takes 劣弱 as referring to the state of health of the man, rather than describing the limpness of the penis.

45. Yeh emends *Ishimpō* 彭享 to 彭亨 with ample justification.

46. The combination 妖孽 means unaccountable disaster or evil monster. Levy's "die early" seems to confuse this with the next taboo which foretells 夭殘, and H.V.G.'s "monstrously wild" describes the child rather than the fate that will befall him or her.

47. Levy takes 莖脉 as "passage" and H.V.G. as "stem veins." It is difficult to know if the term refers to blood vessels, meridians, or the duct, but on balance the duct or channel seems most likely.

48. Yeh changes 當令不合 in *Ishimpō* to 當合不合. Again, it is difficult to know if we are looking at emendation or erratum, but the change certainly does not help the sense.

49. This list is introduced as the "seven taboos" 七忌, but the section closes by calling them the "seven injuries" 七傷. It does not correspond to the "seven injuries" in the SNF and is unique among lists of "taboos," "disasters," "injuries," and "ills" in combining the consequences to the perpetrator and the offspring.

50. Tamba gives an interlinear 市中 after 市人 in the text, which Yeh accepts as an emendation. Levy's "townspeople" rejects the suggestion, but unfortunately 市人 actually means "merchants," making the phrase 傷死市人 very difficult to manage. I intuit some sympathetic connection between sex by candlelight and death in "broad daylight" in the marketplace.

51. Yeh changes 所合 to 所食, which is a justifiable emendation if ever there was one.

52. I cannot explain why Yeh inverts the two characters in *Ishimpō* 藏胞 to give us 胞藏. H.V.G. avoid translating the verb 過, but I endorse Levy and WHM's interpretation of the line. I am aware of the custom of burying the afterbirth of sons in a hole under the bed and that of daughters outside the window, but what was the norm from which the present practice deviates I cannot say. Tamba's suggestion that 裏 is a mistake for 裹 offers little comfort.

53. For 陰垣下入地七尺 I agree with Levy's "bury it beneath a shaded wall, putting it seven feet into the ground," but reject H.V.G.'s "buried it within seven feet of a shadowy wall."

54. Levy and H.V.G.'s translations of 多變 as "undergo frequent changes" and "undergo many changes" do not do justice to the Chinese nuance of 事變 connoting unforeseen or uncontrollable calamity.

55. Neither Levy's "ill-omened of mouth and tongue" nor H.V.G.'s "encounter misfortune" adequately convey the sense of 口舌不祥, which I feel describes a child whose tongue will get him in trouble. The term 口舌 is another name for the constellation 箕宿, but this probably is a coincidence, and I know of no particularly inauspicious associations with it.

56. WHM alone takes 三五 as "the fifteenth," and thus concludes that East and West concur in their understanding of fertility cycles.

57. I agree with Levy's translation of 二七 as "fourteen," but H.V.G.'s "twenty-seven" ignores standard usage. There may or may not be any significance to the number fourteen being the traditional age of female puberty.

58. The character 麗 in the combination 麗面 is not listed in either CW or TH, and I cannot therefore account for the specificity of Levy's "pockmarked face," V.G.'s "coarse face," or H.V.G.'s "wrinkled face." My own rendering is deliberately vague and should not imply privileged knowledge.

59. The two characters 槌項 are not a standard compound that has stood the test of time. Interpretations run the gamut: V.G., "elongated neck"; Levy, "mallet neck"; and H.V.G., "short neck." Because the syntactical pattern in this passage seems to be based on phrases of four, I take 槌項結喉 as a unit expressing the idea of long neck and protruding larynx. However, as I can find no independent confirmation of the long or the short of it, I am simply retaining the literal image in translation.

60. The characters 麥齒 are the same as those in the expression for the second degree of vaginal depth, although there seems no doubt that here they describe a condition of the teeth. Levy's "dark teeth" and Humana's "grain-color slabs" take color as the point of departure, whereas V.G.'s "irregular teeth" and H.V.G.'s "teeth resembling grains of wheat" are based on arrangement or shape. I feel confident that the image refers to a dental pattern suggestive of helter-skelter grains of wheat.

61. Tamba gives 人多逆生 with an interlinear note suggesting 交 for 人, which Yeh accepts as an emendation, although this contributes little to clearing up the ambiguity. The term 逆生 is a well-established combination meaning to go against the normal course of nature, but the question remains as to whether this applies to the woman as a whole or the pattern of hair growth. H.V.G. throw out the line, but Levy's "in most cases they grow inversely" and V.G.'s "such women are harmful to a man" reflect this split. In the end, I am most swayed by 逆毛不御 in the next paragraph and 陰毛多而且強又生逆毛此相不可皆賊命損壽也 in FCPI.

62. The phrase 常從高就下 contains nothing but the most elementary words in the language, but it is one of the most imponderable in the work. Levy's "her constant accord with the high and affixing to the low likewise cannot be controlled" and H.V.G.'s "aloofness and assumed airs before condescending" are a

fraud, but V.G.'s "women who have inclinations for low-class men" not only is more plausible, but he is honest enough to add parenthetically that his translation is "uncertain." My own interpretation agrees with WHM and CKYSTPS.

63. All but Levy throw out the expression 氣高, though his "high spirited" may not be sufficiently pejorative in its connotation. CW defines 氣高 as "vaulting sky and fresh air," which is obviously not to the point. The term 氣高 is paired with 男聲 as a four character unit, and remembering that in Chinese medicine the male is ruled by ch'i and the woman by blood, a woman manifesting an excess of ch'i is then a "tomboy" or masculinely assertive. I am in agreement with WHM and CKYSTPS.

64. V.G. ignores the phrase 不快善, but Levy's "inauspicious overhastiness" is a lapse into the wrong century. Although I cannot find the combination 快善 as such, I believe it is the sum of the basic meanings of the independent characters: happy and good. This is not far from H.V.G.'s "[a disposition] not pleasantly amiable."

65. Maspero suggests emending "forty" to thirty to make this consistent with earlier statements. I am inclined to think that thirty as an outside limit may be a bit extreme in this context.

66. In interpreting the phrase 生淫水不御, there is a consensus that 淫水 refers to vaginal secretions: V.G., "excessive vaginal secretions"; Levy, "produces lewd liquids"; and H.V.G., "fluid oozing from the female organ." As vaginal secretions during intercourse (heretofore 精 or 精液) are prized so highly, there must be a qualitative or contextual distinction between these and 淫水. The use of 媱津 in THT in the positive sense of vaginal secretions during sex makes it appear that the distinction is one of timing. I surmise that 淫水 here refers to inappropriate discharge occasioned by improper thoughts.

67. I ching, "Great Commentary," Part I, Chapter 11.

68. V.G. hits 消息 on the head with "flux and influx of Yin and Yang in the cosmos," but Levy's "mundane world" and H.V.G.'s "arousing" miss by a mile.

69. Yeh interprets Ishimpō 社穗 as 社穗. Both Levy and V.G. translate it as if it were 社稷. I agree on the grounds that 穗 and 稷 are easily confused in cursive script, that 社稷 is both a familiar and appropriate compound here, and 社穗 is neither. H.V.G.'s "near

grains and crops" shows how dangerous is a little bit of learning.

70. I can live with V.G.'s "kitchen fire" and H.V.G.'s "kitchen stove," but Levy's "kitchen range" shows him asleep at the wheel of history again. Although modern cooking devices are sometimes called "ranges" by their manufacturers and others, this use of the word hardly can be considered appropriate for translating a pre-T'ang text.

71. I take 腎源 as synonymous with 真陽, 陽火, 元陽, 真火, 先天之火, or 命門之火. This is the prenatal physiological fire centered in the *ming-men* between the kidneys.

72. H.V.G. incorrectly translate 蛾 as "silkworm."

73. I cannot identify the character 𡤾 in *Ishimpō* 雀𡤾. Yeh interprets it as 㸤, which is defined in CW as "looking like one is about to die." I do not know how both Levy and H.V.G. arrive at "sparrow's eggs" as the only variant of the standard 蛋 I can locate is 旦. However, as sparrow egg whites actually are used in compounding prescriptions and the compound 雀卵 appears in Ma Wang tui, it is a forced option.

Tung Hsüan tzu

1. Four of the most common characters 人之所上, yet what diversity of interpretation: V.G., "of all that makes man prosper"; Levy, "the place for man's being esteemed"; and H.V.G., "sexual desire is the strongest of man's desires." Of the many definitions of 上 as a verb, I feel that the most relevant here is that which takes it as synonymous with 尚, 貴, or 重. WHM agrees.

2. H.V.G omits this last line from the paragraph. This whole paragraph should be compared with later works that insist on role reversal as essential for deriving the benefits of intercourse.

3. The combination 牽引 occurs in a series of seven unequivocal pairs of opposites. It is easy to get the impression from dictionary definitions that the two are synonymous, but two factors militate against this: first the improbability on stylistic grounds of a pair of synonyms in a long list of antonyms, and second, previous contexts in which 牽 meant "pull in" and 引 "draw out." V.G., H.V.G., and Chang have simply refused to translate the expression, whereas Levy has divided the twelve character line into three phrases, giving us "Dragging forward and back" for 進退牽引.

4. Yeh accepts Tamba's suggested emendation of 蜜 to 密. Individually, the two characters in the pair 疏密 can refer to spatial or temporal intervals. The fact that 疏 is used so often in these texts in the sense of slowly or unrushed pulls one toward the temporal interpretation, but the fact that all the other pairs in the series refer to spatial relations pulls the other way. V.G., H.V.G., and Chang all read it as "slow or fast," but I side with Levy's "laxly and tightly" for its sense if not its diction. Of the three citations in CW for 疏密, all refer to space.

5. H.V.G. omit this last line.

6. The character 嗚, translated here as "kiss" and "press mouths together" two lines earlier, is defined in CW as "jovial appearance." My translation, then, is based solely on the present context, which frames the term so tightly as to preclude any other interpretation. Tamba suggests 飲, meaning "to drink," for 嗚, which would give us "drinking from each other's mouths," in other words, "kissing." Yeh emends *Ishimpō* 嘘 to 唖, neither of which appear in CW. Tamba suggests 啑 for 嘘, which denotes birds feeding. I might just add 啀, meaning "to cluck or sip," as another candidate for confusion.

7. Levy's "the woman flows lewdly" is wrong because 媱津 is obviously a variant of 淫水, which is a standard term for vaginal secretions, and because he misses 無 in the text, resulting in him conveying the opposite meaning.

8. I agree with V.G., Levy, and de Smedt's interpretation of 緣病發於內疾形於外矣. H.V.G.'s "there is either a disease in the person or there is some external disturbance" takes a different and misguided tack.

9. The expression 森森然 has two possibly relevant meanings: luxuriant and trembling. The latter is rare, whereas the former works well with the pine tree image. Only V.G. takes 玉門 rather than 玉莖 as the subject of the sentence, translating "that umbrageous region that resembles a cluster of low-growing pine trees in front of a deep grotto." The parallel phrase 峀峀然若巨石之擁深谿, which occurs several lines later, he correctly assigns to "his member." We should also not expect to find a panegyric to pubic hair in a culture whose feminine ideal was hairlessness.

10. The combination 磣勒 recurs frequently in this text, but is not listed in CW. Individually 磣 means sandy, sand, or ugly, whereas 勒 means to bridle, rein in, forcibly control, or carve. My colleagues confidently render it: V.G., "play about"; Levy, "presses in and out"; and H.V.G., "nestling and rubbing."

Perhaps it was a common idiom at the time that eluded the lexicographers, but from all contexts here it cannot be other than a general term for the movements of lovemaking. My best guess is that 磣 may be a mistake for 掺, meaning among other things, to grasp, hold, or bring together. Again, I cannot find this specific combination, but the two work well together. The combination 參差, whose general meaning is irregular or confused, appears in the "Ta le fu" in precisely the same sexual context.

11. Judging from its appearance in all contexts, I cannot but agree with Levy and H.V.G.'s definition of 金溝 as upper part of the vulva. De Smedt's "(umbilicus)" is as improbable as it is unfounded.

12. Again I agree with Levy and H.V.G.'s definition of 璿臺 as glans clitoris.

13. This context provides fairly good confirmation that 玉理 is indeed the lower part of the vulva where the labia meet (commissura labiorum posterior).

14. Between the end of this phrase and the beginning of the next, H.V.G. interpolate, "now beside her curling vine bush," which corresponds to nothing in the original text. Neither Yeh nor any other translator shares this hallucination.

15. The curious term 辟雍 originally referred to an imperial college established during the Western Chou in the form of a circular island surrounded on all sides by water. Levy's "left and right sides of the vulva" seems reasonable, but H.V.G.'s "carina urethralis vaginae" (elevated ring of flesh surrounding the opening of the urethra) seems too inconspicuous a feature to merit such an elegant term.

16. The *Ishimpō* provides a note at this point saying, "The preceding is foreplay without penetration."

17. Today 子宮 is used exclusively for uterus, and H.V.G. and Levy translate accordingly. Only V.G.'s "vagina" acknowledges the many examples in these sexology texts that prove the possibility of premodern multiple meanings.

18. Only V.G. makes the mistake of attributing this climax to the man. Although the absence of a stated subject makes the author of 快洩其精津液同流 ambiguous, nevertheless, the fact that the man remains at the height of his power and proceeds undaunted, giving the "enemy" no quarter, makes any other conclusion unlikely. He is also enjoined not to become "excited" and in the end to leave the field in full possession of his potency. If, in fact, the whole paragraph is descriptive of one episode, and not a collage of several sessions, a case could be made based on the language for multiple female orgasms, although I find no precedent for this in the classical literature.

19. I accept Levy and H.V.G.'s interpretation of 神田 as "prepuce of the clitoris."

20. I accept Levy and H.V.G.'s interpretation of 幽谷 as "vestibular fossa."

21. No one has difficulty with the line 求死求生乞性乞命 except Levy, who again forgets his century, translating the second half as, "begs for sex and destiny." The character 性 had nothing to do with sex until the twentieth century, and surely 命 is better rendered "life" here than "destiny." If nothing else, the combination 性命 should have alerted him.

22. Levy and H.V.G. render 陽臺 "glandula vestibuli major." In my view, that degree of specificity is unjustified, but from context here and in the fourteenth posture, the depth of penetration is considerable.

23. V.G. and Levy take 氣 as the subject of 出入 in the phrase 廿一息候氣出入, and H.V.G. give that role to the man's penis. In this paragraph alone 出入 appears once unambiguously in the sense of love movements, 入 twice and 出 once. The passage is far from cut and dried, but in the end I am most swayed by the parallelism with 候女動搖 in the next line and by the phrase 候息出入勻調 in Ch'en P'u's *Ch'en hsien-sheng nei-tan chüeh*. What prevents me from being totally comfortable with this decision, however, is that the *Tung Hsüan tzu* most closely resembles an "Ars Amatoria" and least resembles a medical or yoga manual.

24. Everyone omits the phrase 自不煩, except Levy, who mistranslates it, "he himself is untroubled," despite its repeated use throughout these texts in the sense of sexual excitation.

25. V.G., de Smedt, and Levy agree that the phrase 細細抽拔 refers to the action of carefully and gently withdrawing the penis from the vagina. H.V.G.'s "all the while maintaining a gentle probing and pulling action" pursues a mistaken tangent.

26. Following the title of the fourth posture, *Ishimpō* gives us 已上四勢之外遊戲皆是一等也, which only V.G. interprets as, "Next to these four basic positions there are the following playful variations." I can only surmise that this results from taking 之外 as 以外 instead of reading the phrase 外遊戲 as the operative unit.

27. V.G., Levy, Chang, and Humana all interpret 蠶纏綿 as silkworms "spinning" or "reeling." I agree rather with H.V.G. and de Smedt's "intertwined" for the following reasons: first, it is bad enough that silkworms are required to spin silk for us, but to ask them to reel it off as well is adding insult to injury; second, spinning, in any event, is a solitary exercise; and third, no dictionary defines 纏綿 as having anything to do with silkworms spinning. In fact, it most often is used in the sense of emotional entanglement.

28. Everyone concurs in some variation of "turning" or "twisting" for 龍宛轉, but Humana's "Forcing the Dragon" and H.V.G.'s "the dragon yields" either ignore the basic subject-verb structure of the phrase or misinterpret the meaning of 宛轉. As they stand, the two characters are a standard compound, but one could perhaps make a case for their being a variant of 婉轉, which means inseparable or entwined.

29. Only de Smedt interprets 翡翠 as "emerald" instead of "kingfisher," and, of course, "the mating of emerald" makes no sense.

30. The various translations differ so widely—excising what is difficult and supplying words not in the original—that it would take pages to compare and criticize them. I have attempted to cleave as closely to the language of the text as possible, while not pretending to have made total sense of it.

31. Only de Smedt and H.V.G. fall for 翻 as "somersault," something butterflies are not so famous for as flying. Perhaps they are influenced by the colloquial 翻筋斗, but actually this title is further confirmation of our interpretation of 龍翻.

32. The only legitimate difference of opinion on 背飛鳧 should be whether the subject is singular or plural; that is, whether both are flying or only the party on top. De Smedt's "the wild duck flies away"; Levy's "Rear-flying wild duck"; and H.V.G., "wild duck flying backward" either take the wrong semantic tack or are inconceivable as images in English.

33. V.G., de Smedt, and H.V.G. all take 向上 as raising her crossed feet. I agree with Levy that the meaning indicates that the toes are pointing upward, in other words, that the woman is supine. My reasoning is that the concept of physically raising a body part is never expressed with the words 向上 and that mutual embrace could be accomplished only if the crossed feet encircled the man, which the text does not specify.

34. The title 臨壇竹 has provoked some honest differences of opinion. Everyone takes 壇 as "altar" except H.V.G. who translate "Bamboo on terrace border." The word 壇 refers to altars used for state religious ceremonies or raised earth platforms used for public oath taking by entire armies. There is no association between this sort of space and bamboos and very little resonance between the highly public nature of its function and the sex act. On the other side, supporting the "terrace" thesis is the strong association between bamboo and private flower terraces 花壇.

35. For some reason H.V.G. translate 深投 as "brushes."

36. The phrase 於丹穴 occurs twice in this paragraph. The second time makes perfect grammatical and physical sense, but the first fails on both counts. Tamba suggests a scribal error. My fellow translators uniformly ignore the first, but I have attempted to preserve it without doing too much violence to the English.

37. Levy, H.V.G., and HMF correctly interpret this posture as a threesome; V.G. and de Smedt do not. Based on internal evidence, the man cannot logically be both "facing up" and in "winnowing basket" pose simultaneously, and the phrase 攻擊上下 clinches the image of alternately penetrating two partners. On comparative grounds, Posture 8 in the SNML precisely parallels this one in vocabulary and grammatical constructions, but leaves no room for ambiguity. This would seem a difficult manoeuver to accomplish accepting the CW and TH definitions of 箕坐. V.G.'s "cross-legged" is not much better. Kneeling would facilitate the horizontal approach of the penis to the task.

38. I agree with Levy and HMF in reading this posture as a threesome involving two males and one female. Everyone translates 小男 as "small man," whereas I agree with CW's definition of "boy." The HMF colloquial Chinese paraphrase suggests simultaneous vaginal and anal penetration by the two males. For me, the two man interpretation turns on the phrase 共交, which would be redundant if applied only to the more familiar configuration.

39. For *Ishimpō* 右右肩 Yeh gives just 右肩. Levy and HMF translate, "left and right," whereas V.G. and H.V.G. simply "shoulders." De Smedt takes Yeh at face value, accepting that both feet are placed on one shoulder. I agree with Tamba's suggestion

that the original intention was 左右 "left and right."

40. Here is a very clear example of 子宮 as vagina. See also Posture 21.

41. Only V.G. seems to appreciate that 山羊 is not "mountain goat," as everyone else has rendered it, but simply "goat," the 山 serving to distinguish it from sheep.

42. HMF translates 箕坐 as 盤坐, agreeing with V.G.'s "cross-legged," although the accompanying photograph shows the man kneeling. I know that goats are capable of sitting on their rumps with rear legs outstretched on the ground, but have never seen one cross legged.

43. I apologize for vagueness in the rendering of 鷿鷄, but CW defines it as "crane," "phoenix," "chicken," or "large bird." Accordingly, V.G. gives us "Jungle Fowl"; Levy, "Gamecock and Fowl"; H.V.G., "Jungle Fowl"; and de Smedt inexplicably, "cicada." The term 臨場 does indeed mean to approach a battlefield, which tends to support the cockfight image. What is unique about this posture is that a second woman positions herself behind and assists the movements of the first. This may suggest the role of a trainer or "second." In the absence of a conclusive reading of 鷿鷄 I prefer not to carve guesswork in stone.

44. What distinguishes 蹲 from 跪 is that in the former the knees do not touch the ground. What distinguishes 胡蹲 from the indigenous Chinese style of 蹲 or 跪, according to CW, is that in the former the right knee is placed on the ground while the left knee is elevated with' the lower leg planted perpendicular. To his credit, Levy provides a note to similar effect, but everybody else evades the issue, except V.G. whose "cross-legged" seems even less likely here than for 箕坐.

45. The language of this paragraph is ambiguous enough to admit of several interpretations. V.G. has the "young girl" as principal partner, receiving the "stalk" herself, with the second woman in a supporting role behind the first. H.V.G. likewise has the young girl as principal, but with the "older woman" helping fore and aft. HMF makes the man responsible for his own insertion, with the "more experienced" woman helping from behind. Based on syntax and diction, I come closest to agreeing with Levy's interpretation, which has the young woman insert the "jade stalk" into the other woman's "jade gate" and then circle around to assist her movements. In the end, I feel that a careful reading of the text reveals three women, one receiving the "jade stalk,"

and one each assisting the principals. This actually lends credence to the "gamecock" theory, giving each of the contestants a second.

46. Everyone translates 玄溟 as "sea," except H.V.G., who gives us "mysterious lake." I cannot find the compound 玄冥 as such, but the only definition of 溟 is "sea."

47. It seems clear from this context that 箕坐 can be only "legs outstretched" or "cross legged," and I think the use of the supporting hand favors the former.

48. Only H.V.G. agree with my interpretation of 又男 as indicating another man. Everyone else translates as if one man takes the inferior and superior positions sequentially. HMF offers the novel solution of man and woman locking tightly and rolling over and over. The two-man interpretation not only is grammatically defensible, but the only configuration that fulfills the promise of the title. There is no precedent for giving a single title to what would then be two postures. If one objects that two men and one woman duplicates "Female Phoenix Tends Her Fledgling," it is possible to point out other examples of minimal distinction.

49. V.G. takes 三春 as "three years old"; Levy, "Early, Mid, and Late Spring"; H.V.G., "late spring"; and HMF, "spring." CW defines 三春 as "the three months of spring" or "three years"; TH adds, "the third month of spring." My interpretation follows *Su wen*, "Ssu-ch'i t'iao-shen ta-lun" 春三月.

50. H.V.G. follow Tamba's suggestion that 秋狗 should be 三秋狗.

51. I feel that only V.G.'s "bucking through a stream" captures the image of the horse jumping into the stream, rather than over it, as H.V.G. and de Smedt imply. While fording the stream, the horse negotiates the irregular bottom, clambering up on shallow rocks, and swimming the deeper stretches.

52. I concur in Yeh's suggestion that there is a lacuna of one character before 波.

53. V.G. and H.V.G. take 鴉臼 as "mortar." I feel that the image of a sparrow pecking leftover grains of rice in a husking mortar works well enough, but CW clearly defines 鴉臼 as "crow's nest," citing four quotations from literature. De Smedt takes "crows" as the subject of the sentence, second only to H.V.G.'s "woodpecker" for implausibility. Woodpeckers eat only insects.

54. I cannot make sense of this image. V.G. makes a valiant attempt by pluralizing the subject, "deep and shallow strokes in steady

succession, like large stones sinking into the sea." Everyone else agrees that the force of 投 is "thrown" or "tossed," rather than "sinking," and that the subject is singular. There seems no way of conceptualizing the toss or sinking of a rock into the sea so as to produce the double image of shallow and deep.

55. The term 狡兔 is a standard combination, which everyone correctly renders "crafty," "elusive," and so on, except H.V.G. who give us "running."

56. De Smedt, H.V.G., and Chang take 帆 as "junk," "sailboat," and "sailing boat," respectively. V.G. and Levy both translate it as "sail." Given the verb 擡 and the storm conditions described, I feel the operative image concerns the boat as it is heaved up and let down by the swells rather than the sails being raised and lowered. Moreover, the boat itself makes a more plausible correlative for the human body than its sail.

57. The character 擡 in the phrase 下擡玉理上衝金溝 is a bit unusual. CW's first definition of 擡 is 動 and the second the more familiar 舉. It cites two classical lexicons that define it as 動 or 動振. I think the 擡 here, then, is not so much literally to lift up, but to probe, prod, or "raise" in the sense of stimulate.

58. I agree with H.V.G., de Smedt, and Chang's interpretation of 五鎚 as "five hammers." V.G.'s "a hammer" and Levy's "iron hammered five times" reflect some discomfort, perhaps, with the image of five hammers representing one penis, but this objection may be overcome by poetic license.

59. The line 玄圃天庭兩相磨搏其勢若兩崩巖之相欽 is one of special interest. It features the only appearance of the terms 玄圃 and 天庭, which Levy and H.V.G. define respectively as "prepuce of clitoris" and "vestibular fossa." Neither of them explain the incongruity of these two parts of the female genitalia colliding with one another as both diction and image require. I feel external parallelism and internal syntax should lead us to interpret the two terms as representing man and woman. Chang is so convinced of this apparently that he translates 玄圃 and 天庭 directly as "jade peak" and "jade gate." V.G. and de Smedt simply translate or transliterate the names, and even V.G.'s note is noncommittal as to the referent, although it appears that both assumed two parties. CW informs us that 天庭 is the highest peak in the mythical K'un-lun Mountains and 玄圃 either the lower slopes or the eastern quarter. De Smedt's "two

shepherds come face to face" for the last part of the line is a far cry from any conceivable interpretation of the language of the text.

60. There is a rather abrupt transition in this paragraph from the first line, which explains the timing for ejaculation, to the balance, which describes the techniques of ejaculation control. Neither Levy, de Smedt, H.V.G., nor Chang is thrown off by the lack of a clear bridge, but opinion is very divided on the last line, 十分之中只得洩二三矣. I strongly disagree with de Smedt and H.V.G., who interpret this to mean that one should somehow restrict the volume of ejaculate to 20–30 percent. Even if this could be accomplished, it is ruled out by the statement in the previous paragraph which says, "when ejaculating there should be complete evacuation."

61. The phrase 舌柱下腭 is immediately reminiscent of 舌抵上腭 repeated in nearly every meditation text, ancient and modern. The use of the verb 柱, which specifically means to support from below as a post or column, also seems to suggest a confusion of 下 for 上. Although I cannot find the compound 下腭, CW citing the *Tzu hui* defines 腭 as 齒內上下肉, which indicates that the floor of the mouth may indeed be called 下腭. Therefore without stronger evidence, I hesitate to emend the original as V.G. has done. Levy and H.V.G. make the best of an uncomfortable predicament, but de Smedt's "position his head immediately above his tongue" is simply incomprehensible.

62. It is worth noting here for our understanding of "returning the *ching*" that at the end of a very specific list of ejaculation control techniques, which does not include manual compression of the perineum, we are told 精便自上 "the *ching* will rise of itself."

63. For the phrase 損精力 Levy translates "injures the strength of the emission." *Ching* is *ching* and not "emission."

64. "Lao tzu" 老子 is used generically here and does not represent the putative author of the *Tao te ching*. The advice here contradicts most other pronouncements on the subject of eugenic timing.

65. The combination 服餌 means to take drugs, especially longevity tonics. Simply looking up 餌 in a dictionary produces such ludicrous results as Levy, "eat dumplings" and H.V.G., "not eat candies or cookies except with meals."

66. V.G. says, "Autumn: lie with the head pointing north," and omits winter altogether.

67. The Celestial Stem days for each season   *261*

are those corresponding to the cardinal element of that period; hence, wood for spring, fire for summer, metal for autumn, and water for winter. This correspondence makes them auspicious for intercourse, not "harmful" as Levy says.

68. Yeh mistakes 呂 (written 呂 in *Ishimpō*) for 臣. V.G. inverts the given name 敬大 transliterating "Ta-ching."

69. Primary definitions of 疹 all have to do with skin disorders; secondary meanings include "affliction" and "chronic disease." Levy and H.V.G.'s "pain" may be unnecessarily vague, and V.G.'s "vaginal disease" misleading.

70. I agree with Levy and H.V.G.'s interpretation of the line 無敵不可服. V.G.'s "one will be invincible" must be based on a misreading of 服 here in the sense of "surrender."

71. V.G.'s translation of 白蜜 as "wax" is wrong.

72. For *Ishimpō* 五丸 Yeh gives 五九. V.G. accepts Yeh's emendation (or error), translating "five or nine days." If one wished to go this way, "forty-five" might be a better choice. The typical prescription pattern includes quantity of medicine per dose, the number of doses per day, and the number of days in the program. If one emends the text to 五九, it leaves no instructions as to the quantity of dosage per administration. From the point of view of punctuation, 日再 is a more likely unit than 再以知爲度.

73. The text says 四分, which should be perfectly clear. V.G.'s "four grams" is incorrect because the ancient value of the *fen* is 0.3125 grams; Levy's "four parts" is incorrect because the *fen* is a specific unit; and H.V.G.'s "4 *liang*" is incorrect because the text says 分 not 兩.

74. Interpretations of 五分匕 also are various. V.G.'s "five gr. in a square spoon" and Levy's "five portions in square teaspoonfuls" suffer from the same misapprehensions as in the previous note. I can almost agree with H.V.G.'s "one-half cubic inch spoonful" but for the fact that the unit in question is "square" not "cubic."

75. I agree with H.V.G.'s "born in the first month of the year," rather than Levy's "blended in the first (lunar) month."

76. V.G. and H.V.G. choose not to translate the words 急小. Levy's "making it urgent, small" would have been better off not trying, although when he meets 急 again in the next paragraph he interprets it correctly.

Medical Manuals and Handbooks for Householders

"Health Benefits of the Bedchamber"

1. In the Taoist pharmacopoeia, powdered mica was thought to contribute to a state of superior health.

2. The phrase 未經生乳 provides another opportunity to disagree with V.G.'s and WHM's interpretation of "undeveloped breasts." Apart from the reasons discussed in earlier notes, the use of 未經 here, I feel, would be inappropriate for a process that does not happen overnight, but works perfectly with "childbirth."

3. The phrase 槌項結喉 appeared earlier in the YFPC, and occurs just so in the *Tao tsang* version of this text. V.G.'s 頂 for 項 seems to be an error either on his part or in the text he was copying.

4. The expression here 慎密 is from the *I ching*, "Great Commentary."

5. V.G.'s interpretation of the phrase 久用不止陰氣逾陽陽則轉損 is fundamentally different from my own: "If the contact lasts too long, the Yin essence (absorbed by the man) will grow stronger than his own Yang essence, whereby the latter will be harmed." First, the words 陰家 in the previous phrase clearly indicate that the subject is man and woman and not *yin* and *yang* within the body of the man, and, second, V.G.'s version implies an entirely novel theory, which is found nowhere else in this literature.

6. I disagree with V.G.'s punctuation of the passage: 若不數交。交而即瀉。則不得益瀉之。精氣自然生長. I would shift one period to read: 若不數交。交而即瀉。則不得益。瀉之精氣自然生長.

7. Here is another context from which to determine the meaning of 握固. Remembering that Maspero and Needham previously have translated the expression as "hold the penis" and "compress the perineum," respectively, we can see the impossibility of simultaneously attending to those parts and thrashing about with the hands in all directions. V.G.'s "firmly control himself" also ignores the technical nature of this term.

8. V.G. translates the characters 縮下部及吸腹 as "constraining the lower part of his body so that he breathes with his abdomen." I believe that the two words 吸腹 mean to draw or suck in the abdomen and not to "breathe" with the abdomen. It is nearly impossible to

maintain the tension of the anal sphincter while simultaneously moving the diaphragm.

9. In a note explaining the location and significance of this point, V.G. states: "Secondly, we saw above that the handbooks of sex advise to prevent emission of semen during the act by compressing the urethra. Sun, however, states that the same effect is obtained by pressing the *P'ing-i Point.* . . . The *P'ing-i* point is located about one inch above the nipple of the right breast, and is also defined as '*yin* present inside *yang* (*yang-chung yu yin*).'" Porkert gives six alternates for the point located on the perineum best known as 會陰 or 海底. Two of them are 平翳 and 屏翳, both pronounced *p'ing-i*. V.G. suggests that we consult G. Soulie de Morant's *L'acuponcture chinoise* for further details on acupuncture, so this may be assumed to be his source. I can find no primary text or informant placing any such point anywhere near that neighborhood. I also do not know Porkert's source for this particular alternate, but the coincidence is very convincing. Another interesting coincidence is the point on the stomach meridian located in the area of the breast known as 屋翳.

10. V.G. translates 以左手握持 as, "Then the man should press (the P'ing-i Point) with the fingers of his left hand." Though the verb has no stated object, the verb itself 握持 so clearly means to grasp or hold that to parenthetically supply the words "P'ing-i Point" is unjustified. When it is mentioned just two lines earlier it is with the appropriate verb 抑, to press. My parenthetical "penis" also is speculative, of course, but what else is there to "hold" after all?

11. V.G. is obviously uncomfortable with the phrase 思在丹田中有赤氣。內黃外白 and attempts to resolve the apparent contradiction with, "There is a bright, red essence, yellow inside and red and white outside." Whatever the limits of our own imaginations, there can be no justification for translating 外白 as "red and white." This visualization is a variation of the technique known as "absorbing the radiance of the sun and moon" 服日月芒法 described in many works on Taoist meditation. In some texts one is advised to visualize a "red orange" 朱橘.

12. *Ni-yüan* 泥垣 is an alternate of *ni-wan* 泥丸 especially favored in Buddhist texts.

13. V.G.'s translation of the passage 凡人氣力。自有盛而過人者, "Man's passion naturally has its periods of great abundance. Therefore, even superior men can not [sic] bear a protracted abstention from sexual in-

tercourse." His first mistake is taking 氣力 as "passion" when it so clearly means general strength or vitality. Then ignoring his own punctuation, he reads 過人 as a noun, "superior men," when it obviously modifies 氣力 in the sense of surpassing the norm. Interpreting 亦 as "even" also takes the phrase in a direction never intended by the author.

"The Dangers and Benefits of Intercourse with Women"

1. Approximate quote from *Lao tzu*, Chapter 12.

2. Needham translates the phrase 閉精守一, "retain his *ching* entirely and guard it." The term 守一 is a common Taoist expression for maintaining concentration, centeredness, and wholeness; in short, for preserving 真一. Needham's reading takes 守一 as if it were 守之.

3. As it stands, the phrase 精動而正 is untenable. My translation assumes that 正 is a mistake for 止.

4. Maspero emends 九十三 to 九十二, suggesting that it be interpreted as 9 times 12, or 108. The whole passage in which this occurs, consisting of five lines of text, appears verbatim in FCPI where the number also is 93. Admittedly, it is a strange number, but if the author of the present text did not see fit to emend it, I feel compelled to be at least as conservative.

5. A minister of the Yellow Emperor.

6. Because this line does not appear in the work known as the *Lao tzu*, "Lao tzu" may mean something like the elders, old ones, or wise ones.

7. It seems likely that there is an error here, as 81, the product of 9 times 9, normally is regarded as the penultimate *yang* number.

8. This also is absent from the *Lao tzu*.

The Wondrous Discourse of Su Nü

1. The expression 三清 refers to three gods of the Taoist pantheon or three realms of the immortals.

2. The term 金匱 represents a safe place for keeping precious books.

3. "Yellow and white" represent gold and silver, which in turn stand for the alchemical arts.

4. The place where the Yellow Emperor cast a great caldron and ascended into heaven.

5. The *Shen-hsien chuan* records that when King Liu An of Huai Nan achieved immortal-

ity, his dogs and chickens licked the remains of his elixir and thus accompanied him into heaven.

6. Birthplaces of Mencius and Confucius, respectively.

7. There are many versions of the "four elements" 四大 in Buddhist and Taoist metaphysics, but in meditation manuals specifically, it usually refers to the four constituents of the physical body conceived of as earth, water, wind, and fire.

8. *I ching*, "Great Commentary," Part 1, Chapter 5.

9. *Lao tzu*, Chapter 42.

10. The 如意 is not really a "scepter" in the sense of a symbol of imperial authority, but rather an ornate implement, originally a back scratcher, raised to an art form.

11. This is the unique occurrence of the term 紅毬, which seems to indicate the vulva.

12. This line echoes the parable in *Chuang tzu*, "Autumn Flood," of the turtle who preferred the safety of his humble origins to the dangers of imperial favor.

13. V.G. considers this the unique example of sex involving two women partners simultaneously. This is because he failed to recognize the same in Postures 15 and 16 of the *Tung Hsüan tzu* or see the parallel grammatical constructions that link this passage to the earlier work.

14. The character 菱 in the combination 菱齒 seems almost certainly to be an error for 麥, which it closely resembles. I can discover nothing about the water caltrop 菱 that warrants its association with "teeth" 齒, and still less with a woman's privates. The appearance of the term 麥齒 in Ma Wang tui suggests a compound of considerable antiquity and durability. Nevertheless, I have stopped short of a positive emendation.

15. The combination 昆戶 is almost certainly an error for 昆石, which appears in the earlier texts, although emendation might be premature given the ambiguities surrounding the term 昆石 itself. The appearance of 磧石 in "The Highest Tao" some day will play a vital role in finally resolving this difficulty.

16. Fever due to *yin* deficiency, as if heat originated in the bones. The condition often is seen in pulmonary tuberculosis.

17. Fever that rises and falls at regular intervals like the tides.

18. The "three internal parasites," written here 三彭, but more often seen as 三尸, is not a medical term, but rather the Taoist belief that three spirits, variously named and lo-

cated, afflict us from within and even report our transgressions to the Lord of Heaven on our birthdays as we sleep.

19. The "three commencements" 三元, which should not be confused with the 三元 encountered elsewhere in these texts as the "three primary vitalities," refers to the fifteenth day of the first, seventh, and tenth months.

20. Celebrated at the beginning of the four seasons, equinoxes, and solstices.

21. The term 月祓 in the text must be a mistake for 月破.

22. The "five sacred peaks" 五岳 represent the four cardinal directions and center of China: Mount T'ai in Shantung, Mount Heng in Hunan, Mount Hua in Shensi, Mount Hung in Hopeh, and Mount Sung in Honan.

23. The condition expressed here as 火盛水枯 also is known in Chinese medicine as 命門火旺. The kidney stores the primal *yin* (the semen) and primal *yang* (the fire of the *ming-men*). When the semen is deficient, the fire of desire rages out of control, resulting in the "reckless activity of the ministerial fire" 相火妄動.

24. In Chapter 3 of this work, the author warned against penetration to the "valley seed" (five inches) because of the danger of injuring the liver.

25. Bound feet were said to resemble the lily bud in size and shape.

26. V.G. surely errs in translating 桃 "prune."

27. The four pairs of Celestial Stems and Terrestrial Branches, representing the hour, date, month, and year of a person's birth, used to determine a couple's compatibility.

28. V.G. translates 郎中 as "Boy," interpreting 郎 as "boy" and 中 perhaps as "among," although he does not use the word. Context permits no interpretation here other than "penis," but dictionary definitions give only "an official rank," "physician," or "card shark." Although such expressions are seldom glossed, I believe it is a play on words alluding to the male private parts as literally "the man's middle."

29. The five medicinal minerals mentioned by Ko Hung in the *Pao P'u tzu* are cinnabar, realgar, alum, azurite, and loadstone. However, one cannot rule out the possibility that 五石 refers to the 五石 cited in the *Shih chi* as containing actinolite, stalactite, loadstone, azurite, and diamond.

30. Whether V.G.'s error or a mistake in the edition from which he copied, the charac-

ter 述 in the expression 好述 obviously should be 述.

31. *I ching*, *T'ai* (Peace).

32. According to Shao Yung's square arrangement of the sixty-four hexagrams, *Ch'ien* (heaven, man) is located in the northwest (lower right), and *K'un* (earth, woman) is located in the southeast (upper left).

True Classic of Perfect Union

1. The second character in the compound 交姤 clearly is a mistake for 媾.

2. "Fiendish forces" 魔兵 is a Buddhist term for the "army of Mara," the temptress.

3. V.G. translates the phrase 撮住谷道 as "compressing the seminal duct between the fingers." Although the verb 撮 does mean "to pinch," the action actually is effected by the muscles of the anal sphincter itself and not the hand as an external agent. Sphincter constriction is a very common technique in both Indian and Chinese yoga and is recommended frequently in these sexology texts under such verbs as 提 and 縮.

4. The combination 氣精 as it appears in V.G.'s copy of the original text presents three possibilities: it is either a scribal error faithfully reproduced without emendation, a fresh error introduced to the public for the first time, or one of the very rare examples of its intended use. Although a scribal inversion of 精氣 seems likely, it perhaps is worthwhile exploring the alternative. Maspero interprets the 氣精 in the title of Ssu-ma Ch'eng-chen's 服氣精義論 as "Breath and Essence," with Needham following suit. From context and other sources, I believe that the operative compound in this case is actually 精義. A bona fide example appears in the 性命圭旨, where 氣精 in the phrase 上藥三品神與氣精 clearly refers to "*ch'i* and *ching*." Not having seen the original from which V.G. copied, however, I hesitate to initiate an emendation.

5. "After Completion" (*Chi-chi*) is the sixty-third hexagram in the *I ching*, consisting of the trigrams *Li* (fire) under *K'an* (water), and symbolizing the perfect interaction of the two trigrams and the optimum distribution of *yin* and *yang* lines. In "pure practices" meditation, this hexagram represents the harmonization of heart and kidneys; and in the sexual school, the most beneficial relationship of partners.

6. V.G. translates the term 髓海 (literally, "marrow sea") as "marrow," though it is a well-established compound for brain. This is not surprising as the brain, marrow, and bones all participate in the "kidney" 腎 system, and the *Ling shu* states: "The brain is the sea of the marrow."

7. The *jen* 仞 is equal to approximately eight feet.

Exposition of Cultivating the True Essence

1. The sixteenth day of the fifth lunar month.

2. I cannot find a specific gloss for the expression 四脉, but I suspect it may be equivalent to 四肢 or 四維, meaning the "four limbs."

3. The combination 肩鼓 that appears in V.G.'s copy is problematic. It is not a standard compound and the literal meaning, "shoulder the drum," is less than clear. I suspect that 肩 may be a mistake for 扇, meaning to "fan" or excite, just as 鼓 means to "drum" or excite. Unfortunately, I cannot find a gloss for the hypothetical compound 扇鼓 either, but the sense of executing fanning or drumming movements seems appropriate.

4. In "pure practices" texts the "mysterious gate" 玄關 usually refers to the space between the eyebrows where enlightenment takes place or the "*ch'i* point" (*ch'i-hsüeh*) below the navel, but here and in other "sexual school" texts, the "gate" that guards the male *ching* or female vagina may also be so designated.

5. The term translated here as "jade terrace" (*ch'iung-t'ai*) 瓊臺, and clearly denoting a male part, should be distinguished from "jade terrace" (*hsüan-t'ai*) 璿臺, which appears in the *Tung Hsüan tzu* for a female part. In both cases, the precise location is yet to be positively established, but context here seems to point to the male member.

6. There is no other example in these texts, nor can I find a gloss, for the expression 兩道白脉. That the concept existed in some quarters of the rising *ch'i* dividing at this point in its orbital circulation is attested to by the phrase in the *Huan hsien-sheng fu nei-yüan-ch'i chüeh*: "Now imagine two courses of white *ch'i*, which are both drawn up through the *chia-chi* and penetrate the *ni-wan*."

7. The character 真, translated "True," is not a philosophical abstraction, but a state of primal purity of body and mind.

8. The "red tide" 赤潮 refers to the menses.

9. I believe that *yin* 陰 here refers to the female organ and the feminine secretions and essence associated with it.

10. I feel that the character 閑 here is a scribal error for 閉.

11. "Yellow court" 黃庭 should not be confused with the meditation point of the same name, but refers here, I believe, to the earth.

The Elixir Literature of Sexual Alchemy

Seeking Instruction on the Golden Elixir

1. This curious circumlocution is undoubtedly based on *Lao tzu* (chapter 41), "When the inferior scholar hears of the true *tao*, he laughts."

2. Sung philosopher, Shao Yung 邵雍 (1011–1077), based his teachings on the *I ching* and considered number as fundamental to understanding cyclical processes in the natural world. The passage quoted here also appears in the *Wu-chen p'ien*, Part I, Verse 43.

3. *Lao tzu*, Chapter 55.

4. *I ching*, "Hsi-tz'u chuan" (Great Commentary), Part 1, Chapter 4.

5. I cannot determine the *locus classicus* for this model of conception, but it appears four times with interesting variations in the sexology corpus. In this text it is the first essence to arrive that is surrounded by the second, and the inner essence that determines the sex of the offspring. In the *Exposition of Cultivating the True Essence*, Chapter 20, by contrast, the first to arrive surrounds the second, but similarly it is the inner that determines the sex. The *Essentials of the Women's Golden Elixir Method* agrees with this present text in the first instance, asserting that the first arrival is surrounded by the second. *The Wondrous Discourse*, Chapter 5, does not mention the order of arrival, but states simply that, when the blood surrounds the *ching*, it results in male offspring and vice versa for female. Speculations on sex determination in Ma Wang tui and *Ishimpō* are formulated in terms of the precise day following the cessation of menses on which conception takes place. The *Exposition* describes both systems in the same chapter, but does not attempt to reconcile or synthesize them.

6. *I ching*, *Fu* (Return), "T'uan" (Commentary on the decision).

7. *Ts'an-t'ung ch'i*, Chapter 4.

8. Ibid., Chapter 5.

9. There are many interpretations of the term *ssu-hsiang* 四象 ("four images"), but in view of the context created by the term "*chi* earth," I believe it refers to metal, wood, water, and fire.

10. *Ts'an-t'ung ch'i*, Book 1, Chapter 1.

11. Ibid., Chapter 5.

12. *Ch'a-nü* 姹女 ("beautiful maiden") refers here not to the female partner, but to the *yin* line in the middle of *Li*, or the male *ching*.

True Transmission of the Golden Elixir

1. Located in Shensi Province and one of the "five sacred mountains" of China.

2. A prefecture in Shansi Province.

3. The brother of King Wu, the first ruler of the Chou dynasty, and one of the most respected figures in the Confucian school. Here he symbolizes a very august personality.

4. Peking was the Ming capital at this time, having been moved in 1403 from Nanking.

5. Capital of Honan province.

6. The "*Ch'ien* body" 乾體, like the trigram and hexagram of the same name, is pure *yang*, having replaced the weak middle of *Li* with a strong line from *K'an*.

7. *Kuei* and *jen* are the tenth and ninth Celestial Stems, respectively. *Kuei* is associated with the menses and *jen*, perhaps, with the stage just prior to puberty or the onset of each period, the *yang* stage that precedes the fall into *yin* materiality.

8. "Two" and "four" refer to the first two and second four stages of the "six stages" 六候 of the elixir refining process.

9. This gloss on "refining the self" 煉己 differs from the interpretation of the "pure practices," or nonsexual, school. Both identify the object of "refining" as *Li*, or mercury, but the nonsexual takes *Li* as the "heart," and the sexual as the "true mercury," or semen. A corollary to this issue is the interpretation of the character 己 in the expression 煉己. Although translating it here somewhat diffidently as "self," I would like to acknowledge an alternative interpretation set forth by the Ch'ing scholar, Li Tao-p'ing, who reads the *Ts'an-t'ung ch'i* as expounding a system of correspondences matching the eight trigrams and ten Celestial Stems so that *Li* matches 己 and *K'an* matches 戊. This provides a possible explanation for the terms "*chi* earth" and "*wu* earth" representing mercury and lead, respectively.

10. This is a reverse quotation from the *Lao tzu*, Chapter 28.

11. *Lao tzu*, Chapter 28.

12. "Flourishing wood" 木旺 is a designation for the period following the vernal equinox.

13. "Fire advent" 火相 refers to the period beginning with the first month of summer.

14. The period in question is "white dew" 白露 and is the sixteenth of the Twenty-Four Climatic Periods.

15. Chang Tzu-yang 張紫陽 was the author of the *Wu-chen p'ien* and First Patriarch of the Southern School of Taoism.

16. I interpret *"K'un* male" 坤男 to be synonymous with 嬰兒, the *yang* line in the middle of *K'an*; and *"Li* female" 離女 to equal 姹女, or the *yin* line in the middle of *Li*.

17. The heart.

18. Quotation from *I ching*, "Great Commentary," Part I, Chapter 4.

19. The term "three realms" 三界 is variously defined in Taoism and Buddhism as heaven, earth, and man; the realms of desire, form, and formlessness; past, present, and future; or heaven, earth, and water; desire, form, and formlessness; past, present, and future; the infinite, ultimate and manifest realms; or simply this world. In this context, the term refers, perhaps, in a general way to the universe in all its dimensions.

20. Mount Wu-i 武夷 is a mountain in Fukien and the focus of various legends concerning the attainment of immortality by a certain Ch'ien Chien. It also is the sixteenth of the "thirty-six cave paradises" in Taoism.

21. The surnames of four Taoist immortals. Of the scores of Taoist immortals and notables named Chang, perhaps the most famous are Chang Tao-ling, Chang San-feng, and Chang Tzu-yang. My choice here would be Tzu-yang. Of those named Ko, by far the best known is Ko Hung. Chung is undoubtedly Chung Li-ch'üan, and Lü, Lü Tung-pin.

Summary of the Golden Elixir

1. Three levels of practice in Taoism, also reflected in the tripartite organization of the *Tao tsang*.

2. The five ranks of immortals from highest to lowest are heavenly, godly, earthly, human, and ghostly.

3. A god variously described in different sources, but generally associated with the east, wood, fatherhood, and stewardship of the male immortals. Often mentioned as the counterpart of the Queen Mother who rules the west.

4. The 三華 are *ching*, *ch'i*, and spirit.

5. A phrase from the *Ts'an-t'ung ch'i* interpreted by the sexual school to mean a human being of the opposite sex.

6. The 兩儀 are *yin* and *yang*.

7. The 地戶 indicates the region of the perineum.

8. I cannot find relevant definitions of 四門. Most of the very specific meanings clearly are inapplicable, but the "four directions" 四方 may indicate in a general way a withdrawal from all distractions.

9. The term 黃庭 generally is understood to refer to the very center of the body in the region of the spleen, but another tradition identifies three "yellow courts," being the centers of the brain, heart, and spleen, respectively.

10. I cannot find a gloss for 丹府, but take it as a synonym for *tan-t'ien*.

11. According to Ko Hung, the 明堂 is located between the eyebrows at a depth of one inch.

12. Among the many meanings of 三元, the most relevant for this context is *"ching, ch'i, and spirit."* However, because the context calls for a concrete locus, and in the absence of independent gloss, I can only speculate that it may refer to the "three *tan-t'ien*" as the centers of *ching*, *ch'i*, and spirit. I feel that "sources" here conveys simultaneously the sense of locus and primary element.

13. The expression 踵息 undoubtedly originates with Chuang tzu's, "The sage breathes from his heels." In a broad sense it refers to deep breathing (as if from one's very heels), but also to various techniques for circulating the *ch'i* from the "bubbling spring" point in the ball of the foot through the legs to the *tan-t'ien*.

14. The continuous circuit formed by circulating the *ch'i* up the *Tu* and down the *Jen* meridians.

15. Placing the thumb of the right hand within the circle formed by the thumb and index finger of the left.

16. The term 王府 has not been encountered before, but I surmise it is another cover for *tan-t'ien*.

17. Point at the ball of the foot.

18. The term 元海 is yet another cover for the *tan-t'ien*.

19. I feel that the character 紐, which appears in the text, is a mistake for 扭.

20. "Casting the sword" 鑄劍 refers to various practices, with or without the benefit of partner, for strengthening and gaining supernormal control over the male reproductive

organs. The present text advocates "casting the sword" by "entering the stove," though this is is condemned by the "pure practices" school.

21. A figure of speech for older men having intercourse with young women.

22. The "crucibles" 鼎, of course, refer to female partners, and the "weight" is an obvious reference to their age.

23. A figure of speech, here, from the former imperial examination system.

24. The term 太虛 refers to heaven or *ch'i* in its primordial, undifferentiated state.

25. The term 玄牝 has many interpretations. The expression first appears in the *Lao tzu*, where it usually is interpreted to refer to *yin* and *yang* as the bipolar power of creation and transformation. In later inner alchemy texts, such as the *Huang-t'ing ching* and *Chin-tan ssu-pai tzu*, it comes to indicate the water region, or physiological North Pole of the body, the kidneys or lower *tan-t'ien*.

26. A point just above the space between the eyebrows, also called the 天庭.

27. I am interpreting "mysterious valley" 玄谷 here on my own initiative as a synonym for "heavenly vale" 天谷 in the center of the head.

28. *Yin* and *yang*.

29. "Stove" 爐 in this context refers to the female partner.

30. The term 潮候, originally denoting high tide and similar to 潮信, is applied here to the approach of menses.

31. The moon and its phases are intimately associated with the woman's menstrual cycle and enshrined in such expressions as 月經, 月事, and 月信.

32. Either the saliva or sexual secretions of the female partner, but I cannot determine which with certainty.

33. In the phrase 休折臨落花 I am interpreting the character 休 as a negative imperative, but cannot make a positive identification of 落. One possibility is that "flowers" approximates the phenomenon of ovulation and that "fallen flowers" thus are the menses.

34. The expression 沒弦琴 is reminiscent, of course, of 琴弦 in our earliest texts; and although I can find no independent gloss or parallel text, I believe it refers to the female vulva.

35. Again, not the sort of term one finds glossed, but I feel confident it refers to the penis.

36. The Southern and Northern Schools of Taoism each have their own "Five Patriarchs" 五祖. Because of the association of sexual practices with the Southern School, one can assume that these were Chang Tzu-yang 張紫陽, Shih Hsing-lin 石杏林, Hsüeh Tao-kuang 薛道光, Ch'en Ni-wan 陳泥丸, and Pai Tzu-ch'ing 白紫清.

37. There are also two sets of "Seven Adepts," which on the southern side includes the "Five Patriarchs," plus Liu Yung-nien 劉永年, and P'eng Ho-nien 彭鶴年.

38. "Post-natal" 後天, here is used in the special sense of postpubescent.

39. The term 河車 here should not be confused with the same combination used elsewhere in the sense of microcosmic orbit meditation.

40. The seventh of the Celestial Stems, *keng* 庚, is associated with the direction west and the element metal. Metal, in turn, signifies the middle line in *K'an*, which is the basis for restoring *Li* to *Ch'ien*, or the "golden elixir." Twice "seven" is fourteen years, or 5,048 days, the time of the first menses or the opening of the connection between heart and kidneys in the woman.

41. The expression "white tiger" 白虎 has a number of other related associations, including a divinity of the western quarter, a group of seven constellations in the western sky, and in the vernacular, a woman without pubic hair.

42. The "five facial features" 五官 are eyebrows, eyes, ears, nose, and mouth.

43. The K'ai-yüan catalogue of the Chinese Buddhist canon, or *Tripitika*, contains 5,048 items.

44. The term "yellow path" 黃道, originally referred to the ecliptic of the sun, but here, as in a reference in the *Wu-chen p'ien*, it seems to indicate the central region of the body.

45. These definitions of 螺, 紋, 鼓, 角, and 脉 are similar to, but differ in some details from the Buddhist 五種不女. Medical sources use the same nomenclature and closely parallel definitions.

46. This list, too, approximates, but differs somewhat from the Buddhist 五種不男. Some medical sources give an alternative list, 天, 漏, 犍, 怯, and 變, defined as genital deformity, spermatorrhea, castration, impotence, and hermaphroditism.

47. One *ch'ien* 錢 is equal to a tenth of a *liang*, or approximately 3.125 grams.

48. Almost certainly the vagina rather than the oral cavity.

49. In Chinese medicine the term 刀圭 refers to a small measuring spatula with a capacity of one-tenth of a "square inch spoon," and also as a synecdoche for the science of herbal medicine itself.

50. The text gives 鏽劍 here instead of 鑄劍, raising suspicions of either a shortage of type or a practical joke, as the error produces the rather humorous meaning "rusty sword."

51. In Taoist mythology 火棗 is a name for one of the fruits of immortality. In "pure practice" inner alchemy it is one of many covers for lead, or *K'an*. I cannot determine with certainty whether it represents the energetic or liquid aspect of the woman's sexual response here.

52. The term "*kuei* water" 癸水 usually refers to the menses, but here it seems to signify a first stage of female secretions following sexual stimulation.

53. The difficulty here in interpreting the meaning of *jen* 壬 is that in the present context it appears to follow *kuei* 癸, whereas in the system of Celestial Stems from which they are borrowed, the order is *jen* (nine) and *kuei* (ten). Among the Stems, both *jen* and *kuei* are associated with the direction north, the element water, and the female functions of conception and menses. The five pairs of Celestial Stems are each assigned to an organ and divided according to *yin* and *yang*. *Jen* and *kuei* are associated with the kidneys, the *jen* being *yang* and representing the *ch'i* aspect, and the *kuei* being *yin* and representing the fluid aspect.

54. I take 珠 as "mysterious pearl" 玄珠, a cover for the elixir.

55. The phrase 光透簾帷 is a standard meditation metaphor for an enlightening flash of brilliance that penetrates the eyelids from within.

56. The second character in the combination 火苻 that appears in the text is an error, I believe, for 符. "Fire tally" 火符 is the *yang-ch'i* that rises up the spine during microcosmic orbit practice, being the counterpart of "*yin* tally," the descending arc.

57. The term 太玄關 is an alternate for *wei-lü*, denoting here the center of sexual energy. It is a synonym for 玄機 in HCYI.

58. I cannot discover what more specific meaning the term 清仙仙客 may have.

59. Tzu 子 is the first of the Terrestrial Branches and represents, in terms of the diurnal cycle, the Chinese hour 11:00 PM to 1:00 AM, when the sun passes its nadir and the *yang* force returns. In the microcosm of the human male, the "hour of the living *tzu*" 活子時 manifests as erection of the penis, which like *tzu* is located due north.

60. Kung Chien Lao Jen reduces these complex calculations to the period beginning with the tenth day after the cessation of menses and ending with the twenty-second and a half day. I feel this is based on a Western estimate of the cycle of female fertility rather than actually cracking the code of the original text. I am not prepared to be more specific at this point, but clearly the time frame is much narrower.

Secret Principles of Gathering the True Essence

1. The character 碧 in the phrase 風生帆碧落 is unintelligible. The same phrase appears later in the text, this time with 必 instead of 碧, which makes perfect sense and suggests a safe emendation.

2. There is an erratum in the text involving 蜜 for 密.

3. "Column of jade" 玉柱 is a standard term in mediation texts describing the phenomenon of a nasal secretion accompanying deep stages of absorption.

4. "West Pond" 西池 is more a poetic conceit than a specific geographic location.

5. I cannot decipher the significance of these numbers.

6. I cannot ascertain the special significance of "seven" 七 here. Elsewhere seven is considered the "proper" 正 *yang* number, "the origin of heaven, earth, man and the four seasons," and a symbol for fire, the south, the west, and the trigrams *Chen* or *Li*.

7. According to a gloss in the *Huang-t'ing ching*, the "gate of heaven" 天門, refers to the point between the eyebrows at a depth of one inch, also called the "bright hall" 明堂. The commentary here associates the "gate of heaven" with the "northwest," which is the seat of *Ch'ien* in the King Wen arrangement of the trigrams.

8. The "living *tzu*" is the *yang-ch'i* within the human body.

9. The text gives 念 here instead of 驗.

10. It should be borne in mind that the esoteric theory underlying this paradoxical couplet is that the woman contributes the "*yang* essence" and the man is "impregnated."

11. The text mistakenly gives 認便 here instead of 忍便.

12. I believe that 提扳 in the text here should be 提拨.

13. Again 拨 makes more sense here than the 扳 given in the text.

14. During microcosmic orbit meditation, half of the cycle is called "advancing the *yang* fire" 進陽火, and symbolized by the six Terrestrial Branches from *tzu* to *chi*; and the other half, "withdrawing the *yin* tally," 退陰符 from *wu* to *hai*. The former is accentuated on the inhalation and the latter on the exhalation. Sometimes, the cycle is applied to one mediation session or an entire series.

15. *Tzu* 子 and *wu* 午 are the first and seventh of the Terrestrial Branches, representing the hours 11:00 PM to 1:00 AM and 11:00 AM to 1:00 PM, the solstices, and the poles of the body (fundament and head) traversed by the *ch'i* during microcosmic orbit. *Yin* 寅 and *hsü* 戌 are the third and tenth of the Terrestrial Branches.

16. Some authorities specify synchronization of meditation practice with such macrocosmic manifestations of the incipient *yang* force as midnight and the winter solstice. Most, however, emphasize the microcosmic movement of *yin* and *yang* as determined by the individual's own "biological clock" rather than the sun, moon, and stars. The significance of *tzu* and *wu* in meditation has been discussed in note 13; *mao* 卯 (the fourth Terrestrial Branch) and *yu* 酉 (the tenth) traditionally are called 沐浴, literally "to bathe," but in this context rest periods. These are the "equinoxes" during which the state of "advance" or "retreat" remains stable and no new phase is initiated.

17. The "fire" of *yang-ch'i* is controlled chiefly by the mind and breath. The terms "civil" 文 and "martial" 武 usually are interpreted to mean the application of gentle or forceful breathing. The martial is employed during "advancement of the *yang* fire" and the civil during "withdrawal of the *yin* tally."

18. The "one *yang*" 一陽 is the single *yang* line in the middle of *K'an*, representing the masculine in the midst of the feminine.

19. The term "central extremity" 中極 refers to the Pole Star. As the epicenter of the northern sky, I believe this represents the "northern" or lower portion of the body, and thus the *tan-t'ien*. In acupuncture, it is the point on the *Jen* meridian just below the 關元.

20. Clearly, "white tiger's tail" 白虎尾 and "moon cave" 月窟 metaphorically represent the female parts, whereas "green dragon's head" 青龍頭 and "heavenly root" 天根 represent the male.

"The Rootless Tree"

1. The character in *Chang San-feng ch'üan-chi* 張三丰全集 and *Chang San-feng t'ai-chi lien-tan pi-chüeh* 張三丰太極煉丹秘訣 is *nieh* 臬, which makes no sense here. *Li* 梨 is the standard character in this familiar phrase, an example of which may be found in *The Exposition of Cutivating the True Essence*.

2. *K'en liao* 肯了 in *Chang San-feng t'ai-chi lien-tan pi-chüeh* does not read as well as *pei liao* 背了 in the *Ch'üan-chi* and is obviously a scribal error.

3. The *yen-yüeh lu* 偃月爐 is a cover for the vulva.

4. *Shunyata* is emptiness and *samsara* the mundane world. Their equation here is the standard Ch'an Buddhist statement indicating that *nirvana* is not outside of but immanent within the everyday world.

Women's Practices

Queen Mother of the West's Ten Precepts

1. Lu Fu, a provincial governor of the Three Kingdoms period befriended and took counsel with ten eminent and virtuous men in his province.

2. A paradise of the immortals.

3. Two points on the bladder meridian on either side of the spinal column at about the level of the third thoracic vertebra.

4. I suspect that Wei Yüan-chün 魏元君 is Wei Fu-jen 魏夫人, a woman of the Chin dynasty believed to have attained immortality and honored with the title Yüan-chün, indicating a female immortal.

5. I can find no gloss for the expression "yellow leaves" 黃葉, but from context it seems to indicate a simple folk remedy for a minor malady.

6. *I ching*, Hexagram 2, *K'un* (The Receptive). "Yellow" is the color of earth and of the center.

7. I can only take "stream sea" 溪海 as equivalent to "breast stream" 乳溪. The *Su wen*, "Ch'i-hsüeh lun" says, "Great convergences of flesh are *ku* 谷; small convergences are *hsi* 溪."

8. The "palace" is the "crimson palace," or heart.

9. The characters as they appear in the text, 桃核, are undoubtedly an inversion of 核桃. From the context it almost certainly is not an

error for 桃孩, which is the ruling spirit of the *ming-men*.

10. The two characters that appear in the text 民相 are unusual in two respects. First, one would expect the more familiar combination 君相, but if this is not an error, then placing 民 before 相 is highly irregular. Second, if 民 indeed is intended, the concept of a "popular fire," although not unknown (it appears in the *Hui-ming ching*), actually is quite rare. Because the passage in the *Hui-ming ching* states: "Within the cavity is the 'monarchial fire' 君火, at its opening the 'ministerial fire' 相火, and throughout the body the 'popular fire' 民火," it seems unlikely that the trio would be broken up and the last two be given alone, especially in inverted form. Despite this and the obvious ease of confusing 君 and 民 in a handwritten manuscript, I would stop short of recommending a positive emendation. A slightly different version can be found in the *Chen-hsien mi-chuan huo-hou-fa* that designates the fires of the heart, kidneys, and bladder as "ruler, minister, and people."

11. Although I cannot find the specific combination 腸紅, based on the medical expression 腸風便血, I take it to mean bright red blood discharged from the rectum just before moving the bowels.

12. Viscous red discharge from the vagina attributed in Chinese medicine to excessive "fire" in the heart and liver.

13. A kind of vicarious menses, occurring cyclically just prior to, during, or after the normally anticipated period, which takes the form of retching blood or nosebleed.

14. I believe there is an inversion in the three characters, 溪歸海, that should read 歸溪海. What appears here is grammatically awkward, difficult to interpret, and the expression 歸溪海 appears in the previous chapter.

15. The 三山 are three mountains of the immortals rising from the sea.

16. A paradise of the immortals located in the K'un-lun Mountains.

17. Originally *gao* indicated the area immediately below the heart and *huang* the area between the heart and diaphragm. Later it came to mean a deeply seated and incurable disease. The text mistakenly gives 盲 instead of 肓. The use of the terms here should be distinguished from the acupuncture point, *kao-huang* 膏肓, Bladder 43.

18. Thin body fluids circulating between the muscles and skin, which serve to warm and lubricate the skin.

19. More precisely, the term 三伏 refers to the third and fourth *keng*, 庚, days after the summer solstice, plus the first *keng* day after the first day of autumn. The 三伏, then, is a collective term for the warmest part of the year.

20. I can find no gloss for 心罡, but interpret it as a fusion of 天心 and 天罡, both of which refer in astronomy to the Big Dipper or central region of the sky and, according to the *Hui-ming ching*, to the "true consciousness" in inner alchemy.

21. The *Ch'ing-ching ching* says: "Contemplate the mind within to discover that the mind does not exist; contemplate phenomena without to discover that phenomena do not exist; contemplate forms at a distance to discover that forms do not exist."

22. The first of the "three pure realms," 三清, being that reserved for sages.

23. The "true seeds" 真種子 is a metaphor for the appearance of "true *ch'i*," "true *ching*," or "medicine" during meditation.

24. Quote from *Analects*, "Tzu Han."

25. Approximate quote from *Chuang tzu*, "T'ien-hsia."

26. "T'ien-ku" 天谷, literally "vale of heaven," is a cover for the "upper *tan-t'ien*" in the head.

27. The term 南無 (Sanskrit, *namah*; Pali, *namo*) is an expression of submission, reverence, or devotion used as a formula of faith in Buddhist liturgy, incantations, and so forth.

28. I can find no gloss for 紅孩兒.

29. *Kung-an* 公案, better known by the Japanese pronunciation, "koan," originally meant "legal cases," but in Ch'an (Zen) Buddhist usage, it refers to hypothetical problems formulated by masters for students to ponder as a means to enlightenment.

30. I cannot identify this term.

31. I cannot identify this term.

32. The word "Tara" (Chinese 哆囉) has many definitions, but the most relevant here refers to certain female deities of the Tantric school. The origin of the term is ascribed by some to the root *tar*, meaning "to cross"; hence she who aids seekers to cross the sea of mortality.

33. I cannot identify this term.

Essentials of the Golden Elixir Method for Women

1. In external alchemy, "yellow sprouts" 黃芽 generally refers to unoxidized bright

lead, but in internal cultivation the term is used for the appearance of yellow light during meditation. Neither definition seems perfectly applicable here.

2. Most classical authorities place the "gate of life" 命門 either in the right kidney, the two kidneys, or a point between the two, but in any event on the dorsal side. This text agrees with the minority nomenclature, as seen in such works as the *Huang-t'ing ching*, which place it near the navel. Even rarer traditions identify it with the *wei-lü* or the eyes.

3. In this, as in most sources, the "secluded pass" 幽闕 is identified with the kidneys.

4. The three most important ventral points from navel to pubis are 丹田, 氣海, and 關元, but their location, dimensions, and order differ in various sources.

5. In medical terminology, "empty orifice" 空竅 refers to those orifices that open to the outside.

6. The term 月信 is a standard for menstrual period, although the author provides a new interpretation here.

7. This differs from the male location of the 炁穴, which is synonymous with the lower *tan-t'ien*.

8. The 玉宇 is the abode of the Emperor of Heaven.

9. This should be compared with the statement in the SNML: "If the *yin* blood surrounds the *yang-ching*, a male child will be born; if the *yang-ching* surrounds the *yin* blood, a girl child will be born."

10. An ancient unit of weight variously defined at different periods, but including one twenty-fourth or one forty- eighth of a *liang*. Here, if one *chu* is produced every 12 days for 180 days to equal one *liang*, it would seem that the author took the *chu* as one-fifteenth of the *liang*.

11. The "white tiger" 白虎 is a cover term for the *ch'i*.

Master Li Ni-wan's Precious Raft of Women's Dual Practice

1. This is from the *I ching*, Hexagram 61, "Inner Truth" (*Chung fu*) and generally is interpreted to mean that the fowl's cry rises to heaven but the bird itself is earth bound. The implication is that calamity results from overstepping the limits of one's preparation.

2. *Yu* 酉 is the tenth Terrestrial Branch, represented by the chicken or cock.

3. The expression 閻浮, Chinese for Jambudvipa, refers to a tree giving its name to one

of the island paradises surrounding the fabled Mount Meru.

4. The ocean of the *bhutatathata*, or all-embracing immaterial nature of the *dharmakaya*.

5. I feel fairly confident that 轆轤, "wind-lass," is a metaphor for the shoulders, particularly in view of the verb 聳, which invariably is used for exercises involving rhythmically hoisting and releasing the shoulders.

6. The text gives 未 here instead of 末 in the expression 末後. The same phrase 末後大著 appears correctly in Chapter 5 of this work.

7. A popular novel with many fanciful elements describing the adventures of a Buddhist monk and his three disciples during a pilgrimage to India.

8. Ch'en Ying-ning, editor of *Correct Methods for Women's Practice*, included in this anthology, tells us in his Preface that the original title of the work was *Expanded Instructions of the Golden Flower on the Correct Methods of Women's Practice* (*Tseng-pu chin-hua chih-chih nü-kung cheng-fa*), the core characters of which are the same as this title. Ch'en mentions finding the original in eleven chapters, two addenda, and sixteen verses, which conflicts with the "eighteen" in this title. I have not discovered an independent version or listing of the original title to determine a possible relationship.

9. Heaven, earth, and man; from the *I ching*, "Discussion of the Hexagrams."

10. The Pancha parisad, 無遮會 in Chinese, was a great Buddhist assembly, which took place every five years for confession, penance, and so on.

11. In Buddhism, the cause of all phenomena, or the content of the "seed-store" of consciousness from which all phenomena spring, the *alayavijnana*.

12. The 天龍八部 are the *devas*, *nagas*, *yakshas*, *gandharvas*, *asuras*, *garudas*, *kinaras*, and *maroragas*.

13. The expression 乾元 appears in the *I ching*, Hexagram 1, "The Creative."

14. I believe that 頂 refers here to the summit or crown of the head.

15. The expression 坤元 appears in the *I ching*, Hexagram 2, "The Receptive."

16. The term 牝 denotes the female gender, or as synonymous with 陰 and 坤, may refer to the feminine aspect. Here, I believe, the female reproductive system is intended.

17. The combination 真常 is a Buddhist term for the eternal reality, or Buddha-truth.

18. I believe that the "two fives" 二五 refer to the five *yang* (odd) and five *yin* (even) numbers described in the *I ching*, "Great Commentary," Part I, Chapter 9: "The numbers of heaven are five and the numbers of earth are five." Their various combinations and interactions symbolize the myriad phenomena.

19. *Dharmakaya* 法身 is the embodiment of Truth and Law in Buddhism, the spiritual or true body.

20. *Rupakaya* 色身 is the physical body, as contrasted with *dharmakaya*.

21. An expression that indicates redundancy.

22. The text mistakenly gives the character 按 here instead of 安.

23. This differs from the more familiar formulation, which regards men as *yang* on the outside and *yin* on the inside, and women as vice versa.

24. This also is contrary to the "paired practice" formulation, which considers man *Li* and woman *K'an*.

25. The text gives 乘 here instead of 乖.

26. *Lao tzu*, Chapter 25.

27. *Lao tzu*, Chapter 21.

28. A Buddhist mataphor for *nirvana*.

29. The chief texts of the Hua-yen, Ch'an, and T'ien-t'ai sects of Buddhism in China.

30. Three islands inhabited by the immortals.

31. Ten islands inhabited by the immortals.

32. The 火記 is a work on the stages of progress toward immortality mentioned in the *Ts'an-t'ung ch'i*.

33. In Buddhist terminology, 大千 is a major chiliocosm, consisting of 3,000 great chiliocosms.

34. The "three realms" 三界 in Buddhism are sensuous desire 欲; form 色; and spirit 無色界.

35. From the *Odes*, "Songs of Yung." This ode traditionally is interpreted to be a criticism of Hsüan Chiang, who appeared lavishly attired at the funeral of her husband, Duke Hsüan of Wei, instead of looking appropriately mournful. Premodern interpretations of her "misfortune" emphasize her lack of wifely virtue, but some contemporary critics feel her forced marriage and enforced chastity in the prime of life constituted her misfortune.

36. The doctrine in such Buddhist sects as the Hua-yen, T'ien-t'ai, an Chen-yen that all things proceed from the *dharmakaya* and that all phenomena are of the same essence as noumena.

Correct Methods for Women's Practice

1. The 五漏 are "leakages" from the eyes, nose, tongue, ears, and pores, associated with the Five Viscera (liver, lungs, heart, kidneys, and spleen), respectively. The "three passes," here, are not the more familiar *wei-lü, chia-chi,* and *yü-chen,* but the ears, eyes, and mouth.

2. I cannot find a gloss for 金室, and have not encountered it previously in the literature. The distinction here among 神, 性, and 意 makes the matter somewhat more problematic. Triangulating from the direct objects of the verbs and extrapolating in light of the possibility of parallelism with the woman's three "elixir fields"—breasts, navel, and uterus—the best guess would be navel, or middle *tan-t'ien.*

3. A Buddhist term for the ocean of Buddha-wisdom.

4. I cannot find an independent gloss for *tan-kung* 丹宮, but I am assuming it is a synonym for *tan-t'ien* 丹田.

5. Another name for Queen Mother of the West.

6. Editor Ch'en Ying-ning points out the confusion of terminology in the text, which equates "tip of the nose" with "tail of the nose" and designates it as "root of the mountain" 山根. In Chinese physiognomy, the 山根 refers to the upper portion of the nose between the eyebrows. This is a reflection of the debate within Buddhist meditation circles as to whether the "end of the nose" 鼻端 indicates the tip or the bridge and which is the proper focal point of concentration.

7. In Buddhism, the five components of a sentient being, especially human: *rupa* 色, physical form related to the five organs of sense; *venana* 受, functioning of the senses or mind in relation to affairs; *sanjna* 想, mental function of conception or discerning; *samskara* 行, mental judgments of like and dislike, good and evil, and so on; and *vijnana* 識, mental faculty of perception and cognition.

8. The text gives 治 instead of the obviously intended 始.

9. The lower pole of the body being north, I take 北海 to be synonymous with "sea of *ch'i*" 氣海.

10. The editor tells us in a note at the end of this verse that other works give "two breasts" instead of "two palms."

11. The "five dragons" 五龍 are the five spirits of the Five Phases, often designated

273

with the names of the five notes of the Chinese pentatonic scale.

12. Avalokitesvara, "Goddess of Mercy," the center of whose cult in China is a sacred island, P'u-t'o, off of Ningpo.

13. This differs from the more familiar "six character transmission," which uses the following sounds and organ centers: *hsü* 嘘 (liver); *ho* 呵 (heart); *ssu* 呬 (lungs); *ch'ui* 吹 (kidneys); *hu* 呼 (spleen); and *hsi* 嘻 (triple heater).

14. The Chinese concept of soul consists of a *yang* aspect, *hun* 魂, which belongs to heaven, and a *yin* aspect, *p'o* 魄, which belongs to earth.

15. The Chinese transliteration of the Sanskrit *om* or *aum*.

16. From a story in the *Hua-yen sutra*.

17. An error in the text gives 腎 for 賢.

18. A Sung monk who transported the materials and constructed a large temple edifice with his own hands.

Bibliography

Note: Volume and page numbers for Tao tsang *(Taoist canon) entries, indicated by TT, refer to Li I-mang, ed.,* Tao tsang *(Peking: Wen-wu Press, 1987). Various editions of the same work found in the* Tao tsang *are not separately noted, but are included in the page citations.*

Akagi Koichi 赤木幸一. *Hsien-jen hui-ch'un ch'iang-ching shu* 仙人回春強精術 (Methods of the immortals for rejuvenation and sexual strengthening). Taipei: Wu-ling ch'u-pan-she, 1983.

Andersen, Poul. *The Method of Holding the Three Ones: A Taoist Manual of Meditation of the Fourth Century* A.D. London and Malmö: Curzon Press, 1980.

Bennett, Steven. "Patterns of the Sky and Earth: A Chinese Science of Applied Cosmology." *Chinese Science*, 3 (1978): 1–26.

Beurdeley, Michel, ed. *The Clouds and the Rain: The Art of Love in China.* Frebourg: Office du Livre; London: Hammond and Hammond, 1969. Also published as *Chinese Erotic Art.* Hong Kong: Chartwell Books.

Blofeld, John. *The Secret and the Sublime: Taoist Mysteries and Magic.* New York: E. P. Dutton, 1973.

Chai Ch'ang li 翟昌禮 and Liu Ming 柳明. *Yang-sheng yü ch'ang-shou* 養生與長壽 (Health practices and longevity). Peking: K'o-hsüeh p'u-*chi* ch'u-pan-she, 1985.

Chang chün-fan 張君房, ed. *Yün-chi ch'i-ch'ien* 雲笈七籤 (Seven bamboo tablets of the cloud bookcase). TT, vol. 23, pp. 1–849.

Chang Chung-yüan. *Creativity and Taoism: A Study of Chinese Philosophy, Art and Poetry.* New York: Harper and Row, 1970.

Chang, Jolan [Chung-lan]. *The Tao of Love and Sex: The Ancient Chinese Way to Ecstasy.* New York: E. P. Dutton, 1977.

Chang Jung-ming 張榮明. *Chung-kuo ku-tai ch'i-kung yü hsien-ch'in che-hsüeh* 中國古代氣功與先秦哲學 (Ancient Chinese yoga and pre-Ch'in philosophy). Shanghai: Shang-hai jen-min ch'u-pan-she, 1987.

Chang Po-tuan 張伯端. *Wu-chen p'ien* 悟真篇 (Essay on realizing the true). TT, vol. 2, pp. 910–1030; vol. 3, pp. 1–16; vol. 4, pp. 711–749.

Chang San-feng 張三峯. *Chin-tan chieh-yao* 金丹節要 (Summary of the golden elixir). In *San-feng tan-chüeh* and *Tao-tsang ching-hua*, series 4, no. 6, vol. 2.

———. *Ts'ai-chen chi-yao* 採真機要 (Secret principles of gathering the true essence). In *San-feng tan-chüeh* and *Tao-tsang ching-hua*, series 4, no. 6, vol. 2.

———. "Wu-ken shu" 無根樹. In *San-feng tan-chüeh, Chang San-feng ch'üan-chi*, and *Chang San-feng t'ai-chi lien-tan pi-chüeh.*

Chang San-feng t'ai-chi lien-tan pi-chüeh 張三丰太極煉丹秘訣 (Secret transmissions of Chang San-feng on the Great Ultimate cultivation of the elixir). In *Tao-tsang ching-hua.*

Chang Shih-ling 張石齡. *Hui-ch'un pu-shen mi-fang* 回春補腎秘方 (Secrets of rejuvenation and sexual strengthening). Hong Kong: Tsung-heng ch'u-pan-she, n.d.

Chang, Stephen. *The Tao of Sexology: The Book of Infinite Wisdom.* San Francisco: Tao Publishing, 1986.

Ch'en Hua 陳華. "Chung-i yü hsing" 中醫與性 (Chinese medicine and sex). Unpublished, n.d.

Ch'en Ping 陳兵. *Tao-chiao ch'i-kung pai-wen*

道教氣功百問 (One hundred questions on Taoist yoga). Peking: Chin-jih chung-kuo ch'u-pan-she, 1989.

Ch'en Ying-ning 陳櫻寧. *Tao-chiao yü yang-sheng* 道教與養生 (Taoism and health). Peking: Hua-wen ch'u-pan-she, 1989.

Ch'en Kuo-fu 陳國符. *Tao-tsang yüan-liu k'ao* 道藏原流考 (A study of the origins of the *Tao tsang*). Shanghai: Chung-hua, 1949; Peking: Chung-hua, 1963.

Chen, Linda. "Traditional Chinese Concepts of Sex and the Body." Unpublshed, 1974.

Ch'en Ying-ning 陳櫻寧, ed. *Nü-kung cheng-fa* 女功正法 (Correct methods of women's practice). In *Tao-tsang ching-hua*, series 4, no. 5.

Ch'i-kung ching-hsüan 氣功精選 (Selected articles on Chinese yoga). Peking: Jen-min t'i-yü ch'u-pan-she, 1981.

Chia, Mantak. *Taoist Secrets of Love: Cultivating Male Sexual Energy.* New York: Aurora Press, 1984.

Chia, Mantak and Maneewan Chia. *Healing Love through the Tao: Cultivating Female Sexual Energy.* Huntington: Healing Tao Books, 1986.

Chiao Kuo-jui 焦國瑞. *Ch'i-kung yang-sheng hsüeh kai-yao* 氣功養生學概要 (Outline of Chinese yogic hygiene). Fuchow: Fu-chien jen-min ch'u-pan-she, 1984.

Ch'ien-ku mi-wen lu 千古秘聞錄 (Record of secrets of the ages). Hong Kong: Mei-pao ch'u-pan-she, n.d.

Ch'iu Ling 邱陵. *T'u-chieh chung-kuo liu-hsing ch'i-kung* 圖解中國流行氣功 (Illustrated popular Chinese yoga). Hong Kong: Wan-li shu-tien, 1987.

Chou Ch'ien-ch'uan 周潛川. *Ch'i-kung yao-erh liao-fa yü chiu-chih p'ien-ch'a shou-shu* 氣功藥餌療法與糾治偏差手術 (Yogic and herbal therapies and corrective methods). T'ai-yüan: Shen-hsi jen-min ch'u-pan-she, 1984.

Chou, Eric. *The Dragon and the Phoenix: Love, Sex and the Chinese.* New York: Arbor House, 1971.

Chu Chien-p'ing 竹劍平, et al. *Chung-kuo ku-tai yang-sheng ch'ang-shou mi-fa* 中國古代養生長壽秘法 (Secrets of ancient Chinese health and longevity). Hangchow: Che-chiang k'o-hsüeh chi-shu ch'u-pan-she, 1987.

Chung-i ming-tz'u shu-yü hsüan-shih 中醫名詞術語選釋 (Dictionary of traditional Chinese medical terms and expressions). Peking: Jen-min wei-sheng ch'u-pan-she, 1973.

Dai, Bingham. "Culture and Delusional Systems of Some Chinese Mental Patients." *International Journal of Social Psychiatry* 2 (1965): 59–69.

Douglas, Nik, and Penny Slinger. *Sexual Secrets.* New York: Destiny Books, 1979.

Eberhard, Wolfram. *Guilt and Sin in Traditional China.* Berkeley and Los Angeles: University of California Press, 1967.

Edwardes, A. *The Jewel in the Lotus: A Historical Survey of the Sexual Culture of the East.* New York: Julian Press, 1959.

———, and R. E. L. Masters. *The Cradle of Erotica: The Definitive Study of Exotic Afro-Asian Sexual Behaviour.* New York: Lancer Books, 1962.

Fischman, Walter, and Frank Warren. *Sexual Acupuncture.* New York: E. P. Dutton, 1978.

Fu Chin-ch'üan 傅金銓, ed. *Nü chin-tan fa-yao* 女金丹法要 (Essentials of the golden elixir method for women). In *Tao-tsang ching-hua*, series 5, no. 5.

Gichner, Lawrence. *Erotic Aspects of Chinese Culture.* Washington, D.C.: privately printed, 1957.

de Groot, J. M. M. *Sectarianism and Religious Persecution in China.* Taipei: Ch'eng-wen Publishing Co. (reprint), 1970.

van Gulik, R. H. *Erotic Colour Prints of the Ming Period.* Tokyo, privately printed, 1951.

———. *Sexual Life in Ancient China.* Leiden: E. J. Brill, 1961.

Harper, Donald. "The Sexual Arts of Ancient China as Described in a Manuscript of the Second Century B.C." *Harvard Journal of Asiatic Studies* 47, no. 2 (1987): 539–593.

Hasegawa Gorō 長谷川五郎. Hsiao Ching-ling, trans. *Hsing-kan ching-hsüeh chien-k'ang fa* 性感經穴健康法 (Health through sexual acupoints). Taipei: Ta-chan ch'u-pan-she, 1990.

Ho Lung-hsiang 賀龍驤, and P'eng Han-jan 彭瀚然, eds. *Tao-tsang chi-yao* 道藏輯要 (Essentials of the Taoist canon). Chengtu: Erh-hsien ssu, 1906.

Homann, Rolf., trans. *Pai wen p'ien, or the Hundred Questions.* Leiden: E. J. Brill, 1976.

Hsia, Emil, Ilza Veith, and Robert Geertsma. *The Essentials of Medicine in Ancient China and Japan: Yasuyori Tamba's Ishimpō.* Leiden: E. J. Brill, 1986.

Hsiao T'ien-shih 蕭天石, ed. *Nei-wai kung t'u-shuo chi-yao* 內外功圖說輯要 (Collection of illustrated manuals of internal and external techniques of self-cultivation). Taipei: Tzu-yu ch'u-pan-she, 1982.

————. *Tao-chia yang-sheng hsüeh kai-yao* 道家養生學概要 (Outline of Taoist health practices). Taipei: Tzu-yu ch'u-pan-she, 1979.

————. *Tao-hai hsüan-wei* 道海玄微 (Mysteries of the sea of *tao*). Taipei: Tzu-yu ch'u-pan-she, 1981.

Hsieh Yü-ping 謝語冰. *Chung-hua ch'i-kung ching-hsüan* 中國氣功精選 (The best of Chinese yoga). Peking: Ch'ing-kung-ye ch'u-pan-she, 1989.

Hsing mi-fang chih pai-ping 性秘方治百病 (Sexual secrets for curing all illnesses). n.p., n.d.

Hsü Chih-wei 徐志偉. *Tao te ch'i-kung chien-shen fa* 道的氣功健身法 (Yogic health methods of the *tao*). Hong Kong: Hsing-lien ch'u-pan-she, 1988.

Huang Chao-han 黃兆漢. *Ming-tai tao-shih Chang San-feng k'ao* 明代道士張三丰考 (A study of the Ming dynasty Taoist, Chang San-feng). Taipei: Hsüeh-sheng shu-chü, 1989.

————. *Tao-chiao yen-chiu lun-wen chi* 道教研究論文集 (Studies on Taoism). Hong Kong: Chung-wen ta-hsüeh ch'u-pan-she, 1988.

Huang-ti nei-ching su-wen 黃帝內經素問 (Yellow Emperor's classic of internal medicine), and *Huang-ti nei-ching ling-shu* 黃帝內經靈樞 (Vital axis of the Yellow Emperor's classic of internal medicine). TT, vol. 21, pp. 1–484.

Huang-t'ing nei-ching yü-ching 黃庭內景玉經 (Jade classic of the inner radiance of the yellow court). TT, vol. 4, pp. 835–868; vol. 5, pp. 907–912; vol. 6, pp. 499–540.

Huang-t'ing wai-ching yü-ching 黃庭外景玉經 (Jade classic of the outer radiance of the yellow court). TT, vol. 4, pp. 869–878; vol. 5, pp. 913–915; vol. 6, pp. 541–543.

Humana, Charles, and Wang Wu. *The Chinese Way of Love*. Hong Kong: CFW Publications, 1982.

Ishihara Akira, and Howard Levy. *The Tao of Sex*. Yokohama: Shibundo, 1968.

Ishihara Akira 石原明, et al. *Ishimpō kan dai-jijūhachi, bōnai* 醫心方卷第廿八房內 (The twenty-eighth chapter of the *Ishimpō*, art of the bedchamber). Tokyo: Shibundo, 1970.

Ko Hung 葛鴻. *Pao P'u tzu nei-p'ien* 抱樸子內篇 (Inner chapters of the Master Who Embraces Purity). TT, vol. 28, pp. 171–333.

Kobler, Fritz. "Description of an Acute Castration Fear Based on Superstition." *Psychoanalytic Review* 35 (1948): 285–289.

Kung-chien Lao-jen 公鑑老人. *Chung-kuo yang-sheng ts'ai-pu shu* 中國養生採補術 (Chinese health and sex practices). Hong Kong: Mei-pao ch'u-pan-she, n.d.

Kuo Chou-li 郭周禮. *Chung-hua ch'i-kung fa-chan shih* 中華氣功發展史 (History of the development of Chinese yoga). Peking: T'ien-tse ch'u-pan-she, 1989.

Lagerway, John. *Taoist Ritual in Chinese Society and History*. New York and London: Macmillan, 1987.

Li Hsi-yüeh 李西月, ed. *Chang San-feng ch'üan-chi* 張三丰全集 (The complete works of Chang San-feng). In Ho Lung-hsiang, P'eng Han-jan, et al., eds. *Tao-tsang chi-yao*.

Li I-mang 李一氓, ed. *Tao tsang* 道藏 (Taoist canon). Peking: Wen-wu ch'u-pan-she, 1987.

Li Ni-wan 李泥丸 [Li Weng 李翁]. *Ni-wan Li tsu-shih nü-tsung shuang-hsiu pao-fa* 泥丸李祖師女宗雙修寶筏 (Master Li Ni-wan's precious raft of women's dual practice). In *Tao-tsang hsü-pien, ch'u-chi*, 20.

Li Shou-k'ang 李壽康. *Ch'i-kung chih-liao yü pao-chien* 氣功治療與保健 (Chinese yoga therapy and prevention). Hong Kong: Hsiang-kang te-li shu-chü, 1974.

Li Yüan-kuo 李遠國. *Ch'i-kung ching-hua chi* 氣功精華集 (The best of Chinese yoga). Chengtu: Pa-shu shu-she, 1987.

————. *Tao-chiao ch'i-kung yang-sheng hsüeh* 道教氣功養生學 (Taoist yogic health practices). Chengtu: Ssu-ch'uan-sheng she-hui k'o-hsüeh ch'u-pan-she, 1988.

Lin Chung-p'eng 林中鵬, ed. *Chung-hua ch'i-kung hsüeh* 中華氣功學 (Chinese yoga). Peking: Pei-ching t'i-yü hsüeh-yüan ch'u-pan-she, 1988.

Liu Chan-wen 劉占文. *Chung-i yang-sheng hsüeh* 中國養生學 (Health practices of traditional Chinese medicine). Shanghai: Shang-hai chung-i hsüeh-yüan ch'u-pan-she, 1988.

Liu Shao-pai 劉少白. *Ch'i-kung liao-fa* 氣功療法 (Chinese yoga therapy). Tainan: Ch'eng-ta shu-ssu, n.d.

Liu, Tsun-yan. "Lu Hsi-hsing, A Confucian Scholar, Taoist Priest and Buddhist Devotee of the Sixteenth Century." *Asiatishe Studien* 18/19 (1966).

277

————. "Lu Hsi-hsing and His Commentaries on the Ts'an-t'ung ch'i." *The Tsing Hua Journal of Chinese Studies* 7 (1968).

————. "Taoist Self-Cultivation in Ming Thought." In Wm. Theodore de Bary, ed., *Self and Society in Ming Thought.*" New York: Columbia University Press, 1970.

Liu Wu-yüan 劉悟元. *Wu-ken shu chieh* 無根樹解 (Commentary to "The Rootless Tree"). In *Tao-shu shih-erh chung.* Shanghai: Chiang-tung shu-chü, 1913.

Lu K'uan-yü. *Taoist Yoga: Alchemy and Immortality.* New York: Samuel Weiser, 1970.

————. *The Secrets of Chinese Meditation.* New York: Samuel Weiser, 1972.

Lü Chi-t'ang 呂繼唐. *Ching-kung yang-sheng te li ho fa* 靜功養生的理和法 (The theory and practice of meditation for health). Shanghai: Shang-hai fan-i ch'u-pan kung-ssu, 1985.

Lü Kuang-jung 呂光榮. *Chung-kuo ch'i-kung ching-tien* 中國氣功經典 (Chinese yoga classics). Peking: Jen-min t'i-yü ch'u-pan-she, 1990.

Lü Yen 呂品. *Hsi Wang Mu nü-hsiu cheng-t'u shih tse* 西王母女修正途十則 (Queen Mother of the West's ten precepts on the correct path of women's practice). In *Tao-tsang hsü-pien, ch'u-chi,* 19.

————. *Ch'un-yang yen-cheng fu-yu ti-chün chi-chi chen-ching* 純陽演正孚祐帝君旣濟真經 (All-merciful Savior Lord Ch'un-yang's true classic of perfect union). In van Gulik, *Erotic Colour Prints of the Ming Period.*

Ma Chi-jen 馬濟人. *Chung-kuo ch'i-kung hsüeh* 中國氣功學 (Chinese yoga). Sian: Shen-hsi k'o-hsüeh chi-shu ch'u-pan-she, 1983.

Ma I-ming 馬一鳴, ed. *Chung-kuo ku-tai yang-sheng ch'ang-shou mi-fa* 中國古代養生長壽秘法 (Secret ancient Chinese methods of health and longevity). Hangchow: Che-chiang k'o-hsüeh chi-shu ch'u-pan-she, 1989.

Maspero, Henri. "Les Procédés de 'Nourir le Principe Vital' dans la Religion Taoist Ancienne." *Journal Asiatique* 229 (1937).

————. *Le Taoïsme.* Paris: Publications du Musée Guimet, 1950.

Nan Huai-chin 南懷錦. *Ching-tso hsiu-tao ch'ang-sheng pu-lao* 靜坐修道長生不老 (Meditation and longevity). Taipei: Lao-ku wen-hua shih-yeh kung-ssu, 1982.

Needham, Joseph. *Science and Civilization in China,* vol. 2, pp. 146–152; and vol. 5, pp. 184–218. Cambridge: Cambridge University Press, 1962, 1986.

Palos, Stephan. *The Chinese Art of Healing.* New York: McGraw-Hill, 1971.

Pan Ku 班固. *Ch'ien Han shu* 前漢書 (History of the former Han). Taipei: I-wen Press (reproduction of 1900 woodblock edition).

Porkert, Manfred. *The Theoretical Foundations of Chinese Medicine: Systems of Correspondence.* Cambridge, Mass.: MIT Press, 1979.

Reich, Wilhelm. *The Function of the Orgasm: Sex-Economic Problems of Biological Energy,* Vincent Carfango, trans. New York: Farrar, Straus and Giroux, 1973.

Rin, Hsien. "A Study of the Aetiology of Koro in Respect to the Chinese Concept of Illness," *International Journal of Social Psychiatry* 2 (1965): 7–13.

Robinet, Isabelle. *Méditation Taoïste.* Paris: Dervy Livres, 1979.

Saso, Michael. *The Teachings of Taoist Master Chuang.* New Haven and London: Yale University Press, 1979.

————. *Taoism and the Rite of Cosmic Renewal.* Seattle: Washington State University Press, 1972.

Schipper, Kristofer. "Science, Magic and Mystique of the Body." In M. Beurdeley, ed. *The Clouds and the Rain: The Art of Love in China.*

————. "The Taoist Body," *History of Religions* 17 (1978): 355–386.

————. *Le Corps Taoïste.* Paris: Fayard, 1982.

Scruton, Roger. *Sexual Desire.* New York: The Free Press, 1986.

Seidel, Anna. "A Taoist Immortal of the Ming Dynasty: Chang San-feng." In Wm. Theodore de Bary, ed. *Self and Society in Ming Thought.* New York and London: Columbia University Press, 1970.

Shang-ch'ing huang-shu kuo-tu i 上清黃書過度儀 (Salvation ritual of the yellow book, a *shang-ch'ing* scripture). TT, vol. 32, pp. 735–742.

Shen Chih-ch'iang 申志強, ed. *Chung-i shen-tsang-ping hsüeh* 中國腎臟病學 (Kidney pathology in traditional Chinese medicine). Chengchow: Ho-nan k'o-hsüeh chi-shu ch'u-pan-she, 1990.

Shen Chin-ao 沈金鰲. *Fu-k'o yü-chih* 婦科玉尺 (Jade ruler of gynecology). Shanghai: Shang-hai k'o-hsüeh chi-shu ch'u-pan-she, 1983.

Sivin, Nathan. *Chinese Alchemy: Preliminary Studies*. Cambridge, Mass.: Harvard University Press, 1968.

Sheng Wu-shan [Cheng Wou-chan]. *Érotologie de la China: Tradition Chinoise de l'Érotisme*. Paris: Pauvert, 1965.

de Smedt, Marc. *Chinese Eroticism*. New York: Crescent Books, 1981.

Su Nü ching 素女經 (Classic of Su Nü). Preface by Jih-pen hsing-i-hsüeh yüan yen-chiu-she 日本性醫學院研究社. Hong Kong: Hsiang-kang i-hsüeh-yüan yen-chiu-she, n.d.

Su Nü ching ta-ch'üan 素女經大全 (The complete *Classic of Su Nü*). Taipei: Sheng-huo ch'u-pan-she, 1978.

Sun Ju-chung 孫如忠. *Chin-tan chen-chuan* 金丹真傳 (True transmission of the golden elixir). In *Tao-tsang ching-hua*, series 2, no. 7.

Sun Kuang-jung 孫光榮, ed. *Chung-i yang-sheng ta-ch'üan* 中醫養生大全 (Complete health practices of traditional Chinese medicine). Peking: Pei-ching k'o-hsüeh chi-shu ch'u-pan-she, 1990.

Tamba Yasuyori 丹波康賴. *Ishimpō* 醫心方 (The essence of medical prescriptions). Originally compiled 982, first printed 1854. Tokyo: Kodansha, 1973; Taipei: Hsin wen-feng ch'u-pan kung-ssu, 1966.

Takafuji Sōichirō 高藤聰一郎. Ts'ai Chen-jen, trans. *Ch'iang-ching pu-shen* hui-ch'un shu 強精補腎回春術 (The art of rejuvenation through sexual strengthening). Hong Kong: Tsung-heng ch'u-pan-she, n.d.

T'an Chin-ch'ung 譚金崇, ed. *Yang-sheng pi-tu* 養生必讀 (Essential readings in traditional Chinese health sciences). Hsien-ning: Hu-pei k'o-hsüeh chi-shu ch'u-pan-she, 1988.

T'ao Hsiung 陶雄, et al., eds. *Ch'i-kung ching-hsüan hsü-pien* 氣功精選續編 (More selected articles on Chinese yoga). Peking: Jen-min t'i-yü ch'u-pan-she, 1987.

T'ao Hung-ching 陶弘景 (also attributed to Sun Ssu-miao). *Yang-hsing yen-ming lu* 養性延命錄 (Record of nourishing nature and lengthening life). TT, vol. 18, pp. 474–484.

T'e-hsiao mi-fang 特效秘方 (Marvelous prescriptions). San-chung-shih: Shih-hsin ch'u-pan-she, 1982.

Teng Hsi-hsien 鄧希賢. *Tzu-chin kuang-yao ta-hsien hsiu-chen yen-i* 紫金光耀大仙修真演義 (Exposition of cultivating the true essence by the Great Immortal of the Pur-

ple Gold Splendor). In van Gulik, *Erotic Colour Prints of the Ming Period*.

Ts'ao Hsi-ling 曹希亮. *Chung-i chien-shen shu* 中醫健身術 (Health practices of traditional Chinese medicine). Sian: Shen-hsi k'o-hsüeh chi-shu ch'u-pan-she, 1983.

Ts'ao Yüan-yü 曹元宇. "Chung-kuo ku-tai chin-tan-chia te she-pei chi fang-fa" 中國古代今丹家的設備及方法 (Apparatus and procedures of the ancient Chinese alchemists). In Wang Chin 王璡 et al., eds., *Chung-kuo ku-tai chin-shu hua-hsüeh chi chin-tan-shu* 中國古代金屬化學及金丹術, pp. 67–86. Shanghai: Chung-kuo k'o-hsüeh t'u-shu i-ch'i kung-ssu, 1955.

Tseng Tsao 曾慥. *Tao shu* 道樞 (Axial principles of the *tao*). TT, vol. 20, pp. 610–858.

Ts'ui Hsi-fan 崔希範. *Ju yao ching* 入藥鏡 (Mirror of absorbing the medicine). TT, vol. 5, pp. 881–886. Also in *Tao-tsang chi-yao*, *Tao-hai chin-liang*, and *Tao-tsang ching-hua*.

Unschuld, Paul. *Medicine in China: A History of Ideas*. Berkeley: University of California Press, 1985.

Waley, Arthur. *Three Ways of Thought in Ancient China*. London: George Allen and Unwin, 1939.

———. "Notes on Chinese Alchemy, Supplementary to Johnson's 'Study of Chinese Alchemy'," *Bulletin of the London School of Oriental and African Studies* 6 (1930).

Wang Erh-feng 王爾峰 et al., eds. *Chin-tan* 金丹 (The golden elixir). Peking: Chung-kuo fu-nü ch'u-pan-she, 1990.

Wang Hsün 王勳, ed. *Ku-chin nan-nü yang-sheng ching-yao* 古今男女養生精要 (Essential ancient and modern health practices for men and women). Peking: Kuo-chi wen-hua ch'u-pan-she, 1988.

Wang Pu-hsiung 王卜雄. *Chung-kuo ch'i-kung hsüeh-shu fa-chan shih* 中國氣功學術發展史 (History of the development of Chinese yoga). Changsha: Hu-nan k'o-hsüeh chi-shu ch'u-pan-she, 1988.

Wang Lien 王廉. *Tao-yin yang-sheng shu* 導引養生術 (Yogic health practices). Hong Kong: Tsung-heng ch'u-pan-she, n.d.

Wang Mu 王沐. *Nei-tan yang-sheng kung-fa chih-nan* 內丹養生功法指南 (Guide to inner elixir health techniques). Peking: Tung-fang ch'u-pan-she, 1990.

Wang Tsao-li 王早立 et al., eds. *Shih-yung chien-shen yang-sheng ta-ch'üan* 實用健身養生大全 (Complete practical system of health and self-cultivation). Peking:

Chung-kuo k'o-hsüeh chi-shu ch'u-pan-she, 1990.

Watts, Alan. *Nature, Man and Woman: A New Approach to Sexual Experience*. London: Thames and Hudson; New York: Pantheon, 1958.

Weakland, John. "Orality in Chinese Conceptions of Male Genital Sexuality," *Psychiatry* 19 (1956): 237–247.

Wei Po-yang 魏伯陽. *Chou-i ts'an-t'ung ch'i* 周易參同契 (Harmony of the three). TT, vol. 20, pp. 63–311.

Welch, Holmes. *Taoism: The Parting of the Way*. Boston: Beacon Press, 1965.

————, and Anna Seidel, eds. *Facets of Taoism: Essays in Chinese Religion*. New Haven and London: Yale University Press, 1979.

Wong, Bruce. *TSFR: The Taoist Way to Total Sexual Fitness for Men*. Princeton, N.J.: Golden Dragon Publishers, 1982.

Wu Hsiu-ming 吳修明 *Yü-fang pi-chüeh* 玉房秘訣 (Secrets of the jade chamber). Taipei: Hsin-feng wen-hua shih-yeh kung-ssu, n.d.

Wu Ming-hsiu 吳明修. *Su Nü ching chin-chieh* 素女經今解 (Contemporary commentary on the *Classic of Su Nü*). Tainan: Chen-p'ing wen-hua ch'u-pan-she, 1972.

Wu T'ieh-mei 吳鐵梅, et al., eds. *Ma Wang tui Han-mu po-shu* 馬王堆漢墓帛書 (Silk manuscripts from the Han tomb of King Ma), vol. 4. Peking: Wen-wu ch'u-pan-she, 1985.

Yeh Te-hui 葉德輝. *Shuang-mei ching-an ts'ung-shu* 雙梅景闇叢書 (Shadow of the double plum tree collection). Changsha, 1903.

Yü Ying-shih. "Life and Immortality in the Mind of Han China," *Harvard Journal of Asiatic Studies* 25 (1964–65): 80–122.

Appendix:
Dates of the Dynasties

Hsia:	approximately twenty-first to sixteenth centuries B.C.	Sui:	581–618
		T'ang	618–907
Shang:	approximatley sixteenth to eleventh centuries B.C.	Five Dynasties Ten King-	
Chou:	1066–221 B.C.	doms:	907–979
Ch'in:	221–206 B.C.	Sung:	960–1279
Han:	206 B.C.–220 A.D.	Liao:	907–1125
Three King-		Western Hsia:	1032–1227
doms:	220–280	Chin:	1115–1234
Chin:	263–316	Yüan:	1279–1368
Period of North-South		Ming:	1368–1644
		Ch'ing:	1644–1911
Division:	317–581		

Index